AF516070

The UTTARARĀMACHARITA of *Bhavabhūti*

Edited with the Commentary of Viraraghava, Various Readings, Introduction, a Literal English Translation, Exhaustive Notes and Appendices by

M.R. Kale

MOTILAL BANARSIDASS PUBLISHERS
PRIVATE LIMITED • DELHI

Reprint : Delhi, 1982, 1988, 2003, 2006, 2010
Fifth Edition: Delhi, 1934

ISBN: 978-81-208-0519-4 (Cloth)
ISBN: 978-81-208-0520-0 (Paper)

MOTILAL BANARSIDASS
41 U.A. Bungalow Road, Jawahar Nagar, Delhi 110 007
8 Mahalaxmi Chamber, 22 Bhulabhai Desai Road, Mumbai 400 026
203 Royapettah High Road, Mylapore, Chennai 600 004
236, 9th Main III Block, Jayanagar, Bangalore 560 011
Sanas Plaza, 1302 Baji Rao Road, Pune 411 002
8 Camac Street, Kolkata 700 017
Ashok Rajpath, Patna 800 004
Chowk, Varanasi 221 001

Printed in India
By Jainendra Prakash Jain at Shri Jainendra Press,
A-45, Naraina Phase-I, New Delhi 110 028
and Published by Narendra Prakash Jain for
Motilal Banarsidass Publishers Private Limited,
Bungalow Road, Delhi 110 007

CONTENTS

PREFACE TO THE THIRD EDITION.

The second edition of this book was out of print for a long time, but as I had other works on hand, and as I was unwilling to bring out a fresh edition of it without submitting it to as complete a revision as the time at my disposal would allow me to do, I could not bring out the third edition until now In this edition the Sanskrit rendering of the Prákrit passages has been printed along with the text, as in the case of similar editions of other Sanskrit plays brought out by me. I have made a few changes in and additions to the Commentary, suited to the wants of the class of students for whom this edition is intended. Considerable additions have been made to the Notes, while the whole of the Introduction has been recast and in part re-written. In this revision work I have often consulted the editions of this play by Profs Belvalkar and Káne the latter more frequently, and to which I am indebted for a few quotations. I have not always been able to agree with them, and in such cases I have tried to give my reasons. I thankfully acknowledge this assistance derived from them. Any suggestions &c. for further improving this edition will be cordially welcomed.

May 1924. M. R. KA'LE.

INTRODUCTION.

I. THE SANSKRIT DRAMA.[1]

We shall begin with a brief outline of the general structure and arrangement of the Sanskrit Drama, without a knowledge of which the technical remarks on the construction of the present play here, as well as those made in the Notes, will not be intelligible to the general reader.[2] Poetry in Sanskrit, from its inherent nature, as apart from its intrinsic merit, is divided into two kinds—दृश्य 'what is capable of being seen or exhibited', and श्रव्यं 'what can only be heard or chanted.' The drama falls under the first division. 'Rúpaka' is the general term in Sanskrit for all dramatic compositions, which also comprises a subordinate class called *Uparúpaka*. The 'Rupaka',[3] which has Rasa or Sentiment for its substratum, is divided into ten classes, *viz.*, नाटकं सप्रकरणं भाणः प्रहसनं डिमः । व्यायोगसमवकारौ वीथ्यङ्केहामृगा इति ॥. Of the Uparûpakas or Minor Dramas there are eighteen species, the most important of which are *Nâṭakas*, such as the Ratnâvalî, Viddhaśálabhañjiká &c., *Troṭakas* such as the Vikramorvaśîya, and *Saṭṭakas* such as the Karpûramañjarî,—all differing very little from the general features of a *Nâṭaka*.

Having thus disposed of the divisions into which the whole of the scenic art is capable of falling, we turn to the principle of division among the *Rúpakas* themselves, which is threefold:[4]—(1) वस्तु or the Plot of the play; (2) नेता or the Hero; (3) and रस or the Sentiment. These three are the essential constituents, nay, the very life-blood, of every dramatic piece. Each of these we shall succinctly deal with in its order.

---

1 The first two Sections are almost the same as those prefixed to our S'âkuntala.

2 The information given here has been mainly culled from the Daśarúpaka. The minor particulars not noticed here will be found in my Sâhityasârasaṃgraha (Nir. Ed.).

3 अवस्थानुकृतिर्नाट्यं रूपं दृश्यतयोच्यते । रूपकं तत्समावेशाद्दशधैव रसाश्रयम् ॥ D.-R.; रूप्यतेऽभिनयैर्यत्र वस्तु तद्रूपकं विदुः । नाटकाद्यैर्दशविधम् । *Nâṭya* is another and perhaps a wider term for the drama or the dramatic art, and is so called because it represents the different situations in (the scenes presented by) life. The sage Bharata is the founder of the science of music and dramaturgy and his work is styled the *Nâṭya-S'âstra*. *Nâṭya* is also *Rûpa*, inasmuch as it has *dṛiśyatá* or the capability of being seen, and *Rûpaka* inasmuch as its subject-matter is represented by actors assuming particular characters.

4 वस्तु नेता रसस्तेषां भेदकः ।

(A) VASTU OR THE PLOT.

Vastu is primarily of two kinds: अधिकारिक or 'Principal' and प्रासङ्गिक or 'Accessary.' The Principal is that which relates to the chief characters or the persons concerned with the essential interest of the piece, and pervades the whole arrangement. The Accessary is that which appears in furtherance of the main topic, and is concerned with characters other than the Hero or the Heroine. This latter is of two kinds; *viz. Patáká* and *Prakarî*. The 'Patâká' or 'Banner' is an episode by which the progress of the plot is illustrated, furthered or hindered (so as to give additional interest to it). It is of considerable length, and sometimes extends to the very end of a play. The 'Prakarî' is also an episodical incident–of limited duration and minor importance–one in which the principal characters take no part. Besides these two, there are three other elements requisite for the development of the plot. These are बीज or the seed, बिन्दु or the drop, and कार्य or the final issue. *Bîja* is the circumstance leading to the ultimate end briefly stated, which, as the plot develops, bears multifarious results[1], and which is as it were the seed of the plot. *Bindu*[2] is what cements a break in the plot caused by the introduction of some other incident. *Kârya* is the final object of the plot, which being attained the whole is finished. These five are technically called Arthaprakṛitis (अर्थप्रकृतयः).

The *Vastu*, which is thus divided into five classes, may again be divided into three classes according to the source of its derivation. It may be borrowed from history or tradition, or it may be fictitious, or mixed, *i. e.* partly drawn from history and partly the creation of the poet's fancy. A *Nâṭaka* belongs to the first class, a *Prakaraṇa* to the second.

As regards its development a dramatic plot has five stages or conditions called *Avasthâs*. They are–(1) आरम्भ beginning or setting on foot of the enterprise, (2) यत्न efforts, (2) प्राप्त्याशा prospect of success, (4) नियताप्ति certain attainment through the removal of obstacles, and (5) फलागम obtainment of the desired object. While these five stages are in progress there must be some links to connect them with the principal and subordinate parts of the main action (the episodes and incidents). These are called the *Saṃdhis*. They are five in number, answering to the five *Arthaprakṛitis*, each of which they join with its

---

1 स्वल्पोद्दिष्टस्तु तद्धेतुर्बीजं विस्तार्यनेकधा ।

2 अवान्तरार्थविच्छेदे बिन्दुरच्छेदकारणम् ।

corresponding stage, *viz.* मुख, प्रतिमुख, गर्भ, अवमर्श and निर्वहण (also called उपसंहृति or उपसंहार). Thus *Mukha saṃdhi* is the combination of the Bîja and A'rambha, *i. e.* wherein the seed is sown, so to speak, with all its *Rasas.* In the *Pratimukha* there is the means (*yatna*) to the chief end, as originally implied by the Bîja in the Mukha which herein sprouts up. In the *Garbha* there is attainment and non-attainment of the desired end, implying a further sprouting up of the original Bîja. There are impediments, but the main plot gains ground under resistance. The *Avamars'a saṃdhi* is that in which the seed attains a more luxuriant growth than in the *Garbha,* being accompanied by *Niyatápti* of the end, but whose final result is postponed further off by fresh impediments of various sorts (as in the Śákuntala the King's forgetting Sakuntalà after marriage owing to Durvàsas' curse). The *Nirvahaṇa* or consummation is the harmonious combination of all the aforesaid parts in the final catastrophe.

The subject-matter, whether historical, fictitious or mixed, is, from its inherent nature, capable of a twofold division. It is divided into—(1) सूच्य deserving to be suggested or implied only, as being of a dry or otherwise unfit character; and (2) दृश्यश्रव्य fit to be represented and heard as being highly sentimental and pleasing. The suggestions or implications are made in five ways, विष्कम्भचूलिकाङ्कास्याङ्कावतारप्रवेशकैः ॥ (1) For *Vishkambha* see Notes, Act II. (2) *Chúliká* is the suggestion of some incident from behind the scenes (नेपथ्ये). (3) An अङ्कास्य[1] is one wherein is suggested by the actors at the time of their departure the connexion between the Act finished and the one to be commenced, which otherwise would look disconnected, as the speech of Kámandakî and others at the end of the 3rd Act of the Mál.-Màdh. (4) अङ्कावतार[2] consists in casting the seed of the subject-matter of an Act in the previous Act before it has drawn to its close, so that the Act following is a continuation of the one preceding; *e. g.* the sixth Act of the Śák., the germ of which is implanted at the end of the fifth Act; *cf.* also Mâlav. II. and Mál-Mâdh. II. (5) A प्रवेश or 'Introducer' is one which being interposed

---

1 अङ्कान्तपात्रैरङ्कास्यं छिन्नाङ्कस्यार्थसूचनात् ।

2 अङ्कावतारस्त्वङ्कान्ते पातोऽङ्कस्याविभागतः । The distinction, however, between an Aṅkásya and an Aṅkávatára is considered by some to be merely imaginary. Vis'vanátha actually supplants the latter by Aṅkamukha which he defines as that where, in one Act, the substance of all the other Acts is suggested.

between any two Acts suggests like the Vishkambhaka some past or future event to show the connexion between the parts of the story through the conversation of *low* characters. It can never introduce the first Act. According to Jagaddhara, the language in a प्रवेशक is generally Śauraseni or any similar dialect as opposed to the Sanskrit found in a Śuddhavishkambhaka.

The subject-matter is further divided into three kinds—सर्वश्राव्यं or प्रकाशं, अश्राव्यं or स्वगतं, and नियतश्राव्यम्. The terms are explanatory of themselves. The last is of two kinds, जनान्तिकं and अपवारितकं (which are explained in the Notes). Independent of these divisions, there is one called आकाशभाषितं (आकाशे) or 'Speech from the void.'

(B) NETA' OR THE HERO.

The Hero is required to be modest, decorous, comely, munificent, civil, of sweet address, eloquent, sprung from a noble family, &c.[1] Heroes are mentioned to be of four kinds; *viz.* धीरोदात्त, धीरललित, धीरशान्त and धीरोद्धत. '*Dhîrodátta*' or the Hero of sublime qualities, is one who is magnanimous, patient, not given to boasting, self-possessed, of firm resolve, whose high spirit is concealed and who is true to his engagements. We are not concerned with the other three classes of Heroes here. Each of these Heroes may be of one or other of four sorts. He may be दक्षिण or 'gallant,' *i. e.* equally devoted to many women though principally attached to one; or शठ 'sly', *i. e.* one, who being attached to one lady, covertly acts in a way unpleasant to her; or he may be धृष्ट 'bold', openly making his professions to another, and not ashamed even when reproached; or lastly, he may be अनुकूल 'favourable,' devoted to one Heroine only. The धीरोदात्त hero has eight manly qualities—शोभा, विलास, माधुर्य, गाम्भीर्य, धैर्य, तेजस् , लालित्य and औदार्य.

Among the assistants of the Hero, the principal is पीठमर्द, the hero of the Patákà or episode, clever in discourse, devoted to his master, and a little inferior to him in qualities. Next comes the Vidúshaka, his constant companion, whose business consists in the repartees of wit, in helping his friend in his love-intrigues and thus assisting in the general *dénouement* of the play. The third, and of equal rank with the Vidúshaka, is Viṭa, who

---

1 नेता विनीतो मधुरस्त्यागी दक्षः प्रियंवदः। रक्तलोकः शुचिर्वाग्मी रूढवंशः स्थिरो युवा ॥ बुद्ध्युत्साहस्मृतिप्रज्ञाकलामानसमन्वितः। शूरो दृढश्च तेजस्वी शास्त्रचक्षुश्च धार्मिकः ॥ भेदैश्चतुर्धा ललितशान्तोदात्तोद्धतैरयम् ॥

knows one art only and is thereby useful to the Hero. The Hero thus equipped may still take into his service ministers of state and ministers of religion, ascetics, allies, &c. as well as eunuchs, mutes, barbarians (Yavanas) &c. Sometimes there may be a Rival-Hero called प्रतिनायक, who is avaricious, bold, impetuous, criminal and of evil conduct.

The Nâyikâ or the Heroine, who must be possessed of qualities similar to those of the Hero, is of three kinds[1]. She may be the wife of the hero (स्वीया), as Sîtâ in the Uttar., or one belonging to another (अन्या परकीया), or a common woman (सामान्या or साधारणस्त्री) as Vasantasenâ in the Mṛich. The परकीया (so called because she is in the power of her guardian) may be a maiden or the wife of another. But the latter must not be introduced as the Heroine in a play[2]. The maiden's love, however, better helps the *rasa* and is, therefore, the most favourite theme with many Sanskrit poets. Further divisions and subdivisions of the *Náyiká* are not introduced here, as they have very little to do with the construction of the drama. For her assistants the Heroine may have a सखी, दासी, धात्रेयी, प्रतिवेशिका and others, possessing qualities corresponding to those of the friends of the Hero.

(C) RASA OR SENTIMENT.

Rasa is that lasting impression or feeling produced to his overwhelming delight in a man of poetic sensibility by the proper action of the *Vibhávas*, and *Anubhávas*, as well as the *Sáttvika-bhâvas* and the *Vyabhichâribhávas*[3]. Bhâva or Feeling is the complete pervasion of the heart by any emotion, whether of pleasure or of pain, arising from the object under sight. Vibhâva or an Excitant is that which being perceived nourishes the main sentiment. It is divided into *Âlambana*, that which is, as it were, the support or substratum of the *Rasa*, the person or thing with reference to which a sentiment arises— such as the Hero or the Heroine, and *Uddîpana*, or what excites or enhances (adds to the development of) the senti-

---

1 स्वान्या साधारणस्त्रीति तद्गुणा नायिका त्रिधा ।

2 अन्यस्त्री कन्यकोढा च नान्योढाङ्गिरसे क्वचित् ।

3 विभावैरनुभावैश्च सात्त्विकैर्व्यभिचारिभिः । आनीयमानः स्वाद्यत्वं स्थायीभावो रसः स्मृतः ॥ सुखदुःखादिकैर्भावैर्भावस्तद्भावभावनम् । ज्ञायमानतया तत्र विभावो भावपोषकृत् ॥ आलम्बनोद्दीपनत्वप्रभेदेन स च द्विधा । अनुभावो विकारस्तु भावसंसूचनात्मकः ॥

ment, such as the moon, the beauties of the vernal season &c., beauty, decorations &c. of the principal characters, in the case of शृङ्गार. *Anubháva* or an Ensuant is the outward manifestation of internal feeling through the eyes, face &c. The Sáttvika or natural *bhávas* are a subdivision of *Anubháva*, and are mentioned as eight in number—स्तम्भप्रलयरोमाञ्चाः स्वेदो वैवर्ण्यवेपथू । अश्रुवैस्वर्यमित्यष्टौ ।. The *Vyabhichárís* or the Accessaries are those Bhâvas which are not strictly confined to any *Rasa*, but appearing and disappearing, like waves in the ocean, they serve as feeders to the prevailing sentiment and strengthen it in different ways. *Stháyibháva* (स्थायिभाव) or the Permanent Sentiment of a composition is one—the ocean melting all salt into water—which, not being interrupted by any sentiment contrary or akin to its nature occurring at intervals, converts all of them into its owu nature[1]. Now a *Rasa* would prove contrary to another if the आश्रय or substratum of both were the same. But as अङ्गि (principal) and अङ्ग (subordinate) a रस may be mixed with one or more of others.

There are eight Stháyibhávas, रति, हास, शोक, क्रोध, उत्साह, भय, जुगुप्सा and विस्मय, on which are based respectively the eight sentiments-शृङ्गार the Erotic, हास्य the Comic, करुण the Pathetic, रौद्र the Furious, वीर the Heroic, भयानक the Terrible, बीभत्स the Loathsome, and अद्भुत the Marvellous. There is a ninth sentiment, that of शान्त the Quietistic, having शम or tranquillity for its Stháyibháva. But it is not suited to dramatic purposes and rarely occurs as a main sentiment in a drama. Of these eight sentiments, शृङ्गार and हास्य, वीर and अद्भुत, बीभत्स and भयानक, and रौद्र and करुण are akin to each other, as they proceed from the same condition of the mind. As we are concerned with the Erotic alone, that being the prevailing sentiment in Kâlidâsa's plays, we shall say something about it here. शृङ्गार is mainly divided into विप्रलम्भ or Love in-separation, and संभोग or Love-in-union. The former, the Das'arûpaka subdivides into two kinds, अयोग the Non-consummation of marriage, and विप्रयोग the Separation of the lovers deep in love after marriage. The former, which arises from the dependent position of one or the other of the parties, or through distance, or through the intervention of adverse fate, has ten stages, अभिलाष, चिन्ता &c. mentioned in the com.; चिन्ता 'anxiety' occurs through मान, प्रवास or some such cause. मान, 'jealous anger', arises from a breach in the duties of love (प्रणयभङ्ग) and may be on both sides (rarely, however, the Nâyaka is *mânî*).

1 विरुद्धैरविरुद्धैर्वा भावैर्विच्छिद्यते न यः । आत्मभावं नयत्यन्यान्स स्थायी लवणाकरः ॥

This मान has several varieties, such as ईर्ष्यामान, आनुमानिकमान, &c. It is capable of being dispelled in six ways—सामा भेदेन दानेन नत्युपेक्षारसान्तरैः—and is called गुरु, लघु or मध्यम according to the greatness or the smallness of the effort required to make the Nâyiká give it up. संभोग is when the two lovers are in the enjoyment of each other's company, engaged in looking at each other, kissing each other &c.

(D) THE GENERAL CONDUCT OF THE NÂTAKA.

Every dramatic piece opens with a prelude or prologue (प्रस्तावना) which is itself introduced by what is called the *Nándî*. This Nándî, according to some, must suggest the gist of the whole plot. The Sûtradhâra may sometimes retire after the recital of the Nândî, in which case another actor called स्थापक (for he *establishes* as it were the topic of the play) takes his place. In the Prelude, which may begin with a brief allusion to the poet's literary attainments, his genealogy, &c., the Sútradhára or the Sthâpaka suggests the subject in the form of the Bîja, or by a simple beginning, or by naming the character about to enter (as in the Śákuntala). He must please the audience with sweet songs descriptive of some season and couched in the Bhâratî vṛitti. The प्रस्तावना is of two kinds—(1) प्ररोचना as in the Ratn., and (2) आमुख in which the Sútradhâra holds conversation with the actress or his assistants, bearing on the subject to be introduced. This latter is of three kinds, of which one is प्रयोगातिशय . When the entry of a character is directly indicated by the Sútradhâra saying 'Here he enters,' that is Prayogâtiśaya.

The Prelude being over the piece is commenced, being hereafter arranged and exhibited in the manner indicated in the three foregoing Sections. The whole matter should be well determined and divided into Acts and Scenes. A Náṭaka may consist of from five to ten Acts. The Hero should be Dhírodátta. The prevailing sentiment should be शृङ्गार or वीर (or sometimes करुण), others being introduced as conducive to its development. Nothing should be introduced in the play which either misbeseems the Hero or is discordant with the main sentiment. An Act must not be tiresomely long, should be full of *Rasa*, and introduced by *Vishkambhaka*, &c. according to necessity. Its close is marked by the exit of all characters. Such incidents as journeys, massacres, wars, &c., should not be represented in a play; they may only be indicated. The death of the

Hero must never be exhibited. This accounts for the somewhat monotonous character of Sanskrit plays and the absence of tragedies in Sanskrit.[1] The play should end, as it began, with a benediction or prayer, called the Bharatavákya, as it is repeated by the principal personage in his character of an actor, and contains an expression of wishes for general prosperity and happiness. The Unity of interest or action must be maintained throughout. As regards the language to be used in a piece, the Hero and the higher characters speak in classical Sanskrit, while females and other minor characters speak in the different Prakrit dialects.

The student will have seen from the foregoing sketch, that the characteristic peculiarities of the Indian drama are mainly three:—(1) its peculiar structure; (2) the absence of the distinction between Comedy and Tragedy; and (3) the diversity of languages to be spoken by the characters. The above-mentioned general characteristics of a Náṭaka belong with certain modifications to the other divisions of the Rúpaka as well. Of these we may notice the Prakaraṇa and the Troṭaka. The plot of a प्रकरण should be fictitous and drawn from real life in a respectable class of society. The Hero, who must be धीरप्रशान्त, may be of ministerial rank, or a Bráhmaṇa, or a merchant (Vaiśya). The Heroine may be a maiden of a noble family, or a courtesan. The most appropriate sentiment is the Erotic. Gamblers and other low characters should be introduced. There should be ten Acts. The Mál.-Mádh. and the Mṛich. belong to this species. A Troṭaka may consist of 5,7,8 or 9 Acts. The characters to be represented should be celestial as well as human (as in the Vik.). The Vidúshaka should take a prominent part in it and be present in every Act. The prevailing sentiment should be शृङ्गार. In other particulars it does not differ from the Náṭaka.

---

1 Wilson observes—"They (the Hindu plays) never offer a calamitous conclusion, which, as Johnson remarks, was enough to constitute a Tragedy in Shakespeare's days; and although they propose to excite all the emotions of the human breast, terror and pity included, they never effect this object by leaving a painful impression upon the mind of the spectator. The Hindus in fact have no Tragedy............The absence of tragic catastrophe in the Hindu dramas is not merely an unconscious omission; such a catastrophe is prohibited by a positive rule. The conduct of what may be termed the classical drama of the Hindus is exemplary and dignified. Nor is its moral purport neglected; and one of their writers declares, in an illustration familiar to ancient and modern poetry, that the chief end of the Theatre is to disguise by the insidious sweet the unpalatable but salutary bitter, of the cup."

II. THE POET.

(1) His Date.

The problem of settling with exactness the date of a Sanskrit author is, in general, a very vexed one, as all students of antiquarian research are aware. Sanskrit writers rarely make any direct statements about themselves, which would enable us to fix the periods during which they flourished; their dates are as a rule to be arrived at by indirect evidence collected from a mass of inscriptional and literary records; and, as these are often conflicting, the result cannot always be declared as satisfactory and convincing. Even now scholars are not agreed about the date of Kálidása, the premier poet of India; it is not surprising, therefore, that the dates of many poets of lesser fame should be shrouded in hazy obscurity. Fortunately for us the gloom is comparatively lifted from the date of Bhavabhúti, and it can be safely affirmed that he lived and flourished towards the close of the seventh century. This result is arrived at with the help of a quotation from Kalhaṇa's Rájataraṃgiṇî which asserts that Bhavabhúti was patronized by King Yaśovarman of Kányakubja (modern Kanoj): कविर्वाकपतिराजश्रीभवभूत्यादिसेवितः । जितो ययौ यशोवर्मा तद्गुणस्तुतिवन्दिताम् ॥ (Rájat. IV. 144). The date of Yaśovarman is fixed by Dr. Stein as being somewhere near 736 A D. Kalhaṇa's quotation also mentions Vákpatirâja as a court-poet of Yaśovarman; this Vákpatirâja is the author of a long Prâkrit poem called *Gauḍavaho*, in which occurs (799) the following verse :—

भवभूइजलहिणिग्गदकव्वामयरसकणा इव फुरन्ति ।
जस्स विसेसा अज्ज वि वियडेसु कहाणिवेसेसु ॥
(भवभूतिजलधिनिर्गतकाव्यामृतरसकणा इव स्फुरन्ति ।
यस्य विशेषा अद्यापि विकटेषु कथानिवेशेषु ॥)

"In his vast narrative-structures there shine even now excellences, like drops of the liquid nectar of poetry from the ocean of Bhavabhûti." This note of personal admiration proves that Vâkpatirâja was a student of Bhavabhûti's writings, to which he was indebted for whatever merits might lie in his own work. The words अज्ज वि ("even now") in the stanza must be interpreted to mean, as is shown by Dr. Belvalkar, that "Bhavabhúti's connexion with the court of Yaśovarman fell in the earlier part of that monarch's reign, and that the dramatist was somewhat earlier than Vâkpatirâja."

The date which we thus obtain for Bhavabhûti is also further supported by ample collateral evidence, both of a negative and of a positive character. Bhavabhûti's works show abundant traces of the influence of Kálidâsa, in the domain of language as well as of ideas; this easily places him later than Kâlidàsa, who himself cannot be later than the fifth century. Again, Bâṇa, the author of the *Kâdambarî*, who flourished at about 610 A. D. and was a court-poet of Harsha, mentions a number of poets in the introduction to his *Harshacharita*; therein we find Bhása and Kálidása eulogized, but the name of Bhavabhûti does not occur. The omission of the name of such an illustrious writer tends to show that Bhavabhûti was unknown to and therefore later than Báṇa. The first definite mention of Bhavabhûti in literature occurs in the play *Bâlarâmâyaṇa*, whose author Râjaśekhara calls himself an *Avatára* of Bhavabhûti:—

बभूव वल्मीकभवः कविः पुरा ततः प्रपेदे भुवि भर्तृमेण्ठताम् ।
स्थितः पुनर्यो भवभूतिरेखया स वर्तते संप्रति राजशेखरः ॥ (I. 16)

As Rájaśekhara's date is known to be about 900 A. D., this becomes the latest limit for Bhavabhûti's date, who can be well imagined to have lived some two centuries earlier to merit such spiritual elevation at the hands of the not over-modest author of the Bálarâmâyaṇa. A large number of writers, including Kshemendra, Dhanaṃjaya (author of the Daśarûpaka) and Mahimabhṭṭa (author of the Vyaktiviveka) have quoted Bhavabhûti in their works; their evidence, however, is superfluous after the unmistakable reference by Râjaśekhara quoted above.

(2) His Personal History.

What we have said before as regards the dates of Sanskrit poets applies with even greater force to the problem of reconstructing their biographies; on this point there is even a greater lack of information, and collateral evidence, too, is more meagre and more untrustworthy. If a poet is modest about himself, we know next to nothing about his personal history, as has happened in the case of Kálidása; sometimes an author does give us a few details of an autobiographical kind, as has been done by Bhavabhûti; we have indeed to be thankful that he has not imitated his predecessor, Kálidása, in observing a studious silence about himself. In the Prologue to each of his three plays Bhavabhûti gives some account of himself and his family. This account is the fullest in the *Mahávíracharita*, which was probably his earliest work. It is therein stated that his ancestral home was a city called Padmapura "in the south" (दक्षिणापथे). This is belived to have been in the Berars, though the exact location of the town is yet uncertain; some have tried to identify it with Padmávatî, a city which the poet has rather minutely described in the Mâlatî-Mâdhava ;but the grounds for such an identification are meagre and uncovincing.* Bhavadhûti gives Udumbara as the surname of his family; the Udumbaras were descendants of the sage Kas'yapa; they were followers of the Taittirîya school of the Black Yajurveda. They were pious and devout Brahmaṇas, well versed in Brahmalore ("ब्रह्मवादिन:") and keeping the fivefold sacred fire. In this family there was one Mahâkavi, and Bhavabhúti was fifth in descent from him, his grandfather's name being Bhaṭṭa Gopála and that of his father Nîlakaṇṭha†. His mother's name was Jâtukarṇî. His tutor was one Jñânanidhi, who must have

---

*As Bhavabhu ti has stated that his family belonged to the Deccan and followed the Taittirya S'âkhâ, Dr. Bhâṇḍârkar conjectures that his native place must have been somewhere near Chândâ in the Central Provinces, "where there are still many families of Marâṭhî Des astha Brâhmaṇas of the Taittirîyasa'khâ,......and in the country to the south and south-east of which there are families of Tailaṅga Brâhmaṇas following the same Veda." (Vide his notes on Mâl.-Mâdh. I. I. 31) He also conjectures, from Bhavabhúti's vivid descriptions of the scenes near and around Goda'varí, that his native place must have been near that river.

† About Bhavabhúti's own name there is some controversy. It appears that Bhavabhúti was his real (original) name, and that later on the title 'S'rî-Kaṇṭha' was given to him by friendly admirers. This seems to be the straightforward sense of the words श्रीकण्ठपदलाञ्छनः भवभूतिर्नाम (see p. 3 of this ed.). It is surprising to find that Dr. Belvalkar considers S'rî-kaṇṭha to be the original name and Bhavabhûti to be the title. In this he follows some commentators who give various fanciful explanations of the word Bhava-bhúti, (see Vîra.'s com., p. 4 of this ed.); but these explanations seem to be later inventions to explain the formation of the word somehow; the disagreement among the commentators themselves is a sufficient proof of this.

been, indeed, a veritable 'store of learning', if we are to judge from the varied accomplishments of his distinguished pupil. Bhavabhúti had acquired thorough proficiency in the various branches of knowledge which then formed the usual curriculum of Bráhmaṇic study. He gives proofs of his vast erudition in the course of his works. He had mastered the Vedic lores, the six systems of philosophy, grammar, rhetorics, &c. &c. His knowledge of the Yoga philosophy he displays in Mál.-Mádh. (Act V.) and in Mv. (Act III.). That he was familiar with the literature of the Upanishads is shown by his reference to the doctrine of *Vivarta* in more than one place in the Uttar. (III. 47 ; IV. 15), by his description for the *Vairâja Lokas* (II. 12), and by his allusion to the *Asúrya Lokas* (Act IV. p. 103). Bhavabhûti was in fact one of the most profound scholars of his time with a masterly skill as poet and dramatist. Fortune does not appear to have smiled upon him; but he won through, uphill though the fight must have been. He has referred in defiant terms to his detractors in the well-known verse ये नाम केचिदिह नः प्रथयन्त्यवज्ञां &c. (Mâl.-Mâdh. I. 8); that his self-confidence and proud boast were justifiable has been shown by the verdict of posterity. He must have been a man of fine sensibility, and gentle and optimistic by temperament. His references to love, children, friendship and such-like topic show that he must have enjoyed family life to the full and appreciated it at its highest. It is not unfair to conclude, from such sentiments as are expressed in प्रेयो मित्रं बन्धुता वा समग्रा...... स्त्रीणां भर्ता धर्मदाराश्च पुंसां (Mál.—Mádh. VI. 18), that Bhavabhúti's conjugal life must have been a happy union of twin souls.

We might note in passing that various stories are current among the Pandits making Bhavabhúti a contemporary of Kàlidâsa. Thus in the *Bhojaprabandha* it is stated that on one occasion the goddess Bhuvaneśvarî herself gave a decision in favour of Bhavabhûti when there was a dispute as regards the comparative merits of a number of rival poets including Kàlidàsa, Bhavabhúti, Bâṇa and Mayûra. Another well-known legend relates how Kálidâsa improved upon Bhavabhúti's original line अविदितगतयामा रात्रिरेवं व्यरंसीत् (Utt. I. 27) by removing the dot over व and reading रात्रिरेव व्यरंसीत्. The untrustworthiness of such anecdotes is abundantly established by the different dates of the poets referred to; they prove nothing historically.

(3) His Works

Bhavabhûti is known to have written three plays, the Mahávîracharita, the Málatî-Mádhva and the Uttararámacharita. The Mahávîracharita seems to have been his earliest production, because, as Dr. Sir Bhandarkar has remarked, "it does not exhibit that power and felicity of expression and insight into the human heart that the other two display, and is often heavy and uncouth." The biographical details about the poet are given more fully in the Mv. than in the other two plays, which also would indicate that when he wrote the Mv., Bhavabhúti was an author unknown to the public; later on, when he wrote his last play, the Uttararámacharita, he abridges all this account into barely one line. The Mahávîracharita is a play in seven Acts; it deals with Râma's history as narrated in the Rámáyaṇa, and the predominent sentiment is Heroic (वीर रस). The story covers Râma's life from his very childhood to his return to Ayodhyâ after his victory over Râvaṇa. As a first work it shows great skill in dramatic construction, though it lacks Bhavabhúti's mature command over expression. His Málatîmádhava must be placed second in chronological order; his bitter reference to his critics in ये नाम केचिदिह नः &c. (I. 8) seems to point to the fact that his earlier work did not meet with their approbation. Possibly the critics were justified then. But the dazzling splendour of his new romance, teeming with realistic pictures and flowing with a forceful majesty of language, must have silenced all detractors. For in his last work (Utt.) we find the poet at peace with his critics, and describing himself as "शब्दब्रह्मविद् परिणतप्रज्ञ कवि" (VII. 20). The Málatîmádhava is a romantic play in ten Acts, dealing with the love-story of Mádhava, the son of Devaráta who was a minister of the king of Berar, and Málatî, the daughter of Devaráta's friend Bhûrivasu The couple fall in love at first sight, and after going through several trials are united happily in the end. As a love-play the composition merits comparison with the Śâkuntala. Bhavabhúti's exuberant genius is seen here flowering into graceful fancies and entrancing situations through which the audience sits spell-bound till the final dénouement. There are critics who prefer the Mál.-Mādh.

to tha Uttara. as the best work of Bhavabhúti. In the Uttara. Bhavabhúti narrates in seven Acts the story of Ráma and Sîtâ after their return to Ayodhyâ; it is thus a sort of supplement to the Mv. We shall deal with this play in detail in a subsequent Section; we merely notice it here as being the last in chronological order.

Bhavabhúti is not known to have written any other works. In ancient anthologies, such as the Śârṅgadharapaddhati and the Rasikajîvana, we find stanzas quoted as Bhavabhúti's which are not to be found in any of his known works; the total number of such stanzas is about twelve. It is probable that Bhavabhúti might have written other plays or poems which are no more extant, and from which these quotations might have been made; the probability, however, is rather a remote one, since the anthologists, by their inconsistency in ascribing a particular stanza to a particular author, vitiate the reliability of their own statements.

(4) A LITERARY ESTIMATE OF BHAVABHU'TI.

In the galaxy of Sanskrit poets, Bhavabhúti is a star of the first magnitude, ranking with Bhása, Kálidása, Báṇa and other master-artists. Sanskrit critics have assigned him a very high place in the company of poets and have sung his praises in many laudatory stanzas. Thus Govardhanácharya, himself a poet of no mean order, has said :—

भवभूतेः संबन्धाद्भूधरभूरेव भारती भाति ।
एतत्कृतकारुण्ये किमन्यथा रोदिति ग्रावा ॥ (A'ryás. I. 36)

wherein he refers to the height of pathos to which the genius of the poet has attained in composing the Uttararámacharita. Kshemendra has referred to the fondness of our poet for the Śikhariṇí metre:—

भवभूतेः शिखरिणी निरर्गलतरङ्गिणी ।
रुचिरा घनसंदर्भे या मयूरीव नृत्यति ॥ (Suv. III. 33);

while Dhanapála, in his *Tilakamañjarî* says :—

स्पष्टभावरसा चित्रैः पदन्यासैः प्रवर्तिता ।
नाटकेषु नटस्त्रीव भारती भवभूतिना ॥ (Introd. verse 30),

wherein Bhavabhúti's plays are complimented on their clear delineation of emotions (*bháva*) and sentiments (*rasa*) and on their wonderful felicity of literary expression.

European critics, too, have appreciated the high claim of Bhavabhúti as a dramatic author and poet. Thus in the language of the Málatîmádhava, Prof. Wilson finds "extraordinary beauty and power." It is not difficult to understand the vogue of Bhavabhúti and the popularity he enjoys as a Sanskrit poet. As we shall see in the next Section, he is a master, supreme and without rival, in the art of portraying pathos. "करुणस्य मूर्तिरथ वा शरीरिणी," which are his own words (III. 4) in describing Sîtâ, might well stand as a description of his own poetic genius, so far as the Uttararámacharita is concerned. It is in the Málatimádhava, however, that we see the display of his creative skill at its best; therein his genius gets wider scope owing to the variety of situations and the rapidly moving action. He scorns conventionality of description, the tame and tepid atmosphere of love-in-a-harem, and all the delicate trappings like the cuckoo's song and the mango's blossom with which Sanskrit poets habitually invest their descriptions of love. His imagination takes large strides, and he prefers to dwell on the grand and the sublime, rather than on the trivial and the mild. He is one of the few poets who have given us impressive descriptions of vast forests, big mountain ranges, rushing water falls and panoramic scenery. Kálidása is admitted by all as a master in the description of Nature's beauties; his muse, however, loves to dwell upon its gentler aspects. For gorgeous scenery adequately described we must go to Bhavabhúti and read verses like एते ते कुहरेषु गद्गदनदद्गोदावरीवारयो &c. (Utt. II. 30) or जृम्भाजर्जरडिम्बडम्बरघनश्रीमत्कदम्बद्रुमाः &c. (Mál.-Mádh. IX. 16) or सोत्साहं धृतशासनैः सकुतुकैर्वृक्षौकसां नायकैः &c. (Mv. VII. 10). Bhavabhúti was a great stylist and had a wonderful command over language; he was skilled in adjusting the sound of his verse so as to be an echo to the sense; witness the effect produced by reading aloud the verse उत्फुल्लार्जुनसर्जवासितवहत्पौरस्त्यझञ्झामरुत् &c. (Mál.-Mâdh. IX. 17) which describes a sudden rain-storm, or the verse किमपि किमपि मन्दं (Utt. I. 27) which describes lovers talking sweet, indistinct nothings to each other, or the verse अवनिरमरसिन्धुः &c. (Utt. III. 48) which pronounces a blessing. The chief merit of Bhavabhúti's plays, apart from questions of language, lies, however, in their high moral tone. Even in describing ordinary human love, Bhavabhúti never wanders into the sensuous; he has probed the depths of romantic passion without descending to appeals to mere lust. He maintains* a dignified gravity throughout; his ideal of a lover is one who obliterates self; his ideal of a king is also one who is ready to sacrifice self at the altar of public good; and in describing these ideals his imagery is elevated and his conceits ethereal.

Bhavabhûti is a great writer whose merits far outweigh his faults; this analysis would not, however, be complete without some mention of the latter. The defects, such as they are, of his literary style are apparent even on a cursory observation. His words are often harsh and unfamiliar, and his expressions lack the smooth polish and easy intelligibility to be found in the works of Kàlidâsa. He uses long, formidable compounds in his prose, and they are sometimes (*e. g.* in the Málatî-Mâdhava Act III.) more involved than even those in Báṇa's *Kádambarî*. He has a habit of repeating words, phrases, and even stanzas, a practice which palls upon the reader when too frequently indulged in. As observed by Mr. Káne, there are at least *seventeen verses* in the Uttar. which are to be found already used either in the Mv. or in the Málati-Mádhava! As a constructive artist he neglects to observe the unities of time and place. This is never serious so long as it does not mar the interest of the play; and we may say to the credit of Bhavabhûti that, excepting one or two lapses, he manages to keep the interest unflagging in all his three dramas. A graver charge is that he is not an adept in the skilful handling of his incidents or in the judicious and gradual development of his plot. There is some truth in this charge, and it is no good excuse to say that the poet was handicapped by his choice of a subject from the Rámáyaṇa. Whatever the source may be, it is always left to the dramatist so to wield his materials and invent dramatic action as to present a piece throbbing with pertinent interest and full of arresting situations. Even

* It may be remarked here that humour, or gaiety of any kind, is notably absent from Bhavabhûti's plays; and that the Vidûshaka or the Buffoon, who is a regular figure in most Sanskrit dramas, is nowhere employed by our author. The interest that piquant jokes and witty sallies impart to a play (e. g. the Mṛichchakaṭika) is lacking in the compositions of Bhavabhûti, which is a serious drawback from the spectator's point of view.

a third-rate poet like Râmabhadra-Dîkshita has managed to make his *Jánakipariṅaya* unusually interesting because he possessed a fertile inventive faculty. We might admit therefore that Bhavabhûti had no eye for incidents; the spectators who merely looked for the story might doubtless find it dull on the stage.

(5) BHAVABHU'TI AND KA'LIDA'SA.

As a dramatic artist Bhavabhûti naturally invites comparison with his renowned predecessor, the author of the *S'a'kuntala.* Although as a poet on the whole we may place Kálidása above Bhavabhúti, as a dramatic poet the palm is certainly disputed with him by the latter. Nay, the tide of opinion among the Pandits once ran so high as to decidedly declare in favour of Bhavabhúti, as the author of the *Uttara-rámacharita**. These two poets are justly regarded as the leading dramatists in Sanskrit. Both are most original poets gifted with genius of the highest order. Both are masters of the natural style of poetry and both are equally happy in their choice of words. It is true that Bhavabhûti's style is rather elaborate, and in a few places marked by long compounds; but in that the poet was, in our opinion, unconsciously yielding to the tendency of his age. If Kâlidâsa has more fancy and imagination, Bhavabhûti is more sentimental and passionate. Kâlidâsa excels in depicting the sentiment of love (शृंगार), while Bhavabhûti is at his best when depicting Pathos (करुण) and Heroism (वीर). Neither, however, is much inferior to the other in depicting what may be called the other's *forte.* As Dr. Sir Bhandarkar has remarked, "the former (K.) *suggests* or *indicates* the sentiment which the latter (Bh.) *expresses* in forcible language. In the language of Sanskrit critics, Kâlidâsa's *rasa* is conveyed or *abhivyakta* by the *lakshya* or *vyaṅgya* sense of words, while Bhavabhûti's is conveyed by the *váchya* sense." Kálidása's may be described as the synthetical method of poetry, as opposed to Bhavabhúti's which is analytical. We shall give a few quotations in illustration of what we have said above. When Dushyanta sees Śakuntalā after love has wounded his heart, he simply

* *Cf.* the memorable line उत्तरे रामचरिते भवभूतिर्विशिष्यते ।. For an interesting anecdote which makes the two poets exist contemporaneously with each other, vide Dr. Sir Bhandarkar's preface to his ed. of the Mâl.-Mâdh., pp. x-xi.

says—' अये लब्धं नेत्रनिर्वाणम् (P. 67; see also our note on this) but compare Bhavabhu'ti (Ma'l.-Ma'dh. III. 16)—

अविरलमिव दाम्ना पौण्डरीकेण नद्धः
स्नपित इव च दुग्धस्रोतसा निर्भरेण ।
कवलित इव कृत्स्नश्चक्षुषा स्फारितेन
प्रसभममृतमेघेनेव सान्द्रेण सिक्तः ॥

Here the feeling is the same, but the different forms of it are forcibly described. Compare the scene between Dushyanta and Śakuntalá when left alone, with what Mâdhava says when Ma'latî embraces him in the disguise of her friend Lavaṅgiká (VII. 12)—

एकीकृतस्त्वचि निषिक्त इवावपीड्य
निर्भुग्नपीनकुचकुड्मलयाऽनया मे ।
कर्पूरहारहरिचन्दनचन्द्रकान्त-
निष्यन्दशैवलमृणालहिमादिवर्गः ॥

Compare also, and as an instance of Bhavabhúti's forcible style, the first effect produced on Mádhava on seeing Málatî. He says (I. 30) परिच्छेदातीतः सकलवचनानामविषयः &c. Compare further the meeting of Dushyanta and Śakuntalá (p. 82 भवतु । मोक्ष्यामि &c.) with that of Mádhava and Mālatī (ततः प्रविशतः &c. माधवः-(सानन्दम् ।) दलयति परिशुष्यत् &c., निश्वातेन्ते सुतनु &c. (VIII I. 2) अयि निरनुरोधे । जीवयन्निव &c. (VII. I. 3) and दुग्धं चिराय &c. (VIII. 4). We have compared Śák. and Mál.-Mádh. because both are love-plays. It may be, as Sir Bhandarkar remarks, that Bhavabhúti modelled the love of Mádhava and Málatî upon that of Dushyanta and Sakuntalá. But the love of Mádhava is more ethereal than that of Dushyanta, and perhaps Bhavabhúti as a poet is more ethereal than Kálidása.

In the realm of pathos, however, Bhavabhúti's mastery is truly unrivalled (cf. कारुण्यं भवभूतिरेव तनुते). Kálidása, who had splendid opportunity of delineating pathos in the fifth Act of the Śákuntala, relies almost solely on suggestion; and when it comes to actual description, he contents himself by merely stating—

सा निन्दन्ती स्वानि भाग्यानि बाला
बाहूत्क्षेपं क्रन्दितुं च प्रवृत्ता । (V. 30)

In the Vikramorvaśîya, the wailings of the mad king Purûravas fail to excite any corresponding emotion in the spectators, first because they feel that it is all a bit unreal, as the king is insane, and secondly because most of his speeches merely describe in felicitous language the magnificent scenery around him. In the Uttararámacharita the poet keeps his audience enthralled throughout the seven Acts by the situations as well as by his inspired expressions. Let the student read:—

सीता—किमेताभ्यामनाथाभ्याम् ।
रामः—हृदय वज्रमसि ।
भागी॰—कथं त्वं सनाथाऽप्यनाथा ।
सीता—कीदृशं मेऽभाग्यायाः सनाथत्वम् । (Act. VII.)
Or वासन्ती—(सकरुणम् ।) देव देव
अस्मिन्नेव लतागृहे त्वमभवस्तन्मार्गदत्तेक्षणः
सा हंसैः कृतकौतुका चिरमभूद्गोदावरीसैकते । &c.
सीता—दारुणासि वासन्ति दारुणासि ।......
रामः—अयि चण्डि जानकि इतस्ततो दृश्यसे नानुकम्पसे ।
हा हा देवि स्फुटति हृदयं &c. (Act III.)

Bhavabhúti's play would make his audience weep copiously; Kálidása's would simply excite sympathy. As a poet of nature and as a describer of the picturesque, again, Bhavabhúti would hardly count as inferior to Kálidāsa. His description of Janasthána (Act II.) is not less vivid than Kálidása's description of the Kumáravana in Vikr. (Act IV.) He can rival Kálidàsa in all the points where the latter is said to excel; he can describe with flowing grace (cf. कठोरपारावतकण्ठमेचकं वपुर्वृषस्कन्धसुबन्धुरांसकम् &c. VI. 25), and when necessary he can write with incisive force (cf. सिद्धं ह्येतद्वाचि वीर्यं द्विजानां बाह्वोर्वीर्यं यत्तु तत्क्षत्रियाणाम् &c. V. 32). The plays of Kálidása on the whole do not much aim at giving a realistic picture of the life of the society of his age; Bhavabhúti's do. The characters of Kálidása are more romantic and idealistic in their conception, those of Bhavabhúti's more realistic and varied. The idealism of one is almost equally balanced by the realism of the other, and herein each reader must finally judge for himself where the superiority lies.

III. THE PLAY.

(1) THE PLOT.

The Uttararámacharita is based on the well-known story of the Rámáyana, with certain changes introduced by the poet. We summarize below the plot of the play as developed in its seven Acts, for convenient and ready reference :—

Act I. After the Benediction and the announcement of the title of the play, with a few words about the author, the audience is informed in the Prelude (*Prastávaná*) that the monkey chiefs the holy sages, and other guests assembled in Ayodhyá for the coronation of Ráma after his victory over Râvaṇa, were allowed to return to their respective homes after festivities in their honour. There is an incidental allusion to a scandalons rumour about Sítá and a suggestion that evil might come to her by reason of it. The audience are further told that Râma has just repaired to the inner apartments to console Sîtâ who is depressed at the departure of her father Janaka. It is at this point that the actual play begins. Râma is introduced as trying to comfort the disconsolate Sîtâ, when a messenger arrives from the hermitage of Râma's brother-in-law, Ṛishyaśṛiṅga, with a blessing on Sîtâ from Vasishṭha and a direction from Arundhatî and others to Râma to satisfy the longings of Sîtâ, who was at that time far gone with child. Vasishṭha sends word to Râma to preserve the glory of his race by looking to the welfare of his subjects. Râma, in accepting the message, vows to sacrifice everything, "*even including Sîtá*," to the general good, thus foreshadowing as it were the abandonment of Sîtâ to please his subjects. Lakshmaṇa enters and proposes as a diversion that they may pay a visit to the picture-gallery, which they accordingly do. They inspect the paintings on the wall which present different scenes in their past lives; the reminiscences thus called up are both painful and delightful. While this is going on a spy employed by Râma to go about in the city to note how his rule was liked by the people comes in and whispers the evil news about the aspersions cast on the purity of Sîtâ. This is a staggering blow to Râma, who is torn by the internal conflict between his deep love for Sîtâ and the necessity of abandoning her to please his people. Finally he resolves to sacrifice her to his sense of duty, and orders Lakshmaṇa to take her to the forest and leave her there. Lakshmaṇa accordingly departs with Sîtâ to fulfil his elder brother's behest.

Act II. An interval of twelve years separates the first Act from the second. By means of an Interlude (*Vishkambhaka*), the poet informs the audience as to the events that have happened since after the close of the first Act. Sîtâ, being abandoned in the forest, gives birth to twin sons, who are taken charge of by Vâlmîki. He names them as Kuśa and Lava, and takes great pains to educate them in the various arts and sciences. In the meantime Râma had begun to perform the Aśvamedha sacrifice, Sîtâ's place as his consort being supplied by a golden image of her. The sacrificial horse was dispatched round the world with a large army having Lakshmaṇa's son, Chandraketu, as its general. The most recent act of Râma was his starting out in search of a Śûdra ascetic named Śambûka whose unauthorized penance had caused the death of a Brâhmaṇa's son. Here ends the Interlude. Then Râma is shown as discovering S'ambúka in the Daṇḍaka forest and killing him with a sword. The Śûdra ascetic appears before Râma in his celestial form and greets him for having raised him to heaven. The sight of the Daṇḍaka forest and Janasthâna reminds Râma of old happenings and arouses painful emotions. Finally he departs in the company of Śambúka to pay his respects to the sage Agastya who lived near by and who had expressed a desire to see him.

Act III. In an Interlude (*Vishkambhaka*) there is a dialogue between two river-goddesses, Tamasâ and Muralâ, which acquaints the audience how Agastya's wife Lopâmudrâ, through her deep affection for Râma, sends word to the goddess Godâvarî to protect Râma in his sad bereavement lest he might do violence to his person, in the midst of his old associations in the Daṇḍaka forest exciting sorrowful memories. Tamasâ tells Muralâ that there was no need of any such precaution, since the goddess Gaṅgâ had come to the river-goddess Godâvarî with Sîtâ whose touch possessed the magic power of reviving Râma from swoon, if need should arise; by the favour of Gaṅgâ Sîtâ was rendered invisible to Râma who therefore would not be aware of her presence. The whole Act is occupied with describing in detail the lamentations of Sîtâ and Râma occasioned by their presence in the forest closely associated with their past life. Râma afterwards returns to Ayodhyâ to finish the horse-sacrifice, and Sîtâ returns to Gaṅgâ to perform the ceremonies connected with the twelfth birth-day anniversary of her twins.

Act IV. In the Interlude (*Vishkambhaka*) the dialogue between two pupils of the sage Vâlmîki informs the audience that great preparations are being made in the penance-grove to welcome with due hospitality the sage Vasishṭha, and Râma's mothers, and Sîtâ's father Janaka, who are all on a short visit to Vâlmîki's hermitage as his guests. Janaka then enters alone, and in a pathetic soliloquy gives vent to his deep grief. Then at the request of Vasishṭha Râma's mother Kausalyâ comes to meet Janaka, and both are overpowered by the same feelings of grief and anguish. Kausalyâ espies at a distance a boy who resembles Râma in his dignity. They all guess as to who he may be, and send the Chamberlain to Vâlmîki to ascertain the truth. The boy is no other than Lava. He salutes the elders who are strangers to him, and tells how his preceptor Vâlmîki has written a history of Râma, the published portion of which ends with the abandonment of Sîtâ, the later part, connected with her exile, being yet unpublished. While they are thus engaged in conversation, the boys in the hermitage run to Lava, their fellow-student, to announce to him the arrival of a horse. They drag off Lava to behold the wonderful animal not seen ever before. An attendant arrives from Vâlmîki and tells Janaka that the sage replies that everything will be disclosed in time. Lava and the boys hasten towards the horse, and Lava, recognizing it to be a sacrificial horse, orders the boys to capture it and lead it to the hermitage. A soldier enters and advises Lava to desist from his foolishness. Lava defies him and welcomes in a truly martial spirit the opportunity thus afforded to challenge the whole hostile army to fight.

Act V. The soldiers are worsted by Lava and find themselves compelled to flee. The timely arrival of their leader Chandraketu fills them with hope of protection. Chandraketu observes Lava fighting like a true warrior, undaunted and undismayed by the vast forces ranged against him. Chandraketu openly commends the valour of Lava and challenges him to a fight. Lava in the meanwhile reduces the whole army to a paralysed silence by means of his magic missile (called *Jṛimbhaka*). This fills Chandraketu with wonder and amazement. He descends from his chariot and the two youths meet face to face. The conversation that ensues happens to turn upon Râma's heroic deeds. Lava makes some slighting remarks which provoke the anger of Chandraketu ; they thereupon hasten to the battle-field to fight out their dispute to the bitter end.

Act VI. In the Interlude (*Vishkambhaka*) between a Vidyâdhara and his wife, the audience are informed that a fierce combat is raging between the two princes. Fire-missiles are met by water-missiles, which are again counteracted by Wind-missiles. In a dreadful and uninterrupted manner the fight continues for some time, when it is arrested by the arrival of Râma on the battle-field. The fight is stopped, and Râma lovingly asks Chandraketu to embrace him, which the latter does. Then Chandraketu, in a true chivalrous spirit, requests his uncle to treat Lava with the same warmth of affection. Râma closely glances at Lava and is impressed with his martial bearing. Lava, on the other hand, is invaded by a sense of calmness and modesty. He learns from Chandraketu who the august personage before him is and salutes him on knowing that he is Chandraketu's uncle, Râma. Râma embraces him, and on being implored to forgive Lava's audacity commends it and asks him to withdraw the charm which had thrown the whole army into a stupor. A conversation goes on as to Lava's history, and the presence of Kuśa is announced. Kuśa learns from Lava that he is in the presence of Ráma, and salutes him. Ráma embraces him, and feels in the embrace a sense of parental affection and finds in the two boys a facial likeness to children of the Raghu race. On closer observation he notices in them a vivid resemblance to the features of Sîtâ ; this leads to a conversation which is painful to Râma in its associations. Râma views from a distance the approach of Vasishṭha, Arundhati

Kausalyâ and Janaka, and is overcome by a deep sense of affliction and shame to be thus brought face to face with Janaka. He hastens to meet them.

Act VII. This Act opens with a dramatic representation arranged to bring about a most touching union between Râma and Sitâ. The plan is Vâlmîki's, who chooses this method of convincing Râma of the spotless purity of Sitâ. The stage-manager announces the play and the cry of Sitâ is heard. The manager tells the audience that Queen Sitâ is about to throw herself into the waters of the Ganges. Râma excitedly calls upon her to stop, when he is reminded by Lakshmaṇa that it was merely a dramatic show. The goddenes Earth and Gaṅgâ try to console Sitâ. The conversation is carried on by the three, revealing step by step how Sitâ gave birth to her sons, and how they were to be brought up by Vâlmîki. The audience is convinced of the purity of Sitâ's married life, and even Râma calls upon his people to testify to it. Then Arundhatî introduces Sitâ in person to bring back to consciousness Râma who was under a deep swoon owing to great grief. Arundhatî then addresses the assembled people, and gently rebukes them for doubting the chastity of Sitâ, who is praised as being purity incarnate by even gods and goddesses. A most happy union takes place, and the customary Benediction (*Bharatavâkya*) ends the play amidst general rejoicings.

It will be noticed that the principal points in the development of the plot are :—(1) the arrival of the spy with the news about the evil rumours concerning Sîtá ; (2) the abandonment of Sîtá near Válmîki's hermitage ; (3) Râma's visit to the Daṇḍaka forest in connexion with Śambúka's austerities ; (4) his being brought in contact with Sîtá who remains invisible ; (5) the Aśvamedha sacrifice commenced by Ráma ; (6) the capture of the sacrificial horse by Lava at the hermitage of Válmîki ; (7) the fight between Lava and Chandraketu ; (8) Râma's arrival on the scene which puts an end to the fight ; (9) Râma's interview with Lava and Kuśa ; (10) the declaration of Sîtá's purity by the Earth, divine Ganges and Arundhatî ; (11) and the happy union of Râma and Sîtâ at the end.

(2) The Sources of the Plot and the Changes Effected by the Poet.

The story of Vâlmîki's Rámáyaṇa, on which Bhavabhûti has based his Uttar., is one that is most popular and held in universal reverence. The incidents of the drama are to be ound in the last Kâṇḍa of the Rámáyaṇa, necessary changes

being freely made to improve the dramatic effect and to ensure dramatic success. The Uttararâmacharita is a sequel to the Mahávîracharita, and the two plays together present a dramatic epitome of the history of Râma. The dramatic form has an advantage over the poetical one in that it produces more telling effect and appeals more to the heart, and thus the story remains firmly fixed in the memory with vivid precision. It is needless to give here a summary of the Rámáyaṇa account, for to the Hindu student the story must be already familiar in all its principal features. We shall therefore proceed to examine in what particulars the poet has departed from the original, and with what justification. He has made one most important change, and several others of a minor significance. The end of the original story is tragic, where Sîtâ is taken to the nether world by the goddess Earth, and Râma soon finishes his earthly career. But conforming to the canons of Sanskrit dramaturgy which prohibit a tragic end the poet changes the original and makes the play end with the happy meeting of Ráma, Sîtâ, and their sons, after a period of long, sorrowful separation. The Râmâyaṇa describes that there was a fight between Râma on one hand and his sons on the other, wherein Ráma was worsted; but Bhavabhûti does not wish to make his noble hero suffer martially at the hands of his sons, and he, therefore, arranges that the fight should be between Chandraketu and Lava, the status of the fighting princes being equal. Râma's meeting with Vásantî and the invisible presence of Sîtâ while he was in the Daṇḍaka forest are two inventions of the poet which enable him to describe the pathetic distress of his hero when separated from his beloved and to exhibit how deep-seated and changeless their affection was. The visit of the sage Vasishṭha with Arundhatî and Râma's mothers is not to be found in the original, but is invented by the poet, as their presence was necessary for bringing about the final catastrophe as conceived by him.

The influence of Válmîki's Râmâyaṇa is abundantly visible throughout this play, which contains actual quotations even from the famous epic (VI. 31, 32, 36). There is no reason, therefore, to doubt that he had the Râmâyaṇa before him; the question arises, however, whether there is any other version of the Ráma's story which he had access and which he utilized for the purposes of his play. The story of Ráma is given also in the Padma-puráṇa, in three different places; and, as the version given in the Pâtâla-Khaṇḍa has many points of similarity between Acts IV.–VI. of the Uttar., Dr. Belvalkar has come to the conclusion that probably Bhavabhûti derived his material from that source. We think, however, that there are not sufficient grounds for holding such a belief until the present Padma-purâṇa is shown to be definitely anterior to Bhavabhûti in date. The purâṇas have undergone various amplifications and sweeping revisions at various periods, and it is exceedingly doubtful whether their current recensions are identical with those that were extant fifteen centuries ago. The Padma-puráṇa, in particular, has long sections which bear close similarity to Kâlidása's *Raghuvaṃs'a* and *Śâkuntala*; they would appear to be the work of some one who was familiar with and admired the the works of India's most famous poet. Dr. Belvalkar himself seems to have been conscious of this characteristic of the puráṇas, for, after stating that "more probably, however, Bh. derived his material from......the Padma-puráṇa," he immediately states in the next paragraph that Bhavabhûti's source "must undoubtedly have been some account *like that in the Padma-puráṇa*."* [The italics are ours]. It should also be noticed that even the Padma-puráṇa account does not exactly tally with Bhavabhûti's, and the learned doctor himself has pointed out the variations. In view of these facts it is impossible to accept the Padma-puráṇa categorically as the basis of our play. Doubtless several forms of the Râma-history were current in ancient India, and Bhavabhûti might have derived supplementary material from these.

(3) Technical Remarks.

The Uttararámacharita is a *nâṭaka* proper among the various kinds of dramatic compositions. As regards the three principal requisites, the वस्तु or Plot is प्रख्यात or historical; the नेता or Hero is धीरोदात्त; and the नायिका (Sîtá) is स्वीया. There is no प्रतिनायक or प्रतिनायिका as in some other plays. The prevailing sentiment is करुण, infused with वीर and शृङ्गार on occasions. The student need not enter into the minor distinctions and divisions of अर्थप्रकृति, संधि &c., some of

*See pp. lvii—lviii of his Introd. to the Uttar. (Vol. XXI. of the Harvard Oriental Series).

which have been pointed out in their proper places in the commentary (*e. g.* बिन्दु on p. 45, चूलिका on p. 55, तोटक on p. 92 &c.).

As regards its external features, it opens with the customary नान्दी or Benediction, which is of the द्वादशपदा variety. Then in the प्रस्तावना or Prelude, the Sútradhára informs the audience of the title of the play, with some account of the author, and imparts some preliminary information, before the play properly begins with the entry of Ráma who is shown seated in company of Sîtá whom he is consoling. Then each of the three succeeding Acts has a विष्कम्भक or Interlude whose purpose is to acquaint the audience with what has occurred during the interval since the last Act. The fifth Act, which follows immediately after the fourth, does not possess any such Interlude; the sixth is provided with one; while in the seventh its purpose its served by the long speech of Lakshmaṇa in the beginning. In the seventh Act there is a short play within the play; it belongs to the variety of the one-act kind known as प्रेक्षणक. And finally there is the भरतवाक्य as usual.

(4) Time–Analysis of the Play.

The action comprised in the Uttar. is spread over a period of twelve years. It begins at a time when Sîtá had far gone with child (कठोरगर्भा p. 7). The first act begins early in the after-noon of some day before which the elders had left Ayodhyá to visit the hermitage of Ṛishyaśṛiṅga, who had commenced a sacrifice lasting for twelve years, and on which Janaka had left for his country. Sîtá was disconsolate at the departure of her father, and Ráma is shown as consoling her (p. 9); and this he does after leaving his judgement-seat (धर्मासनाद्विशति &c. p. 9) which he could do after mid-day; see Vik. II. 1. At the end of the Act Sîtâ starts for the forest in the company of Lakshmaṇa who had to abandon her there under Ráma's orders. There is an interval of about twelve years and three months between this Act and the second, as is clear from the words of A'treyî (संप्रति तु परिसमाप्तं तद् द्वादशवार्षिकं सत्रम् p. 52). Sîtá had given birth to twin sons soon after her abandonment, and these sons are now twelve years old. (*Cf.* अद्य खल्वायुष्मतोः कुशलवयोर्द्वादशस्य जन्मसंवत्सरस्य संख्यामङ्गलग्रन्थिरभिवर्तते । p. 66). The events of the third Act therefore happen exactly on their twelfth birth-day anniversary. The time of the second act seems to be the second watch of the early morning, the third Act following the same afternoon. Between the third Act and the next there does not appear to be any interval longer than that of a day. For we are told in the interclude to the sixth Act that Râma puts a stop to the fight between Chandraketu and Lave; and Râma could not have spent more than a day at Agastya's hermitage. The forth Act begins soon after the visit of Vasishṭha, Arundhatî &c. to Válmîki, which was referred to in Act II. (p. 53). The fifth Act immediately follows on the same day as the fourth; it is rather a continuation of it, and there is not an interval of more than an hour or so between the two. The sixth Act, too, follows immediately, as is shown by the fact that the fight between Chandraketu and Lava is still raging, the Vidyádhara witnessing it with his mate (p. 140). The seventh Act must follow soon after, probably the next day; for after Ráma was introduced to Kuśa and Lava in the sixth Act, not much time could be allowed to elapse before explanations were demanded of, and given by, Válmîki. It is not possible to fix the days of these Acts with any greater accuracy, as there are no references anywhere in the play to seasons or months.

(5) Critical and General Remarks.

The *Uttararámacharita* occupies a very high place in the dramatic literature of the Hindus, and it is accepted by common consent as a masterpiece of the author. Bhavabhúti appears to have possessed all the requisites of the true dramatist and poet,—active imagination, an exuberant fancy, the appreciation of the sublime and the beautiful, high power in characterization, a thorough knowledge of the workings of the human heart, and a ready sympathy with suffering humanity. In addition to that he has a most enviable command over language, and the rhythm and music of his verses is almost matchless in its fascinating power. He is a master in the art of depicting the different emotions of the human heart, and he displays everywhere a profound knowledge of the best situations calculated to enhance the impression of his delineations of such sentiments. His Uttararámacharita is essentially a drama of Pathos, and his indirect boast that the one sentiment of Pathos is depicted by him in many colours and varied phases (एको रसः करुण एव &c. III. 47) is not at all unmerited. Every Act adds to the impression produced upon the mind, and the reader is irresistibly moved to tears to hear the lamentations of Ráma, Sîtá, Janaka and other dignified personages suffering under the blows dealt by destiny. The melting tenderness of Râma's heart contrasted with his stern composure of mind when discharging what he conceives to be his kingly duty is supremely pathetic in effect, and justifies the author's observation that the hearts of the great are harder than adamant and softer than flower (II. 7).

In the construction of the play as a whole, the poet has shown considerable skill. In the first Act the introduction of the scene of the picture-gallery is very happily conceived, and the observations on the various scenes portrayed are most felicitous. In the second Act the dialogue between A'treyî and Vásantî and the description of the forest-scenery arousing painful memories of the past furnish matter of touching interest. The third Act is a masterly achievement of the creative imagination of the poet and stands unparalleled for its pathos. The whole situation is so exquisitely brought about that the lamentations of Ráma in the very presence of Sítá, her occasional contact reviving him and intensifying his grief, and Sîtá's majestic bearing even under the weight of grief and her idealistic womanly behaviour, all profoundly evoke the sympathy of the audience, impressing them with the painful seriousness of the occasion and adding a thousand-fold to the dramatic effect of the play. The fourth Act introduces elderly and holy personages; the audience looks upon them with deep feelings of reverence and adoration and weeps with them in their sorrow, consequent on the supposed loss of Sîtá. Towards the end a welcome diversion is created by the young boys who come trooping in and carry off Lava to witness a horse. The fifth Act is martial in its setting, and herein our author shows himself as great an adept in portraying heroism as he was in depicting pathos; the dignified and chivalric behaviour of Chandraketu and Lava, the defiance they hurl at each other, and their mutual courtesy and generosity in appreciating the good points of the antogonist—all these act as an exhilirating tonic after the preceding mournful incidents. The sixth Act is the weakest among all; it merely serves as a preliminary to the *dénouement*, and prepares the audience to witness the imminent union of Ráma with his queen. In the seventh Act, use is made of a theatrical representation arranged by Válmîki as a contrivance to bring about the desired union. Sîtá's chastity is once more established in the presence of deities and holy personages, and there is an end to her misfortunes. This play within a play is a most ingenious device, and puts one in mind of a similar contrivance in Shakespeare's *Hamlet*.

The one serious charge that can be brought against the play is its lack of dramatic action. The reader must have noticed that the story moves little, if at all, through the second and the third Acts, which are full of psychological interest as containing fine analysis of emotion, but help little towards the *dénouement*. The same can be said of the battle-scene in the fifth Act, which provides good reading and might possess spectacular interest, but does not bring us any the nearer to the catastrophe. This lack of dramatic action has made Dr. Macdonell describe the work as "rather a dramatic poem than a play," and there is some justification, as we have shown, for this remark. Indeed, as one critic has pointed out, the poet could well have omitted the second and the fifth Acts, and given us a shorter Náṭaka in five Acts, without much marring the beauty or the interest of the piece.

(6) THE PRINCIPAL CHARACTERS.

RA'MA

The Hero of Válmîki's Rámáyaṇa is the cherished idol of millions of worshipping Hindus, who regard him as the seventh incarnation of God and to whom he is the embodiment of every social and domestic virtue. He is endeared to their hearts by his glorious self-negation and sense of filial duty when he renounced the kingdom and repaired to the forest in order that his father's promise should be observed in word and deed. He is still more endeared to them by his excellent rule after he became a king, when his sole concern was to keep the people contented and happy, so that Ráma-Rájya ("the rule of Ráma") came to be in popular parlance a term descriptive of an idealistically perfect government. In the Uttar. the poet has dwelt on this part of his character, and has shown him as an ideal husband and father, and a model of domestic virtues. Ráma is the most illustrious example of what may be called the faithfulness of the husband to his wife. His love for Sîtá is genuine and pure and deep rooted. It is true that he had to abandon her, and he did abandon her to the sacrifice of his domestic bliss and mental peace, but therein we note the exemplary sacrifice of affection to duty. This kingly trait of his character is fully expressed when he declares—

स्नेहं दयां च सौख्यं च यदि वा जानकीमपि ।
आराधनाय लोकानां मुञ्चतो नास्ति मे व्यथा ॥ (I. 12)

To ensure the good of his subjects he considered his *highest duty,* and to it must be sacrificed all questions of personal happiness. Sitá was as much his life and soul as his own individuality. (*Cf.* त्वं जीवितं त्वमसि मे हृदयं द्वितीयं &c. III. 26), but he was prepared to surrender everything, nay his very life, to secure the contentment of his people; and manfully he did it, though as a gentle-hearted and affectionate husband he could not but weep, and weep bitterly, for the loss of his wife whom he knew he was abandoning for no fault of hers. Her purity and chastity were beyond doubt, so far as he himself was concerned; but if they were questioned by his subjects, he must take immediate steps to satisfy them, even by giving her up who was his life and soul. Critics of Ráma's abandonment of Sîtá, among whom might be counted Vàsantî in the play (*cf.* अयि कठोर यशः किल ते प्रियं किमयशो ननु घोरमतः परम् &c. III. 27), have found fault with Ràma for his undue solicitude for the happiness of his over-nice subjects. In this they are chiefly influenced by their sympathy for the helplessness of Sitá, but they miss the very beauty of Ràma's character when they take such a narrow view of his action. Judged by the ideal standard of duty, Ráma deserves our approbation for his unparalleled self-sacrificing act rather than condemnation for his seemingly cruel behaviour; and to the great no standard of duty is acceptable except the ideal one, as they cannot tolerate any compromise where the question of duty comes in. No one was more conscious of the cruelty of his act than Ráma himself, as is evident from his utterances in the drama; but, as he lived for his people, he was bound to please them at any cost. And he was not so cruel, after all, for he took care to see that Sîtá was not left in the tenantless desert as a prey to wild animals; she was abandoned near the hermitage of Vàlmîki by Lakshmaṇa, who must have done so not without specific instructions from Ràma.

Many other minor traits of his character are beautifully exemplified in the drama. Observe how he shows his inborn humility by his silently ignoring one of the most famous episodes of his career, *viz.* his encounter with Paraśuráma, when his attention was being particularly drawn to it by Lakshmaṇa (p. 21); even Sîtá is struck by the विनयमाहात्म्य of her lord, whom she openly compliments on the same (*cf.* सुट्ठु शोभसे आर्यपुत्र एतेन विनयमाहात्म्येन p. 21). Again, note the noble generosity and forgivingness of his disposition which is illustrated when Lakshmaṇa begins to refer to another noted episode, *viz.* the evil machinations of Kaikeyî and Manthará to accomplish his exile to the forest (p. 23). With characteristic largeness of heart Râma wishes to pass it over and is ready to forgive and forget the evil others have wrought unto him. The incidents of his sending Śatrughna against Lavaṇa and himself starting to pursue another evil-doer, *viz.* Śambûka, illustrate further how ready he was to subordinate personal grief to the welfare of his subjects. His faithfulness in conjugal life is peculiarly brought to the notice of the audience when they learn that Ráma did not marry again after he lost Sîtá, the requirement of sacrificial ceremonies being met by keeping a golden image of his wife by his side (p. 53). The first two Acts bring out all the essential characteristics of Ráma's nature, and the succeeding Acts tend to strengthen the impression created by the first two, particularly bringing to our notice his tenderness and easy sensibility as well as his fortitude in the face of calamities. In brief, Válmîki's hero has not suffered in the least at the hands of our poet-dramatist ; he is the same idealized type of individual and kingly virtues.

SÎTA'.

Sîtá, the heroine of the Rámáyaṇa, is one of those charming pictures of feminine excellence of which the ancient history of India furnishes numerous examples. She belongs to the noble company of ladies like Sávitrî, Damayantî, Draupadî and others, who have been the Hindu ideals of womanly virtues, and who have exalted womanhood to the height of divine perfection. It is a noteworthy coincidence that all of them were subjected to very severe tests in which their purity, courage, patience, and other virtues were severely tried, and nobly did they come out through those tests. Whenever we think of the glory of A'ryan womanhood exhibited in the lives of those ladies, the meek and sorrowful figure of Sítá presents itself prominently before our mental eye and evokes our heart-felt sympathy and admiration. Sítá seems to have been the most unfortunate of these women; ill-luck pursued her since her very childhood, and her life presents a tragic tale of uncommon and prolonged misery, of dark and unmerited suspicions, of days passed in the wilderness and of time spent in captivity.

Bhavabhúti has dwelt on one particular episode in all this tale of woe, *viz.* her abandonment by Ráma immediately after his coronation. This enforced separation is the cruellest blow to one of her affectionate nature; how loving and trusting she was and how she worshipped her lord and hung upon his every word of his is most vividly shown by the poet in the first Act. (*Cf.* अत एव राघवकुलधुरंधर आर्यपुत्रः । p. 15; अयि देव एवं मम कारणात्क्लान्त आसीः । p. 28; आर्यपुत्र युष्माभिरपि तत्र गन्तव्यम् । p. 33; तस्मै कोपिष्यामि यदि तं प्रेक्षमाणा आत्मनः प्रभविष्यामि । p. 46). The same qualities of Sítá are shown in greater relief in the third Act during the mysterious meeting between herself and Ráma. She considers herself to blame for the seeming cruelty of Ráma in abandoning her, and would not tolerate that even a privileged person like Vásantí should find fault with Ráma for that (*cf.* प्रियार्हः खलु सर्वस्यार्यपुत्रो विशेषतो मम प्रियसख्याः । p. 81). She is ever ready to merge her individuality into that of her lord; it is *his* happiness which is foremost in her mind, and not her own. A'ryan women are from time immemorial distinguished for their disinterested love and self-abnegation, and Sítá is an unrivalled embodiment of these virtues. The perfect love that existed between the pair has been put in immortal words by the author of the Rámáyaṇa, which even Bhavabhúti could not improve upon; so he is content to quote them (*vide* प्रकृत्यैव प्रिया सीता &c. VI. 31, 32). And he has succeeded pre-eminently in his endeavour to picture this perfect ideal of wedded love.

CHANDRAKETU.

Chandraketu, the son of Lakshmaṇa, is introduced as the commandant of the army accompanying the sacrificial horse.

He is a prince, heroic, courtly in demeanour, frank, sensible to the merits of others, and free to appreciate them. Though young he is fired with the true martial spirit of a Kshatriya warrior, and the very responsible duty entrusted to him of guarding the sacrificial horse bespeaks the high confidence placed in his valour by Ráma. When he sees Lava fighting with his whole army single-handed, he was filled with wondering admiration, and is frank enough to admit the superior bravery of the boy-warrior who, in no wise daunted by the fearful odds against him, is dealing deadly arrows with great martial activity. Notice the deep tone of irony which pervades his speech which censures his followers for making a combined rush against one who is fighting single-handed (संख्यातीतैः...धिग्वो धिगस्मान् V. 12). Chandraketu gives ample proof of his chivalry and sense of martial justice when he declines to fight from his chariot and descends on the ground (p. 134). The dialogue that follows is worthy of the youthful and bold spirit of the two heroes. Chandraketu's regard for his uncle Ráma is highly characteristic, and Lava's attitude of defiance is not marred by any want of respect for the head of the solar race. Chandraketu's request (p. 144) that Ráma may look upon Lava with fatherly affection is a further proof of the magnanimity of his heart which is free from all traces of jealousy even though Lava had proved his own superiority by the use of the Jṛimbhaka missiles.

LAVA AND KUS'A.

The twin brothers are portrayed as being in every respect worthy of their illustrious father. Brought up in the midst of wholesome surroundings under the direct guardianship of Válmiki, they display all the virtues of Kshatriya princes in the highest degree. From the description of Lava (IV. 19, 20) it is seen that he is represented as following the life of a क्षात्रियब्रह्मचारिन् (a boy-warrior); he is modest, childlike and guileless, resembling in every respect his parent in his features and outward form, having, as Janaka puts it (IV. 22), the same voice, the same modesty and the same natural dignity. In the fifth Act we are brought face to face with Lava's martial spirit, and the dignified opposition which he offers even to the hero of the Rámáyaṇa excites our admiration. Sumantra describes (p. 136) his nature as an admixture of दर्प (boldness) and सौजन्य (humility), and the description is aptly fitting. In the presence of his elders, Lava is humble and reverent; compare how dutifully he bows to Janaka, Arundhatî &c. in Act IV. (p. 115). But as a proud warrior he could not brook the overbearing attitude of his rival, however great he might be; he was not to be frightened by any flaunting vanity on the other side (see IV. 28). In the mouth of Ráma the poet has put a happy śloka (VI. 9) which exactly portrays Lava's martial dignity. Lava's tender feelings are aroused in the presence of his parent; he bows down in childlike simplicity at the feet of the latter, and gives evidence of his good breeding, all the while remaining unaware of the real relation subsisting between him and himself.

Kuśa is brought on the stage for a comparatively short space of time; but even then he proves himself a worthy elder brother of the intrepid Lava. His very entrance is a sufficient proof of the martial fire that is burning within him (*see* VI. 18, दत्तेन्द्राभयदक्षिणै &c.). Ráma has described his appearance in exceedingly choice words in the well-known śloka हरिस्तृणीकृतजगत्त्रयसत्त्वसारा &c. (VI. 19). Like Lava, Kuśa too is overcome by the same feeling of reverence for Ráma; his hostile attitude quickly vanishes, and he salutes Ráma with proper humility.

VA'LMÎKI.

This exalted sage takes more than common interest in the family of the Raghus, and is tenderly attached to Ráma and Sîta. He is endowed with prophetic vision; and though remaining in the background he endeavours in a very special manner to establish the chastity of Sîtá and to bring about the union of the separated royal pair. Though a sage distinguished for his deep piety and meditation of the Supreme Brahma, he is not insensible to the promptings of the heart; he is ever tender and kind-hearted, and exercises a purifying influence over all.

DRAMATIS PERSONS

—:o:—

MALES.

सूत्रधार—The chief manager of the play.
नट—An actor.
राम—The King of Ayodhyá (Hero).
कञ्चुकिन्—A chamberlain.
गृष्टि (कञ्चु०)—Name of Daśaratha's chamberlain.
अष्टावक्र—A Bráhmaṇa ascetic.
लक्ष्मण—Ráma's brother.
दुर्मुख—A spy employed by Ráma.
शम्बूक—A Śúdra ascetic.
दाण्डायन, सौधातकि—Two pupils of Válmíki.
जनक—King of Videha, father of Sítâ.
लव, कुश—The twin sons of Ráma.
चन्द्रकेतु—Lakshmaṇa's son.
सुमन्त्र—Chandraketu's charioteer.
वाल्मीकि—A sage, the author of the Rámáyaṇa.
विद्याधर—A semi divine being.
बटवः—Boys (in Act IV.).
पुरुषः—A man from Chandraketu's army.

FEMALES.

सीता—Râma's wife and Queen (Heroine).
अरुन्धती—Wife of Vasishtha.
कौसल्या—Râma's mother.
तापसी (आत्रेयी)—A female ascetic.
वनदेवता (वासन्ती)—A sylvan goddess.
मुरला, तमसा—Two rivers (personified).
पृथिवी—Sîtâ's mother, the Earth (personified).
गङ्गा—The river Ganges (personified).
विद्याधरी—The mate of the Vidyádhara.
प्रतीहारी—A door-keeper.

OTHER PERSONS MENTIONED.

वसिष्ठ—A sage, the preceptor of the Raghu family.
ऋष्यशृङ्ग—Râma's brother-in-law.
And many other characters from the Rámáyaṇa, *e. g.* Sugrîva, Máruti, Ûrmilá &c &c.

SCENE.

Act I., Ayodhyâ; Act II., Daṇḍakáraṇya (Janasthána); Act III., Daṇḍakáraṇya (Pañchavaṭî); Acts IV.—VII., the region near and around Vâlmîki's hermitage.

———

IMPORTANT ABBREVIATIONS.

A. G.—Apte's Guide to Sanskrit Composition.

A.-K.—Amarakośa.

Bg—Bhagavadgîtâ.

Bh—Bhartṛihari's Śatakas.*

Bhaṭṭ—Bhaṭṭikâvya.*

Bṛih.-Up—Bṛihadâraṇyakopanishad.

Br.-Sû.—Brahmasûtras.

Chhán.-Up.—Chhândogyopanishad.

Com.—Commentary; commentator.

D.-K—Daśakumáracharita.*

D.-R.—Daśarûpaka.

Gh.—Ghanaśyâma (com. on Uttara.)

Gît.—Gîtagovinda.

Hitop.—Hitopadesa.*

Kád.—Kádambarî.*

Kám.-Nît.—Kâmandaka's Nîtisara.

Káv.-D.—Kávyâdarśa.

Káv.-S.—Kávyálaṃkára-Sútras of Vámana.

Kir.—Kirátárjunîya.*

K.-P.—Kávya-Prakáśa.

Kum.—Kumárasaṃbhava.*

Mah.-. Bh-Mahábhárata.

Málav.—Málavikágnimitra.*

Malli.—Mallinâtha.

Mál.-Mádh—Málatî-Mádhava.*

Megh.—Meghadûta*.

Mṛich.—Mṛichchhakaṭika.*

M.-S.—Manusmṛiti.

Mud.—Mudrárákshasa.*

Mv.—Mahávîracharita.

M.-W.—Sir Monier-Williams.

Nág.—Nágánanda.*

Páṇ.—Páṇini's Ashṭádhyâyî.

Pt.—Pañchatantra.*

Ragh.—Raghuvaṃśa.*

Râmá.—Rámáyaṇa.

Ratn.—Ratnâvalî.*

Ṛig-V.—Ṛig-Veda.

Ṛitu.—Ṛitusaṃhára.*

S'âk.—Śákuntala.*

S.-D.—Sáhitya-Darpaṇa.

Sid.-K.—Siddhánta-Kaumudî.

S'is'.—Śiśupálavadha.

Up.—Upanishad.

Uttar.—Uttararámacharita.*

Várt.—Várttika.

Veṇî.—Veṇîsaṃhára.*

Vik.—Vikramorvaśîya.*

Vîra.—Vîrarághava (Com. on Uttara.)

V.-P.—Vishṇu-Puráṇa.

---

* Annotated by the Editor.

भूमिका ।

भवभूतेः संबन्धाद्भूधरभूरेव भारती भाति ।
एतत्कृतकारुण्ये किमन्यथा रोदिति ग्रावा ॥

—आचार्यगोवर्धनस्य ।

इह खलु सकलविद्याकलाकलापादिपीठेऽस्मिन्भारते वर्षे निजयशःसुरभीकृतदिगन्तरालाः प्रतिभाशालिनः परःशताः कवीश्वरा भासकालिदासादयः स्वकृत्याभरणैर्वाग्देवी रुचिरं मण्डयन्ति स्म । तेषु चैकतमः श्रीभवभूतिर्नाटकचक्रवर्ती **महावीरचरितमालती-माधव-उत्तररामचरिता**ख्यरूपकत्रयस्य प्रणेता प्रधानपदमारूढ इति सर्वैर्विपश्चिद्भिरभ्युपपन्नम् । स चायं कविः कान्यकुब्जाधिपस्य यशोवर्मणः सदसमलंचकारेत्यत्र विषये " कविर्वाक्पतिराजश्रीभवभूत्यादिसेवितः । जितो ययौ यशोवर्मा तद्गुणस्तुतिबन्दिताम् ॥ " इति राजतरङ्गिणीस्थं पद्यं मानम् । स च यशोवर्मा ख्रिस्तीयसप्तमशतकोत्तरार्धे राज्यमकरोदिति यूरोपीयविदुषां निर्णयो येन भवभूतेरपि समयः ख्रिस्तीयसप्तमशतकान्तपातीति सुव्यक्ततया प्रतीतिमारोहति । अनेन च कविना स्वरचितप्रबन्धानां प्रस्तावनास्वात्मनो वंशादिकं किंचिदितिवृत्तमुपनिबद्धं तद्यथा । आसीद्दक्षिणापथे पद्मपुरं नाम नगरम् । तत्र केचित्तैत्तिरीयाः काश्यपाश्चरणगुरवः पङ्क्तिपावनाः पञ्चाग्नयो धृतव्रताः सोमपीथिन उदुम्बरनामानो ब्रह्मवादिनः प्रतिवसन्ति स्म । तदीयवंशे महाकविर्नाम कश्चिद्वाजपेययाजी द्विजः समजनि यस्मात्पञ्चमः पुरुषो भवभूतिः । भवभूतेः पिता नीलकण्ठः पितामहो भट्टगोपालो जननी जतुकर्णी गुरुश्च ज्ञाननिधिः । यथार्थनाम्नो ज्ञाननिधेः सकाशादधीतवानयं कविर्व्याकरणतर्कमीमांसादीनि शास्त्राणि । अस्य भवभूतिरिति पितृकृतं नामासीत्पश्चाच्च श्रीकण्ठ इति वाक्संपदधिष्ठानतया नामान्तरमस्य संबभूवेति भाति । केचित्तु भवभूत्यभिधानं ' साम्बा पुनातु भवभूतिपवित्रमूर्तिः ' इत्यन्तं, ' गिरिजायाः स्तनौ वन्दे भवभूतिसिताननौ ' इत्यन्तं वा पद्यमुपरचितवतोऽस्य कवेर्जातं श्रीकण्ठाख्यैवास्य पितृकृतेति मन्यन्ते । ' अस्मै कवय ईश्वर एव भिक्षुरूपेणागत्य भूतिं दत्तवानिति वदन्ति । एवं च भवात् भूतिर्यस्येति भवभूतिरित्यन्वर्थः ' इत्यपि केचिदाहुः । उपरिनिर्दिष्टरूपकत्रयं विहाय नान्यः कोऽपि भवभूतिरचितः प्रबन्धः समुपलभ्यते । शार्ङ्गधरपद्धत्यादिषु भवभूतिकृततया निवेशितानि कानिचित्स्फुटपद्यानि वर्तन्ते यान्युपर्युक्तनाटकत्रये न चक्षुर्गोचरीभवन्ति । तस्माद्भवभूतिनाऽन्येऽपि केचिद्ग्रन्थाः प्रणीयन्तेति नासंभावनीयम् ।

भवभूतिप्रबन्धेषु " श्लेषः प्रसादः समता माधुर्यं सुकुमारता । अर्थव्यक्तिरुदारत्वमोजः कान्तिसमाधयः ॥" इति दण्ड्युक्ताः सर्वेऽपि काव्यगुणाः समुल्लसन्तीति व्यक्तमेव प्रेक्षावताम् । " यत्प्रौढित्वमुदारता च वचसां यच्चार्थतो गौरवं तच्चेदस्ति ततस्त-

देव गमक पाण्डित्यवैदग्ध्ययोः ।" इति मालतीमाधवप्रस्तावनायामुपनिबद्धं पद्यार्धमेव सुयुक्ततयापवर्णयति कवेरस्य गुणविशेषशालिनीं निबन्धनचातुरीम् । रसभावादीनां तेषु तेषु स्थलेषु निपुणमुपन्यासेन प्रतिभाया दिगन्तसंचारिविशालत्वेनार्थानुरूपशब्दरचनया सर्वाङ्गीणमनोज्ञतया च प्रबन्धानां कविरयं सहृदयप्रेक्षकाणां सुतरां श्लाघ्य इति सुविदितमेव सुधियाम् । कविनाऽनेन महावीरचरितमालतीमाधवयोरनुक्रमं वीरशृङ्गारौ प्रधानतयोपवर्णितौ करुणश्च रसोऽत्रोत्तररामचरिते मुख्यत्वेन समुपन्यस्तो यं प्रत्यक्षीकृतवतां रसिकानां श्लाघाभूयिष्ठा निरसूया वाचो निरगच्छन् । आहुश्च पण्डिताः–'उत्तरे रामचरिते भवभूतिर्विशिष्यते' इति । वीररसोऽप्यत्रैव पञ्चमाङ्के लवचन्द्रकेतुसंप्रहारे समुपयुज्यमान आकर्षति चेतः सामाजिकानाम् । रसादिपरिणतिपरीक्षणानुबन्धेनोत्तरचरितं प्रागुक्तनाटकद्वयनिर्माणानन्तरं कविना व्यरच्यतेत्यापाततोऽभिव्यक्तं भवति । एवमेव च महावीरचरितमस्य प्रथमा कृतिरित्यपि सुशक्यं परिज्ञातुम् । अस्मिन्नुत्तरचरिते भगवतो जानकीजाने रामचन्द्रस्य राज्याभिषेकात्परं सीतात्यागमारभ्य चरितांशः प्रायः श्रीवाल्मीकिरामायणकथानुसारेण सप्तस्वङ्केषु विभज्य समुपवर्णितः । अत्र वस्तुभूतस्य रामचरितस्य पद्मपुराणोपवर्णितरामचरितेन किमपि साम्यमालोक्यते यद्विचारयतां प्रादुरासीत्केषांचित्तर्को यदहो पद्मपुराणमेवोत्तरचरितनाटकस्य मूलमिति । किं त्वद्योपलभ्यमानं पद्मपुराणं भवभूतेरर्वाक्तनमुताहो प्राक्कालिकमिति विषये न संख्यावतामैकमत्यमित्यलं मूलान्तरकल्पनोपजल्पैः । अथात्र नाटकोपनिबद्धं कथावस्त्वङ्कानुक्रमेण सारांशतोऽस्माभिः सुलभावबोधार्थमत्रोपक्षिप्यते—

प्रथमोऽङ्कः—नान्दीपठनानन्तरं सूत्रधारप्रवेशे रामचन्द्रस्य राज्याभिषेकोत्सवानन्तरं स्वगृहान्गतेषु प्लवङ्गराक्षसब्रह्मर्षिराजर्षिसमूहेषु गुरुजनोऽपि ऋष्यशृङ्गस्य दशरथजामातुर्द्वादशवार्षिके सत्रे संनिहितो भवितुं कठोरगर्भामपि सीतां विमुच्य प्रयातः । ततो विदेहान्निवृत्ते जनके विमनस्कायाः सीतायाः परिसान्त्वनाय रामभद्रो वासगृहं यास्यतीति कथांशः प्रस्तुतः । ततः सीतारामप्रवेशे दुर्मनायनानां देवीमुपसान्त्वयति रामे ऋष्यशृङ्गाश्रमादष्टावक्रो वसिष्ठसंदेशमादायायोध्यां प्राप्तः । स च संदेशो यथा—"जामातृयज्ञेन वयं निरुद्धास्त्वं बाल एवासि नवं च राज्यम् । युक्तः प्रजानामनुरञ्जने स्यास्तस्माद्यशो यत्परमं धनं वः ॥" इति । तं च रामः "स्नेहं दयां च सौख्यं च यदि वा जानकीमपि । आराधनाय लोकानां मुञ्चतो नास्ति मे व्यथा" इति प्रतिवदन्प्रतिजग्राह । अथ सीताविनोदनार्थं लक्ष्मणविज्ञापनानुरोधेनालेख्यवीथिकाभिदर्शने प्रस्तुते तत्र स्वपूर्वचरितालेख्यानि दृष्ट्वा तत्तद्वृत्तान्तस्मरणेन पूर्वानुभूतानां हर्षविरहशोकादीनां भावानां पुनःसंवेदनं रामचन्द्रस्य जातम् । चित्रगतदण्डकोपान्तवनलक्ष्मीदर्शनेन सीतायाः पुनरपि तासु वनराजिषु विहरणे भागीरथ्यवगाहने च दोहदः समुदपद्यत । तं संपादयितुं रथमुपस्थापयेति रामो लक्ष्मणमाददेश । अत्रान्तरे दुर्मुखो नाम राजापसर्प आगत्य सीताया रावणगृहवासमधिकृत्य जनापवादं रामस्य कर्णेऽकथयद्येन सपद्यसौ मूर्छामवाप । समाश्वस्य च 'सतां केनापि कार्येण लोकस्याराधनं व्रतम्' इति सीतात्या-

गमेव परं कर्तव्यं मन्वानो राजा बहु विलप्य लक्ष्मणाय तादृशीं रह आज्ञां ददौ । सीतालक्ष्मणौ चारण्यं प्रति रथमधिष्ठाय प्रतस्थाते ।

द्वितीयोऽङ्कः—अत्र विष्कम्भके आत्रेयीवासन्तीप्रवेशेऽङ्कद्वयसमयान्तर्वर्ति वृत्तमभिज्ञापितं तद्यथा । लक्ष्मणेन वने परित्यक्ता सीतादेवी दारकद्वयं प्रसूतवती । तच्च यमजं पुत्रद्वयं भगवता वाल्मीकिना धात्रीकर्मतः परिगृह्य सस्नेहं पोषितं रक्षितं सर्वविद्यासु पारगत्वं प्रापितं च । रामेण च सीताया हिरण्मयीं प्रतिकृतिं सहचारिणीत्वेन समुपस्थाप्याश्वमेधः क्रतुः प्रक्रान्तः । मध्याश्वं विसृज्य यथाशास्त्रं तस्य रक्षितॄन्परिकल्प्य लक्ष्मणात्मजेन चन्द्रकेतुना समधिष्ठितं चतुरङ्गसाधनं तमनु प्रहितम् । स्वयं च राजा रामचन्द्रः शम्बूकं नाम कंचित्तपस्यन्तं शूद्रं तपस्यनधिकारित्वाच्छीर्षच्छेद्यमन्विष्यन्संचरतीति । तदनु दण्डकायां शम्बूकं समासाद्य रामस्तं हत्वा तत्रैव कंचित्कालं तत्तत्स्थानावलोकनस्मारितपूर्ववृत्तान्तः स्नेहखेदनिर्वेदाद्यनुभवंश्चचार । ततश्च समीपवर्तिनं भगवन्तमगस्त्यं मुनिं द्रष्टुं प्रायात् ।

तृतीयोऽङ्कः—अत्र विष्कम्भके तमसामुरलासंवादेऽयं वृत्तान्तः परिज्ञापितः । अगस्त्याश्रमात्परापतन्रामः पुनर्दण्डकां प्राप्य तत्र सीताविप्रलम्भशोकसमाकुलः सन्न ज्ञायेत किं विधास्यतीति साशङ्का भगवती भागीरथी सीतासमेता गोदावरीपरिसरे दण्डकारण्यैकदेशमुपागता । सीतादेवी चावनितलवर्तिनी देवताप्रभावात्सर्वेषां भूतानामदृश्याऽवर्ततेति । तदनु यथापूर्वनिरूपितं रामो मूर्छामापन्नः सीता च ससंभ्रमं स्वयमदृश्यैव सती तमात्मकरस्पर्शेन संज्ञां लम्भितवती । साह्लादमुच्छ्वसितो रामचन्द्रस्तु चक्षुषी उन्मील्य यावदवलोकयति तावन्न किमपि तत्र लक्ष्यते । ततः पूर्वपरिचितान्करिकलभकगिरिमयूरहरिणकादीन्दृष्ट्वा संवर्धितमन्युभारो रुदन्रामो वनदेवतया वासन्त्या भृशमुपालब्धः पुनरपि मूर्छामभ्यापन्नः । भूयश्च सीता यथापूर्वमदृश्यैव वर्तमाना तं हृदि ललाटे च स्पृष्ट्वा चेतनां प्रत्यापादयत् । अन्ते च विविधं विलप्य प्रागुपक्रान्तमश्वमेधं क्रतुं समापयिष्यन्रामः पुष्पकं विमानराजमारुह्यायोध्यामभिप्रतस्थे ।

चतुर्थोऽङ्कः—अत्र विष्कम्भके वाल्मीकिच्छात्रयोः प्रवेशेनेदं ज्ञापितं भवति । परिसमाप्तद्वादशवार्षिकसत्रस्य ऋष्यशृङ्गस्याश्रमात्सारुन्धतीको वसिष्ठो राममातृभिरनुगतो भगवतो वाल्मीकेराश्रमपदं प्राप्तः । तत्रैव च विदेहाधिपो जनकोऽपि प्रियसुहृदं वाल्मीकिं द्रष्टुमायात इति । अथ जनकस्तत्र कौसल्यादिभिर्दशरथदारैर्मिलित्वा सर्वं यथावृत्तं संस्मृत्य परं निर्वेदमापन्नः । तेषु च सीतावियोगविमनस्केषु भगवत्याऽरुन्धत्या ‘ सर्वमिदं कल्याणोदर्कं भविष्यति ’ इति वसिष्ठवचनं स्मृतिमुपस्थाप्य तेषां समाश्वासनं विहितम् । अत्रान्तरे तत्रैवाश्रमे रामतनयं महाभागं कुमारलवं दृष्ट्वा तस्य च रामभद्रेणाकृतिद्युतिवाणीविनयादिषु परतरं साम्यमुत्प्रेक्ष्य कोऽयं कुमार इति कुतूहलिभिस्तद्वृत्तं जिज्ञासमानैर्विज्ञापितो वाल्मीकिः ‘ ज्ञातव्यमेतदवसरे भवद्भिः ’ इति संदिदेश । आश्रमवासिनो बटवश्च श्रीमतो रामचन्द्रस्याश्वमेधिकं तुरंगमं स्वाश्रमसंनिकर्षे चरन्तमुपवीक्ष्य हयमात्रस्यादृष्टपूर्वतया तं कमप्यद्भुतं पशुं मन्यमानास्तदवलोक-

नार्थे लवं हठादाकृष्य नीतवन्तः। अश्वमधिकृत्य तस्य रक्षितृगणस्य प्रौढिवादपराण्यक्षराण्युपश्रुत्य लवस्य संदीपनं जातम्। अवमत्य चायुधीयश्रेणीः सज्जीकृतशरासनो लवः क्षत्रियकुमारानुरूपं धीरोद्धतमुपक्रम्याश्वं बलादपहृतवान्।

पञ्चमोऽङ्कः—अथापहृतेऽश्वे तदीयरक्षकसैनिकैः सार्धं लवस्यैकाकिनः संग्रामः संबभूव यस्मिन्स्वीयजृम्भकास्त्राणामद्भुतप्रभावेण लवेनाखिलं तद्बलं क्षणेन निःसंज्ञतां नीतम्। ततश्चन्द्रकेतुः समरभूमिं प्रापत्। आसीच्चास्य लवेन सह वीरपुरुषोचितः परस्परसंलापः। चन्द्रकेतोर्महानुभावस्य प्रसन्नकर्कशाभिर्वीरवचनप्रयुक्तिभिर्लवस्य चेतः समाकृष्यत। चन्द्रकेतोरपि हृदयं विक्रान्ते लवेऽहेतुना पक्षपातेन स्नेहनिगडितं बभूव। किं तु संभाषणवशादुत्तरादुत्तरे संप्रजाते रामचन्द्रस्य चरितमुद्दिश्य लवेनोपक्षिप्तानुपालम्भानक्षाम्यंश्चन्द्रकेतुः स्फुरितक्रोधो युद्धेनैव वादमन्तयितुकामो लवेन सह विमर्दक्षमां भूमिमवतीर्णः।

षष्ठोऽङ्कः—अत्र विष्कम्भके विद्याधरमिथुनमुखेन कविना लवचन्द्रकेतुसमरवर्णनं कृतम्। ततः प्रवृत्त एवानयोः संगरे श्रीमात्रामचन्द्रस्तत्रोपगत्य तयोरायोधनमुपशमितवान्। चन्द्रकेतुर्लवस्य पराक्रमं भृशतया प्रशशंस। रामस्यापि मनस्तस्मिन्कथमपि निमित्तनिरपेक्षमुपस्निग्धमभवत्। ततो रामाज्ञया लवो जृम्भकास्त्राणि यावदुपसंहरति तावत्तस्य ज्येष्ठो भ्राता कुश उद्धतं पराक्रमं तत्रोपस्थितः। ततस्तयोः कुमारयोः स्ववंशसंवादिनीमाकृतिं प्रेक्ष्य किमिमौ जानकीतनयौ स्यातामिति रामस्यापि चित्तं संदेहस्यूतमासीत्। अत्रान्तरे शिशुकलहमाकर्ण्य सभया दशरथमहिष्यो वसिष्ठवाल्मीकादिभिः सार्धं तत्रैवायान्तीति निशम्य रामोऽपि तान्संभावयितुं प्रयुक्तः।

सप्तमोऽङ्कः—अथ वाल्मीकिनिदेशाल्लक्ष्मणो गङ्गायास्तीरे रङ्गभूमिमेकां परिकल्पयामास। तत्रानेनैव मुनिना प्रणीतं लघुनाटकं किमप्यप्सरोभिः प्रयुज्यमानं द्रष्टुं रामादयः सर्वे उपनिमन्त्रिता आसन्। तस्मिंश्च प्रबन्धे कविना सीताया वने परित्यागादनन्तरं यद्वृत्तं तन्निखिलं संक्षेपत उपनिबद्धमभूत्। अथ तत्प्रत्यक्षीकुर्वन्रामः सीताया गङ्गायां स्वदेहार्पणं पुत्रद्वयजननं पृथ्वीभागीरथीभ्यां सीताया रक्षणं पुत्रयोश्च क्षात्रोचितसंस्कारार्थं वाल्मीकिहस्ते निक्षेप इत्यादि निरवशेषं याथातथ्येन ज्ञातवान्। अथास्मिन्लघुनाटके सीता प्रसवानन्तरमदर्शनं गतवती। ततश्च पश्चाद्गङ्गापृथिवीभ्यां सह सलिलाद्बहिः प्राप्य सर्वैः सह समगच्छत। एवं च सर्वेषां समक्षं जातां सीतायाः शुद्धिमुपलभ्य रामोऽपि सहर्षं तां भूयोऽङ्गीचकार सुताभ्यां च संगतोऽतीताखिलशोकशङ्कः परां कोटिमानन्दस्याप्यगच्छत्।

अथ

उत्तररामचरितम् ।

प्रथमोऽङ्कः ।

इदं कविभ्यः पूर्वेभ्यो नमोवाकं प्रशास्महे ।
वन्देमहि च तां वाचममृतामात्मनः कलाम् ॥ १ ॥

अथ तत्रभवान्भवभूतिर्नाम कविकण्ठीरवः 'एकः शब्दः सम्यग्ज्ञातः सुष्ठु प्रयुक्तः स्वर्गे लोके कामधुग्भवति' इत्यादिश्रुत्या परिनिष्ठितशब्दप्रयोगस्य धर्मत्वमवगच्छन् 'काव्यं यशसेऽर्थकृते' इत्यादिना काव्यरूपस्य तस्य प्रकर्षं विभाव्य दृश्यस्य श्रव्यापेक्षया 'देवानामिदमामनन्ति मुनयः कान्तं क्रतुं चाक्षुषम्' (मालविकाग्निमित्रे उक्तमेतत्कविना) इत्युक्तनाट्याश्रयत्वप्रयुक्तप्राधान्यात्प्रकरणादीनां यथायथं रसवस्तुनायकापकर्षोत्तत्प्रकर्षान्नाटकं चिकीर्षुः पूर्वचरितस्य महावीरचरितत्वेन वर्णितत्वादुत्तरं चरितं वर्णयितुमभिसंधाय पूर्वरङ्गप्रधानाङ्गभूतां नान्दीमाह— इदं कविभ्य इति ॥ **इदं** प्रारिप्सितग्रन्थादौ चिकीर्षितत्वेन बुद्धिस्थं मङ्गलं **पूर्वेभ्यः कविभ्यः नमोवाकं प्रशास्महे** । पूर्वकालप्रसिद्धप्राचेतसादिकविविषयकनमउक्तिं निर्दिशाम इति वाक्यार्थः । 'प्रशासनं तु निर्देशः' इति कोशः । 'आङ्शासु इच्छायाम्' इति धातोः आङ्पूर्वकत्वं प्रायिकमित्युक्तेः प्रपूर्वकत्वेनेच्छार्थकत्वं च । 'नमउक्तिर्नमोवाकः' इति कोशः । भावे घञ् । कुत्वम् । अमात्यानुवर्तनपुरःसरराजदर्शनन्यायेन गुणकृतात्मसंस्कारः प्रधानोपकाराय महते प्रभवति । तत्र गुणोऽपि संस्कारमनुभवतीति न्यायेन कविनमस्कारानन्तरं वाणीं नमस्करोति—वन्देमहीति । एतेन अनुग्राहकवाणीनमस्कारात्पूर्वमनुग्राह्यप्राचेतसादिनमस्कारायोगः इत्यपास्तम् । 'भगवद्वन्दनं त्वाद्यं गुरुवन्दनपूर्वकम्' इति विधेश्च । 'मधुमयभणितीनां मार्गदर्शी महर्षिः,' 'काव्यज्ञशिक्षयाभ्यासः' इति च । प्राचेतसादीनां गुरुत्वानपायाच्च । **तां** प्रसिद्धां पूर्वोक्तनमस्कारार्हत्वेन बुद्धिस्थामिति वा । **अमृतां** शाश्वतीम् । 'यज्ञशेषसुधामोक्षेष्वमृतं शाश्वते त्रिषु' इत्यभिधानात् । **आत्मनः** परमात्मनः **कलाम्** अंशभूताम् । विग्रहाध्याये तथा प्रतिपादनात् हयग्रीवांशत्वाच्च । तदुक्तमाचार्यैः—'दाक्षिण्यरम्या गिरिशस्य मूर्तिर्देवी सरोजासनधर्मपत्नी । व्यासादयोऽपि व्यपदेश्यवाचः स्फुरन्ति सर्वे तव शक्तिलेशैः ॥' इति । [**वाचं वन्देमहि** नमस्कुर्याम **च**] अत्र पूर्वार्धे सर्वलोकनमस्कार्याः पूर्वकालप्रसिद्धाः प्राज्ञाः केचिद्दुर्ष्या इति सूच्यते । लोकनमस्कार्या

---

१ गुरुभ्यः. २ सर्वेभ्यः. ३ वाक्यं. ४ वन्दामहे. वाणीं (टी.), विन्देम देवता.

इत्यनेन धूर्तवर्ण्यकभाणादिव्यावृत्तिः । पूर्वेत्यनेन कल्पितवर्ण्यकप्रकरणादिव्यावृत्तिः । भरतस्य च काप्यवर्णनाद्रामलक्ष्मणशत्रुघ्नानां त्रयाणामेव कथांशोपयोगित्वेनात्र बहुवचनस्य कपिञ्जलाधिकरणन्यायेन त्रित्वपर्यवसानमव्याहतम् । कविभ्य इत्यनेन यथा कविषु वाल्मीकेरायत्वेन प्राधान्यम् । अन्येषामानन्तर्यादप्राधान्यम् । एवं तत्सूचितवर्ण्यानां मध्ये रामचन्द्रस्य वर्णनायां ज्येष्ठत्वेन प्राधान्यं लक्ष्मणादेश्चा-प्राधान्यमिति सूचितम् । एवं च नानेकनेतृत्वप्रयुक्तनाटकत्वहानिः । अत एव लक्ष्मणशत्रुघ्नयोरुपसर्जनत्वावगमात् सीतापरित्यागे लक्ष्मणप्रेषणस्य लवणवधार्थं शत्रुघ्नप्रेषणस्य च ध्वननात्प्रथमाङ्कार्थः सूच्यते । उत्तरार्धे प्राज्ञी काचन स्त्री वर्ण्यत इति सूचितम् । आत्मनः कलामित्यनेन तस्या देवतांशसंभवत्वं कस्यचिद्धर्मपत्नी-त्वं च सूच्यते । 'अर्धो वा एष आत्मनो यत्पत्नी' इति पत्न्या अवयवत्वोपचारात् । कलाशब्दस्यावयवाचित्वात् । अत एव नायकस्यापि देवतांशसंभवत्वं सूच्यते । देवतांशसंभूतस्त्रियं प्रति तादृशस्यैव नायकस्यौचित्यात् । अमृतामिति मरणस्य प्रसक्तिपूर्वकप्रतिषेधाद्गङ्गापतनसंभावितस्य सीतामरणस्य गङ्गापृथिवीभ्यां सह नदागमनेन भावनिश्चयरूपो द्वितीयाङ्कप्रभृतिसप्तमाङ्कान्तार्थः सूच्यते । नमस्का-रसमुच्चयेन समप्राधान्यावगमाच्छाकुन्तलादाविव नासाध्याया वर्ण्यत्वम् । अपि तु साध्याया एव वर्ण्यत्वमिति सूच्यत इति सुधियो विभावयन्तु । अस्य श्लोकस्य योजनान्तरमपि—इदमित्यादि । 'इदंकविभ्यः' इत्येकं पदम् । 'नमः' वाकम्' इति च पदद्वयम् । एतेन द्वादशपदत्वसिद्धया न नान्दीनियमहानिः । अयमर्थः—पूर्वेभ्यः प्राचीनेभ्यः इदंकविभ्योऽस्या बुद्धिस्थरामकथायाः कविभ्यः । रामकथासंबन्धिकविभ्य इत्यर्थः । वाल्मीकिवसिष्ठादिभ्य इति तदर्थः । कथाया बुद्धिस्थत्वात् 'पापमभ्यश्च पुनाति वर्धयति च श्रेयांसि सेयं कथा' इत्युपसंहारे वक्ष्यमाणत्वाच्चेदंशब्देन परामर्श इत्युपपन्नम् । प्राथमिककथादर्शित्वरूपमुपकारं ख्यापयितुं पूर्वेभ्य इत्युक्तम् । कथान्तरकविनमस्कारे प्रयोजनाभावादिदंकविभ्य इत्युक्तम् । उच्यतेऽनेनेति वाकमुक्तिसाधनीभूतम् । कवेर्वश्यवाक्त्वेऽपि प्रारि-प्सितग्रन्थसमाप्तौ कविनमस्कारस्य साधनत्वं तात्पर्यम् । करणे घञ् । तस्य चोपदेशाप्रवृत्तावित्यत्रेव बाहुलकत्वम् । अन्यथा ल्युटा भाव्यम् । 'संज्ञायामिति च प्रायिकम् इत्युक्तत्वान्न दोषः । यद्वा उच्यते यत्तद्वाकम् । कर्मणि घञ् । 'अकर्तरि च कारके' इत्यनुशासनात् । वाचिकं नमः प्रशास्महे इच्छामः निर्दिशाम इति वा । तां पूर्वोपस्थितां प्रवृत्तिनिमित्तविधयास्याः कविपदेनोप-स्थितेः अमृतामानुपूर्व्यानित्याम् । शब्दस्य नित्यत्वपक्षे स्वरूपेण नित्यामित्यर्थः । यद्वा अमृतं मोक्षस्तदस्या अस्तीत्यमृताम् । मत्वर्थीयोऽच्प्रत्ययः । तेन स्त्रीत्वोपपत्तिः । प्रयोजकतासंबन्धेन मोक्षवतीमित्यर्थः । रामायणादिना मोक्ष-प्रयोजकत्वं च 'एकैकमक्षरं प्रोक्तं महापातकनाशनम्' इति स्फुटम् । अत्र

(नान्यन्ते ।)

सूत्रधारः—अलमतिविस्तरेण । अद्य खलु भगवतः कालप्रिय-नाथस्य यात्रायामार्यमिश्रान्विज्ञापयामि—एवमत्रभवन्तो विदांकुर्वन्तु । अस्ति खलु तत्रभवान्काश्यपः श्रीकण्ठपदलाञ्छनः पदवाक्यप्रमाणज्ञो भवभूतिर्नाम जातूकर्णीपुत्रः ।

हेतुमाह—आत्मनः कलां परमात्मप्रतिपादकविद्याम् । 'विद्यायां कालभेदे च मुक्तौ शिल्पे कलेति च' इति वैजयन्ती । रामायणादिकं परमात्मप्रतिपादकत्वं च 'वेदवेद्ये परे पुंसि' इत्यादौ स्पष्टम् । रामायणाध्यात्मरामायणरूपां वन्देमहि प्रणमाम । 'विषयमङ्गलद्वयसंग्रहो विजयते' इति बालरामायणनाटके स्फुटम् । अस्यां योजनायां पूर्ववत्काव्यार्थसूचनं बोद्धव्यम् ॥ १ ॥ नान्दीलक्षणं तु—'यत्राष्टभिर्द्वादशभिरष्टादशभिरेव वा ।' इत्यादि दशरूपकादिषु स्फुटम् । नाटकलक्षणं च—'वीरशृङ्गारयोरेकः प्रधानं यत्र वर्ण्यते । प्रख्यातनामकोपेतं नाटकं तदुदाहृतम् ॥' इति । यद्यपि करुणरस एवास्मिन्नाटके प्रधानमिति सर्वजनीनं सूचितं, मरणस्य प्रसक्तिपूर्वकप्रतिषेधो नाटकप्रतिपाद्य इति सूचयता नान्दीस्थामृतपदेन करुण एवास्मिन्नाटके प्रधान इति तथापि वीरशृङ्गारौ प्रायिकौ इत्युक्ते न दोष इत्याहुः । पूर्वरङ्गलक्षणं तु—'यन्नाट्यवस्तुनः पूर्वं रङ्गविघ्नोपशान्तये । कुशीलवाः प्रकुर्वन्ति पूर्वरङ्गः स उच्यते ॥' इति । प्रस्तावनालक्षणं तु—'सूत्रधारो नटीं ब्रूते मारिषं वा विदूषकम् । स्वकार्यप्रस्तुताक्षेपिचित्रोक्त्या यत्तदामुखम् ॥ प्रस्तावना वा तत्र स्यात्' इति । **नान्यन्त इति** । नान्द्याः पूर्वोक्ताया अन्ते समाप्तौ सूत्रधारः प्रविश्याहेति शेषः । तदुक्तम्—'पूर्वरङ्गं विधायादौ सूत्रधारे विनिर्गते । प्रविश्य तद्वदपरः काव्यमासूत्रयेन्नटः ॥' इति । प्ररोचनां प्रस्तोतुं सामाजिकावधानायाह—**अद्य खलु भगवत इति** । भगवतो ज्ञानशक्त्यादिगुणवतः । कालप्रियानाथस्य कालप्रियानामाम्बिकाया नाथः शिवस्तस्य । इयं च कथा पौराणिकी वेदितव्या । यात्रायामुत्सवे आर्याः पूज्या मिश्रा ज्ञानिनस्तथाविधान्विज्ञापयामि । एवं वक्ष्यमाणप्रकारेण अत्रभवन्तः । पूज्या यूयम् । 'अत्रभवत्तत्रभवच्छब्दौ पूज्यार्थौ' इत्युक्तेः । विदांकुर्वन्तु । 'विदांकुर्वन्त्वित्यन्यतरस्याम्' इति सूत्रानुशिष्टोऽयं शब्दः । यात्रायामिति काल उक्तः । **अस्ति खल्विति** । काश्यपः कश्यपगोत्रोद्भवः । ऋष्यण्प्रत्ययः । 'काश्यपः कश्यपो भवति' इति सर्वज्ञतया श्रुतिप्रसिद्धकश्यपवंश्यः । श्रीकण्ठ इति पदं शब्दः लाञ्छनं यस्य स तथोक्तः । श्रीकण्ठनामक इत्यर्थः । 'द्वादशेऽहनि पिता नाम कुर्यात्' इति पैतृकं नामधेयमिदम् । पदवाक्यप्रमाणज्ञः ।

---

१ प्रिया. २ ०छनः भवभूतिर्नाम. ३ क.घि.; जातु०, एतन्नास्ति क्वचित्.

यं ब्रह्माणमियं देवी वाग्वश्येवानुवर्तते।
उत्तरं रामचरितं तत्प्रणीतं प्रयुज्यते ॥ २ ॥

व्याकरणन्यायमीमांसापरिज्ञातेत्यर्थः । भवभूतिर्नाम भवभूतिरिति प्रसिद्ध-नामवान् । एतत्कृत—'साम्बा पुनातु भवभूतिपवित्रमूर्तिः' इति श्लोकश्रवण-संतुष्टो राजा भवभूतिरित्येनं ख्यापयामासेति कथात्रानुसंधेया । किं चास्मै कवये ईश्वर एव भिक्षुरूपेणागत्य भूतिं दत्तवानिति वदन्ति । एवं च भवाद्भगवतो भूतिर्यस्येति भवभूतिरित्यन्वर्थ इत्याहुः । यमिति । ब्रह्माणम् । यजना-दिषट्कर्मनिरतमित्यर्थः । लाक्षणिकोऽयं मुख्यार्थपरत्वे प्रयोजनाभावात् । तथाविधं यं भवभूतिमियं देवताप्रसादादिना साध्यत्वेन प्रसिद्धा वाग्देवी वश्या सत्येव विधिप्रतिषेधार्हा सत्येवान्ववर्ततानुवर्तितवती । यद्वा ब्रह्माणं यमेव वश्या सत्यन्ववर्तत । न त्वन्यमित्यर्थः । पूर्वस्मिन्नर्थे वश्येवान्ववर्तत न त्ववश्यान्व-वर्तत । अलाभेन कालिदासादिषु स्वयमवश्यैव कालिदासप्रभृत्यनुरोधेनागताया वाग्देव्या यदनुवर्तनं तद्यावर्तते । अत्र 'यं ब्रह्माणमियं देवी वाग्वश्ये-वान्ववर्तत' इति द्वितीयान्तब्रह्मशब्देन इवशब्देन च युक्तं पाठान्तरमपि क्वचिद्दृश्यते । तत्रायमर्थः—इयं वाग्देवी यं भवभूतिं ब्रह्माणमिव स्वभर्तारं चतुर्मुखमिव वश्या सत्यन्ववर्ततानुवर्तितवती । देवस्य स्त्री देवी । दीव्यति प्रकाशयति प्रकाशते इति वा देवी । 'देवट्' इति टित्वात् ङीप् । यद्वा—यं देवी यादृशभवभूतिविषयकेच्छावती सती इयं वाग्देवी ब्रह्माणं वश्येवान्वव-र्तत । वश्यानुवर्तनाभिनयमात्रं स्वभर्तरि भावबन्धस्तु भवभूतावेवेति भावः । स्वयंवरं कृतवतीत्यर्थः । दिवुधातोः 'कान्तिगतिषु' इत्युक्तेः इच्छायां वृत्तिः । दीव्यति कामयत इति देवीति कृदन्तदेवीपदयोगेऽपि । परं त्वत्र पाठे व्यवहितान्वयो दोष इत्याहुः । 'उत्तरं रामचरितं यत्प्रणीतं प्रयोक्ष्यते' इति यच्छब्दपाठ इति मत्वा यं वाग्देव्यन्ववर्तत यत्प्रणीतं प्रयोक्ष्यतेऽभि-नेष्यते स भवभूतिर्नाम कविः अस्तीति पूर्वेणान्वयः । यत्तदोर्नित्यसंबन्धात्स इत्यस्य लाभ इति केचित् । परे तु 'तत्प्रणीतम्' इति तच्छब्दयुक्तमेव पाठमुपष्टभ्य 'इयं वाग्देवी यं भवभूतिमन्ववर्तत स भवभूतिर्नाम कविरस्ति । तत्प्रणीतं उत्तरं रामचरितं प्रयोक्ष्यत इत्यन्वयः । अन्यथा विधेयस्य स्फुट-प्रतीत्यनापत्तेश्च' इति वदन्ति । इयं प्ररोचना प्रस्तुता । तदुक्तम्—'निवेदनं प्रयोज्यस्य निर्देशो देशकालयोः । कविकाव्यनटादीनां प्रशंसा तु प्ररोचना' इति ॥२॥

---

१ ब्राह्मणं. २ वश्येवान्ववर्तत (टी.) ३ प्रयोक्ष्यते.

एषोऽस्मि[1] कार्यवशादायोध्यकस्तदानींतनश्च[2] संवृत्तः[3] । (समन्तादवलोक्य ।) भो भो यदि[4] तावदत्रभवतः पौलस्त्यकुलधूमकेतोर्महाराजरामस्यायमभिषेकसमयो[5] रात्रिंदिवमसंहृतानन्दनान्दीकस्तत्किमित्थं[6] विश्रान्तचारणानि[7] चत्वरस्थानानि[8] ।

(प्रविश्य ।)

नटः—भाव प्रेषिता हि[9] ते[10] गृहीतनाम्ना महाराजेन लङ्कासमरसुहृदो

एषोऽस्मीति । कविवशात्कव्यनुरोधेनायोध्यकः । कार्यवशादिति पाठे नाटकप्रयोगानुरोधादित्यर्थ अयोध्यासंबन्धिक इत्यर्थः । 'धन्वयोपधाद्वुञ्' इति सूत्रेण वुञ् । तस्याकादेशश्च । तदानींतनश्च रामपट्टाभिषेककालीनश्च संवृत्तोऽस्मीति योजना । निष्पन्नोऽस्मीत्यर्थः । अयमाशयः—यद्यपि भोजराजगतरीत्या सूत्रधारनटीप्रभृतिभिः प्रकृतदेशकालावलम्बिनीं प्रस्तावनामुक्त्वा सूत्रधारादीनिष्क्रास्य भूमिकां प्रवेश्य प्रवर्तिष्यमाणकाव्याभिनयकथासूचकविष्कम्भो वक्तव्यस्तथापि सूत्रधारस्यैव काव्यकथाघटकदेशकालसंबन्धमङ्गीकृत्य विष्कम्भवर्ण्यकथोपन्यासः सूत्रधारत्वापरित्यागाच्च प्रस्तावनात्वाहानिरिति कवेर्मतम् । तदनुसारेणाहमायोध्यकः संवृत्तोऽस्मीति । अयोध्यासंबन्धित्वं च तस्यां कादाचित्कावस्थानरूपम् । तेन वैदेशिकोऽस्मीति उपरितनग्रन्थेन न विरोधः । **यदि तावदिति** । अत्रभवतः पूज्यस्य पौलस्त्यकुलस्य रावणवंशस्य धूमकेतोरग्निवद्दाहकस्य उत्पातग्रहविशेषस्य वा । महाराजश्चासौ रामश्च इति विग्रहः तस्य । रात्रिंदिवमहर्निशम् । 'अचतुर'—इति सूत्रे निपातितोऽयं शब्दः । असंहृतनान्दीकोऽविच्छिन्नमङ्गलः । 'शेषाद्विभाषा' इति कप् । ह्रस्वप्रतिषेधः । अयं पट्टाभिषेकसमयः यदा पट्टाभिषेकमुहूर्तः यस्मिन्काले । यद्वा समय आचारः पट्टाभिषेकरूप आचारो यदा यस्मिन्काले । इदानीमस्मिन्काले । पट्टाभिषेकसमये चत्वरस्थानान्यङ्गणभागाः विश्रान्तमवसितं चाराणामधिकारिपुरुषाणां चरणं संचरणं येषु तानि । विश्रान्ताश्चाराणामधिकारिपुरुषाणां चरणा अङ्घ्रयो येष्विति वा । चारा निवृत्तव्यापाराः सन्तः चत्वरेषूपविश्य विश्राम्यन्तीति भावः । तत्किमिदानीं पट्टाभिषेककाले चत्वरस्थानानि विश्रान्तचारचरणानीति यत् तत् किमिति योजना । यस्मिन्दिवसे कलशतीर्थसेचनरूपपट्टाभिषेकक्रियाधिकरणमुहूर्तस्तद्दिवसात्प्रभृत्यकदिनानां तदुत्सवकालत्वेन यथायमभिषेकसमय इत्युक्तिरविरुद्धा । सूक्ष्मकालं प्रति स्थूलकालस्याधारत्वात् । प्रासादखट्वापर्यङ्कन्यायोऽत्रानुसंधेयः ॥ **भाव प्रेषिता इति** । महात्मानो महाधैर्याः । सभाजनं सपर्यामुपतिष्ठन्ते प्राप्नुवन्तीति सभाजनोपस्थायिनः । 'सुप्यजातौ' इति णिनिः । इदं च मध्यमणिन्यायेन पूर्वोत्तराभ्यामन्वेति । महर्षयो गौतमविश्वामित्रादयो राजर्षयस्तु जनकप्र-

---

१ षोऽहं. २ ०ध्यिकः. ३ च वैदेशिकः. ४ यदा. ५ पट्टाभि०. ६ आहतानन्द, असंहृतनान्दी०. ७ मित्थमीं. ८ चर०, चारचरणानि (टी.) ९ हीमः. १० श्री मामरराक्षसाः सभा०.

महात्मानः प्लवङ्गराक्षसाः सभाजनोपस्थायिनश्च नानादिगन्तागता ब्रह्मर्षयो राजर्षयश्च यदाराधनायैतावतो दिवसानुत्सवैं आसीत् ।

सूत्रधारः—आं अस्त्येतन्निमित्तम् ।

नटः—अन्यच्च ।

वसिष्ठाधिष्ठिता देव्यो गता रामस्य मातरः ।
अरुन्धतीं पुरस्कृत्य यज्ञे जामातुराश्रमम् ॥ ३ ॥

सूत्रधारः—वैदेशिकोऽस्मीति पृच्छामि । कः पुनरसौ जामाता ।

नटः—

कन्यां दशरथो राजा शान्तां नाम व्यजीजनत् ।
अपत्यकृतिकां राज्ञे लोमपादाय यां ददौ ॥ ४ ॥

भृतयः । देवर्षीणामूर्ध्वदिग्गमनान्नानादिगन्तेत्युक्तिः । यत्समाराधनाय येषां प्लवङ्गमादीनां समाराधनाय पूजनायैतावतो दिवसानेतावत्सु दिवसेषु । अत्यन्तसंयोगे द्वितीया । प्रमोदः । चारगतागतहेतुभूतप्रहर्ष इत्यर्थः । यत्समाराधनाय प्रमोद आसीत् ते प्रेषिता इत्यन्वयः । ' तत्समाराधनाय ' इति तत्पदयुक्तपाठे तु न विश्रान्तचारचरणत्वे हेतुरुक्तो भवतीत्यत्राह—तत्समाराधनायेति । एवं चारचरणहेतुर्गत इति भावः ॥ आं अस्त्येतन्निमित्तम् । आ इति स्मरणवाचकम् । अत एव 'निपात एकाजनाङ्' इति प्रगृह्यत्वात् आ अस्तीति संध्यभावः । 'वाक्यस्मरणयोरङित्' इत्याद्युक्तेः । एतन्निमित्तमस्ति । मया विस्मृतमिति भावः ॥ **वसिष्ठाधिष्ठिता इति** । अरुन्धतीं पुरस्कृत्य वसिष्ठाधिष्ठिता इत्यन्वयः । गुरुपत्नीत्वयुक्तप्राधान्यादरुन्धतीं मुख्यां कृत्वा वसिष्ठेन व्यापारिता इत्यर्थः । वसिष्ठः कर्तव्यं अरुन्धतीमुखमवलोकमानोऽनुशास्ति । ततो देव्योऽरुन्धत्या सह कर्तव्यमनुतिष्ठन्तीति भावः । जामातुरित्येतन्मध्यमणिन्यायेन यज्ञाश्रमाभ्यामन्वेति । यज्ञे यज्ञनिमित्तम् । 'निमित्तात्कर्मसंयोगे' इति सप्तमी । सतीत्यध्याहारेण यज्ञे सति आश्रमं गता इति वार्थः ॥ ३ ॥ वैदेशिको विदेशो देशान्तरं तत्र भवो वैदेशिकः । अध्यात्मादित्वाट्ठञ् । विदेशस्थस्यापि कदाचिदयोध्यास्थितिसंभवादित्याहुः ॥ **कन्यामिति** । व्यजीजनदजनयत् । ' जनी प्रादुर्भावे ' इति धातोर्णिच् । तां शान्तां रोमपादनाम्ने । अपत्यस्य कृतिर्व्यापारो यस्यास्तथाविधाम् । ' शेषाद्विभाषा ' इति कप् । कन्यां ददावित्युक्ते कलत्रार्थमिति प्रतीतेस्तद्वारणायापत्यकृतिकामिति ददौ दत्तवान् ॥ ४ ॥

---

१ सभाजोप०. २ दिगन्तपावनाः. ३ यत्समारा, यत्संभावनाय. ४ प्रमोदः. ५ आसीत् । संप्रति हि वसिष्ठा०. ६ Some read एवमेतत् । संप्रति हि वसिष्ठा &c., नटः—वैदेशिको &c. सूत्र०—कन्यां &c. गतः । तत्किमनेन इ०. ७ राघवमातरः. ८ पुनर्जा०. ९ रोम. १० तां.

विभाण्डकसुतस्तामृष्यश्रृङ्ग उपयेमे । तेन द्वादशवार्षिकं सत्रमारब्धम् । तदनुरोधात्कठोरगर्भामपि वधूं जानकीं विमुच्य गुरुजनस्तत्र गतः ।

सूत्रधारः—तत्किमनेन । एहि । राजद्वारमेव स्वजातिसमयेनोपतिष्ठावः ।

नटः—तेन हि निरूपयतु राज्ञः सुपरिशुद्धामुपस्थानस्तोत्रपद्धतिं भावः ।

सूत्रधारः—मारिष ।

सर्वथा व्यवहर्तव्यं कुतो ह्यवचनीयता ।
यथा स्त्रीणां तथा वाचां साधुत्वे दुर्जनो जनः ॥ ५ ॥

तेन ऋष्यशृङ्गेणे । द्वादश वर्षाणि भविष्यति द्वादशवार्षिकम् । 'तमधीष्टो भृतो भूतो भावी' इत्यधिकृत्य विहितो ठञ् । द्विगुः । 'वर्षाल्लुक् च' इति पाक्षिको लुगभावः । अनुशतिकादित्वादुभयत्र वृद्धिः । न तूत्तरपदवृद्धिमात्रम् । 'अभविष्यति' इति प्रतिषेधात् । न च द्वादशवर्षाणि भूतमित्यर्थोऽस्त्विति वाच्यम् । आरब्धमित्युक्तेरसांगत्यापत्तेः । तदनुरोधात्कठोरगर्भेति नानीता सीतेत्युक्ततया सीतायाः गर्भिणीदशायामेतत्सत्रमारब्धमिति स्पष्टमवगम्यते । एवं द्वितीयाङ्कविष्कम्भे 'ममनन्तरं च गर्भकादशे वर्षे क्षात्रेण कल्पेनोपनीय त्रयीमध्यापितौ' इत्युक्त्या 'संप्रति परिसमाप्तं द्वादशवार्षिकं सत्रम्' इति वक्ष्यमाणतया अत्रत्यद्वादशवार्षिकशब्दस्य द्वादशवर्षाणि भूतमित्यर्थाभ्युपगमेन तद्विरोधापत्तेरिति ध्येयम् । तदनुरोधात्तदनुसरणाद्धेतोः कठोरगर्भा पूर्णगर्भाम् । कठोरशब्दः पूर्णवाची । तदुक्तमुणादिषु वैयाकरणैः–'अयं पूर्णतायामपि' इति । **गतः इति** । 'अनाहूतोऽध्वरं गच्छेत्' इति विधेः किं पुनर्न्यायादिति भावः ॥ **तत्किमिति** । स्वजातिसमयेन स्वजातिमर्यादया । उपतिष्ठावस्तोषयावः । रामस्य 'आत्मानं मानुषं मन्ये रामं दशरथात्मजम्' इति देवतात्वाभावात् 'उपाद्देवपूजा–' इत्यादिना नात्मनेपदम् । तथा च स्वजात्यनुगुणरूपं यत्स्तोत्रं तत् कुर्व इति बोधः ॥ **तेनेति** । स्तोतव्यमिति यत्नेनेत्यर्थः । सुपरिशुद्धां सुष्ठु दोषरहिताम् । स्तुवन्त्यनेनेति स्तोत्रं ग्रन्थः तस्य पद्धतिरानुपूर्वी ताम् । उपस्थानाय गुणिनिष्ठगुणाभिधानाय स्तोत्रपद्धतिमित्यर्थः । समासस्तु षष्ठ्यन्तस्येति बोध्यम् । निरूपयतूत्पादयतु । वदत्वित्यर्थः ॥ ननु यदुक्तं स्तुतिं निरूपयत्विति तदवगच्छामि सुपरिशुद्धामिति नाभ्युपगच्छामि दोषरहितत्वरूपपरिशुद्धत्वस्य प्रयोजनाभावात् । स्तुतिवचनं तु कर्तव्यमेव स्वजातिनियतव्यापारत्वादित्याह—**सर्वथेति** । सर्वेण प्रकारेण सर्वथा व्यवहर्तव्यं व्यवहारः कर्तव्यः । भावे तव्यप्रत्ययः । व्यवहारशब्दः स्तुतिकरणरूपव्याहारपरः । अवचनीयता वचनीयं दोषस्तद्रहितता सुपरिशुद्धतेत्यर्थः ।

---

१ तेन च सांप्रतम्. २ यातः (टी.). ३ व्यवहर्तव्ये.

नटः—अतिदुर्जन इति वक्तव्यम् ।

देव्यामेपि हि वैदेह्यां सापवादो यतो जनः ।
रक्षोगृहेस्थितिर्मूलमग्निशुद्धौ त्वनिश्चयः ॥ ६ ॥

कुतः किमर्थम् । यद्वा कुतः कस्मै । ' सार्वविभक्तिकस्तसिः ' इति चतुर्थ्यर्थे तसिः । अयमाशयः—दोषवत्तया वा दोषरहिततया वा गुणवत्तया वा स्तुतिकरणरूपव्यापारः कर्तव्यः । तस्य स्वजातीयधर्मत्वात्त्वदुक्तसुपरिशुद्धतया तु किम् । तस्याः फलाभावादिति । ननु जनाभिनन्दनमेव तत्फलमस्तु कुतः फलाभाव इत्यत्राह—यथा स्त्रीणामित्यादिना । पूर्वपादस्थहिशब्दस्यात्र संबन्धः । हि यस्माज्जनः स्त्रीणां साधुत्वे दुर्जनस्तस्मादवचनीयता किमर्थेति पूर्वेण संबन्धः । जनः स्त्रीणां साधुत्वे यथा पातिव्रत्यविषय इव वाचां साधुत्वे माधुर्यौज्ज्वल्यादिविषये दुर्जनो दोषदर्शी । दोषदर्शित्वमेव हि दौर्जन्यमिति भावः । यथा स्त्रीणां साधुत्वे जनो दुर्जनस्तथा वाचां साधुत्वेऽपि जनो दुर्जनो हि यस्मात्तस्मादवचनीयता [कस्मात्संभवेदित्यर्थः ।] किमर्थेत्यर्थः ॥ ५ ॥ प्रकृतकथासंगतये यथा स्त्रीणामिति यथेति दृष्टान्त उक्तः । तदुपजीव्य प्रकृतमवलम्बते नटः अतिदुर्जन इति वक्तव्यमिति । तत्र हेतुमाह—देव्या इति । हि यत [देव्यां देवीविषये] इत्यनयोर्यथाक्रमं पूर्वोत्तरार्धयोरन्वयः । हि यस्माद्देव्या दीप्तिमत्या अपि । स्वभावतो दोषप्रतिभटाया अपीत्यर्थः । वैदेह्या विदेहराजपुत्र्याः । संबन्धसामान्ये षष्ठी । जनः सापवादः । अपवादो दोषकथनं तेन सहित इत्यर्थः । तथा च वैदेहिसंबन्ध्यपवादसहित इत्यर्थः । नित्यसापेक्षत्वात्समासः । तदुक्तम्—' संबन्धिशब्दः सापेक्षो नित्यं सर्वः समस्यते । ' इति । यतश्च रक्षोगृहस्थितिः राक्षसगृहावस्थानमात्रम् । न त्वन्यदिति भावः । मूलं दोषकथनहेतुः । अग्निशुद्धौ अनिश्चयस्तु निश्चयाभावश्च । तुशब्दश्चार्थकः । अत्र देव्या इति दोषाभाव उक्तः । रक्षोगृहस्थितिरित्यनेन असाधारणहेत्वभाव उक्तः । अग्निशुद्धावित्यनेन बाधकप्रमाणमुक्तम् । तथा च एतत्सर्वमपि नावलोकितमिति भावः । विषयप्रभावमविगणय्य असतोऽपि दोषस्य कथनं सुतरां दुर्जनकार्यम् । तत्राप्यसाधारणहेतुमप्यदृष्ट्वा विषयप्रभावमप्यविगणय्यासतोऽपि दोषस्य कथनं ततोऽपि दुर्जनकार्यम् । तत्रापि बाधकप्रमाणमप्यविश्वस्यासाधारणकारणमप्यदृष्ट्वा विषयप्रभावमप्यविगणय्यासतोऽपि दोषस्य कथनं ततोऽप्यतिदुर्जनकार्यमिति । अत्र हि यस्मात्सापवादः । यतश्च रक्षोगृहस्थितिर्मूलम् । अग्निशुद्धावनिश्चयश्च जनस्य । तस्माज्जनोऽतिदुर्जन इति वक्तव्यमित्येवं पूर्वे-

१ देव्याः—देवेव्याः (टी.). २ एहे.

सूत्रधारः—यदि पुनरियं किंवदन्ती महाराजं प्रति स्यन्देत ततः कष्टं स्यात् ।

नटः—सर्वथा ऋषयो देवताश्च श्रेयो विधास्यन्ति । (परिक्रम्य ।) भो भोः क्वेदानीं महाराजः । (आकर्ण्य ।) एवं जनाः कथयन्ति—

स्नेहात्सभाजयितुमेत्य दिनान्यमूनि
नीत्वोत्सवेन जनकोऽद्य गतो विदेहान् ।
देव्यास्ततो विमनसः परिसान्त्वनाय
धर्मासनाद्विशति वासगृहं नरेन्द्रः ॥ ७ ॥

(इति निष्क्रान्तौ ।)

प्रस्तावना ।

(ततः प्रविशत्युपविष्टो रामः सीता च ।)

रामः—देवि वैदेहि समाश्वसिहि । ते हि गुरवो न शक्नुवन्ति विहातुमस्मान् ।

किं त्वनुष्ठाननित्यत्वं स्वातन्त्र्यमपकर्षति ।
संकटा ह्याहिताग्नीनां प्रत्यवायैर्गृहस्थता ॥ ८ ॥

णान्वयः ॥ ६ ॥ **यदि पुनरिति** । किंवदन्ती लोकवादः स्यन्देत प्रस्रवेत् । श्रवणविषयीभवेदिति यावत् । अनेन प्रथमाङ्कार्थः सूच्यते । 'सर्वथा ऋषयः' इत्याद्यनेन शेषाङ्कार्थः सूचितः । एष ऋषिकर्तृकश्रेयोविधानरूपबीजन्यासादुपक्षेपो नाम संध्यङ्गमुक्तम् । यथा—'बीजन्यास उपक्षेपः' इति ॥ **आकर्ण्येति** । इदमाकाशभाषितमुच्यते । तदुक्तम्—'अप्रविष्टैः सहालापो भवेदाकाशभाषितम्' इति । **स्नेहादिति** । सभाजयितुं पूजयितुम् । उत्सवेन हर्षजनकव्यापारेण । विमनसो दुःखितहृदयायाः परिसान्त्वनाय तद्दुःखापनयनक्षममधुरवचनप्रयोगाय । 'तुमर्थाच्च' इति चतुर्थी । धर्मासनात् । क्षत्रियधर्मभूतराज्यपरिपालनार्थसिंहासनादित्यर्थः । वासगृहं स्वावासगृहम् । विशति प्रविशति ॥ ७ ॥ एवं प्रस्तावना प्रस्तुता । अथाङ्कः प्रस्तूयते—**ततः प्रविशतीत्यादिना** । अङ्कलक्षणं तु—'प्रत्यक्षनेतृचरितो बिन्दुव्याप्तिपुरस्कृतः । अङ्को नानाप्रकारार्थसंविधानरसाश्रयः ॥' इति । विश्वसिहि संतोषं प्राप्नुहि । 'समाश्वसिहि' इति पाठान्तरम् । विहातुं त्यक्तुम् । **किं त्विति** । किं तु अनुष्ठानस्य नित्यनैमित्तिकादिकर्मकलापनिर्वर्तनस्य नित्यत्वं नियतता । अनुष्ठानाभाव-

---

१ स्यात्, सृशोन, परिस्पन्देत्; प्रतिष्ठेत ततः कष्टतरं. २ स्वस्ति करिष्यन्ति. ३ आसनो॰ ४ वियोक्तुम्; न एव; न ते हि गुरवश्चिरं शक्नुवन्त्यस्मान् विमोक्तुम्. ५ नित्यत्वात्.

सीता—जानामि आर्यपुत्र जानामि। किं तु संतापकारिणो बन्धुजनविप्रयोगा भवन्ति। (क)

रामः—एवमेतत्। एते हि हृदयमर्मच्छिदः संसारभावा येभ्यो बीभत्समानाः संत्यज्य सर्वान्कामानरण्ये विश्राम्यन्ति मनीषिणः।

(प्रविश्य।)

कञ्चुकी—रामभद्र—(इत्यर्धोक्ते साशङ्कम्।) महाराज—

रामः—(सस्मितम्।) आर्य ननु रामभद्र इत्येव मां प्रत्युपचारः शोभते तातपरिजनस्य। तद्यथाभ्यस्तमभिधीयताम्।

कञ्चुकी—देव ऋष्यशृङ्गाश्रमादष्टावक्रः संप्राप्तः।

सीता—आर्य ततः किं विलम्ब्यते। (ख)

रामः—त्वरितं प्रवेशय।

(कञ्चुकी निष्क्रान्तः।)

(क) जाणामि अज्जउत्त जाणामि। किंदु संदावआरिणो बन्धुजणविप्पओआ होन्ति।

(ख) अज्ज तदो किं विलम्बीअदि।

विरहस्यानियम इत्यर्थः। स्वातन्त्र्यं स्वैरावस्थानमपकर्षति न सहते। संकटा हीति। हि यस्मात् आहिताग्नीनां गृहस्थता गृहस्थाश्रमः प्रत्यवायैर्विहितानाचरणजन्यपातकैः संकटा निबिडा दुःखरूपा वा। जाग्रत्प्रत्यवायेत्यर्थः॥ ८॥ एवमिति। येभ्य इति संसारभागेभ्यः संसारेऽवश्यानुभाव्यभागेभ्य इत्यर्थः। संसारो हि शरीरसंबन्धानुबन्धिसुखदुःखसमुदायः। तथा च गुरुबन्धुवियोगादीनां तदेकदेशत्वं संगतम्। बीभत्समाना जुगुप्समानाः। एतद्दोषानुबन्धजनितचित्तवृत्तिनिवृत्तियुक्ता इत्यर्थः। बीभत्सायां जुगुप्सावस्थायिकत्वादित्थं व्याख्यातम्। अत एव बीभत्समाना इत्यस्य 'जुगुप्साविराम—'—इत्यादिना पञ्चमी। 'बन्ध बन्धने' इत्यस्मात्स्वार्थे सनि रूपमिदम्। 'बधेश्चित्तविकारे' इति वार्तिकादस्य चित्तविकारे वृत्तिः। काम्यन्त इति कामाः। कर्मणि घञ्। गृहक्षेत्रपुत्रादयस्तानित्यर्थः। [कञ्चुकीति—'अन्तःपुरचरो वृद्धो विप्रो गुणगणान्वितः। सर्वकार्यार्थकुशलः कञ्चुकीत्यभिधीयते॥' इत्युक्तलक्षणः।] उपचारो व्यवहारः। यथाभ्यस्तमभ्यस्तमनतिक्रम्य। यथार्थत्वात्समासः। अभिधीयताम्। अष्टावक्रस्तदाख्यः। अष्टौ वक्राणि अस्येति विग्रहः। योगरूढशब्दः। 'अष्टनः संज्ञायाम्' इति दीर्घः। हास्यानु-

---

१ भिदः. २ भागाः (टी.), भोगाः. ३ एतन्नास्ति क्वचित्. ४ तातपाद. ५ यथाभ्यासमुच्यताम्. ६ गुरुजनस्य.

(प्रविश्य ।)

अष्टावक्रः—स्वस्ति वाम् ।

रामः—भगवन् अभिवादये । इत आस्यताम् ।

सीता—भगवन् नमस्ते । अपि कुशलं सजामातृकस्य गुरुजनस्यार्यायाश्च शान्तायाः । (क)

रामः—निर्विघ्नः सोमपीथी आवुत्तो मे भगवानृष्यशृङ्ग आर्या च शान्ता ।

सीता—अस्मान्वा स्मरति । (ख)

अष्टावक्रः—(उपविश्य ।) अथ किम । देवि भगवान् वसिष्ठस्त्वामिदमाह—

विश्वंभरा भगवती भवतीमसूत
राजा प्रजापतिसमो जनकः पिता ते ।
तेषां वधूस्त्वमसि नन्दिनि पार्थिवानां
येषां कुलेषु सविता च गुरुर्वयं च ॥ ९ ॥

(क) भअवं णमो दे । अवि कुसलं सजामातुअस्य गुरुअणस्स अज्जाए अ सन्ताए । (ख) अम्हे वा सुमरेदि ।

प्रवेशार्थमष्टावक्रप्रवेशः ॥ सजामातुअस्स सजामातृकस्य । 'प्रायो लुककगजतदयपवाम्' इति सूत्रेण ककारलोपः । तस्मिन्नवशिष्टाकारस्येषत्स्पृष्टयकारश्रुतिश्च प्राकृतव्याकरणसिद्धा । **निर्विघ्न इति** । सोमपीथी । सोमपा इत्यर्थः । भावुकः पूज्यः । शान्तापतित्वादिति भावः । **विश्वंभरेति** । नन्दिनि गुणपूर्णे । 'टुनदि समृद्धौ' इत्यस्मात् भावे घञि 'अत इनिठनौ' इति इनिप्रत्ययः । एकाक्षरात्कृतोऽजाताविति निषेधस्तु प्रायिकः । ब्रह्यादिणिनिर्वा । नान्तत्वात् ङीप् । नन्दिनि पुत्रि । संबोधनम् । इदं च 'अस्माकं तु जनकसुता दुहितैव' इति वक्ष्यमाणरीत्या दशरथमतानुसारेण । भगवती षाड्गुण्यपरिपूर्णा विश्वंभरा भूमिः । भूरित्याद्यनुक्त्वा विश्वंभरोक्तिः क्षान्तिप्रधानतासूचनाय । भवतीं पूज्यां त्वामसूत सूतवती । 'षूङ् प्राणिप्रसवे' । लङ् । शपो लुक् । विश्वंभराशब्दस्तु 'संज्ञायां भृतृ—' इत्यादिना खच्प्रत्ययमुमागमाभ्यां निष्पन्नः । प्रजापतिना ब्रह्मणा समः । स्वाभ्यायादिना ब्रह्मतुल्य इत्यर्थः । मान्धातारमपारसंसदि महद्भावे यशोराशिषु इत्युक्तरीत्या ब्रह्मवत् माहात्म्यशालीति वा । राजा राजते दीप्यते इति । 'कनिन् युवृषितक्षि (उ० १.१५६)—' इत्यादिना कनिन्प्रत्ययः ।

---

१ आर्य. २ एतन्नास्ति क्वाचित्. ३ ०पीती. ४ भावुकः (टी.) ५ कुलगुरुः. ६ गृहेषु, कुले च. ७ सकलस्स, समग्गस्स० ८ अपि.

तत्किमन्यदाशास्महे । केवलं वीरप्रसवा भूयाः ।

रामः—अनुगृहीताः स्मः ।

लौकिकानां हि साधूनामर्थं वागनुवर्तते ।
ऋषीणां पुनराद्यानां वाचमर्थोऽनुधावति । १० ॥

अष्टावक्रः—इदं च भगवत्यारुन्धत्या देवीभिः शान्तया च भूयो

ब्रह्मज्ञानपरिपूर्णतया नैष्ठिकवभिरतिशयदीतियुक्त इत्यर्थः । यद्वा ज्ञानभक्तिवैराग्यैरस्मदादीनपि रञ्जयतीति राजा । धातूनामनेकार्थत्वादिति । जनकः पूर्वोक्तप्रकारेण श्रुतिषु प्रसिद्धः । 'जनको ह वैदेहः,' 'कर्मणैव हि संसिद्धिमास्थिता जनकादयः' इत्यादिषु प्रसिद्ध इत्यर्थः । ते पिता । येषां राज्ञां कुलेष्विति बहुत्वं पूजायाम् । उद्भूतावयवविवक्षया कुलं ब्युत्पादकप्रबन्धः । सर्वं जगत्सुवति कर्मानुष्ठाने प्रेरयतीति वा सविता सूर्यो गुरुः पिता । वयमहम् । 'अस्मदो द्वयोश्च' इति एकत्वे बहुवचनम् । 'सविशेषणस्य प्रतिषेधः' इति तु न विधेयविशेषणविषये । 'ततोऽनु त्वं प्रेयान्वयमपि हताशाः प्रियतमाः ।' इत्यादिप्रयोगात् । 'यद्वा वसिष्ठाङ्गिरसौ ऋषी प्राचेतसस्तथा ।' इति वक्ष्यमाणरीत्या वाल्मीकेः जृम्भकास्त्रसंप्रदायेन विश्वामित्रस्य वामदेवादेश्च ग्रहणात् वयमिति बहुवचनम् । गुरुरित्यनुषक्तस्य वचनविपरिणामात् । गुरवो हितोपदेष्टारः । गृणातीति गुरुः । 'कृग्रोरुच' इत्यौणादिकसूत्रेण निष्पन्नोऽयं शब्दः । 'गुशब्दस्त्वन्धकारः स्यात् रुशब्दस्तन्निवर्तकः' इति निरुक्त्या अज्ञाननिवर्तक इत्यर्थः । गुरवः पितर इत्येव वार्थः । 'स हि विद्यातस्तं जनयति' इति स्मृतेः । 'पुत्रका इति होवाच' इत्यादि पुराणाच्च । तेषां पार्थिवानाम् । 'सर्वा पूर्वमियं येषामासीत्कृत्स्ना वसुंधरा ।' इत्युक्तमुख्यपृथिवीपतिस्वधर्माणां वधूरसि स्नुषासि ॥ ९ ॥ **तदिति** । तस्मात् अन्यत्किं वक्ष्यामाणादितरत्किमाशास्महे । 'आङ्शासु इच्छायाम्' इति धातोर्लट् । अयं भावः—तव गुणातिशयो नाशास्यस्तस्य 'विश्वंभरा भगवती' इत्युक्तमातृसंबन्धादेव तत्सिद्धेः । नापि ज्ञानभक्तिवैराग्यादिकम् । तस्य ब्रह्मविसमजनकसंबन्धादेव तल्लाभात् । न वा हितग्राहित्वमैश्वर्यं भर्तृसंबन्धप्रयुक्तनिकर्षाभावश्च प्रार्थ्यः । तेषां सद्गुरुसंबन्धशालिमहाराजमहाकुलप्रसूतराजकुलस्नुषात्वादेव सिद्धत्वात् । अत एतेषां नाशास्यत्वं किं तु वीरप्रसवत्वस्येति । एष ऋषिभ्रेयोविधानभूतवसिष्ठानुग्रहरूपबीजस्य बहूकरणात्परिकरः । तदुक्तम्—'बीजस्य बहूकरणं परिकरः' इति ॥ **अनुगृहीता इति** । एतन्मनुष्यानुग्रहरूपबीजाङ्गीकरणरूपं समाधानं नाम संध्यङ्गमुक्तम् । तदुक्तम्—'बीजाङ्गीकरणं समाधानम्' इति । **लौकिकानामिति** । लौकिकानामित्यतो व्यतिरेकनिर्देशाल्लौकिकान्यस्य वेदस्यैव इतिहस्युपस्थितेः ऋषीणा-

---

१ सर्वेषां. २ आर्याणां. ३ अनुवर्तते.

भूयः संदिष्टम्। यः कश्चिद्गर्भदोहदोऽस्या भवति सोऽवश्यमचिरान्मानयितव्य इति।

रामः—क्रियते यदेषा कथयति।

अष्टावक्रः—ननान्दुः पत्या च देव्याः संदिष्टमृष्यशृङ्गेण—वत्से कठोरगर्भेति नानीतासि। वत्सोऽपि रामभद्रस्त्वद्विनोदार्थमेव स्थापितः। तत्पुत्रपूर्णोत्सङ्गामायुष्मतीं द्रक्ष्याम इति।

रामः—(सहर्षलज्जास्मितम्।) तथास्तु। भगवता वसिष्ठेन न किंचिदादिष्टोऽस्मि।

अष्टावक्रः—श्रूयताम्।

जामातृयज्ञेन वयं निरुद्धास्त्वं बाल एवासि नवं च राज्यम्।
युक्तः प्रजानामनुरञ्जने स्यास्तस्माद्यशो यत्परमं धनं वः। ११।

मित्युक्तम्। ऋषीणां पुनः। तपस्विनामित्यर्थः। वाचमर्थोऽनुवर्तते वागधीनोऽर्थो भवति। तपस्विनामुक्तिर्हि तपःप्रभावेनानासन्नमप्यर्थमुत्पादयतीति भावः। यद्वा 'ऋष गतौ' इत्यस्य बुद्ध्यर्थत्वात्कालत्रयवर्तिवस्तुसाक्षात्कर्तृत्वं ऋषिपदप्रवृत्तिनिमित्तम्। तथा च भाविनमर्थं दृष्ट्वा ते वदन्ति। ततः स्वकाले प्राप्तं सोऽर्थस्तामनुसरतीति भावः। हि यस्मात् एवं तस्मादनुगृहीता वयमित्यन्वयः। एतत् ऋषिश्रेयोवितरणरूपबीजगुणवर्णनात् विलोभनं नाम संध्यङ्गमुक्तम्। यदुक्तम्—'बीजगुणवर्णनं विलोभनम्' इति ॥ १० ॥ **इदं चेत्यादि**। गर्भस्य दौहदलक्षणम्। 'स कीचकैर्मारुतपूर्णरन्ध्रैः' इतिवत् विशेष्यमात्रपरम्। अन्यथा दौहदशब्दस्यैव गर्भचिह्नवाचित्वात्। तच्च विशिष्टवस्तुविषयाभिलाषादिरूपम्। तस्योदय आविर्भावः। मानयितव्यः संभावयितव्यः। तथा संपादनेन सफलीकार्य इति भावः॥ **क्रियत इति**। एषा कथयति यदि क्रियत इत्यन्वयः॥ **ननान्दुरिति**॥ ननान्दुः। शान्ताया इत्यर्थः। देव्या इत्यस्य पूर्वोत्तराभ्यां संबन्धः। तथा च देवीसंबन्धिननान्दृपतिना देव्याः संदिष्टम्। देवीं प्रति संदिष्टमित्यर्थः। पुत्रपूर्ण उत्सङ्गोऽङ्को यस्या इति बहुव्रीहिः। यद्वात्र पूर्णपदेन यमावित्यपि सूच्यते। अन्यथा पुत्रवदुत्सङ्गामिति वक्तुं शक्यत्वात्। द्रक्ष्याम इति। एतत् बीजानुगुणप्रयोजनविभावनारूपा युक्तिर्नाम संध्यङ्गमुक्तं भवति। तदुक्तम्—'बीजानुगुणप्रयोजनविभावना युक्तिः' इति॥ **जामात्रिति**। ऋष्यशृङ्गेति वक्तव्ये जामात्रित्युक्तं पूज्यतास्फोरणाय। एवं च तदिङ्गितं ज्ञात्वैवास्माभिस्तत्रासितव्यम्। किं पुनस्तत्कृतबहुनिर्बन्धे सतीत्यत आह—निरुद्धा इति। अनेन सर्वप्रकारेणापि नगरं प्रत्यागमने

१ स्वगर्भदोहदोदयः. २ संपादयितव्यः. ३ यदेषा. ४ चाभिहितम्. ५ एतन्नास्ति क्वचित्. ६ द्रक्ष्यामि. ७ सोत्सुक्यस्मि० ८ अस्ति। श्रू०.

रामः—यथा समादिशति भगवान्मैत्रावरुणिः ।

स्नेहं दयां च सौख्यं च यदि वा जानकीमपि ।
आराधनाय लोकस्य मुञ्चतो नास्ति मे व्यथा ॥ १२ ॥

त्वरातिशयो वसिष्ठस्येति व्यज्यते । ननु कुत ईदृशस्त्वरातिशय इत्यत आह—त्वं बाल एवासीति । ननु राज्यतन्त्रविचारोपमर्दाभिज्ञ इत्यर्थः । किं च दशरथजामातरमृष्यशृङ्गं जामातेति निर्दिशन्वसिष्ठः स्वस्य दशरथस्थानीयतामभिप्रैति । तच्च रामबुद्ध्या स्वबुद्ध्या च । एवं चात्रत्यबालशब्दः पुत्रत्वाभिप्रायमूलकः । ततश्च ननु यद्यत्राचार्यकं प्रस्तुतं स्यात् । इति तदागमने त्वरातिशय इति । न केवलमहमाचार्यः किं तु त्वद्बुद्ध्या दशरथस्थानीयश्च । तथा च त्वदीयराज्यतन्त्रविषयकास्थानानर्थशङ्का मामसंनिकृष्टं बाधत इत्याह—त्वं बाल एवासि । न त्वन्यादृशरघुकुलराजवत् शिष्य इत्यर्थः । तथा च तव शिष्यमात्रत्वे पौरोहित्यादिकं वामदेवादयो निर्वक्ष्यन्तीति तदर्थं नास्माकं त्वरा । किं तु तत्पुत्रत्वात् त्वां युवराजीकृत्य महाराजस्थानीयेन मया राज्यतन्त्रो विचारयितव्यः । अन्यथा न मामतिशङ्का मुञ्चतीति भावः । नन्वस्त्वेवम् । तथापि युद्धादिषु लब्धवर्णस्य यौवराज्यस्य पालने सहायापेक्षा नास्तीत्यत्राह—राज्यमिति । नवं च नवमेव । न तु युद्धादिवत् परिचितपूर्वमित्यर्थः । ननु तर्हि किं कर्तव्यमित्यत्राह—युक्त इति । युक्तः संनद्धः । ‘ योगः संनहने ’ इति कोशात् । स्वस्मादात्मन आत्मीयाद्वा । परमं सर्वोत्कृष्टं प्रसिद्धधनस्य क्षयित्वमिति तद्व्यावृत्तिः परमशब्देन विवक्षिता । धनं लब्धांशपरिपालनालब्धांशार्जनाभ्यां धनतुल्यमित्यर्थः ॥ ११ ॥ यथेति । मैत्रावरुणिः मित्रावरुणयोरपत्यमित्यर्थे बाह्वादित्वादिञ्प्रत्ययः । ‘ देवताद्वन्द्वे च ’ इत्यानङ् । इयं च कथा पौराणिकी वेदितव्या । समादिशत्याज्ञापयति । तथा करोमीति शेषः । स्नेहमिति । स्नेहो हि सुखरूपः सुखान्तरहेतुश्च । किं च ‘ शरीरं वसु विज्ञानं मित्रार्थे संपरित्यजेत् ’ इत्युक्तरीत्या सर्वापेक्षया प्रशस्तश्च । अपि च ‘ अहेतुः पक्षपातो यस्तस्य नास्ति ’ इत्युक्तरीत्या दुर्निवर्त्यश्च । तथा च तत्परित्यागोऽपि मम न दुःखायेति भावः । स्नेहस्य व्यवस्थितविषयत्व एव गुणत्वमन्यथा तु दोषत्वमस्तीति निष्कर्षः । दया तु सर्वविषयापि गुणत्वं न मुञ्चति । यथा ‘सर्वभूतेषु सर्वत्र संतुष्टया येन केनचित् । सर्वेन्द्रियोपशान्त्या च तुष्यत्याशु जनार्दनः ॥’ इत्युक्त्या धर्मरूपतया च । किं च परदुःखाधीनसत्ततया तन्निवृत्तिं विना दुर्निवर्त्या । तामपि मुञ्चतो मम न व्यथेति भावः। एतेषां व्यतिरेकेऽप्यात्मनो न व्यतिरेक इत्यस्यापकर्षः। सीता तु ‘प्राणेभ्योऽपि गरीयसी’ इत्युक्तरीत्या जीवितं प्रत्यपि प्रधानभूता । किंच ‘अद्यावसितं रामस्य जीवितप्रयोजनम् ’ इति वक्ष्यमाणरीत्या मद्व्यतिरेकप्रयोजनव्यतिरेकवती । पूर्वोक्तस्नेहदयासौख्यैः संतुष्टोऽहं तामवलम्ब्य । तथाभूतामपि मुञ्चतो मम न व्यथेति भावः। सीतामित्यनुक्त्वा जानकीमित्युक्तिर्लोकाराधनापेक्षया ब्रह्मवित्तमजनकानुरोधोऽप्यकिंचित्कर इति सूचयति । लोके हि अभिमतवस्तुपरित्यागात्पूर्वकाले तस्य संनिधानात्

१ आह. २ तथा. ३ लोकानां.

सीता—अत एव राघवकुलधुरंधर आर्यपुत्रः । (क)

रामः—कः कोऽत्र भोः । विश्राम्यतामष्टावक्रः ।

अष्टावक्रः—(उत्थाय परिक्रम्य च ।) अये कुमारलक्ष्मणः प्राप्तः । (इति निष्क्रान्तः ।)

(प्रविश्य ।)

लक्ष्मणः—जयति जयत्यार्यः । आर्य तेन चित्रकारेणास्मदुपदिष्टमार्यस्य चरितमस्यां वीथिकायामभिलिखितम् । तत्पश्यत्वार्यः ।

रामः—जानासि वत्स दुर्मनायमानां देवीं विनोदयितुम् । तत्कियन्तमवधिं यावत् ।

लक्ष्मणः—यावदार्याया हुताशने विशुद्धिः ।

रामः—शान्तं पापम् । (ससान्त्ववचनम् ।)

(क) अदो जेव्व राहवकुलधुरंधरो अज्जउत्तो ।

न दुःखभूयस्त्वम् । परित्यागात्परमपि तस्यातीतत्वान्न दुःखभूयस्त्वम् । तत्परित्यागकाले तु भवति दुःखभूयस्त्वम् । तावद्वर्तमानत्वात् । मम तु वर्तमानकालेऽपि न दुःखमिति वर्तमानार्थकमुक्तत इति पदशो लभ्यते । व्यथेति सामान्यशब्देन मनोव्याधिरपि नेत्यर्थः ॥ १२ ॥ राघवधुरंधरः । रघुवंशश्रेष्ठ इत्यर्थः । राघवपदोपादानं साभिप्रायकम् । शरणागतसंरक्षणभूतदयालोकाराधनैकपररघुवंशजस्य तवेदमनुरूपमित्यभिप्रायः ॥ विश्राम्यताद्विश्रमं प्राप्नोतु । आशिषि परस्मैपदलोटस्तातङ् । 'विश्राम्यताम्' इति पाठे तु परिजनैरिति शेषः । विश्रमवान्क्रियतामित्यर्थः । णिजन्तात्कर्मणि लोट् ॥ अर्जुनेन तन्नाम्ना । वीथ्यां चित्रमयश्रेण्याम् । दुर्मनायमानां दुःखितमनस्काम् । जनकस्य स्वदेशं प्रति गमनादिति भावः । 'कर्तुः क्यङ् सलोपश्च' । ङित्वादात्मनेपदम् । शानच् । विनोदयितुं दुःखविस्मरणपूर्वकं संतोषं प्रापयितुम् । 'नुद प्रेरणे' उपसर्गबलेन उक्तार्थलाभः । तत्कियानवधिः । तदित्यव्ययम् । तस्येत्यर्थः । अवधिरन्तः कियान् । किंप्रमाणक इत्यर्थः । अनेकसंख्याकेषु मद्व्यापारेषु कीदृशसंख्यायुक्तोऽस्मद्व्यापारः । अस्य चित्रस्यावधिरित्यर्थः ॥ **यावदिति** । हुताशनेन शुद्धिरिति विग्रहः । यावच्छब्दोऽवधारणार्थकः । हुताशनशुद्धिर्यावत् । हुताशनशुद्धिरेवावधिरित्यर्थः । अवधिरिति पूर्वस्मादनुषङ्गः ॥ **शान्तं पापमिति** । योऽयमलीकोपन्यासस्तस्य पीडाहेतुभूतपापशान्तिकरो भवत्विति तात्पर्यम् । लोकोक्तिरियमिष्टजनं प्रत्यनिष्टवचनाक्षमजनाशीर्वचनरूपा । ससान्त्ववचनम् । अत्यर्थमधु-

---

१ विश्राम्यतात्. २ अर्जुनेन चित्रकारेण (टी.) ३ वीथ्याम्. ४ कियानवधिः (टी.). ५ राहवधु०.

उत्पत्तिपरिपूतायाः किमस्याः पावनान्तरैः ।
तीर्थोदकं च वह्निश्च नान्यतः शुद्धिमर्हतः ॥ १३ ॥

देवि देवयजनसंभवे प्रसीद । एष ते जीवितावधिः प्रवादः ।

कष्टं जनः कुलधनैरनुरञ्जनीय-
स्तन्नो यदुक्तमशिवं न हि तत्क्षमं ते ।
नैसर्गिकी सुरभिणः कुसुमस्य सिद्धा
मूर्ध्नि स्थितिर्न चरणैरवताडनानि ॥ १४ ॥

स्वाक्यसहितमित्यर्थः ॥ **उत्पत्तीत्यादि** । उत्पत्त्या परिपूतायाः परिशुद्धायाः कृत्रिमत्वनिरासार्थमिदम् । स्वभावतो दोषप्रतिभटाया इत्यर्थः । अस्याः सीतायाः । पावयन्तीति पावनानि । नन्द्यादित्वाल्ल्युप्रत्ययः । अन्यानि पावनानि पावनान्तराणि । तैरित्यर्थः । किम् । न किमपीत्यर्थः । शुद्धिर्हि दोषनिर्हरणम् । अविद्यमानदोषायाः कथं शुद्धिरिति भावः । किंच अन्तरशब्देन दोषरहितमात्रस्य पावकवस्त्वपेक्षा नास्ति पावकस्य तु तन्नैरपेक्ष्यं कैमुतिकम् । इयं च केवलं दोषरहिता न । किंतु पावका चेति सूच्यते । 'अपि मां पावयेत्साध्वी स्नात्वेतीच्छति जाह्नवी' इति न्यायात् । उक्तमर्थमुत्तरार्धेन दर्शयति—तीर्थोदकमिति । गङ्गादिपावनजलम् । तीर्थशब्दो विशेषणमात्रपरः । यथाश्रुते तीर्थशब्दस्यैव परिशुद्धोदकवाचित्वात् । यद्वा तीर्थानां गुरूणामुदकं पादावनेजनाम्भः । 'आपः पादावनेजनीर्द्विषन्तं नाशयन्तु मे' इति श्रुतेः । वह्निश्च अन्यतः शुद्धिमन्यहेतुकशुद्धिं नार्हतः । यथा पावकत्वाविशेषात्तीर्थोदकवह्न्योरितरापेक्षा नास्ति तद्वदस्या अपि पावकत्वाविशेषेण तदपेक्षा नास्तीत्यतिस्फुटम् । किंच विनिगमनाविरहात् वह्नेर्वा सीतासंबन्धतः शुद्धिः किं न स्यादित्याशयः । अग्निप्रवेशानुमतिर्मूढप्रत्यायनार्था वा । अग्निप्राशस्त्यार्था वा ॥ १३ ॥ **जीवितावधिरिति** । जीवितस्यावधिर्यस्येति बहुव्रीहिः । यदीयावधिः जीवितावधिः । स इत्यर्थः । प्रसीद । **क्लिष्ट इति** । यद्यस्मात्कारणात्क्लिष्टो जनो दुःखितो जनो जनैरनुरञ्जनीयः । क्लेशं विस्मार्य लालनीय इत्यर्थः । नतु पूर्वानुभूतदुःखस्मारणेन क्लेशयितव्य इत्यर्थः । तत्तस्मात् । अशुभममङ्गलम् । 'अशिवम्' इति पाठान्तरम् । ते त्वद्विषये । शेषे षष्ठी । न आवयोः । 'अस्मदो द्वयोश्च' इति द्वित्वे बहुवचनम् । यदुक्तम्—'अस्मत्कर्तृकं यद्वचनम्' इत्यर्थः । 'नपुंसके भावे क्तः' । 'यावदार्याया हुताशनशुद्धिः' इत्युक्तलक्ष्मणवचनमित्यर्थः । अत्र लक्ष्मणवचनस्य रामस्य स्वोक्तितैक्याभिसंधिना । 'रामस्य दक्षिणो बाहुर्नित्यं प्राणो बहिश्चरः' इत्युक्तेः । तत् । वचनमित्यनुषज्यते । नः त्वदेकजीवितयोस्तव निर्दोषतां च जानतोरित्यर्थः । न क्षमं नोचितम् । अयं भावः—बन्धुत्वमित्रत्वानादरेण जनत्वरूपसामान्यधर्म एवानुरञ्जनीयानुरञ्जकभावे पर्याप्तो हेतुः । तत्र 'प्रेयो मित्रं बन्धुता वा समग्रा सर्वे कामाः संपदो जीवितं वा । स्त्रीणां भर्ता धर्मदा-

१ सीते इत्यधि० २ प्रणामः. ३ कष्टो, क्लिष्टो जनः किल जनैः (टी.) ४ तन्मे. ५ दुरुक्तं. ६ न च. ७ मुसलैः. ८ नाडिनानि.

सीता---भवत्वार्यपुत्र भवतु । एहि । प्रेक्षामहे तावत्ते चरितम् । (इत्युत्थाय परिक्रामतः ।) (क)

लक्ष्मणः---इदं तदालेख्यम् ।

सीता---(निर्वर्ण्य ।) क एते उपरिनिरन्तरस्थिता उपस्तुवन्तीवार्यपुत्रम् । (ख)

लक्ष्मणः---एतानि तानि सरहस्यानि जृम्भकास्त्राणि यानि भगवतः कृशाश्वात्कौशिकमृषिमुपसंक्रान्तानि तेन च ताटकावधेप्रसादीकृतान्यार्यस्य ।

रामः---वन्दस्व देवि दिव्यास्त्राणि ।

(क) होदु अज्जउत्त होदु । एहि । पेक्खह्म दाव दे चरिदम् ।

(ख) के एदे उवरिणिरन्तरट्ठिदा उवत्थुवन्दि विअ अज्जउत्तम् ।

राश्च पुंसाम् ' इत्युक्तरीत्या सर्वप्रकारप्रियतमायास्तव विषये तथाविधानामस्माकं पूर्वानुभूतदुःखस्मारणमहापराधो नोचित एव तत्राप्यलीकनिर्बन्धतत्स्मारणं तु सुतराम् । किंच निर्दोषतां च जानतोरावयोस्तत्कथनं तु दूरोत्सारितमिति । सुरभिणः कुसुमस्य सुगन्धप्रधानस्य पुष्पस्य मूर्ध्नि स्थितिः नैसर्गिकी निसर्ग एव । विनयादित्वात्स्वार्थे ठक्प्रत्ययः । सिद्धा प्रसिद्धा । चेतनाचेतनसाधारण्येन प्रसिद्धा । चेतनैरवचूडरूपेणाचेतनैः शाखाग्रे च धारणात् । चरणैरवताडनानि न । न दृष्टानीत्यर्थः । अयं भावः---त्रिविधानि तावत्कुसुमान्यवगन्तव्यानि । कान्तिप्रधानानि सौरभ्यप्रधानानि उक्तोभयप्रधानानि चेति । तत्र कान्तिप्रधानानि शाल्मलीकुसुमादीनि सौरभ्यप्रधानानि दमनकादीनि उभयप्रधानानि मालतीप्रभृतीनि । तत्र सौरभ्यमात्रप्रधानस्यापि न चरणावताडनार्हत्वम् । तस्य घ्राणैकनिरन्तरानुभाव्यत्वात् । एवं नाद्यस्यापि । तस्य दर्शनैकानुभाव्यत्वात् । उभयप्रधानस्य तु सुतरां न चरणावताडनार्हत्वमिति । सुरभिणः कुसुमस्येति पदद्वयोपादानादित्थं व्याख्यातम् । अत्र ' न मुसलैः ' इति केचित्पठन्ति । ॥ १४ ॥ प्रेक्षामहे पश्याम इत्यर्थः । आलेख्यं चित्रम् । उपरिनिरन्तरास्थिता अविरलं स्थिता अनुपविष्टा इत्याशयः । तेषां दिव्यास्त्रत्वादुपरिस्थितिर्युक्तेत्युपरिलेखनम् । उपस्तुवन्ति स्तोत्रं कुर्वन्ति । सरहस्यानि । प्रयोगप्रतिसंहारोपयिकमन्त्रादयो रहस्यानि । तत्सहितानीत्यर्थः । जृम्भकास्त्राणि भृशाश्वात्तन्नाम्नो मुनेः कौशिकं विश्वामित्रमुपसंक्रान्तानि प्राप्तानि । उपसंक्रान्तानीति कर्तृप्रत्ययेन स्वयमेव तानि कौशिकं प्राप्तानीति लभ्यते । तथा च---' भृशाश्वः परःसहस्रपरिवत्सरान्तेवासिने कौशिकाय ' इति वक्ष्यमाणं परःसहस्रपरिवत्सरान्तेवासित्वं जृम्भकास्त्ररूपफलगुरुत्वमपेक्ष्यासत्कल्पमिति हृदयम् । तेन च विश्वामित्रेण प्रसादीकृतानि । प्रसादतत्कार्यजृम्भकास्त्रयोरभेदाध्य-

---

१ ०क्रामतिः. २ तावद्. ३ देवि ए०. ४ सरहस्यजृ. ५ भृशा (टी.) ६ ०मृषिं विश्वस्य मित्रं विश्वामित्रम्. ७ एतन्नास्ति क्वचित्. ८ के वाणिं.

ब्रह्मादयो ब्रह्महिताय तप्त्वा परःसहस्राः शरदः तपांसि ।
एतान्यपश्यन्गुरवः पुराणाः स्वान्येव तेजांसि तपोमयानि ॥ १५ ॥

सीता—नम एतेभ्यः । (क)

रामः—सर्वथेदानीं त्वत्प्रसूतिमुपस्थास्यन्ति ।

सीता—अनुगृहीतास्मि । (ख)

लक्ष्मणः—एष मिथिलावृत्तान्तः ।

सीता—अहो दलन्नवनीलोत्पलश्यामलस्निग्धमसृणमांसलेन देहसौभाग्येन विस्मयस्तिमिततातदृश्यमानसौम्यसुन्दरश्रीरनादरखण्डितशंकरशरासनः शिखण्डमुग्धमुखमण्डल आर्यपुत्र आलिखितः । (ग)

(क) णमो एदाणम् । (ख) अणुग्गहीदह्मि ।

(ग) अह्महे दलन्तणवणीलुप्पलसामलसिणिद्धमसिणमंसलेण देहसोहग्गेण विह्मअत्थिमिदताददीसन्तसोम्ममुन्दरासिरी अणादरखंडिदसंकरसरासणो सिहण्डमुद्धमुहमण्डलो अज्जउत्तो आलिहिदो ।

वसायादित्थमुक्तम् । केवलप्रसादेन दत्तानीत्यर्थः । **ब्रह्मादय इति** । पुराणा ब्रह्मादयश्चतुर्मुखप्रभृतयः । गुरवस्तपउपदेष्टारः । तमोनिवर्तका इत्यर्थः । ' शरदस्तपांसि ' इति वा पाठः । तपांस्यन्तःकरणनैर्मल्यापादनद्वारा भगवत्साक्षात्कारहेतुभूतकायशोषणव्रतानि । परःसहस्रम् । सहस्रात्परा इत्यर्थः । ' कर्तृकरणे कृता बहुलम् ' इति बहुलग्रहणात्समासः । सुप्सुपेति वा । परस्परादित्वात्सहस्रशब्दस्य सुडागमः । सहस्रसंख्याधिकसंख्याका इत्यर्थः । ' विंशत्याद्याः सदैकत्वे सर्वाः संख्येयसंख्ययोः ' इत्यनुशासनादेकत्वम् । शरदः संवत्सरान् । अत्यन्तसंयोगे द्वितीया । तथा च सहस्रसंख्याधिकसंवत्सरेषु निरन्तरं तप्त्वेत्यर्थः । ब्रह्म परमात्मा प्रधानं च । तत्कार्यत्वाज्जगत ब्रह्मशब्देनोच्यते । तदुक्तम्—'तादर्थ्यादुपचारोऽस्ति क्वचित्स्वस्वामिभावतः । अङ्गाङ्गिभावतात्कर्म्याद्वैपरीत्यादपीष्यते ॥ ' इति । तस्य हिताय तदपेक्षितेष्टानिष्टप्राप्तिपरिहारसाधनाय तपःफलभूतजृम्भकोपदेशेन राजभिर्विरोधिनिरसनेन जगतः पुरुषार्थसाधननिर्वर्तनसिद्धेरिति भावः । अथवा ब्रह्म वेदस्तस्य हिताय धारणाय । धारणार्थकधाञ्धातोर्नपुंसके भावे क्तः । 'दधातेर्हिः' इति हिभावश्च । अनुत्सादायेति भावः । तपोमयानि तपःस्वरूपाणि । स्वार्थिको मयट् । स्वानि स्वकीयानि तेजांसि एतानि

---

१ परःसहस्रं शरदाम्. २ अदर्शन्. ३ मुनयः. ४ ०थैतानि. ५ प्रसवं. ६ णमो णमो ७ मसिणसोहमाण. ८ अनाआस. ९ क्खु-थु-डिद (त्रुटित). १० मुद्धमण्डणो.

लक्ष्मणः—आर्ये पश्य पश्य ।

संबन्धिनो वसिष्ठादीनेष तातस्तवार्चति ।
गौतमश्च शतानन्दो जनकानां पुरोहितः ॥ १६ ॥

[रा]मः—द्रष्टव्यमेतत् ।

जनकानां रघूणां च संबन्धः कस्य न प्रियः ।
यत्र दाता ग्रहीता च स्वयं कुशिकनन्दनः ॥ १७ ॥

अदर्शञ्जृम्भकास्त्राण्यपश्यन् । कार्यकारणनिबन्धनमिदं सामानाधिकरण्यम् । 'दृशिर् प्रेक्षणे' इति धातोः लुङ् । तथा च । बहुतरतपःकार्यभूतानामेतेषां केवलगुरुप्रसादसाध्यत्वम् । नतु शुश्रूषादिसाध्यत्वमिति भावः ॥ १५ ॥ त्वत्प्रसूतिं त्वत्प्रसवम् । त्वत्पुत्रावित्यर्थः । 'द्विधागर्भग्रन्थिस्तदनुदिवसैः' इति वक्ष्यमाणरीत्या यमलत्ववत्पुंप्रजात्वमपि निर्णीतमिति सूच्यते । अन्यथा स्त्रीप्रजात्वे जृम्भकाभ्यनुज्ञानमसंगतं स्यात् । उपस्थास्यन्ति प्राप्स्यन्ति । मामिव स्तोष्यन्तीति वार्थः । **अह्मह इति** । दलितनीलोत्पलवच्छ्यामलं स्निग्धं च चाकचक्ययुक्तम् । मांसलं स्फीतं तेन । तथाविधेनेत्यर्थः । विशेषणसमासः । देहसौभाग्येन देहसौन्दर्येण । विस्मित आश्चर्ययुक्तः । अत एव स्तिमितो निश्चलो यस्तातस्तेन दृश्यमाना सौम्या आह्लादकरी सुन्दरश्रीर्यस्य स तथोक्तः । प्राकृते आत्मनेपदाभावाद्दीसन्तेत्युक्तिः । त्रुटितं भग्नं शरासनं येन स तथोक्तः ॥ **संबन्धिन इति** । जनकानां जनकापत्यभूतानाम् । लाक्षणिकोऽयं शब्दः । पुरोहितो गौतमो गौतमपुत्रः । 'ऋष्यन्धकवृष्णिकुरुभ्यश्च' इत्यण्प्रत्ययः । शतानन्दस्तन्नामा । तथा च—एष तव तातो वसिष्ठादीन्संबन्धिनोऽर्चति पूजयति । जनकानां पुरोहितो गौतमः शतानन्दश्चार्चतीत्यनुषङ्गः । यथाक्रमं तव तातो जनकः संबन्धिनो दशरथप्रभृतीनर्चयति । जनकानां पुरोहितो गौतमः शतानन्दश्च वसिष्ठादीनर्चयति चेत्यन्वयः ॥ १६ ॥ **सुश्लिष्टमिति**[1] । हेमारविन्दपरिमलन्यायादिति भावः । **जनकानामिति** । जनकानां जनकवंशोद्भवानां रघूणां रघुवंशोद्भवानां च । लाक्षणिकोऽयं शब्दः । संबन्धो अपत्यसंबन्धः । कस्य न प्रियः । सर्वस्यापि प्रिय इत्यर्थः । यत्र संबन्धे कुशिकनन्दनो विश्वामित्रः स्वयं दाता स्वयं प्रतिग्रहीता च । दशरथं प्रति दाता. जनकं प्रति प्रतिग्रहीता चेत्यर्थः । अयं भावः—तव मम च परिणयरूपोऽयं संबन्धो जनकदशरथयोरावयोर्जनानां च मध्ये कस्यचिदपि नाप्रियः । तथा हि—जनकानां रघूणामित्यनेन रघुवंश्याञ्जनकवंश्यान्प्रति नाप्रियत्वमिति लभ्यते । अत्र निमीनामित्यनुक्त्वा जनकानामिति पदोपादानेन 'कर्मणैव हि संसिद्धिमास्थिता जनकादयः' इति जनके प्रसिद्धं कर्मभोगशीलत्वमिह स्फोर्यते । एवं काकुत्स्थानामित्यनुक्त्वा रघूणामित्युक्त्या

---

१ सुश्लिष्टं (टी.).

सीताः—एते खलु तत्कालकृतगोदानमङ्गलाश्चत्वारो भ्रातरो विवाहदीक्षिता यूयम्। अहा जानामि तस्मिन्नेव काले प्रदेशे तस्मिन्नेन वर्ते। (क)

रामः—

समयः स वर्तत इवैष यत्र मां
　समनन्दयत्सुमुखि गौतमार्पितः।
अयमागृहीतकमनीयकङ्कण-
　स्तव मूर्तिमानिव महोत्सवः करः॥ १८॥

(क) एदे क्खु तक्कालकिदगोदाणमङ्गला चत्तारो भादरो विआहदिक्खिदा तुह्मे। अह्मो जाणामि तस्सिं जेव्व पदेसे तस्सिं जेव्व काले वत्तामि।

'श्रुतस्य यायादयमन्तमर्भकस्तथा परेषां युधि चेति पार्थिवः' इत्यादि कालिदासनिरुक्त्या 'लङ्घिबंह्योर्नलोपश्च' इत्यनुशासनेन च लब्धया लङ्कते जानाति सर्वमिति व्युत्पत्त्या 'मनुरिक्ष्वाकवेऽब्रवीत्' इत्यैक्ष्वाकवं रघुकुलासाधारणज्ञानयोगशीलत्वं सूच्यते। तथा चान्यादृशजनकविषये जातोऽपत्यसंबन्धः संबन्धिनामित्यभिमतो भवति। तत्र क्षीरशर्करावदन्योन्यसंपर्करमणीयज्ञानकर्मशीलजनकविषयत्वे तु तस्य हेमारविन्दपरिमलन्यायेनातिश्लाघ्यत्वमिति तान्प्रत्यप्रियत्वव्यावृत्तिः। अत एव चावां प्रत्यपि नाप्रियत्वम्। यत्र दातेत्यादिनापि जनकदशरथौ प्रत्यप्रियत्वं व्यावर्त्यते। तत्र दशरथं प्रत्ययाचितोपनतत्वाज्जनकं प्रति दुष्करधनुर्भङ्गप्रतिज्ञानिवर्तनरूपमहोपकारकरणाच्च गुर्वनुज्ञाप्राप्तत्वान्महर्षिकारितत्वाच्च नावां प्रत्यप्रियत्वम्। स्वयमित्यनेनाग्रहादिमूलकत्रिशङ्कुयाजनहरिश्चन्द्रोपप्लवव्यावृत्तिः। अत एव जनान्प्रत्यप्रियत्वं निरस्तम्। शिष्टानुमतस्य धर्मत्वे शिष्टकारिते तस्य कैमुतिकसिद्धत्वात्। तथा चापस्तम्बस्मृतिः—'यत्त्वार्योः क्रियमाणं तं प्रशंसन्ति स धर्मः' इति। ब्रह्मर्षिर्विश्वामित्र इत्याद्यनुक्त्वा कुशिकनन्दन इति पदोपादानं विश्वामित्रः स्वब्रह्मर्षित्वमविगणय्य भूतपूर्वगत्या क्षत्रियत्वं स्वीकृत्य बन्धुभावेनास्मत्संबन्धिभावेनास्ति असतिसंबन्धे ब्रह्मर्षिकृत्यानीति व्यञ्जयति॥ १७॥ **एदे क्खु इति**। गोदानमङ्गलं क्षौरकर्म तस्य मङ्गलार्थत्वान्मङ्गलत्वम्। विवाहेन दीक्षिता विवाहदीक्षिता इति विवाहहेतुकव्रतवन्त इत्यर्थः। 'दीक्षमौण्ड्येज्योपनयनव्रतादेशेषु' इति दीक्षिधातोः कर्तरि क्तः। तस्मिन्नेव प्रदेश इति प्रत्यभिज्ञादार्ढ्यमिति॥ **समय इति**। यत्र समये गौतमार्पितः पुरोधसा शतानन्देन प्रतिपादित आगृहीतकमनीयकङ्कणः। समन्तादृहीतकमनीयवलयः तथापि मूर्तिमान् महोत्सव इव स्थितः समनन्दयत् स एष समयो वर्तत इव। स्मृतिवैशद्यमिदम्। अत्र सुमुखि 'आगृहीतकमनीयकङ्कणः' इत्युक्त्या सिद्धसाध्यसमभि-

---

१ ०मुद्गृहीत, स्वयमागृहीत. २ रोचि.

लक्ष्मणः—इयमार्या । इयमप्यार्या माण्डवी । इयमपि वधूः श्रुतकीर्तिः ।

सीता—वत्स इयमप्यपरा का । (क)

लक्ष्मणः—(सलज्जस्मितम् । आत्मगतम् ।) अये ऊर्मिलां पृच्छत्यार्या । भवतु । अन्यतः संचारयामि । (प्रकाशम् ।) आर्ये दृश्यतां द्रष्टव्यमेतत् । अयं च भगवान्भार्गवः ।

सीता—(ससंभ्रमम् ।) कम्पितास्मि । (ख)

रामः—ऋषे नमस्ते ।

लक्ष्मणः—आर्ये पश्य पश्य । अयमसावार्येण—(इत्यर्धोक्ते ।)

रामः—(साक्षेपम् ।) अयि वत्स बहुतरं द्रष्टव्यम् । अन्यतो दर्शय ।

सीता—(सस्नेहबहुमानं निर्वर्ण्य ।) सुष्ठु शोभसे आर्यपुत्र एतेन विनयमाहात्म्येन । (ग)

लक्ष्मणः—एते वयमयोध्यां प्राप्ताः ।

(क) वच्छ इअं वि अवरा का । (ख) कम्पिदम्हि ।

(ग) सुट्ठु सोहसि अज्जउत्त एदिणा विणअमाहप्पेण ।

व्याहारन्यायेनागृहीतकमनीयकङ्कणत्वं प्रति सीताया वदनकमलसौन्दर्यातिशयो हेतुरित्यवगम्यते । अन्यथा 'पाणिं गृह्णीष्व पाणिना' इत्युक्तपाणिपीडनस्य प्रकोष्ठवर्तिमणिवलयग्रहणासंगतेः । तथा च—सीतामुखचन्द्रदर्शनानन्दपारवश्येन सम्यक्करग्रहणाभावात्संवृत्तस्तथात्व एव स पाणिर्मूर्तिमान्महोत्सव इव स्थितः । सम्यक्स्पर्शो तु निःसीमानन्दकर इति व्यज्यते । आगृहीताः सम्यग्गृहीताः शृङ्गारमूलकसात्त्विकभावविशेषरूपत्वेन स्पृहणीयाः कङ्कणाः स्वेदजलबिन्दवो यस्मिन्स तथोक्त इत्यप्याहुः । आगृहीतवैवाहिकप्रतिसर इत्यपि केचित् ॥ १८ ॥ इयमार्या माण्डवीति भरतभार्यात्वात्, इयमपि वधूरिति शत्रुघ्नभार्यात्वात् स्नुषात्वेन ग्रहणम् ॥ **अयमिति** । भार्गवः परशुरामः ॥ कम्पितास्मि । येनेति शेषः ॥ **अयमार्येणेत्यादि** । अत्र वैष्णवं धनुरारोपय्य समाकृष्टतेजस्क इति वक्तुमुद्युक्तवान् लक्ष्मणः । तावदात्मप्रशंसामसहमानो रामः प्रतिषिद्धवानित्याशयः । साक्षेपं सप्रतिषेधम् । 'क्षिपु निरसने' इत्यस्मात् भावे घञ्प्रत्ययः । अन्यतो दर्शय । अन्यत्र लिखितं दर्शयेति भावः ॥ विनयमाहात्म्येन विनयस्य स्वोत्कर्षतानाविष्करणरूपस्य स्वस्मिन्निकर्षानुसंधानरूपस्य वा माहात्म्यं भूयस्ता तेनेत्यर्थः । एते वयमयोध्यां प्राप्ताः । तथा-

---

१ सलज्जा०. २ अपवार्य. ३ ससाध्वसं. ४ एतन्नास्ति क्वचित्. ५ भीदह्मि (भीतास्मि).

रामः—(सास्रम् ।) स्मरामि हन्त स्मरामि ।

जीवत्सु तातपादेषु नवे दारपरिग्रहे ।
मातृभिश्चिन्त्यमानानां ते हि नो दिवसा गताः ॥ १९ ॥

इयमपि तदा जानकी

प्रतनुविरलैः प्रान्तोन्मीलन्मनोहरकुन्तलै-
र्दशनमुकुलैर्मुग्धालोकं शिशुर्दधती मुखम् ।
ललितललितैर्ज्योत्स्नाप्रायैरकृत्रिमविभ्रमै-
रकृत मधुरैरम्बानां मे कुतूहलमङ्गकैः ॥ २० ॥

लिखिता इत्यर्थः ॥ जीवत्स्विति । तातपादेषु । पितरीत्यर्थः । पूजायां पादशब्दो बहुवचने । 'उत्तमानां स्वरूपं तु पादशब्देन भण्यते' इति । जीवत्सु सप्राणे । 'यस्य च भावेन' इति सप्तमी । दारसंग्रहे नूतने सति मातृभिश्चिन्त्यमानानां नस्ते दिवसा गता इत्यन्वयः । गता दिवसास्ते हीति स्मरणाकारप्रदर्शनं वा । अबन्धोरपि रक्षकस्य जीवनमानन्दाय । सर्वविधसंरक्षणशीलस्य पितुर्जीवनं तु निरवधिकाह्लादजनकम् । किं च दाराणां सततपरिचर्येऽपि प्रियैकवेषत्वं नूतनसंग्रहे तु अमन्दानन्दहेतुत्वम् । स्वरूपसत्येव माता निरतिशयसौख्यकारिणी । तत्रापि सा लोकप्रसिद्धसर्वविधसंरक्षणानि कृत्वा ततोऽप्यधिकानि चिन्तयति चेत् निःसीमानन्दलाभः । एवमपरिच्छिन्नानन्दकन्दलहेतुत्वाद्दिवसानां तच्छब्देन निर्देशः । तातपादजीवनादीनां मध्य एकैकमेवानन्दहेतुः । समुदितानि तु सुतरामिति भावः ॥ १९ ॥ 'नूतने दारसंग्रहे' इत्युक्तं विशिनष्टि—इयमपि तदेत्यादिना । प्रतन्विति । शिशुः शैशवान्तवती । शिशुप्रायेत्यर्थः । 'पतिसंयोगसुलभं वयो दृष्ट्वा च मे पिता' इत्युक्तेः । पतनेन प्रस्थितदशनपतनेन । प्रान्तोन्मीलदित्युक्तेः । विरलैः सान्तरालैः । प्रान्तेत्याद्यत्र उन्मीलच्छब्दः प्ररोहद्दन्तपरः । दशनकुसुमैरिति रूपकसाहचर्यात् । तथा च उन्मीलदेव उद्यन्नूतनदशनाङ्कुर एव मनोहरकुड्मलमुन्मीलन्मनोहरकुड्मलम् । प्रान्ते उन्मीलन्मनोहरकुड्मलं येषामिति बहुव्रीहिः । यद्वा कुड्मलशब्दो मुकुलसदृशदशनपरः । प्रान्तोन्मीलन्ति मनोहरकुड्मलानि येषामित्यर्थः । रूपकातिशयोक्तिरलंकारः । दशनकुसुमैरिति तु रूपकमुपमा वेति संकर इत्यपि वदन्ति । दशना एव कुसुमानि तैर्धावल्यशिखरित्वादिसादृश्याद्रूपणमुपमा वा । हेतुभिः मुग्धः सुन्दर आलोको यस्य तत्तथोक्तम् । यद्वा दशनकुसुमैरिति इत्थंभूतलक्षणे तृतीया । दशनकुसुमैरुपलक्षितमित्यर्थः । मुग्धालोकं सुन्दरकटाक्षं मुखं दधती इयं सीता ललितादपि कुसुमादपि ललितैः सुकुमारैः । यद्वा ललितं नाम हासाद्यन्यतमविशेषः । तदुक्तम्—'सुकुमाराङ्गविन्यासो ललितं परिकीर्तितम् ।' इति । तेन ललितैः । विलसितैरित्यर्थः । 'लड विलासे' कर्तरि क्तः । लडयोरेकत्वम् । ज्योत्स्नाप्रायै

---

१ नूतने दारसंग्रहे. २ पतन (टी.) ३ कुड्मलैः (टी.) ४ कुसुमैः (टी.) ५ मन्दालोकं. ६ अङ्गानाम्.

लक्ष्मणः—एषा मन्थरा ।

रामः—(सत्वरमन्यतो दर्शयन् ।) देवि वैदेहि

इङ्गुदीपादपः सोऽयं शृङ्गवेरपुरे पुरा ।
निषादपतिना यत्र स्निग्धेनासीत्समागमः ॥ २१ ॥

लक्ष्मणः—(विहस्य । स्वगतम् ।) अये मध्यमाम्बावृत्तमन्तरितमार्येण ।

सीता—अहो एष जटासंयमनवृत्तान्तः । (क)

लक्ष्मणः—

पुत्रसंक्रान्तलक्ष्मीकैर्यद्वृद्धेक्ष्वाकुभिर्धृतम् ।
धृतं बाल्ये तदार्येण पुण्यमारण्यकव्रतम् ॥ २२ ॥

(क) अह्मो एसो जडासंजमणवुत्तन्तो ।

ज्योत्स्नासदृशैः । यद्वा ज्योत्स्ना कान्तिः । लावण्यमिति यावत् । तत्प्रायैः । तत्प्रचुरैरित्यर्थः । प्रायशब्दः प्रचुरवाची । जलप्रायो देश इतिवत् । लावण्यस्वरूपं तु 'भूयिष्ठं तेज एवाद्भिर्बहुलाभिर्मृदूकृतम् । चक्षुरानन्दजननं लावण्यमिति कथ्यते ॥' इति । अकृत्रिमाः स्वाभाविका विभ्रमा विलासा येषां तानि । तैरित्यर्थः । विभ्रमशब्दो गोबलीवर्दन्यायेन माधुर्यललितान्यपरः । यद्वा 'विभ्रमस्त्वरया कालभूषास्थान' इत्युक्तविभ्रमपरः । सोऽकृत्रिमो येषु तथोक्तैरित्यर्थः । प्रियैरित्यर्थः । 'अभूषणेऽपि रम्यत्वं माधुर्यमिति कथ्यते' इत्युक्तमाधुर्ययुक्तैरित्यर्थः । अनुकम्पितैरङ्गैरङ्गकैः । 'अनुकम्पायाम्' इति कन्प्रत्ययः । अतिसुकुमारतया गाढालिङ्गनादिषु दयनीयैरित्यर्थः । तदाह कालिदासः- 'सदयं सुन्दरि गृह्यते रसोऽस्य' 'पीतं मया सदयमेव रतोत्सवेषु' इति । यद्वा अल्पैरङ्गैरङ्गकैः । 'अल्प' इतिसूत्रेण कन्प्रत्ययः । अल्पत्वं चेह तनुत्वमभिप्रेतम् । तदुक्तम्— 'स्वभावावतनुका नूनम्' इति । अनेन 'सुश्लिष्टसंधिबन्धत्वं सौन्दर्यमिति कथ्यते' इत्युक्तसौन्दर्यमप्युक्तं भवति । तेन विना तनुत्वस्य दोषत्वात् । मेऽङ्गानां कुतूहलमकृत कृतवती । 'डुकृञ् करणे' । सिचो लोपः । कर्त्रभिप्राय आत्मनेपदेन रामाङ्गकुतूहलकरणफलं सीताया इत्यवगम्यते । 'अद्वैतं सुखदुःखयोः' इति वक्ष्यमाणत्वात् । केचित्तु 'अम्बानाम्' इति पाठ इत्याहुः ॥ २० ॥ मन्थरावृत्तान्तस्तत्प्रयत्नफलपट्टाभिषेकान्तरायरूपः ॥ **इङ्गुदीति** । स्निग्धेन स्नेहवता निषादपतिना गुहेन समागमः संबन्धः ॥ २१ ॥ मध्यमाम्बावृत्तान्तमिति क्लीबत्वं प्रामादिकम् । अन्तशब्दं त्यक्त्वा मध्यमाम्बावृत्तमन्तर्हितमिति पठनीयमित्याहुः ॥ जटासंयमनं जटाबन्धनम् ॥ **पुत्रेति** । पुत्रेषु संक्रान्ता स्वयमेवाश्रयशैथिल्यादागता । स्वतः संक्रान्तेत्यर्थः । गत्यर्थादिसूत्रेण कर्तरि क्तः । तथाविधा लक्ष्मीर्येषां ते तथो-

१ मुग्धा मन्थ०, एष मन्थरावृत्तान्तः. २ अनुत्तरमन्यतो गत्वा. ३ वृत्तान्तोऽन्तरितः. ४ कृतम.

सीता—एषा प्रसन्नपुण्यसलिला भगवती भागीरथी । (क)

रामः—देवि रघुकुलदेवते नमस्ते ।

तुरगविचयव्यग्रानुर्वीभिदः सगराध्वरे
कपिलमहसामर्षात्प्लुष्टान्पुरां प्रपितामहान् ।
अगणिततनूतापं तप्त्वा तपांसि भगीरथो
भगवति तव स्पृष्टानद्भिश्चिरादुददीधरत् ॥ २३ ॥

सा त्वमम्ब स्नुषायामरुन्धतीव सीतायां शिवानुध्यानपरा भव ।

लक्ष्मणः—अयमसौ भरद्वाजावेदितश्चित्रकूटयायिनि वर्त्मनि वनस्पतिः कालिन्दीतटे वटः श्यामो नाम ।

रामः—(सस्पृहमवलोकयति ।)

सीता—स्मरति वैतं प्रदेशमार्यपुत्रः । (ख)

रामः—अयि कथं विस्मर्यते ।

(क) एसा पसण्णपुण्णसलिला भअवदी भाईरही ।

(ख) सुमेरेदि वा एदं पदेसं अज्जउत्तो ।

क्तास्तैः । उरःप्रभृतित्वात्कप् । वृद्धाश्च ते इक्ष्वाकवश्चेति इक्ष्वाकुवंश्या इत्यर्थः । तैर्यद्व्रतं धृतं तत्पुण्यं व्रतमार्येण बाल्ये धृतमिति योजना । आरण्यकानां व्रतम् । अरण्यचरमनुष्यसंबन्धि व्रतमित्यर्थः । अत्र पुत्रसंक्रान्तलक्ष्मीकैरित्यनेन पुत्रवत्त्वमुपभुक्तराज्यत्वं वृद्धेत्यनेन वार्धकं चावगम्यते । एवं चैतेषां समुदितानां सत्त्व एव पूर्वेषामारण्यकव्रतधारणं न तु यत्किंचित्सत्त्वे । रामस्य तु एतेषां सर्वेषामभावेऽप्यारण्यकव्रतधारणम् । बाल्ये इत्यनेन पुत्रवत्त्वोपभुक्तराज्यकत्वशरीरशैथिल्यवार्धकाभावानां लाभात् । पुण्यमिति । विशेषणं प्रसिद्धव्यावृत्त्यर्थम् । तद्धि अनुष्ठातुरेव पुण्यफलसाधनम् । इदं तु सकलभुवनाभीष्टसाधनमिति । आर्येणेत्यनेनासामर्थ्यनिबन्धनलोकवादभीत्यादिना न कृतम् । किं तु वैदिकश्रद्धामूलमित्यवगम्यते ॥ २२ ॥ प्रसन्नपुण्यसलिला स्वच्छपरिशुद्धजला ॥ **तुरगेति** । सगराध्वरे तुरगस्येन्द्रापहताश्वस्य विचयेऽन्वेषणे व्यग्रान्ससंभ्रमान् । अत एवोर्वीभिदो भूमिखानिनः । भिदेः क्विप् । कपिलमहसा तन्नामकमुनितेजसा रोषाद्धेतोः प्लुष्टान्दग्धान् । 'प्लुष दाहे' । कर्मणि क्तः । तवाद्भिः स्पृष्टानुदतीतरदुत्तारयति स्म । तरतेर्णिचि लुङ् ॥ २३ ॥ शिवे मङ्गलेऽनुध्यानं यस्या इति विग्रहः । एतेन बीजानुगुणप्रोत्साहनरूपं भेदो नाम संध्यङ्गमुक्तम् । तदुक्तम्—'बीजानुगुणप्रोत्साहनं भेदः' इति । वनस्पतिरपुष्पत्वे सति फलवान् । वटः श्यामो नाम

---

१ रोषात्. २ पितुश्च पितामहान्; पितॄन्प्रपितामहान् (टी.) ३ पातं. ४ उदतीतरत्. ५ ०ध्याना. ६ एषः. ७ तटवटः.

अलसलुलितमुग्धान्यध्वसंजातखेदा-
दशिथिलपरिरम्भैर्दत्तसंवाहनानि ।
परिमृदितमृणालीदुर्बलान्यङ्गकानि
त्वमुरसि मम कृत्वा यत्र निद्रामवाप्ता ॥ २४ ॥

लक्ष्मणः—एष विन्ध्याटवीमुखे विराधसंरोधः ।

सीता—अलं तावदेतेन । प्रेक्षे तावदार्यपुत्रस्वहस्तधृततालवृन्तातपत्रनिवारितातपमात्मनो दक्षिणारण्यप्रवेशारम्भम् । (क)

रामः—

एतानि तानि गिरिनिर्झरिणीतटेषु
वैखानसाश्रिततरूणि तपोवनानि ।

(क) अलं दाव एदिणा । पेक्खामि दाव अज्जउत्तसहत्तधरिदतालवुन्तादवत्तनिधारिदादपं अत्तणो दक्खिणारण्णप्पवेसारम्भम् ।

तथा प्रसिद्धिमान् ॥ **अलसेत्यादि** । अध्वनि मार्गे संपातः सम्यग्गमनम् । रामलक्ष्मणापेक्षया त्वरितगमनमिति भावः । 'अग्रतस्ते गमिष्यामि मृद्नन्ती कुशकण्टकान्' इत्युक्तत्वात् । तेन यः खेद आयासस्तस्माद्धेतोरलसललितमुग्धान्यलसानि प्रसरणाकुञ्चनासमर्थानि ललितानि मृदूनि मुग्धानि सुन्दराणि । स्वभावतः सौन्दर्यसौकुमार्ययोः सत्त्वेऽप्यध्वसंपातखेदादलसललितमुग्धानीत्युक्त्या मार्गगमनायासेन तयोर्द्विगुणीभाव इति भावः । 'तथापि दृशोः प्रिया' इत्युक्तेः । अशिथिलपरिरम्भैर्दृढतरालिङ्गनैः । बहुवचनमालिङ्गनावृत्त्यभिप्रायकं कामतन्त्रप्रसिद्धालिङ्गनभेदबाहुल्याभिप्रायकं वा । दत्तानि संवाहनानि येभ्य इति चतुर्थीबहुव्रीहिः । संवाहनं नामाङ्गानां गमनादिजनितायासशमनौपयिकदृढतमस्पर्शविशेषः । परितः साकल्येन मृदिता निष्पीडिता या मृणाली तद्वद् दुर्बलानि स्वस्वधारणसामर्थ्यरहितान्यङ्गकानि । 'अनुकम्पायाम्' इति कन्प्रत्ययः । त्वं ममोरसि कृत्वा यत्र यस्मिन्प्रदेशे निद्रामवाप्ता स कथं विस्मर्यत इति योजना । अयं भावः—पूर्वमध्वसंपातखेदः, ततो ललितत्वसौकुमार्यद्विगुणीभावः, ततस्तद्दर्शनवशादशिथिलालिङ्गनबाहुल्यम्, ततश्च तत्संवाहनता, ततः स्वधारणसामर्थ्यविरहदौर्बल्यम्, ततो रामवक्षःस्थल एव लग्नता, ततस्तदीयसौकुमार्यपारवश्यात्तत्रैव निद्रावाप्तिरिति ॥ २४ ॥ स्वहस्तधृततालपत्रमेव तालवृन्तं तदेवातपत्रं यस्मिन्निति विग्रहः । आत्मनोऽत्याहितं जीवितनिरपेक्षक्रियारूपम् । दक्षिणारण्ये पथिकत्वमिति विग्रहः ॥ **एतानीति** । येषु तपोवनेषु । अतिथिषु विषये साधुरातिथेयोऽतिथिसत्कारः परमः येषां ते पुण्या

---

१ ललित. २ संपात (टी.). ३ संवाध:. ४ ०उत्तहत्थ. ५ तालवेण्टादवत्तं. ६ ०वत्तं अत्तणो दक्खिणारण्णपहिअत्तणम् (०पत्रमात्मनो दक्षिणारण्यपाथिकत्वं) टी.; अत्तणो अच्चाहितं (अत्याहितं) अच्छिहि (अक्षिभ्यां) इ. पा.

येष्वातिथेयपरमाः शमिनो भजन्ते
नीवारमुष्टिपचना गृहिणो गृहाणि ॥ २५ ॥

लक्ष्मणः—अयमविरलानोकहनिवहनिरन्तरस्निग्धनीलपरिसरारण्यपरिणद्धगोदावरीमुखरकन्दरः सततमभिष्यन्दमानमेघमेदुरितनीलिमा जनस्थानमध्यगो गिरिः प्रस्रवणो नाम।

रामः—

स्मरसि सुतनु तस्मिन्पर्वते लक्ष्मणेन
प्रतिविहितसपर्यासुस्थयोस्तान्यहानि।
स्मरसि सरसनीरां तत्र गोदावरीं वा
स्मरसि च तदुपान्तेष्वावयोर्वर्तनानि ॥ २६ ॥

किं च।

इत्यर्थः। यमिन इति द्वितीयान्तम्। पक्वान्नाधिकारिणो यतीन् भजन्ते। सेवन्ते। किं च नीवारमुष्टेः पचनं यैस्ते गृहिणो गृहाणि भजन्ते। यद्वा यमिन इति गृहिविशेषणपदं प्रथमान्तम्। यमवन्तः। इदं धर्मादीनामप्युपलक्षणम्। आतिथेयपरमा गृहिणो गृहस्था गृहाणि भजन्त इत्यन्वयः। यद्वा आतिथेयपरमा आतिथ्यापेक्षिणो नीवारमुष्टेः पचनं येभ्य इति तथोक्ता यमिनः पक्वान्नाधिकारिणः कर्तारो गृहिणो गृहस्थस्य गृहाणि भजन्ते। तानि वैखानसैर्मुनिभिराश्रितास्तरवो येषु तथोक्तानि एतानीत्यन्वयः ॥ २५ ॥ **अयमविरलेत्यादि**। अरण्यपरिणद्धा गोदावरी मुखेषु येषां तानि कन्दराणि यस्य स तथोक्तः। पर्वतानां स्वतोऽपि नीलत्वान्मेदुरितेत्युक्तम्। **स्मरसीति** ॥ हे सुतनु शोभना तनुर्यस्या इति विग्रहः। तनूरित्यूङन्ताद्वा संबुद्धौ ह्रस्वः। तस्मिन्पर्वते। प्रस्रवण इत्यर्थः। विहिताश्च ताः सपर्याश्च विहितसपर्याः। विहितसपर्यासु विहितसपर्यासु प्रतिविहितसपर्यम्। वीप्सायामव्ययीभावः। तत्र आसमन्तात्सुखेन स्थितयोरित्यर्थः। 'सुः पूजायाम्' इति कर्मप्रवचनीयत्वात् षत्वाभावः। यद्वा प्रतिविहिताभिः। प्रत्युपकारीकृताभिरित्यर्थः। अस्मत्कृतवनानुगमनानुज्ञामहोपकारस्येति शेषः। आवयोरित्याकृष्यते। सरसनीरां स्वाभाविकमधुररसयुक्तजलवतीम्। अनेन समुद्रसंगमसमीपस्थजलं व्यावर्त्यते। तत्रास्याः क्षारप्रसिद्धेर्वा किमित्यर्थः। अत एव पूर्वोत्तरयोः किमिति लभ्यते। अत्र प्राथमिकत्वाद्बाह्यत्वाच्च प्रथमं तान्यहानीति दिनस्योक्तिः। आनन्तर्याद्रहस्यत्वाच्च आवयोर्वर्तनानीत्यस्यानन्तरोक्तिः। तदुभयोपकारित्वाद्गोदावर्या मध्योक्तिरिति ध्येयम् ॥ २६ ॥

---

१ यमिनः. २ लानेकानोकह. ३ मुखरक०. ४ मध्यमः. ५ स्वस्थयोः. ६ सरसतीराम्.

किमपि किमपि मन्दं मन्दमासत्तियोगा-
दविरलितकपोलं जल्पतोरक्रमेण ।
अशिथिलपरिरम्भव्यापृतैकैकदोष्णो-
रविदितगतयामा रात्रिरेवं व्यरंसीत् ॥ २७ ॥

लक्ष्मणः—एषा पञ्चवट्यां शूर्पणखा ।

सीता—हा आर्यपुत्र एतावत्ते दर्शनम् । (क)

रामः—अयि विप्रयोगत्रस्ते चित्रमेतत् ।

सीता—यथा तथा भवतु । दुर्जनोऽसुखमुत्पादयति । (ख)

रामः—हन्त वर्तमान इव [मे] जनस्थानवृत्तान्तः प्रतिभाति ।

(क) हा अज्जउत्त एत्तिअं दे दंसणम् ।
(ख) जहा तहा होदु । दुज्जणो असुहं उप्पादेदि ।

किमपीति । आसक्तिः रत्यभिनिवेशो विषयानुभूत्यानवस्थानलक्षणस्तस्या योगात् संबन्धाद्धेतोः अविरलितौ निरन्तरीकृतौ कपोलौ यस्मिन्कर्मणि तथोक्तम् । मन्दं मन्दमतिसूक्ष्माक्षरं यथा तथा । अक्रमेणान्योन्यस्वभावविरुद्धप्रक्रियया । किमपि किमपि । इदं च गुप्तकथनम् । जल्पतोः । अशिथिले गाढे परिरम्भे व्यापृतमेकैकं दोः ययोरिति पूर्वस्मादनुषङ्गः । शेषे षष्ठीयम् । अविदितं यथा तथा गता यामा यस्या-स्तथाविधा रात्रिरेव व्यरंसीत् विरमति स्म । नैवासक्तियोगविस्रम्भसंलापक्रीडादय इत्यर्थः । 'व्याङ्परिभ्यो रमः' इति परस्मैपदम् । 'यम रम—' इति सगिटौ । अत्र अविदितगतेति वाविदितगतनाडीति वा अकृत्वा यामपदोपादानादयमाशयोऽवगम्यते । * * * तथाहि किमपि किमपीत्यस्य सुरतकालीनवक्तव्यजातमेवार्थः । गुप्तकथना-देवं च किमपि किमपि जल्पतोरित्यत्र मन्दं मन्दमविरलितकपोलमित्युभयत्र जल्पनेऽन्वेति । अक्रमेणेत्यपि तथा । एवं च सुरतकालीनजल्पनस्य मान्यातिशयोक्तिकथनादार्द्रवाक्त्वं सीताया गम्यत इत्युक्ताद्रतिविशेषात्फुल्लजृम्भिताख्यबन्धविशेषौ सूच्येते । तदुक्तं काञ्ची-नाथेन—'उत्फुल्लजृम्भितयोः स्त्रिया आर्द्रवचो न क्रोधः' इति । तल्लक्षणं तु अविरलित-कपोलत्वमुपविष्टयोरेव सुलभमिति । एवं कतिपयैरेव बन्धविशेषै रात्रेरेवाव-सितत्वाद्बहूनां क्रीडाविशेषाणां तद्धेतुभूतासक्तियोगस्य वाविरतत्वाद्रात्रिरेव व्यरंसीदि-त्युक्तम् । इदमेवाभिसंधाय 'बिन्दुमात्रं विशिष्यते' इति कालिदासेनोक्तम् । वस्तुतस्तु संलापादिबाह्यसंभोग एव स्वारस्यमिति सुधियो विभावयन्तु ॥ २७ ॥ **एष इति** । शूर्पणखाविवादः । रामेण लक्ष्मणं प्रति तेन रामं प्रति प्रेषणा-दिरिति भावः । 'नखमुखात्संज्ञायाम्' इति ङीषो निषेधः । 'पूर्वपदात्'

१ अविचलित. २ सपुलक. ३ रेवं. ४ एष......शूर्पणखावि-सं-वादः. ५ ज्ञेय (एव) दे,

लक्ष्मणः—

अथेदं रक्षोभिः कनकहरिणच्छद्मविधिना
तथा वृत्तं पापैर्व्यथयति यथा क्षालितमपि ।
जनस्थाने शून्ये विकलकरणैरार्यचरितै-
रपि ग्रावा रोदित्यपि दलति वज्रस्य हृदयम् ॥ २८ ॥

सीता—(साम्रमात्मगतम् ।) अयि देव रघुकुलानन्द एवं मम कारणात्क्लान्त आसीः । (क)

लक्ष्मणः—(रामं निर्वर्ण्य । साकूतम् ।) आर्य किमेतत् ।

अयं ते बाष्पौघस्त्रुटित इव मुक्तामणिसरो
विसर्पन्धाराभिर्लुठति धरणीं जर्जरकणः ।
निरुद्धोऽप्यावेगः स्फुरदधरनासापुटतया
परेषामुन्नेयो भवति च भराध्मातहृदयः ॥ २९ ॥

(क) अयि देव रहुकुलाणन्द एव्वं मम कालणादो किलन्तो आसि ।

इति णत्वम् । **वियोगत्रस्तेति** ॥ वियोगात् तत इति विग्रहः । 'पञ्चमी' इति योगविभागात्समासः ॥ असुखं दुःखम् ॥ **अथेति** । अथ विकलकरणैरार्यचरितैः । यथा ग्रावापि रोदिति वज्रस्यापि हृदयं दलति तथा पापै रक्षोभिर्जनस्थाने शून्ये सति कनकहरिणच्छद्मविधिना वृत्तमिदं क्षालितमपि व्यथयतीत्यन्वयः । अथ शूर्पणखाचित्रदर्शनानन्तरम् । यथा येन प्रकारेण विकलानि स्वस्वव्यापारशून्यानि करणानि चक्षुरादीनि येषु तथोक्तैरार्यचरितैर्मूर्छाप्रभृतिव्यापारैर्ग्रावापि शिलापि रोदिति रोदनं करोति । 'रुदादिभ्यः' इतीट् । वज्रस्यापि वज्रादन्येनाभेद्यस्य हृदयं मध्यप्रदेशो दलति द्विधा भिन्नं भवति तथा तेन प्रकारेण वृत्तमिति संबन्धः । जनस्थाने पापै रक्षोभिः शून्ये सति । खरदूषणादिवधानन्तरमित्यर्थः । कनकहरिणच्छद्मविधिना स्वर्णमारीचमायिकमृगव्याजकरणेन वृत्तं निष्पन्नमिदमिति । सीताहरणादेश्चित्रस्याङ्गुल्या निर्देशः । क्षालितमपि प्रतिकृतमपि व्यथयति दुःखं जनयति शूर्पणखानन्तरं सीताहरणं लिखितमिति भावः । अत्र ग्रावापि रोदितीत्यादिकं नायोगे योगकल्पनम् । किं तु वास्तवमेव । 'अपि वृक्षाः परिम्लानाः' इतिवदुपपत्तेः । एवं स्मृत्वायापि रोदितीत्यवगम्यते ॥ २८ ॥ **आर्येति** । एतद्वक्ष्यमाणम् ॥ **अयं तावदिति** । त्रुटितः छिन्न आवेगो दुःखातिशयः । अधरश्च नासापुटश्चेति विग्रहः । तयोर्द्वन्द्वश्च । अतो न नासाशब्दे ह्रस्वः । उन्नेयोऽनुमेय आध्मातहृ-

---

१ करुणैः, करुणकरुणैः. २ तावद्वाष्पः. ३ गलति. ४ चिरमा०,—च चिरा०, च तथा०; विरसाध्मा०. ५ कलिदोसि (क्लिष्टोसि); अह्मो दिणअरकुलाणन्द एव्वंपि एत्तिअं महत्तकालणादो किलन्दो आसि (अहो दिनकरकुलानन्द एवमपि एतावत् मम कारणात् क्लान्त आसीः ।).

रामः—वत्स

तत्कालं प्रियजनविप्रयोगजन्मा
तीव्रोऽपि प्रतिकृतिवाञ्छया विसोढः ।
दुःखाग्निर्मनसि पुनर्विपच्यमानो
हृन्मर्मव्रण इव वेदनां करोति[1] ॥ ३० ॥

सीता—हा धिक् हा धिक्। अहमप्यतिभूमिं गतेन रणरणकेनार्यपुत्रशून्यामिवात्मानं पश्यामि[2] । (क)

लक्ष्मणः—(स्वगतम्।) भवतु। अन्यतः क्षिपामि। (चित्रं विलोक्य। प्रकाशम्।) अथैतन्मन्वन्तरपुराण[3]गृध्रराजस्य तत्रभवतस्तातजटायुषश्चरित्रविक्रमोदाहरणम् ।

सीता—हा तात निर्व्यूढस्तेऽपत्यस्नेहः । (ख)

रामः—हा तात काश्यप शकुन्तराज किं[4] नु खलु पुनस्त्वादृशस्य महतस्तीर्थस्य[5] साधोः संभवः ।

लक्ष्मणः—अयमसौ जनस्थानपश्चिमतश्चित्रकुञ्जवान्[6]नाम दनुकबन्धाधिष्ठितो दण्डकारण्य[7]भागः । तदिदमृष्यमूकपर्वते मतङ्गस्या[9]श्रमपदम् । इयं च[10] श्रमणा नाम सिद्धा[11] शबरतापसी । तदेतत्पम्पाभिधानं पद्म[12]सरः ।

(क) हद्धी हद्धी । अहंवि अदिभूमिं गदेण रणरणएण अज्जउत्तसुण्णं विअ अत्ताणं पेक्खामि । (ख) हा ताद णिव्वूढो दे अवच्चसिणेहो ।

दयो गद्गदशब्दयुक्तकण्ठः । 'ध्मा शब्दे' इति धातोः कर्मणि क्तः । नेदं चित्रकथनं किं तु तादात्विकवास्तवावस्थाकथनमेव । तत्कथयेत्यादिप्रतिवचनानुरूप्यात् ॥ २९ ॥ **तत्कालेति** । प्रतिकृतिषु प्रतिक्रियासु वाञ्छयादरेण विपच्यमानः । स्वयमेव परिपाकमाश्रित्येत्यर्थः । कर्मणः कर्तृत्वविवक्षया 'कर्मवत्कर्मणा' इत्यातिदेशिकयगात्मनेपदम् । इदं च मध्यमणिन्यायेन पूर्वोत्तराभ्यामन्वेति । तनोति । विस्तारयतीत्यर्थः ॥ ३० ॥ भूमिमतिक्रान्तोऽतिभूमिः । 'अत्यादयः क्रान्ताद्यर्थे द्वितीयया' इति समासः । भावप्रधानो निर्देशः । अतिभूमित्वं गतेनेत्यर्थः । वैपुल्यं प्राप्तेनेति यावत् । रणरणकेन भयसंभ्रमेण । आक्षिपाम्यन्यतो मनःप्रवर्तनेन पूर्वोक्तं

---

१ तनोति. २ प्रेक्षे. ३ पुराणस्य. ४ क्व पुनः. ५ तीर्थभूतस्य. ६ वान्नाम पर्वतः, ०स्थानपश्चिमः. ७ भूमागः. ८ अमुष्य परिसरे. ९ मतङ्गा०. १० तत्र. ११ सिद्धशबरी. १२ सरः.

सीता—अत्र किलार्यपुत्रेण विच्छिन्नामर्षधीरत्वं प्रमुक्तकण्ठं रुदितमासीत्। (क)

रामः—देवि रमणीयमेतत्सरः।

पतस्मिन्मदकलमल्लिकाक्षपक्ष-
व्याधूतस्फुरदुरुदण्डपुण्डरीकाः।
बाष्पाम्भःपरिपतनोद्गमान्तराले
संदृष्टाः कुवलयिनो भुवो विभागाः ॥ ३१ ॥

लक्ष्मणः—अयमार्यो हनूमान्।

सीता—एष स चिरनिर्विण्णजीवलोकप्रत्युद्धरणगुरूपकारी महानुभावो मारुतिः। (ख)

(क) एत्थ किल अज्जउत्तेण विच्छिण्णामरिसधीरत्तणं पमुक्ककण्ठं रुण्णं आसि।

(ख) एसो सो चिरणिव्विण्णजीवलोअपच्चुद्धरणगुरुओवआरी महानुभावो मारुदी।

विस्मारयामि। **अथैतदिति**। अन्यो मनुर्मन्वन्तरम्। मयूरव्यंसकादित्वात्समासः। मन्वन्तरात्पुराणस्येति विग्रहः। सुप्सुपेति समासः। तातजटायुषः पितृसखत्वात्तातपदव्यपदेशः। चरित्रं स्ववृत्तम्। विक्रमः शौर्यम्। उदाहरणम्। सदृशचित्रलेखनमिति भावः। **हा तातेति**। काश्यपः कश्यपपौत्रः। तीर्थभूतस्य हितोपदेष्टुः ॥ **एतस्मिन्निति**। मदेन कलं कूजितं येषां ते तथोक्ताः। तथाविधानां मल्लिकाक्षाणां हंसविशेषाणां [हंसास्तु श्वेतगरुतश्चक्राङ्गा मानसौकसः। राजहंसास्तु ते चञ्चुचरणैर्लोहितैः सिताः ॥ मलिनैर्मल्लिकाक्षास्त। इत्यमरः।] पक्षैर्गरुद्भिर्व्याधूताः कम्पिताः स्फुरन्त उरवो दण्डा येषां तानि पुण्डरीकाणि येषु ते तथोक्ताः। कुवलयिनश्च विभागाः प्रदेशा बाष्पाम्भसः परिपतनोद्गमनयोरन्तराले मया संदृष्टाः। निरन्तरं दृष्टा इत्यर्थः। तथा कुवलयिन इत्यत्र प्रशंसायां मतुपा प्रशस्तकुवलययुक्ता इत्यर्थलाभेन रात्रौ दृष्टा इति सूच्यते। केचित्तु मदकलमल्लिकाक्षपक्षव्याधूतस्फुरदुरुदण्डपुण्डरीका विभागा बाष्पाम्भःपरिपतनोद्गमान्तराले कुवलयिनो दृष्टा इत्यन्वयमुक्त्वा बाष्पाम्भःप्रसरणमलिनीकृतपुण्डरीकाः कुवलयवन्तो दृष्टा इत्यर्थमाहुः। परे तु मदकलमल्लिकाक्षपक्षव्याधूतस्फुरदुरुदण्डपुण्डरीकाः कुवलयिनश्च विभागाः। विभज्यन्त इति विभागाः परस्परं संकीर्णप्रदेशाः। बाष्पाम्भःपरिपतनोद्गमान्तराले संदृष्टा एकीकृत्य दृष्टाः। समित्येकीकारे। अविभागेन दृष्टा इत्याहुः। इतरे तु—'ननु रमणीयमेतत्पद्मसरः' इत्युक्तं त्वया तत्कथमुपपद्यते विरहोद्दीपककलकूजितयुक्तहंसाधिष्ठितपुण्डरीकयुक्तस्य सरसो द्रष्टुमशक्यत्वादित्यत्राह—एतस्मिन्मदकलेति। मत् अकलेति पदच्छेदः। मदिति पञ्चम्येकवचनम्। पृथक्पदं समस्तं वा। मन्मन्निमित्तं विरहव्यथातुरमद्धेतोर्न विद्यते कलं कूजितं येषां ते तेषां मल्लिकाक्षाणां हंस-

---

१ परं रम०. २ मया (टी.). ३ आर्ये. ४ विच्छड्डिदा (विच्छर्दिता०); विसज्जिता० विसृष्टा०). ५ परुण्णं (प्ररुदितं). ६ णिव्वूढ (निर्व्यूढ). ७ महाभाओ (महाभागः).

रामः—

दिष्ट्या सोऽयं महाबाहुरञ्जनानन्दवर्धनः ।
यस्य वीर्येण कृतिनो वयं च भुवनानि च ॥ ३२ ॥

सीता—वत्स एष कुसुमितकदम्बतरुताण्डवितबर्हिणः किंनामधेयो गिरिर्यत्रानुभावसौभाग्यमात्रपरिशेषधूसरश्रीर्मूर्छैस्त्वया प्ररुदितेनावलम्बितस्तरुतल आर्यपुत्र आलिखितः । (क)

(क) वच्छ एसो[1] कुसुमिदकद तरुताण्डविअबंहिणो किंणामहेओ गिरी जत्थ अणुभावसोहग्गमेत्तपरिसेसधूसरसिरी मुच्छन्दो तुए परुदिएण अवलम्बिदो तरुअले अज्जउत्तो आलिहिदो ।

विशेषाणां पक्षैर्व्याधूतानि । कम्पितानीति यावत् । अत एव स्फुरदुरुदण्डानि निवृत्ताधारतया चलदुरुदण्डानि पुण्डरीकाणि येषु तथोक्ताः कुवलयिनः पुण्डरीकवद्विवा विकासाद्यभावेनाकिंचित्करत्वाद्धंसैरव्याधूततया कुवलयसत्तामात्रवन्तः । एतस्मिन्विभागा बाष्पाम्भःपरिपतनोद्गमान्तराले संदृष्टाः सम्यग्दृष्टाः । परिहाससंभावितत्वादवस्थितिव्यतिरेकनिश्चयपर्यन्तं दृष्टा इत्यर्थः । निवृत्तोपप्लवतया सम्यग्दृष्टा इति भावः । मल्लिकाक्षाः खलु विरहोद्विग्नस्य मम कृते स्वयं विरहसमुद्दीपकं कूजितं त्यक्त्वा तदुद्दीपकानि पुण्डरीकाण्यप्यनाशयन् । ततोऽहं निवृत्तोपप्लवतया नान्तरीयकतयावस्थितिपर्यन्तं तान्विहंगान्दृष्टवानिति भावः । युक्तं चैतत् । विरहखिन्नं रामं प्रति मल्लिकाक्षाणाम् 'अपि ग्रावा रोदिति' इति न्यायेन करुणायाः संभवात् । दत्तचक्रवाकशापदर्शनेन चक्रवाकशापदाता रामोऽस्माकमपि शापं दास्यतीति भीत्या शब्दासंभवात् । 'कण्ठेषु स्खलितं गतेऽपि शिशिरे पुंस्कोकिलानां रुतम् ।' इत्यादिविषयविशेषैस्तिरश्चामपि विरहिजनानुरोधः प्रसिद्धश्चेति वदन्ति ॥ ३१ ॥ **एष इति** । चिरान्निर्व्यूढं निष्पादितं यज्जीवलोकप्रत्युद्धरणं तेन गुरु यथा भवति तथा । उपकरोतीत्युपकारी । दशमासपरिमितरावणगृहवासस्यातिभूयस्त्वाभिसंधिना चिरादित्युक्तम् । स्वसत्तयैव जीवलोकममतासंभावनया स्वोद्धरणेन तदुद्धरणसंभावनया च जीवलोकप्रत्युद्धरणमित्युक्तम् ॥ **दिष्ट्येति** । दिष्ट्येत्यानन्दे । **यस्य वीर्येणेत्यादि** । वयम् । लक्ष्मणभरतशत्रुघ्नसीताविभीषणसुग्रीववानराः अहं चेत्यर्थः । कृतिनः सुकृतिनः । यद्वा कृतमुपकारस्तद्वन्तः । उपकृता इत्यर्थः । अन्योन्यवृत्तान्तकथनेन सीतारामयोः, स्वानवधानप्रयुक्तसीताविरहपरिहारेण लक्ष्मणस्य, वह्निप्रवेशपरिहारेण भरतशत्रुघ्नयोः, शरणागतस्वपरिग्रहसिद्धान्तेन बिभीषणस्य, सुखोत्पादनेन सुग्रीवस्य, मधुवनभङ्गापराधवारणेन वानराणाम्, स्वसंजीवनादिना भुवनानां च कृतित्वमिति यथायथमूहनीयम् ॥ ३२ ॥ अनुभावः प्रभावः । सौभाग्यं सौन्दर्यम् । प्ररुदितेन

१ एसो सो. २ ज्ञन्वर. ३ मुह्रुत्तं मु०.

लक्ष्मणः—

सोऽयं शैलः ककुभसुरभिर्माल्यवान्नाम यस्मि—
नीलः स्निग्धः श्रयति शिखरं नूतनस्तोयवाहः ।

रामः—

वत्सैतस्माद्विरम विरमातः परं न क्षमोऽस्मि
प्रत्यावृत्तः पुनरिव स मे जानकीविप्रयोगः ॥ ३३ ॥

लक्ष्मणः—अतः परमार्यस्य तत्रभवतां कपिराक्षसानां चासंख्यातान्युत्तरोत्तराणि कर्माश्चर्याणि । परिश्रान्ता चेयमार्या । तद्विज्ञापयामि विश्राम्यतामिति ।

सीता—आर्यपुत्र एतेन चित्रदर्शनेन प्रत्युत्पन्नदोहदाया अस्ति मम विज्ञाप्यम् । (क)

रामः—नन्वाज्ञापय ।

सीता—जाने पुनरपि प्रसन्नगम्भीरासु वनराजिषु विहरिष्यामि पवित्रसौम्यशिशिरावगाहां भगवतीं भागीरथीमवगाहिष्य इति । (ख)

रामः—वत्स लक्ष्मण ।

लक्ष्मणः—एषोऽस्मि ।

रामः—वत्स अचिरं संपादनीयोऽस्या दोहद इति संप्रत्येव गुरुभिः संदिष्टम् । तदस्खलितसुखसंपातं रथमुपस्थापय ।

(क) अज्जउत्त एदिणा चित्तदंसणेण पच्चुप्पण्णदोहलाए अत्थि मए विण्णवम् ।

(ख) जाणे पुणोवि पसण्णगम्भीरासु वणराइसु विहरिस्सं पवित्तसोम्मसिसिरावगाहां भअवदिं भाईरहिं ओगाहिस्सं ति ।

रोदनकर्त्री । 'आदिकर्मणि क्तः' । रोदनप्रारम्भ एव । अवलम्बितः पतन् । यथा धारित इति ॥ **सोऽयमिति** । ककुभा वृक्षविशेषास्तेषां पुष्पैः सुरभिः । 'पुष्पमूलेषु बहुलम्' इति लुप् । विप्रयोगः वियोगः । प्रत्यावृत्तः पुनरागतः ॥ ३३ ॥ अपरिसंख्यानि परिसंख्या निषेधः । अवधिरिति यावत् । तद्रहितानि संख्याशून्यानीति वा ॥ प्रत्युत्पन्नदोहदायाः । उत्पन्नाभिलाषाया इत्यर्थः । उत्पन्नमनोविकाराया इति वा ॥ **वत्स अचिरेत्यादि** । एष गूढप्रकाशनादुद्भेदः ॥

---

१ आर्येणास्मिन् **as part of Lak.'s speech; रामः**–विरम. २ पुनरपि. ३ अपरिसंख्यानि (टी.). ४ अचिरादेव. ५ दौर्हृदं. ६ आज्ञप्तम्. ७ विण्णवणिज्जं (विज्ञापनीयं). ८ विहरिअ (विहृत्य). ९ पवित्तणिम्मलासिसिरसलिलं (पवित्रनिर्मलशिशिरसलिलां).

सीता—आर्यपुत्र युष्माभिरपि तत्र गन्तव्यम् । (क)

रामः—अयि[1] कठिनहृदये एतदपि वक्तव्यमेव[2] ।

सीता—तेन हि प्रियं मे । (ख)

लक्ष्मणः—यथा[3]ज्ञापयत्यार्यः । (इति निष्क्रान्तः ।)

रामः—प्रिये अत्र वाता[4]यनोपकण्ठे मुहूर्तं संविष्टौ[5] भवावः ।

सीता—एवं भवतु । अपह्रिये खलु परिश्रमजनितया निद्रया । (ग)

रामः—तेन हि निरन्तरमवलम्बस्व मा[6]मत्र शयनाय ।

जीवयन्निव ससाध्वसश्रमस्वेदबिन्दुरधिकण्ठमर्प्यताम् ।
बाहुरैन्दवमयूखचुम्बितस्यन्दिचन्द्रमणिहारविभ्रमः ॥ ३४ ॥

(तथा कारयन्सानन्दम् ।) प्रिये किमेतत् ।

विनिश्चेतुं शक्यो न सुखमिति वा दुःखमिति वा
प्र[7]मोहो निद्रा वा किमु विषविसर्पः किमु मदः ।
तव स्पर्शे स्पर्शे मम हि परिमूढेन्द्रियगणो
विकारश्चैतन्यं भ्रमयति च संमील[8]यति च ॥ ३५ ॥

(क) अज्जउत्त तुह्मेहिं वि तहिं गन्दव्वम् । (ख) तेण हि पिअं मे[9] । (ग) एव्वं होदु । ओहीरिज्जा[10]मि क्खु परिस्समजणिदाए णिद्दाए ।

जीवयन्निति । साध्वसं भयम् । आधिकण्ठम् । कण्ठे इत्यर्थः । इन्दोरमी ऐन्दवाः । चन्द्रमणिश्चन्द्रकान्तशिला । जीवयन्नर्प्यतामिवेत्यन्वयः । इवशब्दः ईषदर्थकः । जीवयन्निति च 'लक्षणहेत्वोः' इति शतृ । तथा च मत्संजीवनफलकं यदीषदर्पणं तत्कर्म क्रियतामित्यर्थः । अथ वा एतद्विरहे 'न जीवेयं क्षणमपि' इत्युक्तम् । अत्र ऐन्दवेत्यादिना सादृश्यमुक्त्वा जीवयन्निवेति विशेषस्योक्तेः व्यतिरेकालंकारः । 'व्यतिरेको विशेषश्चेदुपमानोपमेययोः ।' इति ॥३४॥ **तथा कारयन्निति** । 'सहजलज्जाजडदृशः' इति वक्ष्यमाणरीत्या लज्जयाविष्टायां तस्यां स्वयं तथा कारयन्नित्यर्थः । पूर्वोक्तश्रमवशाच्च स्वयमेव तथा कारयतीत्युक्तम् ॥ **विनिश्चेतुमिति** । अत्रत्यसुखदुःखशब्दौ प्रियाप्रियमित्रशत्रुसंश्लेषादिजन्यमानससुखदुःखपरौ शारीरसुखदुःखमदविषविसर्पयोः पृथग्ग्रहणात् । सुखदुःखयोः शारीरमानसत्वाविभागस्तु 'कर्माणि च येन संस्पर्शात्कर्तुः शरीरसुखम्' इति सूत्रतद्व्याख्यानयोः स्पष्टः ।

---

१ अयि, अति–कठिने. २ वक्तव्यम्. ३ यदा. ४ वातायनावर्तके. ५ संविष्टा भव. ६ मामनुगमनाय. ७ प्रबोधः. ८ संमोहयति; भ्रमयति समुन्मीलयति च; स्थगयाति च संमीलयाति च. ९ पिअं मे पिअं मे. १० ओहरिदह्मि परिस्समणिद्दाए (अपहृतास्मि परिश्रमनिद्रया).

सीता—स्थिरप्रसादा यूयमित इदानीं किमपरम्। (क)

रामः—

म्लानस्य जीवकुसुमस्य विकासनानि
संतर्पणानि सकलेन्द्रियमोहनानि।

(क) स्थिरप्पसादा तुह्मे इदो दाणिं किमवरम्।

अत्र सीत इति संबुद्ध्यन्तमध्याहार्यम्। तवेत्युक्तेः। हे सीते तव स्पर्शे स्पर्शे त्वदीययावत्स्पर्शेषु परिमूढः स्वस्वविषयग्रहणासमर्थ इन्द्रियगणश्चक्षुरादीन्द्रियसमूहः येन स तथोक्तो मम विकार आन्तरावस्थाविशेषः। चैतन्यमन्तःकरणावच्छिन्नचैतन्यम्। जीवचैतन्यमिति यावत्। अद्वैतमतप्रक्रिययेदमुक्तम्। मदन्तरात्मानमिति फलितोऽर्थः। भ्रमयति प्रतिकूलतया भासमानः सन् क्षुब्धं करोति संमीलयति च अनुकूलतया भासमानः सन् उल्लासयति च। अयमित्यध्याहार्यम्। अयं विकारः सुखमिति विनिश्चेतुं न शक्यः दुःखमिति वा विनिश्चेतुं न शक्यः। प्रमोहो वा प्रकृष्टमूर्छात्वेन संशयितुं योग्यो निद्रा वा सुषुप्तित्वेन संशयितुं योग्यः। विषविसर्पः किमु। विषेण विसृप्यत इति विग्रहः। कर्मणि घञ्। विषप्रसरणजन्यत्वेन संशयितुं योग्य इत्यर्थः। मदः किमु। मदत्वेन संशयितुं योग्य इत्यर्थः। अस्य विकारस्य स्पर्शजन्यत्वात्परिमूढेन्द्रियगणत्वादन्तरात्मक्षोभकरत्वाच्च तथाविधशात्रवादिस्पर्शजन्यमानसदुःखत्वेन संशययोग्यत्वम्। एवं स्पर्शजन्यत्वात्परिमूढेन्द्रियगणत्वादन्तरात्मोल्लासकारित्वाच्च तथाविधमित्रादिस्पर्शजन्यमानससुखत्वेन संशयार्हत्वम्। भवति च मित्रादिस्पर्शजन्यसुखं परिमूढेन्द्रियगणम्। 'नीवीं प्रति प्रणिहिते तु करे प्रियेण सख्यः शपामि यदि किंचिदपि स्मरामि' इत्युक्तेः। एवं स्पर्शजन्यत्वात्परिमूढेन्द्रियगणत्वादन्तरात्मक्षोभकरत्वाच्चास्य दण्डाद्यभिघातजन्यपरिमूढेन्द्रियगणत्वान्तरात्मक्षोभकरत्वविशिष्टसूक्ष्मप्राणसंचाररूपमूर्छात्वेन संभावनार्हत्वम्। एवमस्य विकारस्य स्पर्शजन्यत्वात्परिमूढेन्द्रियगणत्वादन्तरात्मानुकूलत्वाच्च मृदुतरतल्पादिस्पर्शजन्यत्वनिवृत्तेन्द्रियव्यापारत्वपरमात्मसुपरिष्वङ्गप्रयुक्तसुखरूपत्वविशिष्टनिद्रात्वेन संशयार्हत्वम्। एवमस्य स्पर्शजन्यत्वात्परिमूढेन्द्रियगणत्वादन्तरात्मप्रतिकूलत्वाच्च तथाविधविषस्पर्शजन्यविकारत्वेन संशयार्हत्वम्। एवमस्य स्पर्शजन्यत्वात्परिमूढेन्द्रियगणत्वादन्तरात्मानुकूलत्वात्तथाविधमदत्वेन संशययोग्यत्वम्। मदस्य क्षीरसुराद्याप्यायकवस्त्वायत्तत्वात्स्पर्शजन्यत्वं परिमूढेन्द्रियगणत्वमन्तरात्मानुकूलत्वं च। तदुक्तम्—'मदिरादिकृतो मोहहर्षव्यतिकरो मदः।' इति। सर्वमिदं सीताया भोग्यताप्रकर्षे तात्पर्यमाविष्करोति। हिशब्दः प्रसिद्धौ। तथा च मदीयोऽयं विकारस्त्वयापि ज्ञायत इति व्यज्यते ॥ ३५ ॥ **म्लानस्येति**। म्लानस्य हर्षक्षयवतो जीवकुसुमस्य जीव एव कुसुमं तस्य विकासनानि वि-

१ तुम्हे किं एत्थ अच्चरिअं; धीरप्पसादा तुह्मेत्ति एत्थ दाणिं अच्चरिअं (धीरप्रसादा यूयमित्यत्रेदानीमाश्चर्यम्).

एतानि ते सुवचनानि सरोरुहाक्षि
कर्णामृतानि मनसश्च रसायनानि ॥ ३६ ॥

सीता—(विहस्य ।) प्रियंवद एहि । संविशावः । (क)

(इति शयनाय समन्ततो निरूपयति ।)

रामः—अयि किमन्वेष्टव्यम् ।

आविवाहसमयाद् गृहे वने शैशवे तदनु यौवने पुनः ।
स्वापहेतुरनुपाश्रितोऽन्यया रामबाहुरुपधानमेष ते ॥ ३७ ॥

(क) पिअंवद एहि । [3]संविसह्म ।

कामजनकानि हर्षोत्पादकानि संतर्पणानि तृप्तिजनकानि भोग्यान्तरापेक्षानुत्पादकानि अत एव सकलानामिन्द्रियाणां मोहनानि स्वव्यापारनिरोधीनि कर्णयोरमृतानि। यथाऽमृतस्य 'दृष्ट्वा तृप्यन्ति' इति दर्शनमात्रेण तृप्तिजनकत्वम् । तद्वदेषामर्थपर्यालोचनं विनापि रमणीयत्वमिति भावः। मनसश्च रसायनानि रसायनं नाम अनेकरसवस्तुसमुदायात्मकरसवस्तुविशेषो वाग्भटे प्रसिद्धः । बहुवचनेनानेकरसायनसदृशानीति व्यज्यते। किं चानेकरसायनवस्त्वास्वादनेन सर्वेषां रसानां तत्रोपालम्भः। एवं शब्दान्तरश्रवणजन्यसुखानामेतद्वचनैर्लाभ इति व्यज्यते । अपि च यथा रसायनस्य रसमयत्वाद्रोम्यत्वम्, औषधात्मकत्वाद्रोगनिवर्तकत्वं च, एवमेतेषामपि प्रियत्वं हितत्वं चेति व्यञ्जयितुं रसायनत्वोक्तिः । सरोरुहाक्षि आयामत्वविपुलत्वाभ्यां सादृश्यमभिप्रेतम् । एवं च स्वस्या अपि स्ववचनवैलक्षण्यप्रयुक्तविस्मयातिशयाचक्षुषोरायतत्वविपुलत्वद्विगुणीभाव इति भावः । ते सुवचनानि स्वकीयवचनवैलक्षण्यातिशयतः सीतायाः स्ववचनेषु स्वीयतासंशयः स्यादिति ते इत्युक्तिः । सुशब्देन सीतावचनेष्वपि एतादृशं सौभाग्यं नानुभूतपूर्वमिति व्यज्यते । 'क्षणे क्षणे यन्नवतामुपैति तदेव रूपं रमणीयतायाः ।' इति न्यायेन न दोषः ॥ ३६ ॥ प्रियंवद प्रियवादिन् । 'प्रियवशे वदः खच्' । संविशावः । 'स्वप्नः संवेश इत्यपि' इत्यमरः ॥ अपि संदेष्टव्यम् । संदेश उक्तिः । भ्रुकुटीभटोऽयं सूचयितव्यः । किमर्थमुक्तिप्रयास इति भावः । यद्वा यथा शयनदशायामुपधानादीनामुपकरणत्वं तद्वन्ममापीति विधिर्वा किमर्थ इति भावः ॥ उपकरणत्वमेवाह--आविवाहेति । आविवाहसमयाद्विवाहसमयादारभ्येत्यर्थः । गृहे शैशवे यौवने च स्वापहेतुः वने पुनर्यौवने स्वापहेतुरित्यन्वयः । न तु यथासंख्यम् । अन्ययानुपाश्रितः स्वापहेतुतयानुपाश्रित इत्यर्थः । अतः 'जुष्टं परमनारीणां भुजैः परमसुन्दरैः । ' इत्यनेन न विरोधः । चेटीविषयासंवाहने तात्पर्यात् । 'न रामः परदारान्वै चक्षुर्भ्यामपि पश्यति' इत्युक्तेः । मद्बाहुरुपधानमित्यनुक्त्वा रामबाहुरित्युक्तिः प्रसिद्धि-

१ सरोरुहाक्ष्याः; एतानि तानि वचनानि सरोरुहाक्ष्याः २ अपि संदेष्टव्यम्. ३ सइस्सं (शयिष्ये).

सीता——(निद्रां नाटयन्ती ।) अस्त्येतत् । आर्यपुत्र अस्त्येतत् । (इति स्वपिति ।) (क)

रामः——कथं प्रियवचैना मे वक्षसि प्रसुप्तैव । (निर्वर्ण्य ।)

इयं गेहे लक्ष्मीरियममृतवर्तिर्नयनयो-
रसावस्याः स्पर्शो वपुषि बहुलश्चन्दनरसः ।
अयं बाहुः कण्ठे शिशिरमसृणो मौक्तिकसरः
किमस्या न प्रेयो यैदि परमसह्यस्तु विरहः ॥ ३८ ॥

(प्रविश्य ।)

प्रतीहारी——देव उपस्थितः । (ख)

रामः——अयि कः ।

प्रतीहारी——आसन्नपरिचारको देवस्य दुर्मुखः । (ग)

रामः——(स्वगतम् ।) शुद्धान्तचारी दुर्मुखः । स मया पौरजानपै-दानपसर्तुं प्रहितः । (प्रकाशम् ।) आगच्छतु ।

(प्रतीहारी निष्क्रान्ता ।)

(**क**) अत्थि एदम् । अज्जउत्त अत्थि एदम् । (**ख**) देव उवट्ठिदो । (**ग**) आसण्णपरिआरओ देवस्स दुम्मुहो ।

द्योतनार्थौ । 'उपधाय भुजं तस्य' इत्यादिवचनात् ॥ ३७ ॥ **इयमिति** । इयं गेहे लक्ष्मीर्लक्ष्मीसदृशी । इयममृतवर्तिर्नयनयोः । तथा नयनानन्दकरीत्यर्थः । किमेतत्पर्यन्तानुधावनवचनेन । एतदीयमेव यत्किंचिन्मम पर्याप्तमित्याह——असावस्या इति । वपुषि प्रसिद्धचन्दनव्यावृत्तिः । अस्याः किं न प्रेयः । एतत्संबन्धि किं न प्रियम् । सर्वमपि प्रियमेवेत्यर्थः । अत्र सीतापेक्षया तत्संबन्ध्येव प्रियमिति रामचन्द्रमतमिति कवेराशयोऽवगम्यते । उपसंहारे किमस्या न प्रेय इत्युक्तवान् । इतरथा कथमेषेत्येव न वदेत् । भर्तृमीढश्च——'मनसिजरुजः सा वा दिव्या ममालमपोहितुं रहसि लघयेदारब्धा वा तदाश्रयणी कथा' इत्याह । अत्र रामबाहुरुपधानमिति सीतां प्रति स्वबाहोरुपधानत्वमुक्त्वा 'अयं बाहुः कण्ठे शिशिरमसृणो मौक्तिकसरः' इत्युक्तं रामेण । तदिदं वैलक्षण्यातिशयकार्यम् । अत्र 'इयं गेहे लक्ष्मीः' इत्यादिभिरेकस्या एव सीतायाः गृहविषये दीपकलिकाकार्यकारित्वं चक्षुर्विषये ज्योत्स्नादिकार्यकरत्वं कण्ठे हारकार्यकारित्वं च व्यज्यते । रूपकमुल्लेखो वा अलंकारः ॥ ३८ ॥ आसन्नपरिचारको दुर्मुखस्तन्नामा । अपसर्पो गूढचरः । प्रहितः प्रेषितः प्रयुक्तः । न तु वास्तव्य इत्यर्थः ।

---

१ प्रियवचनैव. २ यदि पुनरसह्यस्तु, किमपरमसह्यस्तु. ३ पदेष्वपसर्पः (**Two MSS.** and टी.).

(प्रविश्य)

दुर्मुखः—(स्वगतम् ।) हा कथं सीतादेव्या ईदृशमचिन्तनीयं जनापवादं देवस्य कथयिष्यामि। अथ वा नियोगः खल्वीदृशो मे मन्दभाग्यस्य। (क)

सीता—(उत्स्वप्नायते ।) हा आर्यपुत्र सौम्य कुत्रासि । (ख)

रामः—अये सैवेयं[1] रणरणकदायिनी चित्रदर्शनाद्विरहभावना[2] देव्याः स्वप्नोद्वेगं[3] करोति । (सस्नेहमङ्गमस्याः परामृशन् ।)

अद्वैतं सुखदुःखयोरनुगुणं[4] सर्वास्ववस्थासु य-
द्विश्रामो हृदयस्य यत्र जरसा यस्मिन्नहार्यो रसः ।
कालेनावरणात्ययात्परिणते यत्स्नेहसारे[5] स्थितं
भद्रं तस्य[6] सुमानुषस्य कथमप्येकं हि तत्प्रार्थ्यते[7] ॥ ३९ ॥

(क) हा कहं सीतादेइए ईदिसं अचिन्तणिज्जं जणाववादं देव्वस्स कहइस्सं । अहवा णिओओ क्खु इदिसो मे[9] मन्दभाअस्स ।

(ख) हा अज्जउत्त सोम्म कहिं सि ।

रणरणकदायिनी विक्षोभकारिणी । विरहभावना वियोगध्यानम् । चित्रदर्शनादिति स्मरणहेतुरुक्तः । स्वप्ने निद्रायामुद्योगं वचनादिप्रयत्नम् । 'उद्वेगम्' इति पाठे भयसंभ्रममित्यर्थः । अङ्गमस्याः परामृशन् । एतेनोपरितनश्लोकस्यापत्यविषयत्वकल्पना परास्ता । तथा सति उदरमस्याः परामृशन्निति वक्तव्यतापत्तेः । न च 'मयैवादौ ज्ञातः करतलपरामर्शकलया द्विधा गर्भग्रन्थिः' इति वक्ष्यमाणानुवादस्य पुरोवादसापेक्षतया अत्रेत्याङ्गशब्दस्य तद्विशालोदरपरत्वं कवेः संमतमिति वाच्यम् । तत्र 'सहजलज्जाजडदृशः' इति जागरप्रतीतेः । अत्र च सुषुप्तिप्रतीतेस्तदयोगादिति ध्येयम् । **अद्वैतमिति** । यत्सर्वास्ववस्थासु सुखदुःखयोरद्वैतमनुगतम् । जाग्रत्स्वप्नसुषुप्त्यादिसर्वावस्थासु ये सुखदुःखे तयोः संबन्धि यदद्वैतमभिन्नत्वं तदनुगतम् । तद्विशिष्टमित्यर्थः । सर्वास्ववस्थास्वभिन्नसुखदुःखापादकमित्यर्थः । द्वयोर्भावो द्वैतम् । इदमेवाद्वैतं चक्रवाकमिथुनवर्णनव्यपदेशेन नवेन कविना व्याख्यातम्—'भुक्तं तद्बिमृणालयोर्मिथुनयोः पीतं द्विराजीवयोः सुप्तं तद्विफलाशयोरविरलं संश्लिष्टयोर्यद्यपि । पर्यायात्समयद्वयेन विरुतं भिन्नप्रयत्नेन वा मूर्तिद्वैतवशान्मतिर्मिथुनमित्यद्वैतमेवानयोः ॥' इति । पर्यायादिति पर्यायशब्दमन्तर्भाव्य न विरुद्धमिति ल्यब्लोपे पञ्चमी व्याख्येया । नातः समयद्वय इत्यनेन पौनरुक्त्यम् । यत्र दाम्पत्ये हृदयस्य गुरुकुलशिष्टमनस इत्यर्थः । विश्रामः श्रमापनयनकसुखविशेषानुभवः । अत्र 'विश्राम इत्यपाणिनीयम् । नोदात्तेति वृद्धिप्रतिषेधात्' इति वैयाकरणाः । श्रीहर्षस्तु 'विश्रामो विश्रमश्च' इति द्विरूपकोश उक्तवान् ।

---

१ मैव. २ विभावना. ३ उद्योगं (टी.). ४ अनुगतं. ५ प्रेम (टी.) ६ प्रेम. ७ प्रार्थ्यते (टी). ८ दाणीं देवीमन्तरेण. ९ मह मन्दभाअहेअस्स एसो (मम मन्दभागधेयस्यैषः).

दुर्मुखः—(उपसृत्य ।) जयतु देवः । (क)

रामः—ब्रूहि यदुपलब्धम् ।

दुर्मुखः—उपस्तुवन्ति देवं पौरजानपदा विस्मारिता वयं महाराजदशरथस्य रामभद्रेणेति । (ख)

रामः—अर्थवाद एषः । दोषं तु मे कंचित्कथय येन स प्रतिविधीयते ।

दुर्मुखः—(सास्रम् ।) शृणोतु देवः । (कर्णे ।) एवमिव इति । (ग)

रामः—अहह तीव्रसंवेगो वाग्वज्रः । (इति मूर्छति ।)

(क) जेदु देव्वो । (ख) उवत्थुवन्ति देवं पौरजाणपदा विसुमरिदा अह्मे महाराअदसरहस्स रामभद्देणेत्ति । (ग) सुणादु देओ । एव्वं विअ । इति ।

यस्मिन्दाम्पत्ये रसः स्पृहारूपो जरसा जरया अहार्यो हर्तुमशक्यः । यद्वा यस्मिन्सति रस आह्लादो जरसाप्यहार्यः । आवरणात्ययात् । पदद्वयमिदम् । वरणं विवाहः, अत्ययः शरीरसंपातः, वरणं चात्ययश्चेति समाहारद्वन्द्वः । आवरणात्ययात् । वरणात्ययमभिव्याप्येत्यर्थः । वरणमारभ्य शरीरपातपर्यन्तं वर्तमानेन कालेन परिणते उपचयं प्राप्ते प्रेमसारे उत्कृष्टप्रेम्णि स्थितं स्थितिमत् । 'मालत्याः प्रथमावलोकदिवसादारभ्य विस्तारिभिर्भूयः स्नेहविचेष्टितैर्मृगदृशो नीतस्य कोटिं पराम् ।' 'परां कोटिं स्नेहपरिचयविकासादधिगते' इत्यादि समानार्थकम् । 'कालेनावरणात्ययात्परिणते यत्प्रेमसारे स्थितम्' इति वाक्यं वेदितव्यम् । केचित्तु आवरणात्ययात्प्रतिबन्धकनिवृत्तेरिति व्याचक्षते । प्रेम्ण उत्कृष्टत्वं च परकीयावेश्योपपत्याद्यविषयकत्वम् । तस्य सुमानुषस्य दाम्पत्यस्य । 'सुमानुषं तु दाम्पत्यम्' इत्यभिधानात् । इति प्राञ्च आहुः । अत एवैतद्विकृतिभूतादाम्पत्यार्थकमनिच्छातिशब्दस्य द्रविडभाषाप्रसिद्धिरपि । अन्ये तु 'प्रकरणानुगुण्याद्विशेषणस्वारस्यात्तच्छब्देन दाम्पत्ये लब्धे सुमानुषस्येति तद्विशेषणतया योजनीयम् । शोभनो मानुषो येन' इत्याहुः । केचित्तु 'सुमानुषस्य सौजन्यस्य' इत्याहुः । कथमपि सर्वप्रकारेणापि तत्प्रसिद्धमेकं मुख्यं भद्रं क्षेमं प्रार्थ्यते प्रकर्षेण याच्यते । अभिलष्यते वा । हि यस्मात्सुमानुषस्य भद्रमेकं प्रार्थ्यते तस्मात् सैव रणरणकदायिनीत्यादिपूर्वेणान्वयः । अनर्थशङ्कीनि बन्धुमित्रहृदयानीति न्यायेनेति भावः । प्रेमसारे स्थितमित्यनेन मधुकटाहनिक्षिप्तरसालफलसादृश्यं व्यज्यते । अत्र फलविषयकौत्सुक्यप्रतिपादनादारम्भ उक्तः । तदुक्तम्—'औत्सुक्यमात्रमारम्भः फललाभाय भूयसे' इति ॥ ३९ ॥ **कर्णे एवमिवेति** । 'अर्थस्त्वेकेन विज्ञेयः पश्चाज्ज्ञात्वा

---

१ एवैषः २ अनितीमोयं. ३ जआदि; जअवि जअदि, जेदु जेदु. ४ ०पदा जहा (यथा) ५ महाराअं दसरहं रामदेव्वेणेत्ति (महाराजं दशरथं रामदेवेनेति). ६ महाराओ. ७ एव्वं.

दुर्मुखः—आश्वसितु देवः। (क)

रामः—(आश्वस्य।)

हा हा धिक्परगृहवासदूषणं य-
द्वैदेह्याः प्रशमितमद्भुतैरुपायैः।
एतत्तत्पुनरपि दैवदुर्विपाका-
दालर्कं विषमिव सर्वतः प्रसृतम्॥ ४०॥

तत्किमत्र मन्दभाग्यः करोमि। (विमृश्य सकरुणम्।) अथ वा किमन्यत्।

सतां केनापि कार्येण लोकस्याराधनं व्रतम्।
यत्पूरितं हि तातेन मां च प्राणांश्च मुञ्चता॥ ४१॥

संप्रत्येव च भगवता वसिष्ठेन संदिष्टम्। अपि च।

यत्सावित्रैर्दीपितं भूमिपालै-
र्लोकश्रेष्ठैः साधु शुद्धं चरित्रम्।
मत्संबन्धात्कश्मला किंवदन्ती
स्याच्चेदस्मिन्हन्त धिङ्मामधन्यम्॥ ४२॥

(क) आस्ससदु देव्वो।

प्रसक्ततः। कर्णे एवमिवेत्युक्त्वा काव्यबन्धे प्रयुज्यते॥' इत्युक्तत्वात्॥ **हा हेति**। परगृहवास एव दूषणम्। नान्यदिति भावः। आलर्कं श्वसंबन्धि। प्रसक्तम् पाठान्तरे 'प्रसृतम्' इति वा। एकत्र स्पर्शः कालान्तरेण सर्वतः प्रसरणमिति भावः॥ ४०॥ मन्दभाग्योऽल्पभाग्यः। **सतामिति**। केनापि कार्येण। 'स्नेहं दयां च सौख्यं च यदि वा जानकीमपि' इत्युक्तरीत्या लोकस्याराधनं लोकस्य प्रीतिजनकव्यापारः। सतां धर्मशास्त्रस्मृत्यादीनां परं धर्मः श्रेष्ठत्वेनाभिमतः। तथा चापस्तम्बः—'यत्त्वार्याः क्रियमाणं प्रशंसन्ति स धर्मः' इति। न चेदमननुष्ठानपराहतमित्याह—तत्प्रतीतमिति। 'अवश्यं पितुराचारः' इति। स्फोरणार्थमिदम्। मां च मुख्यतममत्परित्यागानुषङ्गिकः तातस्य स्वप्राणत्याग इत्याह—प्राणांश्चेति। मुञ्चतेति हेतौ शतृ। प्राणत्यागहेतुकं पूरणमित्यर्थः॥ ४१॥ **संप्रत्येव संदिष्टमिति**। 'युक्तः प्रजानामनुरञ्जने स्याः' इति संदिष्टमिति भावः। **यदिति**। सावित्रैः सवितुः पुत्रैः। 'तस्यापत्यम्' इत्यप्रत्ययः। अनेनाभिजन उक्तः। भूमिपालैरित्यनेन क्षत्रधर्मभूतभूमिपालनात्मकवृत्तमुक्तम्। परिशेषाल्लोकश्रेष्ठैरित्यनेन विद्योक्ता। एवमभिजनविद्यावृत्तैः सर्वाभ्यर्हमनुप्रभृतिराजभिर्दीपितं प्रकाशितं स्वयमनुष्ठितमनुष्ठापितं च चित्रमाश्चर्यभूतम्।

---

१ प्रसक्तम्. २ अद्य. ३ एतत्. ४ परम्. ५ पूजितं; तत्प्रतीतं (टी.). ६ चित्रम्. ७ संबन्धा, संबद्धा.

हा देवि देवयजनसंभवे हा स्वजन्मानुग्रहपवित्रितवसुंधरे हा निमि[1]जनकनन्दिनि हा पावकवसिष्ठारुन्धतीप्रशस्तशील[2]शालिनि हा राम[3]मयजीविते हा महारण्यवासप्रियसखि हा तातप्रिये हा स्तोक[4]वादिनि कथमेवंविधायास्तवायमीदृशः परिणामः ।

त्वया जगन्ति पुण्यानि त्वय्यपुण्या जनोक्तयः ।
नाथवन्तस्त्वया लोकास्त्वमनाथा विपत्स्यसे ॥ ४३ ॥

कश्मला हेया । किंवदन्ती लोकवादः ॥ ४२ ॥ स्वतो निर्दोषेत्याह–हा देवि । उत्पत्तिवंशदोषोपि नास्तीत्याह—देवयजनसंभवे । स्वोत्पत्तिभूमेरपि शुद्धिजननीत्याह—स्वजन्मेति । संपर्कवशदोषोपि नास्तीत्याह—मुनिजनकेति । नन्दिनीत्यनेन औरसकन्यापेक्षयाभिमतेति व्यज्यते । गुरुदेवताभिमतेत्याह—पावकवसिष्ठेति । शीलेन वृत्तेन शाल्यते श्लाघ्यत इति शीलशालिनि । 'शाॄ श्लाघायाम्' इत्यस्माद्बाहुलकात्कर्मणि णिनिः । डलयोरेकत्वम् । तद्विवृणोति—राममयेति । अनेन रावणस्मरणमपि दूरोत्सारितमिति व्यज्यते । रामस्य रावणस्मरणगन्धासहत्वात् त्विदमनुमेयं न । किं त्वनुष्ठानेन प्रकटितमित्याह—महारण्येति । प्रियत्वविशेषणम् । निर्बन्धलोकवादादिव्यावृत्तिः । सखीत्यनेन दण्डकारण्यगमने पत्नीत्वप्रयुक्तप्राधान्यं नाङ्गीकृतम् । किं तु पुरुषसिंहरामसमप्रधानत्वमेवेति । 'समानं ख्यायते इति सखा' इति व्युत्पत्तेरुपलक्षणमिदम् । रामापेक्षया प्राधान्यस्यापि । 'अग्रतस्ते गमिष्यामि मृद्नती कुशकण्टकान्' इत्युक्तत्वात् । तातस्य प्रिये अभिमते 'वधूचतुष्केपि' इत्यादिवक्ष्यमाणरीत्येति भावः । स्तोकं मितं वदन्तीत्यर्थः । 'सत्याय मितभाषिणाम्' इत्युक्तरीत्या । निमित्तलेशाभावेपि कथमयं परिणाम इति भावः । **त्वयेति** । त्वया जगन्ति पुण्यानि पुण्यवान्ति । मत्वर्थीयाच्प्रत्ययः । 'पापानां वा शुभानां वा वधार्हाणां प्लवङ्गम । कार्यं करुणमार्येण न कश्चिन्नापराध्यति ॥' इति त्वन्मतानुसारेण पापपुण्ययोरनुग्रहतौल्यादिति भावः । जनानामुपजीव्यविरोध इत्याह—त्वय्यपुण्या जनोक्तयः । अत्र त्वया जगन्ति पुण्यानीति भुवनानां पुण्यत्वमुक्त्वा जनोक्तय इति जनशब्दोपादानान्नैवं लोकान्तरस्थानामुपजीव्यविरोध इति व्यज्यते । उक्तिपदेन वस्तुस्थित्यभावाद्विषयप्रभवाच्च । इत्थं मनसा संभावनमपि नोचितम् । सुतरां बहिस्तदुक्तिः सापि जातेति व्यज्यते । जनानामुक्तय इति विग्रहाद्यः कश्चिदित्थं प्रलपतीत्यपि न किं तु बहुजना एवं वदन्तीति व्यज्यते । षष्ठीबहुवचनेन विग्रहे प्रमाणं—'रे रे पौरजानपदाः न खलु भवतां देव्याः स्थानं गृहेऽभिमतं ततः' इत्यादिवक्ष्यमाणरामवचनम् । तेऽपि कदाचिदित्युक्त्वा विरमन्तीत्यपि न बहुकृत्वो वदन्तीति बहुवचनार्थः । अपुण्या इति व्यतिरेकोक्त्या कश्चिदपि कदाचिदपि न यथार्थं प्रत्येति नापि वक्तीति व्यज्यते । नाथवन्त इति । अहं लोकानामधीशः, मम त्वं नाथा । तथा

---

१ मुनिजनक. २ शीले. ३ रामैक. ४ प्रियस्तोक०.

(दुर्मुखं प्रति ।) दुर्मुख ब्रूहि लक्ष्मणम् । एष ते नूतनो राजा रामः समाज्ञापयति । (कर्णे ।) एवमेवम् । इति ।

दुर्मुखः—हा कथमिदानीमग्निपरिशुद्धाया गर्भस्थितपवित्ररघुकुलसंतानाया देव्या दुर्जनवचनादेवमनार्यमध्यवसितं देवेन (क)

रामः—शान्तम्[1] । कथं दुर्जनाः[2] पौरजानपदाः ।

इक्ष्वाकुवंशोऽभिमतः[3] प्रजानां
जातं च दैवाद्वचनीयबीजम् ।
यच्चाद्भुतं कर्म विशुद्धिकाले
प्रत्येतु कस्तद्यदि[4] दूरवृत्तम् ॥ ४४ ॥

तद्गच्छ ।

दुर्मुखः—हा देवि । (इति निष्क्रान्तः ।) (ख)

(क) हा कहं दाणीं अग्गिपरिसुद्धाए गब्भट्ठिदपवित्तरहुउलसंताणाए देइए दुज्जणवअणादो एवं[6] अणज्जं अज्झवसिदं देव्वेण । (ख) हा देई ।

च—'यस्यैते तस्य तद्धनम्' इति न्यायेन लोकानामपि त्वमेव नायिकेत्याशयः । यद्वा त्वं मध्यात्मतयावस्थिता, अहं च त्वयि तथावस्थितः । आह च हनूमान्—'अस्या देव्या मनस्तस्मिंस्तस्य चास्यां प्रतिष्ठितम् । तेनेयं स च धर्मात्मा मुहूर्तमपि जीवति ॥' इति । तथा च लौकिकैर्मयि प्रतिपद्यमानं लोकनाथत्वं त्वदीयमित्यर्थः । इत्याद्यूहनीयम् । त्वमनाथेति । त्वत्सत्तामात्रं मम लोकनाथत्वे प्रयोजनम्, अहं तु त्वत्कृते व्यर्थ इति भावः । विपत्स्यसे विपन्ना भविष्यसि । पूर्ववियोगोऽपि रावणवधेप्सितत्वादसत्कल्प इति न तस्मिंस्त्वं विपन्ना । अस्य तु वियोगस्य 'सौमित्रेरपि पत्रिणामविषये तत्र प्रिये क्वासि मे' इति वक्ष्यमाणरीत्या पूर्वोपायाविषयत्वात् इतः परमेव विपन्ना भविष्यसीति लृटा व्यज्यते । पूर्वार्धे विभावनाविशेषोऽलंकारः । 'विरुद्धात्कार्यसंपत्तिर्दृष्टा काचिद्विभावना' इति लक्षणात् ॥ ४३ ॥ **इक्ष्वाकुवंश इति** । विशुद्धिकाले यदद्भुतं कर्म तद्यदि तदस्तीति यद्युच्यते दूरवृत्तं कः प्रत्येति । न कोऽपीत्यर्थः ॥ ४४ ॥ **हा कष्टमिति** । नृशंसः । क्रूरः । अतिबीभत्सकर्मेति प्रसिद्धनृशंसाद्व्यावृत्तिः । **शैशवादिति** । शैशवात्प्रभृति पोषितां बाल्यमारभ्य वर्धिताम् । अनेन 'विषवृक्षोऽपि संवर्ध्य स्वयं छेत्तुमसांप्रतम्' इति न्यायः स्फोर्यते । ननु स्वाप्रियत्वे त्याज्यत्वमित्यत्राह—प्रियामिति । ननु तथापि दोषप्रसक्तौ का गतिरित्यत्राह—अपृथगाश्रयामिति । पृथगाश्रयरहितामित्यर्थः ।

१ शान्तं पापं. २ दुर्जना नाम पौरजानपदाः. ३ शोद्भवतः. ४ तद्यदि दूर० ५ परिप्फुडिद (परिस्फुरित). ६ इदं ववसिदं देव्वेण (इदं व्यवसितं देवेन); अज्जेण एवं.

रामः—हा कष्टम् । अतिबीभत्सकर्मा नृशंसोऽस्मि संवृत्तः ।

शैशवात्प्रभृति पोषितां प्रियां
सौहृदादपृथगाश्रयामिमाम् ।
छद्मना परिददामि मृत्यवे
सौनिको गृहशकुन्तिकामिव ॥ ४५ ॥

तत्किमस्पर्शनीयः पातकी देवीं दूषयामि । (इति सीतायाः शिरः स्वैरमुन्नमय्य बाहुमाकर्षन् ।)

अपूर्वकर्मचण्डालमयि मुग्धे विमुञ्च माम् ।
श्रितासि चन्दनभ्रान्त्या दुर्विपाकं विषद्रुमम् ॥ ४६ ॥

ननु तथापि मनोवृत्तिरन्यत्रेत्यत आह—सौहृदादिति । इमामितीदंपदेन तात्कालिकान्तर्वत्नीत्वनिद्रावत्त्वादिकं परामृश्यते । छद्मना व्याजेन । सीताभिलषितवनप्रस्थापनव्याजेनेत्यर्थः । मृत्यवे परिददामि । देयसाकल्याद्दानसाकल्यम् । तदिमाम् । गर्भस्थशिशुद्वयं चेत्यर्थः । सौनिके जीवहिंसाजीविनि । 'कर्मणा यमभिप्रैति स संप्रदानम्' इति चतुर्थ्यर्थे सप्तमी । प्रथमान्तपाठोऽप्यस्ति । गृहशकुन्तिकाम् । 'अनुकम्पायां कन्' ॥ ४५ ॥ **अपूर्वेति** । अत्र मुग्धे विमुञ्च मामिति सिद्धसाध्यसमभिव्याहारन्यायेन अद्यतनमोचनप्रसञ्जकवतीत्यर्थो लभ्यते । मौग्ध्यस्य मोचनप्रसञ्जकत्वं च तदापादकसंपर्कोपादनद्वारा । स च संबन्धो रावणप्रत्याख्यानपूर्वको लङ्कादेशीय एव । तथा हि—भवितव्यः परगृहवासो जातस्तथापि नैतावता ममात्यहितं प्रसज्जति । रावणो न मां बलात्कर्तुमर्हति । ततश्च तदभिमततदसंपादनेनैव कालयापनं सुकरम् । प्रत्याशया च स मां न हनिष्यति । रामस्तु इदानीं मां निर्दोषां परीक्ष्यानुमन्यमानोऽपि कदाचित्कस्यचिद्वचनमनुसरँल्लोकाराधनश्रद्धया मामरण्ये परित्यजेदित्यादिको विचारः सीतायाः स्यात् । तदा नैवंविधदुःखानुभवप्रसक्तिरिति तदिदं मौग्ध्यस्याद्यतनविपत्प्रयोजकत्वमित्याशयः । सर्वमिदं निर्वेदातिशयद्योतकम् । अपूर्वश्चासौ कर्मचण्डालश्चेति विग्रहः । चण्डालो हि क्रूरतमः । कर्मचण्डालस्तु सुतराम् । यस्तत्रापूर्वो विलक्षणः अहं कर्मचण्डालो रावणादपि क्रूर इति भावः । स हि रावणो न सीतायाः प्राणहानिकरोऽभवत् । अहं तु तत्कारी भवामीति । पूर्वोक्तमौढ्यहेतुकरामसंश्रयणमेवाह—श्रितासीति । द्रुमत्वोक्तिर्भूयस्त्वाभिप्रायात् । दुर्विपाकत्ववचनमत्यन्तक्रौर्यातिशयप्रतिपत्त्यर्थम् । चन्दनभ्रान्त्येत्येतद्दुःखभूयस्त्वादर्जनीयत्वख्यापनार्थम् । अन्यभ्रान्तौ प्रवृत्तिमान्द्यादिकं स्यात् । असीत्यनेनाद्यापि न मुञ्चसीत्यपि व्यज्यते । श्रितेति कर्तृवाचकनिष्ठान्तम् । तेन श्रयणस्य लङ्कादेशीयत्वलाभः । अयमाशयः—लोके हि फलवज्जातीयानामपि वृक्षाणामफलत्वे छेद एवोचितः । अनर्थावहत्वे तु सुतराम् । विषवृक्षस्य तु छेदे का प्रतिहतिः । तस्यापि

---

१ प्रियैः, पालिता प्रियैः, ०श्रयां प्रियाम्. २ अपृथगाशयाम्. ३ सौनिके (टी.).

(उत्थाय ।) हन्त[1] विपर्यस्तः संप्रति जीवलोकः । पर्यवसित[2]मद्य जीवितप्रयोजनं रामस्य । शून्यमधुना जीर्णारण्यं जगत् । असारः संसारः । कष्ट[3]प्रायं शरीरम् । अशरणोऽस्मि । किं करोमि का गतिः । अथ वा

दुःखसंवेदनायैव रामे चैतन्यमाहितम्[4] ।
मर्मोपघातिभिः[5] प्राणैर्वज्रकीलायितं हृदि ॥ ४७ ॥

दुर्विपाकत्वे सर्वथा छेद्यत्वमेव । तथापि 'विषवृक्षोऽपि संवर्ध्य स्वयं छेत्तुमसांप्रतम्' इति न्यायेन यदि छेदप्रतिषेधः तर्हि तस्य परित्यागे का प्रतिहतिः । अत्र क्रूररामकर्मकसंश्रयणप्रतिबिम्बस्य सीताप्रस्तुतकर्तृकदुर्विपाकविषद्रुमाश्रयणस्य वर्णनाल्ललितालंकारः । 'प्रस्तुते वर्ण्यवाक्यार्थप्रतिबिम्बस्य वर्णनम् । ललितम्' इति लक्षणात् ॥ ४६ ॥ हन्तेति दुःखे । संप्रति सीताविरहे । विपर्यस्तोऽन्यथाभूतः । साहित्ये 'यस्तया सह स स्वर्गो निरयो यस्तया विना' इति रामायणोक्तरीत्या जीवलोकस्य स्वर्गत्वम् वियोगे तु नरकत्वमेवेति । स्वर्गान्यस्य नरकस्यैव स्वारसिकत्वात्प्राणिनां नरकप्राप्तावपि नात्मवस्तुनाशः । मम तु सीतामयजीवितत्वात्तन्नाशे जीवितनाश इति । अद्यावसितमिति समाप्तं जीवितमेव प्रयोजनम् । जीवितमिति वक्ष्यमाणमिहानुसंधेयम् । सीताविरहितजीवितं निष्प्रयोजनमित्यर्थः । यत एवं ततोऽधुना जीर्णारण्यं जगत्स्वर्गादिकं ह्यात्मनः स्थिरत्वे कालान्तरानुभाव्यं स्यात् । 'अनादौ संसारे' इति न्यायात् । आत्मवस्तुनाशे तु स्वानुपभोगात् जीर्णारण्यत्वम् । सीतासाहित्ये हि अरण्यस्यापि पञ्चवट्याः 'यस्यां ते दिवसाः' इति रीत्या स्वगृहत्वात् तदयोगे तु स्वगृहस्यापि जीर्णारण्यत्वमित्याशयः । असारः शून्यः । काष्ठप्रायं शरीरम् । 'ज्योत्स्नेव हिमदीधितेः' इत्युक्त्या यथा चन्द्रस्य कौमुद्यभावे काष्ठप्रायता तद्वत्स्वस्येति भावः । अथ पूर्ववत् । 'सुग्रीवं शरणं गतः' 'सागरं शरणं गतः' इत्यादिकस्य नावकाश इत्याह—अशरणोऽस्मीति । पूर्ववत्सेतुबन्धनादि कर्तव्यं नास्तीत्याह—किं करोमीति । अथ पूर्ववद्रावणवधादिरूपप्राप्यं नास्तीत्याह—का गतिरिति । गम्यत इति गतिः । यतश्चैवं ततः क्व गच्छामि, किमरण्यं गच्छामि, उत पातालविवरम्, किं वा मरणं गच्छामि इति विकल्पाशयः । न तूक्तः कल्पः सर्वोऽपि न कल्पत इत्याह—अथ वेति । पूर्वोक्ताक्षेपकः । दुःखेति चैतन्यमात्मा ज्ञप्तिर्वा । दुःखसंवेदनायैव रामे आगतम् । आगतमित्यनेन दुर्मुखवाक्यश्रवणानन्तरं गतं चैतन्यं पुनरागतमिति व्यज्यते । यद्वा शक्तिप्रहारादिषु गतं पुनरागतमिति वा । पट्टाभिषेकदिनान्तरीयकसुखं तु असत्कल्पमिति हृदयम् । 'अर्पितम्,' 'आहितम्' इति पाठयोस्तु आदितः प्रभृति 'राज्याद्भ्रंशो वने वासः सीता नष्टा द्विजो हतः । ईदृशीयं ममालक्ष्मीर्निर्दहेदपि पावकम् ॥' इत्युक्तरीत्या दुःखानुभवायैव

---

१ हन्त हन्त. २ अद्यावसितं; अद्येति नास्ति क्वचित्. ३ काष्ठ. ४ अर्पितं; आगतम्. ५ स्थिरैः

हा अम्ब अरुन्धति हा भगवन्तौ वसिष्ठविश्वामित्रौ हा भगवन्पावक हा देवि भूतधात्रि हा तात जनक हा तात मातरः हा प्रियसखे सुग्रीव हा सौम्य हनूमन् हा परमोपकारिन् लङ्काधिपते बिभीषण हा सखि त्रिजटे परिमुषिताः स्थ परिभूताः स्थ रामहतकेन। अथ वा को नाम तेषामहमिदानीमाह्वाने।

ते हि मन्ये महात्मानः कृतघ्नेन दुरात्मना।
मया गृहीतनामानः स्पृश्यन्त इव पाप्मना॥ ४८॥

योऽहम्

विस्रम्भादुरसि निपत्य लब्धनिद्रा-
मुन्मुच्य प्रियगृहिणीं गृहस्य शोभाम्।
आतङ्कस्फुरितकठोरगर्भगुर्वी
क्रव्याद्भ्यो बलिमिव निर्घृणः क्षिपामि॥ ४९॥

सीतायाः पादौ शिरसि कृत्वा।) देवि देवि अयं पश्चिमस्ते रामशिरसो पादपङ्कजस्पर्शः। (इति रोदिति।)

चैतन्यसद्भाव इति भावः। स्वर्गिणां चैतन्यं दुःखासंभिन्नसुखानुभवाय। जनानां दुःखमिश्रसुखानुभवाय। मम सुखासंभिन्नदुःखानुभवाय। तस्मात्पातालविवरगमनेऽप्यपरिहार्यं दुःखमिति भावः। तर्हि मरणं गमिष्यामीति कल्पः कल्प्यतामित्याह—मर्मोपघातिभिरिति। मर्म हृदयादिप्रदेशानुपघ्नन्तीति विग्रहः। 'सुप्यजातौ–' इति णिनिः। न केवलं दुःखानुभवापादकाः किं तु स्वयमपि दुःखप्रदा इति भावः। वज्रकीलवद्दृढतया स्थिरीभूयते। भङ्गानर्हत्वेन वा सादृश्यम्। तथा च मरणमपि दुर्लभमित्यर्थः॥ ४७॥ **हेति**। अरुन्धति। अरुन्धतीकृतसीतापातिव्रत्यानुमोदनं न प्रमाणीकृतमिति भावः। भगवन्ताविति। भवतां ज्ञानशक्तिमपि खला न पश्यन्तीति भावः। **पावकेति**। तव वचनप्रवेशौ व्यर्थाविति भावः। भूतधात्रि त्वत्सुतायामनिमित्तदोषवादिनो जनान्कथं बिभर्षि इति भावः। **सौम्येति**। सीतावृत्तान्तकथनजनितानन्दाप्रयुक्तमत्कृतालिङ्गनमद्विज्ञातशरीरसौभग भवदीयप्रयासो व्यर्थ इति भावः। परिमुषिताः मुषितद्रव्यकाः। **ते हीति**। कृतं उपकारं हन्तीति कृतघ्नः। एतत्कृतपूर्वोपकारविस्मरणादिति भावः॥ ४८॥ **विस्रम्भादिति**। विस्रम्भादन्तरङ्गत इति ज्ञानादिति भावः। गृहस्य लक्ष्मीं शोभां तदलंकारभूताम्। कठोरगर्भः पूर्णगर्भः। गुर्वीमित्यनेन यमलत्वं सूचयति। क्रव्याद्भ्यो मांसभक्षकेभ्यः। क्रव्यं मांसमदन्ति

---

१ मातः. २ ०सख महाराज. ३ महोप०. ४ मुषि०, दूषिता. ५ कश्च. ६ जात. ७ लक्ष्मीम्. ८ दारुणः. ९ शिरसि.

(नेपथ्ये ।)

अब्रह्मण्यमब्रह्मण्यम् ।

रामः——ज्ञायतां भोः किमेतत् ।

(पुनर्नेपथ्ये ।)

ऋषीणामुग्रतपसां यमुनातीरवासिनाम् ।
लवणत्रासितः स्तोमः शरण्यं त्वामुपस्थितः ॥ ५० ॥

रामः——आः कथमद्यापि राक्षसत्रासः । तद्यावदस्य दुरात्मनो[2] कुम्भीनसीपुत्रस्यो[3]न्मूलनाय शत्रुघ्नं प्रेषयामि । (कतिचित्पदानि गत्वा[4] पुनर्निवृत्य ।) हा देवि कथमेवंगता भविष्यसि । भगवति वसुंधरे सुश्लाध्यां दुहितरमवेक्षस्व जानकीम् ।

जनकानां रघूणां च यत्कृत्स्नं गोत्रमङ्गलम् ।
यां[6] देवयजने पुण्ये पुण्यशीलामजीजनः ॥ ५१ ॥

(इति रुदन्निष्क्रान्तः ।)

सीता—हा सौम्य आर्यपुत्र कुत्रासि । (सहसोत्थाय ।) हा धिक् हा धिक् दुःस्वप्नेन विप्रलब्धाहमार्यपुत्रमाक्रन्दामि । (विलोक्य ।) हा धिक् हा धिक् एकाकिनीं मां प्रसुप्तामुज्झित्वा गत आर्यपुत्रः । किमिदानीमेतत् ।

खादन्तीति विग्रहः । ' क्रव्ये च ' इति विट् ॥ ४९ ॥ अब्रह्मण्यं ब्राह्मणानामत्याहितम् । ' अब्रह्मण्यमवध्योक्तौ ' इत्यमरः ॥ **ऋषीणामिति** । लवणो नाम राक्षसस्तेन त्रासित ऋषीणां स्तोम इत्यन्वयः ॥ ५० ॥ **कथमित्यादि** । निःशेषितराक्षसकुलत्वात् ; स्वस्येति भावः । यद्वा कथमद्य राक्षसत्रासोऽपीत्यन्वयः । न केवलं सीताविश्लेषदुःखप्राप्तिः किं तु राक्षसभयं चेति समुच्चयार्थः । कथमिति विस्मये । पूर्ववदेवोभयं मिलितमिदमाश्चर्यमिति भावः । दुरात्मनो दुर्बुद्धेः । माधुरस्य मधुरेश्वरस्य । कुम्भीनसी नाम तन्माता । उन्मूलनाय मूलेन सहोत्पाटनाय । यावत् प्रेषयामि प्रेषयिष्यामि । ' यावत्पुरानिपातयोर्लट् ' । एवंविधा मया वञ्चिता गर्भिणी सती कथं गमिष्यसीति भावः । भगवति सर्वज्ञे । सुश्लाघ्यां निर्दोषां निरुपप्लवां वा । **जनकानामिति** । यत्कृत्स्नं गोत्रमङ्गलम् । यदिति विधेयापेक्षया क्लीबम् । अजीजनः । उत्पादितवत्यसीत्यर्थः ॥५१॥ अत्र बिन्दुर्नाम संध्यङ्गमुक्तम् । दाम्पत्यविशेषविच्छेदहेतुत्वात्पुनरच्छेदकारणत्वाच्च । तदुक्तम्— अवान्तरार्थविच्छेदे बिन्दुरच्छेदकारणम् ' इति ।

---

१ त्रातारम्. २ दुरात्मनो माधुरस्य. ३ कुमारस्य. ४ परिक्रम्य. ५ एवंविधा गमिष्यासि (टी.) ६ ताम्.

भवतु तस्मै कोपिष्यामि यदि तं प्रेक्षमाणाऽऽत्मनः प्रभविष्यामि। कोऽत्र परिजनः। (क)

(प्रविश्य।)

दुर्मुखः—देवि कुमारलक्ष्मणो विज्ञापयति सज्जो रथ आरोहतु देवीति। (ख)

सीता—इयमारोहामि। (उत्थाय परिक्रम्य।) परिस्फुरतीव मे गर्भ-भारः। तच्छिथिलं गच्छावः। (ग[1])

दुर्मुखः—इत इतो देवी। (घ)

सीता—नमस्तपोधनेभ्यो नमो रघुकुलदेवताभ्यो नम आर्यपुत्रच-रणकमलेभ्यो नमः सकलगुरुजनेभ्यः। (ङ)

(इति निष्क्रान्ताः सर्वे।)

इति महाकविश्रीभवभूतिविरचिते उत्तररामचरिते
चित्र[2]दर्शनो नाम प्रथमोऽङ्कः।

(क) हा सोम्य अज्जउत्त कहिंसि। हद्धी हद्धी दुस्सिविणेण[3] विप्पलद्धा अहं अज्ज-उत्तं आक्कंदामि। हद्धी हद्धी एआइणिं मं पसुत्तं उज्झिअ [4]गदो अज्जउत्तो। किं दाणी एदं। होदु से कुप्पिस्सं जइ तं पेक्खन्ती अत्तणो पहविस्सं। को एत्थ परिअणो।

(ख) देइ कुमारलक्खणो विण्णवेदि सज्जो रहो आरुहदु देइ त्ति।

(ग) इअं आरुहामि[5]। [6]परिप्फुरदि विअ मे गब्भभारो। ता सिहिलं गच्छह्म।

(घ) इदो इदो देइ। (ङ) णमो तपोधणाणं णमो रहुउलदेअदाणं णमो अज्जउत्तचरणकमलाणं णमो सअलगुरुअणाणं।

कोऽत्र परिजनः। परिजनस्य मध्ये कोऽत्र संनिहित इत्यर्थः। परिजनस्येति निर्धारणे षष्ठ्येकवचनान्तम्। निर्धारणे षष्ठीप्रयोगोऽप्यस्ति। सज्जो गमनाय संनद्धः। रघुकुल-देवते लक्ष्मीनारायणाविति प्रसिद्धमेव। तन्नमस्कारो यात्राकाले विहितः। 'आदित्य-मण्डलं विष्णुं ध्यात्वा यात्रां प्रवर्तयेत्।' इति स्मरणात्॥

दाशरथिवंशजनुषो भूसारजवीरराघवार्यस्य।
उत्तररामचरित्रव्याख्याङ्केष्वादिमः प्रायात्॥

इति श्रीवाधूलवीरराघवविरचितायां भवभूतिभावतलस्पर्शिनी-समाख्यायामुत्तररामचरितव्याख्यायां प्रथमोऽङ्कः॥

---

१ प्र०... . २ ०दर्शनं. ३ ०विणविप्प०, दुस्सिविणरणरणअविप्पलद्धा अज्जउत्तसुण्णं विअ अत्ताणं पेक्खामि (दुःस्वप्नरणरणकविप्रलब्धा आर्यपुत्रशून्यमिवात्मानं पश्यामि). ४ कहिं गदो णाहो (कुत्र गतो नाथः।). ५ आरूढह्मि (आरूढास्मि). ६ फुरइ मे गब्भभारो सणिअं ग० (स्फुरति मे गर्भभारः शनैर्गच्छामः).

द्वितीयोऽङ्कः ।

(नेपथ्ये ।)

स्वागतं तपोधनायाः[1] ।

(ततः प्रविशत्यध्वगवेषा तापसी ।)

तापसी—अये वनदेवतेयं फलकुसुमपल्लवार्घ्येण[2] मामुपतिष्ठते ।

(प्रविश्य ।)

वनदेवता—(अर्घ्यं विकीर्य[3] ।)

यथेच्छं[4] भोग्यं वो वनमिदमयं मे सुदिवसः
सतां सद्भिः सङ्गः कथमपि हि पुण्येन भवति ।
तरुच्छाया तोयं यदपि तपसो[5] योग्यमशनं[6]
फलं वा मूलं वा तदपि न पराधीनमिह वः ॥ १ ॥

नेपथ्य इति । 'कुशीलवकुटुम्बस्य स्थली नेपथ्यमिष्यते' इत्युक्ततिरस्करिणीतिरोहितनर्तनभूमिकापरिग्रहौपयिकस्थानविशेषः ॥ **वनदेवतेति** । पल्लवार्घ्येण पल्लवयुक्तपूजाद्रव्येण दूरात् प्रविष्टा सती उपतिष्ठते पूजयति । देवतात्वारोपादात्मनेपदम् । दूरादित्यपादाने पञ्चमी । यद्वा मामुपतिष्ठते संगता भवति । 'गङ्गायमुनामुपतिष्ठते' इतिवत् उभयत्रापि 'उपाद्देवपूजा–' इत्यादिना तङ् । अर्घ्यं वितीर्य दत्त्वा । **यथेच्छमिति** । इदम् । मदीयमित्यर्थः । वनं वनमेव न तु स्पृहणीयपुरप्रासादादिकमित्यपरितोषो व्यज्यते । तथापि 'अविद्यमाने कर्णोऽपि' इति न्यायेन यथाधिकारं सभाजयितव्यमेवेत्याह—यथेच्छाभोग्यं इच्छामनतिक्रम्य यथेच्छम् । यथेच्छं आभोग्यमिति विग्रहः । इच्छानिवृत्तिपर्यन्तमसंकोचेनोपभोगार्हमित्यर्थः । व इति पूजायां बहुवचनम् । अतिथिसामान्याभिप्रायकं वा । अयं मे सुदिवसः साधुजनसंपर्कादिति भावः । सतां विद्यमानामेव न तु प्रसादनादि कुर्वतामित्यर्थः । सद्भिः साधुभिः सह सङ्गः संपर्कः कथमपि कृच्छ्रेण पुण्येन भवति । साधुजनसंपर्कलाभः प्रणिपातादिसाध्यो भवति । तदभाववतां तु दुष्टहेत्वभावात् केवलादृष्टसाध्यो भवतीति भावः । यद्वा कथमपि सतां येन केन प्रकारेण वर्तमानानाम् । कामचारे स्थितानामित्यर्थः । सद्भिः ब्रह्मविद्भिरित्यर्थः । 'अस्ति ब्रह्मेति चेद्वेद सन्तमेनं ततो विदुः ।' इति श्रुतेः । सङ्गः संपर्कः पुण्येन हि भवति । अयमाशयः—'तस्मादेवंविदा नासीत' इति श्रुत्या ब्रह्मज्ञानवतां तच्छून्यैः सहवासादिकं प्रतिषिद्धम् । एवं च तेषां तैः सङ्गः पुण्यैकसाध्य इति । इदं च स्वनिकर्षभावनाकार्यम् । फलं वा मूलं वा इतोऽन्यदपि तपसां योग्यमशनम् । नीवारपाण्डु-

---

१ ०नायै. २ कुसुमगर्भेण...दूरान्मां. ३ वितीर्य. ४ यथेच्छाभोग्यं. ५ तपसां. ६ भोग्यं, भोज्यम्.

तापसी—किमत्रोच्यते ।

प्रियप्राया वृत्तिर्विनयमधुरो वाचि नियमः
प्रकृत्या कल्याणी मतिरनवगीतः परिचयः ।
पुरो वा पश्चाद्वा तदिदमविपर्यासितरसं
रहस्यं साधूनामनुपधि विशुद्धं विजयते ॥ २ ॥

(उपविशतः ।)

वनदेवता—कां पुनरत्रभवतीमवगच्छामि ।

तापसी—आत्रेय्यस्मि ।

वनदेवता—आर्ये आत्रेयि कुतः पुनरिहागम्यते । किंप्रयोजनो[1] वा दण्डकारण्यप्रचारः[2] ।

आत्रेयी—

अस्मिन्नगस्त्यप्रमुखाः प्रदेशे भूयांस उद्गीथविदो वसन्ति ।
तेभ्योऽधिगन्तुं निगमान्तविद्यां वाल्मीकिपार्श्वादिह पर्यटामि ॥ ३ ॥

वातजलादिकमित्यर्थः । तदपि तच्च पराधीनं नेति ॥ १ ॥ **प्रियेति** । प्रियप्राया प्रियप्रचुरा युक्ता चेत्यर्थः । वृत्तिः कायिकव्यापारः । तथापि वाक्कौर्ये महान्दोष इत्यत आह—विनयमधुरो वाचि नियमः । विनयेन स्वनिकर्षभावनारूपेण स्वोत्कर्षाननुसंधानरूपेण वा मधुरः प्रियः वाचि नियमः सत्याय मितभाषित्वम् । तथापि मनोवृत्तिदौष्ट्यं स्यादत आह—प्रकृत्या कल्याणी मतिः । प्रकृत्या स्वभावतः कल्याणी श्रेयस्विनी । तथाप्यसत्सङ्गवशाद्वैपरीत्यं स्यादत आह—अनवगीतः । अनिन्दित इत्यर्थः । तदिदं वृत्तिवाचिनियमादिपरिचयसमुदायरूपं विजयते सर्वोत्कर्षेण वर्तते । तत्कथंभूतमित्याह—पुरो वा पश्चाद्वा भूतभविष्यत्कालयोः । तत्तत्पुरुषसंनिधानयोरिति वार्थः । अविपर्यासितरसं अन्यूनस्वभावम् । रसपदेन प्रियत्वं व्यज्यते । अनुपधि निर्व्याजं विशुद्धं प्रामादिकदोषरहितं रहस्यम् । 'शीलं संवसता ज्ञेयम्' इति न्यायेन चिरकालशुश्रूषादिभिरेव ज्ञातुं शक्यं न तु दाम्भिकवृत्तिवत्स्वयं प्रकटमित्यर्थः । तथाविधं तदिदं विजयत इति योजना ॥ २ ॥ अवगच्छामि जानामि ॥ **किंप्रयोजन इति** । प्रचारः संचारः ॥ **अस्मिन्निति** । अगस्त्यप्रमुखा अगस्त्यप्रभृतयो भूयांसो बहव उद्गीथविदः। 'ओमित्युद्गीथमुपासीत' इति परस्मिन् ब्रह्मणि उद्गीथदृष्टिं कुर्वन्त इत्यर्थः । दहरविद्यादीनामुपलक्षणम् । सकलवेदान्ततात्पर्यपर्यालोचनशीला इति भावः । तेभ्यः अधिगन्तुं तत्कृतव्याख्यानेन ज्ञातुम् । आख्यातोपयोगे' इति पञ्चमी । [निगमान्तः वेदान्तः ।] पर्यटामि । 'अटगतौ' ॥ ३ ॥

---

१ प्रयोजनं...रण्यप्रवेशस्य. २ प्रवेशः, रण्योपवनप्रचारः.

वनदेवता—यदा तावदन्येऽपि मुनयस्तमेव हि पुराणब्रह्मवादिन प्राचेतसमृषिं ब्रह्मपारायणायोपासते तत्कोऽयमार्याया दीर्घप्रवासप्रयासः ।

आत्रेयी—तत्र[1] महानध्ययनप्रत्यूह इत्येष दीर्घप्रवासोऽङ्गीकृतः ।

वनदेवता—कीदृशः ।

आत्रेयी—तस्य भगवतः केनापि देवताविशेषेण सर्वप्रकाराद्भुतं स्तन्यत्यागमात्रके वयसि वर्तमानं दारकद्वयमुपनीतम् । तत्खलु[2] न केवलमृषीणामपि तु चराचराणां भूतानामान्तराणि तत्त्वान्युपस्नेहयति ।

वनदेवता—अपि तयोर्नामसंविज्ञानमस्ति ।

आत्रेयी—तयैव किल देवतया तयोः कुशलवाविति नामनी प्रभावश्चाख्यातः ।

वनदेवता—कीदृशः प्रभावः ।

आत्रेयी—तयोः किल सरहस्यानि जृम्भकास्त्राण्याजन्मसिद्धानीति ।

वनदेवता—अहो[3] नु भोश्चित्रमेतत् ।

आत्रेयी—तौ च भगवता वाल्मीकिना धात्रीकर्म[4] वस्तुतः परिगृह्य पोषितौ परिरक्षितौ च । निर्वृत्त[5]चौलकर्मणोश्च तयोस्त्रयीवर्जमितरास्तिस्रो

तावदिति । पुराणश्चासौ ब्रह्मवादी चेति विग्रहः । ब्रह्म परमात्मानं वेदान्वा वदतीति । णिनिः । पुराणत्वे प्राचेतसमिति हेतुकथनम् । ब्रह्मपारायणाय वेदान्तविद्याध्ययनाय । पारायणं नाम आदित आरभ्यान्तादविच्छेदेनाध्ययनमुपासते । **तदिति** । प्रवासो देशान्तरगमनम् । **तस्मिन्निति** । प्रत्यूहः विघ्नः ॥ **तस्येति** । स्तन्यत्यागमात्रं यस्मिन्निति बहुव्रीहेः कप्प्रत्ययः । दारकद्वयं शिशुद्वयम् । **तदिति** । तस्य वाल्मीकेः संनिधानीकरोति ॥ **अपीति** । नाम्नोऽभिलापकशब्दस्य संज्ञानं संकेतसंबन्धकरणम् ॥ **तयोरिति** । जन्मसिद्धानि जन्मना ज्ञातानि न तूपदेशेन ॥ **तौ चेति** । धात्रीकर्मत उपमातृव्यापारेण । पोषितौ क्षीरादिना वर्धितौ । रक्षितौ । पिपीलिकादिभ्य इति भावः । **निर्वृत्तेति** । निर्वृत्तं निष्पन्नम् । त्रयीवर्जं त्रयीं वर्जयित्वा । अङ्गान्यपीति शेषः । इतराः—"आयुर्वेदो धनुर्वेदस्तथा गान्धर्वनामकः" इत्युक्ता इत्यर्थः ।

---

१ तस्मिन्हि. २ केवलं तस्यापि तु–तिरश्चामप्यन्तःकरणानि;–सचराचराणां भूतानाम०. ३ इति हि भोश्चित्रम्. ४ कर्मतः (टी.); ०कर्मवत्सलताम्. ५ वृत्तचूडौ च त्रयीवर्जमितरा विद्याः सावधानेन परिपाठितौ.

विद्याः सावधानेन परिनिष्ठापिताः । समनन्तरं च गर्भैकादशे वर्षे क्षात्रेण कल्पेनोपनीय गुरुणा त्रयीविद्यामध्यापितौ । न ह्येताभ्यामतिप्रदीप्तप्रज्ञामेधाभ्यामस्मदादेः सहाध्ययनयोगोऽस्ति । यतः ।

वितरति गुरुः प्राज्ञे विद्यां यथैव तथा जडे
न च खलु तयोर्ज्ञाने शक्तिं करोत्यपहन्ति वा ।
भवति च पुनर्भूयान्भेदः फलं प्रति तद्यथा
प्रभवति शुचिर्बिम्बग्राहे मणिर्न मृदां चयः ॥ ४ ॥

वनदेवता—अयमसावध्ययनप्रत्यूहः ।

आत्रेयी—अन्यश्च ।

वनदेवता—अथापरः कः ।

आत्रेयी—अथ स ब्रह्मर्षिरेकदा माध्यंदिनसवनाय नदीं तमसामनुप्रपन्नः । तत्र युग्मचारिणोः क्रौञ्चयोरेकं व्याधेन विध्यमानं ददर्श । आकस्मिकप्रत्यवभासां च देवीं वाचमव्यतिकीर्णवर्णामानुष्टुभेन छन्दसा परिणतामभ्युदैरयत् ।

मा निषाद प्रतिष्ठां त्वमगमः शाश्वतीः समाः ।
यत्क्रौञ्चमिथुनादेकमवधीः काममोहितम् ॥ ५ ॥

सावधानेन । वाल्मीकिनेति शेषः । परिनिष्ठापिताः सम्यङ् निष्पादिताः । **तदनन्तरमिति** । एकादशानां पूरणं एकादशम् । 'तस्य पूरणे' इति डट्प्रत्ययः । गर्भात् गर्भवर्षात् एकादशं गर्भैकादशं तस्मिन्नित्यर्थः । 'गर्भैकादशे राजन्यम्' इति स्मृतेः । कल्प्यतेऽनुष्ठीयतेऽनेनेति कल्पः अनुष्ठानपरिपाटीप्रकाशकग्रन्थः । **न त्वेताभ्यामिति** । दीप्तिः प्रतिभा । प्रज्ञा ज्ञानं उत्कार्थग्रहणम् । **वितरतीति** । तयोः प्राज्ञजडयोः ज्ञाने शक्तिं न करोति प्राज्ञस्य ज्ञाने अपूर्वां शक्तिं न जनयति जडस्य ज्ञाने शक्तिं नापहन्ति जडस्य ज्ञाननिष्ठां शक्तिं न नाशयति । बिम्बग्राहे प्रतिबिम्बज्ञानोत्पादने मणिः वज्रं रत्नसामान्यं वा । मृदादयः आदिपदात् वृक्षपाषाणलोष्टग्रहणम् ॥ ४ ॥ अथेति प्रश्ने ॥ **अथेति** । माध्यंदिनसवनाय मध्यंदिनसंबन्धिकर्मणे । अनुप्रपन्नः प्राप्तः । **तत्रेति** । युग्मं द्वन्द्वं यथा तथा चरत इति युग्मचारिणौ तयोः क्रौञ्चयोः पक्षिविशेषयोः । व्याधेन पुलिन्देन । ददर्श अपश्यत । आकस्मिकप्रत्यवभासां निर्हेतुकाविर्भावाम् । आनुष्टुभेन छन्दसा । स्वार्थिकोऽण्प्रत्ययः । **मा निषादेति** । प्रतिष्ठां तु अम गमः इति पदचतुष्टयं निषादपक्षे बोध्यम् । एवं च माङ्योगेऽडागमानिषेध उपपद्यते । अमेत्यस्य न विद्यते मा लक्ष्मीः

---

१ भगवतैकादशे—omitting गुरुणा. २ अतिदीप्तिप्रज्ञाभ्याम्. ३ तु. ४ हि. ५ तयोः. ६ बिम्बोद्ग्राहे. ७ मृदादयः. ८ मध्यंदिनसमये–सवने; अथ श्रूयताम् । एकदा तमसामनुप्रपन्नो भगवान्प्राचेतसस्तत्र युग्म०. ९ बध्यमानम्. १० अव्यतिकीर्णां; एतन्नास्ति क्वचित्. ११ परिच्छिन्नाम्.

वनदेवता—चित्रमाम्नायादन्यो नूतनच्छन्दसामवतारः ।

आत्रेयी—तेन खलु[1] पुनः समयेन तं भगवन्तमाविर्भूतशब्दब्रह्मप्रकाशमृषिमुपसंगम्य भगवान्भूतभावनः पद्मयोनिरवोचत्—'ऋषे प्रबुद्धोऽसि वागात्मनि ब्रह्मणि तद्ब्रूहि रामचरितम् । अव्याहतज्योतिरार्षं ते प्रातिभं[2] चक्षुः । आद्यः कविरसि' इत्युक्त्वान्तर्हितः । अथ स भगवान्प्राचेतसः प्रथमं मनुष्येषु शब्दब्रह्मणस्तादृशं विवर्तमितिहासं रामायणं प्रणिनाय ।

वनदेवता—हन्त तर्हि मण्डितः[3] संसारः ।

आत्रेयी—तस्मादेवोचं[4] तत्र हि महानध्ययनप्रत्यूह इति ।

वनदेवता—युज्यते ।

आत्रेयी—विश्रान्तास्मि भद्रे । संप्रत्यगस्त्याश्रमस्य पन्थानं ब्रूहि ।

वनदेवता—इतः पञ्चवटीमनुप्रविश्य गम्यतामनेन गोदावरीतीरेण ।

यस्येति विग्रहः । एवं च अलक्ष्मीकेति निषादं प्रति मन्युर्गम्यते । अत एव भगवन्तं प्रति रावणवधजनितप्रीत्यतिशयेन मानिषादेति सलक्ष्मीकत्वप्रतिपादनम् । भगवत्परत्वे मा लक्ष्मीः निषीदत्यस्मिन्निति मानिषादः । बाहुलकादधिकरणे घञ् । तस्य संबुद्धिः । निषेधार्थमाशब्देन अडागमसमर्थनं तु क्लिष्टम् । प्रतिष्ठा आस्पदम् । व्याधपक्षे मा गमः न गच्छेः भगवत्पक्षे अगमः प्राप्तवानिति । समाः संवत्सरान् । अत्यन्तसंयोगे द्वितीया ॥ ५ ॥ आम्नायात् वेदात् ॥ **तेनेति** । तेन समयेन कालेन । भूतेन प्रजाः भावयति उत्पादयतीति विग्रहः । यद्वा भूतं सत्यम्, निर्निरोधमिति वा । भावना अध्यवसायः यस्येति वा । पद्मयोनिः भगवन्नाभिकमलजातः । अनेन पूर्वोक्तभूतभावनत्वप्रयुक्तपरत्वशङ्का निराकृता । प्रबुद्धोऽसि प्रकृष्टज्ञानवानसि । वागेव आत्मा यस्य तस्मिन् ब्रह्मणि शब्दब्रह्मणि । वाचो वैपुल्याभिप्रायकं ब्रह्मत्वरूपणं ब्रह्मतत्त्वमेव शब्दरूपेण भातीत्यर्थ इति कैयटमतानुसारेण वा । अव्याहतज्योतिः अप्रतिहतप्रकाशं आर्षं ऋषिसंबन्धि योगजन्यज्ञानं चक्षुः नेत्रं ज्ञानमिति फलितोऽर्थः । 'तत्सर्वं मत्प्रसादेन विदितं ते भविष्यति' इत्यादि रामायणे द्रष्टव्यम् । आद्यः कविरसीत्युक्त्वा अनुगृह्य । अन्तर्हितः परोक्षतां गतः ।

---

१ हि. २ प्रतिभाचक्षुः; ते चक्षुः; प्रतिभातु; आर्षमव्याहतज्योतिः प्रतिभाचक्षुरस्तु ते । आद्यः कविरसीत्युक्त्वा तत्रैवान्तरधीयत ॥ इ. पा. ३ पण्डितः. ४ तस्मादेव हि ब्रवीमि; तस्मादवोचं तदनुरोधान्नस्तत्र हि.

आत्रेयी—(सास्रम् ।) अप्येतत्तपोवनम् । अप्येषा पञ्चवटी । अपि सरिदियं गोदावरी । अप्ययं गिरिः प्रस्रवणः । अपि जनस्थानवनदेवता वासन्ती त्वम् ।

वनदेवता—अस्त्येतत्सर्वम् ।

आत्रेयी—हा वत्से जानकि ।

स एष ते वल्लभबन्धुवर्गः प्रासङ्गिकीनां विषयः कथानाम् ।
त्वां नामशेषामपि दृश्यमानः प्रत्यक्षदृष्टामिव नः करोति ॥ ६ ॥

वासन्ती—(सभयम् । स्वगतम् ।) कथं नामशेषामित्याह । (प्रकाशम् ।) आर्ये किमत्याहितं सीतादेव्याः ।

आत्रेयी—न केवलमत्याहितं सापवादमपि । (कर्णे ।) एवमेवम् ।

वासन्ती—अहह दारुणो दैवनिर्घातः । (इति मूर्च्छति ।)

आत्रेयी—भद्रे समाश्वसिहि समाश्वसिहि ।

वासन्ती—हा प्रियसखि हा महाभागे ईदृशस्ते निर्माणभागः । हा रामभद्र । अथ वा अलं त्वया । आर्ये आत्रेयि अथ तस्मादरण्यात्परित्यज्य निवृत्ते लक्ष्मणे सीतादेव्याः किं वृत्तमिति काचिदस्ति प्रवृत्तिः ।

आत्रेयी—नहि नहि ।

वासन्ती—हा कष्टम् । अरुन्धतीवसिष्ठाधिष्ठितेषु रघुकुटुम्बकेषु जीवन्तीषु च प्रवृद्धासु राज्ञीषु कथमिदं जातम् ।

आत्रेयी—ऋष्यशृङ्गाश्रमे गुरुजनस्तदासीत् । संप्रति तु परिसमाप्तं तद्द्वादशवार्षिकं सत्रम् । ऋष्यशृङ्गेण च संपूज्य विसर्जिता गुरवः । ततो भगवत्यरुन्धती नाहं वधूविरहितामयोध्यां गमिष्यामी-

स इति। [बन्धूनां वर्गः बन्धुवर्गः वल्लभश्चासौ बन्धुवर्गश्च] दृश्यमानः दृष्टिविषयीभूतः। प्रासङ्गिकीनां प्रसक्त्यनुप्रसक्त्या जातानां कथानां प्रश्नप्रतिवचनरूपाणां वाक्यसंदर्भाणां विषयः प्रतिपाद्यः वल्लभशाखिनां स्वयं वर्धितत्वात् अत्यर्थप्रीतिविषयाणां वृक्षाणाम् । शाखिनामिति वचनं सीताकरस्पर्शप्रयुक्तस्फीतत्वाभिप्रायकम् ॥ ६ ॥ दैवनिर्घातः दैवप्रहारः । दारुणः तीव्रः ॥ **हा प्रियसखीति**। निर्माणभागः सृष्टिफलम् । अथ वेति जनवाक्पिधानस्य दुःशकत्वादिति भावः । किं वृत्तमिति निष्पन्नमिति । प्रवृत्तिः वार्ता । आसीत् अभूत् । किमिति काक्वा योजनीयम् । **संप्रति परिसमाप्तमिति** । इदमेवाभिसंधाय पूर्वोक्तव्याख्यानमिति न विस्म-

१ सबाष्पम्. २ तथैव तत्सर्वम्. ३ शाखि. ४ दृश्याम्. ५ हा. ६ एतन्नास्ति क्वचित्. ७ सीतायाः. ८ आसीत्. ९ आर्यारुन्धती. १० रघुकुलक०, रघुकुटुम्बकेषु, अधिष्ठिते रघुकुले. ११ सत्रे. १२ गच्छामीति.

त्याह । तदेव राममातृभिरनुमोदितम् । तदनुरोधाद्भगवतो वसिष्ठस्य[1] परिशुद्धा वाचो वाल्मीकितपोवनं गत्वा तत्र वत्स्याम इति ।

वासन्ती—अथ स[2] राजा किमाचार[3]: संप्रति ।

आत्रेयी—तेन राज्ञा क्रतु[4]रश्वमेधः प्रक्रान्तः ।

वासन्ती—हा[5] धिक् परिणीतमपि ।

आत्रेयी—शान्तं[6] पापम् । नहि नहि ।

वासन्ती—का तर्हि यज्ञे सहधर्मचारिणी ।

आत्रेयी—हिरण्मयी सीताप्रतिकृ[7]तिः ।

वासन्ती—हन्त भोः ।

वज्रादपि कठोराणि मृदूनि कुसुमादपि ।
लोकोत्तराणां चेतांसि को नु[8] विज्ञातुमर्हति ॥ ७ ॥

आत्रेयी—विसृष्टश्च वामदेवाभिमन्त्रितो मेध्योऽश्वः । उपक्ल्पि[9]ताश्च यथाशास्त्रं तस्य रक्षितारः । तेषामधिष्ठाता च लक्ष्मणात्मजश्चन्द्रकेतुरवाप्त[10]दिव्यास्त्रसंप्रदायश्चतुरङ्गसाधना[11]न्वितोऽनुप्रहितः ।

र्तव्यम् । वधूविरहितां स्नुषाविरहिताम् । **तदन्विति** । तदनुरोधात् तदनुसरणात् । श्रद्धा निश्चयः ॥ **अथेति** । किमाचारः कीदृशव्यापारवान् । **तेनेति** । राजक्रतुः राज्ञां साधारणो यः क्रतुः क्रतुराजो वा अश्वमेधः । राजदन्तादित्वात् परनिपातः ॥ **सीतेति** । सीतायाः प्रतिकृतिः प्रतिमा । गृहिणीकृता धर्मपत्नीकृता ॥ **वज्रादपीति** । अयमाशयः—निर्दोषायां सीतायां रामहृदयस्य मृदुत्वमेव स्वाभाविकम् । कठोरत्वं तु मूर्खलोकानुसरणार्थत्वादागन्तुकमिति प्रकृतिकरणादवगम्यत इति । न च 'यस्य भार्या विदूरस्था यदि सा दूषितापि वा । अनिच्छुः प्रतिकूला च तस्याः प्रतिकृतौ क्रिया ॥' इति स्मरणात् प्रकृतिकरणं मृदुत्वानुपपादकमिति वाच्यम् । तस्य परिणयान्तराशक्तनिरवकाशक्रियाविषयत्वात् । अश्वमेधादेः सावकाशत्वात् परिणयान्तरशक्तत्वात् । किं च सीतासदृशप्रतिमाकरणं मृदुत्वापादकमेव । एतादृशविचारसाध्यत्वात् 'को हि विज्ञातुमर्हति' इति तज्ज्ञानस्वरूपयोग्यतापि दुर्लभेत्युक्तम् । अत्रार्थान्तरन्यासालंकारः ॥ ७ ॥ वामदेवेन अनुमन्त्रितः अनुज्ञातः वसिष्ठासंनिधानादिति भावः । मेध्याश्वः यज्ञियाश्वः । प्रक्लृप्ता इति यथाशास्त्रं शास्त्रोक्तन्यायेन । तेषामिति 'चतुःशता रक्षन्ति यज्ञस्याघातये' इत्यादिश्रुतिमनुल्लङ्घ्य अधिष्ठाता नियामकः अनुप्रहितः [प्रेषितः] ॥

---

१ वसिष्ठस्यापि श्रद्धा वाल्मीकिवनं गत्वा. २ रामभद्रः. ३ किमारम्भः (टी.). ४ राजक्रतुः. ५ अहह. ६ शान्तम्. ७ प्रतिकृतिर्गृहिणीकृता. ८ हि. ९ प्रक्लृप्ताः, प्रयुक्ताः. १० दत्त. ११ बलान्वितः; चतुरङ्गेति नास्ति क्वचित्; अश्वसाध०.

वासन्ती—(सस्नेहकौतुकास्नम् ।) कुमारलक्ष्मणस्यापि पुत्रः । हन्त मातर्जीवामि ।

आत्रेयी—अत्रान्तरे ब्राह्मणेन मृतं पुत्रमुत्क्षिप्य राजद्वारे सोरस्ताडमब्रह्मण्यमुद्घोषितम् । ततो न राजापचारमन्तरेण प्रजानामकालमृत्युः संचरतीत्यात्मदोषं निरूपयति करुणामये रामभद्रे सहसैवाशरीरिणी वागुदचरत्—

शम्बूको नाम वृषलः पृथिव्यां तप्यते तपः ।
शीर्षच्छेद्यः स ते राम तं हत्वा जीवय द्विजम् ॥ ८ ॥

इत्युपश्रुत्यैवाकृष्टकृपाणपाणिः पुष्पकं विमानमारुह्य सर्वा दिशो विदिशश्च शूद्रतापसान्वेषणाय जगत्पतिः संचरितुमारब्धवान् ।

वासन्ती—शम्बूको नाम धूमपः शूद्रोऽस्मिन्नेव जनस्थाने तपश्चरति । तदपि नाम रामभद्रः पुनरपीदं वनमलंकुर्यात् ।

आत्रेयी—भद्रे गम्यतेऽधुना ।

वासन्ती—आर्य आत्रेयि एवमस्तु । कठोरीभूतस्तु दिवसः ।

कण्डूलद्विपगण्डपिण्डकषणोत्कम्पेन संपातिभि-
र्घर्मस्रंसितबन्धनैः स्वकुसुमैरर्चन्ति गोदावरीम् ।

अत्रान्तर इति । अब्रह्मण्यमिति वचनमुद्घोषितमुच्चैरुच्चारितम् । **तत इति** । राजापचारं राजदोषम् । निरूपयति मीमांसमाने । करुणामये परदुःखदुःखित्वरूपानुकम्पाप्रचुरे । उदचरत् उद्गतवती ॥ **शम्बूक इति** । तपः तप्यते तपश्चरति । 'तप ऐश्वर्ये वा' इति तङ् । दिवादित्वात् श्यन् । शीर्षच्छेद्यः शिरश्छेदार्हः । 'शीर्षच्छेदाद्यच्च' इति यत्प्रत्ययः ॥ ८ ॥ दिशः प्राच्यादयो विदिश आग्नेयादयः ॥ अपि नामेति अलंकुर्यादित्यनेनान्वयः । संभावनायामपिशब्दः ॥ **कण्डूलेति** । कण्डूलानां कण्डूमतां द्विपगण्डपिण्डानां पिण्डाकारगजकपोलानां कषणेन संघट्टनया आकम्पेन अत्यर्थचलनेन संपतन्तीति संपातीनि तथाविधैः । घर्मेण निदाघौष्ण्येन स्रंसितबन्धनैः शिथिलितवृन्तैः । छायायां अनातपे अपस्किरमाणाः भक्षार्थं चञ्च्वा भूमिं लिखन्तः । 'किरतेर्हर्षजीविकाकुलायकरणेष्विति वाच्यम्' । 'अपाच्चतुष्पाच्छकुनिष्वालेखने'

---

१ सहर्ष०. २ पुत्र इति मातरः. ३ आरोप्य राजद्वारि. ४ राजापराधम्. ५ प्रजानां; प्रजायाम्. ६ उपश्रुत्य कृपाणपाणिः. ७ पुष्पकमधिरुह्य. ८ संचारम्. ९ नामाधोमुखो. १० कठोरश्च. ११ गण्डमण्डलकषो०; कषणाकम्पेन.

छायापस्किरमाणविष्किरमुखव्याकृष्टकीटत्वचः
कूजत्क्लान्तकपोतकुक्कुटकुलाः कूले कुलायद्रुमाः ॥ ९ ॥
(इति परिक्रम्य निष्क्रान्ते ।)
इति शुद्धविष्कम्भः ।

(ततः प्रविशति पुष्पकस्थः सदयोद्यतखड्गो रामः ।)

रामः—

रे हस्त दक्षिण मृतस्य शिशोर्द्विजस्य
जीवातवे विसृज शूद्रमुनौ कृपाणम् ।
रामस्य गात्रमसि दुर्वहगर्भखिन्न-
सीताविवासनपटोः करुणा कुतस्ते ॥ १० ॥

इति सूत्राभ्यां तद्युटौ । तथाविधानां विष्किराणां वायसादीनां मुखैः व्याकृष्टा कीटत्वक् येषामिति विग्रहः । कपोताः पारावताः कुक्कुटाः चरणायुधाश्च ते कूजन्तः क्लान्ताश्च येष्विति विग्रहः । कूले । तीरवर्तिन इत्यर्थः । कुलायद्रुमाः पक्षिनीडयुक्ता द्रुमाः स्वकुसुमैः गोदावरीमर्चन्ति पूजयन्ति इति संबन्धः । अत्र वृक्षवर्णनया वैदिकशिरोमणीनां गृहमेधिनां मध्याह्नकालवृत्तान्तः प्रतीयते । कण्डूलेत्यादिविशेषणेन द्रव्याणां दुरूहशास्त्रार्थसंदेहनिर्णयार्थमुपसन्नैः तैः तत्कृतोऽपदेशानिवृत्तसंशयतया संतुष्टैः भूमिपतिभिः समर्पितत्वं प्रतीयते । घर्मस्रंसितैरित्यनेन तेषां 'कषाये कर्मणि पक्व' इति निवृत्तकामलोभादितया द्रव्याणां देवताराधनतया प्रतिहतप्रदानं प्रतीयते । छायापस्किरमाणेत्यनेन तेषां गृहेषु अतिथयः स्वयमागत्य भोज्यानि भुञ्जत इति प्रतीयते । कूजत्क्लान्तेत्यनेन तेषां मध्याह्नकालप्रयुक्तश्रान्तियुक्तनानाशाखाध्येतृनानाबटुसमाजपौष्कल्यं प्रतीयते । कुलायेत्यनेन तेषामनेककुटुम्बभरणं प्रतीयत इति सहृदया विदांकुर्वन्तु ॥ अत्र कुसुमपतनस्य गोदावरीपूजात्वोत्प्रेक्षा कृता । सा च गम्या वाचकशब्दप्रयोगाभावात् । 'तस्य भगवतः केनापि' इत्यारभ्य 'अयमध्ययनप्रत्यूहः' इत्यन्तेन अष्टावक्रप्रवेशात् लक्ष्यस्य सीतावनप्रापणेनालक्ष्यस्य बीजस्योद्भेदात् प्रतिमुखसंधिरयम् । 'लक्ष्यालक्ष्यस्य बीजस्य व्यक्तिः प्रतिमुखं मतम् ।' इति लक्षणात् । 'अप्येतत्तपोवनम्' इत्यारभ्य दृष्टनष्टपदार्थानुसरणरूपपरिसर्प उक्तः । 'हा रामभद्र' इति प्रमुखनिष्ठुरवचनरूपं वज्रमुक्तम् । 'सीताप्रतिकृतिः' इत्यादिनानुरागप्रकाशनरूपप्रगम उक्तः । 'वज्रादपि' इत्यत्रारत्युपशमनात्मकः शम उक्तः । 'विसृष्टश्च वामदेवानुमन्त्रितः' इत्यारभ्य 'जनस्थान एव तपश्चरति' इत्यन्तेन ब्रह्मक्षत्रियशूद्राणां कीर्तनात् वर्णसंकर उक्तः । इयं चूलिका । तदुक्तम्—'नेपथ्यान्तःस्थितैः पात्रैश्चूलिकार्थस्य सूचनम्' इति ॥ ९ ॥ उद्यतः उन्नमितः ॥ **हे हस्तेति** । दक्षिणहस्त अपसव्यहस्त कृपाणं खड्गं शूद्रमुनौ विसृज विमुञ्च । निर्भरः पूर्णः । विवासनं निष्कासनम् । पटोरित्यनेन 'छद्मना परिददामि' इत्येतद्विवक्षितम् ।

१ अवस्किरमाण, शाखाप०. २ क्रान्त. ३ ०भद्रः. ४ हे. ५ बाहुः. ६ निर्भर. ७ प्रवासन.

(कथंचित्प्रहृत्य ।) कृतं रामसदृशं कर्म । अपि जीवेत्स ब्राह्मणपुत्रः[1] ।

(प्रविश्य ।)

दिव्यपुरुषः—जयतु जयतु देवः ।

दत्ताभये त्वयि यमादपि दण्डधारे
संजीवितः शिशुरसौ[2] मम चेयमृद्धिः ।
शम्बूक एष शिरसा चरणौ नतस्ते
सत्सङ्गजानि निधनान्यपि तारयन्ति ॥ ११ ॥

रामः—द्वयमपि प्रियं नः । तदनुभूयतामुग्रस्य तपसः फलम्[3] ।

यत्रानन्दाश्च मोदाश्च यत्र पुण्याश्च[4] सपदः ।
वैराजा नाम ते लोकास्तैजसाः सन्तु ते शिवाः[5] ॥ १२ ॥

शम्बूकः—युष्मत्प्रसादादेवैष[6] महिमा । किमत्र तपसा[7] । अथ वा महदुपकृतं तपसा ।

अन्वेष्टव्यो यदसि भुवने भूतनाथः शरण्यो
मामन्विष्यन्निह वृषलकं योजनानां शतानि ।

अत्र विध्यलंकारः ॥ १० ॥ प्रहृत्य प्रक्षिप्येत्यर्थः । इदं चिन्त्यम्—'दूराध्वानं वधम्' इत्यारभ्य एतान्युद्वेगकारित्वात् प्रयोगानुचितानि इति तन्निषेधात् । अत्रानिष्टवस्तुविक्षेपात् विधूतम् । **कृतमिति** । रामसदृशं कर्म न तु दशरथसदृशं कर्म । दशरथो ह्यबुद्धिपूर्वकं शूरतापसवधं कृतवान् । तथा च 'पितुः शतगुणं पुत्रः' इति न्यायेन दोषविषय एव न तु गुणविषय इति स्वोपालम्भ इह व्यज्यते । **अपि जीवेदिति** । अपिः संभावनायाम् । अशरीरवाण्या शिशुजीवननिश्चयेऽपि पावकवचनेन सीतायाः निर्दोषत्वनिश्चयेऽपि फलाभाववत् स्वीयदैवविपर्ययेणात्रापि तथा स्यादित्याशयः ॥ **प्रविश्येति** । दिव्यपुरुषः शम्बूकशरीरं विहाय देवत्वेनेति भावः । **दत्ताभय इति** । यमादपि दत्ताभये त्वयि दण्डधारे सतीत्यन्वयः । यमहेतुकभयनिवारणदातरि यमशासितरि त्वयि सति असौ शिशुः बुद्धिस्थो ब्राह्मणशिशुः । निधनानि मरणानि तारयन्ति । संसाराब्धिमिति शेषः ॥ ११ ॥ **तदिति** । आनन्दाः आत्मानुभवजन्या हर्षाः । मोदाश्च दिव्यविषयानुभवजन्या हर्षाः । संपदः अणिमादिविभूतयः । वैराजा नाम वैराजा इति प्रसिद्धाः ॥ १२ ॥ **युष्मत्प्रसादेति** । 'धातुः प्रसादान्महिमानमीदृशम्' इति श्रुतिः प्रत्यभिज्ञायते । किमत्र तपसा । तपसा किमत्रेत्यर्थः । **अथ वेति** । तपःकर्तृको महोपकार इति भावः । तदुपपादयति—**अन्वेष्टव्य इति** । यदसीति प्रसिद्धवन्निर्देशात् 'सोऽन्वेष्टव्यः' इति श्रुतिः प्रत्यभिज्ञायते । अनेन कारणत्वमप्युक्तम् । 'कारणं तु ध्येयः' इति श्रुतेः । न केवलं प्रधानहिरण्यगर्भादिवत् कारणत्वम्, किं तु निरुपाधिकस्वामित्वं स्वीकृतमित्याह—लोकनाथ इति ।

---

१ शिशुः. २ अयम्. ३ परिपाकः. ४ पुण्या हि; पुण्याभिसंभवाः. ५ ध्रुवाः. ६ स्वामिन्युष्मत्प्रसादोपायः, वः प्रसादापादानः; युष्मत्पादप्रसादनोपायः. ७ तपसः फलम्. ८ भुवनैः. ९ लोके .

क्रान्त्वा प्राप्तः स इह तपसां संप्रसादोऽन्यथा चेत्
क्वायोध्यायाः पुनरुपगमो दण्डकायां वने वः ॥ १३ ॥

रामः—किं नाम दण्डकेयम् । (सर्वतोऽवलोक्य ।) हां कथम् ।

स्निग्धश्यामाः क्वचिदपरतो भीषणाभोगरूक्षाः
स्थाने स्थाने मुखरककुभो झांकृतैर्निर्झराणाम् ।
एते तीर्थाश्रमगिरिसरिद्गर्तकान्तारमिश्राः
संदृश्यन्ते परिचितभुवो दण्डकारण्यभागाः ॥ १४ ॥

शम्बूकः—दण्डकैवैषा । अत्र किल पूर्वं निवसता देवेन

चतुर्दश सहस्राणि रक्षसां भीमकर्मणाम् ।
त्रयश्च दूषणखरत्रिमूर्धानो रणे हताः ॥ १५ ॥

'एष सर्वभूताधिपतिः' इति श्रुतिः प्रत्यभिज्ञायते । पूर्वोक्तान्वेष्टव्यत्वादिफलमाह—शरण्य इति । 'एष सर्वभूतपालः' इत्यादयः श्रुतयः प्रत्यभिज्ञाप्यन्ते । न हि पालनसामर्थ्यमृते सर्वेश्वरत्वहानिरित्युपबृंहणात् हरहिरण्यगर्भादीनां रक्षकत्वशङ्कानिरासः । इदं च घण्टाकर्णादिविषये स्पष्टम् । वृषलकं अज्ञातो वृषलो वृषलकः तम् । अज्ञाते कन्प्रत्ययः । अनेन प्रयासेनान्वेषणीयत्वं स्वस्य सूच्यते । अन्विष्यन् । न तु चारादिनान्वेषयन्निति भावः । योजनानां शतानि अयोध्यादण्डकयोः योजनेयत्तानिश्चयेऽपि एवमुक्तिः कृत्स्नभूमण्डलान्वेषणानन्तरं अत्र प्राप्त इति सूचयति । तन्मूलं तु 'पृथिव्यां तप्यते तपः' इति अशरीरवाण्या पृथिव्यामिति सामान्योक्तिः । प्राप्तः । न तु मां दूतैः प्रापितवानित्यर्थः । वृषलक इत्यत्र वृषं धर्मं लुनातीति वृषल इति व्युत्पत्त्या 'शुश्रूषा शूद्रस्य' इत्युक्तस्वधर्मच्छेदेन स्वतन्त्रतपश्चरणरूपस्वदोषाधीनत्वं विवक्षितम् । तपसां संप्रसादः तपःकृतानुग्रहः । पुनरित्यनेन अपूर्ववनविलोकनस्पृहयान्यथासिद्धिर्वारिता । वनपदं दण्डकायामपि गमनप्रदेशत्वसूचनार्थम् । एवं सर्वप्रकारेणापि दुर्घटभवदागमनसंघटकत्वात् तपसां प्रसाद इति भावः ॥ १३ ॥ **स्निग्धेति** । श्यामाः नीलाः । आभोगः विपुलावकाशः । रूक्षाः चित्तक्षोभकराः । गर्ताः अवटाः ॥ १४ ॥ **चतुर्दशेति** । दूषणखरत्रिमूर्धान इति समासान्तविधेरनित्यत्वात् । 'द्वित्रिभ्यां ष मूर्ध्नः' इति षप्रत्ययाभावः । केचित्तु दूषणखरत्रिमूर्धा नः इति पदद्वयं कृत्वा नः अस्माकं रणे दूषणखरत्रिमूर्धाः हता इति षप्रत्ययान्तमेव समर्थयन्ते । अस्माकमिति रामेण समाधिना दिव्यपुरुषवचनं पक्षैक्याभिप्रायकम् । वस्तुतस्तु नोशब्दः पृथक्पदमित्याश्रित्य अत्र निवसता देवेन दूषणखरत्रिमूर्धा हताः । नो किमिति काक्वा योजनीयम् ।

---

१ तु. २ आः; हा कथं—आम्. ३ सरिद्गर्भ; मिश्राः—सान्द्राः. ४ चतुर्दश च राक्षसाः. ५ निपातिताः.

येन सिद्धक्षेत्रेऽस्मिञ्जनस्थाने मादृशामपि जानपदानाम्[1]कुतोभयः संचारो जातः[2]।

रामः—न केवलं दण्डकैव[3] जनस्थानमपि।

शम्बूकः—बाढम्। एतानि खलु सर्वभूतरोमहर्षणान्युन्मत्तचण्डश्वापदकुल[4]संकुलगिरिगह्वराणि जनस्थानपर्यन्त[5]दीर्घारण्यानि दक्षिणां दिशमभिवर्तन्ते। तथा हि।

निष्कूजस्तिमिताः क्वचित्क्वचिदपि प्रोच्चण्डसत्त्वस्वनाः
स्वेच्छासुप्तगभीरघोर[6]भुजगश्वासप्रदीप्ताग्नयः।
सीमानः प्रदरोदरेषु विल[7]सत्स्वल्पाम्भसो यास्वयं
तृष्यद्भिः प्रतिसूर्यकैरजगरस्वेदद्रवः पीयते॥ १६॥

रामः—

पश्यामि च जनस्थानं भूतपूर्वखरालयम्।
प्रत्यक्षानिव[8] वृत्तान्तान्पूर्वाननुभवामि च॥ १७॥

(सर्वतोऽवलोक्य।) प्रियारामा[9] हि सर्वथा वैदेह्यासीत्। एतानि तानि नाम कान्ताराणि। किमतः परं भयानकं[10] स्यात्। (सास्रम्।)

त्वया सह निवत्स्यामि वनेषु मधुगन्धिषु।
इतीहारमतैवासौ[11] स्नेहस्तस्याः स तादृशः॥ १८॥

इयं च प्रत्यभिज्ञापनशैली गौरव्यविषयेष्वनुभवसिद्धा॥ १५॥ **येनेति**। सिद्धक्षेत्रे सिद्धिप्रदपुण्यक्षेत्रे अकुतोभयः नास्ति कुतो भयं यस्येति विग्रहः॥ **एतानीति**। रोमहर्षणानि रोमाञ्चजनकानि। **निष्कूजेति**। निर्गताः कूजाः कूजितानि येभ्य इति विग्रहः। कूजितशून्या इत्यर्थः। 'कूज अव्यक्ते शब्दे' इत्यस्मात् भावे घञ्प्रत्ययः। सत्त्वानां जन्तूनाम्। प्रदरोदराणि गुहामध्याः। प्रतिसूर्यकैः वक्रकृकलासकैः॥ १६॥ **पश्यामीति**। भूतपूर्वो यः खरालयः तथाविधमित्यर्थः। भूतपूर्वः खरालयः खरगृहं यस्मिन्निति वा। प्रत्यक्षानिव पुरोवर्तमानानिव। अनुभवामि स्मृतिवैशद्येन प्रत्यक्षीकरोमि॥ १७॥ कान्ताराणि दुर्गमवर्त्मानि। भयानकं भयजनकम्। **त्वयेति**। मधुगन्धः एषु अस्तीति मधुगन्धीनि तेषु वनेषु इह कान्तारेषु आरमतेव प्रीतिं प्राप्तवत्येव। कुत इत्यत आह—स्नेहस्तस्याः स तादृश इति। 'हृदयं त्वेव जानाति प्रीतियोगं परस्परम्' इत्युक्तरीत्या परिच्छेदातीत इत्यर्थः॥ १८॥

---

१ भीरुजान०, भीरुजनानाम्. २ संवृत्तः. ३ दण्डकेयं किं तु. ४ कुलाक्रान्तविकट. ५ पर्यन्तानि. ६ घोष, भोग. ७ विरस; विरलस्वच्छ. ८ प्रत्यक्षमिव. ९ प्रिया रामा; प्रियरामा १० भयानकस्य. ११ इति हाऽरमतैवासौ; इनि था रमतीवासौ; इति चारमतीवासौ; इति चारमते सीता (वासौ); इतीवारमतेहासौ.

न[1] किंचिदपि कुर्वाणः सौख्यैर्दुःखान्यपोहति ।
तत्तस्य किमपि द्रव्यं यो हि यस्य प्रियो जनः ॥ १९ ॥

शम्बूकः—तदलमेभिर्दुरासदैः[2] । अथैतानि मदकलमयूरकण्ठकोमलच्छविभिरवकीर्णानि पर्यन्तै[3]रविरलनिविष्टनीलबहल[4]च्छायतरुणतरुषण्डमण्डितान्यसंभ्रान्तविविधमृगयूथानि पश्यतु महानुभावः[5] प्रशान्तगम्भीराणि मध्य[6]मारण्यकानि ।

इह समदशकुन्ताक्रान्तवानीरवीरुत्[7]-
प्रसवसुरभिशीतस्वच्छतोया वहन्ति ।
फलभरपरिणामश्यामजम्बूनिकुञ्ज-
स्खलनमुखरभूरिस्रोतसो निर्झरिण्यः ॥ २० ॥

अपि च ।

दधति कुहरभाजामत्र भल्लूकयूना-
मनुरसितगुरूणि स्त्यानमम्बूकृतानि ।
शिशिरकटुकषायः स्त्यायते सल्लकीना-
मिभदलितविकीर्णग्रन्थिनिर्ष्यन्द[8]गन्धः ॥ २१ ॥

नेति । यस्य प्रियः प्रीतिमान् प्रीतिविषयो वा यः जनः किंचिदपि न कुर्वाणः सन् किंचित्कारलेशेनापि शून्यः सन् सौख्यैः स्वीयमुखैः करणैः दुखान्यपोहति नाशयति । तत् दुःखनाशहेतुभूतो जनः । विधेयप्राधान्यात् नपुंसकत्वम् । तस्य अपोहनीयदुःखवतः पुरुषस्य किमपि विलक्षणं द्रव्यं भव्यवस्तु । 'द्रव्यं च भव्ये' इत्यनुशासनम् । यद्वा सौख्यैरिति इत्थंभूतलक्षणे तृतीया । तथा च सौख्यैः विशिष्टः सुखितः प्रियः इष्टः यः जनः यस्य न किंचिदपि कुर्वाणः स्वरूपातिरेकिव्यापारलेशशून्यः सन् दुःखानि अपोहति तदित्यादि पूर्ववत् । दुःखनिवृत्तिहेतुव्यापारलेशशून्यः सन्नपि स्वीयसुखविशिष्टः यः स्वरूपेणैव यद्दुःखनिवृत्तिं प्रति कारणं तं प्रति तस्य निस्तुलभव्यद्रव्यत्वमिति भावः । एवं चाहं सीताविषये किंचित्कारलेशशून्योऽपि सुखितः सन् तद्दुःखनिवर्तक इति कान्तारगमनं युक्तमेवेति हृदयस्थितोऽर्थः ॥ १९ ॥ **अथेति** । पर्यन्तैः अभ्यर्णप्रदेशैः । छायाप्रधानाः तरवः छायातरवः । प्रशान्तानि अनुद्वेगजननानि । **इहेति** । शकुन्ताः पक्षिणः वानीराः वेतसविशेषाः । मुखराणि शब्दवन्ति भूरीणि स्रोतांसि यासां ताः ॥ २० ॥ **दधतीति** । कुहरभाजां गुहावर्तिनां भल्लूकयूनां ऋक्षाणां अनुरसितेन अनुरणनेन गुरूणि महान्ति अम्बूकृतानि निष्ठीवनशब्दाः स्त्यानं वृद्धिं वैपुल्यं वा दधति

---

१ अकिं०. २ दुःसहैः. ३ पर्वतैः. ४ बहुल; तरुणेति नास्ति क्वचित्; षण्ड–खण्ड. ५ महाभागः. ६ श्वापदकुलशरण्यानि महारण्यानि. ७ मुक्त. ८ निष्पन्द.

रामः—(सबाष्पस्तम्भम् ।) भद्र शिवास्ते पन्थानो देवयानं प्रतिपद्यस्व पुण्येभ्यो लोकेभ्यः ।

शम्बूकः—यावत्पुराणब्रह्मवादिनमगस्त्यमृषिमभिवाद्य शाश्वतं पदमनुप्रविशामि । (इति निष्क्रान्तः ।)

रामः—

एतत्तदेव हि वनं पुनरद्य दृष्टं
यस्मिन्नभूम चिरमेव पुरा वसन्तः ।
आरण्यकाश्च गृहिणश्च रताः स्वधर्मे
सांसारिकेषु च सुखेषु वयं रसज्ञाः ॥ २२ ॥

एते त एव गिरयो विरुवन्मयूरा-
स्तान्येव मत्तहरिणानि वनस्थलानि ।
आमञ्जुवञ्जुललतानि च तान्यमूनि
नीरन्ध्रनीलनिचुलानि सरित्तटानि ॥ २३ ॥

मेघमालेव यश्चायमारादपि विभाव्यते ।
गिरिः प्रस्रवणः सोऽयं यत्र गोदावरी नदी ॥ २४ ॥

अस्यैवासीन्महति शिखरे गृध्रराजस्य वास-
स्तस्याधस्ताद्वयमपि रतास्तेषु पर्णोटजेषु ।
गोदावर्याः पयसि विततश्यामलानोकहश्री-
रन्तःकूजन्मुखरशकुनो यत्र रम्यो वनान्तः ॥ २५ ॥

अत्रैव सा पञ्चवटी यत्र निवासेन विविधविश्रम्भातिप्रसङ्गसाक्षिणः

भजन्ति । निष्यन्दः स्वरसस्रवः । स्त्यायते वर्धते विसरति वा ॥ २१ ॥ देवयानाः देवयाननामकाः । ते च ' अग्निर्ज्योतिरहः शुक्लः षण्मासा उत्तरायणम् ' इत्युक्ताः । लोकेभ्यः लोकाननुभवितुम् ॥ **एतदिति** । गृहिणः गृहमेधिन । सांसारिकेषु जन्मफलभूतेषु ॥ २२ ॥ **एत इति** । विरुवन्मयूराः कूजद्बर्हिणः ॥ २३ ॥ **मेघमालेति** । मेघमालेव मेघमालासदृशः यः अयं पुरोवर्तिपदार्थः आरादिव समीपस्थ इव विभाव्यते ज्ञायते । यत्र गिरौ गोदावरी नदी स प्रस्रवणो गिरिः ॥ २४ ॥ **अस्यैवेति** । [रताः सुखेन स्थिता इत्यर्थः । वितता प्रसृता श्यामला च अनोकहश्रीः वृक्षशोभा यस्मिन् । अन्तः कूजन्तः अत एव मुखराः शकुनाः पक्षिणो यस्मिन् । वनान्तः वनोद्देशः ।] मुखरशकुनः कूजत्पक्षियुक्तः अत एव अन्तःकूजन् स्वयं कूजन्निव स्थितः ॥ २५ ॥ **यत्रेति** । विश्रम्भाः स्वैरविलासाः ।

---

१. देवयानाः २ प्रलीयस्व;–पुण्येषु लोकेषु; प्रतिष्ठस्व. ३ पुराणब्रह्मर्षिमगस्त्यम्. ४ एतत्पुनर्वनमहो कथमद्य. ५ रुतानि; आमन्द्रमञ्जुलरुतानि. ६ नीप. ७ यः श्याम आरादपि. ८ सोऽयमत्र. ९ विनत, विततानोकहश्यामल. १० मधुर.

प्रदेशाः प्रियायाः प्रियसखी च वासन्ती नाम वनदेवता । किमिदमापतितमद्य रामस्य । संप्रति हि ।

चिराद्वेगारम्भी प्रसृत इव तीव्रो विषरसः
कुतश्चित्संवेगात्प्रचल इव शल्यस्य शकलः ।
व्रणो रूढग्रन्थिः स्फुटित इव हृन्मर्मणि पुन-
र्घनीभूतः शोको विकलयति मां मूर्छयति च ॥ २६ ॥

तथापि तान्पूर्वसुहृदो भूमिभागान्पश्यामि । (निरूप्य ।) अहो अनवस्थितो भूमिसंनिवेशः । तथा हि ।

पुरा यत्र स्रोतः पुलिनमधुना तत्र सरितां
विपर्यासं यातो घनविरलभावः क्षितिरुहाम् ।
बहोर्दृष्टं कालादपरमिव मन्ये वनमिदं
निवेशः शैलानां तदिदमिति बुद्धिं द्रढयति ॥ २७ ॥

हन्त । परिहरन्तमपि मामितः पञ्चवटीस्नेहो बलादाकर्षतीव । (सकरुणम् ।)

यस्यां ते दिवसास्तया सह मया नीता यथा स्वे गृहे
यत्संबन्धिकथाभिरेव सततं दीर्घाभिरास्थीयते ।

चिरादिति । तीव्रः स्पर्शदशायामपि दुस्सहः । अनेन अज्ञातस्पर्शविषविशेषव्यावृत्तिः । चिरात् भूयांसं कालं शमित्वा । वेगं वेदनाशैघ्र्यं आरम्भयति उत्पादयतीति वेगारम्भी । अनेन पूर्वोक्तविषविशेषव्यावृत्तिः । प्रसृतः यत्राङ्गुल्यादौ स्पर्शः ततोऽन्यत्र सर्वाङ्गेषु प्रसृतः दलनादिना दुःसहप्रसरणः यः विषरसस्तत्सदृश इत्यर्थः । रसशब्देन विशेषोत्कर्षो विवक्षितः । कुतश्चित् यस्मात् कस्माच्चित् संवेगात् संभ्रमादिजन्यात् निर्घातात् प्रचलः शल्यस्य बाणाग्रस्य शकलः खण्ड इव स्थितः । स हि मरणभयादनुद्धृत एव तिष्ठति । रूढाः प्रादुर्भूताः ग्रन्थयः उपव्रणाः यस्मात् स तथोक्तः । स्फुटितः दलितः हृन्मर्मणि व्रण इव हृदयमर्मवर्तिव्रणसदृशः । क्वाचित्कस्पर्शसार्वत्रिकप्रसरणाभ्यां प्रथमः दृष्टान्तः । प्रतिकार्यत्वशङ्काव्युदासाय द्वितीयः । स्वल्पकालत्वव्यावृत्तये तृतीयः । विशेषमाह—नूतन इवेति । विकलयति शून्यं करोति ॥ २६ ॥ अनवस्थितो भूतसंनिवेशः अनियता पदार्थस्थितिः । **पुरेति** । बहोः कालात् दृष्टं बहुकालमदृष्ट्वा दृष्टम् । ल्यब्लोपे पञ्चमी । यद्वा पूर्वदर्शनकालबहुविप्र[illegible]काले दृष्टम् । 'सप्तमीपञ्चम्यौ' इति पञ्चमी । तदिदमिति बुद्धिं प्रत्यभिज्ञाम् । अत्र प्रस्तुतवृत्तान्तवर्णनात् अप्रस्तुतप्राणिकुटुम्बोपचर[illegible]चयपरिस्फूर्तिरिति कुवलयानन्दकृत् ॥ २७ ॥ **यस्यामिति** । स्वे गृहे यथा यस्यां ते दिवसाः

---

१ प्रतिवसति इत्यधि०. २ तत्किमिदम्. ३ रामहतकस्य. ४ चिरोद्वे. ५ चलित, निहित. ६ पुराभूतः. ७ नूतन इव, विकलयति संमूर्च्छ०, विदलयति, विफलयति, शकलयति (घन०). ८ तथाविधानपि तावत्. ९ भूत. १० अभवत्. ११ हन्त हन्त. १२ स्नेहात् (टी.). १३ पुनः. १४ संबन्ध. १५ आस्थीयते.

**एकः संप्रति नाशितप्रियतमस्तामद्य रामः कथं
पापः पञ्चवटीं विलोकयतु वा गच्छत्वसंभाव्य वा ॥ २८ ॥**

शम्बूकः—जयतु जयतु देवः। देव भगवानगस्त्यो मत्तः श्रुतमवत्संनिधानस्त्वामाह—परिकल्पितविमानावतरणमङ्गला प्रतीक्षते वत्सला लोपामुद्रा सर्वे चै महर्षयः। तदेहि संभावयास्मान्। अथ प्रजविना पुष्पकेण स्वदेशमुपगम्याश्वमेधाय सज्जो भविष्यसीति।

रामः—यथाज्ञापयति भगवान्।

शम्बूकः—ईतस्तर्हि देवः प्रवर्तयतु पुष्पकम्।

नीताः निरुपप्लवत्वरामणीयकादिभिः स्वगृहतुल्यायां यस्यां पञ्चवट्यां नीताः अतिवाहिताः। न केवलं रात्रयो नीताः किं तु दिवसा अपि नीता इति दिवसपदेन व्यज्यते। तेन स्वगृहापेक्षया वैलक्षण्यमपि पञ्चवट्याः। तत्र हि–राज्यतन्त्रादिना दिवसेषु न सहावस्थानं घटते। तया सह मयेति वान्वयः। स्वे गृहे गुरुसंनिधितिरोहितप्रणयपारतन्त्र्यासंकोचात् स्वगृहाद्विशेषः। यत्संबन्धकथाभिः। कर्त्रीभिः। आस्थीयत। तस्थेर्भावे लङ्। एवकारेण वाग्व्यापारान्तरप्रतिषेधः। यत्कथाभिः इत्यनुक्त्वा यत्संबन्धकथाभिरित्युक्तेः पञ्चवटीपरिसरवर्तिनामपि रामणीयकं व्यज्यते। अत्र 'स्मरन्कमलपत्राक्षीं रामः संध्यामुपागमत्' इत्युक्तरीत्या सर्वकालं बुद्धिस्थत्वात् तथेत्युक्तम्। तामेव न तु यां कांचिदित्यर्थः। वियोगे हि रमणीयवस्तुदर्शनमात्रं दुःसहम्, किं पुनः सहानुभूतरमणीयदर्शनं दुःसहमिति। एकः केवलः। सीताशून्य इति भावः। ननु राज्ञः शुद्धान्त एव स्थित्यर्हायाः कथं सहगमनं घटते। पुरं प्रति गमने तु सुलभमेव तद्दर्शनमिति किमिहात्याहितमिति अत्राह—नाशितप्रियतम इति। नाशितत्वमपि दैवाधीनं चेत् कथंचित् सह्यत एव न तु तथा। किं तु मदधीन एव नाश इति दुःखातिशयो व्यज्यते। ननु तर्हि यत्र सा तत्रैव गम्यतामित्यत्राह—पाप इति। मरणप्रतिबन्धकपापवानित्यर्थः। 'तथाप्येष प्राणः स्फुरति न तु पापो विरमति' इत्युक्तेः। असंभाव्य असंमान्य रामः पञ्चवटीं विलोकयतु। वेत्यन्यादृशशैल्यात् सर्वथा न मत्स्वरूपं विलोकनमसंभाव्यगमनं वेति व्यज्यते। संप्रति नाशितप्रियतम इत्यनेन आर्द्रदुःखत्वं व्यज्यते। सर्वथा प्रियारामेत्यारभ्य एतच्छ्लोकपर्यन्तमनुरागप्रकाशनविशिष्टवचनरूपं पुष्पं नाम संध्यङ्गमुक्तम् ॥ २८ ॥ **भगवानिति**। मत्तः श्रुतं संनिधानं त्वत्सामीप्यं येन सः। मत्त इति रामागमनाख्यातुः दिव्यपुरुषस्यागस्त्यं प्रति गुरुप्रायत्वं कवेरभिमतमिति व्यज्यते। 'आख्यातोपयोगे' इति पञ्चमीविधानात्। **परिकल्पितेति**। आवरणमङ्गलं नीराजनादिकम्। लोपामुद्रा अगस्त्यपत्नी प्रतीक्षते कृतक्षणा तिष्ठति। त्यक्तसर्वव्यापारा तिष्ठतीत्यर्थः। अथ प्रजविना प्रकृष्टवेगवता। एकदेशिनेति ज्ञापनात्

---

१ एव. २ परिकलिता–वरण–भरण. ३ चागस्त्यायनाः. ४ अश्वमेधसज्जो भव. ५ इत इतो, इत इत एतु, देवः.

रामः—(पुष्पकं प्रवर्तयन् ।) भगवति पञ्चवटि गुरुजनोपरोधात्क्षणं क्षम्यतामयमतिक्रमो रामस्य ।

शम्बूकः—देव पश्य पश्य ।

कूंजत्कुञ्जकुटीरकौशिकघटाघूत्कारवत्कीचक-
स्तम्बाडम्बरमूकमौकुलिकुलः क्रौञ्चावतोऽयं गिरिः ।
एतस्मिन्प्रचलाकिनां प्रचलतामुद्वेजिताः कूजितै-
रुद्वेल्लन्ति पुराणरोहिणतरुस्कन्धेषु कुम्भीनसाः ॥ २९ ॥

अपि च ।

एते ते कुहरेषु गद्गदनदद्गोदावरीवारयो
मेघालम्बितमौलिनीलशिखराः क्षोणीभृतो दाक्षिणाः ।
अन्योन्यप्रतिघातसंकुलचलत्कल्लोलकोलाहलै-
रुत्तालास्त इमे गभीरपयसः पुण्याः सरित्संगमाः ॥ ३० ॥

(इति निष्क्रान्तौ ।)

पञ्चवटीप्रवेशो नाम द्वितीयोऽङ्कः ।

कर्मधारयादिनिः । प्रवर्तयन् गमयन् । गुरुजनस्य अगस्त्यस्य आदेशोपरोधादाज्ञानुसरणाद्धेतोः । अतिक्रमः असंभाव्यगमनरूपः । अत्रेष्टजनानुनयात् पर्युपासनं नाम संध्यङ्गमुक्तम् ॥ गुञ्जदिति । कुञ्जा एव कुटीराः । गुञ्जन्तः अव्यक्तशब्दवन्तः कुञ्जकुटीराः येषां ते । कौशिकघटाः घूकपंक्तयः तासां घुत्काराः एषु सन्तीति तद्वन्तः कीचकाः तेषां रन्ध्रवतां वेणुविशेषाणां स्तम्बाः काण्डाः तेषामाडम्बरः संभ्रमः तेन मूकानि जोषमासीनानि मौकुलिकुलानि यस्य स तथोक्तः । क्रौञ्चाभिधोऽयं तन्नामकोऽयं गिरिः । प्रचलाकिनां मयूराणाम् । रोहिणतरवः हरिचन्दनवृक्षाः । कुम्भीनसाः सर्पाः । उद्वेल्लन्ति वेपन्ते । 'वेल्ल चलने' ॥ २९ ॥ एत इति । कुहरेषु गुहासु गद्गदं यथा तथा नदन्ति शब्दवन्ति गोदावरीवारीणि येषु तथोक्ताः । शिखराग्रं मौलिः । पर्वताग्रं शिखरमिति इह भेदः । क्षोणीभृतः पर्वताः । दाक्षिणाः दक्षिणदिशावर्तिनः । एते ते पूर्वं भवता दृष्टाः । अन्योन्यप्रतिघातेन परस्परप्रत्यास्फालनेन संकुलाः निबिडाः चलन्तः कल्लोलाः तरङ्गाः तेषां कोलाहलैः कलकलैः उत्तालाः उल्बणाः सरित्संगमाः नदीसंगमाः ॥ ३० ॥

वाधूलवंशजनुषो भूसारजवीरराघवार्यस्य ।
उत्तररामचरित्रव्याख्यायामवसितो द्वितीयोऽङ्कः ॥

इति श्रीवाधूलवीरराघवविरचितायां भवभूतिभावतलस्पर्शिनी-
समाख्यायामुत्तररामचरितव्याख्यायां द्वितीयोऽङ्कः ॥

---

१ गुरुजनानुरोधात्; गुरुजनादेशोपरोधात्. २ गुञ्जत्. ३ घुत्कार. ४ क्रौञ्चाभिधः. ५ चन्दन, रोहित, रौहिण. ६ मेघालंकृत, मेघालंबित. ७ दक्षिणाः. निष्क्रान्ताः सर्वे. ९ इति महाकविश्रीभवभूतिप्रणीते उत्तररामचरितनाटके पञ्च०.

तृतीयोऽङ्कः ।

(ततः प्रविशति नदीद्वयम् ।)

एका——सखि मुरले किमसि संभ्रान्तेव ।

मुरला——सखि तमसे प्रेषितास्मि भगवतोऽगस्त्यस्य पत्न्या लोपामुद्रया सरिद्वरां गोदावरीमभिधातुम् । जानास्येव यथा वधूपरित्यागात्प्रभृति

अनिर्भिन्नो गभीरत्वादन्तर्गूढघनव्यथः ।
पुटपाकप्रतीकाशो रामस्य करुणो रसः ॥ १ ॥

तेन च तथाविधेष्टजनकष्टविनिपातजन्मना प्रकर्षगतेन दीर्घशोकसंतापेन संप्रत्यतितरां परिक्षीणो रामभद्रः । तमवलोक्य कम्पितमिव मे सबन्धनं हृदयम् । अधुना च प्रतिनिवर्तमानेन रामभद्रेण नियतमेव पञ्चवटीवने वधूसहवासविस्रम्भसाक्षिणः प्रदेशा द्रष्टव्याः । तेषु च निसर्गधीरस्याप्येवंविधायामवस्थायामतिगम्भीराभोगशोकक्षोभसंवेगात्पदे पदे महान्ति प्रमादस्थानानि शङ्कनीयानि रामभद्रस्य । तद्भगवति गोदावरि तत्र त्वया सावधानया भवितव्यम् ।

वधूपरित्यागात् स्नुषापरित्यागात् । **अनिर्भिन्न इति** । करुणो रसः इष्टजनवियोगजन्यदुःखातिशयात्मकरसः । पुटपाकप्रतीकाशः लोहादिमयसंपुटान्तर्वर्तिसंतापनसदृश इत्यर्थः ॥ १ ॥ **तेनेति** । तथाविधेष्टजनस्य सीतायाः कष्टविनिपातात् दुःखमयविक्षेपात् जन्म उत्पत्तिः यस्य तथोक्तेन । प्रकृष्टोऽधिकः गद्गदशब्दः येन तथोक्तेन । 'प्रकर्षगद्गदेन' इति पाठे प्रकर्षेण गद्गदो यस्मिन्निति विग्रहः । दीर्घशोकसंतानेन दीर्घदुःखपरिवाहेण परिक्षीणः कार्श्यदौर्बल्यादियुक्तः । कुसुमेन समं बन्धनं यस्येति विग्रहः । कुसुमसमबन्धनम् । तद्वत् सुच्छेदमित्यर्थः । **अधुनेति** । वधूसहनिवासे ये विस्रम्भाः स्वैरलीलाः तत्साक्षिणः तत्साक्षात्कर्तारः प्रदेशाः वनोद्देशाः । नियतमित्यसंदेहवाचि । **तत्रेति** । गम्भीरः आभोगः आयामः यस्य तथोक्तः यः शोकः तेन जातस्य क्षोभस्य प्रकृतिविपर्यासस्य संवेगात् वेगातिशयात् । महान् प्रमादः अनवधानता येषु तथोक्तानि । संज्ञाच्छेदकारीणीत्यर्थः । शोकस्थानानि जगतां शोकनिमित्तानि । रामात्याहितानीति भावः । सावधानया अवधानं मनसो

---

१ तमसा मुरला च इत्यधि. २ भगवति. ३ अनिर्भिन्नगभीरत्वात्. ४ गुरु. ५ कष्टपरीपाक. ६ प्रकर्षतां–प्रकृष्टतां–गतेन, प्रकृष्टगद्गदेन(टी०). ७ संतानेन. ८ नितराम्. ९ कुसुमसमबन्धनं (टी.). १० सहनिवास. ११ तत्र, तेन. १२ महाप्रमादानि शोकस्थानानि. १३ तत्रभवत्या.

वीचीवातैः शीकरक्षोदशीतैराकर्षद्भिः पद्मकिञ्जल्कगन्धान् ।
मोहे मोहे रामभद्रस्य जीवं स्वैरं स्वैरं प्रेरितैस्तर्पयेति ॥ २ ॥

तमसा—उचितमेव दाक्षिण्यं स्नेहस्य । संजीवनोपायस्तु मौलिकं एव रामभद्रस्याद्य संनिहितः ।

मुरला—कथमिव ।

तमसा—श्रूयताम् । पुरा किल वाल्मीकितपोवनोपकण्ठात्परित्यज्य निवृत्ते लक्ष्मणे सीतादेवी प्राप्तप्रसववेदनमतिदुःखसंवेगादात्मानं गङ्गाप्रवाहे निक्षिप्तवती । तदैव तत्र दारकद्वयं प्रसूता । भगवतीभ्यां पृथ्वीभागीरथीभ्यामभ्युपपन्ना रसातलं च नीता । स्तन्यत्यागात्परेण च दारकद्वयं तस्याः प्राचेतसस्य महर्षेर्गङ्गादेवी स्वयमर्पितवती ।

मुरला—(सविस्मयम् ।)

ईदृशानां विपाकोऽपि जायते परमाद्भुतः ।
यत्रोपकरणीभावमायात्येवंविधो जनः ॥ ३ ॥

तमसा—इदानीं तु शम्बूकवृत्तान्तेनानेन संभावितजनस्थानागमनं रामभद्रं सरयूमुखादुपश्रुत्य भगवती भागीरथी यदेव भगवत्या लोपामुद्रया स्नेहादाशङ्कितं तदेवाशङ्क्य सीतासमेता केनचिदिव गृहाचारव्यपदेशेन गोदावरीं विलोकयितुमागता ।

विषयान्तरसंचारविमुखता तत्सहितया ॥ **वीचीति** । शीकराणां सूक्ष्मांशैः पद्मकिञ्जल्कानामरविन्दकेसराणां गन्धान् सौरभ्याणि आकर्षद्भिः हरद्भिः । शीकरक्षोदेत्यनेन शैत्यमुक्तम् । पद्मकिञ्जल्कगन्धानित्यनेन सौरभ्यमुक्तम् । आकर्षद्भिरित्यनेन मान्द्यमुक्तम् । वहनाशक्तावेव कर्षणसंभवात् । स्वैरं निःशङ्कम् । अत्र स्वैरमित्युक्त्या सुरभिशीतलमृदुवाता अपि विरहिणामनर्थकारिण इति न शङ्क्यम् । विरहिणां चैतन्यदशायामेव दुःसहा इमे । मूर्च्छितानां तु प्राणप्रतिष्ठापनकारा एव । नातस्त्वयातिशङ्का कर्तव्येति व्यज्यते ॥ २ ॥ **उचितमिति** । दाक्षिण्यं सामर्थ्यं, ऊहापोहात्मकज्ञानवत्त्वं वा । मूलतः । सीताङ्कुरात् मूलमिति सीतोच्यते । मौलिक इति पाठेऽप्यर्थः प्रागिव ॥ **वाल्मीकीति** । प्राप्तप्रसववेदनं जातप्रसवदुःखम् । आत्मानं स्वम् । दारकद्वयं शिशुद्वयम् । अभ्युपपन्ना संगता । स्तन्यत्यागात्परेण स्तन्यत्यागानन्तरम् । **ईदृशानामिति** । विपाकः दशा [परिणामः] । उपकरणीभावमुपकरणत्वम् ॥ ३ ॥ **इदानीं त्विति** । उपश्रुत्याकर्ण्य । तत् सर्वं श्रूयतामित्यारभ्य ऋषिश्रेयोवितरणरूपबीजस्य अन्वेषणाद्गर्भसंधिरयम् । ' गर्भस्तु दृष्टनष्टस्य बीजस्यान्वेषणं मुहुः '

---

१ प्रेषितैः, तर्पय-स्तंभय. २ मूलतः. ३ सर्वं श्रूयताम्. ४ अस्ति खलु. ५ गते, प्रतिनिवृत्ते. ६ ०वेदना. ७ प्रासूत. ८ ०भ्यामप्युभाभ्याम्. ९ सुतद्वयं. १० गङ्गादेव्या स्वयमर्पितम्; समर्पितं स्वयम्. ११ पावनाद्भुतः. १२ ०कवध०. १३ स्थानगमनं. १४ गोदावरीमुपागता.

मुरला—सुचिन्तितं भगवत्या भागीरथ्या राजधानीस्थितस्यास्य खलु तैस्तैर्जगतामाभ्युदयिकैः कार्यैर्व्यापृतस्य रामभद्रस्य नियताश्चित्तविक्षेपाः। अव्यग्रस्य पुनरस्य शोकमात्रद्वितीयस्य पञ्चवटीप्रवेशो महाननर्थ इति। तत्कथमिदानीं सीतादेव्या रामभद्र आश्वासनीयः स्यात्।

तमसा—उक्तमत्र भगवत्या भागीरथ्या—'वत्से देवयजनसंभवे सीते, अद्य खल्वायुष्मतोः कुशलवयोर्द्वादशस्य जन्मसंवत्सरस्य संख्यामङ्गलग्रन्थिरभिवर्तते। तदात्मनः पुराणश्वशुरमेतावतो मानवस्य राजर्षिवंशस्य प्रसवितारं सवितारमपहतपाप्मानं देवं स्वहस्तावचितैः पुष्पैरुपतिष्ठस्व। न च त्वामवनिपृष्ठचारिणीमस्मत्प्रभावाद्वनदेवता अपि द्रक्ष्यन्ति किं पुनर्मर्त्याः' इति। अहमप्याज्ञापिता—'तमसे त्वयि प्रकृष्टप्रेमैव वधूर्जानकी। अतस्त्वमेवास्याः प्रत्यनन्तरीभव' इति। साऽहमधुना यथादिष्टमनुतिष्ठामि।

मुरला—अहमप्येतं[12] वृत्तान्तं भगवत्यै लोपामुद्रायै निवेदयामि। रामभद्रोऽप्यागत एवेति तर्कयामि।

तमसा—तदियं गोदावरीह्रदान्निष्क्रम्य[13]

इत्युक्तेः। केनचिदिव गृह्याचारव्यपदेशेनेत्यत्र प्रस्तुतोपयोगिच्छद्माचरणरूपं अभूताहरणं नाम संध्यङ्गमुक्तम्। **सुष्ठु इति**। राजनीतिस्थितस्य क्षत्रियोचितराज्यपरिपालनात्मकधर्मनिष्ठस्य। अभ्युदयाय भवन्तीत्याभ्युदयिकानि इति विग्रहः। तैः आभ्युदयिकैः। चित्तविक्षेपाः हृदयतोदाः। अव्यग्रस्य व्यापारान्तरशून्यस्य। अनर्थः तद्दुःखहेतुः। एष तत्त्वार्थानुकीर्तनरूपो मार्ग उक्तः। द्वादशस्य जन्मवत्सरस्य संख्यामङ्गलग्रन्थिरभिवर्तते संख्यापूर्तिहेतुकमङ्गलग्रन्थिः। वत्सरे वत्सरे शिशूनां जन्मनक्षत्रे शान्त्युत्सवं कृत्वा मङ्गलार्थं करे पटसूत्रादिना स्त्रियो ग्रन्थिं कुर्वन्ति। स तु करे वलयरूपेण तिष्ठतीत्युपदेशः। मानवस्य मनुसंबन्धिनः। प्रसवितारं जनकम्। अपहतपाप्मानं निरस्तसमस्ताविद्यादिदोषगन्धम्। देवं जगत्सृष्ट्यादिलीलाशालिनम्। अत्र 'एष सर्वेभ्यः पाप्मभ्य उदेति' इत्यन्तरादित्यविद्याप्रत्यभिज्ञापिता। तत्र च कप्यासश्रुत्या नारायण एव प्रतिपाद्य इति स्पष्टमेव। उपतिष्ठस्व सेवस्व। **अत इति**। प्रत्यनन्तरीभव अनु-

१ राजनीति. २ इति शङ्के. ३ सीतया रामभद्रोयम्. ४ उक्तमेव, उक्तमद्य. ५ भागीरथीदेव्या. ६ द्वादशजन्म॰, द्वादशसंवत्सरस्य, द्वादशस्य संवत्सरस्य संख्यामङ्गलग्रन्थिरभिसंबध्यते. ७ अभिबध्यते, वर्धते. ८ पृष्ठवर्तिनीम्. ९ किमुत. १० वधूर्वत्सा. ११ प्रत्यन्तरी॰. १२ प्यमुं. १३ निर्गत्य.

परिपाण्डुदुर्बलकपोलसुन्दरं
दधती विलोलकबरीकमाननम् ।
करुणस्य मूर्तिरथ वा शरीरिणी
विरहव्यथेव वनमेति जानकी ॥ ४ ॥

मुरला—इयं हि सा ।

किसलयमिव मुग्धं बन्धनाद्विप्रलूनं
हृदयकुसुमशोषी दारुणो दीर्घशोकः ।
ग्लपयति परिपाण्डु क्षाममस्याः शरीरं
शरदिज इव घर्मः केतकीगर्भपत्रम् ॥ ५ ॥

(इति परिक्रम्य निष्क्रान्ते ।)

शुद्धविष्कम्भः ।

(नेपथ्ये ।)

प्रमादः प्रमादः ।

(ततः प्रविशति पुष्पावचयव्यग्रा सकरुणौत्सुक्यमाकर्णयन्ती सीता ।)

सीता—अह्महे जानामि प्रियसखी मे वासन्ती व्याहरतीति । (क)

(क) अम्हहे जाणामि पिअसही मे वासन्दी वाहरदित्ति ।

चरीभव ॥ **रामभद्र इति** । तर्कयामि अनुमिनोमि ॥ **परिपाण्डु इति** । करुणस्य इष्टवियोगजन्यदुःखातिशयस्य मूर्तिः आकारो वा । विरहव्यथा । विरहजन्यसंतापादिरूपा ॥ ४ ॥ **किसलयमिति** । परिपाण्डु उक्तरीत्या अतिम्लानत्वेऽपि लावण्याविरोधिपाण्डुतोक्ता । ग्रीष्मविरहतापयोरयमेव विशेषः यत् ग्रीष्मस्य लावण्यनाशकत्वं विरहस्य तु तदभाव इति । तथा च कालिदासः— ' समस्तापः कामं मनसिजनिदाघप्रसरयोर्न तु ग्रीष्मस्यैवं सुभगमपराद्धं युवतिषु । ' इति । एवं सुभगं न । एवं लावण्यापरित्यागेन रमणीयं न भवतीत्यर्थः । तथाह भगवान् वाल्मीकिः—' ज्योत्स्ना तुषारमलिना पौर्णमास्यां हि लक्ष्मण । सीतेव चातपश्यामा दृश्यते न च शोभते ॥ ' इति । ग्रीष्मस्यातपश्यामेति लावण्यनाशकत्वम् । क्षामं कृशं ग्लपयति म्लानं करोति । शरदिजः शरत्कालजः । ' प्रावृट्शरत्— ' इत्यादिसूत्रेणालुक् । अत्र लिङ्गादभ्यूहनरूपं अनुमानं नाम संध्यङ्गमुक्तम् ॥ ५ ॥ **शुद्धविष्कम्भ इति** । संस्कृतात्मकविष्कम्भ इत्यर्थः । विष्कम्भस्वरूपं तु—' वृत्तवर्तिष्यमाणानां कथांशानां निदर्शकः । संक्षेपार्थस्तु विष्कम्भो मध्यपात्रप्रयोजितः ॥' इति ।

---

१ मूर्तिरिव वा. २ विरहव्यथैव. ३ कमल; शोषी-दाही. ४ जात जात. ५ व्यग्रहस्ता.

(पुनर्नेपथ्ये ।)

सीतादेव्या स्वकरकलितैः सल्लकीपल्लवाग्रै-
रग्रे लोलः करिकलभको यः पुरा वर्धितोऽभूत् ।

सीता—किं तस्य । (क)

(पुनर्नेपथ्ये ।)

वध्वा सार्धं पयसि विहरन्सोऽयमन्येन दर्पा-
दुद्दामेन द्विरदपतिना संनिपत्याभियुक्तः ॥ ६ ॥

सीता—(ससंभ्रमम् । कतिचित्पदानि गत्वा ।) आर्यपुत्र परित्रायस्व परित्रायस्व मम तं पुत्रकम् । (स्मृतिमभिनीय । सवैक्लव्यम् ।) हा धिक् हा धिक् । तान्येव चिरपरिचितान्यक्षराणि पञ्चवटीदर्शनेन मां मन्दभागिनीमनुबध्नन्ति । हा आर्यपुत्र । (इति मूर्च्छति ।) (ख)

(प्रविश्य ।)

तमसा—वत्से समाश्वसिहि । समाश्वसिहि ।

(नेपथ्ये ।)

विमानराज अत्रैव स्थीयताम् ।

सीता—(समाश्वस्य । ससाध्वसोल्लासम् ।) अह्महे जलभरभरितमेघमन्थरस्तनितगम्भीरमांसलः कुतो न्वेष भारतीनिर्घोषो भ्रियमाणकर्णविवरां मामपि मन्दभागिनीं झटित्युच्छ्वासयति । (ग)

(क) किं तस्स ।

(ख) अज्जउत्त परित्ताहि परित्ताहि मह तं पुत्तअम् । हद्धी हद्धी । ताइं ज्जेव्व चिरपरिचिदाइं अक्खराइं पञ्चवटीदंसणेण मं मन्दभाइणिं अणुबन्धन्ति । हा अज्जउत्त ।

(ग) अह्महे जलभरभरिअमेहमन्थरत्थणिअगम्भीरमंसलो कुदो णु एसो भारईणिग्घोसो भरन्तकण्णविवरं मं वि मन्दभाइणिं झत्ति उस्सासेदि ।

केवलसंस्कृतप्रायः शुद्ध इति ॥ व्याहरति वदति ॥ **सीतेति** । स्वकरकलितैः स्वकराभ्यां दत्तैरित्यर्थः । वध्वा सार्धं स्त्रिया सह । उद्दामेन उत्कटेन संनिपत्य स्वयमापत्य । अभियुक्तः प्रत्यर्थितया संगतः ॥ ६ ॥ **आर्यपुत्रेति** । परित्रायस्वेति । एष ह्यपकारिजनात् भीतिरूप उद्वेग उक्तः । **तानीति** । अक्षराणि आर्यपुत्रेति वर्णाः । अनुबध्नन्ति अनुसरन्ति । मन्दभागिनीमल्पपुण्यफलाम् ॥ **जलेति** । मांसलः स्फीतः । भारतीनिर्घोषः वर्णोच्चारणध्वनिः ।

---

१ पोषितः. २ वेगात्. ३ दधती. ४ विचिन्त्य. ५ ससाध्वसोत्कंपो०. ६ ०णेण पुणोवि मं (पुनरपि मां). ७ अणुरुन्धन्ति. ८ जलभरिदमेहत्थणिद. ९ भरन्तो (भरन्). १० उस्सुआवेइ (उत्सुकापयति).

तमसा—(सस्नेहास्रम् ।) अयि वत्से

अपरिस्फुटनिक्वाणे कुतस्त्येऽपि त्वमीदृशी ।
स्तनयित्नोर्मयूरीव चकितोत्कण्ठितं स्थिता ॥ ७ ॥

सीता—भगवति किं भणस्यपरिस्फुटेति । मया पुनः स्वरसंयोगेन प्रत्यभिज्ञातमार्यपुत्र एव व्याहरतीति । (क)

तमसा—श्रूयते तपस्यतः किल शूद्रस्य दण्डधारणार्थमैक्ष्वाको राजा जनस्थानमागत इति ।

सीता—दिष्ट्या अपरिहीनराजधर्मः खलु स राजा । (ख)

(नेपथ्ये ।)

यत्र द्रुमा अपि मृगा अपि बन्धवो मे
यानि प्रियासहचरश्चिरमध्यवात्सम् ।
एतानि तानि बहुनिर्झरकन्दराणि
गोदावरीपरिसरस्य गिरेस्तटानि ॥ ८ ॥

सीता—(दृष्ट्वा ।) हा कथं प्रभातचन्द्रमण्डलापाण्डुरपरिक्षामदुर्बलेनाकारेणायं निजसौम्यगम्भीरानुभावमात्रप्रत्यभिज्ञेय आर्यपुत्र एव । भगवति तमसे धारय माम् । (इति तमसामाश्लिष्य मूर्च्छति ।) (ग)

तमसा—(धारयन्ती ।) वत्से समाश्वसिहि समाश्वसिहि ।

(क) भअवदि किं भणासि अपरिप्फुडेत्ति । मए उण सरसंजोएणे पच्चभिआणिदं अज्जउत्तो एव्व वाहरदित्ति ।

(ख) दिट्ठिआ अपरिहीणराअधम्मो वखु सो राआ ।

(ग) हा कहं पहादचन्दमण्डलापण्डुरपरिक्खामदुब्बलेन आआरेण अअं णिअसोम्मगम्भीराणुभावमेत्तपच्चहिजाणिज्जो अज्जउत्तो एव्व । भअवदि तमसे धारेहि मम् ।

उत्सुकापयति उत्कण्ठितां करोति ॥ स्वरसंयोगेन स्वरसंदर्भेण प्रत्यभिजानामि तदिदमिति वेद्मि ॥ **श्रूयत इति** । तपस्यतः तपश्चरतः । कण्ड्वादिरयम् । दण्डधारणार्थम् अपराधानुगुणशिक्षणार्थम् । ऐक्ष्वाकः इक्ष्वाकुवंश्यः । 'दाण्डिनायन—' इत्यादिसूत्रेण टिलोपः ॥ अपरिहीनधर्मः अन्यूनधर्मः ॥ **यत्रेति** । अध्यवात्सम् उषितवानास्मि । 'उपान्वध्याङ्वसः' इति कर्मत्वम् । एतानीति । गोदावरीपरिसरस्य गोदावरीसमीपवर्तिनः ॥ ८ ॥ परिक्षामदुर्बलेन दुर्बलायमानेन । पाठान्तरम् 'परिक्षामधूसरेण' इति । अतिकृशेन दुर्बलेन चेत्यर्थः ॥

---

१ सस्मिता०. २ किमव्यक्तेपि निनदे, किमव्य... कुतस्ते प्रीतिरीदृशी. ३ उत्कण्ठिता. ४ दण्डकारण्यम्. ५ सरसंजोएण पच्चभिजाणामि णं अज्जउत्तेण एव्व एदं वाहरिदं (स्वरसंयोगेन प्रत्यभिजानामि ननु आर्यपुत्रेणैवैतद्व्याहृतम् ।). ६ लावप०...क्खामधूमधूसरेण. ७ अअं सो. ८ पच्चभिआणिदो अज्जउत्तो एव्व ता मं धारेहि (प्रत्यभिज्ञात आ० एव तन्मां धारय). ९ ता भ० धारेहि मं धारेहि मं.

(नेपथ्ये ।)

अनेन पञ्चवटीदर्शनेन

अन्तर्लीनस्य दुःखाग्नेरद्योद्दामं ज्वलिष्यतः ।
उत्पीड इव धूमस्य मोहः प्रागावृणोति माम् ॥ ९ ॥

हा प्रिये जानकि ।

तमसा—(स्वगतम् ।) इदं तदाशङ्कितं गुरुजनेन[१] ।

सीता—(समाश्वस्य ।) हा कथमेतत् । (क)

(पुनर्नेपथ्ये ।)

हा देवि दण्डकारण्यवासप्रियसखि विदेहराजपुत्रि । (इति मूर्च्छति ।)

सीता—हा धिक् हा धिक् । मां मन्दभागिनीं व्याहृत्यामीलन्नेत्रनीलोत्पलो मूर्च्छित एव । हा कथं धरणिपृष्ठे निरुद्धनिःश्वासनिःसहं विपर्यस्तः । भगवति तमसे परित्रायस्व परित्रायस्व । जीवयार्यपुत्रम् । (इति पादयोः पतति ।) (ख)

तमसा—

त्वमेव ननु कल्याणि संजीवय जगत्पतिम् ।
प्रियस्पर्शो हि पाणिस्ते तत्रैष[३] निरतो जनः ॥ १० ॥

(क) हा कहं एदम् ।

(ख) हद्धी हद्धी । मं मन्दभाइणिं वाहरिअ[४] ओमीलंतणेत्तणीलुप्पलो मुच्छिदो एव्व[५] । हा कहं धरणिपिट्ठे णिरुद्धणिस्सासणीसहं[७] विपल्हत्थो । भअवदि तमसे परित्ताएहि परित्ताएहि । जीवावेहि अज्जउत्तम् ।

अनुभावमात्रप्रत्यभिज्ञेयः प्रभवेन केवलं प्रत्यभिज्ञातुं शक्यः ॥ **अन्तर्लीनस्येति** । अन्तर्लीनस्य अन्तर्गूढस्य । उद्दामं उल्बणं यथा तथा अद्य ज्वलिष्यतः एतदव्यवहितोत्तरक्षणभाविज्वलनवतः धूमस्य उत्पीड इव धूमसंबन्धिसंघात इव संमर्द इवेति वा । मोहः मूर्च्छा प्राक् ज्वलनात् पूर्वम् । आवृणोति संछादयति ॥ ९ ॥ **इदमिति** । गुरुजनेन । लोपामुद्राप्रभृतिनेत्यर्थः । एष संचितार्थप्राप्तिरुपक्रम उक्तः ॥ **हेति** । धरणीपृष्ठे भूतले निरुद्धनिःश्वासनिःसहं निरुद्धः प्रवृत्तिहीनः निःश्वासः यस्मिन् कर्मणि तद्यथा भवति तथा निःसहं दुर्बलं विपर्यस्तः ॥ **त्वमेवेति** । त्वमेव ननु कल्याणीत्यस्यायं भावः । त्वयैवायं संजीवनीयः इति चिरंतनी प्रसिद्धिः । 'आनीतवातं स्वधया तदेकम्' इति श्रुत्यायमर्थोऽवगम्यते । एकं जगतां प्रलीनत्वादसहायमतो निर्व्यापारम् । तत् परं ब्रह्म स्वधात्वं सिद्धिस्त्वम्, स्वधा स्वाहा इति स्वधाशब्दवाच्यया लक्ष्म्या आनीतजीवम् इति । एवं च अद्य कथमहं वैदेशिकी जीवयामि त्वमेव जीवयेति । अत्र

---

१ तावद्. २ नापि. ३ यत्रैष, यत्रैव, तत्रैव निरतो भरः (भवः); तत्रैव नियतो भवः; नियता भव. ४ उद्दिसिअ. ५ अ'मीलिद. ६ एव्व अज्जउत्तो. ७ निरुस्साहणीसहं (णिरुत्साहणिःसहं).

सीता—यद्भवतु तद्भवतु । यथा भगवत्याज्ञापयति । (इति ससंभ्रमं निष्क्रान्ता ।) (क)

(ततः प्रविशति भूम्यां निपतितः सास्रया सीतया स्पृश्यमानः साह्लादोच्छ्वासो रामः ।)

सीता—(किंचित्सहर्षम् ।) जाने पुनः प्रत्यागतमिव जीवितं त्रैलोक्यस्य । (ख)

आश्च्योतनं नु हरिचन्दनपल्लवानां
निष्पीडितेन्दुकरकन्दलजो नु सेकः ।
आतप्तजीवितपुनःपरितर्पणोऽयं
संजीवनौषधिरसो नु हृदि प्रसिक्तः ॥ ११ ॥

अपि च ।

स्पर्शः पुरा परिचितो नियतं स एव
संजीवनश्च मनसः परिमोहनश्च ।
संतापजां सपदि यः परिहृत्य मूर्च्छा-
मानन्दनेन जडतां पुनरातनोति ॥ १२ ॥

सीता—(ससाध्वसोत्कम्पमुपसृत्य ।) एतावदेवेदानीं मे बहुतरम् । (ग)

रामः—(उपविश्य ।) न खलु वत्सलया सीतादेव्याभ्युपपन्नोऽस्मि ।

सीता—हा धिक् हा धिक् । किमिति मामार्यपुत्रो मार्गिष्यति । (घ)

(क) जं होदु तं होदु । जह भअवई आणवेइ ।
(ख) जाणे उण पच्चाअदं विअ जीविअं तेलौअस्स ।
(ग) एत्तिअं एव्व दाणिं मे बहुदरम् ।
(घ) हद्धी हद्धी । किंति मं अज्जउत्तो मग्गिस्संदि ।

मां मन्दभागिनीमित्यारभ्य परित्रायस्वेत्यन्तसंदर्भेण शङ्कात्रासरूपसंभ्रम उक्तः ॥ १० ॥ आह्लादः आनन्दः उच्छ्वासः श्वाससंचारः ताभ्यां सहितं यथा तथा ॥ **जान इति**। प्रत्यागतं पुनरागतम् । त्रयाणामपि लोकानां राममयजीवितत्वात् रामजीवने तज्जीवनमिति भावः । तदुक्तम्—'रामो रामो राम इति प्रजानामभवन्कथाः । रामभूतं जगदभूद्रामे राज्यं प्रशासति ॥' इति ॥ **आश्च्योतनमिति** । हरिचन्दनपल्लवानां आश्च्योतनं नु कल्पतरुकिसलयरसक्षरणाद् द्रवीकरणं किम् । कन्दलजः अङ्कुरजः ॥ ११ ॥ **स्पर्श इति** । संजीवनश्च प्राणधारणहेतुभूतश्च परितोषणश्च आह्लादजनकश्च । मूर्च्छां प्रज्ञाशून्यतां आनन्दनेन जडतां आनन्दाधिक्यप्रयुक्तप्रज्ञाशून्यतामातनोति आ समन्तात् विस्तारयति ॥ १२ ॥ एतावदेव मत्स्पर्शो पुरा परिचितत्वकथनमेव । इदानीं वियोगसमये ॥ वत्सलया प्रीतिमत्या मदीयदोषं सहमानया वा । अभ्युपपन्नोऽस्मि अनुगृहीतोऽस्मि । इदं इष्टजनातिसंधानात्मकम-

---

१ सहर्षं स्वगतम्. २ प्रश्चो. ३ तरोः; जीवित-जीवन-मनः०. ४ परितोषणः. ५ प्रतिहत्य. ६ ससाध्वसकरुणम्. ७ सीतेति नास्ति क्वचित्. ८ पुणो वि. ९ तेलोअणाहस्स (त्रिलोकनाथस्य). १० णिन्दिस्सादि (निन्दिष्यति).

रामः—भवतु । पश्यामि ।

सीता—भगवति तमसे अपसरावस्तावत् । मां प्रक्ष्यानभ्यनुज्ञातेन संनिधानेन राजाऽधिकं कोपिष्यति । (क)

तमसा—अयि वत्से भागीरथीप्रसादाद्वनदेवतानामप्यदृश्यासि संवृत्ता ।

सीता—आम् अस्ति खल्वेतत् । (ख)

रामः—हा प्रिये जानाकि[1] ।

सीता-(समन्यु[2]गद्गदम्।)आर्यपुत्र असदृशं खल्वेतद्वचनमस्य वृत्तान्तस्य। साम्रम् ।) अथ वा किमिति वज्रमयी जन्मान्तरेष्वपि पुनरसंभावितदुर्लभदर्शनस्य मामेव मन्दभागिनीमुद्दिश्य वत्सलस्यैवंवादिन आर्यपुत्रस्योपरि निरनुक्रोशा भविष्यामि । अहमेतस्य हृदयं जानामि ममाप्येषः । (ग)

रामः—(सर्वतो[3]ऽवलोक्य । सनिर्वेदम् ।) हा न[4] किंचिदत्र ।

(क) भअवदि तमसे ओसरह्म दाव । मं पेक्खिअ अणब्भणुण्णादेण संणिहाणेण राआ अहिअं कुप्पिस्सदि ।

(ख) आम् अत्थि खु एदम् ।

(ग) अज्जउत्त असरिसं क्खु एदं वअणं इमस्स वुत्तन्दस्स । अह वा किंत्ति वज्जमेई जम्मन्तरेसु वि पुणो असंभाविअदुल्लहदंसणस्स मं एव्व मन्दभाइणिं उद्दिसिअ वच्छलस्स एव्वंवादिणो अज्जउत्तस्स उवरि णिरणुक्कोसा भविस्सम् । अहं एदस्स हिअअं जाणामि ममावि एसो ।

तिबलं नाम संध्यङ्गमुक्तम् ॥ अनभ्यनुज्ञातेन अननुमतेन । संनिधानेन समीपस्थित्या ॥ **आर्यपुत्रेति** । एतत् प्रियेत्यामन्त्रणम् । अस्य वृत्तान्तस्य । परित्यागरूपस्येत्यर्थः । वज्रमयी अत्यन्तकाठिन्ययुक्ता । मन्दभाग्यां मामुद्दिश्य वत्सलस्य निर्दोषत्वनिश्चयपूर्वकं मयि प्रीतिमतः निरनुक्रोशा निर्दया । अनुक्रोशपदेन रामदशामिमां दृष्ट्वा मुक्तकण्ठं मया रोदितव्यम् । तत् किमेवं कठिना भवामीति व्यज्यते । 'अनुक्रोशाति

---

१ ननु प्रिये जानाकि इत्यधिकम्. २ ससाध्वस०, ससाध्वसम्. ३ विलोक्य. ४ कथमत्र न कश्चिदपि; न काचिदत्र. ५ ओसरम्ह । जइ दाव मे पेक्खिस्सदि तदो (यदि तावन्मां प्रेक्षिष्यते तदा). ६ अहिअदरं, आहिअं पि—मम राआ महारओ कुविस्सदि (अधिकतरं, अधिकमपि-मम राजा महाराजः कोपिष्यति). ७ एतन्नास्ति क्वचित्. ८ भगवदि ९ ०वज्जमई विव. १० जम्मन्तरे संभाविद. ११ अहं एव्व.

सीता—भगवति तमसे तथा निष्कारणपरित्यागिनोऽप्येतस्यैवं-विधेन दर्शनेन कीदृश इव मे हृदयानुबन्ध इति न जानामि। (क)

तमसा—जानामि वत्से जानामि।

तटस्थं नैराश्यादपि च कलुषं विप्रियवशा-
द्वियोगे दीर्घेऽस्मिञ्झटितिघटनात्स्तम्भितमिव।
प्रसन्नं सौजन्याद्दयितकरुणैर्गाढकरुणं
द्रवीभूतं प्रेम्णा तव हृदयमस्मिन्क्षण इव॥ १३॥

रामः—देवि

प्रसाद इव मूर्तस्ते स्पर्शः स्नेहार्द्रशीतलः।
अद्योप्यानन्दयति मां त्वं पुनः क्वासि नन्दिनि॥ १४॥

(क) भअवदि तमसे तहा णिक्कारणपरिच्चाइणो वि एदस्स एव्वंविधेण दंसणेण कीदिसो विअ मे हिअआणुबन्धोत्ति ण आणामि।

मुक्तकण्ठं रोदित्यनेनेति अनुक्रोशः' इत्यमरव्याख्या। कीदृशी मे हृदयावस्था। आर्यपुत्र परित्रायस्व मम पुत्रकमित्यारभ्य ममाप्येष इत्यन्तेन संदर्भेण प्रतिपादिता मम हृदयावस्था कीदृशीत्यर्थः। **तटस्थमिति**। तव हृदयमस्मिन् क्षणे नैराश्यात् तटस्थमिवेत्यादि-विभिन्नवाक्यतया योजना। नैराश्यात् प्रत्याशाभावात् तटस्थं प्रसादकालुष्यादिरहि-तम्। विप्रियवशात् कलुषं परित्यागरूपादप्रियाद्धेतोः कलुषं क्रोधयुक्तम्। दीर्घे अस्मिन् वियोगे आमरणान्तभावित्वेन ज्ञातेऽस्मिन् विरहे झटितिघटनात् आकस्मिकसंघटनात् स्ताम्भितमिव विस्मयास्तिमितमिव सौजन्यात् प्रकृत्या कल्याणत्वात् प्रसन्नं भविष्यतानुसंधानेन निवृत्तकालुष्यम्। दयितकरुणैः रामस्य दुःखात्मकावस्था-विशेषैः गाढकरुणं परदुःखदुःखित्वरूपकरुणासान्द्रम्। प्रेम्णा प्रणयेन द्रवीभूतं विलीनम्। अत्र तटस्थं नैराश्यादित्यनेन तान्येव चिरपरिचितान्यक्षराणीति वाक्याभिमता सीतावस्था प्रतिपादिता। अपि च कलुषं विप्रियवशादित्यनेन असदृशं खल्वमुष्य वृत्तान्तस्येत्येतद्वाक्याभिमतावस्था प्रतिपादिता। वियोगे दीर्घेऽस्मिन्नित्यनेन कथं प्रभातचन्द्रमण्डलेत्यादिविवक्षितावस्था प्रतिपादिता। कथमित्यस्य विस्मयार्थकत्वात्। प्रसन्नं सौजन्यादित्यनेन अथ वा किमिति वज्रमयीवेत्यादिप्रतिपादितावस्था दर्शिता। दयितकरुणैर्गाढकरुणमित्यनेन हा धिक् इदं मां मन्दभागिनीं व्याहृत्येत्यादिवाक्य-विवक्षितावस्था प्रतिपादिता। द्रवीभूतं प्रेम्णेत्यनेन उत्सुकयति उत्कण्ठितं स्थितमित्यादिवाक्यप्रतिपादितावस्थोक्ता॥ १३॥ **प्रसाद इति**। स्नेहा-र्द्रशीतलः स्नेहार्द्रश्चासौ शीतलश्चेति विग्रहः। स्नेहहेतुकत्वात् स्नेहार्द्रत्वम्॥ १४॥ प्रत्ययेन विश्वासेन। शल्यितोऽपि शल्यवान्कृतोऽपि। 'तदस्य संजा-

---

१ घटनोत्तम्भितम्. २ अद्याप्येवार्द्रयति. ३ कीलिसी मे हिअआवत्था (कीदृशी मे हृदयावस्था).

सीता—एते खलु तेऽगाधदर्शितस्नेहसंभारा आनन्दनिष्यन्दिनः सुधामया आर्यपुत्रस्योल्लापाः । येषां प्रत्ययेन निष्कारणपरित्यागशल्यितोऽपि बहुमतो मम जन्मलाभः । (क)

रामः—अथ वा कुतः प्रियतमा । नूनं संकल्पाभ्यासपाटवोपादान एष रामभद्रस्य भ्रमः ।

(नेपथ्ये ।)

अहो महान्प्रमादः प्रमादः । ('सीतादेव्याः स्वकरकलितैः' इत्यर्धं पठ्यते ।)

रामः—(सकरुणौत्सुक्यम् ।) किं तस्य ।

(पुनर्नेपथ्ये । 'वध्वा सार्धं' इत्युत्तरार्धं पठ्यते ।)

सीता—क इदानीमभियोक्ष्यते । (ख)

रामः—क्वासौ क्वासौ दुरात्मा यः प्रियायाः पुत्रकं वधूद्वितीयमभिभवति । (इत्युत्तिष्ठति ।)

(प्रविश्य संभ्रान्ता ।)

वासन्ती—कथं देवो रघुनन्दनः ।

सीता—कथं प्रियसखी मे वासन्ती । (ग)

वासन्ती—जयतु जयतु देवः ।

रामः—(निरूप्य ।) कथं देव्याः प्रियसखी वासन्ती ।

वासन्ती—देव त्वर्यतां त्वर्यताम् । इतो जटायुशिखरस्य दक्षिणेन सीतातीर्थेन गोदावरीमवतीर्य संभावयतु देव्याः पुत्रकं देवः ।

सीता—हा तात जटायो शून्य त्वया विनेदं जनस्थानम् । (घ)

(क) एदे क्खु ते अगाधदंसिदसिणेहसंभारा आणन्दणिस्सन्दिणो सुहामआ अज्जउत्तस्स उल्लावा । जाणं पच्चएण णिक्कालणपरिच्चाअसल्लिदोवि बहुमदो मह जम्मलाहो ।

(ख) को दाणिं अहिउज्जिस्सदि । (ग) कहं पिअसही मे वासन्ती ।

(घ) हा ताद जडाओ सुण्णं तुए विणा इदं जणट्ठाणम् ।

तम्' इति सूत्रेणेतच् ॥ **नूनमिति** । संकल्पाभ्यासस्य स्मृतिसंतानस्य पाटवं स्फूर्तिः तदेव उपादानं कारणं यस्य तथोक्तः भ्रमः । सीता पृष्टवतीत्याकारकान्यथाज्ञानम् ॥ **अहहेति** । हृदयमर्माणि छिन्दन्तीति विग्रहः । कथोद्घाताः

---

१ ०ल्पावभास; एष विभ्रमः. २ वोत्पादितः. ३ तस्य वत्सस्य. ४ आः क्वासौ दुरा०. ५ शिखरिंदक्षिणेन; जटायुगिरिशिखरस्य हस्तं-हस्त-दक्षिणेन. ६ अगाधमाणस (अगाधमानस). ७ सुदा मए (श्रुता मया). ८ अभिजुज्जइ (अभियुज्यते). ९ अज्ज (अद्य) सुण्णं.

रामः—अहह हृदयमर्मच्छिदः[1] खल्वमी कथोद्धाताः।

वासन्ती—इत इतो देवः।

सीता—भगवति सत्यमेव वनदेवता अपि मां न प्रेक्षन्ते। (क)

तमसा—अयि वत्से सर्वदेवताभ्यः प्रकृष्टमैश्वर्यं[2] मन्दाकिनी-देव्यास्तत्किमित्याशङ्कसे।

सीता—ततोऽनुसरावः। (इति परिक्रामति।) (ख)

रामः—भगवति गोदावरि नमस्ते।

वासन्ती—(निरूप्य।) देव मोदस्व विजयिना वधूद्वितीयेन दे-व्याः पुत्रकेण।

रामः—विजयतामायुष्मान्।

सीता—अहो ईदृशो मे पुत्रकः संवृत्तः। (ग)

रामः—हा देवि दिष्ट्या वर्धसे।

> **येनोद्गच्छद्बिसकिसलयस्निग्धदन्ताङ्कुरेण**
> **व्याकृष्टस्ते सुतनु लवलीपल्लवः कर्णमूलात्[3]।**
> **सोऽयं पुत्रस्तव मदमुचां वारणानां विजेता**
> **यत्कल्याणं वयसि तरुणे भाजनं तस्य जातः॥ १५॥**

सीता—अवियुक्त इदानीमयं दीर्घायुरनया सौम्यदर्शनया भवतु। (घ)

रामः—सखि वासन्ति पश्य पश्य कान्तानुवृत्तिचातुर्यमपि शि-क्षितं वत्सेन।

> **लीलोत्खातमृणालकाण्डकवलच्छेदेषु संपादिताः[4]**
> **पुष्यत्पुष्करवासितस्य[5] पयसो गण्डूषसंक्रान्तयः।**

(क) भअवदि सच्चं एव्व वणदेवदा वि मं ण पेक्खंन्दि[6]।

(ख) तदो अणुसरह्म। (ग) अह्मेहे ईदिसो[7] मे पुत्तओ संवुत्तो।

(घ) अविउत्तो दाणिं अअं दीहाऊ इमाए सोम्मदंसणाए होदु।

पुरावृत्तोपन्यासाः॥ **अयीति**। प्रकृष्टमुत्कृष्टम्। अत्र प्रस्तुतोत्कर्षाभिधानरूपोदा-हृतिरुक्ता॥ **येनेति**। तरुणे वयसि यत् कल्याणं अङ्गनापरिष्वङ्गरूपं मङ्गलं तस्य भाजनं पात्रं जातः॥ १५॥ **लीलेति**। लीलया उत्खाता उद्धृता मृणालकाण्डा एव कवला ग्रासाः तेषां छेदेषु अवसानेषु। पुष्यद्भिः वर्धमानैः पुष्करैः पद्मैः

---

१ मर्माविधः. २ प्रकृष्टतमं. ३ कर्णपूरात्. ४ संपातिताः. ५ पुष्यत्. ६ पेक्खदि (प्रेक्षते). ७ एदिसो एसो संवुत्तो.

सेकः शीकरिणा करेण विहितः कामं विरामे पुन-
र्यत्स्नेहादनरालनालनलिनीपत्रातपत्रं धृतम् ॥ १६ ॥

सीता—भगवति तमसे अयं तावदीदृशो जातः। तौ पुनर्न जानामि कुशलवावेतावता कालेन कीदृशौ संवृत्ताविति। (क)

तमसा—यादृशोऽयं तादृशौ तावपि।

सीता—ईदृश्यहं मन्दभागिनी यस्या न केवलं निरन्तरमार्यपुत्रविरहः पुत्रविरहोऽपि। (ख)

तमसा—भवितव्यतेयमीदृशी।

सीता—किं वा मया प्रसूतया येन तादृशमपि मम पुत्रकयोरीषद्विरलकोमलधवलदशनोज्ज्वलकपोलमनुबद्धमुग्धकाकलीविहसितं निबद्धकाकशिखण्डकममलमुखपुण्डरीकयुगलं न परिचुम्बितमार्यपुत्रेण। (ग)

तमसा—अस्तु देवताप्रसादात्।

सीता—भगवति तमसे एतेनापत्यसंस्मरणेनोच्छ्वसितप्रस्नुतस्तनी तयोश्च पितुः संनिधानेन क्षणमात्रं संसारिण्यस्मि संवृत्ता। (घ)

(क) भअवदि तमसे अयं दाव ईरिसो जादो। दे उण ण आणामि कुसलवा एत्तिएण कालेण कीरिसो[1] संवुत्तेत्ति। (ख) ईदिसी[2] अहं मन्दभाइणी जाए ण केवलं णिरन्तरं[3] अज्जउत्तविरहो पुत्तविरहो वि। (ग) किं वा मए पसूदाए जेण तादिसंपि मह पुत्तआणं[4] ईसिविरलकोमलधवलदसणुज्जलकपोलं[5] अणुबद्धमुद्धकाअलीविहसिदं णिबद्धकाकसिहण्डअं अमलमुहपुण्डरीअजुअलं[6] ण परिचुम्बिअं अज्जउत्तेण।

(घ) भअवदि तमसे एदिणा अवच्चसंसुमरणेण उस्ससिदपण्हुदत्थणी ताणं[7] अ पिदुणो संणिहाणेण खणमेत्तं संसारिणीह्मि संवुत्ता।

वासितस्य सुरभितस्य पयसः जलस्य गण्डूषसंक्रान्तयः पयःसंबन्धिगण्डूषसंक्रमणानि संपादिताः निर्व्यूढाः। अथ वा पुष्यति उपचयवति पुष्करे शुण्डाग्रे वासितस्य संजातवासस्य पयसः जलस्य गण्डूषसंक्रान्तयः। लीलोत्खातमृणालकाण्डरूपकवलच्छेदेषु कवलार्धखण्डेषु। अधिकरणे सप्तमी। संपादिताः निर्व्यूढाः। तत्र हि 'अच्छिद्राणि भूयांसि' इति भावः। अनरालं अवक्रम्॥१६॥ अनुबद्धमुग्धकाकलीविहसितमुत्पन्नसूक्ष्म-

---

१ कीदिसा विअ होन्ति (कीदृशाविव भवतः). २ ईरिसी ह्मि म० अहं. ३ ०न्तरो, णिःसहो. ४ तारिसाणं (तादृशयोः). ५ विरलधवलदसणकुम्हलुज्जलं (०दशनकुड्मलोज्ज्वलम्). ६ णिच्चुज्जलं (नित्योज्ज्वलं) मुहपुण्डरीअ०. ७ दाणिं वच्चाणं (इदानीं वत्सयोः).

तमसा—किमत्रोच्यते । प्रसवः खलु प्रकर्ष[1]पर्यन्तः स्नेहस्य । परं चैतदन्योन्यसंश्लेषणं पित्रोः ।

अन्तःकरणतत्त्वस्य दम्पत्योः स्नेहसंश्रयात् ।
आनन्दग्रन्थिरेकोऽयमपत्यमिति बध्यते[2] ॥ १७ ॥

वासन्ती—इतोऽपि देवः पश्यतु ।

अनुदिवस[3]मवर्धयत्प्रिया ते
  यमचिरनिर्गतमुग्धलोलबर्हम् ।
मणिमुकुट इवोच्छिखः कदम्बे
  नदति स एष वधूसखः शिखण्डी ॥ १८ ॥

सीता—(सकौतुक[4]स्नेहास्रम् ।) एष स एष सः । (क)

रामः—मोदस्व वत्स मोदस्व[5] ।

सीता—एवं भवतु । (ख)

भ्रमिषु कृतपुटान्तर्मण्डलावृत्ति[6]चक्षुः
  प्रचलितचटुल[7]भ्रूताण्डवैर्मण्डयन्त्या ।
करकिसलयतालैर्मुग्धया नर्त्यमानं
  सुतमिव मनसा त्वां वत्सलेन स्मरामि ॥ १९ ॥

(क) एसो सो एसो सो । (ख) एवं[8] होदु ।

मधुरास्फुटध्वनिमुग्धस्मितम् । देवताप्रसादाद्देवतानुग्रहात् । **प्रसव इति** । पर्यन्तः परा कोटिः । अन्योन्यसंश्लेषणं अविनाभावहेतुभूतम् । तदुभयमपीत्याह--**अन्तःकरणेति** । दम्पत्योः जायापत्योः अन्तःकरणतत्त्वस्य हृदयवस्तुनः स्नेहसंश्रयात् । स्नेहः प्रीतिः । संश्रयः संश्रयणम् । अविश्लेष इति यावत् । स्नेहश्च संश्रयश्चेति समाहारद्वन्द्वः । तस्मान्निमित्तादित्यर्थः । अन्नाद्धेतोर्वसतीत्यत्र अन्नफलको वास इति बोधः । तद्वदत्रापि स्नेहसंश्रयणफलकआनन्दग्रन्थिरिति । आनन्दग्रन्थिः आनन्दमयग्रन्थिः । आनन्दपदेन ग्रन्थ्यन्तरव्यावृत्तिः । अपत्यमिति पठ्यते परिभाष्यते॥ १७॥ **अनुदिवसमिति** । अचिरनिर्गतमुग्धलोलबर्हं प्रत्यग्रोत्पन्नसुन्दरचलत्पिच्छं यं अवर्धयत् स एष शिखण्डी वधूसखः सन् कदम्बे वृक्षे मणिमुकुट इव । आनुपूर्व्यात् पृथुकृशत्वात् नानावर्णत्वाच्च रत्नमयकिरीटसादृश्यम् । नदति केकां करोति ॥ १८ ॥ **भ्रमिष्विति** । मण्डलं यथा भवति तथा आवृत्तिः मण्डलावृत्तिः । पुटे अन्तः पुटान्तः । पुटान्तः मण्डलावृत्तिः पुटान्तर्मण्डलावृत्तिः । भ्रमिषु भ्रमणेषु । मयूरस्य मण्डलाकारनाट्यचारिष्विति यावत् । कृता रचिता पुटान्तर्मण्डलावृत्तिः ययोस्तथोक्ते चक्षुषी यैस्तथोक्तानि कृतपुटान्तर्मण्डलावृत्तिचक्षूंषि । प्रचलितयोः चटुलयोः सुन्दरयोः भ्रुवोः ताण्डवानि नर्तनानि । कृतपुटान्तर्मण्डलावृत्ति-

---

१ प्रकृष्ट. २ पठ्यते. ३ अतरुणमदताण्डवोत्सवान्तेष्वयमचिरोद्गतमुग्धलोलबर्हः. ४ सकौतुकास्त्रम्. ५ वयमद्य वर्धामहे. ६ वृत्त. ७ चतुर. ८ एव्वं होदु एव्वं होदु.

रामः हन्त तिर्यञ्चोऽपि परिचयमनुरुध्यन्ते ।

कतिपयकुसुमोद्गमः कदम्बः
प्रियतमया परिवर्धितोऽयमासीत् ।

सीता—(निरूप्य सास्रम् ।) सुष्ठु प्रत्यभिज्ञातमार्यपुत्रेण । (क)

रामः—

स्मरति गिरिमयूर एष देव्याः
स्वजन इवात्र यतः प्रमोदमेति ॥ २० ॥

वासन्ती—अत्र तावदासनपरिग्रहं करोतु देवः ।

(राम उपविशति ।)

वासन्ती—

एतत्तदेव कदलीवनमध्यवर्ति
कान्तासखस्य शयनीयशिलातलं ते ।
अत्र स्थिता तृणमदाद्बहुशो यदेभ्यः
सीता ततो हरिणकैर्न विमुच्यते स्म ॥ २१ ॥

रामः—इदं तावदशक्यमेव द्रष्टुम् । (इत्यन्यतो रुदन्नुपविशति ।)

सीता—सखि वासन्ति किं त्वया कृतमार्यपुत्रस्य मम चैतद्दर्शयन्त्या । हा धिक् हा धिक् । स एवार्यपुत्रस्तदेव पञ्चवटीवनं सैव प्रियसखी वासन्ती त एव विविधविस्रम्भसाक्षिणो गोदावरीकाननोद्देशास्त एव जातनिर्विशेषा मृगपक्षिपादपाः सैव चाहम् । मम पुनर्मन्द-

---

(क) सुट्ठु पच्चहिआणिदं अज्जउत्तेण ।

चक्षूंषि च प्रचलितचटुलभ्रूताण्डवानि चेति विग्रहः । तैः । तदुक्तं कनककविना—'किं चाधस्तादुपरि च नयन्त्यानतोन्निद्रपक्ष्मा चक्राकारं भ्रमयति मुहुर्विश्वमावर्तयन्ती' इति । करकिसलयतालैः करसंघट्टनजाततालध्वनिभिः । जातिभेदाभिप्रायकं बहुवचनम् । वत्सलेन सस्नेहेन ॥ १९ ॥ अनुरुध्यन्ते अनुसरन्ति । **कतिपय इति** । कतिपयकुसुमानामुद्गम उत्पत्तिः यस्मिन्निति विग्रहः । **स्मरतीति** । एष गिरिमयूरः गिरिप्रियो मयूरः गिरिमयूरः । शाकपार्थिववत्समासः । गिरेः प्रियत्वं उन्नतत्वनिरुपल्लवत्वादिना । अत्र अस्मिन् प्रियतमापरिवर्धितकदम्बवृक्षे स्वजन इव स्वबन्धुविषय इव यतः यस्मात्कारणात् प्रमोदं प्रीतिमेति प्राप्नोति । तस्मादेष देव्याः स्मरति । सीतां स्मरतीत्यर्थः ॥ २० ॥ [कदलीवनस्य मध्ये वर्तते इति] ॥ २१ ॥

---

१ य आसीत्. २ अस्मात्परं—'एतत्तु देवस्य–देव्याः–आश्रमपदम्' इत्यधिकम्. ३ नीरन्ध्रबाल. ४ अदाद्वनगोचरेभ्यः.

भाग्याया दृश्यमानमपि सर्वमेवैतन्नास्तीति तदीदृशो जीवलोकस्य परिवर्तः । (क)

वासन्ती—सखि सीते कथं न पश्यसि रामभद्रस्यावस्थाम् ।

नवकुवलयस्निग्धैरङ्गैर्ददन्नयनोत्सवं
सततमपि नः स्वेच्छादृश्यो नवो नव एव यः ।
विकलकरणः पाण्डुच्छायः शुचा परिदुर्बलः
कथमपि स इत्युन्नेतव्यस्तथापि दृशोः प्रियः ॥ २२ ॥

सीता—प्रेक्षे सखि प्रेक्षे । (ख)

तमसा—पश्यन्ती प्रियं भूयाः ।

सीता—हा दैव एष मया विनाऽहमप्येतेन विनेति स्वप्नेऽपि केन संभावितमासीत् । तन्मुहूर्तमात्रं जन्मान्तरादिव लब्धदर्शनं बाष्पसलिलान्तरेषु प्रेक्षे तावद्वत्सलमार्यपुत्रम् । (इति पश्यन्ती स्थिता ।) (ग)

तमसा—(परिष्वज्य सास्रम् ।)

विलुलितमतिपूरैर्बाष्पमानन्दशोक-
प्रभवमवसृजन्ती तृष्णयोत्तानदीर्घा ।

(क) सहि वासन्दि किं तुए किदं अज्जउत्तस्स मह अ एदं दंसअन्तीए । हद्धी हद्धी । सो एव्व अज्जउत्तो तं एव्व पञ्चवटीवणं सा एव्व पिअसही वासन्दी दे एव्व विविहविस्सम्भसक्खिणो गोदावरीकाणणुद्देसा दे एव्व जादणिव्विसेसा मिअपक्खिपाअवा सा ज्जेव्व चाइम् । मह उण मन्दभाइणीए दीसन्तं वि सव्वं एव्व एदं णत्थित्ति ता ईदिसो जीवलोअस्स परिवट्टो । (ख) पेक्खामि सहि पेक्खामि ।

(ग) हा देव्व एसो मए विणा अहंवि एदेण विणेत्ति सिविणेपि केण संभाविदं आसि । ता मुहुत्तमेत्तं जम्मन्तरादो विअ लद्धदंसणं बाहसलिलन्तरेषु पेक्खामि दाव वच्छलं अज्जउत्तम् ।

नवेति । विकलकरणः शून्यचक्षुरादिकरणः शुचा दुःखेन परिदुर्बलः स्वधारणेऽप्यसमर्थः । बलं हि धारणसामर्थ्यम् । उन्नेतव्यः अनुमेयः । तथापि दृशोः प्रियः । अनुपहतलावण्यकत्वादिति भावः ॥२२॥ **हा इति** । केन संभावितमासीत् । केन हेतुना संभावितं उत्पादितम् । त्वयेति शेषः । दुर्लभलब्धदर्शनं यदृच्छया लब्धदर्शनमिति व्याख्यातारः ॥ **विलुलितमिति** । 'विलुठितम्' इति पाठान्तरम् । अतिपूरैः अतिशयितस्रोतोभिः विलुलितं विकीर्णमानन्दशोकप्रभवमानन्दशोकहेतुकं बाष्पमश्रु अवसृ-

---

१ कुवलयदलस्निग्धैः; ददत्—ददौ. २ ते...नवं नवमेव. ३ सः. ४ पाण्डुः सोऽयम्. ५ कृशाम्. ६ पुत्रि पश्य०; पश्य प्रियं भूयः. ७ सतृष्णं पश्यति. ८ सस्नेहास्रं परिष्वज्य. ९ पक्ष्मलोत्तान. १० परिणामो संवुत्तो. ११ मुहुत्तअं (मुहूर्तकम्). १२ अणुलद्ध; दुल्लहलद्ध (दुर्लभलब्ध).

स्नपयति हृदयेशं स्नेहनिष्यन्दिनी ते
धवलबहलमुग्धा दुग्धकुल्येव दृष्टिः ॥ २३ ॥

वासन्ती—

दधतु तरवः पुष्पैरर्घ्यं फलैश्च मधुश्चुतः
स्फुटितकमलामोदप्रायाः प्रवान्तु वनानिलाः ।
कलमविरलं रज्यत्कण्ठाः क्वणन्तु शकुन्तयः
पुनरिदमयं देवो रामः स्वयं वनमागतः ॥ २४ ॥

रामः—एहि सखि वासन्ति नन्वितः स्थीयताम् ।

वासन्ती—(उपविश्य सास्रम् ।) महाराज अपि कुशलं कुमारलक्ष्मणस्य ।

रामः—(अश्रुतिमभिनीय ।)

करकमलवितीर्णैरम्बुनीवारशष्पै-
स्तरुशकुनिकुरङ्गान्मैथिली यानपुष्यत् ।
भवति मम विकारस्तेषु दृष्टेषु कोऽपि
द्रव इव हृदयस्य प्रस्तरोद्भेदयोग्यः ॥ २५ ॥

जन्ती उत्पादयन्ती । पक्ष्मला च सा उत्ताना च सा दीर्घा च इति विग्रहे विशेषणसमासः । उत्तानविपुला । स्नेहस्य अनुरागस्य निष्यन्दः यस्यामस्तीति विग्रहः । दुग्धकुल्येव सुधामयकृत्रिमाल्पसरिदिव स्नपयति स्नानं करोति । आदन्तत्वात् पुगागमे 'ग्लास्नावनुवमां च' इति वैकल्पिको ह्रस्वः ॥ २३ ॥ **दधत्विति** । मधूनि मकरन्दानि श्चोतयन्ति क्षरन्तीति विग्रहः । 'श्चुतिर् क्षरणे' इत्यस्मादन्तर्भावितण्यर्थात् कर्तरि क्विप्प्रत्ययः । यद्वा मधुभिः मकरन्दैः श्चयोतन्ति आर्द्रीकुर्वन्तीति विग्रहः । 'श्च्युतिर् आसेचने' इत्यस्मात् क्विप् । इदं च वनानिलानां विशेषणम् । तृतीयान्तपाठे फलविशेषणं पुष्पविशेषणं वा । 'च्यु च्यवने' इत्यस्मात् भावे क्तप्रत्यये मधूनां च्युतं च्यवनं येभ्य इति पुष्पपक्षे । फलपक्षे तु कर्मणि क्तप्रत्ययेन मधुभ्यः च्युतैरिति पञ्चमीतत्पुरुषः । पुष्परससमृद्धौ तात्पर्यम् । तदेवं पक्षत्रये—आद्यः शकारचकाराभ्यां युक्तः पाठः । द्वितीयः शकारचकारयकारैर्युक्तः । तृतीयस्तु चकारयकाराभ्यामिति विवेकः । रज्यत्कण्ठा रागयुक्तकण्ठाः । क्वणन्तु गीतवाद्यभेदेन शब्दं कुर्वन्तु । अत एव कूजन्त्विति नोक्तम् ॥ २४ ॥ अनाकर्णनं आकर्णनाभावम् । **करकमलेति** । करकमलवितीर्णैः करकमलदत्तैः अम्बुनीवारशष्पैः नीवारो धान्यविशेषः शष्पं बालतृणं

---

१ मधुर. २ अविकलम्. ३ रत्युत्कण्ठाः. ४ अनाकर्णनम्. ५ प्रस्रव; प्रश्रव.

वासन्ती—महाराज ननु पृच्छाम्यपि कुशलं कुमारलक्ष्मणस्येति ।

रामः—(आत्मगतम् ।) अये महाराजेति निष्प्रणयमामन्त्रणपदं सौमित्रिमात्रे च बाष्पस्खलिताक्षरः कुशल[1]प्रश्नः । तथा मन्ये विदित-सीतावृत्तान्तेयमिति । (प्रकाशम् ।) आं कुशलं कुमार[2]स्य ।

वासन्ती—(रुदती ।) अयि देव किं परं दारुण[3]ः खल्वसि ।

सीता—सखि वासन्ति किं त्वमेवंवादिनी भवसि । प्रियार्हः खलु सर्वस्यार्यपुत्रो विशेषतो मम प्रियसख्याः । (क)

वासन्ती—

त्वं जीवितं त्वमसि मे हृदयं द्वितीयं
त्वं कौमुदी नयनयोरमृतं त्वमङ्गे ।
इत्यादिभिः प्रियशतैरनुरुध्य मुग्धां
तामेव शान्तमथ वा किमिहो[4]त्तरेण ॥ २६ ॥

(इति मू[5]र्च्छति ।)

(क) सहि वासन्दि किं तु[6]मं एव्वंवादिणी होसि । पिआरु[7]हो क्खु सव्वस्स अज्जउत्तो विसेसदो मह पिअसहीए ।

तैः । अपुष्यत् अवर्धयत् । अत्राम्बुना तरून् अम्बुनीवाराभ्यां शकुनीन् अम्बुनीवारशष्पैः कुरङ्गानिति विवेकः । तेषु दृष्टेषु सत्सु प्रस्रवोद्भेदयोग्यः प्रसरणोत्पत्तियोग्यः द्रव इव कोऽपि विकारः मम हृदयस्य भवति उत्पद्यते ॥ २५ ॥ महाराजेत्यामन्त्रणपदं संबोधनशब्दः । आः इति सोपालम्भाङ्गी-कारे । **त्वमिति** । त्वं जीवितं प्राणाः । त्वं मे द्वितीयं हृदयमसि । त्वं नय-नयोः कौमुदी तद्वदानन्दिनी । ' कौ मोदन्ते जना यस्मात्तेनेयं कौमुदी मता । ' इति कौमुदीपदनिरुक्तेः । त्वमङ्गे विषये अमृतं पीयूषम् । तद्वज्जराप्रतिबन्धेन नित्ययौवनावहेत्यर्थः । अत्र प्राणाः प्राणा एव हृदयं हृदयमेव कौमुदी कौमुद्येव अमृतं अमृतमेव । त्वं तु प्राणा हृदयं कौमुद्यमृतमेतत् सर्वमिति प्राणाद्यपेक्षया वैलक्षण्यमपि सूच्यते । देवतायाः स्वरया अपि ज्ञातुं वक्तुं चा-शक्यत्वादाह—**इत्यादिभिरिति** । प्रियाणां प्रियवचनानां शतैः । अनन्तवाची शतशब्दः । ' शतं सहस्रमयुतं सर्वमानन्त्यवाचकम् ' इत्युक्तेः । मुग्धां अनुरुध्य । ' उदययौवना मुग्धा ' इति लक्षणलक्षितां सुन्दरीम् । त्वत्कौर्यमजानतीमिति वार्थः । अनुरुध्य अनुनीय । तामेव पूर्वोक्तानुनयविषयभूतामेवात्र कथं त्यक्तवानसि । नाशितवानसीति वा । वाक्यशेषस्य दुःखातिशयेन वक्तुमशक्यतया प्रकरणाद्यनुग्र-हेणार्थाध्याहारवादे विवक्षितार्थलाभासंभवात् शब्दाध्याहारवादे तस्य सुलभत्वात्

---

१ कुशलानुप्रश्नः. २ कुमारलक्ष्मणस्य; इति रोदिति इत्य०. ३ किमिति दारुणः, -दारुणो दारुणः. ४ किमतः परेण. ५ मूर्च्छति. ६ तुमं सि. ७ पूआरुहो (पूजार्हः).

तमसा[1]—स्थाने वाक्यनिवृत्तिर्मोहश्च ।

रामः—सखि समाश्वसिहि समाश्वसिहि ।

वासन्ती—(समाश्वस्य ।) तत्किमिदमकार्यमनुष्ठितं देवेन ।

सीता—सखि वासन्ति विरम विरम । (क)

रामः—लोको न मृष्यतीति ।

वासन्ती—कस्य[2] हेतोः ।

रामः—स एव जानाति किमपि ।

तमसा—चिरा[3]दुपालम्भः ।

वासन्ती—

अयि कठोर यशः किल ते प्रियं किमयशो ननु घोरमतः परम् ।
किमभवद्विपिने हरिणीदृशः कथय नाथ कथं बत मन्यसे ॥ २७ ॥

सीता—त्वमेव सखि वासन्ति दारुणा कठोरा च यैवमार्यपुत्रं प्रदीप्तं प्रदीपयसि । (ख)

तमसा—प्रणय एवं व्या[4]हरति शोकश्च ।

रामः—सखि किमत्र मन्तव्यम् ।

त्रस्तैकहायनकुरङ्गविलोलदृष्टे-
स्तस्याः परिस्फुरितगर्भभरालसायाः ।
ज्योत्स्नामयीव मृदुबालमृणालकल्पा
क्रव्याद्भिरङ्गलतिका नियतं विलुप्ता ॥ २८ ॥

सीता—आर्यपुत्र ध्रियये एषा ध्रियये । (ग)

रामः—हा प्रिये जानकि क्वासि ।

(क) सहि वासन्दि विरम विरम । (ख) तुमं एव्व सहि वासन्दि दारुणा कठोरा अ जा एव्वं अज्जउत्तं पलित्तं पदीवेसि ।

(ग) अज्जउत्त धरामि एसा धरामि ।

प्रयोगे हेतुभूततत्स्मरणेन मूर्च्छोत्पत्तेश्चाह—मुह्यतीति । अथ वेति पूर्वोक्ताक्षेपे शान्तम् । त्वामुपलभ्यालम् । अतः परेण किम् । अतिक्रान्तत्वादिति भावः ॥ ॥ २६ ॥ २७ ॥ **त्रस्तेति** । ज्योत्स्नामयीव ज्योत्स्नाविकृतिरिव स्थिता क्रव्याद्भिः विलुप्ता । नाशितेति भावः । नियतमिति संभावनायाम् । अत्र प्रकरणे

---

१ रामः. २ तत्कस्य. ३ उचितस्तदुपालम्भः. ४ व्याहारयति. ५ च. ६ मुग्ध, ७ प्रलुप्ता. ८ एव्वं विलपन्ती; एव्वं पलवन्तं पलावेसि (प्रलपन्तं प्रलापयसि).

सीता—हा धिक् हा धिक् । अन्य इवार्यपुत्रः प्रमुक्तकण्ठं रोदिति । (क)

तमसा—वत्से सांप्रतिकमेवैतत् । कर्तव्यानि खलु दुःखितैर्दुःखनिर्वापणानि ।

पूरोत्पीडे तटाकस्य परीवाहः प्रतिक्रिया ।
शोकक्षोभे च हृदयं प्रलापैरेव धार्यते ॥ २९ ॥

विशेषतो रामभद्रस्य यस्य बहुतरप्रकारकष्टो जीवलोकः ।

इदं विश्वं पाल्यं विधिवदभियुक्तेन मनसा
प्रियाशोको जीवं कुसुममिव घर्मो ग्लपयति ।
स्वयं कृत्वा त्यागं विलपनविनोदोऽप्यसुलभ-
स्तदद्याप्युच्छ्वासो भवति ननु लाभो हि रुदितम् ॥ ३० ॥

रामः—कष्टं भोः कष्टम् ।

दलति हृदयं गाढोद्वेगं द्विधा तु न भिद्यते
वहति विकलः कायो मोहं न मुञ्चति चेतनाम् ।
ज्वलयति तनूमन्तर्दाहः करोति न भस्मसा-
त्प्रहरति विधिर्मर्मच्छेदी न कृन्तति जीवितम् ॥ ३१ ॥

सीता—एवं न्विदम् । (ख)

(क) हद्धी हद्धी । अण्णो विअ अज्जउत्तो पमुक्ककण्ठं रोइदि ।
(ख) एवं ण्णेदं ।

उपायापायशङ्काभ्यां कार्यसंभवरूपप्राप्त्याशा प्रतिपादिता ॥ २८ ॥ अन्य इव पृथग्जन इव । **पूरोत्पीड इति** । पूरोत्पीडे स्रोतोभूयस्त्वे । परीवाहः जलनिःसारणम् । प्रतिक्रिया प्रतीकारः चिकित्सा । शोकक्षोभे शोकाधिक्यप्रयुक्तप्रकृतिविपर्यासे । प्रलापैः परिदेवनैः ॥ २९ ॥ बहुप्रकाराणि कष्टानि बहुविधानि दुःखानि यस्मिन् तथोक्तः । **इदमिति** । अभियुक्तेन तत्परेण । विधिवत् यथाशास्त्रम् । विलपनं चासौ विनोदश्चेति विग्रहः । उच्छ्वासः प्राणधारणम् ॥ ३० ॥ **दलतीति** । दलति स्फुटति । द्विधा न भिद्यते । पृथक्कारेण शकलद्वयं न भवतीत्यर्थः । न कृन्तति न छिनत्ति ॥ ३१ ॥ **न किलेति** । देव्याः सीतायाः गृहे स्थानं गृहस्थितिः न चाप्यनुशोचिता । तत्परित्यागहेतुकशोकोऽपि युष्माकं नेति भावः । भावाः अभिप्रायाः तथा द्रवयन्ति वाचामगोचरं यथा तथा विलापयन्ति । 'परिद्रवयन्ति' इत्यपि पाठः । रुद्यते रोदनं करोमि । भावे

---

१ सांप्रतं युक्तान्येवैतानि कर्तव्यानि यतो रोदनान्येष दुःखितस्य दुःखनिर्वापणानि भवन्ति. २ निर्धारणानि. ३ प्रलापैरव०. ४ ०भद्रस्य बहु०-; बहुम०. ५ क्रमयति. ६ गाढोद्वेगात्; शोकोद्वेगात्. ७ परुण्णो होदि (प्ररुदितो भवति).

रामः—हे भवन्तः पौरजानपदाः ।

न किल भवतां देव्याः स्थानं गृहेऽभिमतं तत-
स्तृणमिव वने शून्ये त्यक्ता न चाप्यनुशोचिता ।
चिरपरिचितास्ते ते भावाः परिद्रवयन्ति मा-
मिदमशरणैरद्यास्माभिः प्रसीदत रुद्यते ॥ ३२ ॥

वासन्ती—(स्वगतम् ।) अतिगम्भीरमापूरणं मन्युसंभारस्य । (प्रकाशम् ।) देव अतिक्रान्ते धैर्यमवलम्ब्यताम् ।

रामः—सखि किमुच्यते धैर्यमिति ।

देव्या शून्यस्य जगतो द्वादशः परिवत्सरः ।
प्रनष्टमिव नामापि न च रामो न जीवति ॥ ३३ ॥

सीता—मोहितास्म्येतैरार्यपुत्रवचनैः । (क)

तमसा—एवमेव वत्से ।

नैताः प्रियतमा वाचः स्नेहार्द्राः शोकदारुणाः ।
एतास्ता मधुनो धाराः श्चोतन्ति सविषास्त्वयि ॥ ३४ ॥

रामः—अयि वासन्ति मया खलु

यथा तिरश्चीनमलातशल्यं
प्रत्युप्तमन्तः सविषश्च दंशः ।
तथैव तीव्रो हृदि शोकशङ्कु-
र्मर्माणि कृन्तन्नपि किं न सोढः ॥ ३५ ॥

(क) मोहिदह्मि एदेहिं अज्जउत्तवअणेहिं ।

लट् । प्रसीदत प्रसादं कुरुत ॥३२॥ मन्युभारस्य कोपातिशयस्य आपूरणमाविष्करणम् । अतिगभीरमतिगूढम् । अवलम्ब्यतां आश्रीयताम् । त्वयेति शेषः ॥ **देव्या इति** । द्वादशानां पूरणः द्वादशः । 'तस्य पूरणे डट्' । परिवत्सरः संवत्सरः । रामः न जीवतीति न । जीवत्येवेत्यर्थः । जीवनाभावोऽन्याय्य इति व्यज्यते ॥ ३३ ॥ **नैता इति** । प्रियतमा इष्टतमाः स्नेहार्द्रा अनुरागशीतलाः शोकदारुणा दुःखेन रूक्षा एता वाचो न । किं तु एताः सविषा मधुनो धाराः श्चोतन्ति स्रवन्ति । अत्रापह्नुतिरलंकारः ॥ ३४ ॥ **यथेति** । तिरश्चीनं तिर्यग्भूतं प्रत्युप्तं निखातं अलातशल्यमुल्कामयं लोहकीलाग्रं सविषो दन्तश्च यथा तीव्रः तथैव तीव्रो मर्माणि हृदयादीनि कृन्तन् सन्नपि छिन्दन् सन्नपि हृदि शोकशङ्कुः दुःखात्मककीलं किं न सोढः न व्यसह्यत किम् । सहतेः कर्मणि क्तः ॥ ३५ ॥

---

१ वाप्य. २ स्त्वेते. ३ तथा; परिभ्रमयन्ति. ४ ०द्याप्येवं, किमिह शरणं नाद्याप्येवम्. ५ अवपूरणं शोकसागरस्य. ६ लुप्तं—न च—सीतेति नामापि. ७ दन्तः. ८ ओहरामि अ मोहिआ विअ…०उत्तस्स पिअवअणेहिं (अपहृिये च मोहितेव……पुत्रस्य प्रियवचनैः); सोहिदह्मि (शोभितास्मि).

सीता—एवमस्मि मन्दभागिनी पुनरप्यायासकारिण्यार्यपुत्रस्य । (क)

रामः—एवमतिनिष्कम्पस्तम्भितान्तःकरणस्यापि मम संस्तुततत्तत्प्रियवस्तुदर्शनादुद्दामोऽयमावेगः । तथा हि ।

वेलोल्लोलक्षुभितकरुणोज्जृम्भणस्तम्भनार्थं
यो यो यत्नः कथमपि मयाऽऽधीयते तं तमन्तः ।
भित्त्वा भित्त्वा प्रसरति बलात्कोऽपि चेतोविकार-
स्तोयस्येवाप्रतिहतरयः सैकतं सेतुमोघः ॥ ३६ ॥

सीता—एतेनार्यपुत्रस्य दुर्वारदारुणारम्भेण दुःखसंक्षोभेण परिमुषितनिजदुःखं किमपि प्रमुग्धं मे हृदयम् । (ख)

वासन्ती—(स्वगतम् ।) कष्टमभ्यापन्नो देवः । तदन्यतः क्षिपामि तावत् । (प्रकाशम् ।) चिरपरिचितानिदानीं जनस्थानभागानवलोकनेन मानयतु देवः ।

रामः—एवमस्तु । (इत्युत्थाय परिक्रामति ।)

(क) एव्वंह्मि मन्दभाइणी पुणोवि आआसआरिणी अज्जउत्तस्स ।

(ख) एदिणा अज्जउत्तस्स दुव्वारदारुणारम्भेण दुःखसंखोएण परिमुंसिअणिअदुक्खं किंपि पमुद्धं मे हिअअं ।

वेलेति । वेलाया मर्यादाया उल्लोलः उद्गतः । अतिवेल इत्यर्थः । क्षुभितः प्रवाहभूयस्तया नदीवत् क्षोभवांश्च यः करुणः प्रियजनविश्लेषजन्यदुःखातिशयः तस्य उज्जृम्भणमभिवृद्धिः तस्य स्तम्भनं प्रतिहतिः तदर्थम् । 'करणोज्जृम्भणस्तम्भनार्थम्' इति पाठे वेलोल्लोलं वेलातिक्रान्तं क्षुभितं क्षोभः यस्य तथोक्तस्य करणस्य । हृदयादेरित्यर्थः । कथमपि प्रयासेन समाधीयते उत्पाद्यते । चेतोविकारः संभ्रमातिशयः । ओघः दीर्घप्रवाहः ॥ ३६ ॥ **आर्यपुत्रस्येति** । दुर्वारो दुर्निवर्त्यः दारुणानां क्रूरमूर्च्छासंतापादीनामारम्भ उपादानं येनेति विग्रहः । परिमुषितं निजदुःखं स्वीयदुःखं यस्येति तथोक्तम् । स्फुटति दलति । आक्षिपामि । अन्यत्र नयामीत्यर्थः । **संदीपन इति** । विनोदनोपायः चिरपरिचितजनस्थानाभोगावलोकनरूपः दुःखस्य संदीपन एव

---

१ विष्कम्भ, गूढ०. २ संस्तुतप्रिय०; संस्तुतबहुनरप्रियदर्शनात्. ३ अयायमावेगः. ४ वेलो०, हेलो०. ५ करणो०. ६ समाधीयते. ७ अन्यासक्त:. ८ ०तानामिदानीं जनस्थानभागानामवलोकनेनात्मानमानन्दयतु देवः; चिरपरिचितानिताञ्जनस्थानभागानवलोकयतु देवः. ९ एव्वंवि ... अहं जा पुणोवि. १० पप्फुरिदणिअदुक्खं विअ आकंपिदं (प्रस्फुरितनिजदुःखमिवाकम्पितं); विअ वेवदि मे हि०; ०दुक्खं पमुक्कजीविअं मे हिअअं फुट्टइ (प्रमुक्तजीवितं मे हृदयं स्फुटति).

सीता—संदीपन एव दुःखस्य प्रियसख्या विनोदनोपाय इति तर्कयामि । (क)

वासन्ती—(सकरुणम् ।) देव देव

अस्मिन्नेव लतागृहे त्वमभवस्तन्मार्गदत्तेक्षणः
सा हंसैः कृतकौतुका चिरमभूद्गोदावरीसैकते ।
आयान्त्या परिदुर्मनायितमिव त्वां वीक्ष्य बद्धस्तया
कातर्यादरविन्दकुड्मलनिभो मुग्धः प्रणामाञ्जलिः ॥ ३७ ॥

सीता—दारुणासि वासन्ति दारुणासि यैतैर्हृदयमर्मगूढशल्यसंघट्टनैः पुनः पुनरपि मां मन्दभागिनीमार्यपुत्रं च संतापयासि । (ख)

रामः—अयि चण्डि जानकि इतस्ततो दृश्यस इवं न चानुकम्पसे ।

(क) संदीवैंण एव्व दुःखस्स पिअसहीए विणोदणोवाओ त्ति तक्केमि ।

(ख) दालुणासि वाँसन्ति दालुणासि जा एदेहिं हिअअमम्मगूढसल्लसंघट्टेनेहिं पुणो पुणोवि मं मन्दभाइणिं अज्जउत्तं अ संदाँवेसि ।

उद्दीपनहेतुरेवेति तर्कयामि जानामि ॥ **अस्मिन्निति** । अस्मिन्नेव लतागृहे त्वं अभवः स्थितवान् । तन्मार्गे सीताया आगमनमार्गे दत्तं ईक्षणं नेत्रं येन तथोक्तः । हंसैः कृतमुत्पादितं कौतुकं हर्षः यस्यास्तथोक्ता । गोदावरीसैकते पुलिनोच्चये । आयान्त्या आगच्छन्त्या तया सीतया परिदुर्मनायितमिव परिकुपितमनस्कमिव स्थितम् । न तु वस्तुतः कुपितहृदयामित्यर्थः । त्वां वीक्ष्य कातर्यात् अपराधप्रतिसंधानजनितसाध्वसात् अरविन्दकुड्मलनिभः पद्मकोशसदृशो मुग्धः सुन्दरः प्रणामाञ्जलिः । मस्तकन्यस्तकरसंपुटादिप्रणामाङ्गभूताञ्जलिरित्यर्थः । अथ वा 'नामयत्यपि वा देवं प्रह्वीभावयति ध्रुवम् । प्रह्वीभवति नीचे हि परो नैच्यं विलोकयन् ॥ अतो वा नमउक्तीदं यत्तं नामयति स्वयम् । वाचा नम इति प्रोच्य वपुषा मनसा च यत् ॥' इति भगवच्छास्त्रोक्तरीत्या प्रणामः । कोपोद्धतरामहृदयनमनहेतुभूतोऽञ्जलिरित्यर्थः । उक्तं च—'अञ्जलिः परमा मुद्रा क्षिप्रं देवप्रसादिनी' इति । अत एव रामायणे—'कृतापराधस्य हि ते नान्यत्पश्याम्यहं क्षमम् । अन्तरेणाञ्जलिं बद्धा लक्ष्मणस्य प्रसादनात् ॥ ' इति । बद्धः घटितः ॥ ३७ ॥ **दारुणेति** । हृदयमर्मोद्धाटितशल्यस्य हृदयमर्मणि स्थितकीलाग्रस्य संघट्टनैः संचलनैरेतैः पुरावृत्तान्तकथनैरार्यपुत्रं मां च स्मरयसि । मद्विषयकस्मृतिमार्यपुत्रस्य जनयसीत्यर्थः । या स्मरयसि सा त्वं दारुणेति पूर्वेणान्वयः । चण्डि कठिने जानकि जनकपुत्रि नानुकम्पसे दयां न करोषि ।

---

१ स्थिर. २ एतन्नास्ति क्वचित्. ३ संदीवणाइं...पिअसही पिणोदणोवाओ त्ति मण्णदि (संदीपनानि...प्रियसखी विनोदनोपाय इति मन्यते). ४ सहि वासन्ति. ५ मम्मुग्घाडिअसल्ल (मर्मोद्धाटितशल्य). ६ सुमरावेसि (स्मरयसि), सल्लसरिसेहिं...अजज्उत्तं वि दुणावेसि (शल्यसदृशैः...आर्यपुत्रमपि दुनोषि).

हा हा देवि स्फुटति हृदयं ध्वंसते देहबन्धः
शून्यं मन्ये जगदविरतज्वालमन्तर्ज्वलामि ।
सीदन्नन्धे तमसि विधुरो मज्जतीवान्तरात्मा
विष्वङ्मोहः स्थगयति कथं मन्दभाग्यः करोमि ॥ ३८ ॥

(इति मूर्च्छति ।)

सीता—हा धिक् हा धिक् पुनरपि प्रमूढ आर्यपुत्रः । (क)

वासन्ती—देव समाश्वसिहि समाश्वसिहि ।

सीता—आर्यपुत्र मां मन्दभागिनीमुद्दिश्य सकलजीवलोकमङ्गलाधारस्य ते वारं वारं संशयितजीवितदारुणो दशापरिणाम इति हा हतास्मि । (इति मूर्च्छति ।) (ख)

तमसा—वत्से समाश्वसिहि समाश्वसिहि । पुनस्त्वत्पाणिस्पर्श एव संजीवनोपायो रामभद्रस्य ।

वासन्ती—कथमद्यापि नोच्छ्वसिति । हा प्रियसखि सीते क्वासि संभावयात्मनो जीवितेश्वरम् ।

(सीता ससंभ्रममुपसृत्य हृदि ललाटे च स्पृशति ।)

वासन्ती—दिष्ट्या प्रत्यापन्नचेतनो रामभद्रः ।

(क) हद्धी हद्धी पुणोवि पमूढो अज्जउत्तो ।

(ख) अज्जउत्त मं मन्दभाइणिं उद्दिसिअ सअलजीवलोअमङ्गलाधारस्स दे वारं वारं संसइदजीविअदालुणो दसापरिणामो त्ति हा हदह्मि ।

जानकीत्युक्त्या परमदयालुजनकराजपुत्र्यास्तवेदं निर्दयत्वं नोचितमिति व्यज्यते । **हाहेति** । हाहाशब्दो दुःखातिशयद्योतकः । हृदयं स्फुटति दलति । देहबन्धः शरीरावयवानां संधिः । जातावेकत्वम् । ध्वंसते विशीर्णो भवति । जगत् लोकं शून्यं असत्कल्पम् । अभावप्रतियोगीति यावत् । मन्ये जानामि । अविरला अविच्छिन्ना ज्वाला यस्मिन् कर्मणि तत्तथोक्तम् । अन्तः शरीरान्तः ज्वलामि । काष्ठवत् ज्वलामीति यावत् । विधुरः ज्ञानादिशून्यः सीदन् विशीर्णीभवन् अन्तरात्मा अन्धे अन्धयति लोकानित्यन्धं तस्मिन् तमसि मज्जति अवगाढो भवति । मोहो मूर्च्छा विष्वक् परितः स्थगयति संछादयति । कथं करोमि किं करोमि । हृदयस्फोटादि निवारयामि उत त्वदागमनार्थं लोकाननुनयामि अथ वा तान्निगृह्य त्वामानेष्यामि वेति भावः ॥ ३८ ॥ पुनरपि मूढो मूर्छितः । वारं वारं पदे पदे संशयितजीवितः संशयितं संशयविषयं जीवितं यस्मिंस्तथोक्तः । मरणपर्यवसायीति भावः । अत एव दारुणः क्रूरः दशापरिणामः दशापरिपाकः । **हा प्रियसखीति** । जीवितेश्वरं प्राणनाथं रामं संभावय संभावितं कुरु । रामासंभवं परिहरस्वेत्यर्थः ।

---

१ स्रंसते. २ अविरल, अविरम. ३ ते पाणि. ४ °लोअमङ्गलिअजम्मलाहस्स (मङ्गल्य–माङ्गलिक–जन्मलाभस्य); °लाधारजम्मलाहस्स.

रामः—

आलिम्पन्नमृतमयैरिव प्रलेपै-
रन्तर्वा बहिरपि वा शरीरधातून्।
संस्पर्शः पुनरपि जीवयन्नकस्मा-
दानन्दादपरविधं तनोति मोहम्॥ ३९॥

(आनन्दनिमीलिताक्ष एव।) सखि वासन्ति दिष्ट्या वर्धसे।

वासन्ती—देव कथमिव।

रामः—सखि किमन्यत्। पुनः प्राप्ता जानकी।

वासन्ती—अयि देव रामभद्र क सा।

रामः—(स्पर्शसुखमभिनीय।) पश्य नन्वियं पुरत एव।

वासन्ती—अयि देव किमिति मर्मच्छेददारुणैरेभिः प्रलापैः प्रियसखीदुःखदग्धामपि मां पुनर्मन्दभाग्यां दहसि।

सीता—अपसर्तुमिच्छामि। एष पुनश्चिरसद्भावसौम्यशीतलेना-

हृदि ललाटे च स्पृशति। इदं च लोकेऽनुभवसिद्धम्। **दिष्ट्येति**। दिष्ट्येत्यानन्दे। प्रत्यापन्ना पुनरागता चेतना प्रज्ञा यस्य स तथोक्तः। **आलिम्पन्निति**। अमृतमयैः अमृतस्वरूपैः। चिन्मयमित्यादाविव स्वार्थिको मयट् प्रत्ययः। प्रकृष्टो लेपः यैस्ते। लेपसाधनद्रव्यैः अन्तर्वा बहिरपि वा अन्तर्बहिश्च शरीरं धातूंश्च। नाडीश्च अन्तर्नाडीः बहिः शरीरमिति विवेकः। आलिम्पन्निव। सर्वाङ्गीणलेपनकर्तेति संभावनीयः। जीवयन् प्राणप्रतिष्ठाहेतुभूतः अकस्मात् निर्हेतुकः संस्पर्शः पुनरपि आनन्दात् आनन्दमुत्पाद्यापरं मोहं दुःखहेतुकपूर्वमूर्छातिरिक्तमूर्छाम्। आनन्दादिति ल्यब्लोपे पञ्चमी। यद्वा आनन्दादिति हेतौ पञ्चमी। तथा च दुःखजन्यपूर्वमूर्छातिरिक्ताम्। आनन्दहेतुकां मूर्छामादधातीव उत्पादयतीव। अन्ये तु परो न भवतीत्यपरः। अनन्य इत्यर्थः। आनन्दादपरं मोहं आनन्दात्मकमूर्छामित्याहुः॥ ३९॥ सानन्दमुन्मीलिताक्ष एव उन्मीलिते त्यक्तमुकुलीभावे अक्षिणी यस्य तथोक्तः। अत्र हृदि ललाटे चेत्यादिना इष्टार्थोपायानुसरणात्मकाक्षेप उक्तः। **अयीति**। मर्मच्छेदवत् हृदयावयवक्षतिवत् दारुणैः दुःसहैः प्रलापैः अनर्थकवचोभिः दहसीत्यत्रान्वयः। प्रियसख्याः सीतायाः विपत्त्या विपदा यद्दुःखं तेन दग्धां भस्मीक्रियमाणाम्। **अपसर्तुमिति**। चिरस्य बहुकालरूढस्य प्रणयस्य स्नेहस्य भारेण

१ ०दपरमिवादधाति. २ सानन्दमुन्मीलिताक्षः (टी०). ३ पुनरपि. ४ देव रामभद्र. ५ अनिमलापैः. ६ विपत्तिदुःख (टी०). ७ पुनः पुनः; पुनर्मन्दभागिनीं दहसि माम्.

र्यपुत्रस्पर्शेन दीर्घदारुणमपि झटिति संतापं हरता वज्रलेपोपनिबद्ध इव स्विद्यन्निःसहविपर्यस्तो वेपनशीलोऽवश इव मे हस्तः । (क)

रामः—सखि कुतः प्रलापाः ।

गृहीतो यः पूर्वं परिणयविधौ कंकणधर-
श्चिरं स्वेच्छास्पर्शैरमृतशिशिरैर्यः परिचितः ।

सीता—आर्यपुत्र स एवेदानीमसि त्वम् । (ख)

रामः—

स एवायं तस्यास्तुहिनकिरौपम्यसुभगो
मया लब्धः पाणिर्ललितलवलीकन्दलनिभः ॥ ४० ॥

(इति गृह्णाति ।)

सीता—हा धिक् हा धिक् । आर्यपुत्रस्पर्शमोहितायाः प्रमादः खलु मे संवृत्तः । (ग)

(क) ओसरिदुं इच्छम्मि । एसो उण चिरसंभावसोम्मसीअलेण अज्जउत्तप्फरिसेण दीहदारुणंवि झत्ति संदावं हरन्तेण वज्जलेवोवणिवद्धो विअ सिज्जन्तणीसहविपल्हत्थो वेअणसीलो अवसो विअ मे हत्थो । (ख) अज्जउत्त सो एव्व दाणिं सि तुमम् । (ग) हद्धी हद्धी । अज्जउत्तप्फरिसमोहिदाए पमादो क्खु मे संवुत्तो ।

अतिशयेन हेतुना सौम्यः आह्लादकरः शीतलः शीतश्च तथाविधेन । दीर्घश्चासौ दारुणश्चेति विग्रहः । खञ्जकुब्जादिवत् समासः । तथाविधं संतापं झटिति उल्लाघयता लघूकुर्वता आर्यपुत्रस्पर्शेन वज्रलेपेन उपनद्ध इव घटित इव पर्यस्तव्यापारः । निष्पन्द इत्यर्थः । मे अग्रहस्तः आसाञ्जित इव लग्न इव । प्रलापैरिति वासन्तीवाक्यस्योत्तरमाह—'सखि कुतः प्रलापाः' इति ॥ **गृहीत इति** । यः करः परिणयविधौ विवाहविधौ कंकणधरः गृहीतः यः करः सुधाया अमृतस्य सूतिरुत्पत्तिः यस्मात्तस्य चन्द्रस्य अमृतशिशिरैः सुधाशीतलैः पादैः किरणैः परिचितः संश्लिष्टः । उक्तविशेषणसाम्यादाह—आर्यपुत्र स एवेदानीं त्वमसि इति । यः करः कंकणधरो गृहीतः यः सुधासूतेः पादैः परिचितः स एव त्वमिदानीमित्यर्थः । उभयत्रापि परिणयविधौ कंकणधरत्वं लावण्यसंश्लिष्टत्वरूपसुधासूतिकिरणपरिचितत्वं चावशिष्टमिति कृत्वा सीतावाक्यं प्रवृत्तम् । राम आह—स एवायमिति । ललितेन सुकुमारेण लवलीकन्दलेन लवलीनामकलताङ्कुरेण निभः सदृशः तदितरकरेण गृहीतान्यकरेण औपम्येन सादृश्येन सुभगः मनोज्ञः । सव्यकरसादृश्यं दक्षिणकरस्य तथा दक्षिणकरसादृश्यं सव्यकरस्येति भावः । तस्याः स एव पाणिः मया लब्धः ॥ ४० ॥

---

१ सुधासूतेः पादैः (टी०). २ तुहिनकरकौपम्य; तदितरकरौ०. ३ चिरप्पणअस्सभाव... वोवणद्धो प्पणअसंभार (प्रणयसंभार). ४ संदावं उल्लाहअन्तेण वज्जलेहोवणद्धो विअ परिअद्धवावारो आसंजिओ विअ मे अग्गहत्थो (संतापमुल्लाघयता वज्रलेपोपनद्ध इव पर्यस्तव्यापार आसञ्जित इव मेऽग्रहस्तः).

रामः—सखि वासन्ति आनन्दनिमीलितेन्द्रियः साध्वसेन परवानस्मि । तत्त्वं तावदेनां धारय ।

वासन्ती—कष्टमुन्माद एव ।

(सीता ससंभ्रमं हस्तमाक्षिप्यापसर्पति ।)

रामः—हा धिक् प्रमादः ।

करपल्लवः स तस्याः सहसैव जडो जडात्परिभ्रष्टः ।
परिकम्पिनः प्रकम्पी करान्मम स्विद्यतः स्विद्यन् ॥ ४१ ॥

सीता—हा धिक् हा धिक् । अद्याप्यनवस्थितास्तिमितमूढघूर्णन्नयमो न पर्यवस्थापयत्यात्मानम् । (क)

तमसा—(सस्नेहकौतुकस्मितं निर्वर्ण्य ।)

सस्वेदरोमाञ्चितकम्पिताङ्गी जाता प्रियस्पर्शसुखेन वत्सा ।
मरुन्नवाम्भःप्रविधूतसिक्ता कदम्बयष्टिः स्फुटकोरकेव ॥ ४२ ॥

सीता—(स्वगतम् ।) अम्हहे अवशेनैतेनात्मना लज्जापितास्मि भगवत्या तमसया । किमिति किलैषा मंस्यत एष ते परित्याग एषोऽभिषङ्ग इति । (ख)

रामः—(सर्वतोऽवलोक्य ।) हा कथं नास्त्येव । नन्वकरुणे वैदेहि ।

(क) हद्धी हद्धी । अज्जवि अणवत्थिदत्थिमिदमूढघुण्णन्तणअणो ण पज्जवत्थावेदि अत्ताणअं । (ख) अम्हहे अवसेनं एदेण अत्ताणएण लज्जाविदह्मि भअवदीए तमसाए । किंत्ति किल एसा मण्णिस्सदि एसो दे परिच्चाओ एसो अहिसङ्गोत्ति ।

गृह्णाति ग्रहणमभिनयति । प्रमादः अनवधानम् । प्रियास्पर्शसाध्वसेन प्रियायाः सीतायाः स्पर्शेन यत् साध्वसं शृङ्गारजं भयं तेन परवान् परवशः । उन्मादः चित्तविभ्रमः । हस्तमाक्षिप्य रामहस्तं निरस्य ॥ **करपल्लव इति** । प्रकम्पी चञ्चलः स्विद्यन् स्वेदवान् तस्याः स करपल्लवः परिकम्पिनः चञ्चलात् [स्विद्यतः] जडात् मम करात् अनवधानतो जडात्मनो मम करात् सहसा परिभ्रष्टः परिच्युतोऽभवत् ॥ ४१ ॥ अनुबद्धा उत्पन्ना बह्वी घूर्णमाना उद्गच्छन्ती वेदना यस्य तमात्मानं न संस्थापयामि न स्थिरं करोमि । [**सस्वेदेति** । वत्सा प्रियस्पर्शसुखेन सस्वेदानि च रोमाञ्चितानि संजातपुलकानि च कम्पितानि च अङ्गानि यस्याः सा तथोक्ता जाता । केव । मरुता नवाम्भसा प्रविधूता चासौ सिक्ता च तादृशी । स्फुटकोरका कदम्बयष्टिरिव । उपमालंकारः ।] ॥ ४२ ॥ कथं नास्त्येवेति व्यक्तम् । स्फुटमित्यर्थः । कथमन्यथा वासन्ती न पश्येत् । अन्यथा सीताया अस्तित्वे वासन्ती कथं कस्माद्धेतोः न पश्येत् । स्वस्य भ्रान्तिशङ्कया

---

१ आनन्दमीलितः प्रियास्पर्शसा०. २ तत्त्वमपि धारयेमाम्. ३ जडात्मनः. ४ सस्नेहहासकौतुकं; सस्नेहम्. ५ स्पर्शवशेन बाला. ६ अणुबद्धबहुअघुम्मन्तवेअणं ण संठावेमि (अनुबद्धबहुघूर्णमानवेदनं न संस्थापयामि). ७ अवसं गएण (अवशं गतेन).

सीता—सत्यमकरुणाऽस्मि यैवंविधं त्वां प्रेक्षमाणा जीवाम्येव । (क)

रामः—क्वासि देवि प्रसीद । न मामेवंविधं परित्यक्तुमर्हसि ।

सीता—अयि आर्यपुत्र विपरीतमिवैतत् । (ख)

वासन्ती—देव प्रसीद प्रसीद । स्वेनैव लोकोत्तरेण धैर्येण संस्तम्भयातिभूमिगतंविप्रलम्भमात्मानम् । कुतोऽत्र मे प्रियसखी ।

रामः—व्यक्तं नास्त्येव । कथमन्यथा वासन्त्यपि तां न पश्येत् । अपि खलु स्वप्न एष स्यात् । न चास्मि सुप्तः । कुतो रामस्य निद्रा । सर्वथा स एवैष भगवाननेकवारपरिकल्पनानिर्मितो विप्रलम्भः पुनः पुनरनुबध्नाति माम् ।

सीता—मयैव दारुणया विप्रलब्ध आर्यपुत्रः । (ग)

वासन्ती—देव पश्य पश्य ।

(क) सच्चं अकरुणह्मि जा एव्वंविहं तुमं पेक्खन्दी जीवेमि एव ।

(ख) अयि अज्जउत्त विवरीदं विअ एदम् ।

(ग) मए एव्व दारुणाए विप्पलद्धो अज्जउत्तो ।

वनदेवतायाः प्रमितिप्रकर्षं विभाव्य वासन्तीत्युक्तम् । एवं योग्यानुपलम्भेन सीताया नास्तित्वं निश्चित्य पूर्वोक्तस्पर्शनस्य भ्रमरूपत्वं मीमांसते । अपि खलु स्वप्न एष स्यात् । एष सीतास्पर्शः स्वप्नः स्यात् । स्वाप्निकज्ञानविषयः स्यादिति संभावनां । यद्वा एष सीतास्पर्शः स्वप्नः स्यात्स्वप्नावस्थोत्पादितः किमु । स्वप्नावस्थायां हि 'संध्ये सृष्टिराह हि' इति सूत्रप्रामाण्यात् तत्पुरुषानुभाव्यतत्तत्पदार्थसृष्टिः परमात्मकर्तृकाभ्युपगम्यते । विस्तरस्तूत्तरमीमांसायां द्रष्टव्यः । स्वप्नं प्रति सुप्तेः कारणत्वादाह—न चास्मि सुप्त इति । तदुपपादयति—कुतो रामस्य निद्रेति । 'अनिद्रः सततं रामः' इति सीतावियोगे रामस्य निद्रा नास्तीति प्रसिद्धमेवेति ननूपपत्तिरिति भावः । पर्यवसितमाह—सर्वथेत्यादिना । मम वासन्त्याश्चानुपलम्भान्निद्राया अभावेन स्वाप्नानुपपत्तेश्च सर्वप्रकारेणापि सीतास्पर्शनं भ्रमरूपमिति भावः । विप्रलम्भः भ्रमः । भगवानित्यनतिलङ्घनीयत्वप्रयुक्तपूज्यताख्यापनार्थम् । अनुबध्नात्यनुसरति । दारुणया

---

१ क्वासि प्रिये । देवि प्रसीद. २ अतिभूमिं गतमात्मा०. ३ प्रिय० मे सीता. ४ निद्रा स्यात्; अथ वा कुतो रामस्य स्वप्नः. ५ परिकल्पित; ०ल्पितनिर्माता. ६ णं, धरामि एव्व जीविदं (ननु, धराम्येव जीवितम्). ७ विप्पदीवं विअ (विप्रतीपमिव).

पौलस्त्यस्य जटायुषा विघटितः कार्ष्णायसोऽयं रथ-
स्ते चैते पुरतः पिशाचवदनाः कङ्कालशेषाः खराः ।
खड्गच्छिन्नजटायुपक्षतिरितः सीतां चलन्तीं वह-
न्नन्तर्व्याकुलविद्युदम्बुद इव द्यामभ्युदस्थादरिः ॥ ४३ ॥

सीता—(सभयम् ।) आर्यपुत्र तातो व्यापाद्यतेऽहमप्यपाह्रिये । तस्मात्परित्रायस्व परित्रायस्व । (क)

रामः—(सवेगमुत्थाय ।) आः पाप तातप्राणसीतापहारिन् क्व यासि ।

वासन्ती—अयि देव राक्षसकुलप्रलयधूमकेतो किमद्यापि ते मन्युविषयः ।

सीता—अहो अहमप्युद्भ्रान्तास्मि । (ख)

रामः—अन्य एवायमधुना विपर्ययो वर्तते ।

उपायानां भावादविरतविनोदव्यतिकरै-
र्विमर्दैर्वीराणां जगति जनितात्यद्भुतरसः ।
वियोगो मुग्धाक्ष्याः स खलु रिपुघातावधिरभू-
त्कथं तूष्णीं सह्यो निरवधिरयं त्वप्रतिविधः ॥ ४४ ॥

(क) अज्जउत्त तादो वावादीअदि अहं वि अवहरिज्जामि । ता परित्ताहि परित्ताहि ।

(ख) अह्मो अहंवि उब्भत्तह्मि ।

कठिनया । विप्रलब्धः वञ्चितः । भ्रान्त इति वा ॥ **पौलस्त्यस्येति** । अयं दृश्यमानः । उद्देश्यसमर्पकमिदम् । कृष्णायसविकारः कार्ष्णायसः । लोहमय इत्यर्थः । जटायुषा विघटितः प्रध्वंसितः । पौलस्त्यस्य रावणस्य रथः स्यन्दनम् । विधेयसमर्पकमिदम् । एते पुरतः पुरोवर्तमानाः कङ्कालशेषाः शरीरास्थिरूपशिष्टांशाः । ते पिशाचवदनाः खरा रावणस्यन्दनीयाः पिशाचमुखा रासभाः । खड्गेन छिन्ना कृत्ता च सा जटायुपक्षतिश्चेति समानाधिकरणसमासः । इतः अत्र पक्षतिः पक्षमूलम् । अन्तर्व्यापृता अन्तश्चलन्ती विद्युत्तडिद्यस्य तथोक्तः । अनेन दृष्टान्तेन रावणस्पर्शवशाद्दोषो नास्तीति सूचितम् । अरिः रावणः । द्यां खमभ्युदस्थादभ्युद्गतवान् । इत इत्यस्माद्देशादिति वा ॥ ४३ ॥ आः **पापेत्यादि** । अत्र रोषसंभ्रमवचनरूपं तोटकं नाम संध्यङ्गमुक्तम् । प्रलयधूमकेतो प्रलयसूचकधूमकेतुनामकग्रहसदृशेति भावसंबुद्धिः । यद्वा राक्षसकुलस्य प्रलये धूमकेतुरग्निः । राक्षसकुलदाहे प्रलयाग्निसदृशेत्यर्थः । मन्युविषयः क्रोधविषयः । अन्य एव पूर्वसीतावियोगाद्विलक्षण एव विपर्ययः सीतावियोगरूपविपर्यासः । वैलक्ष्ण्यमेवाह—**उपायाना-**

---

१ पर्यंत. २ ज्वलन्तीम्. ३ व्यापृत. ४ ०हारिन् लङ्कापत. ५ यास्यसि; यासि तिष्ठ तिष्ठ. ६ अद्यापि. ७ अन्वर्थ एवायमधुना प्रलापो वर्तते. ८ अविरल. ९ व्यतिकरः. १० जनितजगदत्यद्भुतरसः ११ कटुः. १२ रयं तु प्रविलयः-प्रविरहः; रिदानीं तु विरहः. १३ उम्मत्तिअह्मि संवुत्ता (उन्मत्तास्मि संवृत्ता).

सीता—निरवधिरिति हा हतास्मि मन्दभागिनी । (क)

रामः—हा कष्टम्[1] ।

व्यर्थं यत्र कपीन्द्रसख्यमपि मे वीर्यं हरीणां वृथा
प्रज्ञा जाम्बवतोऽपि[2] यत्र न गतिः पुत्रस्य वायोरपि ।
मार्गं यत्र न विश्वकर्मतनयः कर्तुं नलोऽपि क्षमः
सौमित्रेरपि पत्रिणामविषये[3] तत्र प्रिये क्वासि मे[4] ॥ ४५ ॥

सीता—बहुमानितास्मि तं पूर्वविरहम् । (ख)

(क) णिरवधित्ति[5] हा हदह्मि मन्दभाइणी[6] ।

(ख) बहुमणाविदह्मि[7] तं पुव्वविरहं ।

मिति । उपायानां सेनासंनाहसेतुबन्धादिसाधनानां भावात्सत्त्वादविरलाः संतता विनोदानां दुःखविस्मरणहेतूनां व्यतिकराः संबन्धा येषु तथोक्ताः तथाविधैः वीराणां सुग्रीवप्रभृतीनां विमर्दैः परस्परसंप्रहारैर्जनित उत्पादितो जगतामत्यद्भुतरसो वीररसमयरसो येनेति तथोक्तः । वीररसादद्भुतरसस्योत्पत्तिरिति रसविदः । तदुक्तम्—'हास्यो भवति शृङ्गारात्करुणो रौद्रकर्मणः । अद्भुतश्च तथा वीराद्बीभत्साच्च भयानकः॥' इति । मुग्धे सुन्दरे अक्षिणी यस्या इति बहुव्रीहिः । ' न त्वामिहस्थां जानीते रामः कमललोचने । तेन त्वां नानयत्याशु शचीमिव पुरंदरः ॥ ' इत्युक्तम् । स वियोगः पूर्वकालिकविरहः रिपुघातावधिरभूद्रावणसंहारपर्यन्तोऽभूत् । कटुः क्रूरः । तूष्णीं सह्यः उपायाद्यभावात् जोषंभावेन सह्यः । अयं तु प्रविलय इदानींतनवियोगः । पुनर्दर्शनाभावाभिप्रायेण वियोगस्य प्रलयत्वोक्तिः । निरवधिः [निर्गतः अवधिर्यस्मात्] यावज्जीवभावीत्यर्थः ॥ ४४ ॥ बहुमानितास्मि पूर्वविरहहेतुकबहुमानवत्यस्मि । रिपुघातावधिरिति रावणसंहारस्य तन्मूलकत्वोक्तेरिति भावः । ' न त्वदर्थं मया कृतम् ' इति हि पूर्वं रामेणोक्तम् । निरवधिरिति हा हतास्मि । अस्य वियोगस्य निरवधित्वोक्तेः प्रत्याशा छिन्नेति भावः । **व्यर्थमिति** । यत्र प्रदेशे कपीन्द्रसख्यं सुग्रीवमैत्र्यम् । इदमुपलक्षणं सुग्रीवापेक्षयोपसर्जनत्वस्यापि । तदुक्तं रामायणे—'लोकनाथः पुरा भूत्वा सुग्रीवं नाथमिच्छति ' इति । ' स रामो वानरेन्द्रस्य प्रसादमभिकाङ्क्षते ' इति च । व्यर्थं निरर्थकम् । हरीणां वानराणां वीर्यं पराक्रमः यत्र वृथा निष्प्रयोजनः । जाम्बवतः प्रज्ञा युक्तायुक्तकुशलता यत्र न सार्थिकेत्यध्याहारः । वायोः पुत्रस्य हनूमतः गतिरपि न सार्थिका । मार्गं सेतुम् । न क्षमः न योग्यः । सौमित्रेरपि लक्ष्मणस्य । अपिशब्दात् स्वस्य । पत्रिणां बाणानामविषये अगोचरे तत्र तथाविधे

---

१ कष्टं भोः. २ जाम्बवतो न. ३ अविषयः. ४ भोः. ५ अस्मात्पूर्वं—बहुमाणिदह्मि (बहुमानितास्मि) ०धित्ति. ६ इति रोदिति इत्य० ७ बहुमाणिदह्मि पुव्वविरहं.

रामः—सखि वासन्ति दुःखायैव सुहृदामिदानीं रामस्य दर्शनम् । कियच्चिर[1] त्वा रोदयिष्यामि । तदनुजानीहि मां गमनाय ।

सीता—(सोद्वेग[2]मोहं तमसामाश्लिष्य ।) भगवति तमसे कथं गच्छत्येवार्यपुत्रः । (इति मूर्च्छति ।) (क)

तमसा—वत्से[3] समाश्वसिहि समाश्वसिहि[4] । नन्वावा[5]मप्यायुष्मतोः कुशलवयोर्वर्षवर्धनमङ्गलानि[6] संपादयितुं भागीरथीपदान्तिकमेव गच्छावः ।

सीता—भगवति प्रसीद । क्षणमात्रमपि तावद्दुर्लभदर्शनं जनं प्रेक्षे । (ख)

रामः—अस्ति चेदानीमश्वमेधा[7]य सहधर्मचारिणी मे—

सीता—(सो[8]त्कम्पम् ।) आर्यपुत्र का[9] । (ग)

(क) भ[10]अवदि तमसे कहं गच्छदि एव्व अज्जउत्तो ।

(ख) भअवदि पसीद । खणमेत्तं वि दाव दु[11]ल्लहदंसणं जणं पेक्खामि ।

(ग) अज्जउत्त का ।

क कस्मिन्देशे असि भवसि ॥ ४५ ॥ सुहृदां मित्राणां रामदर्शनं दुःखायैव दुःखफलदमेव । रोदयिष्यामि रुदतीं करोमि । अनुजानीहि अनुमतिं कुरु । वर्षर्द्धिमङ्गलानि द्वादशवर्षपूर्तिमङ्गलानि देवतापूजादीनि शुभानि । आयुष्मतोः कुशलवयोः कुशलवोद्देशेन संपादयितुमुत्पादयितुम् । भागीरथ्याः संबन्धद्योतनायेयमुक्तिः । अश्वमेधस्य सहधर्मचारिणीति विग्रहः । दम्पत्योः सहाधिकारत्वात् । अश्वमेधनिरूपितकर्तृकत्ववती जायास्तीति भावः । साक्षेपम् । आक्षेपश्चोदनं तेन सह वर्तत इत्यर्थः । क्रियाविशेषणम् । आर्यपुत्र का सहधर्मचारिणीति शेषः । परिणीतमपि । भावे क्तः । परिणयोऽपि किमिति काक्वा योजनीयम् । सीतापरित्यागानन्तरं न केवलं शरीरधारणं किं तु परिणयोऽपि जातः किमिति समुच्चयार्थः । सीतावियोगे रामस्य शरीरधारणमाश्चर्यमिति प्रसिद्धम् । तदुक्तं हनुमता—'दुष्करं कृतवान्रामो हीनो यदनया प्रभुः । धारयत्यात्मनो देहं न शोकेनावसीदति ॥' इति । 'दुष्करं कुरुते रामो य इमां मत्तकाशिनीम् । विना सीतां महाबाहुर्मुहूर्तमपि जीवति ॥' इति च ॥ नहि नहि । परिणयप्रसक्तिरप्यनिष्टेति द्विरुक्त्या व्यज्यते ।

---

१ तत्कियच्चिरं. २ सोद्वेग.... अवलम्ब्य. ३ वत्से जानकि. ४ अस्मादनन्तरं—विधिस्तवानुकूलो भविष्यति इत्यधि. ५ तदायुष्मनो......वर्षर्द्धिमङ्ग०; वर्षग्रन्थिमङ्गलं. ७ मेधसह०. ८ स्वगतं साक्षेपं (टी०); स्वग० ९ **After this the Com. has**—वासन्ती–परिणीतमपि किमु । रामः–नहि नहि &c. १० हा...तमसे गच्छदि दाणिं अज्जउत्तो । किं करिस्सम. ११ दल्लहं जणं, ०दंसणं अज्जउत्तं.

रामः—हिरण्मयी सीताप्रतिकृतिः।

सीता—(सोच्छ्वासोऽस्रम्।) आर्यपुत्र इदानीमसि त्वम्। अहो उत्खातमिदानीं मे परित्यागलज्जाशल्यमार्यपुत्रेण। (क)

रामः—तत्रापि तावद्बाष्पदिग्धं चक्षुर्विनोदयामि।

सीता—धन्या खलु सा यैवमार्यपुत्रेण बहुमन्यते या चार्यपुत्रं विनोदयन्त्याशानिबन्धनं जाता जीवलोकस्य। (ख)

तमसा—(सस्मितस्नेहोस्रं परिष्वज्य।) अयि वत्से एवमात्मा स्तूयते।

सीता—(सलज्जमधोमुखी। स्वगतम्।) परिहसितास्मि भगवत्या। (ग)

वासन्ती—महानयं व्यतिकरोऽस्माकं प्रसादः। गमनं पुनर्यथा कार्यहानिर्न भवति तथास्तु।

(क) अज्जउत्तो दाणिं सि तुमम्। अह्महे उक्खाणिदं दाणिं मे परिच्चाअलज्जासल्लं अज्जउत्तेण।

(ख) धण्णा खु सा जा एव्वं अज्जउत्तेण बहुमण्णीअदि जा अ अज्जउत्तं विणोदयन्दी आसाणिबन्धणं जादा जीअलोअस्स। (ग) परिहसिदह्मि भअवदीए।

इदानीमसि त्वम्। 'स्वापहेतुरनुपाश्रितोऽन्यया' इत्युक्तरीत्या एकदारव्रतत्वं तवेदानीमेव प्रकटितमिति भावः। परित्याग एव शल्यं परित्यागशल्यम्। निष्कारणपरित्यागस्य प्रत्यवायहेतुत्वप्रयुक्तदुःखजनकत्वाच्छल्यत्वरूपणम्। ननु वास्तवदोषाभावेऽपि दोषवत्ता वृथारूपमित्याभिशस्तिमतां परित्यागो धर्मशास्त्रसिद्ध इति चेन्मैवम्। अग्निप्रवेशादिना मिथ्याभिशस्तेरनवकाशात्। उत्खातितमुद्धृतम्। तत्रापि हिरण्मयसीताप्रतिकृतौ बाष्पदिग्धमश्रुणा लिप्तम्। विनोदयामि विस्मृतदुःखं करोमि। एवं च सीताप्रतिकृतेरश्वमेधसहधर्मचारिणीत्वमानुषङ्गिकम्। मुख्यं तु चक्षुर्विनोदनमिति सूचितम्। यैवं बहुमन्यते चक्षुर्विनोदहेतुत्वप्रयुक्तबहुमानविषयीक्रियते सा प्रतिकृतिर्धन्या यैवमार्यपुत्रं विनोदयन्ती विस्मृतदुःखं कुर्वती जीवलोकस्याशानिबन्धनं रामजीवनप्रत्याशाहेतुत्वात्स्वस्वविषयकाशाहेतुर्जाता सा धन्येत्यन्वयः। परिष्वज्यालिङ्ग्य। एवं 'धन्या खलु सा' इत्यादिपूर्वोक्तरीत्या आत्मा स्तूयते स्तुतिविषयीक्रियते। त्वयेति शेषः। भगवत्या। तमसयेत्यर्थः। अयं व्यतिकर एष समागमः। अस्माकं महान्प्रसादः। अस्मद्विषयानुग्रहप्रयोजित इत्यर्थः। यथा

---

१ सोल्लासं सोच्छ्वासं सा॰ २ हार्द्रम्. ३ प्रमादः. ४ प्रति. ५ आस्तां; कार्यम्. After this some read रामः—तथास्तु. ६ उक्खाइदं (उत्खानितं). ७ परिच्चाअसल्लं.

सीता—प्रतिकूलेदानीं मे वासन्ती संवृत्ता । (क)

तमसा—वत्से एहि गच्छावः ।

सीता—(सकथम् ।) एवं करिष्यावः । (ख)

तमसा—कथं वा गम्यते । यस्यास्तव

प्रत्युप्तस्येव दयिते तृष्णादीर्घस्य चक्षुषः ।
मर्मच्छेदपरैर्यत्नैराकर्षो न समाप्यते ॥ ४६ ॥

सीता—नमो नमोऽपूर्वपुण्यजनितदर्शनाभ्यामार्यपुत्रचरणकमलाभ्याम् । (ग)

तमसा—वत्से समाश्वसिहि समाश्वसिहि ।

सीता—(समाश्वस्य ।) कियच्चिरं वा मेघान्तरेण पूर्णिमाचन्द्रस्य दर्शनम् । (घ)

(**क**) पडिऊला दाणिं मे वासन्दी संवुत्ता । (**ख**) एव्वं करह्म ।

(**ग**) णमो णमो अपुव्वपुण्णजणिददंसणाणं अज्जउत्तचलणकमलाणम् ।

(**घ**) किअच्चिरं वा मेहन्तरेण पुण्णिमाचन्दस्स दंसणम् ।

येन प्रकारेण कार्यस्य कर्तव्यस्य हानिर्लोपो न भवति तथा तेन प्रकारेण गमनं प्रति गमनोद्देशेन कार्यं यत्नः कर्तव्यः । इदानीं वासन्ती मे प्रतिकूला आनिष्टकारिणी संवृत्ता जाता । रामगमनं प्रत्यनुज्ञाकरणादिति भावः । एवं कुर्वः । गच्छाव इत्यर्थः ॥ **यस्यास्तव प्रत्युप्तस्येवेति** । तृष्णया अवलोकनस्पृहया दीर्घस्य आयतस्य । दयिते रामे प्रत्युप्तस्येव स्थितस्य कीलितस्येव स्थितस्य यस्यास्तव चक्षुषो नेत्रस्य संनिकर्षः दयिते संबन्धः । मर्मच्छेदोपमैर्हृदयादिप्रदेशकृन्तनसदृशैर्यत्नैर्निरुध्यते निवर्त्यते । तथाविधया त्वया कथं गम्यत इति पूर्वेणान्वयः । तृष्णादीर्घस्येत्युक्त्या दयिते प्रत्युप्तस्येवेति दयितपदविवक्षितरामस्यामृतसादृश्यं व्यज्यते ॥ ४६ ॥ **नम इति** । प्राकृते चतुर्थीस्थाने षष्ठीद्विवचनस्य बहुवचनत्वम् । सुकृतानि पुण्यानि यैस्ते सुकृतपुण्याः । सुकृतपुण्याश्च ते जनाश्चेति विग्रहे कर्मधारयः । तथाविधैः दर्शनीयाभ्यां सेवितुं शक्याभ्याम् । न तु मादृशपापकृज्जनदर्शनार्हाभ्यामित्यर्थः । ‘ न ते मनुष्या देवास्ते ये चारुशुभकुण्डलम् ’ इत्यादि दशरथोक्तरीत्या पुण्यकृद्दर्शनीयत्वं रामचरणयोरिति भावः । ‘ ममैव दुष्कृतं किंचिन्महदस्ति न संशयः ’ इत्युक्तरीत्या स्वस्याः पापकृत्त्वमिति तात्पर्यम् । अत्र सुष्ठु-

---

१ मर्मच्छेदोपमैर्यत्नैः संनिकर्षो निरुध्यते (टी०) २ णमो सुकिदपुण्णजणदंसणिज्जाणं (सुकृतपुण्यजनदर्शनीयाभ्याम्); अकिदपुण्णजणादंसणिआणं (अकृतपुण्यजनादर्शनीयाभ्याम्). ३ पुण्णचन्दस्स.

तमसा—अहो संविधानकम्।

एको रसः करुण एव निमित्तभेदा-
द्भिन्नः पृथक्पृथगिवाश्रयते विवर्तान्।
आवर्तबुद्बुदतरङ्गमयान्विकारा-
नम्भो यथा सलिलमेव तु तत्समग्रम्॥ ४७॥

कृतं यैस्ते सुकृताः। तथाविधाश्च ते पुण्यजना राक्षसाश्चेति ते विभीषणादयः इति कश्चित्। उक्तरीत्याश्रयणे कृतस्यापि संग्रह इति दिक्। इति मूर्च्छामभिनयति। कियच्चिरं मेघान्तरेण पूर्णचन्द्रदर्शनं मेघमध्ये पूर्णचन्द्रदर्शनम्। 'वीरशृङ्गारयोरेकः प्रधानं यत्र वर्ण्यते।' इत्यौत्सर्गिकस्य शृङ्गारवीरान्यतरप्राधान्यस्य वीरशृङ्गारौ प्रायिकावित्यपवादेऽपि करुणरसप्राधान्यकरणे मानाभावः रसान्तराणां सत्त्वात्। न ह्यत्र विनिगमकमस्ति येन करुणरसस्य प्राधान्यमुपपद्यते। किं च करुणस्य दुःखात्मकत्वेन रसत्वं नास्ति। येन रसप्रधाननाटके तस्योक्तिसंभवः स्यादिति शङ्कां कविस्तमसावाक्यव्याजेन परिहरति—**अहो संविधानकमिति**। अपूर्वरूपकनिर्माणं विस्मयनीयमित्यर्थः। **एक इति**। रस्यते स्वाद्यत इति रसः काव्यानुशीलिनामभ्यासवशविशदीभूतवर्णनीयतन्मयीभवनयोग्यसामाजिकमनोमुकुरभाव्यमानतया निर्भरानन्दसंविद्रूपः। करुण इष्टजनवियोगजन्यदुःखातिशयः। एक एव सन्नपि निमित्तभेदात् व्यञ्जकविभावादिविच्छित्तिविशेषाद्भिन्नः विलक्षणः पृथक्पृथग्विवर्तान् परस्परविलक्षणशृङ्गाराद्यात्मना परिणामान्। 'व्यत्यस्तपरिणामः स्याद्विवर्तः' इति कपिलः। श्रयते भजते। एकस्यानेकधा विकारमात्रे दृष्टान्तमाह—**आवर्तेति**। आवर्तः जलस्य भ्रमः, बुद्बुदः कुड्मलाकारजलसंस्थानविशेषः, तरङ्गः भङ्गः, एतद्रूपान्विकारान्। अवस्थान्तराणीत्यर्थः। तत्समस्तमावर्तादिकं सर्वं सलिलमेव जलमेव। तरङ्गादीनां जलविवर्तत्वाभावाद्विकारमात्रे दृष्टान्तमिदम्। अत एव विवर्तानित्युक्तिः। इदमत्र कवेर्मतम्—'यद्यपि शृङ्गार एक एव रस इति शृङ्गारप्रकाशकारादिमतम्, तथापि प्राचुर्याद्रागिविरागिसाधारण्यात्करुण एक एव रसः। अन्ये तु तद्विकृतयः' इति। करुणस्यानुकार्ये रामादौ दुःखरूपत्वेऽपि सहृदयानामानन्दात्मना परिणमतीत्युक्तरीत्या सामाजिके आनन्दरूपत्वमेव। तर्हि भावकानां करुणात्मककाव्यश्रवणे अश्रुधाराविर्भावः कथमिति चेदत्राहुः—संभोगसमये स्त्रीणामधरदंशनादौ कृत्रिमदुःखानुभवसीत्कारवदत्राप्युपपत्तिः। सुखेऽपि दुःखवदुपचारः कुट्टमितं तल्लक्षणात्। यद्यस्य सहजदुःखात्मकत्वं स्यात् न कोऽपि सामाजिकस्तत्र प्रवर्तेत ततश्च करुणैकरसानां रामायणादीनामुच्छेदप्रसङ्गः स्यात्। तस्माद्रसान्तरवत्करुणस्याप्यानन्दात्मकत्वमेवेति। एवं च रसान्तरापेक्षया प्रकृतित्वमेव करुणस्य प्राधान्ये विनिगमकं शृङ्गारवीरयोः प्रायिकत्वोक्तेस्तदभावे अस्यैवोचितत्वादिति। यद्वा एको रसः रसशब्दवाच्यः। 'अत्र ओदनं पचति' 'अस्य सूत्रस्य पटो वातव्यः' इत्यादाविव भाविनीं वृत्तिमाश्रित्य

१ इव श्रयते. २ हि तत्समस्तम्.

रामः——अयि विमानराज इत इतः ।

(सर्वे उत्तिष्ठन्ति ।)

तमसावासन्त्यौ——(सीतारामौ प्रति ।)

अवनिरमरसिन्धुः सार्धमस्मद्विधाभिः
स च कुलपतिराद्यश्छन्दसां यः प्रयोक्ता ।
स च मुनिरनुयातारुन्धतीको वसिष्ठ—
स्त्वयि वितरतु भद्रं भूयसे मङ्गलाय ॥ ४८ ॥

(इति निष्क्रान्ताः सर्वे ।)

तृतीयोऽङ्कः ।

रसशब्दप्रयोगः । एवम् 'पुटपाकप्रतीकाशो रामस्य करुणो रसः' इत्यत्रापि बोध्यम् । करुणः अनुकार्यरामादिगतेष्टजनवियोगजन्यदुःखातिशयः । एक एव सन्नपि निमित्तभेदात्सखित्वपतित्वपत्नीत्वाद्युपाधिभेदाद्भिन्नः विलक्षण इव पृथक्पृथग् विवर्तान् श्रयते । वासन्तीसीतारामप्रभृतिषु परस्परविलक्षणावस्थाविशेषान्भजति । अत्र विवर्तशब्दो विकारमात्रपरः । एवं दृष्टान्तसामञ्जस्यमुपपद्यते । शेषं पूर्ववत् । अस्मिन् पक्षे रसान्तरसत्त्वे करुणारसप्राधान्यं तूक्तयुक्त्या ग्रन्थाद्बहिः समर्थनीयम् । तथा चैतादृशकरुणरसप्रधानत्वादपूर्वोऽयं कथासंनिवेश इति पूर्वेणान्वयः ॥ ४७ ॥ तमसावासन्त्यौ सीतारामौ प्रति यथासंख्यं प्रति उद्दिश्य । **अवनिरिति** । अवनिर्भूमिः । अमरसिन्धुः गङ्गा । अस्मद्विधाभिः । तमसापक्षे मुरलागोदावरीप्रभृतिभिरित्यर्थः । वासन्तीपक्षे अन्याभिर्देवताभिः सहेत्यर्थः । यश्छन्दसां प्रयोक्ता वेदानां प्रवक्ता आद्यः कुलपतिः स च सूर्यश्च । मुनिर्मननशीलः स प्रसिद्धः । अनुयातानुगता अरुन्धती यमिति विग्रहे द्वितीयाबहुव्रीहिः । शेषाद्विभाषेति कप् । न कपीति ह्रस्वप्रतिषेधः । तथाविधो वसिष्ठः । तव भूयसे प्रचुराय मङ्गलाय भद्रं मङ्गलं वितरतु ददातु । अत्र गर्भबीजस्य ऋषिश्रेयोवितरणरूपस्योद्भेदनादाक्षेपो नाम संध्यङ्गमुक्तं भवति ॥ यदत्रोच्छृङ्खलं किंचित्कविनानेन बध्यते । निरङ्कुशतया तत्तु समाधेयं मनीषिभिः ॥ भावस्य तु गभीरत्वात्स कश्चिदिह कथ्यते । कोशव्याकरणे प्रायेणोच्येते ग्रन्थगौरवात् ॥ ४८ ॥

वाधूलवंशजनुषो भूसारनिवासराघवार्यस्य ।
उत्तररामचरित्रव्याख्यायामवसितस्तृतीयोऽङ्कः ॥

इति श्रीवाधूलवीरराघवविरचितायां भवभूतिभावतलस्पर्शिनीसमाख्यायामुत्तररामचरितव्याख्यायां तृतीयोऽङ्कः ।

---

१ तव. २ श्रेयसे. ३ इति महाकविश्रीभवभूतिप्रणीते उत्तररामचरिते छाया नाम तृ०.

चतुर्थोऽङ्कः ।

(ततः प्रविशतस्तापसौ ।)

एकः——सौधातके दृश्यतामद्य भूयिष्ठसंनिधापितातिथिजनस्य समधिकारम्भरमणीयता भगवतो वाल्मीकेराश्रमपदस्य । तथा हि ।

नीवारौदनमण्डमुष्णमधुरं सद्यःप्रसूताप्रिया-
पीतादभ्यधिकं तपोवनमृगः पर्याप्तमाचामति ।
गन्धेन स्फुरता मनागनुसृतो भक्तस्य सर्पिष्मतः
कर्कन्धूफलमिश्रशाकपचनामोदः परिस्तीर्यते ॥ १ ॥

तत इति । तापसौ तपःशीलौ । एकः । तयोरन्यतर इत्यर्थः । सुधातुरपत्यं सौधातकिः । 'सुधातुरकङ् च' इत्यकङ्ङादेशोऽञ्प्रत्ययः । तस्य संबुद्धिः सौधातके इति । अद्य मध्याह्ने भूयिष्ठं यथा भवति तथा संनिधापितः निकटागामितः अतिथिजनो यस्मिन्निति तथोक्तस्य भगवतो वाल्मीकेः ज्ञानशक्त्यादिपूर्णस्य प्राचेतसस्य यदाश्रमपदं आश्रमस्थानं तस्य समधिकारम्भेण प्रचुरतरमारभ्यमाणातिथिजनसत्कारादिना रमणीयता हृद्यता दृश्यतां चक्षुर्विषयीक्रियताम् । त्वयेति शेषः । **नीवारेति** । तपोवनमृगः तपोवनाश्रयो मुनिसंवर्धितहरिणः । सद्यः समानेऽह्नि । तस्मिन्दिन इत्यर्थः । प्रसूता प्रसववती । कर्तरि क्तः । तथाविधया प्रियया प्रियविषयहरिण्या पीतात् पानं प्राप्य । भावे क्तः । ल्यब्लोपे पञ्चमी । अभ्यधिकं अवशिष्टं प्रचुरं वा हरिणीकर्तृकं वा पानं प्राप्यापि प्रचुरमित्यर्थः । उष्णं च तत् मधुरं च माधुर्ययुक्तं चेति विशेषणसमासः । तथाविधं नीवारौदनमण्डं नीवारो धान्यविशेषः । तत्संबन्ध्योदनस्य यन्मण्डं घनीभूतद्रवविशेषः तत्पर्याप्तं यावदिच्छानिवृत्ति आचामति पिबति । यद्वा सद्यःप्रसूतप्रियापीतादिति हेतौ पञ्चमी । सद्यःप्रसूतप्रियाकर्तृकपानाद्धेतोः अभ्यधिकं यथा भवति तथा प्रचुरं यथा भवति तथा उष्णं मधुरं चेत्यर्थः । अत्र सद्यःप्रसूतत्वमुष्णत्वे हेतुः । उष्णत्वं हि प्रसवविह्वलशरीरतोदपरिहारकम् । प्रियात्वं च मधुरत्वे हेतुः । अत एव मधुरत्वोक्तिः प्रयोजनवती । अन्यथा तस्य माधुर्याव्यभिचारात्तद्वैयर्थ्यं स्पष्टमेव । इदमेवाभिसंधाय 'अम्बुनीवारशष्पैः' इत्यत्र अम्बुना तरून् अम्बुनीवाराभ्यां शकुनीन् अम्बुनीवारशष्पैः कुरङ्गानिति विवेक उक्त इति बोध्यम् । अत एव पर्याप्तं यावदिच्छानिवृत्ति आचामति पिबति । सर्पिष्मतः घृतवतः भक्तस्यान्नस्य स्फुरता प्रसरता गन्धेन सौरभ्येण मनागीषदनुसृतः अनुगतः कर्कन्धूफलमिश्रस्य बदरीफलमिश्रस्य शाकपचनस्य पच्यमानशाकस्य । बदरीफलानि हि आम्लरसार्थं शाकेन सह पच्यन्ते । आमोदः सौरभ्यं परिस्तीर्यते विस्तीर्यते वितितीक्रियते । वायुनेति शेषः । यद्वा परिस्तीर्यते विस्तीर्णो भवतीत्यर्थः । लूयते केदारः स्वयमेवेत्यादाविव कर्मवद्भावाद्यगात्मनेपदे । अथ वा सर्पिष्मतो भक्तस्य स्फुरता गन्धेन कर्त्रा अनुसृतः अनुक्षणं प्रसर्पन् कर्कन्धूफलमिश्रशाकपचनामोदः कर्म अभिव्याप्यत इति व्याख्येयम् ॥ १ ॥

---

१ कतरतम॰. २ हव्यस्य.

सौधातकिः—स्वागतमनेकप्रकाराणां जीर्णकूर्चानामनध्यायकारणानाम् । (क)

प्रथमः–(विहस्य ।) अपूर्वः कोऽपि[1] ते बहुमानहेतुर्गुरुषु सौधातके ।

सौधातकिः—भो दाण्डायन[2] किंनामधेय एष महतः स्त्रीसार्थस्य धुरंधरोऽद्यातिथिरागतः । (ख)

दाण्डायनः—धिक्प्रहसनम् । नन्वयमृष्यशृङ्गाश्रमादरुन्धतीं[3]पुरस्कृतान्महाराजदशरथस्य दारानधिष्ठाय भगवान्वसिष्ठः प्राप्तः । तत्किमेवं प्रलपासि ।

सौधातकिः—हुं वसिष्ठः । (ग)

दाण्डायनः—अथ किम् ।

सौधातकिः—मया पुनर्ज्ञातं व्याघ्रो वृको वैष इति । (घ)

(क) साअदं अणेअपिआराणं जिण्णकुच्छाणं अणज्झाअकालणाणम् ।[4]

(ख) भो दण्डाअण किंणामहेओ एसो महन्तस्स इत्थिऔसत्थस्स[5] धुरंधरो अज्ज[6] अदिही आअदो ।

(ग) हुं वसिठ्ठो । (घ) मए उण जाणिदं वग्घो[7] विओ वा एसोत्ति ।

साअदमिति । स्वागतम् । सकारस्य न लुक् । गकारस्य प्रायो लुक् । 'कगचजतदपयवाम्' इति प्राकृतव्याकरणसूत्रेण लोपः । अकारस्य ईषत्स्पृष्टतया श्रुतिरपि । सूत्रे 'प्रायो' ग्रहणादकारस्य न लुक् । अनेकप्रकाराणाम् । बहुविधानामित्यर्थः । पूर्ववदेव लोपः । यः श्रुतिबोध्यम् । अत्र प्रकारशब्दस्य घञ्वेति प्राकृतव्याकरणसूत्रेण पूर्वस्य वैकल्पिकत्वात् 'पिआर' इति दीर्घः । 'पिआराणं' इति त्वासुपोरिति सूत्रेणानुस्वारः । अनध्ययननिमित्तानामित्यर्थः । शिष्टानध्ययनस्य धर्मशास्त्रसिद्धत्वादिति भावः । जीर्णकूर्चानां शिथिलभ्रूमध्यानाम् । जीर्णशब्दे 'संयोगे च' इति प्राकृतव्याकरणसूत्रेण ह्रस्वः । गुरुषु वसिष्ठादिषु । **भो दण्डाअणेति** । नामधेयं तस्य संबुद्धिः । महतः प्रचुरस्य स्त्रीसार्थस्य अङ्गनासमूहस्य धुरंधरो निर्वापकोऽतिथिरागतः किंनामधेय इत्यन्वयः । दण्डाअणेति स्वरस्य बिन्दवमिति ह्रस्वः । किंणामहेय इत्यत्र 'खघथधभाम्' इति सूत्रेण धकारस्य हकारः । स्त्रीशब्दस्य 'स्त्रीभगिनीदुहितृवनितानां इत्थिबहिणीधूआविलआ' इति प्राकृतसूत्रेण

---

१ खलु तेऽपि बहु०. २ भाण्डायन. ३ तीं पुरस्कृत्य. ४ साअदं अनज्झा ०णाणं विसेसदो जिण्णकुच्चालाणं; कालणाणं तपोधणाणं; आअदं अणज्झाअकारणं सविसेसभूदं अज्ज जिण्णकुच्चाणं (आगतमनध्यायकारणं सविशेषभूतमद्य जीर्णकूर्चानाम्). ५ त्थविर (स्थविर०); थेरीसत्थस्स अग्गधोरिद्धिओ (स्थाविरासार्थस्याग्रधौर्यधरोऽतिथि०). ६ अज्ज चीरधारओ (चीरधारकः). ७ वग्घो वा; वग्घो विअ; वग्घो कोवि एसोत्ति.

दाण्डायनः——आः किमुक्तं भवति ।

सौधातकिः——येन परापतितेनैव सा वराकी कपिला कल्याणी मडमडायिता । (क)

दाण्डायनः——समांसो मधुपर्क इत्याम्नायं बहुमन्यमानाः श्रोत्रियायाभ्यागताय वत्सतरीं महोक्षं[1] वा महाजं वा निर्वपन्ति गृहमेधिनः । तं हि[2] धर्मं धर्मसूत्रकाराः समामनन्ति ।

सौधातकिः——भो निगृहीतोऽसि । (ख)

दाण्डायनः——कथमिव ।

सौधातकिः——येनागतेषु वसिष्ठमिश्रेषु वत्सतरी विशसिता । अद्यैव पर्यागतस्य राजर्षेर्जनकस्य भगवता वाल्मीकिना दधिमधुभ्यामेव निर्वर्तितो मधुपर्कः । वत्सतरी पुनर्विसर्जिता । (ग)

(क) जेणै परावडिदेण एव्व सा वराई कविला कल्लाणी मडमडाइआ ।

(ख) भो णिगिहीदोसि ।

(ग) जेण आअदेसु वसिट्ठमिस्सेसु वच्छदरी विससिदा । अज्ज एव्व पज्जोगदस्स राएसिणो जणअस्स भअवदा वम्मीइणा दहिमहूहिं एव्व णिव्वत्तिदो महुवक्को । वच्छतरी उण विसज्जिदा ।

इत्थिआदेशे कप्रत्ययस्य कलोपः । सत्थस्सेत्यत्र ' संयोगे ' इति ह्रस्वः । धिक्प्रहसनं हासहेतुभूतं त्वदीयवचः । निन्दनीयमिति भावः । अधिष्ठाय । तन्नियामको भूत्वेत्यर्थः । प्रलपसि अनर्थकं वदसि । हुमिति प्रश्ने । अथ किमित्यङ्गीकारे । एष कोऽपि व्याघ्र इति मया ज्ञातमित्यन्वयः । ' संयोगे ' इति ह्रस्वः । किमुक्तं भवति कुत एवमुक्तं भवति । हि तेन वसिष्ठेन हि । वराकी प्रतिकूलदैवा । कपिला नाम गवामवान्तरजातिः । कल्याणी वत्सतरी । द्विहायनीत्यर्थः । बलात्कृत्य मडमडायिता । आलम्भनशब्दानुकरणमिदम् । तथाविधशब्दयुक्ता कृतेत्यर्थः । आलब्धेति यावत् । मडायितेत्यर्थः । ' मृज्नातेर्मड्डपरिहट्टखडववन्नाजचडमल्लमडा ' इति प्राकृतव्याकरणसूत्रेण मृद्धातोर्मड इत्यादेशः । तेन व्याघ्र इति ज्ञातमिति पूर्वेण संबन्धः । आम्नायं धर्मशास्त्रम् । महांश्चासौ उक्षा चेति विग्रहः । निपातनादकारान्तत्वम् । पचन्ति श्रपयन्ति । समामनन्ति उपदिशन्ति । अत्र मया व्याघ्र इत्यादिना गुरुतिरस्कृतिरुद्भव उक्तः । भो निगृहीतोऽसि पराजितोऽसि । **आगतेष्वेवेति** । मिश्रशब्दः पूज्यताद्योतकः । ' एवार्थे एव्व ' इति प्राकृतसूत्रेण एव्वादेशः । दधिमधुभ्यामित्यनेन दधिमधुसंसृष्टमित्यापस्तम्बवचनमभिप्रेतम् । निर्वर्तितः निष्पादितः । वत्सतरी पुनरिति । विसर्जिता मुक्ता

---

१ महोक्षं वा पचन्ति. २ इति हि धर्मं०. ३ तेण; वराई कल्लोडिआ; कल्लाणी बलामोडिअ (बलात्कृत्य). ४ पच्चाअदस्स (प्रत्यागतस्य); पच्चा आअदस्स (पश्चादागतस्य).

दाण्डायनः—अनिवृत्तमांसानामेवं कल्पमृषयो मन्यन्ते । निवृत्तमांसस्तु तत्रभवाञ्जनकः ।

सौधातकिः—किंनिमित्तम् । (क)

दाण्डायनः—स तदैव देव्याः सीतायास्तादृशं दैवदुर्विपाकमुपश्रुत्य वैखानसः संवृत्तः । तथास्य कतिपये संवत्सराश्चन्द्रद्वीपतपोवने तपस्तप्यमानस्य ।

सौधातकिः—ततः किमित्यागतः । (ख)

दाण्डायनः—चिरंतनप्रियसुहृदं भगवन्तं प्राचेतसं द्रष्टुम् ।

सौधातकिः—अप्यद्य संबन्धिनीभिः समं संवृत्तमस्य दर्शनं न वेति । (ग)

दाण्डायनः—संप्रत्येव भगवता वसिष्ठेन देव्याः कौसल्यायाः सकाशं भगवत्यरुन्धती प्रहिता यत्स्वयमुपेत्य वैदेहो द्रष्टव्य इति ।

सौधातकिः—यथैते स्थविराः परस्परं मिलितास्तथावामपि बटुभिः सह मिलित्वाऽनध्यायमहोत्सवं खेलन्तौ संभावयावः । (इति परिक्रामतः ।) (घ)

(क) किंणिमित्तम् । (ख) तदो किंत्ति आअदो ।

(ग) अवि अज्ज संबन्धिणीहिं समं संवुत्तं से दंसणं ण वेत्ति ।

(घ) जह एदे थेविरा परप्परं मिलिदा तह अह्मे वि वडुहिं सह मिलिअ अणज्झाअमहूस्सवं खेलन्तो संभावेह्मो ।

न त्वालब्धेत्यर्थः । **व्याहरन्ति केचिदिति** । केचिद्धर्मशास्त्रकारा आपस्तम्बादयः । एवं कल्पं मांसवर्जं मधुपर्कानुष्ठानपरग्रन्थं व्याहरन्ति वदन्ति । निवृत्तमांसो वर्जितमांसः । **यद्देव्या इत्यादि** । वैखानसः वानप्रस्थः । चन्द्रद्वीपतपोवने तपस्तप्यमानस्य तपश्चरतः कतिपये संवत्सराः । गता इति शेषः । चन्द्रद्वीप इति कश्चिद्द्वीपविशेषः । प्राचेतसं वाल्मीकिम् । संबन्धिनीभिः दर्शनं निवृत्तं न वेति ज्ञायते अपीति योजना अपेः । अयम् । जनक इत्यर्थः । स्नेहाद् द्रष्टव्यः प्रेम्णा दर्शनीयः । स्थविराः वृद्धाः । अनध्यायः अध्ययनाभावः स एव महोत्सवः । आनन्दहेतुत्वादुत्सवत्वरूपणम् । उपास्य परिचर्य ।

---

१ कल्पं व्याहरान्ति; व्याह॰ केचित् (टी॰). २ यद्देव्याः...तदस्य; सीतादेव्याः. ३ संप्रति च प्रि॰. ४ प्रहिता स्वयं॰, उपेत्य स्नेहादयं. ५ इति वक्तुम्. ६ आयि. ७ णिउत्तं, जावं. ८ सवे ह॰; जेरटा. ९ मणेह्म (मानयावः). **After this some read** अह कुत्थ-कहिं-सो जणओ.

दाण्डायनः—तदयं ब्रह्मवादी पुराणराजर्षिर्जनकः प्राचेतसवसिष्ठावुपास्य संप्रत्याश्रमस्य बहिर्वृक्षमूलमधितिष्ठति । य एष

हृदि नित्यानुषक्तेन सीताशोकेन तप्यते ।
अन्तःप्रसृप्तदहनो जरन्निव वनस्पतिः ॥ २ ॥

(इति निष्क्रान्तौ ।)

मिश्रविष्कम्भः ।

(ततः प्रविशति जनकः ।)

जनकः—

अपत्ये यत्तादृग्दुरितमभवत्तेन महता
विषक्तस्तीव्रेण व्रणितहृदयेन व्यथयता ।
पटुर्धारावाही नव इव चिरेणापि हि न मे
निकृन्तन्मर्माणि क्रकच इव मन्युर्विरमति ॥ ३ ॥

कष्टं एवं नाम जरया दुःखेन च दुरासदेन भूयः पराकसांतपनप्रभृतिभिस्तपोभिरात्तरसंधातुरनवष्टम्भो नाद्यापि मम दग्धदेहः पतति । अन्धतामिस्रा ह्यसूर्या नाम ते लोकास्तेभ्यः प्रतिविधीयन्ते य आत्मघातिन

हृदीति । य एषः । जनक इत्यर्थः । हृदि नित्यानुषक्तेन नित्यलग्नेन सीताशोकेन सीतानिमित्तदुःखेन तप्यते तप्तो भवति । जरन् वृद्धः । अन्तःप्रज्वलद्वह्निः । वनस्पतिः पुष्पहीनफलवृक्षः ॥ २ ॥ मिश्रविष्कम्भः । संस्कृतप्राकृतात्मकविष्कम्भ इत्यर्थः ॥ **अपत्य इति** । यस्मात् अपत्ये । सीतायामित्यर्थः । तादृग्दुरितं कौलीनरूपपापं व्यसनं वाभवत् । तीव्रेणातिप्रचुरेण तेन दुरितेन व्यथयता दुःखं प्रापितेन व्रणितहृदयेन विषक्तः प्रसक्तः । पटुः तीक्ष्णः । धारया वहतीति धारावाही । अत्यन्तनैरन्तर्येण प्रवाहीत्यर्थः । चिरेणापि चिरकालेनापि नव इव स्थितः मर्माणि हृदयादीनि निकृन्तन् छिन्दन् क्रकच इव कराल इव स्थितः । मन्युः शोकः कोपो वा न विरमति न शाम्यति ॥ ३ ॥ जरया वयोहान्या । दुरासदेन दुःसहेन दुःखेन सीताविश्लेषजेन । पराको द्वादशदिनोपवासकृच्छ्रम्, सांतपनं चान्द्रायणविशेषः । एवमादिभिः कायशोषकनियमविशेषैः शोषितान्तःशरीरधातोर्मे कथमवष्टम्भ एव पातप्रतिबन्धकावलम्बनमेव । दग्धदेहः हतहृदयमितिवत् निन्दायां दग्धशब्दः । अद्यापि न पततीति योजना । अनेकसामग्रीसमवधानेऽपि पाताभावो विस्मयनीय इति भावः । तर्हि भृगुपतनादिना त्यज्यतामित्यत्राह—**अन्धतामिस्रा इति** । आत्मानं घ्नन्तीति आत्मघातिन इति विग्रहः ।

---

१ प्रसृप्त, प्रदीप्त. २ ज्वलन्. ३ जरसा. ४ रसुपष्टम्भनो न मे; ०धातुरनुपयुज्यमानः; शोषितान्तःशरीरधातोरुपष्टम्भ एव महानद्यापि देहो न पतति (टी०). ५ लोकाः प्रेत्य.

इत्येवमृषयो मन्यन्ते। अनेकसंवत्सरातिक्रमेऽपि प्रतिक्षणपरिभावनास्पष्टनिर्भासः प्रत्यग्रदारुणो इव न मे दुःखसंवेगः प्रशाम्यति। अयि मातर्देवयजनसंभवे सीते ईदृशस्ते निर्माणभागः परिणतो येन लज्जया स्वच्छन्दमाक्रन्दितुमपि न शक्यते। हा पुत्रि

अनियतरुदितस्मितं विराज-
त्कतिपयकोमलदन्तकुड्मलाग्रम्।
वदनकमलकं शिशोः स्मरामि
स्खलदसमञ्जसमञ्जुजल्पितं ते॥ ४॥

भगवति वसुंधरे सत्यमतिदृढासि।

त्वं वह्निर्मुनयो वसिष्ठगृहिणी गङ्गा च यस्या विदु-
र्माहात्म्यं यदि वा रघोः कुलगुरुर्देवः स्वयं भास्करः।

सुप्यजातौ' इति णिनिः। ये बलात्क्रियन्ते तेभ्यः तान् पार्तयितुम्। क्रियार्थे चतुर्थी। असूर्याः सूर्यरहिता अन्धतमसमयास्ते प्रसिद्धा लोका नरकविशेषाः प्रेत्य मरणानन्तरं प्रतिविधीयन्ते इत्येवमृषयो मन्यन्ते। 'असूर्या नाम ते लोका अन्धेन तमसावृताः। तांस्ते प्रेत्याभिगच्छन्ति ये के चात्महनो जनाः॥' इति श्रुतिः। इति धर्मशास्त्रकाराणां मतम्। प्रतिक्षणपरिभावनया संततविचारेण। 'भू अवकल्कने'। अवकल्कनं चिन्तनम्। स्पष्टनिर्भासः विशदप्रकाशः। प्रत्यग्र इव नव्य इव न प्रशाम्यति न नश्यति। निर्माणभागः सृष्टिफलम्। येन निर्माणभागेनाक्रन्दितुमपि रोदितुमपि। अपिशब्दात्क्रियान्तरानर्हत्वं सूच्यते। दोषवादहेतुकत्वात्त्यागस्येति भावः। **अनियतेति**। अनियतरुदितास्मितं अव्यवस्थितरोदनहसनम्। विराजन्तः कतिपये त्रिचतुराः कोमला ललिता दन्ता एव कुड्मलाग्राणि यस्य तथोक्तम्। तेन कुड्मलाग्रशब्दस्य न पूर्वनिपातः न वा दन्तशब्दस्य दतादेशः। स्खलदपूर्णमसमञ्जसं पूर्वापरसंगतिरहितं मञ्जु सुन्दरं जल्पितं वचनं यस्य तथोक्तं ते वदनकमलकं वदनमेव कमलम्। अनुकम्पायां कन्। स्मरामि उत्कण्ठापूर्वकं चिन्तयामि। अत्रानियतरुदितास्मितं स्खलदसमञ्जसमिति विशेषणानुगुण्याद्वदनकमलकमित्यत्र परिणामालंकारः। केवलकमलस्य प्रकृतक्रियान्वयित्वानुपपत्तेः। 'परिणामः क्रियार्थश्चेद्विषयी विषयात्मना' इति लक्षणात्। दन्तकुड्मलाग्रमित्यत्रापि क्रियान्वयविवक्षायां परिणामो रूपकं वा॥ ४॥ **भगवतीति**। अतिदृढासि अतिकठिनासीति सत्यम्। अत्र 'यो वा बिभर्ति काठिन्यं तस्मै भूम्यात्मने नमः' इति वचनं द्रष्टव्यम्। तव वसुंधरात्वप्रयुक्तधैर्येण पुत्रीनाशोऽप्याकिंचित्कर एवेत्युपालम्भो व्यज्यते। **त्वमिति**। यस्याः सीताया माहात्म्यममानुषत्वं त्वं वेत्थ। विदुरित्यस्य विभक्तिवचनयोर्विपरिणामेन योजना। वह्निर्वेद

---

१ भावनया. २ यजनवेदिसं०. ३ देवि सीते. ४ हाहा. ५ मुग्ध. ६ हि.

विद्यां वागिव यामसूत भवती तेव्रत्तु या दैवतं
तस्यास्त्वद्दुहितुस्तथा विशसनं किं दारुणेऽमृष्यथाः ॥ ५ ॥

(नेपथ्ये ।)

इत इतो भगवतीमहादेव्यौ ।

जनकः—— (दृष्ट्वा ।) अये गृष्टिनोपदिश्यमानमार्गा भगवत्यरुन्धती । (उत्थाय ।) कां पुनर्महादेवीत्याह । (निरूप्य ।) हा हा कथमियं महाराजदशरथस्य धर्मदारा: प्रियसखी मे कौसल्या । क एतां प्रत्येति सैवेयमिति ।

आसीदियं दशरथस्य गृहे यथा श्रीः
श्रीरेव वा किमुपमानपदेन सैषा ।
कष्टं बतान्यदिव दैववशेन जाता
दुःखात्मकं किमपि भूतमहो विपाकः ॥ ६ ॥

अयमपरः पापो दशाविपर्यासः ।

य एव मे जनः पूर्वमासीन्मूर्तो महोत्सवः ।
क्षते क्षारमिवासह्यं जातं तस्यैव दर्शनम् ॥ ७ ॥

मुनयो विदुः वसिष्ठगृहिणी अरुन्धती वेद जानाति गङ्गा च वेद जानाति । यदि वा किं च रघोः कुलगुरुः रघुवंशजनकस्तदाचार्यो वसिष्ठो वा । देवः दीप्तशीलः भास्करः स्वयं वेद परानपेक्षं जानाति । अत्र भूम्यादीनामन्योन्यनिरपेक्षप्रामाण्यप्रतिपत्त्यर्थं क्रियैकशेषाकरणाद्विदुरित्यत्र न मध्यमपुरुषः प्रयुक्तः । अत एव पुरुषवचनविपरिणामेन भिन्नानि वाक्यानि । यां प्रसूतवती तस्यास्तथाविधायाः पुनः शुद्धिं गतायाः । अग्निप्रवेशादित्यर्थः । त्वद्दुहितुः सीतायास्तथा विशसनमन्यादृशहिंसनं किममृष्यथाः कथं सोढवत्यसि ॥ ५ ॥ गृष्टिः दशरथकञ्चुकी तेन । निरूप्य हेतुभिर्विचार्य । इयं सैवेति एतां कः प्रत्येति प्रत्यभिजानाति । नाम प्रसिद्धौ । न कोऽपीत्यर्थः । **आसीदिति** । इयं कौसल्या दशरथस्य गृहे श्रीरिवासीदथ वा श्रीरेवासीत् । उपमानत्वबोधकयथाशब्देन किम् । न किमपीत्यर्थः । अत्रोपमालंकारो रूपकालंकार आक्षेपालंकारश्च । सैषा श्रीसदृशी श्रीभूता वा इयं कौसल्या दैववशेन दैवेच्छया अन्यदिव जातान्यद्भूतमिव संवृत्ता । अलक्ष्मीरिव जातेत्यर्थः । अत्रेवेति वर्तते । दुःखात्मकं दुःखैकरसं किमपि वाचामपरिच्छेद्यं भूतं प्राणिविशेषः जाता । साक्षादलक्ष्मीर्जातेत्यर्थः । यथा श्रीः श्रीरेव वेत्यनयोः प्रतिद्वन्द्वभूतमिदमहो विकारः प्राणिनामुपचयापचयरूपागन्तुको विस्मयनीय इत्यर्थः । कष्टं बतेति दुःखातिशये ॥ ॥ ६ ॥ **य इति** । य एष जनः कौसल्या ॥ ७ ॥

---

१ शुद्धिं गतायाः पुनः (टी०). २ त्वम्. ३ का...देवीत्युक्ता. ४ पत्नी. ५ एतत्, एवम्. ६ इति नाम. ७ विकारः.

(ततः प्रविशत्यरुन्धती कौसल्या कञ्चुकी च ।)

अरुन्धती—ननु ब्रवीमि द्रष्टव्यः स्वयमुपेत्यैव वैदेह इत्येष[१] वः कुलगुरोरादेशः । अत एव चाहं प्रेषिता । तत्कोऽयं पदे पदे महानध्यवसायः[२] ।

कञ्चुकी—देवि संस्तभ्यात्मानमनुरुध्यस्व[३] भगवतो वसिष्ठस्यादेशमिति विज्ञापयामि ।

कौसल्या—ईदृशे काले मिथिलाधिपो मया द्रष्टव्य इति सममेव सर्वाणि दुःखानि समुद्भवन्ति । तस्मान्न शक्नोम्युद्वर्तमानमूलबन्धनं हृदयं पर्यवस्थापायितुम् । (क)

अरुन्धती—अत्र कः संदेहः ।

संतानवाहीन्यपि मानुषाणां दुःखानि सद्बन्धुवियोगजानि ।
दृष्टे जने प्रेयसि दुःसहानि स्रोतःसहस्रैरिव संप्लवन्ते ॥ ८ ॥

कौसल्या—कथं नु खलु वत्साया वध्वा एवंगते तस्य राजर्षेर्मुखं दर्शयामः । (ख)

अरुन्धती—

एष वः श्लाघ्यसंबन्धी[४] जनकानां कुलोद्वहः ।
याज्ञवल्क्यो मुनिर्यस्मै ब्रह्मपारायणं जगौ ॥ ९ ॥

कौसल्या—एष स महाराजस्य हृदयानन्दो वत्साया वध्वाः

(क) ईरिसे काले मिहिलाहिवो मए दिठ्ठव्वो त्ति समं एव्व सव्वाइं दुःखाइं समुब्भवन्ति[५] । ता ण सक्कुणोमि उव्वट्टमाणमूलबन्धणं[६] हिअअं पज्जवत्थावेदुम् ।

(ख) कहं णु खु वच्छाए वहूए[७] एवंगेद तस्स राएसिणो मुहं दंसम्ह ।

आदेशः आज्ञा । अनध्यवसायः संशयः । आत्मानं धृतिम् । संस्तभ्य प्रतिहतगतिं कृत्वा । अनुरुध्यस्वानुतिष्ठेत्यर्थः । समं युगपत् । अवतरन्ति प्राप्नुवन्ति । उद्वर्तमानमुद्वृत्तं मूलबन्धनं मूलनियन्त्रणं यस्य तथोक्तम् । शिथिलबन्धनमित्यर्थः । पर्यवस्थापयितुम् ॥ **संतानेति** । संतानेन अविच्छेदेन वाहीनि प्रवहन्त्यपि दुःखानि प्रेयसि जने दृष्टे सतीत्यन्वयः । स्रोतःसहस्रैरनन्तैः स्रोतोभिः । उपलक्षणे तृतीया । संप्लवन्ते महोर्मीभवन्ति ॥ ८ ॥ वध्वाः स्नुषायाः । **एष इति** । यस्मै यं जनकं सार्थयितुम् । 'क्रियार्थो—' इति चतुर्थी । ब्रह्मपारायणं स्वरूपेण गुणैश्च अनवधिकाशयब्रह्मत्वयुक्तपरमात्मप्रतिपादकवेदान्तभागं जगौ उपदिदेश । स एष इति योजना ॥ ९ ॥ हृदयनिर्विशेषः । अन्तरङ्ग इत्यर्थः । सीरः ध्वजे यस्य तथोक्तः ।

१ एवं. २ महानध्य०. ३ संस्तभ्भय. ४ संबन्धि, संबन्ध. ५ ओदरन्ति (अवतरन्ति) (टी०). ६ उग्घट्टमाण (उद्घट्टमान). ७ मे वहुए वनगदाए तस्सा पिदुणो (मे वत्साया वनगतायास्तस्याः पितुः).

पिता राजर्षिः । हा धिक् हा धिक् स्मारितास्म्यनिर्वेदरमणीयान्दिवसान् । हा दैव सर्वमेव तन्नास्ति । (क)

जनकः—(उपसृत्य ।) भगवत्यरुन्धति वैदेहः सीरध्वजोऽभिवादयते ।

यया पूतंमन्यो निधिरपि पवित्रस्य महसः
पतिस्ते पूर्वेषामपि खलु गुरूणां गुरुतमः ।
त्रिलोकीमाङ्गल्यामवनितललीनेन शिरसा
जगद्वन्द्यां देवीमुषसमिव वन्दे भगवतीम् ॥ १० ॥

अरुन्धती—परं ते ज्योतिः प्रकाशताम् । अयं त्वां पुनातु देवः परोरजा य एष तपति ।

जनकः—आर्ये गृष्टे अप्यनामयमस्याः प्रजापालकस्य मातुः ।

कञ्चुकी—(स्वगतम् ।) निरवशेषमतिनिष्ठुरमुपालब्धाः स्मः । (प्रकाशम् ।) राजर्षे अनेनैव मन्युना चिरंपरित्यक्तरामभद्रमुखचन्द्रदर्शनां

(क) एसो सो महाराअस्स हिअआणन्दो वच्छाए वहूए पिदा राएसी । हद्धी हद्धी सुमारिदाह्मि अणिव्वेदरमणीए दिवहे । हा देव्व सव्वं एव तं णत्थि ।

अनिर्वेदाश्च ते रमणीयाश्च । न विद्यते निर्वेदश्चित्तग्लानिर्येषु तथोक्ताः । रमणीया आनन्दहेतवः तथाविधान्दिवसान्स्मारितास्मि दिवसविषयकस्मरणवती कृतास्मि । सर्वमेतदुपलभ्यमानं सर्वं नास्ति असत्कल्पम् । हा दुःख्यते । अभिवादयते । प्रणामेनाशीर्वाचयतीत्यर्थः ॥ **ययेति** । पूतंमन्यः आत्मविषयकपूतत्वप्रकारकज्ञानवान् । त्रिलोकीमाङ्गल्यां लोकत्रयमङ्गलहेतुभूतमुषसमिव प्रातःसंध्यादिदेवतामिव स्थिताम् । अवनितललीनेन शिरसेत्युपलक्षणमष्टाङ्गप्रणामस्य ॥ १० ॥ अक्षरं प्रकृतिपुरुषवत्स्वरूपस्वभावविकाररहितं ज्योतिः स्वयंप्रकाशं प्रकाशतां प्रतिभासताम् । अक्षरमम्बरान्तधृतेर्ज्योतिश्चरणाभिधानादित्यधिकरणद्वयार्थः प्रत्यभिज्ञापितः । देवः जगत्सृष्ट्यादिलीलावान् । रजसां समस्तदोषजातेभ्यः परः । संबन्धसामान्ये षष्ठी । 'परोरजाः' इति वा पाठः । रजसः पर इति विग्रहः । बाहुलकात्समासः । पृषोदरत्वादोकारश्च । य एष तपति स त्वां पुनातु । अनेन अन्तस्तद्धर्मोपदेशादित्यधिकरणार्थः सूचितः । परोरजसामित्यनेन 'उदेति ह वै सर्वेभ्यः पाप्मभ्यः' इति श्रुतिश्चोदिता । अनामयमारोग्यम् । प्रजापालकस्य मातुः राममातुः कौसल्यायाः । इदं च साभिप्रायम् । अनामयमित्यनेन एवं दुःखिनी कियच्चिरं जीवयिष्यतीत्युपालम्भो व्यज्यते । निरवशेषं निःशेषमतिनिष्ठुरं अतिरूक्षम् । अनेनैव मन्युना 'अप्यनामयं प्रजापालकस्य मातुः' इत्यनेन

---

१ मङ्गल्यां. २ लोलेन. ३ अक्षरं. ४ स...परोरजसां. ५ अपि कुशलम्. ६ निर्विशेषम्. ७ अचिर. ८ हिअअणिव्विसेसो...पिदा विदेहराओ सीरद्धओ (हृदयनिर्विशेषः ...पिता विदेहराजः सीरध्वजः). ९ संभाविदह्मि अणुवट्ठिदमहूसवे दिअहे (संभावितास्म्यनुपस्थितमहोत्सवान् दिवसान्); सुमराविदम्हि अणेच्छिदमहूसवे (संस्मारितास्म्यनेच्छिकमहोत्सवान्).

नार्हसि दुःखयितुमतिदुःखितां देवीम् । रामभद्रस्यापि दैवदुर्योगः कोऽपि यत्किल समन्ततः प्रवृत्तबीभत्सकिंवदन्तीकाः पौरजानपदा नाग्निशुद्धिमनल्पकाः प्रतियन्तीति दारुणमनुष्ठितं देवेन ।

जनकः——(सरोषम् ।) आः कोऽयमग्निर्नामास्मत्प्रसूतिपरिशोधने । कष्टमेवंवादिना जनेन रामभद्रपरिभूता अपि वयं पुनः परिभूयामहे ।

अरुन्धती——(निःश्वस्य ।) एवमेतत् । अग्निरिति वत्सां प्रति परिलघून्यक्षराणि । सीतेत्येव पर्याप्तम् । हा वत्से

शिशुर्वा शिष्या वा यदसि मम तत्तिष्ठतु तथा
विशुद्धेरुत्कर्षस्त्वयि तु मम भक्तिं द्रढयति ।
शिशुत्वं स्त्रैणं वा भवतु ननु वन्द्यासि जगतां
गुणाः पूजास्थानं गुणिषु न च लिङ्गं न च वयः ॥ ११ ॥

कौसल्या——अहो उन्मीलन्ति वेदनाः । (इति मूर्च्छति ।) (क)

(क) अहो उम्मीलन्ति वेअणाओ ।

व्यज्यते न क्रोधेन । दैवस्य भवितव्यतायाः दुर्योगः दुःखजननसंनाहः । यत्किल यस्माद्धेतोः प्रवृत्ता प्रसृता बीभत्सा जुगुप्सनीया किंवदन्ती जनश्रुतिः येषां तथोक्ताः । 'किंवदन्ती जनश्रुतिः' इत्यमरः । पौराः पुरे भवाः । तस्माद्दैवदुर्योगः कोऽपीति पूर्वेणान्वयः । अनल्पकाः अत्यल्पाः । अग्निशुद्धिं न च प्रतियन्ति न विश्वसन्ति च । इति पूर्वोक्ताद्धेतोः । दारुणं परित्यागात्मकं रौक्ष्यम् । अग्निशुद्धिरिति क इति योजना । प्रस्ताव इति शेषः । एवंवादिना अग्निशुद्धिरिति वादिना जनेन परिभूयामहे अवमन्यामहे । उपसर्गवशेन भवतेः कर्मणि लकारः । एतत्परिभूयामहे इत्येतत् । एवं जनकोक्तदशासद्भाव एव । लघून्यक्षराणि लाघवापादकंशब्दाः । सीतेत्येव पर्याप्तम् । वह्निसीतयोः पावनत्वे समकक्ष्यत्वात्प्रत्युत सीतायाः प्रकर्षात्सीताशब्द एव परिपूर्ण इति भावः । **शिशुरिति** । त्वं मम शिशुर्वा शिष्या वासीति यत् तत्तिष्ठत्विति योजना । विशुद्धेः निर्दोषताया उत्कर्षः अतिशयः । तथा भक्तिमन्यादृशीं पूजनीयताप्रतिपत्तिं त्वयि मम द्रढयति स्थिरां करोति । शिशुत्वं स्त्रैणं स्त्रीत्वं वा । 'स्त्रीपुंसाभ्यां नञ्स्नञौ' इति नञ्प्रत्ययः । भवतु स्यात् न तु तावता वन्द्यात्वहानिः । जगतां वन्द्यासि अभिवादनीयासि । नन्वित्यवधारणे । गुणाः गुणिषु अहिंसाशौचमस्तेयमित्याद्युक्तगुणवत्सु पूजास्थानमन्वयव्यतिरेकाभ्यां पूजाप्रयोजकाः । लिङ्गजटोपवीतादिकं न पूजाप्रयोजकम ॥ ११ ॥ वेदना दुःखानि । समुन्मीलयन्ति मूलमुत्पाटयन्ति । इति

१ रामभद्रेणापि समन्ततःपरिवर्तितबीभत्स०...अल्पज्ञाः...ष्ठितम्. २ मल्पकाः. ३ प्रातिपद्यन्ते इत्यतः. ४ आग्निर.ग्निः. ५ जनयाति. ६ जगतः. ७ न्ति विअ; समुम्मीलअन्ति विष.

जनकः—हा कष्टं किमेतत् ।

अरुन्धती—राजर्षे किमन्यत् ।

स राजा तत्सौख्यं स च शिशुजनस्ते च दिवसाः
स्मृतावाविर्भूतं त्वयि सुहृदि दृष्टे तदखिलम् ।
विपाके घोरेऽस्मिन्नथ खलु[1] विमूढा तव सखी
पुरंध्रीणां चित्तं[2] कुसुमसुकुमारं हि भवति ॥ १२ ॥

जनकः—हन्त हन्त[3] सर्वथा नृशंसोऽस्मि संवृत्तः । यश्चिरस्य दृष्टान्प्रियसुहृदः प्रियान् दारान्[4] स्निग्धं पश्यामि ।

स संबन्धी श्लाघ्यः प्रियसुहृदसौ तच्च हृदयं
स चानन्दः साक्षादपि च निखिलं जीवितफलम्[5] ।
शरीरं जीवो वा यदधिक[6]मतोऽन्यत्प्रियतरं
महाराजः श्रीमान्किमिव[7] मम नासीद्दशरथः ॥ १३ ॥

मूर्च्छेति मूर्च्छामभिनयति । हन्त किमेतत् । शस्त्राभिघातादिकमन्तरा मूर्च्छा विस्मयनीयेत्यर्थः । अन्यत्किम् । वक्ष्यमाणादन्यन्न किमपीत्यर्थः । **स राजेति** । स राजा तत्सौख्यं स च शिशुजनस्ते च दिवसा इति यत्तदखिलं सुहृदि त्वयि दृष्टे सति स्मृतावाविर्भूतं कस्याप्यंशस्य प्रतोषेण स्मृतिविषयीभूतम् । 'सदृशा दृष्टचिन्ताद्याः स्मृतिबीजस्य बोधकाः ।' इत्युक्तेः । घोरे भयंकरे अस्मिन्विपाके प्रकृतसीतात्यागरूप-दैवपर्यवसाने तव सखी कौसल्या विमूढा नेति । अप्यनामयमस्या इत्यादिभवद्वचन-भङ्ग्याविष्कृतो भवन्मतरीत्या योऽस्या कठिनचित्तताप्रयुक्तमूर्च्छाभावो वा नेत्यर्थः । पुरंध्रीणां चित्तं हि यस्मात्कुसुमवन्मृदुः तस्मान्विमूढा नेति न ॥ १२ ॥ एवमरुन्धत्या बोधितेऽनुतपति—**हन्तेति** । योऽहं चिरस्य दृष्टान् चिराद् दृष्टान्प्रियसुहृदो दशरथस्य प्रियान्मत्प्रीतिविषयान्मयि प्रीतियुक्तान् हि दारान् कौसल्यामस्निग्ध इव शत्रुरिव पश्यामि शत्रुकर्तृकदर्शनवानस्मि । सोऽहं सर्वप्रकारेण क्रूरोऽस्मि हन्त अनुतप्यते । **स संबन्धीत्यादि** । श्रीमान् लक्ष्मीवान्महाराजः सार्वभौमः स दशरथः मम श्लाघ्यः संबन्धी अभूत् । असौ संबन्धिभूतो दशरथः प्रियसुहृदभूत् प्रीतिमान् शोभनहृदयवां-श्चाभूत् । 'सुहृद्दुर्हृदौ मित्रामित्रयोः' इति हृदयशब्दस्य हृदादेशः । तदन्तरङ्गत्वेन प्रसिद्धं हृदयं चाभूत् । चकारेण संबन्धिसुहृत्त्वसमुच्चयः । तदिति दशरथपरं विधेय-प्राधान्यात्क्लीबत्वम् । एवं च तत् संबन्धिसुहृद्भूतदशरथः हृदयं चाभूदिति वा । स पूर्वोक्तत्रयात्मा दशरथः साक्षादानन्दश्च । साक्षाच्छब्देनानन्दहेतावानन्दत्वारोपो व्याव-र्तते । साक्षान्मुख्य इत्यर्थः । निखिलजीवितफलमपि च कर्मज्ञानभक्तिरूपं जीवनप्रयोजनं

---

१ न खलु नः; ननु खलु. २ चेतः. ३ कष्टं कष्टं सर्वथा नृशंसोऽस्मि यश्चि० प्रियदा०. ४ न स्निग्ध इव. ५ पद्यम्. ६ ०तो वा प्रियतमः; प्रियतरः. ७ किमपि.

कष्टमियमेव सा कौसल्या ।

यदस्याः पत्युर्वा रहसि परमं दूषितमभू-
दभूवं दम्पत्योः पृथगहमुपालम्भविषयः ।
प्रसादे कोपे वा तदनु मदधीनो विधिरभू-
दलं वा तत्स्मृत्वा दहति यदवस्कद्य हृदयम् ॥ १४ ॥

अरुन्धती—हा कष्टम् । अतिचिरानिरुद्धनिःश्वासनिष्पन्दं हृदयमस्याः ।

जनकः—हा प्रियसखि । (इति कमण्डलूदकेन सिञ्चति ।)

कञ्चुकी—

सुहृदिव प्रकटय्य सुखप्रदः प्रथममेकरसामनुकूलताम् ।
पुनरकाण्डविवर्तनदारुणो विधिरहो विशिनष्टि मनोरुजम् ॥ १५ ॥

कौसल्या—(आश्वस्य ।) हा वत्से जानकि कुत्रासि । स्मरामि ते नवविवाहलक्ष्मीपरिग्रहैकमण्डनं प्रस्फुरच्छुद्धविहसितं मुग्धमुखपुण्डरीकम् । आस्फुरच्चन्द्रचन्द्रिकासुन्दरैरङ्गैः पुनरपि मे जाते उद्द्योतयोत्सङ्गम् ।

च । चकारः पूर्वसमुच्चायकः । शरीरमभू दुर्लभो मानुषो देह इत्युक्तशरीरं चाभूत् सकलधर्मसाधनत्वाज्जीवो वाभूत् । जीवश्चाभूत्तस्य हि ज्ञानानन्दमयत्वात्प्रेमास्पदत्वमतो जीवादधिकं समस्तकल्याणगुणामृतोदधित्वेनानन्दमयत्वेन च प्रकृष्टं प्रियतरं प्रियो जीवः प्रियतरं ब्रह्म तथाविधं यत्परं ब्रह्म तदभूत् । यत एवं ततः किं नाभूत् । सर्वमप्यभूदित्यर्थः । लोके संबन्धिसुहृदादीनां तत्तन्मात्रत्वमस्य तु सर्वदा सर्वविधत्वमिति भावः ॥ १३ ॥ **यदस्या इति** । अस्या वा पत्युर्दशरथस्य वा यत्परमं त्रायितमभूद्रहसि गुप्तभाषणं विचारो वा जातः । आचारणिजन्तात्कर्तरि क्तः । तत्राहं दम्पत्योर्जायापत्योः पृथगुपालम्भविषयोऽभूवं परस्परपरिहारेण परस्परविषये अयमेवमुक्तवानयमेवं कृतवानियमेवमुक्तवती इयमेवं कृतवतीत्यादिपरस्परापराधकथनपात्रमासम् । 'परमत्याहितमभूत्' इति पाठोऽपि दृश्यते । प्रणयकलहरूपजीवानपेक्षिकमैति तदर्थः । शेषं पूर्ववत् । तदनु उपालम्भान्तरं प्रसादानुष्ठानं कोपानुष्ठानं वा । मदधीनमभूदित्यर्थः । स्मृत्वालम् । तत्स्मरणेन साध्यं नास्तीत्यर्थः । यद्धृदयमवस्कन्द्याक्रम्य दहति भस्मीकरोति । तत्स्मृत्वालम् । कोपप्रसादयोरन्यविषयत्वं च पाठद्वये क्रमाद्विवक्षितम् । तत्र हि परस्परेत्युक्तिरुपलक्षणार्था ॥ १४ ॥ निरुद्धाः संचाररहिताः श्वासाः प्राणवायवो यस्मिन् तथोक्तं निष्पन्दं च । **सुहृदिति** । विधिः प्रथममादौ सुहृदिव मित्रमिव सुखप्रदामेकरसामेकप्रकारामनुकूलतां योगक्षेमहेतुभूतां प्रकटय्य प्रकाशयित्वा पुनरनन्तरमकाण्डेन निर्निमित्तेन विवर्तनेन व्यत्यस्तपरिपाकेन दारुणः सन् क्रूरः सन्मनसो रुजं हृदयपीडां परिशिनष्टि परिशिष्टां करोति । अकाण्डनिवर्तनेन दारुणोऽकाण्डनिवृत्तो भूत्वेत्यप्याहुः सुहृदपि त्यक्त्वा गतश्चेन्मनःपीडां

---

१ त्रायितं; परिमन्तूयितम्. २ चिर. ३ निष्ठुरम्. ४ लुजलेन. ५ सुखप्रदाम्. ६ परि–प्रविशिनष्टि विधिर्मनसो रुजम्.

सर्वदा महाराज एवं भणति । एषा रघुकुलमहत्तराणां वधूरस्माकं तु जनकसुता दुहितैव । (क)

कञ्चुकी—यथाह देवी ।

पञ्चप्रसूतेरपि तस्य राज्ञः प्रियो विशेषेण सुबाहुशत्रुः ।
वधूचतुष्केऽपि यथैवं शान्ता प्रिया तनूजास्य तथैव सीता ॥१६॥

जनकः—हा प्रियसख महाराज दशरथ एवमसि सर्वप्रकारहृदयगमः कथं विस्मर्यसे ।

कन्यायाः किल पूजयन्ति पितरो जामातुराप्तं जनं
संबन्धे विपरीतमेव तदभूदाराधनं ते मयि ।

(क) हा वच्छे जाणइ कहिं सि । सुमरामि दे णवविवाहलच्छीपरिग्गहेकमण्डनं पप्फुरन्तमुद्धविहसिदं मुद्धमुहमुपुण्डरीअं । आप्फुरन्तचन्दचन्दिआसुन्दरेहिं अङ्गेहिं पुणो वि मे जादे उज्जोएहि उच्छङ्गम् । सव्वदा महाराओ एव्वं भणादि । एसा रहुउलमहत्तराणं वहू अह्माणं दु जणअसुदा दुहिदेव्व ।

करोतीति साम्यम् ॥ १५ ॥ नवविवाहलक्ष्म्याः परिग्रहेण एकं मुख्यं मङ्गलं यस्य तथोक्तम् । कौमुद्यां कृत्तिकापौर्णमास्यां भवश्चन्द्रः कौमुदीचन्द्रः । आरोहन्ती प्रादुर्भवन्ती या कौमुदी चन्द्रचन्द्रिका तद्वत्सुन्दरमङ्गं यस्यास्तथोक्ता । उत्सङ्गमङ्कमुद्द्योतय उपवेशेन प्रकाशय । सर्वदा सर्वस्मिन्काले महाराजो दशरथः । एषा सीता रघुकुले महत्तरा ये मनुप्रभृतयस्तेषां वधूः स्नुषा । जनकसुता सीता अस्माकं तु मम तु दुहितैव मदभिप्रायेण दुहितैवेत्येवं भणति । देवी कौसल्या यथाह । तथैवेति शेषः । **पञ्चप्रसूतेरिति** । पञ्चप्रसूतयः पुत्रा यस्य तथोक्तस्य हि । तस्य रा : पङ्क्तिरथस्य सुबाहुशत्रुः रामः विशेषेण प्रिय इष्टः । पञ्चप्रसूतयो यस्मिन् वृन्दे इति वा विग्रहः । निर्धारणे षष्ठी । 'तृतीयादिषु भाषितपुंस्कं पुंवद्गालवस्य' इति पाक्षिकः पुंवद्भावः । पञ्चानां मध्ये रामः प्रिय इत्यर्थः । रामादयश्चत्वारः शान्ता चेति पञ्च । वधूचतुष्केऽपि सीतादिस्नुषाचतुष्टयेऽपि अस्य जनकस्य तनूजा सीता यथा तस्य राज्ञो दशरथस्य प्रिया तथा अन्या ऊर्मिलाप्रभृती राज्ञः प्रिया न । अस्य तनूजा सीतेत्यनेन सीताया एव जनकाभिसंधिना तनूजात्वं नान्यासामिति व्यज्यते । वधूचतुष्केऽपीति निर्धारणे सप्तमीदर्शनात् । ॥ १६ ॥ सर्वैः प्रकारैर्धर्मैः हृदयंगमः । **कन्याया इति** । संबन्धे कन्यावरसंबन्धे । कन्यायाः पितरो जनन्यः जनकाश्च जामातुर्वरस्याप्तं संनिहितबन्धुं जनं पूज-

---

१ राज्ञ आसीत्. २ चतुष्टेऽपि. ३ यथा हि…तथैव नान्या. ४ णवेति नास्ति क्वचित्. ५ मङ्गलं. ६ उप्फुल्लसुद्धहसिदं; संप्फुल्लमुद्धमुहपुण्डरीअं आरुहन्तकौमुदीचन्दसुन्दरं (आरुहन्तकौमुदी०). ७ एहि मे पुणो. ८ जणअसंबन्धेण. ९ दुहिदिआ (दुहितृका).

त्वं कालेन तथाविधोऽस्यपहृतः संबन्धबीजं च त-
द्घोरेऽस्मिन्मम जीवलोकनरके पापस्य धिग्जीवितम् ॥ १७ ॥

कौसल्या—जाते जानकि किं करोमि । दृढवज्रलेपघटितबन्ध-निश्चलं हतजीवितं मां मन्दभागिनीं न परित्यजति । (क)

अरुन्धती—आश्वसिहि राजपुत्रि बाष्पविश्रामोऽप्यन्तरे कर्तव्य एव । अन्यच्च किं न स्मरसि यदवोचदृष्यशृङ्गाश्रमे युष्माकं कुल-गुरुर्भवितव्यं तथेत्युपजातमेव किं तु कल्याणोदर्कं भविष्यतीति ।

कौसल्या—कुतोऽतिक्रान्तमनोरथाया ममैतत् । (ख)

अरुन्धती—तत्किं मन्यसे राजपत्नि मृषोद्यं तदिति । न हीदं सुक्षत्रियेऽन्यथा मन्तव्यम् । भवितव्यमेव तेन ।

आविर्भूतज्योतिषां ब्राह्मणानां
ये व्याहारास्तेषु मा संशयोऽभूत् ।

(क) जादे जाणइ किं करोमि । दिढवज्जलेवघंडिअबन्धणिच्चलं हदजीविदं मं मन्दभाइणीं ण पडिच्चअदि ।

(ख) कुदो अदिकंन्दमणोरहाए मह एदम् ।

यन्ति किल संभावयन्तीति प्रसिद्धम् । तदाराधनं पूजनं ते मयि विपरीतमभूत् । त्वत्कर्तृकमद्विषयकपूजनं सत् प्रतिलोमं जातमित्यर्थः । तथाविधोऽपि त्वं कालेनापहृतः । मया पूज्यमानं भवन्तं द्रष्टुमन्याय्यं तावद्भाग्याभावेऽपि केवलं वा भवन्तं द्रष्टुं मदीयदैवदुर्विपाको नाक्षाम्यदिति भावः । संबन्धबीजं सीता चापहृतम् । लिङ्गविपरिणामः । पूर्वोक्तयोरभावेऽपि तादृशभवदभिमता सीतापि दैवेन नाक्षम्यतेति भावः । घोरे भयंकरे अस्मिन्नेवंविधबहुदुःखभाजने जीवलोकबिले पापस्य पूजनविपर्यासादिहेतुभूतदुरितप्रचुरस्य मम जीवितं प्राणधारणं धिक् । तत्कर्मिका निन्देत्यर्थः । अत्रेदानीं भवत्पूजाद्यभावेऽपि यत्र तल्लाभो लोकान्तरे तत्र गमनस्यापि मदीयजीवनयोनिदुरितं प्रतिबन्धकमिति भावः ॥ १७ ॥ दृढेन वज्रलेपेन बन्धकद्रव्यलेपेन यः प्रतिबन्धो विश्लेषानुत्पादस्तेन निश्चलं हतजीवितं निन्द्यजीवितम् । आश्वसिहि आश्वासं दुःखलघूकरणं प्राप्नुहि । बाष्पस्य दुःखाश्रुणः विश्रामो विच्छेदोऽपि । अपिशब्देन बाष्पादिकं समुच्चीयते । अन्तरेषु मध्ये मध्ये । अन्यच्च बाष्पविश्रामादन्यदपि । यत्कुलगुरुर्वसिष्ठः अवोचत्तन्न स्मरसि किम् । भवितव्यं तथेति परित्यागरूपेण भवनमपरिहार्यमिति हेतोः । उपजातमापातनो जातम् । न त्वन्ततस्तथेत्यर्थः । कल्याणोदर्कं मङ्गलपर्यवसायि भविष्यतीति यदवोचत्तन्न स्मरसि किम् । अतिक्रान्तमनोरथाया असंभाव्याभिलाषविषयायाः । मृषोद्यमिति मिथ्यावचनमिति । **आविर्भूतेति** । आविर्भूत-

१ प्यप०. २ तु. ३ अन्तरेषु, अन्तरा,–ले. ४ गुरुस्तदुपजातमेव. ५ एतन्नास्ति क्वचित् ६ पडिबद्ध–बन्ध०. ७ भअवदि अदिक्कन्तो मणोरहो (अतिक्रान्तो मनोरथः), अदिक्कन्ते० रथे.

भद्रा ह्येषां वाचि लक्ष्मीर्निषक्ता
नैते वाचं विप्लुतार्थां वदन्ति ॥ १८ ॥

(नेपथ्ये कलकलः । सर्वे आकर्णयन्ति ।)

जनकः—अये अद्य खलु शिष्टानध्याय इत्युद्धतं खेलतां बटूनां कलकलः ।

कौसल्या—सुलभसौख्यं तावत् बालत्वं भवति । (निरूप्य ।) अहो एतेषां मध्ये क एष रामभद्रलक्ष्मीपरिशोभितैः सावष्टम्भमुग्धललितैरङ्गैरस्माकं लोचनानि शीतलयति । (क)

अरुन्धती—(अपवार्य सहर्षबाष्पम् ।) इदं नाम तद्भागीरथीनिवेदितरहस्यं कर्णामृतम् । न त्वेवं विद्मः कतरोऽयमायुष्मतोः कुशलवयोरिति । (प्रकाशम् ।)

(क) सुलहसोक्खं दाव बालत्तणं होदि । अह्महे एदाणं मज्झे को एसो रामभद्दलच्छीपरिसोहिदेहिं सावट्टम्भमुद्धललिदेहिं अङ्गेहिं अह्माणं लोअणाइं शीअलावेदि ।

ज्योतिषां परज्योतिर्विषयकपरोक्षज्ञानवतां ब्राह्मणानां विप्राणां ये व्याहारा उक्तयस्तेषु संशयः प्रामाण्यसंदेहो माभूत् नोत्पत्त्यर्हः । हि यस्मादेषां ब्राह्मणानां वाचि भव्या मङ्गलकरी लक्ष्मीः अर्थोपदायकत्वातिशयः । निषक्ता नित्यसङ्गिनी भवति । एते आविर्भूतज्योतिषो ब्राह्मणाः विलुतार्थामसदर्थां वाचमेकामपि गिरं न वदन्ति नोच्चारयन्ति । पूर्वत्र बहुवचनं तदीयसर्ववाचामपि प्रामाण्यबोधनार्थम् । अत्रैकवचनं तु तदीययत्किंचिद्वचोऽप्यप्रामाण्यं नेति बोधनार्थमिति द्रष्टव्यम् । अत्र 'श्लोके सक्तुमिव तितउना पुनन्तो यत्र धीरा मनसा वाचमक्रत । अत्रा सखायः सख्यानि जानते भद्रैषां लक्ष्मीर्निहिताधिवाचि ॥' इति श्रुतिः (ऋ. १०-७१-२) स्फोरिता ॥ १८ ॥ शिष्टागमनप्रयुक्ताध्ययनाभावः शिष्टानध्ययनः । सुलभं सौख्यं यस्मिंस्तथोक्तम् । अनेन 'वृद्धो जनो दुःखशतानि भुङ्क्ते ।' इत्युक्तवार्द्धकनिन्दा व्यज्यते । रामभद्रस्य कौमारलक्ष्म्या चन्द्रवदाह्लादकारिरामशैशवस्य योऽयमवष्टम्भ आलम्बनं तत्सहितैः । लक्ष्मीपदेन शैशवस्य स्पृहणीयत्वं व्यज्यते संबन्धशब्दत्वात्सापेक्षत्वेऽपि समासः । मुग्धललितैः सुन्दरसुकुमारैः । हर्षः इष्टागमात्प्रीतिः । उत्कण्ठा आकारादिविषयाभिलाषः । भागीरथीनिवेदितं गङ्गया कथितं रहस्यं गूढं यत्कर्णयोरमृतवद्भोग्यम् । तदिदं नामायुष्मतोः कुशलवयोर्मध्ये कतरोयऽमिति कुश इति वा लव

१ भव्या. २ नियुक्ता. ३ विप्लुतां व्याहरन्ति. ४ अनध्ययनः—नं. ५ अस्खलितं; यनमिति खेलतां. ६ कोलाहलः. ७ स्वगतं सहर्षोत्कण्ठम्. ८ निवेदितं रहस्यक०; स्यं क०. ९ जनकः. १० दाणीं (इदानीं). ११ रामभद्दस्स कोमारलच्छीसरिसेहिं सावट्टम्भेहिं मु०, कोमारलच्छीसावट्टम्भेहिं मुद्ध…अङ्गेहिं दारको. १२ विलोअणं.

कुवलयदलस्निग्धश्यामः शिखण्डकमण्डनो
बटुपरिषदं पुण्यश्रीकः श्रियेवे सभाजयन्।
पुनरपि शिशुर्भूतो[3] वत्सः स मे रघुनन्दनो
झटिति कुरुते दृष्टः कोऽयं दृशोरमृताञ्जनम् ॥ १९ ॥

कञ्चुकी—नूनं क्षत्रियब्रह्मचारी दारकोऽयमिति मन्ये।

जनकः—एवमेतत्। अस्य[4] हि

चूडाचुम्बितकङ्कपत्रमभितस्तूणीद्वयं पृष्ठतो
भस्मस्तोकेपवित्रलाञ्छनमुरो धत्ते त्वचं रौरवीम्।
मौर्व्या मेखलया नियन्त्रितमधोवासश्च माञ्जिष्ठकं
पाणौ कार्मुकमक्षसूत्रवलयं दण्डोऽपरः पैप्पलः ॥ २० ॥

भगवत्यरुन्धति किमुत्प्रेक्षसे कुतस्त्योऽयमिति।

अरुन्धती—अद्यैवागता वयम्।

जनकः—आर्य गृष्टे अतीव मे कौतुकं वर्तते तद्भगवन्तं वाल्मीकिमेव गत्वा पृच्छ। इमं च बालकं ब्रूहि। वत्स केऽप्येते प्रवयसस्त्वां दिदृक्षव इति।

कञ्चुकी—यदाज्ञापयति देवः। (इति निष्क्रान्तः।)

इति वा न विद्मः न जानामि। 'अस्मदो द्वयोश्च' इत्येकत्वे बहुवचनम्। **कुवलयेति**। शिखण्डकमण्डनः काकपक्षधरो बटूनां ब्रह्मचारिणां परिषदं सदः श्रिया कान्त्या सभाजयन्नलंकुर्वन्। अमृताञ्जनममृतमयमञ्जनं शीतलस्वादिभिः। तद्धि रमणीयमिति कविसमयप्रसिद्धिः ॥ १९ ॥ मन्ये अनुमिनोमि। एतद्भवता संभाव्यमानमेव वस्तुभूतम्। **चूडाचुम्बितेति**। चूडाचुम्बितानि संयुक्ताग्राणि कङ्कपत्राणि बाणपक्षा यस्मिंस्तथोक्तम्। पृष्ठतोऽभितः पृष्ठम्। द्वयोर्भागयोरित्यर्थः। भस्ममयं स्तोकमल्पं पवित्रं पावनं लाञ्छनं पुण्ड्रं यस्य तत्तथोक्तम्। उरः रौरवीमैणेयीं त्वचं धत्ते। मौर्व्यात्मकरशनया नियन्त्रितं माञ्जिष्ठं मञ्जिष्ठरक्तं वासः अधः उरसोऽधस्तात्। क्षत्रियब्रह्मचारिणां मेखलेत्युक्तं माञ्जिष्ठं राजन्यस्य इति च। पाणौ कार्मुकं धनुरक्षसूत्रवलयं जपमालिकावलयम्। अस्तीति शेषः। 'अपरे पैप्पलः' इति पाठे अपरे पाणौ अश्वत्थदण्डः। 'अपरः पैप्पलः' इति पाठे धनुर्दण्डादपरः। अन्य इत्यर्थः ॥२०॥ कुतस्त्यः कस्माद्भवः। अतिशयितं कौतुकं विशिष्टवस्तुजिज्ञासौत्कण्ठ्यम्। प्रवयसो वृद्धाः। दिदृक्षवः द्रष्टुमिच्छवः। यदाज्ञापयतीत्यत्रः तदनुतिष्ठामीति शेषः। एवं भणितः प्रवयसस्त्वां दिदृक्षव इत्युक्तः सन् आगमिष्यति किमिति मन्यध्वे। किं

---

१ मण्डलः. २ श्रियेव. ३ भूत्वा. ४ तथा. ५ स्तोम. ६ किमिनि. ७ अद्यैव वयमप्यागताः. ८ दारकम्. ९ यथा आज्ञापयसि.

कौसल्या—किं मन्यध्व एवं भणित आगमिष्यतीति । (क)

जनकः—भिद्येत वा सद्वृत्तमीदृशस्य निर्माणस्य ।

कौसल्या—(निरूप्य ।) कथं सविनयं निशामितगृष्टिवचनो विसर्जितर्षिदारक इतोऽभिमुखं प्रसृत एव स वत्सः । (ख)

जनकः—(चिरं निर्वर्ण्य ।) भोः किमप्येतत् ।

महिम्नामेतस्मिन्विनयशिशुतामौग्ध्यमसृणो
विदग्धैर्निर्ग्राह्यो न पुनरविदग्धैरतिशयः ।
मनो मे संमोहस्थिरमपि हरत्येष बलवा-
नयोधातुं यत्त्वपरिलघुरयस्कान्तशकलः ॥ २१ ॥

लवः—(प्रविश्य ।) अज्ञातनामक्रमाभिजनान्पूज्यानपि स्वतः कथमभिवादयिष्ये । (विचिन्त्य ।) अयं पुनरविरुद्धः प्रकार इति वृद्धेभ्यः श्रूयते । (सविनयमुपसृत्य ।) एष वो लवस्य शिरसा प्रणामपर्यायः ।

(क) किं मण्णेध एव्वं भणिदो आअमिस्सादित्ति ।

(ख) कहं सविणअं णिसामिदगिद्धिवअणो विसज्जिदइसिदारओ इतोऽहिमुहं पसरिदो एव्व सो वच्छो ।

संदिग्धे । ईदृशस्य लोकोत्तरस्य निर्माणस्याकारस्य । निर्मीयते यन्निर्माणम् । कर्मणि ल्युट् । 'कृत्यल्युटो बहुलम्' इत्युक्तेः । सद्वृत्तं सदाचारो भिद्यते वा । छिन्नं भवति किम्मित्यर्थः । कर्मवत्कर्मणा इति यगात्मनेपदे । सविनयं निशामितं श्रुतं गृष्टिवचनं येन तथोक्तः । एतद्वक्ष्यमाणं किमपि अपूर्वमित्यर्थः । तदाह—**महिम्नामित्यादि** । विनयेन ज्ञानवृद्धशीलवृद्धसंनिधौ स्वनिकर्षपर्यवसाय्यवस्थानेन शिशिरः शीतलः मौग्ध्येन मसृणः पारुष्यरहितः । विदग्धैः सूक्ष्मदर्शिभिर्ग्राह्यो निर्णेयः अविदग्धैः पुनर्न ग्राह्यो निर्णेतुमशक्यः । एतस्मिन्महिम्नामतिशयः लवानिष्ठप्रकृष्टज्ञानतेजःप्रकृतिगुणादिमाहात्म्यानामुत्कर्षः । संमोहेन मूर्च्छया स्थिरमपि काष्ठवन्निष्पन्दमपि मे मनश्चित्तं परिलघुरल्पः अयस्कान्तशकलः अयस्कान्तखण्डः अयोधातुं यद्वल्लोहपिण्डमिव हरति कर्षति । अत्र विनयशिशिरो मौग्ध्यमसृण इत्याभ्यां सलिलहिमोपष्टम्भेन ज्योत्स्नीभवतां सूर्यतेजसां सादृश्यं व्यज्यते ॥ २१ ॥ क्रमः सत्काराद्यानुपूर्व्यं वयः स्थाविरादिकं वयःक्रमस्तस्यौचित्यं प्राप्तवत्ता । ज्ञातं च तद्वयः-

---

१ भिद्यते, वा–किम्. २ शिशिरः. ३ संमोहः,संमोदः. ४ त्येव. ५ भिजात्यान्, अविज्ञातवयःक्रमौचित्यात् पूज्यानपि सतः; अपि नः. ६ भणध (भणथ). ७ ०स्सदि वा ण वेति. ८ सविणअणिसमि० ९ विसज्जिदासेससरिसदारओ (विसर्जिताशेषसदृशदारकः); विसज्जिअ इसिदारए (विसृज्य ऋषिदारकान्). १० अवसारिदो; पराअदो.

अरुन्धतीजनकौ—कल्याणिन् आयुष्मान्भूयाः ।

कौसल्या—जात चिरं जीव । (क)

अरुन्धती—एहि वत्स । (लवमुत्सङ्गे गृहीत्वात्मगतम् ।) दिष्ट्या न केवलमुत्सङ्गश्चिरान्मनोरथोऽपि मे संपूर्णः ।

कौसल्या—जात इतोऽपि तावदेहि । (उत्सङ्गे गृहीत्वा ।) अहो न केवलं दरविकसन्नीलोत्पलश्यामलोज्ज्वलेन देहबन्धेन कवलितारविन्दकेसरकषायकण्ठकलहंसानिनाददीर्घदीर्घेण स्वरेण च रामभद्रमनुहरति । ननु कठोरकमलगर्भपक्ष्मलः शरीरस्पर्शोऽपि तादृश एव वत्सस्य । जात प्रेक्षे तावत्ते मुखपुण्डरीकम् । (चुबुकमुन्नमय्य निरूप्य सबाष्पाकूतम् ।) राजर्षे किं न प्रेक्षसे निपुणं निरूप्यमाणमस्य मुखं वत्साया वध्वा मुखचन्द्रेण संवदत्येव । (ख)

जनकः—पश्यामि सखि पश्यामि ।

(क) जाद चिरं जीव ।

(ख) जाद इदो वि दाव एहि । अह्महे ण केवलं दरविअसन्तणीलुप्पलसामलुज्जलेण देहबन्धेण कवलिदारविन्दकेसरकसाअकण्ठकलहंसणिणाददीहरदीहरेण सरेण अ रामभद्दं अणुहरदि । णं कठोरकमलगब्भपह्मलो सरीरप्पस्सो वि तारिसो एव्व वच्छस्स । जाद पेक्खामि दाव दे मुहपुण्डरीअम् । राएसि किं ण पेक्खसि णिउणं णिरूवज्जन्तं से मुहं बच्छाए वहूए मुहचन्देण संवददि एव्व ।

क्रमौचित्यं तस्याभावः अज्ञातवयःक्रमौचित्यम् । अर्थाभावे अव्ययीभावः । अपञ्चम्या इति प्रतिषेधादम्भावो न । तथा च वयःक्रमौचित्यज्ञानाभावादित्यर्थः । कथमभिवादयिष्ये केन क्रमरूपप्रकारेण नमस्करिष्ये । अविरुद्धः अविपरीतः प्रकारोऽनुष्ठानविशेषः । सामान्यवृद्धविषयकप्रणामकरणरूप इति भावः । सभायां प्रत्येकं न नमस्कुर्यादिति गौतमस्मरणमिहाभिप्रेतम् । उत्सङ्गे अङ्के । दिष्ट्येत्यानन्दे । उत्सङ्गः केवलं न पूरितः किं तु मनोरथोऽपि पूरित इत्यर्थः । जातेति संबोधनम् । विकटमिति विस्तृतवाचिकम् । कन्दोट्टशब्दः कुवलयवाची । घर्घरश्च कांस्यध्वनिस्तद्वदनुकरणं तथाविधेन । अनुसरति अनुकरोति । कठोरस्य समग्रस्य कमलस्य गर्भवदान्तरपत्रवत्पक्ष्मलः स्फीतः तादृश एव रामभद्रस्पर्शसदृश एव । चुबुकमधराधोदेशम् । निपुणं निरूप्यमाणः हेतुभिः पटुतरं विचार्यमाणः । अयमिति शेषः । मुखं चन्द्रेण संवदत्येव । सीतामुखचन्द्रेति यौगिकसादृश्यप्रमाणविषयो भवति । पश्यामि सखि पश्या-

---

१ कृत्वा स्वगतं—अपवार्य. २ पूरितः. ३ क्रोडे कृत्वा. ४ दरविप्पटकन्दोट्टमंसलु०—ट्टसामलुज्ज (दरविस्पष्टकुवलयमांसलोज्ज्व०...श्यामलो०); सामलुण्णदेन (श्यामलोन्नतेन). ५ हंसघोसघग्घराणुणादिणा; हंसघोरघग्घरणिणाददीहरेण. ६ अणुसरेदि. ७ जीव जाद...मुहचन्दं. ८ वज्जन्तो (प्यमाणः) वच्छाए.

कौसल्या—अहो उन्मत्तीभूतमिव मे हृदयं किमपीतोमुखं विप्रलपति । (क)

जनकः—

वत्सायाश्च रघूद्वहस्य च शिशावस्मिन्नभिव्यज्यते
संपूर्णप्रतिबिम्बितेवं निखिला सैवाकृतिः सा द्युतिः ।
सा वाणी विनयः स एव सहजः पुण्यानुभावोऽप्यसौ
हा हा दैवं किमुत्पथैर्मम मनः पारिप्लवं धावति ॥ २२ ॥

कौसल्या—जात अस्ति ते माता स्मरसि वा तातम् । (ख)

लवः—न हि न हि ।

कौसल्या—ततः कस्य त्वम् । (ग)

लवः—भगवतः वाल्मीकेः ।

कौसल्या—अयि जात कथयितव्यं कथय । (घ)

(क) अह्महे उम्मत्तीभूदं विअ मे हिअअं किंपि ए[६]दोमुहं विप्पलवदि ।
(ख) जाद अत्थि दे मादा सुमरसि वा तादम् । (ग) तदो कस्स तुमम् ।
(घ) अयि जाद कहिदव्वं कहेहि ।

मीति आदराद्द्विरुक्तिः । उन्मत्तीभूतमिव विभ्रान्तामिव कुतोमुखं तत्र क्वापि असंभव्य-विषये लग्नमिति यावत् । विलपति परिदेवयति । ' विवलते ' इति च पाठः । **वत्साया इति** । अस्मिन् शिशौ लवे वत्सायाः सीताया रघूद्वहस्य रामचन्द्रस्य च संवृत्तिः संपर्कः । संबन्ध इत्यर्थः । प्रतिबिम्बितेवाभिव्यज्यते अभिव्यक्ता भवति । दर्पणादौ बिम्बवद् दृश्यत इत्यर्थः । निखिला कृत्स्ना आकृतिरवयवस्थानविशेषः सैव सीतारघूद्वहसंबन्धिन्येव । द्युतिर्लावण्यं तयोरेव संबन्धिनी । वाणी लवस्य वाक् सा तयोरेव संबन्धिनी । विनयः प्रश्रयः स एव सहजः स्वाभाविकः । पुण्यश्चासौ पावनश्चासौ अनुभावः समीचीनव्यवसायः । असौ सीतारघूद्वहसंबन्ध्येव । अदूरविप्रकृष्टवाच्योऽदःशब्दः । ' अनुभावः प्रभावे च सतां च मतिनिश्चये ' इत्यमरः । देवि सीते । मम मनः । पारिप्लवं सत् चञ्चलं सत् उत्पथैरमार्गैः धावति अनवस्थितं भवति । हा हा । दुःख्यत इत्यर्थः देवीत्यनेन देवभूयंगतायास्तव कथमिदं संगच्छत इति व्यज्यते । अत एव ह्युत्पथैरित्युक्तम् । अत्र च ' ऋक्पूरब्धूःपथामा–' इति समासान्तः ॥ २२ ॥

---

१ संपृक्ता, संपृक्त, संवृत्तिः (टी०). २ म्यिकेव. ३ देवि, देव. ४ वर्तते. ५ भगवतः सुगृहीतनामधेयस्य. ६ किंवि चिन्तअन्तो बहु (किमपि चिन्तयद्बहु); चिन्तअन्तीए बहु. ७ विलवदि.

लवः—एतावदेव जानामि ।

(नेपथ्ये ।)

भो भोः सैनिका एष खलु कुमारश्चन्द्रकेतुराज्ञापयति न केनचिदाश्रमाभ्यर्णभूमयं आक्रमितव्या इति ।

अरुन्धतीजनकौ—अये मेध्याश्वरक्षाप्रसङ्गादुपागतो वत्सश्चन्द्रकेतुरद्य द्रष्टव्य इत्यहो सुदिवसः ।

कौसल्या—वत्सलक्ष्मणस्य पुत्रक आज्ञापयतीत्यमृतबिन्दुसुन्दराण्यक्षराणि श्रूयन्ते । (क)

लवः—आर्य क एष चन्द्रकेतुर्नाम ।

जनकः—जानासि रामलक्ष्मणौ दाशरथी ।

लवः—एतावेव रामायणकथापुरुषौ ।

जनकः—अथ किम् ।

लवः—तत्कथं न जानामि ।

जनकः—तस्य लक्ष्मणास्ययमात्मजश्चन्द्रकेतुः ।

लवः—ऊर्मिलायाः पुत्रस्तर्हि मैथिलस्य राजर्षेर्दौहित्रः ।

अरुन्धती—(विहस्य ।) आविष्कृतं कथाप्रावीण्यं वत्सेन ।

जनकः—(विचिन्त्य ।) यदि त्वमीदृशः कथायामभिज्ञस्तद्ब्रूहि तावत्पृच्छामस्तेषां दशरथात्मजानां कियन्ति किंनामधेयान्यपत्यानि केषु केषु दारेषु प्रसूतानीति ।

(क) वच्छलक्खणस्स पुत्तओ आणवेदित्ति अमिदबिन्दुसुन्दराइं अक्खराइं सुणीअन्दि ।

कस्य त्वम् । कस्माज्जात इत्यर्थः । सुगृहीतं सुष्ठु प्रतिपादितं नामधेयं यस्य तथोक्तस्य वाल्मीकेस्तस्माज्जातः । सैनिकाः सेनासमवायिनः । अभ्यर्णभूमयः समीपदेशाः ता न क्रामितव्या न केनापि स्प्रष्टव्या इति । आज्ञापयतीत्यर्थः । मेध्याश्वस्य यज्ञाङ्गाश्वस्य प्रसङ्गादवश्यानुरोद्धव्यत्वाद्धेतोः द्रष्टव्य इति सुदिवसः । चन्द्रकेतुदर्शनाच्छोभनदिवसोऽयं विस्मयनीय इत्यर्थः । अमृतबिन्दुसुन्दराण्यक्षराणि सुधापृषत इव भोग्या वर्णाः । दाशरथी दशरथपुत्रौ जानासि किमिति काका योजनीयम् । रामायणकथायाः रामायणनामकवाक्यप्रबन्धस्य पुरुषौ प्रतिपाद्यौ । अथ किमित्यङ्गीकारे । तर्हि ऊर्मिलापुत्रत्वे । मैथिलस्य मिथिलाधिपतेः । आविष्कृतं प्रकाशितम् । वत्सेन लवेन । कथायामभिज्ञस्तत्प्रतिपाद्यार्थज्ञानवान् । किंनामधेयानीत्यारभ्य केषु प्रसूतानीत्यन्तस्य ब्रूहीत्यनेनान्वयः । पश्यामः अस्मज्ज्ञातविषयत्वद्वचनं शृणुम इत्यर्थः ।

---

१ एतदेव. २ भूमिराक्रमितव्येति. ३ तावेव. ४ तत्कथं न जानासि तस्य लक्ष्मणस्यायमात्मजश्चन्द्रकेतुः. ५ ऊर्मिलापुत्रः. ६ कुमारेण. ७ दशरथस्य पुत्राणाम्. ८ एतन्नास्ति क्वचित्. ९ केषु दारेषु.

लवः—नायं कथाप्रविभागोऽस्माभिरन्येन वा श्रुतपूर्वः ।

जनकः—किं न प्रणीत एव कविना ।

लवः—प्रणीतो न[1] प्रकाशितः । तस्यैव कोऽप्येकदेशः संदर्भा[2]न्तरेण रसवानभिनेयार्थः कृतः । तं च स्वहस्तलिखितं मुनिर्भगवान्व्यसृजद्भगवतो भरतस्य मुनेस्तौर्यत्रिकसूत्रकारस्य[3] ।

जनकः—किमर्थम् ।

लवः—स किल भगवान्भरतस्तमप्सरोभिः प्रयोजयिष्यतीति ।

जनकः—सर्वमिदमाकूततरमस्माकम् ।

लवः—महती पुनस्तस्मिन्भगवतो वाल्मीकेरास्था । यतो येषाम[4]न्तेवासिनां हस्तेन तत्पुस्तकं भरताश्रमं प्रति प्रेषितं तेषामनुयात्रिकश्चापपाणिः प्रमादा[5]पनोदनार्थमस्मद्भ्राता प्रेषितः ।

कौसल्या—जात भ्रातापि तेऽस्ति । (क)

लवः—अस्त्यार्यः कुशो नाम ।

कौसल्या—ज्येष्ठ इति भणितं भवति । (ख)

लवः—एवमेतत् । प्रसवा[6]नुक्रमेण स किल ज्यायान् ।

जनकः—किं यमजावायुष्मन्तौ ।

(क) जाद भादावि दे अत्थि । (ख) जेट्ठेत्ति भणिदं होदि ।

कथाविभागः कथैकदेशः । प्रणीतः किं न प्रबद्धः किं नोक्तः किमिति वा न प्रकाशितः न श्रावितो नाध्यापितश्च । तस्य रामायणस्य कोऽपि अनिर्धारितः एकदेशोंऽशः । स च सप्तमे वक्ष्यताणान्तर्नाटकार्थक इति ज्ञेयम् । प्रबन्धान्तरेण श्राव्यप्रबन्धातिरिक्तदृश्यप्रबन्धरूपकरूपेण वा रसवान् करुणाद्भुतरसप्रतिपादकः सर्वाकर्णनादितररसप्रतिपादकः अभिनेयः सत्त्वाङ्गिकादिचतुर्विधाभिनयप्रकाश्योऽर्थः अभिनेयः यस्य तथोक्तीकृतः । मुनिर्वाल्मीकिः । तौर्यत्रिकसूत्रधारस्य नृत्तगीतवादित्रशास्त्राचार्यस्य भरतस्य भावरागतालशास्त्राचार्यत्वमूलकृत्तदाद्यक्षरघटितभरतनामकस्य । तं प्रबन्धं अप्सरोभिः प्रयोज्यकर्तृभिः प्रयोजयिष्यतीत्येतदर्थम् । सर्वमिदं प्रणीतस्याप्रकाशनं प्रबन्धान्तरेण करणं भरतं प्रति प्रेषणं चाकूततरं गूढार्थकम् । आस्था अवश्यकत्वप्रकारकेच्छा । अनुयात्रिकोऽनुचरः प्रमादस्यानवधानप्रयुक्तप्रतीतस्य च्छेदनार्थं निवृत्त्यर्थमस्मद्भ्राता मत्सहजः । आर्यः पूज्यः । ज्येष्ठ इति भणितं भवति । अग्रज इति ध्वनितं भवति । प्रसवानुक्रमेणोत्पत्तिप्रकारेण । ज्यायान् ज्येष्ठः । यमसाधारणपूर्वजानुजत्वव्यवस्थापकजननानुपूर्व्येण ज्येष्ठ इति भावः । अत एव

---

१ न तु. २ प्रबन्धा०. ३ सूत्रधारस्य. ४ यतः केषांचिद० प्रेषितम्. ५ अप्रमादार्थं, प्रमादच्छेदनार्थम्. ६ वक्रमेण.

लवः—अथ किम् ।

जनकः—वत्स कथय कथाप्रबन्धस्य कीदृशः पर्यन्तः ।

लवः—अलीकपौरापवादोद्विग्नेन राज्ञा निर्वासितां देवयजनसंभवा सीतादेवीमासन्नप्रसववेदनामेकाकिनीमरण्ये परित्यज्य लक्ष्मणः प्रतिनिवृत्त इति ।

कौसल्या—हा वत्से मुग्धचन्द्रमुखि क इदानीं ते शरीरकुसुमस्य झटिति दैवदुर्विलासपरिणाम एकाकिन्या निपतितः । (क)

जनकः—हा वत्से

नूनं त्वया परिभवं च वनं च घोरं
तां च व्यथां प्रसवकालकृतामवाप्य ।
क्रव्याद्गणेषु परितः परिवारयत्सु
संत्रस्तया शरणमित्यसकृत्स्मृतोऽस्मि ॥ २३ ॥

लवः—(अरुन्धतीं प्रति ।) आर्ये कावेतौ ।

अरुन्धती—इयं कौसल्या । अयं च जनकः ।

लवः—(सबहुमानखेदकौतुकं पश्यति ।)

जनकः—अहो निर्दयता दुरात्मनां पौराणाम् । अहो रामस्य राज्ञः क्षिप्रकारिता ।

(क) हा वच्छे मुद्धचन्दमुहि को दाणिं दे सरीरकुसुमस्स झत्ति देव्वदुव्विलासपरिणामो एक्काइणीए णिवडिदो ।

पृच्छति—किं यमाविति । कथाप्रपञ्चस्य कथाविस्तरस्य । पर्यन्तोऽवसानम् । यद्वा प्रपञ्चनं प्रकाशनं प्रपञ्चस्तस्य कोऽवधिः । कियत्पर्यन्तं प्रकाशित इत्याशयः । अलीको मिथ्याभूतः पौरापवादः पौरकर्तृकदोषकथनं तेनोद्विग्नेन संभ्रान्तेन राज्ञा रामेण निर्वासितां गृहाच्च्यावितां देवयजनसंभवां यागभूमिजातां परित्यज्य लक्ष्मणः प्रतिनिवृत्त इति यत् एष पर्यन्त इति योजना । शरीरकुसुमस्य कुसुमसदृशशरीरस्य । दैवदुर्विलासस्य दैवदुश्चेष्टितस्य परिणामः फलोपधानम् । क इति दुःखयते । **नूनमिति** । क्रव्याद्गणेषु व्याघ्रादिषु परितः समन्तात्परिवारयत्सु सत्सु । मण्डलीकृत्य व्याप्नुवत्सु । संत्रस्तया त्वयाहं शरणमिति स्मृतः नूनं संभावये ॥ २३ ॥ दुरात्मनां दुर्बुद्धीनाम् । क्षिप्र-

१ प्रपञ्चस्य, कथाप्रबन्धः कीदृशपर्यन्तः. २ कियान्. ३ प्रवाद. ४ देवीं देव० सीतामास०. ५ वचनं, च नवं. ६ अहं. ७ निर्मर्यादता; नि-दु-मे० पौराणां. ८ रामभद्रस्य.

एतद्वैशसवज्रघोरपतनं शश्वन्ममोत्पश्यतः
क्रोधस्य ज्वलितुं धगित्यवसरश्चापेन शापेन वा ।

कौसल्या—(सभयकम्पम् ।) भगवति परित्रायस्व परित्रायस्व । प्रसादय कुपितं राजर्षिम् । (क)

लवः—

एतद्धि परिभूतानां प्रायश्चित्तं मनस्विनाम् ।

अरुन्धती—

राजन्नपत्यं रामस्ते पाल्याश्च कृपणा जनाः ॥ २४ ॥

जनकः—

शान्तं वा रघुनन्दने तदुभयं यत्पुत्रभाण्डं हि मे
भूयिष्ठद्विजबालवृद्धविकलस्त्रैणश्च पौरो जनः ॥ २५ ॥

(प्रविश्य ।)

संभ्रान्ता बटवः—कुमार कुमार अश्वोऽश्व इति कोऽपि भूतविशेषो जनपदेषु श्रूयते । सोऽयमधुनास्माभिः प्रत्यक्षीकृतः ।

(क) भअवदि परित्ताहि परित्ताहि । पसादेहि कुविदं राएसिम् ।

कारिता असमीक्ष्यकारित्वम् । **एतद्वैशसेति** । एतद्वैशसमेव महाव्यसनमेव वज्रस्याशनेर्घोरं पतनं तीक्ष्णपतनं शश्वदुत्पश्यतो मम क्रोधस्य शापेनानिष्टोपघायकसंकल्पेन चापेन च मारकधनुषा च झटिति ज्वलितुमवसरः प्राप्तकालता । राजर्षित्वादिति भावः । प्रसादय प्रसन्नं कुरु ॥ **एतदिति** । परिभूतानामवमतानां मनस्विनां महामनसां प्रायश्चित्तं कोपप्रतीकारः । एतत् प्रसादनमित्यर्थः । अपत्यं रामः कृपणजनाश्च ते पाल्याश्च रक्षणीयाः ॥ २४ ॥ **शान्तं वेत्यादि** । वा अथ वा । शापेन चापेन च ज्वलनाभावे इत्यर्थः । यद्यस्मात्पुत्रभाण्डं मूलधनं पुत्रभूतरामात्मकमूलधनम् । भूयिष्ठानि भूयांसि द्विजाः बालाः शिशवो वृद्धाः स्थाविरा विकला अन्धबधिरादयः स्त्रैणं स्त्रीसमूहः यस्य तथोक्तः पौरो जनश्च । मे हि मदीयाः किल । तस्मात्तदुभयं शापश्चापश्च शान्तं भवतु निवृत्तं भवतु । रुषं न दधे कोपं न धारयामि । यद्वा यद्यस्माद्भूयिष्ठद्विजबालवृद्धविकलस्त्रैणः पौरो जनः । चकारेण रामः समुच्चीयते । तदुभयं पौरजनरामात्मकोभयं मे पुत्रभाण्डं पुत्रात्मकमूलधनवन्मम संरक्षणीयं तत्तस्मात् शान्तं क्रोधेन ज्वलित्वा अलं रुषं न दधे क्रोधं न धारयामि । स्थैर्यद्योतनार्थं द्विः कथनम् ॥ २५ ॥ बटवः प्रविश्य अत्राहुरिति शेषः । भूतविशेषः प्राणिविशेषः । जनपदेषु कोसलादिदेशेषु । आरण्यकत्वादेवमुक्तिः । श्रूयते शाब्दबोधविषयो भवति । प्रत्यक्षीकृतः चक्षुर्विषयी-

---

१ झटि (टी०). २ This is generally read as part of Arundhati's next speech. ३ न रुषं दधे यदुभयं तत्पु०. ४ अरे श्रूयताम् अश्वोऽश्व इति पञ्चसमामायिकः. ५ अनुष्टु०. ६ परित्ताअदु (परित्रायताम्). ७ रुसिदं (रुषितं).

लवः—अश्व इति पशुसमाम्नाये सांग्रामिके च पठ्यते। तद् ब्रूत कीदृशः।

बटवः—श्रूयताम्।

पश्चात्पुच्छं वहति विपुलं तच्च धूनोत्यजस्रं
दीर्घग्रीवः स भवति खुरास्तस्य चत्वार एव।
शष्पाण्यत्ति प्रकिरति शकृत्पिण्डकानाम्रमात्रा-
न्किं व्याऽऽख्यातैर्व्रजति स पुनर्दूरमेह्येहि यामः ॥२६॥

(इत्युपसृत्याजिने हस्तयोश्चाकर्षन्ति।)

लवः—(सकौतुकोपरोधविनयम्।) आर्याः पश्यत पश्यत। एभिर्नीतोऽस्मि। (इति त्वरितं परिक्रामति।)

अरुन्धतीजनकौ—पूर्यतु कौतुकं वत्सः।

कौसल्या—भगवति जानाम्येतमनालोकयन्ती न जीवामीव। अतोऽन्यतो भूत्वा प्रेक्षामहे तावद्गच्छन्तं दीर्घायुषम्। (क)

अरुन्धती—अतिजवेन दूरमतिक्रान्तः स चपलः कथं दृश्यते।

(क) भअवदि जाणामि एदं अणालोअअन्ती ण जीआमि विअ। अदो अण्णदो भविअ पेक्खह्म दाव गच्छमाणं दीहाउम्।

कृतः। पशुसमाम्नाये पशुद्रव्यकयागप्रतिपादकवेदभागे सांग्रामिके युद्धकाण्डे च। कीदृशः किंलक्षणः॥ **पश्चादित्यादि।** सः अश्व इत्युच्यमानः विपुलं पुच्छं पश्चाद्वहति। वनमहिषः कोऽयमुभयतःपुच्छ इत्यारण्यवासनानुरूपेण व्यावृत्त्यर्थे पश्चात्पदम्। अन्यथा पुच्छस्य पश्चाद्वहनाव्यभिचारात्। विपुलमित्यनेन खरव्यावृत्तिः। तस्य हि पुच्छं गोवद्रज्जूकृतं भवति। एवं च वक्ष्यमाणाविशेषणानां तत्साधारणत्वेऽपि न दोषः। धूनोति चालयति। दीर्घग्रीवो भवति आयतकण्ठो भवति। तस्य खुराश्चत्वार एव। नाधिका इत्यर्थः। शष्पाणि बालतृणानि। अत्ति खादति। शकृत्पिण्डकान् पुरीषपिण्डकानाम्रमात्रान् रसालशलाटुपरिमितान् प्रकिरति विक्षिपति। स पुनर्दूरं व्रजति गच्छति ॥ २६ ॥ कौतुकं हर्षः। उपरोधः बलात्क्रियमाणत्वम्। अरण्यगर्भाणां अरण्यचरशिशूनां रूपैरालापैश्च तोषिता यूयम्। अहं तं पश्यन्ती वञ्चितेति जानामि। रामभद्रसंवादेन

---

१ इति नाम. २ अये श्रू०. ३ वा ख्यातैः, व्याख्यानैः. ४ इत्याजिने. ५ कापराध. ६ महत् कौतुकं वत्सस्य. ७ कुतूहलं. ८ एतन्नास्ति क्वचित्. ९ अरण्णगब्भरूवालावेहिं तुह्मे तोसिदा अह्मे अ। भअवदि जाणामि एदं अणालोअअन्ती तं वञ्चआमि—अपेक्खन्ती वञ्चिदा विअ। ता इदो अण्णदा भविअ पेक्खह्म दाव पलायन्तं दीहाउम्। (अरण्यगर्भरूपालापैर्यूयं तोषिता वयं च। भगवति जानामि एतमनवेक्षमाणा वञ्चयेनमपेक्षमाणा वञ्चितेव। तस्मादितोऽन्यतो भूत्वा प्रेक्षामहे तावत्पलायमानं दीर्घायुषम्।) १० अणवेक्खन्ती.

कञ्चुकी—(प्रविश्य ।) भगवान्वाल्मीकिराह ज्ञातव्यमेतदवसरे भवद्भिरिति ।

जनकः—अतिगम्भीरमेतात्किमपि । भगवत्यरुन्धति सखि कौसल्ये आर्ये गृष्टे स्वयमेव गत्वा भगवन्तं प्राचेतसं पश्यामः ।

(इति निष्कान्तो वृद्धवर्गः ।)

(प्रविश्य ।)

बटवः—पश्यतु कुमारस्तदाश्चर्यम् ।

लवः—दृष्टमवगतं च । नूनमाश्वमेधिकोऽयमश्वः ।

बटवः—कथं ज्ञायते ।

लवः—ननु मूर्खाः पठितमेव हि युष्माभिरपि तत्काण्डम् । किं न पश्यथ प्रत्येकं शतसंख्याः कवचिनो दण्डिनो निषङ्गिणश्च रक्षितारः । तत्प्रायमेवं बलमिदं दृश्यते । यदीह न प्रत्ययस्तद्गत्वा पृच्छत ।

बटवः—भो भोः किंप्रयोजनोऽयमश्वः परिवृतः पर्यटति ।

लवः—(सस्पृहमात्मगतम् ।) अये अश्वमेध इति नाम विश्वविजयिनां क्षत्रियाणामूर्जस्वलः सर्वक्षत्रपरिभावी महानुत्कर्षनिष्कर्षः ।

(नेपथ्ये ।)

अयमश्वः पताकेयमथ वा वीरघोषणा ।
सप्तलोकैकवीरस्य दशकण्ठकुलद्विषः ॥ २७ ॥

प्रलोभिताहमिति भावः ॥ कञ्चुकी । गृष्टिरित्यर्थः । अवसरे प्राप्तकाले ॥ एतद्वाल्मीकिवाक्यमतिगम्भीरं गूढाशयं किमपि अपूर्वम् ॥ वृद्धानामरुन्धतीप्रभृतीनां वर्गः समूहः ॥ दृष्टं चक्षुर्विषयीकृतम् । नूनमाश्वमेधिकोऽयमश्व इत्यवगतमनुमितम् । अश्वमेधाय प्रभवत्याश्वमेधिकः । तत्काण्डमश्वमेधप्रतिपादकश्रुतिभागः । बालकाण्डं वा । तत्रापि ह्यश्वमेधः प्रसक्तः । काण्डोऽस्त्रीत्युक्तेः क्लीबत्वम् । शतं कवचिनः शतं निषङ्गिणः शरधिवन्तः । शतमित्यर्थः । शतं दण्डिनः शतं रक्षितार इत्येतन्न पश्यथ किमित्यर्थः । तत्प्रायमेवान्यदपि कवचिप्रभृति सुसदृशं चान्यदपि । अनीकमित्यर्थः । विप्रत्ययो यदि संशयश्चेत् । किंप्रयोजनः किंफलकः । परिवृतः । रक्षितृभिरिति शेषः । पर्यटति परितः संचरति परिगतो गच्छति ॥ अनागते वस्तुनीच्छा स्पृहा । सर्वक्षत्रपरिभावी सकलराजकुलपरिभवजनकः । उत्कर्षनिकषः उपादेयवैलक्षण्यंज्ञापकदृष्टविशेषः । ऊर्जस्वलः बलिष्ठः । अविचाल्यनिकष इत्यर्थः ॥ **योऽयमिति** । योऽयमाश्वमेधिकोऽश्वः । इयम् । अश्व इत्यर्थः । विधेयप्राधान्यात्स्त्रीत्वं पताकात्वं विधेयम् । सप्तावयवेषु लोकेषु एकवीरस्य एकेषु प्रधानेषु वीरयति पराक्रमत इत्येकवीरः तस्य । सप्तलोकेत्यत्र मध्यमपदलोपवत्समासः । पात्रादित्वं वा ।

---

१ किमपि भविष्यति. २ तावदा०. ३ काण्डे. ४ एवान्यदपि. ५ यदि च विप्रत्ययस्तत्. ६ क्षात्रिय. ७ निकषः; निकर्षः. ८ योऽयम.

लवः—(सगर्वमिव[1]।) अहो संदीपनान्यक्षराणि ।

बटवः—किमुच्यते । प्राज्ञः खलु कुमारः ।

लवः—भो भोः तत्किमक्षत्रिया पृथिवी यदेवमुद्घोष्यते[2] ।

(नेपथ्ये ।)

अरे रे[3] महाराजं प्रति कुतः क्षत्रियाः ।

लवः—धिग्जाल्मान्[4] ।

यदि ते[5] सन्ति सन्त्येव[6] केयमद्य बिभीषिका ।
किमुक्तै[7]रेभिरधुना तां पताकां हरामि वः ॥ २८ ॥

भो भो बटवः परिवृत्य लोष्टैरभिघ्नन्तो[8] नयतैनमश्वम् । एष रोहितानां मध्ये वेराकश्चरतु[9] ।

(प्रविश्य सक्रोधदर्पः)

पुरुषः—धिक्चापलं[10] किमुक्तवानसि । तीक्ष्णनीरसा[11] ह्यायुधीयश्रेणयः शिशोरपि दृप्तां वाचं न सहन्ते । राजपुत्रश्चन्द्रकेतुर्[12]रिविमर्दनः । सोऽप्य[13]पूर्वारण्यदर्शनाक्षिप्तहृदयो न याव[14]दायाति तावत्त्वरितमनेन तरुगहनेनापसर्पत ।

वीरैक इत्यापत्तिवारणाय एकेषु वीरयतीति विग्रहोऽङ्गीकृतः । दशकण्ठकुलस्य रावणवंशस्य द्विट् शासिता । तस्य राघवस्य पताका विजयध्वजोऽथ वा पूर्वोक्तातिरेकेण वीरघोषणा वीर इति जगदाकर्णनानुकूलव्यापारः [उच्चैः घोषणमिति यावत्] ॥ २७ ॥ गर्वः परोत्कर्षानादरः । संदीपनानि क्रोधजनकानि । 'मनःप्रज्वलनं क्रोधः' इति ह्युक्तम् । एवं पूर्वोक्तरीत्या उद्घोष्यत इति यावत्तस्मात्किमक्षत्रिया पृथिवीत्यन्वयः । महाराजं प्रति तदौन्मुख्येन कुतः कस्माद्धेतोः क्व वा । धिग्जाल्मानसमीक्ष्यकारिणः । भवद्विषयका निन्देत्यर्थः । अक्षत्रिया इत्यनुषज्यते । क्षत्रिया न सन्तीति भवद्भिरुच्यते यदि सन्त्येवेत्यवगन्तव्यम् । अद्य क्षत्रियसत्ताधिकरणे अस्मिन्दिवसे इयं बिभीषिका भयोत्पादनं का । कीदृशीत्यर्थः । एभिरुक्तैरधुना किम् । न किमपीत्यर्थः । तां वः पताकां हराम्यन्यत्र प्रापयामि ॥ २८ ॥ अभिघ्नन्तस्तर्जयन्तः । रोहितानां मृगविशेषाणाम् । आयुधश्रेणयः शस्त्रपङ्क्तयस्तीक्ष्णतरा हि । त्वत्तोऽपि क्रूरा इत्यर्थः । दृप्तां दर्पयुक्तां वाचं न सहन्ते । शिक्षणाभाववन्तो न भवन्तीत्यर्थः । सोऽपि चन्द्रकेतुरिति योजना । दुर्दान्तोऽमर्षशीलः । अपूर्वारण्यदर्शनेन अननुभूतविपिनावलोकनेनाक्षिप्तहृदयो व्यासक्तमनाः । तरूणां गहनेन दुर्गमसंनिवेशेनापसर्पत पलायध्वम् ।

---

१ सव्यथमिव. २ उद्धतमुद्घो०, उदीर्यते. ३ अरे. ४ जाल्माः. ५ नो. ६ सन्त्येव, अद्य-अन्या. ७ किमुक्तैः संनिपत्यैव-शरसंबाधां-पताकां वो हराम्यहम्. ८ बटवः लोष्टैर्घ्नन्तः परावर्तयत्० ९ ०चरो भवतु. १० चपल. ११ तरा ह्यायुध०. १२ दुर्दान्तः. १३ सौम्यपू० १४ परापतत्यद्यापि तत्त्व०.

बटवः—कुमार कृतमनेनाश्वेन । तर्जयन्ति विस्फुरितशस्त्राः कुमारमायुधीयश्रेणयः । दूरे चाश्रमपदमितस्तदेहि हरिणप्लुतैः पलायामहे ।

लवः—(विहस्य ।) किं नाम विस्फुरान्ति शस्त्राणि । (इति धनुरारोपयन् ।)

ज्याजिह्वया वलयितोत्कटकोटिदंष्ट्र-
मुद्गारिघोरघनघर्घरघोषमेतत् ।
ग्रासप्रसक्तहसदन्तकवक्त्रयन्त्र-
जृम्भाविडम्बिविकटोदरमस्तु चापम् ॥ २९ ॥

(इति यथोचितं परिक्रम्य निष्क्रान्ताः सर्वे ।)

चतुर्थोऽङ्कः ।

कृतं कृतमश्वेनेति । अश्वेन साध्यं किमपि नास्तीत्यर्थः । गर्हायां द्विरुक्तिः । अज्ञानादेव वयमत्र प्रवृत्ता इति भावः । विस्फारितशरासनाः घोषवद्धनुषः तर्जयन्ति भयमुत्पादयन्ति । आश्रमपदं चाश्रमस्थानं च दूरे । विप्रकर्ष इत्यर्थः । हरिणानां यानि प्लुतानि अभूस्पर्शगमनानि । तत्सदृशगमनैरित्यर्थः । पलायामहे परागता भवामः । विस्फुरन्ति घोषयुक्तानि । धनुरारोपयन् । ज्यामिति शेषः । **ज्याजिह्वयेत्यादि** । ज्या मौर्वी सैव जिह्वा रसना तया वलयिता वेष्टिता । उत्कटकोटिरेवोत्तुङ्गाग्रभाग एव दंष्ट्रा यस्य तथोक्तम् । उद्धरयोऽसंख्याता घोरा भयजनका घनाः सान्द्रा घर्घरघोषा यस्य तथोक्तम् । एतच्चापम् । क्लीबत्वं विचारयितव्यम् । सामान्ये नपुंसकत्वं वा । अथ वा भयामृतसकृद्वक्त्रचापाभरणलाञ्छनमिति नपुंसकशशोक्ते क्लीबत्वम् । ग्रासे कवलने प्रसक्तमुद्युक्तं हसत् हासयुक्तमन्तकवक्त्रयन्त्रं व्याघ्रादिमारणयन्त्रसदृशकृतान्तस्य कुहरं तस्य जृम्भाविडम्बि जृम्भानुकारि विकटं विषममुदरं मध्यं यस्य तथाविधमस्तु । अस्य चापस्य तथाभवनं प्राप्तकालमित्यर्थः । जिह्वेव ज्या ज्याजिह्वेत्युपमालंकारो व्याख्येयः । कोटिदंष्ट्रमित्यत्र तु कोट्यात्मकं यद्दंष्ट्रासदृशमिति व्याख्येयम् । विशेष्यविशेषणभावस्य च कामचारत्वान्न दोष इत्यप्याहुः ॥ २९ ॥

वाधुलवंशजनुषो भूसारनिवासराघवार्यस्य ।
उत्तररामचरित्रव्याख्यायामवसितस्तुरीयाङ्कः ॥

इति श्रीवाधूलवीरराघवविरचितायां भवभूतिभावतलस्पर्शिनीसमाख्यायामुत्तररामचरितव्याख्यायां

चतुर्थोऽङ्कः ।

---

१ कृतं कृतम्. २ विस्फारितशरासनाः. ३ उद्धूरि. ४ इति महाकविश्रीभ०ते उत्त०-नाटके कौसल्याजनकयोगे नाम च०.

पञ्चमोऽङ्कः ।

(नेपथ्ये ।)

भो भोः सैनिका जातं जातमवलम्बनमस्माकम् ।

नन्वेष त्वरितसुमन्त्रनुद्यमान-
व्यावल्गत्प्रजवनवाजिना रथेन ।
उद्घातप्रचलितकोविदारकेतुः
श्रुत्वा नः प्रधनमुपैति चन्द्रकेतुः ॥ १ ॥

(ततः प्रविशति सुमन्त्रसारथिना रथेन धनुष्पाणिः साद्भुतहर्षसंभ्रमश्चन्द्रकेतुः ।)

चन्द्रकेतुः—आर्य सुमन्त्र पश्य पश्य ।

किरति कलितकिंचित्कोपरज्यन्मुखश्री-
रविरतगुणगुञ्जत्कोटिना कार्मुकेण ।
समरशिरसि चञ्चत्पञ्चचूडश्चमूना-
मुपरि शरतुषारं कोऽप्ययं वीरपोतः ॥ २ ॥

आश्चर्यमाश्चर्यम् ।

मुनिजनशिशुरेकः सर्वतः सैन्यकाये
नव इव रघुवंशस्याप्रसिद्धः प्ररोहः ।

नेपथ्य इत्यादि । भो भोः सैनिकाः सेनासमवायिनः जातमवलम्बनम् । आश्रयो लब्ध इत्यर्थः । **नन्विति** । सुमन्त्रनुद्यमानाः सुमन्त्रेण प्रेर्यमाणाः प्रोद्वल्गाः प्रकर्षेण चञ्चलाः प्रजविताः प्रकृष्टवेगयुक्ता वाजिनोऽश्वा यस्मिंस्तथोक्तेन । उत्खातेषु निम्नोन्नतप्रदेशेषु प्रचलितकोविदारयुक्तध्वजवान् । प्रधनं युद्धं श्रुत्वा उपैति ननु किल । चूलिका 'नेपथ्यान्तस्थितैः पात्रैश्चूलिकाङ्कस्य सूचनम् ।' इत्युक्तेः ॥ १ ॥ **किरतीति** । कलितेनाहृतेन किंचित्कोपेन ईषन्मन्युना रज्यन्ती रक्तीभवन्ती मुखश्रीराननशोभा यस्य तथोक्तः । अत्र प्रत्यर्थिनामकिंचित्करत्वात्किंचित्कोपेत्युक्तम् । चञ्चत्पञ्चचूडश्चलिताशिखण्डकः कोऽप्यपूर्वोऽयं वीरपोतः वीरशिशुः अविरतं विश्रान्तिरहितं यथा तथा गुणे ज्यायां गुञ्जन्त्यौ अव्यक्तशब्दवत्यौ कोटी अग्रे यस्य तथोक्तेन कार्मुकेण । करणत्वा- त्तृतीया । समरशिरसि युद्धरङ्गे चमूनामुपरि शरतुषारं बाणवर्षं किरति । तुषारो हि अतिसूक्ष्मसलिलवृष्टिः । अत्र रज्यन्मुखश्रीः कार्मुकेण चञ्चत्पञ्चचूड इत्येतैः शरतुषारमित्यनेन च तडित्वतः शक्रचापयुक्तस्य चलिताग्रस्य मेघकिशोरस्य च साम्यं व्यज्यते ॥ २ ॥ **मुनिजनेत्यादि** । एकः असहायः संप्रकोपात्प्रकृष्टमन्युना । लवकोपस्य तद्दृष्ट्याल्पत्वेऽपि चन्द्रकेतुबुद्ध्या महत्त्वारोपः । सर्वतः समन्ताद्दलितानां करिकपोलग्रन्थीनां संधीनां टंकारेण दलनध्वनिना घोरं भयजनकं ज्वलितं शराणां सहस्रं यस्य तथोक्तम् ।

---

१ प्रोद्वल्गप्रजवित. २ उत्खात. ३ संप्राप्तः सपदि कुमारचन्द्रकेतुः. ४ प्रथिततत०; अनवरतनियुञ्जत्. ५ संप्रकोपात् (टी०). ६ ०प्रसिद्धिप्ररोहः.

दलितकरिकपोलग्रन्थिटंकारघोर-
ज्वलितशरसहस्रः कौतुकं मे करोति ॥ ३ ॥

सुमन्त्रः—आयुष्मन् ।

अतिशयितसुरासुरप्रभावं
शिशुमवलोक्य तथैव तुल्यरूपम् ।
कुशिकसुतमखद्विषां प्रमाथे
धृतधनुषं रघुनन्दनं स्मरामि ॥ ४ ॥

चन्द्रकेतुः—मम त्वेकमुद्दिश्य भूयसामारम्भ इति हृदयमपत्रपते ।

अयं हि शिशुरेककः समरभारभूरिस्फुर-
त्करालकरकन्दलीकलितशस्त्रजालैर्बलैः ।
क्वणत्कनककिङ्किणीझणझणायितस्यन्दनै-
रमन्दमददुर्दिनद्विरदवारिदैरावृतः ॥ ५ ॥

सुमन्त्रः—वत्स एभिः समस्तैरपि किमस्य किं पुनर्व्यस्तैः ।

चन्द्रकेतुः—आर्य त्वर्यतां त्वर्यताम् । अनेन हि महानाश्रितजनप्रमोथोऽस्माकमारब्धः । तथा हि ।

आगर्जद्गिरिकुञ्जकुञ्जरघटानिस्तीर्णकर्णज्वरं
ज्यानिर्घोषममन्ददुन्दुभिरवैराध्मातमुज्जृम्भयन् ।

आनन्त्यवाची सहस्रशब्दः । नवः प्रत्यग्रः रघुवंशस्य अप्रसिद्धिप्ररोह इव स्थितः अपख्याताङ्कुरवत्स्थितः । मुनिजनशिशुर्मुनिजनाः शमप्रधानास्तेष्वपि बाल इत्यर्थः । मे कौतुकं हर्षं करोत्युत्पादयति ॥ ३ ॥ **अतिशयितेति** । तथैव तुल्यरूपम् । यथा रामेण तुल्यप्रभावस्तथैव तुल्याकार इत्यर्थः । तथाविधं कुशिकसुतमखद्विषां सुबाहुप्रभृतीनाम् । अत्र कुशिकसुतस्य मखं द्विषन्तीति तेषाम् । स्मृतिमदलंकारः ॥ ४ ॥ अपत्रपते लज्जते । **अयं हीति** । अयमेककः शिशुरेकाकी बालः मदभरेण वीरपानेन समुपजनितमदातिशयेन भूरि अधिकं स्फुरन्ति चलितानि करालानि क्रूराणि करकन्दलीषु करशाखाग्रेषु जटिलानि निबिडानि शस्त्रजालानि येषां तथोक्तैः । क्वणन्तीभिः शब्दवतीभिः कनककिङ्किणीभिर्हेममयक्षुद्रघण्टिकाभिर्झणझणायितैः शब्दविशेषयुक्तैरमन्दमदैरतिशयितदानवारिभिर्दुर्दिनैरन्धकारितैर्द्विरदैर्गजैः करणैः डामरैः भयंकरैर्बलैः सैन्यैरावृतः ॥ ५ ॥ समस्तैः सहितैर्व्यस्तैः पृथक्स्थितैर्नालम् । न पर्याप्तिरित्यर्थः । आश्रितजनानामुपजीविजनानां प्रमारः मारणम् । **आगर्जदिति** । वीरोयं लवः अमन्ददुन्दुभिरवैरतिशायितभेरिशब्दैराध्मातं द्विगुणीकृतम् । आगर्जतां भयवशाद्गाढगर्जनं कुर्वतां गिरिकुञ्जकुञ्जराणां पर्वतगुहावर्तिगजानां घटायै पङ्क्त्यै निस्तीर्णो

---

१ घोरं. २ सहस्रैः. ३ तवैव. ४ इममेकमु. ५ अवष्टम्भः. ६ समररेणु; मदभरेण; भारभूमि॰. ७ जटिल. ८ डामरैः, डम्बरैः. ९ प्रमारः. १० आयुअत्. ११ विस्ती. १२ ज्वरज्या॰

वेल्लद्भैरवरुण्डमुण्डनिकरैर्वीरो विधत्ते भुवं
तृष्यत्कालकरालवक्त्रविघसव्याकीर्यमाणामिव ॥ ६ ॥

सुमन्त्रः—(स्वगतम् ।) कथमीदृशेन सह वत्सस्य चन्द्रकेतोर्द्वन्द्वसंप्रहारमनुजानीमः । (विचिन्त्य ।) अथ वा इक्ष्वाकुकुलवृद्धाः खलु वयम् । प्रत्युपस्थिते रणे च का गतिः ।

चन्द्रकेतुः—(सविस्मयलज्जासंभ्रमम् ।) हन्त धिक् । प्रतिनिवृत्तानि सर्वतः सैन्यानि मम ।

सुमन्त्रः—(रथवेगमभिनीय ।) आयुष्मन् एष ते वाग्विषयीभूतः स वीरः ।

चन्द्रकेतुः—(विस्मृतिमभिनीय ।) आर्य किमस्य नामधेयमाख्यातमाह्वार्यकैः ।

सुमन्त्रः—लव इति ।

चन्द्रकेतुः—

भो भो लव महाबाहो किमेभिस्तव सैनिकैः ।
एषोऽहमेहि मामेव तेजस्तेजसि शाम्यतु ॥ ७ ॥

सुमन्त्रः—कुमार पश्य पश्य ।

विनिर्वर्तत एष वीरपोतः पृतनानिर्मथनात्त्वयोपहूतः ।
स्तनयित्नुरवादिभावलीनामवमर्दादिव दृप्तसिंहशावः ॥ ८ ॥

दत्तः कर्णज्वरो येन तथोक्तश्चासौ ज्यानिर्घोषस्तम् । उज्जृम्भयन्नुल्बणयन्सन् । वेल्लद्भिर्लुठद्भिर्भैरवैर्भयंकरैः । रुण्डखण्डानां शिरःकपालानां निकरैः समूहैर्भुवम् । तृष्यतः कालस्य पिपासितस्य कालस्य मृत्योः करालवक्त्रस्य विघसैर्भुक्तशिष्टैः । 'विघसो यज्ञशेषभोजनशेषयोः' इत्यमरः । व्याकीर्यमाणामिव संस्तीर्यमाणामिव विधत्ते करोति । तृष्यदित्यनेन पिपासयान्यपरेण मृत्युना अर्धजग्धानि मुक्तानीति व्यज्यते ॥ ६ ॥ द्वन्द्वसंप्रहारं द्वन्द्वयुद्धमनुजानीमः अनुज्ञां करोमि । इक्ष्वाकुकुलवृद्धाः खल्वित्यनेन विमृश्यकारित्वमवश्यमिति व्यज्यते । अत्र प्रकाशानुक्तिश्चिन्त्या । अपावृत्तानि पराङ्मुखीभूतानि । आह्वायकैः आह्वानं कुर्वद्भिः । **भो भो इति** । तेजः शौर्यं तेजसि शाम्यतु निर्वाणं भवतु ॥ ७ ॥ **विनिवर्तित इति** । पृतनानिर्मथनात्सेनाप्रहारात् । अपादाने पञ्चमी । उपहूत आहूतः । स्तनयित्नुरवात् मेघध्वनेः सिंहशावः सिंह-

---

१ खण्ड, भ्रूरिरुण्ड. २ भुवः...व्याकीर्यमाणा इव. ३ तृप्यत्. ४ अनुजानीयाम्. ५ स्थिते च का. ६ न्येव; धिक् ०र्तिंतः, अपचितानि; अपावृत्तानि. ७ कृतः; स वीरः-प्रवीरः. ८ आख्यायकैः. ९ महाभाग विनिर्वर्तितः. १० ०र्तिंत; व्यपवर्तत. ११ बालवीरः.

(ततः प्रविशति धीरोद्धतपरिक्रमो लवः ।)

लवः—साधु राजपुत्र साधु । सत्यमैक्ष्वाकः खल्वसि । तदहं परागत एवास्मि ।

(नेपथ्ये महान्कलकलः ।)

लवः—(सावष्टम्भं परावृत्य ।) आः कथमिदानीं भग्ना अपि प्रतिनिवृत्य युद्धाभिसारिणः पर्यवष्टम्भयन्ति मां चमूपतयः । धिग् जाल्मान् ।

> अयं शैलाघातक्षुभितवडवावक्त्रहुतभु-
> क्प्रचण्डक्रोधार्चिर्निचयकवलत्वं व्रजतु मे ।
> समन्तादुत्सर्पन्घनतुमुलसेनाकलकलः
> पयोराशेरोघः प्रलयपवनास्फालित इव ॥ ९ ॥

(संवेगं परिक्रामति ।)

चन्द्रकेतुः—भो भोः कुमार ।

> अत्यद्भुतादसि गुणातिशयात्प्रियो मे
> तस्मात्सखा त्वमसि यन्मम तत्तवैव ।
> तत्किं निजे परिजने कदनं करोषि
> नन्वेष दर्पनिकषस्तव चन्द्रकेतुः ॥ १० ॥

लवः—(सहर्षसंभ्रमं परावृत्य ।) अहो महानुभावस्य प्रसन्नकर्कशा वीरवचनप्रयुक्तिर्विकर्तनकुलकुमारस्य । तत्किमेभिरेनमेव तावत्संभावयामि । (पुनर्नेपथ्ये कलकलः ।)

शिशुरिव निवर्तित इत्येतत्पश्येत्यर्थः ॥ ८ ॥ **ततः प्रविशतीति** । धीरोद्धतस्य युध्युद्धटस्य पराक्रमो यस्येत्यर्थः । धीरोदात्तादयश्चत्वारो नायकाः । प्रसिद्धास्तेषु प्रायेण भटानामेव धीरोद्धतत्वमायाति । सर्वे भग्ना अपि पराजिता अपि पर्यवष्टभ्नन्ति समीपस्थिता भवन्ति । 'अवाच्चालम्बनाविदूर्ययोः' इति षत्वम् । **अयं शैलेत्यादि** । अयमोघः युष्माकं समूहः शैलाघातेन मन्दरसंघट्टेनेन क्षुभितो विपर्यस्तः यः वडवावक्त्रहुतभुग्वाडवमुखाग्निस्तद्वत्प्रचण्डस्य तीक्ष्णस्य क्रोधार्चिर्निचयस्य कोपाग्निज्वालासमूहस्य कवलत्वं भक्ष्यत्वं व्रजतु । क इवेत्यत्राह—पयोराशेरोघः प्रवाह इवेत्यर्थः ॥ ९ ॥ **अत्यद्भुतादिति** । मम त्वं सखा तस्मान्मदीयं यद्वस्तु तत्तवैव त्वदीयमेव । तन्नि[illegible] परिजने किमर्थमेवं कदनं युद्धं करोषि । तव दर्पपरीक्षास्थानमेष चन्द्रकेतुरित्यर्थः ॥ १० ॥ प्रसादवती कर्कशा च कठिना च । आपाततो हृद्या पर्यालोचने तु कठिनेत्यर्थः । वीरवचनप्रयुक्तिः

---

१ त्वरितोद्धत. २ सावेगम्. ३ प्रतिनिवृत्ताः, पृष्ठानुसा० ४ ०ष्टभ्नन्ति, ०भ्नन्ते; पर्यवष्टभ्य निघ्नन्ति. ५ ०द्धन; बल; सेना—हेला. ६ सा०. ७ दपि.

लवः—(सक्रोधनिर्वेदम् ।) आः कदर्थितोऽहमेभिर्वीरसंवादविघ्नकारिभिः पापैः । (तदभिमुखं परिक्रामति ।)

चन्द्रकेतुः—आर्य दृश्यतां द्रष्टव्यमेतत् ।

दर्पेण कौतुकवता मयि बद्धलक्ष्यः
पश्चाद्बलैरनुसृतोऽयमुदीर्णधन्वा ।
द्वेधा समुद्धतमरुत्तरलस्य धत्ते
मेघस्य माघवतचापधरस्य लक्ष्मीम् ॥ ११ ॥

सुमन्त्रः—कुमार एवैनं द्रष्टुमपि जानाति । वयं तु केवलं परवन्तो विस्मयेन ।

चन्द्रकेतुः—भो भो राजानः ।

संख्यातीतैर्द्विरदतुरगस्यन्दनस्थैः पदाता-
वत्रैकस्मिन्कवचनिचितैर्मेध्यचर्मोत्तरीये ।
कालज्येष्ठैरभिर्नववयःकाम्यकाये भवद्भि-
र्योऽयं बद्धो युधि परिकरस्तेन धिग्वो धिगस्मान् ॥ १२ ॥

लवः—(सोन्माथम् ।) कथमनुकम्पते नाम । (विचिन्त्य ।) भवतु । कालहरणप्रतिषेधाय जृम्भकास्त्रेण तावत्सैन्यानि संस्तम्भयामि । (इति ध्यानं नाटयति ।)

वीरवादप्रयोगः । संभावयामि पुरस्करोमि । कदर्थीकृतः अनुचितव्यापारवान्कृतः । वीरसंवादस्य चन्द्रकेतोरुक्तिप्रत्युक्तिकायाः युद्धस्य वा । **दर्पेणेति** । कौतुकवता सामर्थ्यदर्शनेच्छायुक्तेन दर्पेण बलेन मयि बद्धलक्ष्यः दत्तचक्षुर्मयि व्यवसितलक्ष्यत्ववान् । उदीर्णधन्वा उत्क्षिप्तचापः । द्वेधा मयि बले चाभिमुखोऽयं लवः द्वेधा समुद्धतस्य चलितस्य मघवत्संबन्धिचापधरस्य वर्षाकालमेघस्य लक्ष्मीं श्रियं धत्ते ॥ ११ ॥ **संख्येति** । संख्यातीतैरसंख्येयैः । द्विरदतुरगस्यन्दनेषु तिष्ठन्तीति द्विरदतुरगस्यन्दनस्थास्तथाविधैः कवचनिचितैर्वारबाणपिहितैः । अपरवयसि वार्धके ख्यातिकामैः विजयप्रशास्तिकामनावद्भिः कालज्येष्ठैर्वयोधिकैः । न तु शौर्येणत्यर्थः । भवद्भिरेकस्मिन्नसहाये पदातौ पादचारिणि नद्धचर्मोत्तरीयेऽस्मिन् शिशौ विषये योऽयं समभरः एकौघभारः बद्धः तेन वः धिक् । युष्माकमव्यवधानेन निन्दा अस्माकं तु युष्मद्द्वारा ॥ १२ ॥ अनुकम्पते मम दौर्बल्यमाशङ्क्य मद्दुःखं परिजिहीर्षति । कालहरणप्रतिषेधाय कालयापननिवृत्तये संस्तम्भयामि निवृत्तव्यापाराणि

---

१ कदर्थीकृतः. २ एभिर्वारंवारं विघ्नकारिभिर्घोषैः. ३ आर्य आर्य. ४ नद्ध. ५ अचरमवयः०, अवर:-अपरवयसि ख्यातिकामैः (टी०). ६ समभरः. ७ वो धिक्. ८ आः कथं, मय्यप्य० ९ ससंभ्रमं विचिन्त्य.

सुमन्त्रः—तत्किमकस्मादस्मत्सैन्यघोषः प्रशाम्यति ।

लवः—पश्याम्येनमधुना प्रगल्भम् ।

सुमन्त्रः—(ससंभ्रमम् ।) वत्स मन्ये कुमारकेणानेन जृम्भकास्त्रमामन्त्रितमिति ।

चन्द्रकेतुः—अत्र कः संदेहः ।

व्यतिकर इव भीमस्तामसो वैद्युतश्च
प्रणिहितमपि चक्षुर्ग्रस्तमुक्तं हिनस्ति ।
अथ लिखितमिवैतत्सैन्यमस्पन्दमास्ते
नियतममितवीर्यं जृम्भते जृम्भकास्त्रम् ॥ १३ ॥

आश्चर्यमाश्चर्यम् ।

पातालोदरकुञ्जपुञ्जिततमःश्यामैर्नभो जृम्भकै-
रुत्तप्तस्फुरदारकूटकपिलज्योतिर्ज्वलद्दीप्तिभिः ।
कल्पाक्षेपकठोरभैरवमरुद्व्यस्तैरवस्तीर्यते
मीलन्मेघतडित्कडारकुहरैर्विन्ध्याद्रिकूटैरिव ॥ १४ ॥

सुमन्त्रः—कुतः पुनरस्य जृम्भकाणामागमः स्यात् ।

चन्द्रकेतुः—भगवतः प्राचेतसादिति मन्यामहे ।

सुमन्त्रः—वत्स नैतदेवमस्त्रेषु विशेषतो जृम्भकेषु । यतः ।

करोमि । प्रशाम्यन्ति विरमन्ति । प्रगल्भं प्रौढम् । आमन्त्रितमाहूतम् ॥ कः संदेहः । आमन्त्रितमित्यत्र संशयः क इत्यर्थः । मन्ये इत्यस्य संभावनवाचित्वात्तस्याश्चेतिकोटिकसंशयरूपत्वात् । **व्यतिकर इति** । तमःसंबन्धी तामसः विद्युत्संबन्धी वैद्युतश्च । तथाविधो व्यतिकरः संपर्कः प्रणिहितमपि प्रयत्नेन निक्षिप्तमपि । ग्रस्तं च तन्मुक्तं च । खञ्जकुब्जादिवत्समासः । तमसा ग्रस्तज्योतिषा मुक्तम् । तमस्यसत्करूपत्वाद्ग्रस्तत्वं ज्योतिषि च कार्यकरत्वात्ततो मुक्तत्वम् । चक्षुर्हिनस्ति बाधते । नियतं निश्चितम् ॥ १३ ॥ आश्चर्यमभूतपूर्वम् । **पातालेति** । पातालोदरमेव कुञ्जः गुहा तस्मिन्पुञ्जितानि संहतभावं प्राप्तानि यानि तमांसि तद्वत् श्यामैः । उत्तप्तं स्फुरत्तेजिष्ठं च यदारकूटं त्रपुधातुविशेषस्तस्य यत्कपिलं पिशङ्गं ज्योतिस्तद्वज्ज्वलद्दीप्तिभिः । अत एव कल्पाक्षेपे कल्पावसाने कठोरेण दृढेन भैरवेण भीतिजनकेन मरुता व्यस्तैर्वियोजितैर्लीनाम्भोदानि तटित्कडाराणि च कुहराणि एषां तथोक्तैः । कडारः कपिलः । विन्ध्याचलशृङ्गैरिव स्थितैः जृम्भकैर्नभः अभिस्तीर्यते आच्छाद्यते ॥ १४ ॥ कुतः पुनः कस्मात्पुरुषात्पुनरस्य लवस्य । मन्त्रेषु विषये एतदागमनमेवं न त्वन्मतरीत्या न घटते । जृम्भकास्त्रेषु विषये

---

१ अस्माकं बले; उल्लोलाः ०घोषाः प्रशाम्यन्ति. २ इह. ३ अजित. ४ अभि०, अवाकीर्यते. ५ लीना—नीला—०मोद. ६ कास्त्राधिगमः. ७ नेव—नात्र व्यवहारः.

कृशाश्वतनया ह्येते कृशाश्वात्कौशिकं गताः ।
अथ तत्संप्रदायेन रामभद्रे स्थिता अपि ॥ १५ ॥

चन्द्रकेतुः—अपरेऽपि प्रचीयमानसत्वप्रकाशाः स्वयं सर्वं मन्त्रदृशः पश्यन्ति ।

सुमन्त्रः—वत्स सावधानो भव । परागतः प्रवीरः ।

कुमारौ—(अन्योन्यं प्रति ।) अहो प्रियदर्शनः कुमारः । (सस्नेहानुरागं निर्वर्ण्य ।)

यदृच्छासंवादः किमु किमु गुणानामतिशयः
पुराणो वा जन्मान्तरनिबिडबद्धः परिचयः ।
निजो वा संबन्धः किमु विधिवशात्कोऽप्यविदितो
ममैतस्मिन्दृष्टे हृदयमवधानं रचयति ॥ १६ ॥

सुमन्त्रः—भूयसां जीविधर्म एष यद्रसमयी कस्यचित्क्वचित्प्रीतिः यत्र लौकिकानामुपचारस्तारामैत्रकं चक्षूराग इति । तमप्रतिसंख्येयमनिबन्धनं प्रेमाणमामनन्ति ।

एतत्प्राचेतसादधिगम इत्येतद्विशेषत एवं न । न तु मां घटते । **कृ (भृ) शाश्वेति** । भृशाश्वतनया ह्येते एते अस्त्रदेवताविशेषाः कृ-भृ-शाश्वमुनिना आदौ जनिताः । हीति प्रसिद्धौ । कौशिकं विश्वामित्रम् । अथानन्तरं तत्संप्रदायेन विश्वामित्रोपदेशेन ॥ १५ ॥ अपरेऽपि भवदुक्तेभ्योऽन्येऽपि प्रचीयमानसत्त्वप्रकाशाः व्याप्नुवत्संवित्प्रकाशाः । मन्त्रदृशः स्वयमेव संप्रदायेन विनापि । सावधानोऽनन्यमनाः भव । कुमारौ लवचन्द्रकेतू । प्रियं सुखजनकं दर्शनं यस्य तथोक्तः । स्नेहः मैत्री । अनुरागो भोग्यताज्ञानम् । **यदृच्छेति** । यदृच्छया दैवेन संवादः समागमः यस्य तथोक्तः यदृच्छया दैवेन संवाद एकरूपं यस्य तथोक्तो वा । रामादिगुणगणैरेकरूपः इति हृदयम् । तथाविधो गुणगणानामतिशयः किमु पुराणः पुरापि भवः । जन्मान्तरेष्वन्येषु जन्मसु निबिडबद्धः दृढारूढः परिचयो वासना किमु । विधिवशाद्दैवेच्छया अविदितः कोऽपि निजः संबन्धः जननसंबन्धः किमु । यत एवं ततो हृदयं कर्तृ अवधानं व्यापारान्तररहिततां रचयति करोति । अथ वा एतस्मिन्दृष्टे सति मम हृदयं कर्म गुणातिशयादिषु त्रिषु अन्यतमावधानता अवधानं अवहितं करोतीति द्विकर्मणि च ल्युडित्यप्याहुः ॥ १६ ॥ भूयसामित्यादि । यत्र यस्यां प्रतीतौ । तारामैत्री तारा कनीनिका मैत्री प्रेम वा । चक्षूराग आदराद्वीक्षणम् । 'चक्षुःप्रीतिर्भवेद्यत्र' इत्युक्तचक्षूराग इति च लौकिकानां जनानामुपचारो व्यवहारस्तादृशी कस्य-

---

१ भृ०. २ व्यवस्थिताः; स्थिता इति. ३ परमोपचीयमान. ४ हि. ५ ते प्रतिवीरः ६ गुणगणानाम्. ७ बन्धः. ८ ०सां जीविनामेव धर्म एष यत्र स्वरसमयी. ९ स्वरस. १० व्याहारः. ११ त्रकं वा. १२ तदप्रतिसंख्येयनि० प्रेमाणं.

अहेतुः पक्षपातो यस्तस्य नास्ति प्रतिक्रिया।
स हि स्नेहात्मकस्तन्तुरन्तर्मर्माणि[1] सीव्यति ॥ १७ ॥

कुमारौ—(अन्योन्यमुद्दिश्य।)

एतस्मिन्मसृणितराजपट्टकान्ते
मोक्तव्याः कथमिव सायकाः शरीरे।
यत्प्राप्तौ मम परिरम्भणाभिलाषा-
दुन्मीलत्पुलककदम्बमङ्गमास्ते[2] ॥ १८ ॥

किं त्वाक्रान्तकठोरतेजसि गतिः का नाम शस्त्रं विना
शस्त्रेणापि हि तेन किं न विषयो जायेत यस्येदृशः।
किं वक्ष्यत्ययमेवं[3] युद्धविमुखं मामुद्यतेऽप्यायुधे
वीराणां समयो हि दारुणरसः स्नेहक्रमं बाधते ॥ १९ ॥

सुमन्त्रः—(लवं निर्वर्ण्य सास्रमात्मगतम्।) हृदय किमन्यथा परिकल्पसे[4]।

मनोरथस्य यद्बीजं तद्दैवेनादितो हृतम्[5]।
लतायां पूर्वलूनायां प्रसवस्योद्भवः[6] कुतः ॥ २० ॥

च्चित्पुरुषस्य क्वचित्पुरुषे स्वरसमयी अकृत्रिमा वा प्रीतिरिति यत् एषः। विधेयप्राधान्यात्पुंस्त्वम्। भूयसां महीयसां जीविनां प्राणभृतां धर्मस्वभावः। अप्रतिसंख्येयनिबन्धनमविचारणीयमूलं तत्प्रेम प्रमाणं यथार्थानुभवविषयमामनन्ति असकृद्वदन्ति। **अहेतुरिति**। यः अहेतुर्निष्कारणकः पक्षपातः आत्मीयत्वप्रतिसंधानमूलकानुकूलज्ञानरूपस्तस्य अहेतुकपक्षपातस्य प्रतिक्रिया निवर्तकव्यापारः नास्ति न संभवति। स्नेहात्मकः प्रेममयः स तन्तुः भूतानि प्राणिनः अन्तः सीव्यति अन्तःस्यूतानि करोति ॥ १७ ॥ **एतस्मिन्निति**। राजपट्टं नीलरक्तपट्टवस्त्रं तद्वत्कान्ते कमनीये एतस्मिन् लवे चन्द्रकेतौ वा परिरम्भणाभिलाषादालिङ्गनेच्छया। उन्मीलत्पुलककदम्बमुद्यद्रोमाञ्चनिकुरम्बम् ॥ १८ ॥ **किं चेति**। किं च पूर्वोक्तादन्यत्। आक्रान्तकठोरतेजसि आक्रान्तं प्राप्तं कठोरं पूर्णं तेजः पराभिभवनसामर्थ्यं यस्य तस्मिन्विषये शस्त्रं विना का गतिः शस्त्रसाधनकयुद्धात्किं किं कर्तव्यम्। न किमपीत्यर्थः। तर्हि शरीरसौभाग्यानुरोधेन शस्त्रन्यासः क्रियतामित्यत्राह—**शस्त्रेणेति**। यस्य शस्त्रस्य विषय ईदृशः महावीरः न जायेत तेन शस्त्रेणापि किम्। न किमपीत्यर्थः। तर्हि सौकुमार्यवीर्ययोः प्राबल्यदौर्बल्यविचारेण सौकुमार्यानुसारेण शस्त्रन्यासः क्रियतामित्यत्राह—उद्यतेऽप्यायुधे युद्धविमुखं मामयमेव किं वक्ष्यति यत एवं ततः दारुणरसः क्रौर्यैकवेद्यः शूराणां समयः आचारः स्नेहक्रमं स्नेहव्यापारपरिपाटीं बाधते निवर्तयति ॥ १९ ॥ अन्यथा संभाव्यविषयानुसारेण परिप्लवसे चञ्चलीभवसि रामसादृश्यात्तदपत्यं लव इति किं शङ्कसे इति भावः। **मनोरथस्येति**। मनोरथस्य अभिलष्यमाणलवनिष्ठरामापत्यत्वस्य यद्बीजं सीतारूपं तद्दैवादितो हृतं गर्भिणीदशायामेव नष्टम्। 'लूनपूर्वायाम्' इति पाठे पूर्वं लूना छिन्ना तथाविधायाम्। भूतपूर्वनि-

---

१ अन्तर्भूतानि. २ आबद्धोत्पु०. ३ मेवमद्य. ४ परिप्लवसे. ५ हतम्. ६ प्रसूनस्यागमः.

चन्द्रकेतुः—अवतराम्यार्य सुमन्त्र स्यन्दनात् ।

सुमन्त्रः—तत्कस्य हेतोः ।

चन्द्रकेतुः—एकतस्तावदयं वीरपुरुषः पूजितो भवति । अपि च खल्वार्य क्षात्रधर्मः समनुगतो[2] भवति । न रथिनः पादचारमभियुञ्जन्तीति[3] शास्त्रविदः[4] परिभाषन्ते[5] ।

सुमन्त्रः—(स्वगतम् ।) आः कष्टां[6] दशामनुप्रपन्नोऽस्मि ।

कथं न्याय्यमनुष्ठानं[7] मादृशः प्रतिषेधतु ।
कथं वाऽभ्यनुजानातु[8] साहसैकरसां क्रियाम् ॥ २१ ॥

चन्द्रकेतुः—[1]दा तातमिश्रा अपि पितुः प्रियसखमर्थसंशयेष्वार्य-[9]मेव पृच्छन्ति तत्किमार्यो विमृशति ।

सुमन्त्रः—आयुष्मन् एवं यथाधर्ममभिमन्यसे ।

एष सांग्रामिको न्याय एष धर्मः सनातनः ।
इयं हि रघुसिंहानां वीरचारित्रपद्धतिः ॥ २२ ॥

चन्द्रकेतुः—अप्रतिरूपं[10] वचनमार्यस्य ।

इतिहासं पुराणं च धर्मप्रवचनानि च ।
भवन्त एव जानन्ति रघूणां च कुलस्थितिम् ॥ २३ ॥

र्देशात् लूनशब्दस्य पूर्वनिपातः । 'पूर्वलूनायाम्' इति पाठे तु पूर्वस्मिन् काले लूनेत्यर्थः। प्रसवस्य पुष्पस्य ॥ २० ॥ वीरपुरुषः लवः पूजितस्तावद्भवति । द्वयोरवतरणप्रयोजनयोः प्रथमं वीरपुरुषपूजा भवति । क्षत्रधर्मः खल्वपि परिपालितोऽनुष्ठितो भवति । पादचारं पदातिं रथिनो नाभियुञ्जन्तीति शास्त्रविदः क्षत्रधर्मप्रतिपादकार्थशास्त्रज्ञाः परिभाषन्ते नियच्छन्ति । **कथं हीति** । इदमनुष्ठानं राजपुत्रस्य रथादवतरणं प्रतिषेधतु निषिध्यात् । निवर्तयेदित्यर्थः । साहसैकरसां साहसप्रकृत्येकवेषां क्रियां अनुष्ठानमभ्यनुजानातु अनुमन्येत ॥ २१ ॥ तातमिश्रा अपि । मिश्रशब्दः पूज्यवाची । रामादयोऽपि अर्थसंशयेषु अनुष्ठेयाननुष्ठेयसंदेहेषु पितुः प्रियसखं दशरथप्रियसखं त्वां पृच्छन्ति जिज्ञासां बोधयन्ति । यथाधर्मं क्षत्रधर्मानतिक्रमेण । **एष इति** । संग्रामे भवः सांग्रामिकः । एष वीरपुरुषपूजारूपः न्याय्यः उचितः । एष धर्मः क्षत्रधर्मपरिपालनरूपः सनातनश्चिरंतनः । इयं पूर्वोक्तद्वयी वीरचारित्रपद्धतिः वीरव्यापारपरिपाटी ॥ २२ ॥ अप्रतिरूपं निस्तुलम् । **इतिहासमिति** । इतिहासं रामायणभारतादिकम् । पुराणम् 'सर्गश्च प्रतिसर्गश्च' इत्याद्युक्तलक्षणकम् । धर्माः नित्यनैमित्तिकादयः प्रोच्यन्ते प्रकाश्यन्ते एभिरित्यर्थे 'करणाधिकरणयोश्च' इति ल्युट् । मन्वादिस्मृतयस्ता इत्यर्थः ।

---

१ यतः. २ परिपालितः, सम्यगनुगतः, गृहीतः. ३ अभि-आ-योधयन्ति. ४ शस्त्राजीवाः, शस्त्रदेवताः. ५ परिचक्षते. ६ कष्टं बतानु०. ७ हीदं. ८ वाप्य. ९ प्रियं सखायं; धर्मार्थ०. १० प्रतिरूपं.

सुमन्त्रः—(सस्नेहास्रं परिष्वज्य ।)

जातस्य ते पितुरपीन्द्रजितो निहन्तु-
 र्वत्सस्य वत्स कति नाम दिनान्यमूनि ।
तस्याप्यपत्यमनुतिष्ठाति वीरधर्मं
 दिष्ट्या गतं दशरथस्य कुलं प्रतिष्ठाम् ॥ २४ ॥

चन्द्रकेतुः—(सकष्टम् ।)

अप्रतिष्ठे रघुज्येष्ठे का प्रतिष्ठा कुलस्य नः ।
इति दुःखेन तप्यन्ते त्रयो नः पितरोऽपरे ॥ २५ ॥

सुमन्त्रः—अहह हृदयमर्मदारणान्येव चन्द्रकेतोर्वचनानि ।

लवः—हन्त मिश्रीकृतो रसक्रमो वर्तते ।

यथेन्दावानन्दं व्रजति समुपोढे कुमुदिनी
 तथैवास्मिन्दृष्टिर्मम कलहकामः पुनरयम् ।
टणत्कारक्रूरक्वणितगुणगुञ्जद्गुरुधनु-
 र्धृतप्रेमा बाहुर्विकचविकरालोल्बणरसः ॥ २६ ॥

चन्द्र०—(अवतरणं रूपयन् ।) आर्य सावित्रश्चन्द्रकेतुरभिवादयते ।

कुलस्थितिं कुलमर्यादाम् ॥ २३ ॥ **जातस्येति** । वत्स चन्द्रकेतो पितुर्जातस्य त्वत्पितुरस्मच्छिशोरिन्द्रजितो निहन्तुर्वत्सस्य लक्ष्मणस्य अमूनि दिनानि एतावान् जीवितकाल इति यावत् । कति नाम कियन्ति नाम । यद्वा वत्सस्य जातस्यामूनि दिनानि कति नामेत्यन्वयः । वत्सस्य लक्ष्मणस्य यज्जातिं जन्म तत्संबन्धिदिनानि । जन्मप्रभृतिदिनानीत्यर्थः । तस्याप्यपत्यं कर्तृ वीरधर्ममनुतिष्ठति अनुष्ठितं करोति । प्रतिष्ठामागतमास्पदं प्राप्तं माहात्म्यं प्राप्तम् । 'प्रतिष्ठा स्थितिमाहात्म्ये' इति यादवः । दिष्टयेत्यानन्दे ॥ २४ ॥ **अप्रतिष्ठे इति** । कुलज्येष्ठे रामे अप्रतिष्ठे अनास्पदे । अनपत्ये । सतीति यावत् । त्रयः पितरः लक्ष्मणभरतशत्रुघ्नाः ॥ २५ ॥ हृदयमर्मणां हृदयमध्यप्रदेशानां दारणानि छेदकानि । दुःखजनकानीत्यर्थः । **यथेति** । कुमुदिनी कुमुद्वती सरस्योषधिर्वा इन्दौ चन्द्रे समुपोढे सति समुपागते सति यथानन्दं संतोषं व्रजति तथा मम दृष्टिरस्मिन् चन्द्रकेतौ समुपोढे सति आनन्दं व्रजति । एवकारः सादृश्यद्योतनार्थः । रणत्कारेण रणदिति शब्देन क्रूरं भयंकरं क्वणितं घण्टादिरणितं येन तथोक्तेन गुणेन ज्यया गुञ्जदव्यक्तं गुरु महद्यद्धनुस्तस्मिन्धृतः प्रेमा कृता प्रीतिर्येन तथोक्तः । विकचानि विस्तृतानि विकरालानि अतिदृढानि व्रणानि मुखे अग्रे यस्य तथोक्तः । अयं मम बाहुः पुनः बाहुस्तु । दृष्टिवैषम्यार्थः पुनःशब्दः । कलहकामः युद्धकाङ्क्षी । भवतीत्यर्थः । अतो रतिक्रोधस्थायिकयोः शृङ्गारवीरयोर्मेलनान्मिश्रितयोः रसयोः क्रमः परिपाटिर्वर्तत इति पूर्वेण संबन्धः । 'पुंभावं मनसा ययुः' इति न्यायेन कुमुदिनीदृष्टान्तात् शृङ्गाररसोत्पत्तिरिति द्रष्टव्यम् ॥ २६ ॥

---

१ विजेतुः. २ ०वृत्तम्. ३ कुल०. ४ दारुणानि. ५ रसः, मिश्रीकृतक्रमः रसः. ६ र–झणत्कार. ७ विकट–विकरालव्रणमुखः. ८ अयमसावैक्ष्वाकः.

सुमन्त्रः—

अजितं पुण्यमूर्जस्वि ककुत्स्थस्येव ते महः ।
श्रेयसे शाश्वतो देवो वराहः परिकल्पताम् ॥ १७ ॥

अपि च ।

देवस्त्वां सविता धिनोतु समरे गोत्रस्य यस्ते पिता
त्वां मैत्रावरुणोऽभिनन्दतु गरुर्यस्ते गुरूणामपि ।
ऐन्द्रावैष्णवमाग्निमारुतमथो सौपर्णमोजोस्तु ते
देयादेव च रामलक्ष्मणधनुर्ज्याघोषमन्त्रो जयम् ॥ १८ ॥

लवः—कुमार अति[4] हि नाम शोभसे रथस्थ एव । कृतं कृतमत्यादरेण ।

चन्द्रकेतुः—तर्हि महाभागोऽप्यन्यं रथमलंकरोतु ।

लवः—आर्य प्रत्यारोपय रथोपरि राजपुत्रम् ।

सुमन्त्रः—त्वमप्यनुरुध्यस्व वत्सस्य चन्द्रकेतोर्वचनम् ।

लवः—को विचारः स्वेषूपकरणेषु । किं त्वरण्यसदो वयमनभ्यस्तरथचर्याः ।

सुमन्त्रः—जानासि वत्स दर्पसौजन्ययोर्यथोचितमाचरितुम् । यदि पुनस्त्वामीदृशमैक्ष्वाको राजा रामभद्रः पश्येत्तदा तस्य स्नेहेन हृदयमभिष्यन्देत ।

लवः—आर्य सुजनः स राजर्षिः श्रूयते । (सलज्जमिव ।)

अहितस्यैवानभिमतस्यैव पराभवायावमानायादिवराहः प्रलयार्णवमग्नभूमेरुद्धर्ता वराहरूपेणावतीर्णो भगवान् कल्पतां तस्मिन् समर्थो भवतु । [शाश्वतः नित्यः वराहः देवः वराहस्वरूपो विष्णुः श्रेयसे कल्याणाय । विजयलाभायेत्यर्थः । ककुत्स्थस्य इव, अजितमप्रतिहतं पुण्यं ऊर्जस्वि अतिबलवत् मह ओजः परिकल्पतां विदध्यात् ॥ २७ ॥] **देव इति** । देवः सविता सूर्यः धिनोतु प्रीणयतु । मैत्रावरुणः वसिष्ठस्त्वामभिनन्दतु । इन्द्रस्य विष्णोश्च इदं ऐन्द्रावैष्णवम् । 'देवताद्वन्द्वे च' इति आनङ् । अग्नेर्मारुतस्य चेदमाग्निमारुतम् । 'इद्वृद्धौ' इति इत् । सौपर्णं गरुडदेवत्वमोजः पराक्रमः । ज्याघोष एव मन्त्रः । जयं पराभिभवं देयाद्दद्यात् । एतैर्लिङीत्येत्वम् ॥ २८ ॥ शोभसे हृद्यो भवसि । अत्यादरेण कृतम् । अवरोहणं न कार्यमिति भावः । तर्हि मदवरोहणे अनिष्टे । प्रत्यारोपय । राजपुत्रं चन्द्रकेतुम् । त्वमप्यनुरुध्यस्व यथा चन्द्रकेतुस्त्वद्वचनं रथादनवरोहणेनानुरोधितवान् तथा त्वमपि तद्वचनं रथारोहणेनानुसर । स्वेषु स्वीयेषूपकरणेषु रथादिषु । अरण्ये सीदन्ति वसन्तीत्यरण्यसदः । 'सत्सूद्विष'—इत्यादिना क्विप् । अनभ्यस्तरथचर्याः अपरिचितरथगतयः । दर्पसौजन्ययोः यदाचरितं पराक्रमसख्यगत्यानुगुणो य आचारस्तम् जानासीत्यर्थः । अय लवः अस्य राम-

---

१ पुण्यमोजस्वि. The Com. reads for the śloka-अहितस्यैव पराभवाय महानादिवराहः कल्पताम्. २ पतिः. ३ ऐन्द्रं. ४ अतीव. ५ यदाचरितम्. ६ रामः. ७ तदायमस्य...अभिष्यन्दयेत्. ८ मन्ये, मान्यः अन्यच्च चन्द्रकेतो.

वयं[1]मपि न खल्वेवंप्रायाः [2]क्रतुप्रतिघातिनः
क [3]इह न गुणैस्तं राजानं जनो बहु मन्यते ।
तदपि खलु मे स व्याहारस्तुरङ्गमरक्षिणां
विकृतिमखिलक्षत्राक्षेप[4]प्रचण्डतयाऽकरोत् ॥ २९ ॥

चन्द्रकेतुः—(सस्मितम् ।) किं नु भवतस्तातप्रतापोत्कर्षेऽप्यमर्षः ।

लवः——[5]अस्त्वमर्षो मा भूद्वा । [6]एतत्तु पृच्छामि दान्तं हि राजानं राघवं शृणु[7]मः । स किल नात्मना दृप्यति [8]नास्य प्रजा वा दृप्ता जायन्ते । तत्किं मनुष्यास्तस्य राक्षसीं वाचमुदीरयन्ति ।

ऋषयो राक्षसी[9]माहुर्वाचमुन्मत्तदृप्तयोः ।
सा योनिः सर्ववैराणां सा हि लोकस्य नि[10]र्ऋतिः ॥ ३० ॥

इति ह स्म तां निन्दन्ति । अथेतरामभिष्टुवन्ति ।

कामान्दुग्धे विप्रकर्षत्यलक्ष्मीं कीर्तिं सूते दु[11]ष्कृतं या हिनस्ति ।
तां [12]चाप्येतां मातरं मङ्गलानां धेनुं धीराः सूनृतां वाचमाहुः ॥ ३१ ॥

सुमन्त्रः—परिपू[13]तस्वभावो[14]ऽयं कुमारः प्राचेतसान्तेवासी । वदत्ययम[15]भ्युपपन्नमार्षेण संस्कारेण ।

लवः—यत्पुनश्चन्द्रकेतो वदसि किं नु भवतस्तातप्रतापोत्कर्षेऽप्यमर्ष इति तत्पृच्छामि किं व्यवस्थितविष[16]यैः क्षत्रधर्म इति ।

भद्रस्य हृदयमभिष्यन्दयेत् द्रवयेत् । **यदि चेति** । वयमहं क्रतुद्विषतां यज्ञादिघातुकानामरौ शासितरि रामभद्रविषये एवंप्राया यदि प्रेमपात्रभूताश्चेत्क इव को वा तं राजानं रञ्जकं तं रामभद्रं गुणैः शीलादिभिः हेतुभिः न बहु मन्यते । सर्वोऽपि तं संभावयतीत्यर्थः । सौजन्यस्य को विरोध इत्यत्राह——तदपि तथापि अखिलक्षत्राक्षेपः सकलराजतिरस्कारस्तेन प्रचण्डतया क्रूरतया तुरङ्गमरक्षिणामश्वमेधाश्वरक्षकाणां विकृतिं मन्युं सः व्याहारः मे ' तां पताकां हरामि वः ' इत्यादिकः अकरोत् । अथ वा तुरङ्गमरक्षिणां व्याहारः सप्तलोकैकवीरस्येत्युक्तिः मे विकृतिं मन्युमकरोत् ॥ २९ ॥ दृप्ता न जायन्ते । राक्षसीं वाचं दृप्तवाचम् । तदाह—**ऋषय इति** । योनिः कारणम् । निष्कृतिः परिभवहेतुः ॥ ३० ॥ इतरां वक्ष्यमाणाम् । **काममिति** । काममभिलषितं दुग्धे प्रपूरयति । अलक्ष्मीं विप्रकर्षति दूरीकरोति । कीर्तिं गुणवत्ताप्रथां सूते जनयति । दुर्हृदः शत्रून् निष्प्रलाति अतिशयेन नाशयति । सूनृता वागिति शेषः । शुद्धां दोषशून्यां शान्तां कार्कश्यरहितां मङ्गलानां मातरं हेतुं धेनुं स्वरूपेणाभोग्यां धीराः ध्यानशीलाः सूनृतां शुद्धामाहुरिति योज्यम् । इतीतरामभिष्टुवन्तीति पूर्वेणान्वयः ॥ ३१ ॥ अभ्युपपन्नामर्षेण उत्पन्नासहनेन संस्कारेण वासनया । तातप्रतापोत्कर्षेऽप्यमर्ष इति यद्वदसि अत्रोच्यत इति शेषः ।

---

१ यदि च वयमप्येवंप्रायाः क्रतुद्विषनामरौ (टी०). २ क्रतुष्वपि मत्सराः. ३ इव, इह च... न वा बहु. ४ क्षेपः. ५ स्त्विहा०. ६ अन्यदेतत्. ७ राघवमनुशुश्रुम. ८ नाप्यस्य प्रजासु; नास्य प्रजायां दृप्तत्वं जायते; प्रजा ईदृश्यो जा०. ९ ०सीं वाचं वदन्त्यु०. १० निष्कृतिः, निकृतिः. ११ दुर्हृदो निष्प्रलाति-निष्प्रहन्ति. १२ शुद्धां शान्तां (टी.). १३ परिभूतोयं, परिपूर्ण० अपरिप्लुत०. १४ अयं वत्सः. १५ वदत्यभिसंपन्नं, ०पन्नामर्षेण. १६ विषयाः क्षात्र-क्षत्र-धर्माः.

सुमन्त्रः—नैव खलु जानासि देवमैक्ष्वाकं[1] येनैवं वदसि। तद्वि रमातिप्रसङ्गात्[2]।

सैनिकानां प्रमाथेन सत्यमोजायितं त्वया।
जामदग्न्यस्य दमने नै[3] हि निर्बन्धमर्हसि ॥ ३२ ॥

लवः—(सहासम्।) आर्य[4] जामदग्न्यस्य दमनः स राजेति कोऽयमुच्चैर्वादः।

सिद्धं ह्येतद्वाचि वीर्यं द्विजानां
बाह्वोर्वीर्यं यत्तु तत्क्षत्रियाणाम्।
शस्त्रग्राही ब्राह्मणो जामदग्न्य-
स्तस्मिन्दान्ते का स्तुतिस्तस्य राज्ञः ॥ ३३ ॥

चन्द्रकेतुः—(सोन्माथमिव।) आर्य सुमन्त्र कृतमुत्तरोत्तरेण।

कोऽप्येष संप्रति नवः पुरुषावतारो
वीरो न यस्य भगवान्भृगुनन्दनोऽपि।
पर्याप्तसप्तभुवनाभयदक्षिणानि
पुण्यानि तातचरितान्यपि यो न वेद ॥ ३४ ॥

लवः—को हि रघुपतेश्चरितं महिमानं च न जानाति। यदि नाम किंचिदस्ति वक्तव्यम्। अथ वा शान्तम्।

वृद्धास्ते[6] न विचारणीयचरितास्तिष्ठन्तु किं वर्ण्यते
सुन्दस्त्रीमथनेऽप्यकुण्ठयशसो लोके महान्तो हि ते।

व्यवस्थितविषयः रामभद्रमात्रनियताधिकरणकः क्षत्रधर्मः क्षत्रियासाधारणपराक्रमातिशयादिः। अतिप्रसङ्गादनिष्टप्रसञ्जनाद्विरम विरतो भव। 'जुगुप्साविराम-' इति पञ्चमी। **सैनिकानामिति**। प्रमाथेन प्रकृष्टविलोडनेन ओजायितमोजस्वीभूतम्। भावे क्तः। जामदग्न्यस्य दमने परशुरामस्य जेतरि रामभद्रे विषये। निर्बन्धं रूक्षवादम् ॥ ३२ ॥ **सिद्धमिति**। द्विजानां विप्राणां वाचि वीर्यं पराभिभवनसामर्थ्यमिति यत् क्षत्रियाणां बाह्वोर्वीर्यमिति यत्। एतत्सिद्धं प्रसिद्धं किल। जामदग्न्यः शस्त्रग्राही ब्राह्मणः। तस्मिन्दान्ते तस्य राज्ञः तद्दमनकरामभद्रस्य स्तुतिः गुणाभिधानिका का। न किमपीत्यर्थः ॥ ३३ ॥ **कोऽपीति**। यस्य परशुरामश्च वीरो न। यज्ज्ञानाविषयवीरत्ववान् भृगुनन्दनः। यः पुरुषः सप्तानां भुवनानां समाहारः सप्तभुवनं तस्याभयं भयनिवारणं तदेव दक्षिणा प्रत्युपकारनिरपेक्षं स्वाभ्युदयमुद्दिश्य दानं सा पर्याप्ता पूर्णा येषु तथोक्तानि तातचरितानि पुण्यानि रामभद्रवृत्तलक्षणगुम्फकर्माणि शुभकर्माणि तथा तु न वेद न जानाति। एष नवः पुरुषावतारः कोऽपि। क्षेपेऽयं किंशब्दः। अत्र रामचरितलक्षणक्रतूनां जगदभयदानमेव दक्षिणेति वर्णनाद्रूपकालंकारः ॥ ३४ ॥ यदि नाम किंचिदस्ति वक्तव्यम्। वक्तव्यं किंचिदस्ति किमित्यर्थः। **वृद्धा इति**। अविचारणीयचरितास्ते वृद्धास्तिष्ठन्तु। वयोमात्रं तेषां गौरवहेतुरिति भावः। सुन्दस्त्रीमथने ताटकावधेऽपि अकुण्ठयशसः अप्रतिहतकीर्तयः।

१ ऐक्ष्वकम्। तद्विरम. २ विरम; विरम्यताम्. ३ न तु; नैव; नातिनिर्वक्तुम्. ४ आर्य. ५ श्लाघ्यः. ६ वन्द्याः. ७ हुं वर्ण्यते. ८ निधने-दमने-प्यखण्डय०.

यानि त्रीण्यपराङ्मुखान्यपि पदान्यासन्खरायोधने
यद्वा कौशलमिन्द्रसूनुनिधने तत्राप्यभिज्ञो जनः ॥ ३५ ॥

चन्द्रकेतुः—आः तातापवादभिन्नमर्याद अति हि नाम प्रगल्भसे ।

लवः—अये मय्येव भ्रुकुटीधरः संवृत्तः ।

सुमन्त्रः—स्फुरितमनयोः क्रोधेन । तथा हि ।

चूडामण्डलबन्धनं तरलयत्याकूतजो वेपथुः
किंचित्कोकनदच्छदस्य सदृशे नेत्रे स्वयं रज्यतः ।
धत्ते कान्तिमकाण्डताण्डवितयोर्भङ्गेन वक्रं भ्रुवो-
श्चन्द्रस्योद्भटलाञ्छनस्य कमलस्योद्भ्रान्तभृङ्गस्य च ॥३६॥

कुमारौ—तदितो विमर्दक्षमां भूमिमवतरावः ।

(इति निष्क्रान्ताः सर्वे ।)

पञ्चमोऽङ्कः ।

कुतोमुखानि पराङ्मुखानि पदानि पादन्यासपराङ्मुखानीति वाचा वक्तुमपि जुगुप्सया कुतोमुखानीत्युक्तम् । तदिदं शौर्यातिशयकार्यम् अत्रात्यन्तमासन्नो भूत्वा खरः स्थितः तदा रामभद्रश्चापकर्षणार्थं पदत्रयं निवृत्य तं जघानेति प्रसिद्धिः । इन्द्रसूनुनिधने वालिवधे यत्कौशलं नैपुण्यमन्तर्धानपूर्वकत्वरूपं तत्राप्यभिज्ञो जनः वर्तते । हुमिति परिहासे ॥ ३५ ॥ तातापवादिन् रामभद्रविषयदोषवादिन् । भिन्नमर्याद अतिक्रान्तसमुदाचार । भ्रुकुटीमुखः क्रोधप्रयुक्तभ्रूभङ्गयुक्तवदनः । अनयोर्लवचन्द्रकेत्वोः । **क्रोधेनेति** । उद्धता धूताश्चलन्तः कुन्तलाः केशभराः यस्मिन् स तथोक्तः । कोकनदच्छदस्य रक्तारविन्दपत्रस्य रज्यतः रक्तीभवतः । भ्रुवोर्भङ्गेन भीमम् । अनयोरिदं वक्त्रं च । उद्भटलाञ्छनस्य प्रकटलक्ष्मणः चन्द्रस्य उद्भ्रान्तभृङ्गस्य कमलस्य च कान्ति धत्ते । वक्त्रमित्येकवचनोक्तिः संतानैकप्रयुक्तात्यन्तसारूप्यद्योतनाय । निदर्शनालंकारः ॥ ३५ ॥ एह्यागच्छ । विमर्दक्षमां युद्धयोग्यां भूमिमवतरावः । इति निष्क्रान्ताः सर्वे ।

वाधूलवंशजनुषो भूसारनिवासराघवार्यस्य ।
उत्तररामचरित्रव्याख्यायामवसितः पञ्चमोऽङ्कः ॥

इति श्रीवाधूलवीरराघवविरचितायां भवभूतिभावतलस्पर्शिनीसमाख्यायामुत्तररामचरितव्याख्यायां
पञ्चमोऽङ्कः ।

---

१ अकुतो-मुखानि-भयानि. २ ०वादिन्. ३ आः कथं. ४ ०मुखः ५ क्रोधेनोद्धतधूतकुन्तलभरः सर्वाङ्गजः. ६ कान्तिमिदं च वक्त्रमनयोर्भङ्गेन भिन्नभ्रुवोः. ७ उत्कट. ८ लवः—कुमार कुमार एह्येहि । विमर्द &c. ९ इति महा० ते उ ०तनाटके कुमारविक्रमो नाम प०.

षष्ठोऽङ्कः ।

(ततः प्रविशति विमानेनोज्ज्वलं विद्याधरमिथुनम् ।)

विद्याधरः—अहो नु खल्वनयोर्विकर्तनकुरुकुमारयोरकाण्डकलहप्रचण्डयोरुद्द्योतितक्षत्रलक्ष्मीकयोरत्यद्भुतोद्भ्रान्तदेवासुराणि विक्रान्तचरितानि । तथा हि प्रिये पश्य पश्य ।

> **झणज्झणितकङ्कणक्वणितकिङ्किणीकं धनु-**
> **र्ध्वनद्गुरुगुणाटनीकृतकरालकोलाहलम् ।**
> **वितत्य किरतोः शरानविरतस्फुरच्चूडयो-**
> **र्विचित्रमभिवर्तते भुवनभीममायोधनम् ॥ १ ॥**
> **विजृम्भितं च दिव्यस्य मङ्गलाय द्वयोरपि ।**
> **स्तनयित्नोरिवामन्द्रं दुन्दुभेर्दुन्दुमायितम् ॥ २ ॥**

तत्प्रवर्ततामनयोः प्रवीरयोरनवरतमविरलललितविकचकनककमलकमनीयसंहतिरमरतरुतरुणमणिमुकुलनिकरमकरन्दसुन्दरः पुष्पनिपातः ।

विद्याधरी—तत्किमिति पुनरकाण्डविस्फुरिततडिच्छटाकडारमिवाम्बरं झटिति संवृत्तम् । (क)

(क) ता किं ति उण अआण्डविप्फुरिदतडिच्छडाकडारं विअ अम्बरं झत्ति संवुत्तम् ।

युद्धस्य दूराध्वानं वधमिति दृश्यत्वप्रतिषेधाद्विष्कम्भेन तदाह—विद्याधरमिथुनमित्यादिना । विकर्तनः सूर्यः । अकाण्डकलहेन उभयोरप्येकत्वेन वास्तवहेतुरहितवैरेण प्रचण्डयोः क्रूरयोरुद्द्योतिता क्षत्रलक्ष्मीः ययोस्तथोक्तयोः । अत्यद्भुतेनातिविस्मयेन उद्भ्रान्ता देवासुराः यैस्तथोक्तानि विक्रान्तस्य विक्रमस्य विलसितानि । अहो विस्मयनीयानीत्यर्थः । **रणदिति** । रणत्करणेन रणदिति शब्दहेतुव्यास्फालनेन झणझणाकारवत्क्वणितयुक्तम् । ध्वनन् गुरुगुणः ज्या यया तथोक्तया अटन्या धनुष्कोट्या कृतः करालः भीषणः कोलाहलो यस्य तथोक्तं धनुर्वितत्य मण्डलीकृत्य विरतार्य शरानविरतं किरतोर्वर्षतोः लवचन्द्रकेत्वोः ॥ १ ॥ स्तनयित्नोरिव गर्जन्मेघस्येव अमन्ददुन्दुभेर्दुन्दुमायितं दुन्दुमशब्दः जृम्भितं प्रवृत्तम् ॥ २ ॥ अनयोर्लवचन्द्रकेत्वोस्तादर्थ्येन अविरलमिलिता कमलकमनीयसंहतिर्येन तथोक्तः पुष्पनिपातः पुष्पवृष्टिः । तडिच्छटया विद्युज्जालेन कडारं कपिलं आकाशमन्यदिव जातमि-

१ उज्ज्वलन. २ क्षात्र. ३ विलसितानि; विचरणानि. ४ रणात्—रणत्—करणझञ्झण० ५ अविरतं पुनः शूरयोः. ६ जृम्भितं च विचित्राय. ७ अमन्ददु०. ८ प्रवर्त्य०. ९ मिलित, लुलित. १० संततिः; तरुणमुकु०. ११ उण अआण्डतण्डाविदुद्दण्डतरलिदतडित्० (पुनरकाण्डताण्डवितोद्दण्डतरालिततडित्०); पुरो आआसं दुद्दंसतरलतडि०...डारं अवरं विअ झत्ति (पुर आकाशं दुर्दर्शतरलतडि०...डारमपरमिव झटिति).

विद्याधरः—तत्किं नु खल्वद्य

त्वाष्ट्रयन्त्रभ्रमिभ्रान्तमार्तण्डज्योतिरुज्ज्वलः।
पुटभेदो ललाटस्थनीललोहितचक्षुषः॥ ३॥

आं ज्ञातम्। जातक्षोभेण चन्द्रकेतुना प्रयुक्तमस्त्रमाग्नेयम्। यस्यायमग्निच्छटासंपातः। संप्रति हि।

अवदग्धकर्बुरितकेतुचामरै-
रपयातमेव हि विमानमण्डलैः।
दधाति ध्वजांशुकपटाञ्चलेष्विमाः
क्षणकुङ्कुमच्छुरणविभ्रमं शिखाः॥ ४॥

आश्चर्यम्। प्रवृत्त एवायमुच्चण्डवज्रखण्डावस्फोटपटुरवस्फुलिङ्गगुरुरुत्तालतुमुललेलिहानोज्ज्वलज्ज्वालासंभारभैरवः भगवानुषर्बुधः। प्रचण्डश्चास्य सर्वतः संतापः। तत्प्रियामङ्केनाच्छाद्य सुदूरमपसरामि।
(तथा करोति।)

त्यर्थः। तत्किं नु खलु नु किमिति पदद्वयमस्य च वक्ष्यमाणवाक्यद्वयेनान्वयः। **त्वाष्ट्रेति**। त्वष्टृशाणचक्रभ्रमिभ्रान्तमार्तण्डज्योतिः किम्। उज्ज्वलः ललाटस्थनीललोहितचक्षुषः रुद्रललाटनेत्रस्य पुटभेदो नु उन्मीलनं नु। अथ वा किंचित्येकमेव पदम्। मार्तण्डज्योतिरुज्ज्वल इत्येकपदं पुटभेदविशेषणम्। ज्योतिरिवोज्ज्वलतीति तदर्थः॥ ३॥ जातक्षोभेण प्रकृतिविपर्यासवता। आग्नेयमग्निदैवत्यम्। शरसंपातः इषुधारा। **अवदग्धेति**। अवदग्धानि प्रायेण दग्धानि बर्बरितानि यानि दाहजबर्बरध्वनियुक्तानि। केतवः क्षुद्रध्वजाश्चामराणि वालव्यजनानि येषां तथोक्तैः। अपयातम्। भावे क्तः। नवपलाशकुसुमकान्तिसदृशः शिखी अग्निः। ध्वजा महाकेतवः तेषामंशुकानि चीरांशुकानि तान्येव पटाः। सामान्यविशेषशब्दयोः कर्मधारयः। 'उत्तरीये वस्त्रमात्रे सूक्ष्मवस्त्रेऽपि चांशुकम्' इति रत्नमाला। अंशुकपदं सूक्ष्मगात्रपरं गोबलीवर्दन्यायेन। तेषामावलिं ध्वजलक्षणकान्तिव्याजपुञ्जानीति वार्थः। अत्र ध्वजाश्च अंशुकपटाश्चेति विग्रहः। व्याजपर्यायः कपटशब्दः। अंशव एव ध्वजव्याजेन वर्तन्त इति लाभात्तेजिष्ठत्वं ध्वजानां लभ्यते। किं चायमाग्नेयाग्निरग्निमपि दहतीति असंबन्धेऽपि संबन्धादतिशयोक्तिरिति अपह्नवेन सह संकरः॥ ४॥ वज्रखण्डस्याशनिशकलस्य अवस्फोटः स्फुटनं तद्वत्पटु तीक्ष्णं यथा तथा रटन् स्फुलिङ्गगुरुः कणबहुलः। उत्तालतुमुलं यथा तथा अतिशयितसंकुलं यथा तथा लेलिहानः भृशं कवलनपरः। लिहधातोर्यङ्लुकि चानश्। उज्ज्वलज्ज्वालासंभारेण ज्वालातिशयेन भैरवः भयंकरः। उषर्बुधः अग्निः। अस्याग्नेः संपातः सम्यक्पतनम्।

---

१ त्वष्टृ. २ रुज्ज्वलम्. ३ वत्सेन. ४ अप्रतिरूपमाग्नेयमस्त्रम्. ५ अग्निवच्छरसंपातः. ६ बर्बरित. ७ दहति ध्वजांशुकपटावलीमिमां नवकिंशुकद्युतिसविभ्रमः शिखी (टी०). ८ अङ्कुश. ९ रटत्; ०नर. १० स्फुलिङ्ग-निकृतिः-विकृतिः. ११ लोलले लि०, लेलिहानज्वाला. १२ अंशुकेन.

विद्याधरी—दिष्टया एतेन विमलमुक्ताफलशीतलस्निग्धमसृणमांसलेन नाथदेहस्पर्शेनानन्दमन्दमुकुलितघूर्णमानलोचनाया अल्पोदित एवान्तरितो मे संतापः। (क)

विद्याधरः—अयि किमत्र मया कृतम्। अथ वा।

नं किंचिदपि कुर्वाणः सौख्यैर्दुःखान्यपोहति।
तत्तस्य किमपि द्रव्यं यो हि यस्य प्रियो जनः ॥ ५ ॥

विद्याधरी—कथमविरलविलोलघूर्णमानविद्युल्लताविलासमण्डितैर्मत्तमयूरकण्ठश्यामलैरवस्तीर्यते नभस्तलं जलधरैः। (ख)

विद्याधरः—हन्त कुमारलवप्रयुक्तवारुणास्त्रप्रभावः खल्वेषः। कथमविरलप्रवृत्तवारिधारासहस्रसंपातैः प्रशान्तमेव पावकास्त्रम्।

विद्याधरी—प्रियं मे प्रियं मे। (ग)

विद्याधरः—हन्त हन्त भोः सर्वमतिमात्रं दोषाय। यत्प्रलयवातावलिक्षोभगम्भीरगुलुगुलायमानमेघमेदुरान्धकारनीरन्ध्रनद्धमिव एक-

---

(क) दिट्ठिआ एदेण विमलमुत्ताफलसीअलसिणिद्धमसिणमंसलेण णाहदेहप्फंसेण आणन्दमन्दमउलिदघुण्णन्तलोअणाए अप्पोदिदो एव्व अन्दरिदो मे संदावो। (ख) कहं अविरलविलोलघुण्णमाणविज्जुल्लदाविलासमण्डिदेहिं मत्तमोरकण्ठसामलेहिं ओत्थरीअदि णहत्थलं जलहरेहिं। (ग) पिअं मे पिअं मे।

प्रचण्डः अतितीक्ष्णः। विमलमुक्ताशैलवत् निर्दोषमौक्तिकपर्वतवत् शीतलेन स्निग्धेन स्नेहयुक्तेन मसृणेन चाकचक्यवता मांसलेन स्फीतेन। सर्वत्र विशेषणसमासः। आनन्देन संदलिता वर्तिता वेदना यस्मिंस्तथोक्तः। अन्तरितस्तिरोहितः। मया किमत्र कृतम्। न किमपीत्यर्थः। **न किंचिदपीत्यादि**। **पूर्वे** व्याख्यातम् ॥ ५ ॥ विलोलाः वेपमानाः घूर्णमानाः वेष्टमानाः। अवस्तीर्यते आच्छाद्यते। 'अवतीर्यते' इति च पाठः। आग्नेयास्त्रप्रतिद्वन्द्वत्वाद्वरुणास्त्रं प्रयुक्तम्। धारासंपातैर्धारासम्यक्पतनैः प्रशान्तं निर्वापितम्। अतिमात्रं प्रमाणातिक्रान्तं दोषाय। कल्पत इति शेषः। प्रलयवातेन कल्पान्तमारुतेन उत्क्षोभा अतिशयितक्षोभयुक्ता गम्भीरा अनल्पा गुलुगुलायमाना गुलुगुलु इत्याकारकवर्णध्वनियुक्ता ये मेघास्तैर्मेदुरितेन सान्द्रितेन अन्धकारेण नीरन्ध्रमविरलं नद्धमिव बद्धमिव। एकेन वारेण क्षणेन विश्वस्य प्रपञ्चस्य ग्रसनेन कवलनेन। एकवार इहानावृत्तिर्वा।

---

१ आकिंचि०. २ अयि. ३ प्रबलवाता०; ०वातोत्क्षोभ. ४ गुणगुणायमान, गुमगुमायमान. ५ मेदुरित. ६ निबद्ध. ७ मर, मोत्तिअसर, ०सेअ (शैल). ८ आणन्दसंदलिदघुण्णमाणलेअणाए. ९ अद्धोदितो (अर्धोदितः); एतन्नास्ति क्वचित्. १० णभोङ्गणं.

वारविश्वग्रसनविकटविकरालकालमुखकन्दरविवर्तमानमिव युगान्तयोगनिद्रानिरुद्धसर्वद्वारनारायणोदरनिविष्टमिव भूतजातं प्रवेपते । साधु चन्द्रकेतो साधु । स्थाने वायव्यमस्त्रमीरितम् । कुतः ।

विद्याकल्पेन मरुता मेघानां भूयसामपि ।
ब्रह्मणीव विवर्तानां क्वापि विप्रलयः कृतः ॥ ६ ॥

विद्याधरी—नाथ क इदानीमेष ससंभ्रमोत्क्षिप्तकरभ्रमितोत्तरीयाञ्चलो दूरत एव मधुरस्निग्धवचनप्रतिषिद्धयुद्धव्यापार एतयोः कुमारयोरन्तरे विमानवरमवतारयति । (क)

विद्याधरः—(दृष्ट्वा ।) एष शम्बूकवधात्प्रतिनिवृत्तो रघुपतिः ।

शान्तं महापुरुषसंगदितं निशम्य
तद्गौरवात्समुपसंहृतसंप्रहारः ।

(क) णाध को दाणिं एसो ससंभमुक्खित्तकरब्भमिदोत्तरिआञ्चलो दूरदो एव्व महुरसिणिद्धवअणपडिसिद्धजुद्धव्वावारो एदाणं कुमाराणं अन्दरे विमाणवरं ओदरावेदि ।

विकटं निम्नोन्नतं विकरालं विशेषेण भीषणं कालमुखं मृत्युवक्त्रं तस्मिन्विवर्तमानमिव विकुर्वाणमिव । युगान्ते कल्पान्ते योगनिद्रया ध्यानात्मकस्वापेन निरुद्धानि सर्वाणि द्वाराणि यस्य तथोक्तम् । यन्नारायणोदरं समस्तवस्त्वाधारभूतलक्ष्मीनायकोदरम् । तस्मिन्निविष्टमिव भूतम् । जात्येकवचनम् । प्राणिन इत्यर्थः । विपद्यते विपदं प्राप्नोति । वायव्यं वायुदैवत्यम् । 'वाय्वृतु-' इति यत्प्रत्ययः । ईरितं प्रेरितमिति यतः स्थाने युक्तम् । यतः यस्मात् । **विद्येति** । विद्याकल्पेन तत्त्वमस्यादिवाक्यविहिततत्त्वज्ञानसदृशेन मरुता वायुना कर्त्रा भूयसां बहुतराणां मेघानां ब्रह्मणि निर्विशेषसन्मात्रे कूटस्थे चैतन्ये विवर्तानामिव अधिष्ठानविषयसत्ताकव्यावहारिकघटपटादिविकल्पानामिव प्रविलयः निवृत्तिः कृतः । इदं चाद्वैतप्रक्रियया व्याख्यातम् । परमार्थतस्तु विद्याकल्पेन दर्शनसमानाकाराविच्छिन्नस्मृतिसंतानात्मकसद्विद्यादिसदृशेन मरुता ब्रह्मणि निखिलचेतनाचेतनशरीरके समस्तकल्याणगुणाकारे श्रीमति नारायणे विवर्तानामिव विशेषणीभूतचिदचिद्द्वारकविलक्षणविकारभूतदेहेन्द्रियादीनामिव प्रविलयः कृतः । जगदुपादानस्य ब्रह्मणः कार्यत्वनियतनामरूपप्रहाणलक्षणात्यन्तिकलय एव तदपृथक्सिद्धविशेषणभूतजीवस्य मोक्षः । स च 'तमेव विदित्वा-' इत्यादिश्रुतिभिर्भक्तिसाध्य एव मुक्तिः इति । 'ब्रह्मैव सन् ब्रह्माप्येति' इत्युक्तेः ॥६॥ प्रतिषिद्धः निवर्तितः युद्धव्यापारो येन तथोक्तः । अन्तरे मध्ये । प्रतिषेधवाक्येन तयोस्तत्प्रतिघाताय मध्ये रथस्थापनेन तन्निवर्तयतीति भावः । शम्बूकवधात् शम्बूकवधं निर्वर्त्य । ल्यब्लोपे पञ्चमी । **शान्तमिति** । शान्तं कार्कश्यरहितं महापुरुषस्य रामस्य संगदितं वचनं निशम्य । तद्गौरवाद्रामविषयकगरी-

१ विकच. २ कण्ठ, कण्ठमुख. ३ विपद्यते. ४ वत्स चन्द्र०. ५ प्रवि०. ६ दिष्ट्या एष. ७ शब्दं महापुरुषसंविहितम्. ८ पट्टा-ट्टका-ञ्चलो. ९ महुरवअण०. १० मज्झे विमाणं.

शान्तो लवः प्रणत एव च चन्द्रकेतुः
कल्याणमस्तु सुतसंगमेनेन[1] राज्ञः ॥ ७ ॥

तदितस्तावदेहि । (इति निष्क्रान्तौ ।)

मिश्रविष्कम्भः ।

(ततः प्रविशति रामो लवः प्रणतश्चन्द्रकेतुश्च ।)

रामः—(पुष्पकादवतरन् ।)

दिनकरकुलचन्द्र चन्द्रकेतो
सरभसमेहि दृढं[2] परिष्वजस्व ।
तुहिनशकलशीतलैस्तवाङ्गैः
शममुपयातु ममापि चित्तदाहः ॥८॥

(उत्थाप्य[3] सस्नेहास्रं परिष्वज्य ।) अपि नाम कुशलं तत्र दिव्यास्त्रधरदेहस्य ।

चन्द्रकेतुः—कुशलमत्यद्भुतक्रियस्य[4] प्रियदर्शनस्य लवस्य लाभाभ्युदयेन । तद्विज्ञापयामि मामिव विशेषेण वा मत्तः स्निग्धेन[5] चक्षुषा पश्यत्वमुं महावीरप्रकाण्डं तातः ।

रामः—(लवं निरूप्य ।) दिष्ट्या अतिगम्भीरमधुरकल्याणाकृतिरयं[6] वयस्यो वत्सस्य ।

यस्त्वबुद्ध्या समुपसंहृतः निवृत्तः संप्रहारः युद्धं येन तथोक्तः । लवः शान्तः निवृत्तव्यापारोऽभूत् । चन्द्रकेतुश्च प्रणत एव । यत एवं ततः सुताभ्यां लवचन्द्रकेतुभ्यां संगमेनेन समागमेन राज्ञः रामस्य कल्याणमस्तु । विद्याधरेण ज्ञाततत्वात्सुतेत्युक्तिः ॥ ७ ॥ **दिनकरेति** । दिनकरकुलचन्द्र सूर्येण सह तदीयस्यास्मद्वंशस्य आह्लादकप्रसिद्धचन्द्र । सूर्यं प्रति चन्द्रत्वाभावेनास्य तं प्रत्यपि चन्द्रत्वमाधिक्ये पर्यवस्यति । अत एव ममापि चित्तदाह इत्युक्तिः संगच्छते । ममापि एवमत्यन्ततप्तस्यापि मम । अनेन सहस्रभानुतापापेक्षयापि स्वतापस्य भूयस्त्वं गम्यते । शमं निर्वाणमुपयातु प्राप्नोतु ॥ ४ ॥ नूतनदिव्यास्त्रायोधनस्य नूतनामानुष्यास्त्रकरणकयुद्धस्य । नूतनं दिव्यास्त्रैरायोधनं यस्येति बहुव्रीहिः । तवेति शेषः । अनामयमारोग्यम् । अत्यद्भुतस्य आश्चर्यकरस्य प्रियवयस्यस्य लाभ एवाभ्युदयस्तेन । स्निग्धेन स्नेहवता चक्षुषा अनराल्साहसमकुटिलयुद्धादिव्यापारम् ।

---

१ संमिलनेन, पुनरागमनेन. २ मेह्यदयं. ३ **Before this** चन्द्र०—अभिवादये. रामः—अप्यनामयं नूतनदिव्यास्त्रायोधनस्य तव । (टी.); ०मयं नूतनस्य दिव्यास्त्रप्रयोगस्य. ४ ०द्भुतप्रियवयस्यलामा०. ५ शिवेन, शिवतरेण; अविशेषेण मत्तः शिवतरेण; मद्विशेषेण वा मित्रं स्नि०... त्वमुं महा-धीरमनरालसाहसं. ६ ०म्भीराकृतिः; अतिकल्याणाकृतिः.

त्रातुं लोकानिव परिणतः कायवानस्त्रवेदः
क्षात्रो धर्मः श्रित इव तनुं ब्रह्मकोषस्य गुप्त्यै ।
सामर्थ्यानामिव समुदयः संचयो वा गुणाना-
माविर्भूय स्थित इव जगत्पुण्यनिर्माणराशिः ॥ ९ ॥

लवः—(स्वगतम् ।) अहो पुण्यानुभावदर्शनोऽयं महापुरुषः ।

आश्वासस्नेहभक्तीनामेकमालम्ब्यं महत् ।
प्रकृष्टस्येव धर्मस्य प्रसादो मूर्तिसंचरः ॥ १० ॥

आश्चर्यम् ।

विरोधो विश्रान्तः प्रसरति रसो निर्वृतिघन-
स्तदौद्धत्यं क्वापि व्रजति विनयः प्रह्वयति माम् ।
झटित्यस्मिन्दृष्टे किमपि परवानस्मि यदि वा
महार्घस्तीर्थानामिव हि महतां कोऽप्यतिशयः ॥ ११ ॥

अमुं लवम् । अतिगम्भीरा अक्षोभ्या कल्याणी मङ्गलावहा आकृतिराकारो यस्य तथोक्तः । दिष्ट्या आनन्दहेतुः । **त्रातुमित्यादि** । लोकान् चतुर्दशभुवनानि त्रातुं रक्षितुं कायवान्मूर्तिमान् सन् परिणतः जातः अस्त्रवेदः अस्त्रमन्त्रभागस्तद्वत्स्थितः । ब्रह्मकोषस्य ब्रह्माण्डस्य गुप्त्यै रक्षणाय तनुं मूर्तिं श्रितः प्राप्तः क्षात्रो धर्म इव स्थितः । शौर्यवीर्यादिरूपक्षत्रियस्वभाव इव स्थितः । सामर्थ्यानामारब्धकार्यनिर्वहणशक्तीनां समुदय इव स्थितः । गुणानां धैर्यादीनां संचयो वा समूह इव स्थितः । ' वा स्याद्विकल्पोपमयोः ' इति कोशः । जगत्पुण्यनिर्माणानां जगत्पुण्यानुष्ठानानां राशिरिव स्थितोऽयं वत्सस्य वयस्य इति पूर्वेण संबन्धः । आविर्भूय प्रत्यक्षीभूय स्थितः जगत्पुण्यनिर्माणराशिरिव स्थितः । अभूतोपमा ॥ ९ ॥ पुण्ये अनुभावदर्शने यस्य तथोक्तः। अनुभावः प्रभावः । दर्शनं साक्षात्कारः । **आश्वास इति** । भक्तानां स्नेहपूर्वानुध्यानानामाश्वास इव स्थितः । दुःखविस्मरणपूर्वकाह्लाद इव स्थितः । भक्त्योऽन्यत्र हि क्रियमाणा विषयदोषेण दुःखयन्ति तासां रामे क्रियमाणानां विषयसौष्ठवेनाह्लादो जायते । तद्धेतौ तत्त्वारोपः । एकमद्वितीयं महद्विपुलं भक्तीनामायतनं स्थानं च । ' आश्वासस्नेहभक्तीनामेकमालम्बनं महत् ' इति च पाठान्तरम् । आश्वासः द्वेषाभावः । स्नेहः प्रणयः भक्तिः स एव भावनाप्रकर्षेण प्रत्यक्षसमानाकारतामापन्न एव तासां मुख्यविषयभूत इत्यर्थः । प्रकृष्टस्य लोकोत्तरस्य धर्मस्य सुकृतस्य मूर्तिसुन्दरः प्रसाद इव स्थितः महापुरुष इति पूर्वेणान्वयः । उक्तं च ' रामो विग्रहवान्धर्मः ' इति । प्रसाद इह फलप्रदानोन्मुखता ॥ १० ॥ **विरोध इति** । विरोधः वैरम् । विश्रान्तः विरतः । निर्वृतिघन आनन्दसान्द्रः । रस्यते चर्व्यते इति रसः । अपरोक्षावभासरूपः । प्रसरति प्राप्नोति । तद्विपुलमौद्धत्यं दर्पहेतुकसंभावनारूपं क्वापि

---

१ घोषस्य. २ इव. ३ आयतनम् ४ सुन्दरः. ५ किमिति, किमिव.

रामः—तत्किमयमेकपद एव मे[1] दुःखविश्रामं ददात्युपस्नेहयति च कुतोऽपि निमित्तादन्तरात्मानम् । अथ वा स्नेहश्च निमित्तसव्यपेक्षे[2]श्च इति विप्रतिषिद्धमेतत्[3] ।

> **व्यतिषजति पदार्थानान्तरः कोऽपि हेतु-**
> **र्न खलु बहिरुपाधीन्प्रीतयः संश्रयन्ते ।**
> **विकसति हि पतङ्गस्योदये पुण्डरीकं**
> **द्रवति च हिमरश्मावुद्गते चन्द्रकान्तः ॥ १२ ॥**

लवः—चन्द्रकेतो क एते ।

चन्द्रकेतुः—प्रियवयस्य ननु तातपादाः[4] ।

लवः—ममापि तर्हि धर्मतस्तथैव यतः प्रियवयस्य इति[5] भवतोक्तम् । किं तु चत्वारः खलु[6] भवतामेवंव्यपदेशभागिनस्तत्रभवन्तो रामायणकथापुरुषाः । तद्विशेषं ब्रूहि ।

चन्द्रकेतुः—ननु ज्येष्ठतातपादा इत्यवेहि ।

व्रजति । विनयः महाजनसंनिधौ स्वोत्कर्षाननुसंधानरूपः मां प्रह्वयति नमयति । अस्मिन्महापुरुषे दृष्टे सति साक्षात्कृते सति किमिति परवानस्मि कस्माद्धेतोः परतन्त्रोऽस्मि । यदि वा अथ वा तीर्थानामिव गङ्गादिपावनसलिलानामिव महतां पुरुषाणां महार्घः अमूल्यः । श्लाघ्य इति यावत् । अतिशय उत्कर्षः कोऽपि । अन्यादृश इत्यर्थः । इमं च श्लोकं बहवो बहुमन्यन्ते ॥ ११ ॥ एकपद एव एकक्षण एव दुःखविश्रामं दुःखानिर्वृतिं ददाति । कुतोऽपि निमित्तादनिर्धारिताद्धेतोरन्तरात्मानमुपस्नेहयति स्नेहयुक्तं करोति । अथ वा पूर्वोक्तपक्षाभावे । निमित्तसव्यपेक्षः हेतुसापेक्षः स्नेहश्च निमित्तसव्यपेक्षश्चेति यत् स्नेहत्वनिमित्तसापेक्षत्वरूपं विप्रतिषिद्धं व्याहतम् । **व्यतिषजतीति** । कोऽपि हेतुः भवितव्यतारूपः तस्यान्तरत्वमलौकिकत्वं पदार्थानन्तःकरणप्रभृतिवस्तुजातं व्यतिषजति अन्योन्यलग्नान्करोति । अन्तर्भावितण्यर्थोऽयं धातुः । कर्तरि कर्मव्यतिहाराभावान्नात्मनेपदम् । प्रीतयः अत्यन्तानुकूलत्वज्ञानरूपस्नेहः बहिरुपाधीन् बाह्यहेतून्न संश्रयन्ते खलु स्वोत्पादकत्वेन नापेक्षन्त इति प्रसिद्धम् । दृष्टान्तमाह—**विकसतीत्यादि** । पतङ्गस्य सूर्यस्य । चन्द्रकान्तः शिलाविशेषः । अत्र मार्दवस्याप्रयोजकत्वसूचनाय द्वितीयदृष्टान्तः ॥ १२ ॥ धर्मतः पुण्यात् । मित्रस्य पिता स्वस्य पितेति शास्त्रस्यायमर्थः स्वपितृविषये यादृशमनुवर्तनं तादृशं मित्रपितृविषयकं महते श्रेयसे कल्पत इति । एवं च मद्धर्महेतुकपितृत्ववानित्यर्थः । एवं व्यपदेशस्य तातपादशब्दस्य भागिनः स्वामिनः । भागो हि स्वं भागी स्वामी । तातपादशब्दस्य वाच्यतया स्वामिनः अर्थप्रत्ययनार्थत्वाच्छब्दस्य वाच्यशेषत्वं वाचकस्य । तत्रभवन्तः पूजनीयाः

---

१ एतन्नास्ति पुस्तकान्तरे. २ पेक्ष इति. ३ **After this**—तथा हि. ४ ०पादा एते. ५ इत्यात्थ. ६ किल.

लवः—(सोल्लासम् ।) कथं रघुनाथ एव । दिष्ट्या सुप्रभातमद्य यदयं देवो दृष्टः । (सविनयकौतुकं निर्वर्ण्य ।) तात प्राचेतसान्तेवासी लवोऽभिवादयते ।

रामः—आयुष्मन् एह्येहि । (इति सस्नेहमालिङ्ग्य ।) अयि वत्स कृतं कृतमतिविनयेन । अनेकवारमपरिश्लथं परिष्वजस्व माम् ।

परिणतकठोरपुष्करगर्भच्छदपीनमसृणसुकुमारः ।
नन्दयति चन्द्रचन्दननिष्यन्दजडस्तव स्पर्शः ॥ १३ ॥

लवः—(स्वगतम् ।) ईदृशो मां प्रत्यमीषामकारणस्नेहः । मया पुनरेभ्य एवाभिद्रोग्धुमज्ञेन यदायुधपरिग्रहं यावदध्यारूढो दुर्योगः । (प्रकाशम् ।) मृष्यन्त्विदानीं लवस्य बालिशतां तातपादाः ।

रामः—किमपराद्धं वत्सेन ।

चन्द्रकेतुः—अश्वानुयात्रिकेभ्यस्तातप्रतापाविष्करणमुपश्रुत्य वीरायितमनेन ।

रामः—नन्वयमलंकारः क्षत्रस्य ।

न तेजस्तेजस्वी प्रसृतमपरेषां विषहते
स तस्य स्वो भावः प्रकृतिनियतत्वादकृतकः ।
मयूखैरश्रान्तं तपति यदि देवो दिनकरः
किमाग्नेयो ग्रावा निकृत इव तेजांसि वमति ॥ १४ ॥

रामायणकथापुरुषाः रामायणनामकवाक्यप्रबन्धप्रधाननायकाः । तद्विशेषं तेषु विशेषं तातपादस्वव्याप्यरामत्वाद्यन्यतमधर्मविशिष्टत्वं ब्रूहि बोधय । प्राचेतसान्तेवासी वाल्मीकिशिष्यः । **परीति** । परिणतस्य विकसितस्य कठोरस्य समग्रस्य पुष्करस्य पद्मस्य गर्भच्छदवदातपाद्यनभिहतान्तरपत्रवत् पीनः मांसलः मसृणः दन्तुरतारहितः सुकुमारः मृदुलः चन्दननिष्यन्दवत् चन्दनद्रववत् जडः शीतलः । अत्र एकमात्राधिक्यम् । 'चन्दनानिष्यन्दजड' इति संबुद्ध्यन्तपाठेऽपि ॥ १३ ॥ अमीषाम् । रामस्येत्यर्थः । एभ्यः अभिद्रोग्धुमेतद्विषये अपकर्तुम् । 'क्रिया–' इति चतुर्थी । आयुधपरिग्रहः कृतः । बालिशतां मूर्खतां मृष्यन्तां सहन्ताम् । किमपराद्धं कोऽनिष्टाचारः । अश्वस्य मेध्याश्वस्य अनुयात्रिकाः अनुयात्रायां नियुक्तास्तेभ्य इति पञ्चमी । आविष्करणं प्रकाशनमुपश्रुत्याकर्ण्य वीरायितं वीरवदाचरितम् । अयं वीरायितं विधेयप्राधान्यात्पुंस्त्वम् । अलंकारः शोभाकरः । **न तेज इति** । प्रसृतमपरेषां तेजः पराभिभवनसामर्थ्यं न विषहते न सहत इति यत् सः प्रकृतिनियतत्वादुपादानकारण-

---

१ एषः. २ आश्लिष्य; परिष्वज्य. ३ मङ्केन मामप० परिरम्भस्व. ४ अस्मादृशान्. ५ अभिद्रोग्धुमज्ञेनायुधपरिग्रहः कृतः. ६ अत्या०. ७ हि स०, प्रसहते. ८ आग्नेयग्रा०.

चन्द्रकेतुः—अमर्षोऽप्यस्यैव शोभते महावीरस्य । पश्यन्तु हि तातपादाः प्रियवयस्यनिर्युक्तजृम्भकास्त्रनिष्कम्पस्तम्भितानि सर्वतः सैन्यानि ।

रामः—(विलोक्य ।) वत्स लव संह्रियतामस्त्रम् । त्वमपि चन्द्रकेतो निर्व्यापारविलक्षितानि सान्त्वय बलानि ।

लवः—यथाज्ञापयति तातः । (इति प्रणिधानं नाटयति ।)

चन्द्रकेतुः—यथादिष्टम् । (इति निष्क्रान्तः ।)

लवः—तात प्रशान्तमस्त्रम् ।

रामः—वत्स सरहस्यप्रयोगासंहाराण्यस्त्राण्याम्नायवन्ति ।

ब्रह्मादयो ब्रह्महिताय तप्त्वा
परःसहस्राः शरदस्तपांसि ।
एतान्यपश्यन्गुरवः पुराणाः
स्वान्येव तेजांसि तपोमयानि ॥ १५ ॥

अथैतामस्त्रमन्त्रोपनिषदं भगवान्कृशाश्वः परःसहस्रसंवत्सरान्तेवासिने कौशिकाय प्रोवाच । स तु भगवान्मह्यमित्येष गुरुपूर्वानुक्रमः । कुमारस्य कुतः संप्रदाय इति पृच्छामि ।

लवः—स्वतःप्रकाशान्यावयोरस्त्राणि ।

व्याप्तत्वादकृतकः । अनागन्तुकः । स्वो भावः धर्मः । सत्कार्यवादे कारणगुणाः कार्ये उपलभ्यन्ते । मयूखैः किरणैरश्रान्तमविरतमाग्नेयो ग्रावा अग्न्युत्पादकसूर्यकान्तशिला निकृत इव परिभूत इव तेजांसि वमति उद्गिरति । दृष्टान्तालंकारः ॥ १४ ॥ अमर्षोऽपि न केवलं तेजः किं तु मन्युरपि शोभते हृद्यो भवति । स्तम्भितानि निर्व्यापाराणि । संह्रियतामाकृष्यताम् । जृम्भकास्त्रप्रयुक्तपीडाया अननुभूतत्वात् । निर्व्यापारतया विलक्षणानि विस्मयान्वितानि । सान्त्वय मधुरोक्तिभिर्मोदय । प्रणिधानं ध्यानम् । प्रयोगो नियोजनम् । संहार आकर्षणम् । सरहस्यौ अङ्गन्यासाद्यनुष्ठानसहितौ प्रयोगसंहारौ येषां तथोक्तानि । संपद्यन्ते स्थितानि भवन्ति । **ब्रह्मादय इति** । व्याख्यातम् ॥ १५ ॥ अस्त्रमन्त्रोपनिषदं अस्त्रमन्त्रमयीमुपनिषदम् । परःसहस्रं सहस्राधिकसंवत्सरं परिचर्यानिरताय कौशिकाय विश्वामित्राय । भगवान् कौशिकः । पूर्वेषां गुरूणामनुक्रमः परंपरासंप्रदायः गुरुमुखोपदेशः । कुतः कस्मात् । स्वतःप्रकाशानि गुरूपदेशेन विना ज्ञातानि । किं न संभाव्यते । सर्वं संभावितमेवेति

---

१ तात अम०. २ पश्यतु हि तातः. ३ विनिर्मुक्त; नियुक्तेन जृम्भकास्त्रेण विक्रम्य स्तम्भितानि सर्वसै०. ४ (स्वगतम् ।) अहो वत्सस्य ईदृशः प्रभावः । (प्रकाशम् ।) वत्स इ०. ५ निर्दिष्टम्. ६ संहरणानि; ०हारजृम्भकास्त्राणि दिष्ट्या वत्सस्यापि संपद्यन्ते; सरहस्यजृम्भकप्र ७ ०स्त्रं. ८ अथैतन्मन्त्रपारायणोप०. ९ ०हस्रपरिवत्सरा०, सहस्रसंवत्सरपरिचर्यानिरतायान्ते०. १० एष पूर्वा०, एष क्रमः. ११ तु कः, पुनः-तु-कुतः.

रामः—(विचिन्त्य ।) किं न संभाव्यते । प्रकृष्टपुण्यपरिपाकोपादानः कोऽपि महिमा स्यात् । द्विवचनं तु कथम् ।

लवः—भ्रातरावावां यमौ ।

रामः—स तर्हि द्वितीयः कः ।

(नेपथ्ये ।)

दाण्डायन दाण्डायन ।

आयुष्मतः किल लवस्य नरेन्द्रसैन्यै-
रायोधनं ननु किमात्थ सखे तथेति ।
अद्यास्तमेतु भुवनेष्वधिराजशब्दः
क्षत्रस्य शस्त्रशिखिनः शममद्य यान्तु ॥ १६ ॥

रामः—

अथ कोऽयमिन्द्रमणिमेचकच्छवि-
र्ध्वनिनैव बद्धपुलकं करोति माम् ।
नवनीलनीरधरधीरगर्जित-
क्षणबद्धकुड्मलकदम्बडम्बरम् ॥ १७ ॥

लवः—अयमसौ मम ज्यायानार्यः कुशो नाम भरताश्रमात्प्रतिनिवृत्तः ।

रामः—(सकौतुकम् ।) वत्स इत एवाह्वयैतमायुष्मन्तम् ।

लवः—एवम् । (इति परिक्रामति ।)

(ततः प्रविशति कुशः ।)

कुशः—(साकूतहर्षधैर्यं धनुरास्फालयन् ।)

दत्तेन्द्राभयदक्षिणैर्भगवतो वैवस्वताद्वा मनो-
र्दृप्तानां दमनाय दीपितनिजक्षत्रप्रतापाग्निभिः ।

भावः । प्रकृष्टपुण्योपादानकः प्रभूतसुकृतादिकरणकः । द्विवचनं तु आवयोरिति षष्ठीद्विवचनं तु । **आयुष्मत इति** । आयुष्मतः अनुजतया तथोक्तिः । नरेन्द्रसैन्यैः राजसैनिकैरायोधनं ननु युद्धं किम् । तथेत्यात्थ किम् । भुवनेषु राजशब्दः अस्तं नाशमेतु प्राप्नोतु । क्षत्रस्य क्षात्रियजातेः शस्त्राण्येव शिखिनः वह्नयः शमं निर्वाणं यान्तु प्राप्नुवन्तु ॥ १६ ॥ **अथेति** । इन्द्रमणिमेचकच्छावः इन्द्रनीलवन्नीलच्छविः । अथेति प्रश्ने । कदम्बस्येव डम्बरं विभ्रमो यस्येति विग्रहः ॥ १७ ॥ ज्यायानग्रजः । इत एव अत्रैव । एतं कुशम् । सक्रोधं कृतधैर्यं च यथा तथा । **दत्तेति** । अभयमेव दक्षिणा अभयदक्षिणा । इन्द्रस्य अभयदक्षिणा दत्ता यैरिति बहुव्रीहिः । भगवतः

---

१ पुण्योपादानकः. २ यमजौ. ३ कः. ४ भा०. ५ धु च. ६ तर्हि वत्स इत आह्वयेनं. आनय. ७ यदाज्ञापयति तात इति निष्क्रान्तः. ८ साकूत०, सक्रोधं कृतधैर्यं धनुरास्फाल्य ९ दृप्तानां. १० दमनाय.

आदित्यैर्यदि विग्रहो नृपतिभिर्धन्यं ममैतत्ततो
दीप्तास्त्रस्फुरदुग्रदीधितिशिखानीराजितज्यं धनुः ॥ १८ ॥

(इति विकटं परिक्रामति ।)

रामः—कोऽप्यस्मिन्क्षत्रियपोतके पौरुषातिरेकः ।

दृष्टिस्तृणीकृतजगत्त्रयसत्त्वसारा
धीरोद्धता नमयतीव गतिर्धरित्रीम् ।
कौमारकेऽपि गिरिवद्गुरुतां दधानो
वीरो रसः किमयमेत्युत दर्प एव ॥ १९ ॥

लवः—(उपसृत्य ।) जयत्वार्यः ।

कुशः—नन्वायुष्मन् किमियं वार्ता युद्धं युद्धमिति ।

लवः—यत्किंचिदेतत् । आर्यस्तु दृप्तं भावमुत्सृज्य विनयेन वर्तताम् ।

कुशः—किमर्थम् ।

लवः—यदत्र देवो रघुपतिस्तिष्ठति । स च स्निह्यत्यावयोरुत्कण्ठते च युष्मत्संनिकर्षस्य ।

षाड्गुण्यवतः वैवस्वताद्विवस्वत्पुत्रान्मनोः मनुमारभ्य दृप्तानां दमनाय शिक्षणाय दीपितः ज्वलितः निजः असाधारणः क्षत्रप्रताप एवाभिर्यैस्तथोक्तैः । 'दहनाय' इत्यपि च पाठः । आदित्यैः सूर्यवंश्यैः ।'दित्यदित्या'– इति ण्यः । नृपतिभिः विग्रहो यदि विरोधश्चेत्ततः तदा दीप्तानामस्त्राणां स्फुरन्त्यस्तरलाः उग्रास्तीक्ष्णाः या दीधितयस्तासां शिखया कोट्या नीराजिता आर्तीकृता ज्या मौर्वी यस्य तथोक्तम् । ममैतद्धनुः । धन्यं प्रशस्तम् ॥ १८ ॥ विकटं विषमं परिक्रामति । **दृष्टिः इति** । तृणीकृतः अनादृतः जगत्त्रयसत्त्वसारः लोकत्रयबलोत्कर्षो यया सा । धीरोद्धता धीरा चासौ उद्धता चेति विग्रहः । कौमारकेऽपि बाल्येऽपि गिरिवत्पर्वत इव । गिरिर्हि उत्पत्तिप्रभृतिगुरुत्ववान् वृक्षादयस्तु नैवम् । किं तु परिणामविशेषेण गुरुत्वं भजन्ति । किं वीरो रस एति शत्रुकृतापराधादिना प्रज्वलनरूपक्रोधस्थायिकस्वसंवेद्यः प्रकाशविशेषः किमेति । रसालम्बने रसत्वारोपाद्धेत्वलंकारः । दर्पः युद्धकण्डूलता ॥ १९ ॥ आयुष्मन् लवं प्रति सबोधनम् । युद्धं युद्धमिति वार्ता प्रवृत्तिः । युद्धमासीदिति जनवादः श्रूयते स किं सत्य इत्यर्थः । एतद्युद्धं यत्किंचिदल्पकम् । न प्रश्नार्हमित्यर्थः । आर्यस्तु । ज्येष्ठभ्रातृप्रयुक्तपूजाद्योतनाय आर्यशब्दप्रयोगः । दृप्तं भावं दर्पात्मकस्वभावमुत्सृज्य त्यक्त्वा । दृप्तमित्यत्र भावे क्तः । विनयेन निकर्षप्रतिसंधानेन । उपलक्षणे तृतीया । देवः पूज्यः

---

१ नृपतिभिर्वत्सस्य दिष्ट्या ततो. २ दिव्यास्त्र, दृप्तास्त्र. ३ अहो नु खल्वस्मिन्; कोऽप्ययं क्षत्रियपोतः पुरुषातिरेकः. ४ तथा हि इत्यधि०. ५ दृप्तभावमुत्सृज्यार्योऽस्मिन् विनयेन. ६ रघुनन्दनः स्थितः । स रामायणकथानायको ब्रह्मकोषस्य गोप्ता । as part of Lava's speech. Then कुशः—आशंसनीय &c.

कुशः—(सतर्कम् ।) स रामायणकथानायको ब्रह्मकोषस्य गोपायिता ।

लवः—अथ किम् ।

कुशः—आशंसनीयपुण्यदर्शनः स महात्मा । किं तु कथमस्माभिरुपगन्तव्य इति न संप्रधारयामि ।

लवः—यथैव गुरुस्तथोपसदनेन ।

कुशः—कथं हि नामैतत् ।

लवः—अत्युदात्तः सुजनश्चन्द्रकेतुरौर्मिलेयः प्रियवयस्येति सख्येन मामुपतिष्ठते । तेन तत्संबन्धेन धर्मतात एवायं राजर्षिः ।

कुशः—संप्रत्यवचनीयो राजन्येऽपि प्रश्रयः ।

(उभौ परिक्रामतः ।)

लवः—पश्यत्वेनमार्यो महापुरुषमाकारानुभावगाम्भीर्यसंभाव्यमानविविधलोकोत्तरसुचरितातिशयम् ।

कुशः—(निर्वर्ण्य ।)

अहो प्रासादिकं रूपमनुभावश्च पावनः ।
स्थाने रामायणकविर्देवीं वाचं व्यवीवृतत् ॥ २० ॥

रघुनन्दनः रामः अत्र स्थित इति यत्तस्माद्विनयेन वर्तताभिति पूर्वेणान्वयः । ब्रह्मकोषस्य ब्रह्माण्डस्य गोप्ता रक्षकः । स महात्मा अनन्यसामान्यस्वभावः रामः । आशंसनीयमभिलक्षणीयं पुण्यं सुकृतमूलं दर्शनं साक्षात्कारः यस्य तथोक्तः । भवतीति शेषः । ' अस्तिभर्वतिपरः ' इत्युक्तेः । अप्राप्तस्य प्रयोजनस्य प्राप्तुमिच्छा आशंसा । किं तु एवं सत्यपि अस्माभिर्मया कथमुपगन्तव्य इति संप्रधारयामि केन प्रकारेण उपस्थातव्यमिति मीमांसे । **यथैवेति** । यथा गुरुः पिता उपसदनेन समीपानुभजनेन । प्राप्य इति पूरणीयम् । तथैव उपसदनेनात्रापि प्राप्य इत्यध्याहारः । एतद्गुरुवदुपसदनीयत्वं कथं कस्माद्धेतोः । अत्युदात्तः अत्युच्चस्वभावः सुजनः समीचीनजनः । सौजन्यवानिति यावत् । और्मिलेयः ऊर्मिलापुत्रः । स्त्रीभ्यो ढक् । सख्येन सखित्वेन मामुपतिष्ठते संश्लिष्यते । ' उपाद्देव–' इति आत्मनेपदम् । तेन संबन्धेन चन्द्रकेत्वभ्युपगतमैत्रीरूपसंबन्धेन । संप्रति धर्मतस्तातत्वे राजन्ये रामेऽपि प्रश्रयो विनयः अवचनीयो निर्दुष्टः । आकारः महापुरुषलक्षणयुक्तविग्रहसंनिवेशः । अनुभावः गाम्भीर्यमक्षोभ्यत्वमेतैः संभाव्यमानोऽनुमीयमानः विविधः नानाप्रकारः लोकोत्तरो विश्वातिशायी सुचरितानां सुकर्मणामतिशयः उत्कर्षः यस्य तथोक्तः । **अहो इति** । प्रसादः पारुष्यराहित्यं तस्मिन् भवं प्रासादिकम् । प्रसादगुण

---

१ घोषस्य. २ किं तु स. ३ इति संप्र०. ४ उपचारेण. ५ अपि कथं नाम. ६ ०दात्तश्चन्द्र०. ७ संप्रति करणीयो. ८ प्रामोदिकं. ९ अघुण-घ-स्त्, अवीवृतत्.

(उपसृत्य ।) तात प्राचेतसान्तेवासी कुशोऽभिवादयते ।

रामः—एह्येह्यायुष्मन् ।

अमृताध्मातजीमूतस्निग्धसंहननस्य ते ।
परिष्वङ्गाय वात्सल्यादयमुत्कण्ठते जनः ॥ २१ ॥

(परिष्वज्य । स्वगतम् ।) तत्किमपत्यमयं दारकः ।

अङ्गादङ्गात्सृत इव निजस्नेहजो देहसारः
प्रादुर्भूय स्थित इव बहिश्चेतनाधातुरेकः ।
सान्द्रानन्दक्षुभितहृदयप्रस्रवेणेव सृष्टो
गाढाश्लेषे यदमृतरसस्रोतसा सिञ्चतीव ॥ २२ ॥

लवः—तात ललाटंतपो घर्मांशुः । तदत्र सालवृक्षच्छायायां मुहूर्तमासनपरिग्रहं करोतु तातः ।

एवास्य रूपस्य उपादानकारणमिति भावः । रूपं विग्रहः । पावनः स्वसंबन्धानामन्येषामपि शुद्धिहेतुः । अनुभावः व्यवसायविशेषश्च । अहो विस्मयनीयावित्यर्थः । रामायणकविः रामायणप्रणेता वाल्मीकिलक्षणकविः देवीं वाचं वाग्देवीमवीवृधत् इति स्थाने युक्तम् । वृधधातोर्लुङि णिचि चङ् द्वित्वम् ॥ २० ॥ **अमृताध्मातेति** । अमृताध्मातजीमूत इव सुधापूरितकालमेघवत् स्निग्धं संहननं गात्रं यस्य तथोक्तस्य । 'गात्रं वपुः संहननम्' इत्यमरः । ते तव परिष्वङ्गाय आलिङ्गितुमुत्कण्ठते । 'सर्वेन्द्रियसुखास्वादो यत्रास्तीत्यभिमन्यते । तत्प्राप्तीच्छां ससंकल्पामुत्कण्ठां कवयो विदुः ॥' इत्युक्ताभिलाषवान्भवति । अयं जन इत्युक्तेः दर्शनीयत्वरूपवस्तुध्वनिः ॥ २१ ॥ किमित्ययं च दारकः । **अङ्गादङ्गादित्यादि** । अत्र गद्यस्थायंपदस्य पद्यस्थसशब्देन संबन्धात् दारकविशेषणत्वम् । च एवं सोऽयं समस्तविलक्षणो बुद्धिस्थश्च दारकः बालकः । अङ्गादङ्गात् सर्वेभ्योऽङ्गेभ्यः सृतः क्षरितः स्नेहजः स्नेह एव मैत्र्येव स्नेहः द्रवद्रव्यं तस्मिन् जातः निजः नैसर्गिकः । देहे रूपलावण्यसौन्दर्यसमुदायात्मके शरीरे यः सार उत्कृष्टरूपलावण्यसौन्दर्यसमुदाय इव स्थितः । स्वरसग्राहिणो जलादिद्रवद्रव्यं संयोज्यैव स्वरसं गृह्णन्ति । तद्वत्प्रकृष्टेऽपि स्नेहलक्षणद्रवद्रव्यसंबन्धेन गाढाश्लेषरूपसंघट्टनवशाद्बहिःसृतः स्वदेहसार इवेत्युत्प्रेक्षा । स्नेहज इति श्लिष्टरूपकानुप्राणिता च । अत्र 'अङ्गादङ्गात्सभवसि हृदयादभिजायसे' इति श्रुतिः प्रत्यभिज्ञाप्यते । एकः चेतनाधातुश्चैतन्यैकरसे आत्मवस्तुनि एकदेशः बहिः प्रादुर्भूय स्थित इव साक्षात्कारार्हः सन् स्थित इव । सान्द्रानन्दक्षुभितस्य घनतरानन्देन क्षोभं प्राप्तस्य हृदयस्य प्रस्रवेण प्रकृष्टसेकेनावसिक्तः आर्द्रीकृतः गाढः दृढः श्लेष आश्लेषो यस्य तथोक्तः सन् सोऽयं दारकः गाढाश्लेषः सन् हिमच्योतं हिमवर्षमाशंसतीव सूचयतीव । किमिति विस्मये ॥ २२ ॥ ललाटंतपः ललाटं तपतीति विग्रहः ।

---

१ सिंह. २ परिष्वङ्गस्य. ३ तत्किमित्ययं. ४ च्युत, स्रुत ५ निजस्नेहसारस्य, निजो देहजः स्नेहसारः. ६ इत इतश्चे०. ७ एकः. ८ प्रस्रवेणावसिक्तो-सृष्टो; ० नेव मृष्टः, सिक्तः. ९ गात्र-गात्रा-श्लेषे; गात्र-गात्रा-श्लेषः स हि मम हिमश्च्योतमाशंसतीव. १० तपस्तपति. ११ छायायां.

रामः—यदभिरुचितं वत्साय[१] ।

(सर्वे परिक्रम्य यथोचितमुपविशन्ति ।)

रामः—(स्वगतम् ।)

अहो प्रश्रययोगेऽपि गतिस्थित्यासनादयः ।
साम्राज्यशंसिनो भावाः कुशस्य च लवस्य च ॥ २३ ॥
वपुरविहि[२]तसिद्धा एव लक्ष्मीविलासाः
प्रतिक[३]लकमनीयं कान्तिमत्केतयन्ति ।
अमलिनमिव र[४]त्नं रश्मयस्ते मनोज्ञा
विकसितमिव[५] पद्मं बिन्दवो माकरन्दाः ॥ २४ ॥

भू[६]यिष्ठां च रघुकुमारच्छायामनयोः पश्यामि ।

कठोरपारावतकण्ठमेचकं
वपुर्वृषस्कन्धसुबन्धुरांसकं[७]म् ।
प्रसन्नसिंहस्तिमितं च वीक्षितं
ध्वनिश्च माङ्गल्यमृदङ्गमांसलः ॥ २५ ॥

खश्प्रत्यये मुमागमः । मध्याह्नसूर्य इति भावः । तदा हि सर्वासु दिक्षु ललाटातपसंयोगोऽपरिहार्यः । अन्यदा तु न तथा । यथोचितं पितृत्वपुत्रत्वानुगुणम् । **अहो इति** । प्रश्रययोगेऽपि विनयसंबन्धेऽपि । साम्राज्यशंसिनः सार्वभौमत्वसूचकाः गतिस्थित्यासनादयः । आदिशब्देनोक्तिवीक्षणादिपरिग्रहः । भावाः क्रियाः सन्ति । अहो विस्मयनीयम् ॥ २३ ॥ **वपुरिति** । अवियुतसिद्धाः अपृथक्सिद्धाः लक्ष्मीविलासाः लावण्यातिशयाः प्रतिकलकमनीयामनुक्षणरमणीयां कान्तिं चारुतां वपुः शरीरं कर्म । वपुः कान्तिमुद्भेदयन्ति । द्विकर्मकोऽयं धातुः । उत्पादयन्तीत्यर्थः । स्वे स्वीयाः रश्मयः मयूखाः अमलिनं निष्कलङ्कं चन्द्रमिव । माकरन्दाः मकरन्दसंबन्धिनः बिन्दवः कणाः विकसितं त्यक्तमुकुलीभावमरविन्दमिव च वपुःकान्तिमुद्भेदयन्ति ॥ २४ ॥ अनयोः कुशलवयोः भूयिष्ठं अतिशयेन बहु रघुकुलकौमारं रघुवंशसंबन्धिबालत्वम् । **कठोरेति** । कठोरपारावतकण्ठवत् प्राप्तयौवनकपोतकण्ठवन्मेचकं नीलम् । वृषस्कन्धवद्वृषभककुदिव सुबन्धुरं सुन्दरमंसं भुजशिखरं ययोस्तथोक्तयोः । प्रसन्नसिंहवत्कार्कश्यरहितसिंहवीक्षितवत् स्तिमितमतरलम् । माङ्गल्यमृदङ्गवन्मङ्गलार्थमृदङ्गध्वनिवन्मांसलः स्फीतः । हितादित्वाद्यत्प्रत्यये सति प्रज्ञादित्वाणि च आदिवृद्धौ माङ्गल्यशब्दसिद्धिः ॥ २५ ॥ निपुणं निरूपयन् सम्यग्विचारयन् । आकृतिरस्मद्वंशसंवादिनी केवलं न भवति अस्मद्वंशसंवादः अस्मत्कुलसा-

---

१ वत्सस्य. २ अवियुत. ३ प्रतिजन; कमनीयां कान्तिमुद्भेदयन्ति (टी०). ४ चन्द्र रश्मयः स्वे यथा वा (टी०). ५ मरविन्दं (टी०). ६ भूयिष्ठं च रघुकुलकौमारमनयोः. ७ ०सयोः, अबन्धुराशयः–रांसकम्.

(निपुणं निरूप्य ।) अये न केवलमस्मदङ्ग[1]संवादिन्याकृतिः ।

अपि जनकसुतायास्तच्च तच्चानुरूपं
  स्फुटमिह शिशुयुग्मे नैपुणोन्नेयमस्ति ।
ननु पुनरिव तन्मे गोचरीभूतमक्ष्णो-
  रभिनवशतपत्रश्रीमदास्यं प्रियायाः ॥ २६ ॥

मुक्ता[2]च्छदन्तच्छविसुन्द[3]रेयं
  सैवोष्ठमुद्रा स च कर्णपाशः ।
नेत्रे पुनर्यद्यपि र[4]क्तनीले
  तथापि सौभाग्यगुणः स एव ॥ २७ ॥

(विचिन्त्य ।) तदेतत्प्राचेतसाध्युषितमरण्यं यत्र किल देवी परित्यक्ता । इयं चानयोराकृतिर्व[5]यो‍ऽनुभावश्च । यदपि स्वतःप्रकाशान्यस्त्राणीति त[6]त्र विमृशामि । अ[7]पि खलु तच्चित्रदर्शनप्रासङ्गिकर्मस्त्रा[8]भ्यनुज्ञानमुद्भू[9]तं स्यात् । न ह्यसांप्रदायिकान्यस्त्राणि पूर्वेषामप्यनुशुश्रुम । अ[10]यं च संप्लवमानमात्मानं सुखदुःखातिशयो हृदयस्य मे विस्र[11]म्भयते । यमाविति च भू[12]यिष्ठमात्मसंवादः । भूयिष्ठं च मया द्विधा प्रतिपन्नो देव्या गर्भिणीभावे[13] आसीत् । (सास्रम् ।)

दृश्यं सोऽस्य अस्तीति विग्रहः । **अपीति** । तच्च तच्चावयवादिकं गुणजातमेवं च जनकसुतायाः सीतायाः अनुरूपं सदृशं तच्चावयवादिकमिह शिशुयुग्मे कुशलवयोः स्फुटं व्यक्तम् । तच्च गुणजातं च नैपुणेनावहिततया उन्नेयं निश्चयार्हमस्ति विद्यते । क्रियाद्वयान्नैकशेषः । अभिनवशतपत्रस्य नूतनकमलस्य श्रीरिव श्रीर्यस्य तथोक्तमास्यं पुनरक्ष्णोर्गोचरीभूतमिव ननु भूयोऽपि चक्षुर्विषयीभूतमिव ननु संभाव्यते । द्वादशसु संवत्सरेषु चक्षुरगोचरमद्य गोचरतां गतमिति च्विप्रत्ययेन लभ्यते ॥ २६ ॥ शुक्लाच्छदन्तच्छविसुन्दरेयं ओष्ठमुद्रा अधरोत्तरोष्ठसंनिवेशः सैव सीताया एव । कर्णपाशः स एव सीतासंबन्ध्येव । नेत्रे पुनः अनयोः सीतायाश्च दृशौ तु रक्तनीले । यद्यपि अनयोः रक्ते सीताया नीले एव तथापि सौभाग्यगुणः सौन्दर्यगुण स एव एकरूप एव ॥ २७ ॥ प्राचेतसाध्युषितं वाल्मीकिकर्तृकवासाधिकरणम् । यत्रारण्ये । आकृतिरवयवसंस्थानविशेषः । इयमीदृशी । वयः द्वादशवत्सरपरिमितमित्यर्थः । अनुभावश्च प्रभावश्च ईदृश इति शेषः । अस्त्राणि जृम्भकाणि स्वतःप्रकाशानि गुरूपदेशेन विना ज्ञातानीति यत् । तत्रापि चित्रदर्शने प्रासङ्गिकं प्रसङ्गानुप्रसक्तं शस्त्राभ्यनुज्ञानं सर्वथा त्वत्प्रसवमुपस्थास्यन्तीत्यत्र कृतं प्रबुद्धं स्यात्तथा संपादनेन प्रकटं भवेदिति स्मरामीत्यन्वयः । हि यस्मादसांप्रदायिकानि गुरूपदेशक्रमरहितानि अस्त्राणि पूर्वेषामपि मनुप्रभृतीनामपि नेत्यनुशुश्रुम । तस्मात्प्रबुद्धं स्यादिति तत्रापि स्मरामीति पूर्वेण संबन्धः । विस्मये संप्लवमानः

---

१ द्वंश, अस्मत्सं०. २ शुक्ल (टी.). ३ सुन्दरीयं. ४ नेव. ५ वपुश्च, इयं चानयोराकृतिर्वत्सयोः. ६ तत्रापि स्मरामि. ७ तदपि चित्रदर्शनप्रस्तावे अस्त्रा०. ८ शस्त्रा. ९ प्रबुद्धं. १० अयं विस्मयसंप्लवमानसुखदुःखातिशयो हृदयस्य मे विप्रलम्भः; अयं च समप्रथमानसुख०. ११ विप्रलभते; विस्रम्भः. १२ औषद्वयापत्यचिह्नो हि देव्याः. १३ गर्भभार.

पुरा रूढे स्नेहे परिचयविकासादुपचिते
रहो विश्रब्धाया अपि सहजलज्जाजडदृशः।
मयैवादौ ज्ञातः करतलपरामर्शकलया
द्विधा गर्भग्रन्थिस्तदनु दिवसैः कैरपि तया ॥ २८ ॥

(रुदित्वा।) तत्किमेतौ पृच्छामि केनाप्युपायेन।

लवः—तात किमेतत्।

बाष्पवर्षेण नीतं वो जगन्मङ्गलमाननम्।
अवश्यायावसिक्तस्य पुण्डरीकस्य चारुताम् ॥ २९ ॥

कुशः—अयि वत्स

विना सीतादेव्या किमिव हि न दुःखं रघुपतेः
प्रियानाशे कृत्स्नं किल जगदरण्यं हि भवति।
स च स्नेहस्तावानयमपि वियोगो निरवधिः
किमेवं त्वं पृच्छस्यनधिगतरामायण इव ॥ ३० ॥

रामः—(स्वगतम्।) अये तटस्थित आलापः। कृतं प्रश्नेन। मुग्ध-हृदय कोऽयमाकस्मिकस्ते स्नेहपरिप्लवो विकारः। एवं च निर्भिन्नहृदया-

---

मज्जन् सुखदुःखातिशयः हृदयस्य विप्रलम्भः विप्रयोगशृङ्गारः। प्रायेण हि स्वरूपसंतापेन प्रियजनसंयोगविप्रयोगौ सुखदुःखहेतू भवतः। विस्मयसंप्लवमानेत्यनेन विस्मयस्य प्रवाहात्मकत्वं ध्वन्यते। अजले प्लवनासंभवात्। यमाविति द्वाविति। आत्मसंवादः प्रकृतानुभूयमानयमत्वानुरूपस्वपूर्वानुभवः। भूयिष्ठम्। बहुत इत्यर्थः। सामान्ये क्लीबत्वम्। जीवद्द्वयं यदपत्यं तस्य चिह्नं सूचितं यस्मिंस्तथोक्तः। **परामिति**। स्नेहे परिचयस्य संततसाक्षात्कारस्य विकासादतिशयात्परां कोटिमपकर्षासमानाधिकरणोत्कर्षमधिगते प्राप्ते सति। रहो विस्रब्धाया अपि लज्जाविरोधिस्वैरस्थित्यापादकदशाविशेषार्हाया अपि। अर्हे क्तः। सहजलज्जाजडदृशः अपरिहरणीयलज्जागुणेनाधीरलोचनायां आदौ प्रथमं करतलपरामर्शकलया पाण्युदरपरिमार्जनविद्यया। कलाशब्देन सूक्ष्मदर्शनं ध्वन्यते। ग्रन्थिः भङ्गिका द्विधा अपत्यद्वयरूपप्रकारद्वययुक्तः ज्ञातः निश्चितः। तदनु मज्ज्ञानानन्तरं कैर्दिवसैः कतिपयदिवसैस्तयापि ज्ञातः सीतयाप्यवगतः ॥ २८ ॥ केनचिदुपायेन अनिर्धारणीयेन व्याजेन। **बाष्पवर्षेणेति**। जगन्मङ्गलं जगदभ्युदयहेतुभूतं वः आननमवश्यायेन हिमेनावसिक्तस्य पुण्डरीकस्य। विरहपाण्डिम्ना पुण्डरीकत्वोक्तिः। चारुतां शोभां नीतं प्रापितम्। निदर्शनालंकारः ॥ २९ ॥ **विनेति**। सीतादेव्या विना सितावियोगो रघुपतेः किं वा दुःखं न सर्वं दुःखात्मकम्। कृत्स्नं जगत्प्रियानाशे प्रियाया अदर्शने अरण्यं भवति हि। स च स्नेहः सीताविषयकः प्रणयः स तावन्नपरिमितः। वियोगः निरवधिरवसानशून्यः। अनधिगतरामायण इवानधीतरामायण इव पृच्छसि ॥ ३० ॥ तटस्थः अस्मज्जिज्ञासितसीतापुत्रत्वास्पर्शनेन उक्तमित्यर्थः। आकस्मिकः निष्कारणिकः संप्लवाधिकारः प्लुतगमनान्वयः दुर्लभविषयमनोरथा-

---

१ परां कोटिं—दधिगते (टी.). २ केनचिद्. ३ याम्बु. ४ जगादिदम. ५ किमित्येवं. ६ नटस्थः इव. ७ मुग्ध०. ८ पारिप्लवो विकारः; संप्लवाधिकारः (टी०).

वेगः शिशुजनेनाप्यनुकम्पितोऽस्मि । भवतु तावदन्तरयामि । (प्रकाशम् ।) वत्सौ रामायणं रामायणमिति श्रूयते भगवतो वाल्मीकेः सरस्वतीनिष्यन्दः प्रशस्तिरादित्यवंशस्य । तत्र कौतूहलेन यत्किंचिच्छ्रोतुमिच्छामि ।

कुशः—स कृत्स्न एव संदर्भोऽस्माभिरावृत्तः । स्मृतिप्रत्युपस्थितौ तावदिमौ बालचरितस्यान्त्येऽध्याये द्वौ श्लोकौ ।

रामः—उदीरयतु वत्सः ।

कुशः—

प्रकृत्यैव प्रिया सीता रामस्यासीन्महात्मनः ।
प्रियभावः स तु तया स्वगुणैरेव वर्धितः ॥ ३१ ॥
तथैव रामः सीतायाः प्राणेभ्योऽपि प्रियोऽभवत् ।
हृदयं त्वेव जानाति प्रीतियोगं परस्परम् ॥ ३२ ॥

रामः—कष्टमतिदारुणोऽयं हृदयमर्मोद्घातः । हा देवि एवं किल तदासीत् । अहो निरन्वयविपर्यासविरसवृत्तयो विप्रलम्भपर्यवसायिनस्तापयन्ति संसारवृत्तान्ताः ।

वासः किमर्थं इति यावत् । अन्तरयामि छादयामि । सरस्वत्याः वाण्याः निष्यन्दः द्रवः । आदित्यवंशस्य प्रशस्तिः प्रख्यातिहेतुः । रामायणं रामायणमिति श्रूयते । श्रवणबहुत्वाभिप्रायं द्विरुक्तम् । तत्र तदेकदेशं यत्किंचिच्छ्रोतुमिच्छामि । कौतूहलं हर्षः । कृत्स्न एव सकल एव संदर्भः ग्रन्थः आवृत्तः उपाध्यायासहकारेण स्वमात्रेणोच्चारणानुकूलावृत्तिविशेषः कृतः । स्मृतिं प्रत्युपस्थितौ अथ स्मृतिविषयभूतौ । बालचरितस्य बालकाण्डस्यान्ते सर्गान्ते द्वौ श्लोकौ द्वे पद्ये । वत्सौ संबोधनद्विवचनम् । उदीरयतं वदतम् । विधौ लोण्मध्यमाद्विवचनम् । **प्रिया त्विति** । सीता पितृकृतदारा इत्येव रामस्य गुणैः शीलादिभिः । रूपगुणैरभूषितेष्वप्यङ्गेष्विति लक्षणलक्षितरूपप्रभृतिगुणैश्च प्रीतिर्भूयोऽप्यवर्धत ॥ ३१ ॥ **तथैवेति** । तथैव यथा रामस्य सीता प्रिया तथा रामः सीतायाः प्रियोऽभवत् । हृदयं त्वेव । एवकारेण सीतारामयोरपि स्वप्रीतिज्ञानव्यावृत्तिः । प्रीतियोगं प्रीतेरुत्तरोत्तरवृद्धिसंनाहम् । 'योगः संनहन—' इत्युक्तेः । जानाति ॥ ३२ ॥ हृदयमेव मर्म मर्मस्योद्घातः प्रहारः दारुणः दुःसहः । **हा देवीत्यादि** । एतद्वक्ष्यमाणमेवमासीद्वक्ष्यमाणप्रकारेणासीत् । यद्वा 'प्रिया तु—' इत्यादिश्लोकद्वयोक्तमेवमासीद्यथोक्तमभूत् । हा दुःख्यते । **अहो इत्यादि** । निरन्वयविपर्यासे निरन्वयविनाशे । 'अयं तु विप्रलम्भः' इत्युक्तेः विश्लेषस्य

---

१ किंचित्कौतू०. २ अस्माकं विदितं. ३ ०चरितस्यान्ते. ४ रयतां वत्सौ. ५ रामिव०; प्रिया तु सीता रामस्य दाराः पितृकृता इति । गुणै रूपगुणैश्चापि (श्चैव) प्रीतिर्भूयोऽप्यवर्धत ॥ (टी०). ६ मर्मोपघातः, मोद्घाटः. ७ किलैतत्. ८ निरत्यय; ०विपर्यासवृत्तविप्रलम्भस्मृतिपर्यवसायिनसंतापकाः संसा०.

क्व तावानानन्दो निरतिशयविस्रम्भबहुलः
क्व वाऽन्योन्यप्रेम क्व च नु गहनाः कौतुकरसाः ।
सुखे वा दुःखे वा क्व नु खलु तदैक्यं हृदययो-
स्तथाऽप्येष प्राणः स्फुरति न तु पापो विरमति ॥ ३३ ॥

भोः कष्टम् ।

प्रियागुणसहस्राणामेकोन्मीलनपेशलः ।
य एव दुःस्मरः कालस्तमेव स्मारिता वयम् ॥ ३४ ॥

निरन्वयविनाशत्वोक्तिः । दीपस्य निर्वाणजन्यो ध्वंसः निरन्वयविनाशः । तस्यैव उत्तरोत्तरदशासंक्रमणलिङ्गानुमेयो ध्वंसोऽन्यः । सीताया मरणरूपेऽस्मिन्निरन्वयविनाशे विप्रलम्भस्मृतिपर्यवसायिनः । विप्रलम्भश्च स्मृतिश्च विप्रलम्भस्मृती विप्रलम्भो वञ्चन तच्च परेच्छाधीनभ्रमः । स्मृतिर्भूतपूर्वविषयकं ज्ञानम् । तत्पर्यवसायिनस्तद्विषयतामात्रवन्तः दैववञ्चनास्मरणमात्रविषयाः संसारवृत्तान्ताः प्रणयभोगादयः । न तु वस्तुसत्तावन्त इति भावः । यद्वा । निरन्वयविपर्यासात्मको विप्रलम्भः अन्यतरनाशात्मकविरहहेतुकविप्रलम्भशृङ्गारस्तस्मिन् स्मृतिपर्यवसायिनः स्मृतिविषयतामात्रवन्तो भवन्तीत्यर्थः । अभिलाषेर्ष्याप्रवासकलहविरहहेतुत्वेन विप्रलम्भशृङ्गारस्य पञ्चविधत्वात् । 'संभोगो विप्रलम्भश्च शृङ्गारो द्विविधो मतः । संयुक्तयोस्तु संभोगो विप्रलम्भो वियुक्तयोः ।' इत्यादिकमिहानुसंधेयम् । युक्तश्चायमर्थः । नाटकस्य विप्रलम्भशृङ्गारपरत्वस्वारस्यात् । केचित्तु अन्वयश्च विपर्यासश्च अन्वयविपर्यासौ । अन्वयव्यतिरेकावित्यर्थः । तौ न विद्येते येषां ते निरन्वयविपर्यासाः । अन्वयव्यतिरेकशून्या इत्यर्थः । विप्रलभ्यन्ते भ्राम्यन्ते एभिरिति विप्रलम्भाः । बाहुलकः करणे घञ्प्रत्ययः । अन्वयव्यतिरेकशून्यत्वेन सद्विलक्षणतया तुच्छत्वेन विषयतासंबन्धेन भ्रममात्रहेतवः स्मृतिपर्यवसायिनः स्मृतिमात्रविषयातीतघटादिवदर्थक्रियाकारित्वविधुरा इति व्याचक्षते ॥ क्वेति । निरतिशयेनानपकृष्टेन विस्रम्भेण भोगदशायां स्वैरस्थित्युपपादकलज्जानिरोधिज्ञानविशेषेण बहुलः स्फारः स तावानपरिमेयः आनन्दः । क्व गत इति शेषः । अन्योन्यस्य प्रेम परस्परविषयकं परस्पराधिकरणकं च प्रेम प्रणयः क्व । गहना अगाधाः कौतुकरसाः भोगाभिलाषाः क्व । हृदययोः मम तस्याश्च मनसोः सुखे वा दुःखे वा सुखदुःखानुभवकाले तदैक्यमभिन्नत्वं क्व । तच्छब्देन हृदयैक्यस्य दौर्लभ्यं द्योत्यते । तथापि एतेषु सर्वेषु गतेष्वपि पापः मरणप्रतिबन्धकपापवान् । पापगुणसारत्वात्पापत्वव्यपदेशः । एष प्राणः आत्मा स्फुरति न विरमति न नश्यति ॥ ३३ ॥ प्रियेति । प्रियागुणसहस्राणां सौन्दर्यसौजन्याद्यनन्तगुणानाम् । 'संख्यायां द्विबहुत्वे स्तः' इत्युक्तेः बहुवचनम् । क्रमेण उन्मीलनतत्परः प्रकाशनासक्तः यः कालः दुःसहस्तमेव कालं वयं स्मारितास्तद्विषय-

---

१ क्व तेऽन्योन्यं यत्नाः. २ णां क्रमोन्मीलनतत्परः. ३ दुःसहः.

तदा किंचित्किंचित्कृतपदमहोभिः कतिपयै-
स्तदीषद्विस्तारि स्तनमुकुलमासीन्मृगदृशः।
वयःस्नेहाकूतव्यतिकरघनो यत्र मदनः
प्रगल्भव्यापारः स्फुरति हृदि मुग्धश्च वपुषि ॥ ३५ ॥

लवः—अयं च मन्दाकिनीचित्रकूटवनविहारे सीतादेवीमुद्दिश्य रघुपतेः श्लोकः—

त्वदर्थमिव विन्यस्तः शिलापट्टोऽयमग्रतः।
यस्यायमभितः पुष्पैः प्रवृष्ट इव केसरः ॥ ३६ ॥

रामः—(सलज्जास्मितस्नेहकरुणम्।) अति हि नाम मुग्धः शिशुजनः विशेषतस्त्वरण्यचरः। हा देवि स्मरसि वा तस्य प्रदेशस्य तत्समयविस्रम्भातिप्रसङ्गसाक्षिणः। कष्टं भोः कष्टम्।

कस्मरणवन्तः कृताः ॥ ३४ ॥ यदेति। कृतपदं सूचितरेखाकारसंनिवेशं तत् मृगदृशः सीतायाः स्तनमुकुलं कतिपयैरहोभिर्दिवसैरीषद्विस्तारि यस्मिन् काले अभवत्। 'यतः स्नेहाकूत--' इति पाठे स्नेहाकूतयोः अनुरागाभिलाषयोर्व्यतिकरस्य संपर्कस्य घनः मेदुरता यतः। यादृशकालहेतुक इत्यर्थः। 'वयःस्नेहाकूत--' इति पाठे तु-यत्र काले वयसस्तारुण्यस्य स्नेहस्यानुरागस्य आकूतस्याभिप्रायस्य च व्यतिकरेण घनः सान्द्रः। धर्मपरो धर्मिपरश्चायं शब्दो मदनविशेषणम्। मदनः मन्मथः कर्ता हृदि प्रगल्भव्यापारः सन् मनस्यतिशयितशरपातनादिचेष्टायुक्तः सन्वपुषि मुग्धश्च सन्नप्रकटः सन् स्फुरति वर्तते। तमेव कालं स्मारिता वयमित्यन्वयः। अनेन श्लोकेन मुग्धालक्षणं स्फोरितं पादत्रयेण। उदययौवना मुग्धेति दलमुक्तम्। तुरीयपादेन च लज्जाविजितमन्मथेति दलमुक्तम् ॥ ३५ ॥ चित्रकूटवर्त्मनि चित्रकूटपर्वतमार्गे मन्दाकिनीविहारे गङ्गातीरनीरक्रीडायां सीतामुद्दिश्य सीताबोधेच्छया। त्वदर्थमिति। अयं केसरः बकुलवृक्षः यस्याभितः यदीयेषु चतसृषु पार्श्वेषु प्रवृष्ट इव पुष्पकरणकप्रवर्षणकर्तेत्युत्प्रेक्षते। सोऽयमायतः शिलापट्टस्त्वदर्थं विन्यस्त इव। उत्प्रेक्षाद्वयम्। अयमभितः केशरः परितो वर्तमानः केशरवृक्षः। यस्य प्रवृष्ट इव भविष्यत्त्वदुपदेशमूलकयदधिकरणपुष्पवृष्टिकर्तेत्युत्प्रेक्षते। अयं त्वदर्थं विन्यस्त इव। अयं श्लोको रामायणलेखकैः प्रभ्रंशित इति वदन्ति ॥ ३६ ॥ लज्जारहस्यप्रकाशनात् हृदयसंकोचः। स्मितं विस्मयात्। शिशुजनः अतिमुग्धो हि नामेति योज्यम्। अरण्यचरस्तु विशेषतो मुग्धः। तस्य पूर्वानुभूतस्य तस्मिन्समये 'त्वदर्थम्--' इत्यादिश्लोकार्थसमये यो विस्रम्भः लज्जाप्रतिघातेन स्वैरस्थित्यापादकज्ञानविशेषः तेन योऽतिप्रसङ्गः भोगातिमात्रता तस्याभि-

---

१ यदा. २ चित्रकूटमन्दाकिनीपरिसरे; चित्रकूटवर्त्मनि मन्दाकिनीविहारे. ३ शिलापादः. ४ आयतः (टी०). ५ सलज्जितस्ने० ६ मुग्धोऽयं. ७ तस्य तत्समयावि... प्रसङ्गस्य, ०म्भाविम०.

श्रमाम्बुशिशिरीभवत्प्रसृतमन्दमन्दाकिनी-
मरुत्तरलितालकाकुलललाटचन्द्रद्युति ।
अकुङ्कुमकलङ्कितोज्ज्वलकपोलमुत्प्रेक्ष्यते
निराभरणसुन्दरश्रवणपाशमुग्धं मुखम् ॥ ३७ ॥

(स्तम्भित इव स्थित्वा । सकरुणम् ।) अहो नु खलु भोः ।

चिरं ध्यात्वा ध्यात्वा निहित इव निर्माय पुरतः
प्रवासेऽप्याश्वासं न खलु न करोति प्रियजनः ।
जगज्जीर्णारण्यं भवति च विकल्पव्युपरमे
कुकूलानां राशौ तदनु हृदयं पच्यत इव ॥ ३८ ॥

(नेपथ्ये ।)

वसिष्ठो वाल्मीकिर्दशरथमहिष्योऽथ जनकः
सहैवारुन्धत्या शिशुकलहमाकर्ण्य सभयाः ।

त्यर्थः । स्मरसि । 'अधीगर्थदयेशां–' इति कर्मणि षष्ठी । **श्रमाम्बिवति** । श्रमाम्बुशिशिरीभवत् इदं भिन्नं पदं मुखविशेषणम् । सुरतकालजस्वेदसलिलेन शीतलीभवत् । अलकाकुला चूर्णकुन्तलैर्व्याप्ता चन्द्रसदृशललाटद्युतिः यस्य तथोक्तम् । संजातः कलङ्को यस्मिन् कलङ्कितः । कुङ्कुमेन कलङ्कितो न भवतीत्यकुङ्कुमकलङ्कितः । अत एवोज्ज्वलः लावण्यातिरोधानेन प्रकाशमानः कपोलो यस्य तथोक्तम् । कुङ्कुमस्य कलङ्कत्वोक्त्या न केवलमाभरणस्याभरणं किं तु आभरणासहमिति व्यज्यते । निराभरणस्ताटङ्कमौक्तिकगुच्छादिभूषणरहितोऽपि सुन्दरः यः श्रवणपाशः पाशसदृशकर्णसंनिवेशस्तेन मुग्धं सुन्दरमुत्प्रेक्ष्यते संभाव्यते ॥ ३७ ॥ **चिरं ध्यात्वेत्यादि** । अत्र श्लोके स्थितस्य जनस्येत्यध्याहार्यम् । प्रियजनः कर्ता प्रवासे देशान्तरगमने चिरं ध्यात्वा ध्यात्वा स्थितस्य पुरतो निर्माय निहित इव । अनवरतभावनाप्रकर्षयुक्तस्य जनस्य पुरस्तावत्तेन भावनाप्रकर्षेण सृष्ट्वा स्थापित इव । आश्वासं न करोतीति न स्वस्य पुनरागमनेन संतोषं करोत्येव । प्रियजने प्रोषितं ध्यायति सति तदानीमागतः प्रोषितस्तेन ध्यानेन सृष्ट इत्युत्प्रेक्षार्ह इति भावः । कलत्रे ह्युपरते च कलत्रनाशे तु जगत्कर्तृ जीर्णारण्यं शून्यकल्पं भवति । प्रवासवत्पुनरागमनकलङ्काभवेन भावनाप्रकर्षस्यालीकत्वान्नाश्वासहेतुरिति भावः । तदनु जगज्जीर्णारण्यकानन्तरं हृदयं कर्तृ कुकूलानां राशौ तुषाग्निनां समुदाये पच्यत इव पक्वं भवति । कर्मकर्तृलकारोऽयम् । आतिदेशिकयगादयः ॥ ३८ ॥ **वसिष्ठ इति** । दशरथमहिष्यः कौसल्यादयः शिश्वोर्लवचन्द्रकेत्वोः कलहं युद्धमाकर्ण्य जरया वार्द्धकप्रयुक्तशैथिल्येन प्रस्तैर्व्यास्रैर्गात्रैरुपलक्षिताः । सुदूर आश्रमो यस्माद्रणरङ्गात्तथोक्तम् । तस्य भावः

---

१ सौम्यं. २ हि, तु. ३ कलत्र०, कलत्रेऽप्युपरते.

जराग्रस्तैर्गात्रैरथ खलु विदूराश्रमतया[1]
चिरेणागच्छन्ति त्वरितमनसोऽपि[2] श्रमजडाः[3] ॥ ३९ ॥

रामः—कथं भगवत्यरुन्धती वसिष्ठोऽम्बाश्च[4] जनकश्चात्रैव[5] । कष्टं कष्टं खल्वेते द्रष्टव्याः । (सकरुणं विलोक्य ।) अहह तातजनकोऽपि दैवादत्रैवायात इति वज्रेणेव ताडितोऽस्मि मन्दभाग्यः ।

संबन्धस्पृहणीयताप्रमुदितैर्ज्येष्ठैर्[6]वसिष्ठादिभि-
र्दृष्ट्वाऽपत्यविवाहमङ्गलमहे[7] तत्तातयोः संगतम्[8] ।
पश्यन्नीदृशमीदृशे[9] पितृसखं वृत्ते महावैशसे
दीर्ये किं न सहस्रधाऽहमथ वा रामेण किं दुष्करम् ॥ ४० ॥

(नेपथ्ये ।)

भो भोः कष्टं कष्टम् ।

अनुभावमात्रसमवस्थितश्रियं[10]
सहसैव वीक्ष्य रघुनाथमीदृशम् ।
प्रथमप्रबुद्ध[11]जनकप्रबोधना[12]-
द्विधुराः प्रमोहमुपयान्ति मातरः ॥ ४१ ॥

रामः—हा तात हा मातरः हा जनक ।

सुदूराश्रमता तया । चिरेण बहुकालेन ॥ ३९ ॥ कथं द्रष्टव्याः केन प्रकारेण द्रष्टव्याः । तातजनकोऽपि भार्यापितृत्वात्स्वपितृत्वोपचारः । वज्रेणेव अशनिघातेनेव ताडितोऽस्मि व्यथितोऽस्मि । **संबन्धेति** । संबन्धस्यापत्यसंबन्धस्य स्पृहणीयतया श्लाघ्यतया प्रमुदितैः प्रकृष्टमोदयुक्तैः वसिष्ठादिभिः । आदिशब्देन गौतमकौशिकादिपरिग्रहः । अपत्यविवाहमङ्गलविधौ मम तस्याश्च पाणिग्रहणकर्मणि । तत्तातयोस्तथाविधजनकदशरथयोः संगमं संमेलनं दृष्ट्वा महावैशसे वृत्ते सीतात्यागरूपमहाहिंसायां पितृसखं जनकमीदृशमत्यन्तदुःखितमीदृशः पश्यन् वैशसनिमित्तभूतः पश्यन्नहं किं कुतः सहस्रधा अनन्तभागतया न दीर्ये विदारितो न भवामि । अथ वा विदारणाभावे रामेण दुष्करं दारणाभावो वा इतोऽप्यन्यद्वा सर्वं सुकरमिति भावः ॥ ४० ॥ **अनुभावमात्रेति** । अनुभावमात्रेण अनितरसाधारणमहापुरुषत्वेन समवस्थिता समवस्थाहा निश्चयार्हा श्रीरैश्वर्यं यस्य तथोक्तम् । प्रथमप्रबुद्धेन कौशल्याद्यपेक्षया पूर्वोत्पन्नप्रत्यभिज्ञापकेन जनकेन प्रबोधिताः प्रत्यभिज्ञापिताः मातरः अनुभावमात्रसमवस्थितश्रियमीदृशं रघुनाथं वीक्ष्य विधुराः सत्यः शून्यकरणाः सत्यः प्रमोहं प्रकृष्टां मूर्च्छामुप-

---

१ सुदू॰. २ त्वरितगतयः. ३ विश्लथजटाः. ४ अम्बा वाल्मीकिर्ज॰. ५ कोऽप्यत्रैवा॰, वज्रेणैव. ६ ज्येष्ठैः. ७ विधौ; अहो. ८ संगमम्. ९ ईदृशः. १० समुपस्थित. ११ प्रबुद्ध. १२ प्रबोधिताः.

जनकानां रघूणां च यत्कृत्स्नं गोत्रमङ्गलम् ।
तस्मिन्नकरुणे पापे वृथा वः करुणा मयि ॥ ४२ ॥

यावत्संभावयामि । (इत्युत्तिष्ठति ।)

कुशलवौ—इत इतस्तातः ।

(सकरुणाकुलं परिक्रम्य निष्क्रान्ताः सर्वे ।)

इति कुमारप्रत्यभिज्ञानो नाम षष्ठोऽङ्कः ।

यान्ति प्राप्नुवन्तीत्यन्वयः ॥ ४१ ॥ जनकानामिति । जनकानां रघूणां च कृत्स्नं गोत्रमङ्गलमखण्डं कुलश्रेयः । तत्रापि तथाविधसीतायामपि अकरुणे तद्दुःखाधीनदुःखवत्त्वरूपकरुणारहिते मयि वः युष्माकं करुणा मद्दुःखाधीनदुःखवत्ता वृथा । दयया सर्वभूतेषु इत्युक्तादृष्टविशेषमात्ररूपप्रयोजनेनापि शून्येत्यर्थः ॥ ४२ ॥ यावत्संभावयामि अभ्युत्थानाभिवादनादिभिः पुरस्करिष्यामि । यावत्पुरानिपातयोः भविष्यदर्थे लट् । इत्युत्तिष्ठति उत्थानमभिनयति । इत इतस्तातः । अत्रागच्छत्विति शेषः । मार्गदर्शनपरमिदं वाक्यम् । निष्क्रान्ताः । रङ्गस्थानादिति शेषः । सर्वे वसिष्ठाद्येतदङ्काभिनेयभूमिकाधारिण इत्यर्थः ॥

दाशरथिवंशजनुषो भूसारनिवासवीरराघवार्यस्य ।
उत्तररामचरित्रव्याख्यायामवसितोऽङ्कः षष्ठः ॥

इति श्रीवाधूलवीरराघवविरचितायां भवभूतिभावतलस्पर्शिनीसमाख्यायामुत्तररामचरितव्याख्यायां षष्ठोऽङ्कः ।

---

१ तत्राप्य०, तस्याम०. २ ०रुणं. ३ इति महा...प्रणीते उत्त० नाटके कु०,०ज्ञानं.

सप्तमोऽङ्कः ।

(ततः प्रविशति लक्ष्मणः ।)

लक्ष्मणः——भो भो अद्य खलु भगवता वाल्मीकिना सब्रह्मक्षत्रपौरजानपदाः प्रजाः सहास्माभिराहूय कृत्स्न एव सदेवासुरैतिर्यगुरगनायकानिकायः जंगमैः स्थावरश्च भूतग्रामः स्वप्रभावेण संनिधापितः । आदिष्टश्चाहमार्येण——वत्स लक्ष्मण भगवता वाल्मीकिना स्वकृतिमप्सरोभिः प्रयुज्यमानां द्रष्टुमुपनिमन्त्रिताः स्मः । तद्गङ्गातीरमातोद्यस्थानमुपगम्य क्रियतां समाजसंनिवेश इति । कृतश्च मर्त्यामर्त्यस्य भूतग्रामस्य समुचितस्थानसंनिवेशो मया । अयं तु——

राज्याश्रमनिवासेऽपि प्राप्तकष्टमुनिव्रतः ।
वाल्मीकिगौरवादार्य इत एवाभिवर्तते ॥ १ ॥

अथ समग्रप्रयोजनकोडीकाररूपनिर्वहणसंधिः सप्तमेन वक्ष्यन् चमत्कृतिविशेषलाभाय परित्यागानन्तरभाविनीं सीतायाः दशामन्तर्नाटकेन विवक्षुस्तदुपक्षेपिकां लक्ष्मणप्रवेशवतीं रङ्गरचनामाह——**ततः प्रविशति लक्ष्मण इति** । ततः षष्ठाङ्कप्रयोगादनन्तरम् । **भोः किं नु खल्वित्यादि** । भो इति हृदयं प्रति संबुद्धिः । किं नु संनिधापित इति योजना । भगवता षाड्गुण्यवता । ब्रह्म ब्राह्मणाः क्षत्रं क्षत्रियाः पौरा अवशिष्टाः पुरवासिजनाः जानपदाः देशवासिजनाः एतैः सहिताः अस्माभिः सह प्रजा आहूय कृत्स्न एवाखण्ड एव देवा इन्द्रादयः असुरा निर्ऋतिप्रभृतयः तिर्यञ्चः नागादयः एतेषां निकायो वर्गस्तेन सहितः भूतानां प्राणिनां ग्रामः समूहः । सचराचरः सस्थावरजङ्गमः । स्वप्रभावेण स्वतपःशक्त्यतिशयेन किं नु संनिधापितः । किं न्विति विस्मये । आर्येण रामेणादिष्ट आज्ञप्तः । स्वकृतिं स्वग्रन्थम् । अप्सरोभिः उर्वशीप्रभृतिभिः प्रयुज्यमानामभिनीयमानां द्रष्टुमुपनियन्त्रिताः स्मः आवश्यकत्वेनाहूता भवामः । गङ्गातीरं गङ्गाकूलम् । आतोद्यस्य नृत्यगीतवाद्यसमुदायस्य स्थानं प्रवर्तनाधिकरणमुपगम्य प्राप्य समाजस्य सदसः संनिवेशः यथोचितस्थानविभागः क्रियतामित्यादिष्टश्चाहमिति पूर्वेणान्वयः । सीताया गङ्गाजलादुद्गमनसौकर्याय गङ्गातीरस्य रङ्गत्वकल्पनम् । सलिलादुपेतीति वक्ष्यते । मर्त्यः मरणार्हः अमर्त्यः तदनर्हः । मर्त्यश्चासावमर्त्यश्चेति विशेषणयोः समासः । नित्यानित्यात्मकस्येत्यर्थः । भूतग्रामस्य पृथिव्यादिभूतसमुदायस्य समुचितस्थानस्याधिकारानुरूपस्थानस्य संनिवेशः प्रतिष्ठापनम् । पूर्वमाज्ञापनप्रकारकथनमद्य त्वनुष्ठानकथनमिति न पुनरुक्तिः । **अयं तु राज्येति** । राज्यं भूमिपरिपालनात्मकराजकर्म । तदेवाश्रमः स्वैराचारप्रतिबन्धकनियमविशेषः । सुखाल्पत्वदुःखभूयस्त्वाभ्या-

---

१ किं नु खलु. २ प्रजाः सर्वाः. ३ सुरमनुष्यति०...निकायसंतानः. ४ सचराचरो भूत०. ५ नियन्त्रिताः. ६ तद्भागीरथीतीरमनेकस्थानं, तीरमनोहरस्थानम्. ७ स्थानसर्गः, स्थानेषु सम्रुपवेशसङ्गः; कृतं स्थानेषु सम्रुपवेशनं. ८ निवासः.

(ततः प्रविशति रामः ।)

रामः—वत्स लक्ष्मण अपि स्थिता रङ्गप्रेक्षिकाः ।[1]

लक्ष्मणः—अथ किम् ।

रामः—इमौ पुनर्वत्सौ कुशलवौ कुमारचन्द्रकेतुसदृशीं[2] स्थान[3]-प्रतिपत्तिं लम्भयितव्यौ ।

लक्ष्मणः—प्रभुस्नेहप्रत्ययात्तथैव कृतम् । इदं चास्तीर्णं राजासनम्[4] । तदुपविशत्वार्यः ।

रामः—(उपविशति[5] ।)

लक्ष्मणः—प्रस्तूयतां भोः ।

सूत्रधारः—(प्रविश्य ।) भो भो भगवान्भूतार्थवादी प्राचेतसः सस्थावरजङ्गमं जगदाज्ञापयति—यदिदमस्माभिरार्षेण चक्षुषा समुद्वीक्ष्य पावनं[7] करुणाद्भुतरसं च किंचिदुपनिबद्धं तत्र काव्यगौरवादवधातव्यमिति ।

माश्रमत्वरूपणम् । प्राप्तं कष्टं दुःखरूपं मुनिव्रतं येन तथोक्तः । वाल्मीकौ वाल्मीकेर्वा गौरवाद्गुरुत्वप्रतिपत्त्या पूजनीयत्वानुसंधानेन ॥ १ ॥ रङ्गस्य नाट्यस्थानस्य प्राश्निकाः सामाजिकाः रङ्गस्थले राज्ञा सह द्रष्टार इत्यर्थः । प्रश्नं ज्ञातव्यार्थजिज्ञासामर्हन्तीति प्राश्निकाः । तदर्हाधिकारीयष्ठञ् । समस्तशास्त्रनिष्णातहृदया इति भावः । अथ किमित्यङ्गीकारे । इमौ वत्सौ । कुशलवावित्यर्थः । कुमारश्चासौ चन्द्रकेतुश्च तेन समां प्रतिपत्तिं लालनीयत्वादिधियं लम्भयितव्यौ प्रापयितव्यौ । प्रभो राज्ञः । स्नेहेन कुशलवविषयप्रीत्या यः प्रत्ययस्तथैव कार्यमिति व्यवसायः तस्मात् इदं चास्तीर्णं राजासनं सिंहासनस्यास्तीर्णासंभवेऽपि अन्यत्तद्योग्यमासनमास्तीर्णमिति मन्तव्यम् । कृत्स्न एव सदेवासुरेति ब्रह्मेन्द्रादीनामपि तत्र संनिधापितत्वोक्त्या तदैकरूप्याय सिंहासनातिरेकेणास्तीर्णार्हासनस्यैव युक्तत्वात् । एतेनात्र कवेः प्रमादवचनं प्रत्युक्तम् । अत एव 'स चापि रामः परिषद्गतः शनैर्बुभूषयासक्तमना बभूव ह' इति बालकाण्डश्लोके परिषद्गत इति सिंहासनादवरुह्य परिषदि जनानामुत्थानाशङ्कया शनैः स्थित इति व्याख्यातमस्मदाचार्यैः । सर्वे रामादयः इत्यर्थः । प्रस्तूयतामभिनय आरभ्यतामित्यर्थः । सूत्रधारः अन्तर्नाटकीयसूत्रधारः प्रविश्य हेत्यर्थः । भगवान् ज्ञानादिषाड्गुण्यपूर्णः । भूतार्थं सत्यमभिधेयं वदतीति भूतार्थवादी । 'सुप्यजातौ' इति णिनिः । 'युक्ते क्ष्मादावृते भूतम्' इति कोशः । प्रचेतसो वरुणस्यापत्यं पुमान् प्राचेतसः । स्थावरं च तज्जङ्गमं च । विशेषणयोः समासः । आज्ञापयति अकर-

---

१ प्राश्निकाः. २ समां. ३ Om. omits स्थान. ४ तदा०. ५ ०सनमुपवि०. ६ उप०: इमौ-उपविशतः । रा०—प्रस्तूयतां भोः. ७ पावनं वचनामृतम्, पावनकर०.

रामः—एतदुक्तं भवति । साक्षात्कृतधर्माणो महर्षयः । तेषाममृतसाराणि भगवतां परोरजांसि प्रज्ञानानि न क्वचिद्व्याहन्यन्त इति नाभिशङ्कनीयानि ।

(नेपथ्ये ।)

हा आर्यपुत्र हा कुमार लक्ष्मण एकाकिनीं मन्दभागिनीमशरणा-

णदण्डप्रयोजकविधिराज्ञा तां करोतीत्यर्थः । आर्षेणालौकिकेन चक्षुषा दृष्ट्या योगजप्रत्यासत्तिसहकृतपरिशुद्धान्तःकरणेन समुद्वीक्ष्य सम्यगतिशयेन साक्षात्कृत्य । अत्र 'रहस्यं च प्रकाशं च यथावत्संप्रपश्यसि' इत्यादिकं द्रष्टव्यम् । पावनं स्वदर्शनादन्येषां शुद्धिजननम् । अनेन 'काव्यालापांश्च वर्जयेत्' इति निषेधोऽन्यपर इति सूचितम् । वचनरूपममृतं सुधा यस्मिंस्तथोक्तम् । भोग्यत्वेन सादृश्यरूपणम् । करुणश्चाद्भुतश्च करुणाद्भुतौ रसौ यस्मिंस्तथोक्तम् । इष्टजनवियोगजन्यदुःखातिभूमिरूपः शोकः सहकारिभूताविशिष्टदेशकालकाव्यनिपुणनटचेष्टादिवशात्सामाजिकैर्भाव्यमानो निरतिशयस्वप्रकाशानन्दमयरसतां प्रतिपद्यत इति रसविदां संप्रदायः । अद्भुतश्च तथाविधो विस्मयः । गङ्गाप्रवाहपतनं तत्रत्यप्रसववर्णनादिनाऽद्भुतरसयुक्तत्वम् । किंचिन्मार्गे रूपकमित्यर्थः । उपनिबद्धं ग्रथितम् । तत्र रूपके काव्यगौरवात्काव्यस्य रूपकरूपस्य गौरवान्महत्त्वाद्यत्नादवधातव्यं मनसो विषयान्तरसंचाराराहित्यरूपमवधानं कर्तव्यमित्याज्ञापयतीति संबन्धः । साक्षात्कृतो धर्मोऽलौकिकश्रेयःसाधनरूपो यैस्तथोक्ताः । महान्तश्च ते ऋषयः महर्षयः । 'ऋषयः सत्यवचसः' इत्यमरः । 'अमृतं भराणि' इति क्वचित्पाठः । इदं च पदद्वयम् । बिभर्तीति भरम् । पचाद्यच् । त्रिलिङ्गत्वान्नपुंसकबहुवचनोत्पत्तौ भराणीति भवति । अमृतमिति कर्मणि द्वितीया । अमृतकर्मकभरणकर्तॄणीत्यर्थः । 'कर्तृकर्मणोः कृति' इत्यस्यानित्यत्वान्न षष्ठी । तद्व्यापकं तदर्थम् अन्तर्भावेनादर्शनमिति निर्देशद्वयमिति स्पष्टं व्याकरणपरिशीलनशालिनाम् । 'धर्यैरामोदमुत्तमम्' इति भट्टिप्रयोगात् (६·७९) नाप्रयुक्तत्वशङ्का । एतेन 'अमृतं भराणि' इति कवेः प्रमाद इति वदन् व्याख्याता निरस्तः । अमृतभरणकर्तृत्वं चेह मोक्षसाधनत्वरूपम् । यद्वा । ऋतंभराणीति दारमर्थयन्ति । 'ऋतंभरा च मां प्राहुः' इत्युक्तेः संज्ञाशब्दत्वात्संज्ञायां खच्प्रत्ययः । 'ऋतंभराभिधानम्' इत्युक्तेश्च । रजसः पराणि परोरजांसि । परिशुद्धानीत्यर्थः । 'शुद्धनरजस्कं परोरजः' इति कोशः । तेषां भगवतां प्रज्ञानानि प्रमादरहितानि ज्ञानानि न व्याहन्यन्ते । अयथार्थानि न भवन्तीत्येतदुक्तं भवतीति पूर्वेणान्वयः । न हि शङ्कनीयानि । अप्रामाण्यसंशयानर्हाणीत्यर्थः । नेपथ्ये इति । इदं चाङ्काभिनेयसीताप्रवेशाद्युपक्षेपकम् । एकाकिनीमेकाम् । आसन्नप्रसववेदनां समीपागतप्रसूतिव्यथाम् । हताशां व्यर्थमनो-

---

१ अमृतं भराणि, ऋतंभ०. २ इत्यनभि०; न हि शङ्क०.

मरण्य आसन्नप्रसववेदनां हताशाः श्वापदा मामभिलषन्ति । साऽहमिदानीं मन्दभागिनी भागीरथ्यामात्मानं निक्षेप्स्यामि । (क)

लक्ष्मणः—(आत्मगतम् ।) कष्टं बतान्यदेव किमपि ।

सूत्रधारः—

विश्वंभरात्मजा देवी राज्ञा त्यक्ता महावने ।
प्राप्तप्रसवमात्मानं गङ्गादेव्यां विमुञ्चति ॥ २ ॥

(इति निष्क्रान्तः ।)

प्रस्तावना ।

रामः—(सावेगम् ।) [1]देवि देवि [2]लक्ष्मणमवेक्षस्व ।

लक्ष्मणः—[3]आर्य नाटकमिदम् ।

रामः—हा देवि दण्डकारण्यवासप्रियसखि एष ते [6]रामाद्दैवदुर्विपाकः ।

लक्ष्मणः—आर्य [7]दृश्यतां तावत्प्रबन्धार्थः ।

रामः—एष सज्जोऽस्मि वज्रमयः ।

(ततः प्रविशत्युत्सङ्गितैकैकदारकाभ्यां पृथिवीगङ्गाभ्यामवलम्बिता[8] सीता ।)

(क) हा अज्जउत्त हा कुमार लक्खण एआइणिं मन्दभाइणिं असरणं[9] अरण्णे आसण्णप्पसववेअणं हदासा सावदा मं अहिलसन्दि । साहं दाणिं मन्दभाइणी[10] भईरईए अत्ताणं णिक्खिविस्सम्[11] ।

रथ्याम् । श्वापदाः दुष्टमृगाः अभिलषन्ति भक्षितुमिच्छन्ति । भागीरथ्यां गङ्गायामात्मानं निक्षिपामि पातयामि ॥ **विश्वंभरेति** । विश्वंभरात्मजा भूमेः सुता देवी कृताभिषेका । राज्ञा रामेण । प्राप्तः प्रसवः यं प्राप्तप्रसवस्तं [आत्मानम्] । गङ्गा च सा देवी च तस्याम् ॥ २ ॥ **प्रस्तावनेति** । अन्तर्नाटकीयप्रस्तावना वृत्तेत्यर्थः । सावेगं सभयम् । लक्ष्मणमवेक्षस्व मयि सापराधेऽपि त्वत्पुत्रं लक्ष्मणं दृष्ट्वा गङ्गायां न पतितव्यमित्यर्थः । नाटकमिदमुच्यमानगङ्गापतनं नाटकं नाटकप्रयोज्याभिनयात्मकम् । न वास्तवमित्यर्थः । रामाद्विपाकः रामहेतुकः दुःखानुभव इत्यर्थः । दण्डकेति विशेषणं तु साभिप्रायम् । मत्सुखं त्वदधीनं त्वद्दुःखं तु मदधीनमित्यर्थः । आर्ये आश्वस्य दुःखं लघूकृत्य । आर्षः ऋषिप्रणीतः । दर्शनाभावे मुनिः कुप्येदिति हृदयम् । वज्रमयः अत्यन्तकठिनः । सज्जोऽस्मि सीताविपत्तिनाटकं द्रष्टुं बद्धपरिकरोऽस्मि । उत्सङ्गितः उत्सङ्गेन गृहीतः एकैको दारको याभ्यां

---

१ एव दैववशेन. २ हा देवि हा. ३ 'लक्ष्मण', ०णम्. ४ अपि०; क्षमस्व. ५ आर्य आर्य. ६ रामाद्विपाकः. ७ समाश्वस्य दृ० प्रबन्धार्थः; आश्वस्य दृश्यतां प्रबन्धस्त्वार्षः. ८ ०म्बिता प्रमुग्धा. ९ इणिं असरणं...हदासा. १० मन्दाइणीए. ११ णिक्खिवेमि (टी०).

रामः—वत्स लक्ष्मण असंविज्ञातमनिबन्धनमन्धतमसमिव प्रविशामि । धारय माम् ।

देव्यौ—

समाश्वसिहि कल्याणि दिष्ट्या वैदेहि वर्धसे ।
अन्तर्जले प्रसूताऽसि रघुवंशधरौ सुतौ ॥ ३ ॥

सीता–(समाश्वस्य ।) दिष्ट्या दारकौ प्रसूताऽस्मि । हा आर्यपुत्र । (इति मूर्च्छति ।) (क)

लक्ष्मणः—(पादयोर्निपत्य ।) आर्य आर्य दिष्ट्या वर्धामहे । कल्याणप्ररोहो रघुवंशः । (विलोक्य ।) हा हा कथं क्षुभितबाष्पोत्पीड-निर्भरः प्रमुग्ध एवार्यः । (वीजयति ।)

पृथिवी—वत्से समाश्वसिहि ।

सीता—(समाश्वस्य ।) भगवति का त्वमियं च । (ख)

पृथिवी—इयं ते श्वशुरकुलदेवता भागीरथी ।

सीता—भगवति नमस्ते । (ग)

भागीरथी—चारित्रोचितां कल्याणसंपदमधिगच्छ ।

लक्ष्मणः—अनुगृहीताः स्मः ।

(क) दिट्ठिआ दारए प्पसूदम्हि । हा अज्जउत्त ।

(ख) भअवदि का तुमं ईअं अ । (ग) भअवदि णमो दे ।

तथोक्ताभ्यामवलम्बिता धारिता प्रमुग्धा प्रकृष्टमूर्छावती । असंविज्ञातमविदितं पदनिबन्धनं स्थानसंबन्धो यस्मिंस्तथोक्ते । पदनिबन्धनः पादन्यासो वा । मां धारय पतनप्रतिघातं कुरु ॥ **समाश्वसिहीति** । हे कल्याणि मङ्गलवति । संबुद्धिरियम् । वर्धसे श्रेयस्विनी भवसि । दिष्ट्या आनन्देऽयं शब्दः । अन्तर्जले जले अन्तः । प्रसूताऽसि उत्पादितवत्यसि । रघुवंशधरौ रघुसंतानैकदेशौ । दिष्ट्या दैवेन । दुष्टसाधनसंपत्त्यभावात्प्रसूतिप्रतिबन्धकसद्भावाद्दैवमेवात्र कारणमिति भावः । सुन्दरकाण्डस्थदिष्ट्येतिपदस्य दैवेनेत्युत्तानार्थो वर्णितः ॥ ३ ॥ कल्याणः शुभकरः प्ररोहोऽङ्कुरो यस्य तथोक्तः । मुञ्चतं त्यजतम् । लोट्मध्यमद्विवचनम् । मामिति शेषः । श्वशुरकुलस्य पत्युः पितृवंशस्य देवता योगक्षेमनिर्वाहिका भागीरथी । साभिप्रायं नामेह निर्दिष्टम् । चारित्रस्य पातिव्रत्यसच्चरितस्य उचितामनुरूपां कल्याणसंपदं श्रेयःसपत्तिम् । अनुगृहीताः स्मः । रामः सीता अहं च क्षेमोपधायिकाशी-

---

१ ०ज्ञातपदनिबन्धतम इव,–न्धने अन्धे–तमसीवाहमद्य; तम इवाहमान्ध्यं. २ गङ्गा. ३ ०जलं. ४ बाष्पोद्भेद. ५ देव्यौ. ६ ०पचिताम्. ७ तुमं, भअवदीआ का तुझे मं मुञ्चह (भगवत्यौ के युवाम् मां मुञ्चतम्), भगवदीओ के तुम्हे.

भागीरथी—इयं तु जननी ते विश्वंभरा ।

सीता—हा अम्ब ईदृश्यहं त्वया दृष्टा । (क)

पृथिवी—एहि वत्से एहि पुत्रि ।

(इति सीतामालिङ्ग्य मूर्च्छति ।)

लक्ष्मणः—(सहर्षम् ।) दिष्ट्या गङ्गापृथिवीभ्यामभ्युपपन्नार्या ।

रामः—(अवलोक्य ।) करुणतरं खल्वेतद्वर्तते ।

भागीरथी—विश्वंभरापि नाम व्यथत इति जितमपत्यस्नेहेन । यद्वा सर्वसाधारणो ह्येष मनसो मोहग्रन्थिरन्तश्चरश्चेतनावतामनुपप्लवः संसारतन्तुः । देवि भूतधात्रि वत्से वैदेहि समाश्वसिहि समाश्वसिहि ।

पृथिवी—(आश्वस्य ।) देवि सीतां प्रसूय कथमाश्वसिमि ।

सोढश्चिरं राक्षसमध्यवासस्त्यागो द्वितीयस्तु सुदुःसहोऽस्याः ।

भागी०—

को नाम पाकाभिमुखस्य जन्तोर्द्वाराणि दैवस्य पिधातुमीष्टे ॥ ४ ॥

(क) हा अम्ब ईदिसी अहं तुए दिट्ठा ।

विषयीकृता इत्यर्थः । सीताक्षेमे सर्वक्षेम इति हृदयम् । जननी माता । विश्वंभरेति साभिप्रायम् । पुत्र्यां त्वयि एवमलीकवादिनोऽपि जनान् बिभर्तीति क्षमातिशयव्यञ्जनात् । ईदृशी एवमलीकपौरवादेन त्यक्ता विपद्यमाना सती दृष्टा । उभौ सीतापृथिव्यौ । अभ्युपपन्ना अनुगृहीता । एतन्मातापुत्र्योरालिङ्ग्य मूर्च्छारूपं करुणान्तरं मद्दुःखातिरिक्तदुःखम् । अत्रभवती पूज्या विश्वंभरा क्षमाप्रधाना भूमिः व्यथत इति दुःख्यत इति हेतोरपत्यस्नेहेन जितमभिभवः कृतः । अपत्यस्नेहो बलवान्धीरानप्यभिभवतीत्यर्थः । यद्वेति पूर्वकल्पातिरिक्तकल्पद्योतकम् । मनसः हृदयस्य मूढग्रन्थिः मोहात्मको विभागाभावप्रयोजकसंपर्कजनकः । चेतनावतां प्रेक्षावतामान्तरः उपप्लवः अभ्यन्तर उपद्रवः संसारतन्तुः संसारसंधायक एषः अपत्यस्नेहः सर्वसाधारणः । न केवलं विश्वंभरायाः किं तु सर्वेषां समानः । दधातीति धात्री पोषयित्री । यद्वा दधत्येतामिति धात्री । प्राणिनां वर्धयित्रीत्यर्थः । इदं च संबोधनं पृथ्वीं प्रति अभिप्रायगर्भम् । सीतां प्रसूय कथमाश्वसिमि कथं केन प्रकारेणाश्वसिमि क्षीणदुःखा भवामि । मत्सुता संपन्नप्रजेति वा स्वाधीनपतिकेति वा केन हेतुना क्षीणदुःखा भवामीत्यर्थः । **सोढ इति** । राक्षसमध्यवासः चिरं सोढः । भूयांसं कालमनुभूत इत्यर्थः । सुदुःसह इति । अस्याः द्वितीयस्त्यागस्तु अलीकजनवादप्रयुक्तत्यागस्तु

१ ते जननी. २ भगवती वसुंधरा. ३ एहि पुत्रि वत्से सीते. ४ उभे आलिङ्ग्य मूर्च्छतः. ५ कथं; दिष्ट्या खल्वेतत्. ६ करुणोत्तरं–णतरं तु वर्तते. ७ अत्रभवती विश्वंभरा. ८ मानसः. ९ मूढ०, मूढ...रान्तरः... (टी.). १० मम्बि एकः. ११ यश्च, यो हि; सदुभवः. १२ जन्तुः.

पृथिवी—भगवति भागीरथि सदृशमुक्तम् । युक्तमेतद्वा रामभद्रस्य ।

> न प्रमाणीकृतः पाणिर्बाल्ये बालेन पीडितः ।
> नाहं न जनको नाग्निर्नानुवृत्तिर्न संततिः ॥ ५ ॥

सीता—हा आर्यपुत्रं स्मारितास्मि । (क)

पृथिवी—आः कस्तवार्यपुत्रः ।

सीता—(सलज्जास्रम् ।) यथा वाऽम्बा भणति । (ख)

रामः—अम्ब पृथिवि ईदृशोऽस्मि ।

भागी॰—भगवति वसुंधरे शरीरमसि संसारस्य । तत्किमसंविदानेव जामात्रे कुप्यसि ।

> घोरं लोके विततमयशो या च वह्नौ विशुद्धि-
> र्लङ्काद्वीपे कथमिव जनस्तामिह श्रद्दधातु ।
> इक्ष्वाकूणां कुलधनमिदं यत्समाराधनीयः
> कृत्स्नो लोकस्तदिह विषमं किं स वत्सः करोतु ॥ ६ ॥

(क) हा अज्जउत्तं सुमराविदम्हि । (ख) जधा वा अम्बा भणादि ।

सुदु सहः पूर्ववत्सहनानर्ह इत्यर्थः । इदमन्तं पृथ्वीवाक्यमनन्तरं गङ्गावाक्यम् ॥ गङ्गेति । आहेति शेषः । को नाम जन्तुः प्राणी पाकाभिमुखस्य फलोपधानप्रवृत्तस्य दैवस्य सुकृतदुष्कृतात्मकभाग्यस्य द्वाराणि अनुभवमार्गान् पिधातुं रोद्धुमीष्टे समर्थो भवति ॥ ४ ॥ वः रामभद्रस्य युष्मद्वंश्यस्य रामभद्रस्य । अनेन स्वसंबन्धः परिहृत इति ध्वनितम् । एतद्वक्ष्यमाणम् । युक्तं संगतम् । **न प्रमाणीकृत इति** । बाल्ये बालभावे । बालेन स्वेनेति शेषः । पीडितः उद्वाहकर्मणि गृहीतः पाणि न प्रमाणीकृतः युक्तायुक्तविचारे निर्णयहेतुर्न कृतः । गृहीत इत्यनुक्त्वा पीडित इत्युक्तेरयं भावः । सामुद्रिकतन्त्रवेत्ता स्वयं रामो मत्सुतापाणिस्थसाध्वीत्वनिश्चायकं रेखाविशेषं दृष्ट्वा निर्दोषेयं चिरानुभवादेति सूचनाय दृढं पाणिं गृहीतवान् तद्विस्मारेति । अन्यथा पाणिग्रहणस्य दोषवत्यास्त्यागाप्रतिबन्धकत्वादिति मन्तव्यम् । प्रमाणीकृत इत्येतदुत्तरत्र यथालिङ्गं विपरिणमयितव्यम् । वृत्तिः शीलम् । संततिर्वंशः ॥ ५ ॥ यथाम्बा भणति अत्र तथैवेति शेषः । ईदृशोऽस्मि अनार्यपुत्रोऽस्मि । संसारस्य दम्पतिमातृपुत्रस्वसृदुहित्रादिकुटुम्बसंबन्धस्य शरीरमसि शरीरवत्प्रवृत्तिनिवृत्तिनिबन्धनभूतासि । [असंविदाना अजानती] जामात्रे कुप्यसि जामातृविषयकप्रतिकूलप्रतिसंधानरूपमनःप्रज्वलनवती भवसि । 'क्रुधद्रुह–' इति चतुर्थी । **घोरमिति** । अयशः दोषवत्त्वप्रथा । लङ्का चासौ द्वीपश्च लङ्काद्वीपस्तस्मिन् । द्विर्गता आपो यस्मिन्स द्वीपः । 'द्व्यन्त–'

---

१ भगवति सदृ॰. २ युक्तमेतत्सर्वं वो राम॰; युक्तं सदृशमेतद्वा राम॰. ३ युक्तमेतत्सर्वं न वो राम॰. ४ न तु. ५ प्रसीद भग॰. ६ तदिति, तमसि; तदतिगहनं. ७ सुमरीआसि (स्मार्यसे).

लक्ष्मणः—अव्याहतान्तःप्रकाशा हि देवताः सत्त्वेषु[1] ।

भागी[2]०—तथाप्येष तेऽञ्जलिः ।

रामः—अम्ब अनुवृत्तस्त्वया भगीरथ[3]कुले प्रसादः ।

पृथिवी—देवि नित्यं प्रसन्नास्मि वः[4] । किं[5] त्वापातदुःसहस्नेहसंवेगेनैवं ब्रवीमि । न पुनर्न जानामि सीतास्नेहं रामभद्रस्य ।

> दह्यमानेन मनसा दैवाद्वत्सां विहाय सः ।
> लोकोत्तरेण सत्त्वेन[6] प्रजापुण्यैश्च जीवति ॥ ७ ॥

रामः—सकरुणा हि गुरवो गर्भरूपेषु ।

सीता—(रुदती कृताञ्जलिः ।) नयतु मामात्मनोऽङ्गेषु विलयमम्बा । (क)

रामः—किमन्यद्ब्रवीतु ।

भागी०—शान्तम् । अविलीना[7] संवत्सरसहस्राणि भूयाः ।

पृथिवी—वत्से अवेक्षणीयौ[8] ते पुत्रकौ ।

सीता—अनाथास्मि । किमेताभ्याम्[9] । (ख)

(क) णेदु मं अत्तणो अङ्केसु विलअं अम्बा । (ख) अणाधह्मि । किं एदेहिं ।

इति अकारस्य ईकारः । लङ्काद्वीपे या वह्नौ विशुद्धिस्तामिह जनः कथं श्रद्दधातु प्रत्येतु । कृत्स्नो लोकः समाराधनीय इति यदिदमिक्ष्वाकूणां कुलधनं कुलक्रमागतं धनम् । तत्तस्मादिह विषमे एतस्मिन्धर्मसंकटे स वत्सः रामः किं करोतु ॥ ६ ॥ अव्याहतः अकुण्ठितः अन्तःप्रकाशः परोक्षज्ञानरूपः यासां तथोक्ताः । सत्त्वेषु पदार्थेषु । पृथिव्यपि जानात्येवेति भावः । तथापि एवं सत्यपि एषोऽञ्जलिस्ते । 'अञ्जलिः परमा मुद्रा क्षिप्रं देवप्रसादिनी ।' इति । प्रसादन इत्यर्थः । अम्ब भागीरथीति संबुद्धिः । अनुवृत्तः भगीरथप्रभृतिमत्पर्यन्तं संबन्धित इत्यर्थः । तव नित्यं प्रसन्नास्मि नित्यं त्वदीयविषयकमनःकालुष्यरहितास्मि । किमर्थोऽञ्जलिरित्यर्थः । किं त्वेवं प्रसन्नत्वेऽपि स्नेहस्य संवेगस्त्वरा । आपाते श्रवणोत्तरक्षणे दुःसहः सोढुमशक्यः । 'दर्शनक्षण आपातस्तथैवाकर्णनक्षणे ।' इति कोशः । स्नेहेन पुत्रीविषयप्रेम्णा संवेगस्तरलत्वं भयं वा । 'ओविजी भयचलनयोः' इत्यस्माद्भावे घञ्प्रत्ययश्च । 'स्तोः' इति कुत्वं च । रामभद्रस्य सीताविषयकं स्नेहं पुनः प्रेम तु न जानामीति न जानाम्येव । **दह्यमानेनेति** । दह्यमानेन भस्मीक्रियमाणेन मनसा करणेन दैवाद्धेतोः वत्सां सीतां विहाय त्यक्त्वा लोकोत्तरेण सत्त्वेन धैर्येण प्रजानां पुण्यैः सुकृतैश्च जीवति प्राणं धारयति ॥ ७ ॥ गर्भाणामिव रूपं येषां तथोक्तेषु । अस्मास्विति शेषः । गर्भस्य

---

१ भूतेषु; सत्त्वेषु विशेषतो गङ्गा । तदयमञ्जलिस्ते (as Lak.'s speech). २ गङ्गा. ३ गृहे. ४ तव. ५ किं त्वसावापातदुःसहः स्नेहसंवेगः—दुःसहः शोकावेगोऽपत्यस्य । न पुनर्न०. ६ धैर्येण. ७ आविलीना वत्से ०सहस्रं. ८ अवेक्षणीयौ न, अपि रक्षणीयौ. ९ किं एदेहिं अणाहेहिं.

रामः—हृदय वज्रमयमसि।

भागी०—कथं त्वं सनाथाऽप्यनाथा।

सीता—कीदृशं ममाभाग्यायाः सनाथत्वम्। (क)

देव्यौ—

जगन्मङ्गलमात्मानं कथं त्वमवमन्यसे।
आवयोरपि यत्सङ्गात्पवित्रत्वं प्रकृष्यते॥ ८॥

लक्ष्मणः—आर्य श्रूयताम्।

रामः—शृणोतु लोकः।

(नेपथ्ये कलकलः।)

रामः—अद्भुततरं किमपि।

सीता—किमित्यन्तरिक्षं प्रज्वलति। (ख)

देव्यौ—ज्ञातम्।

कृशाश्वः कौशिको राम इति येषां गुरुक्रमः।
प्रादुर्भवन्ति तान्येव शस्त्राणि सह जृम्भकैः॥ ९॥

(नेपथ्ये।)

देवि सीते नमस्तेऽस्तु गतिर्नः पुत्रको हि ते।
आलेख्यदर्शने देवो यथाह रघुनन्दनः॥ १०॥

(क) कीदिसं मम अभाॅगाए सणाधत्तणम्। (ख) किं त्ति अन्तरिक्खं पज्जलदि।

यथा स्वरक्षणीयानर्हत्वं मन्त्ररक्षणीयत्वं तद्वद्गुरूणां वयमित्यर्थः। विलयमदर्शनम्। किं ब्रवीषि। किमिति क्षेपे। संवत्सरसहस्राणि। सहस्रशब्दोऽनन्तवाची। अत्यन्तसंयोगे द्वितीया। अवेक्षणीयौ कटाक्षणीयौ। तदर्थे स्थातव्यमिति भावः। अभाग्यायाः पुण्यरहितायाः। सनाथत्वं नाथवत्त्वम्। **जगन्मङ्गलमिति**। जगन्मङ्गलं जगतां मङ्गलं यस्मादिति बहुव्रीहिः। अनेन मङ्गलदेवतेति समाख्या स्मारिता। अवमन्यसे परिभवसि। यस्य त्वदात्मनः सङ्गात्संपर्कादावयोरपि जगत्पवित्रत्वेन प्रसिद्धयोरपि पवित्रत्वं स्वसंबन्धादन्येषामपि दोषापनोदकत्वं प्रकृष्यते पूर्वापेक्षया अतिशयितं भवति। कर्मकर्तरि लट्॥ ८॥ लोकः शृणोतु। मम हि सीतायाः शुद्धता व्यक्ता कौलीनवादिजन एव शृणोत्वित्यर्थः। **नेपथ्ये इति**। जृम्भकास्त्राणां प्रयोगायोग्यत्वेन तदागमनसूचनार्थं नेपथ्ये इत्युक्तम्। प्रज्वलितं प्रकाशवत्। **भृशाश्व इति**। गुरुक्रमः आचार्यानुपूर्वी। जृम्भकैः सह शस्त्राणि वारुणादीनि प्रादुर्भवन्ति प्रकटीभवन्ति॥ ९॥ **देवीति**। पुत्रकौ नो गतिः अस्माकं प्राप्यौ। आलेख्यदर्शनात्प्रथमाङ्कोक्तचित्रदर्शनात्

---

१ वज्रमासि. २ कथं वत्सौ सनाथावप्यनाथौ. ३ श्रुतम्. ४ आलेख्यदर्शनादेव यथाह्यात्। रघूद्वहः. ५ यदाह. ६ मन्दभाइणीए. ७ किंति सकलः किंति आबद्धकलकलं पज्जलिदं अन्त०.

सीता—दिष्ट्या अस्त्रदेवता एताः । हा आर्यपुत्र अद्यापि ते प्रसादाः परिस्फुरन्ति । (क)

लक्ष्मणः—उक्तमासीदार्येण सर्वथैतानि त्वत्प्रसूतिमुपस्थास्यन्तीति ।

देव्यौ—

नमो वः परमास्त्रेभ्यो धन्याः स्मो वः परिग्रहात् ।
काले ध्यातैरुपस्थेयं वत्सयोर्भद्रमस्तु वः ॥ ११ ॥

रामः—

क्षुभिताः कामपि दशां कुर्वन्ति मम सांप्रतम् ।
विस्मयानन्दसंदर्भजर्जराः करुणोर्मयः ॥ १२ ॥

देव्यौ—मोदस्व वत्से मोदस्व । रामभद्रतुल्यौ ते पुत्रकाविदानीं संवृत्तौ ।

सीता—भगवत्यौ क एतयोः क्षत्रियोचितं कर्म करिष्यति । (ख)

रामः—

एषा वसिष्ठगुप्तानां रघूणां वंशनन्दिनी ।
कष्टं सीताऽपि सुतयोः संस्कर्तारं न विन्दति ॥ १३ ॥

भागी॰—पुत्रि किं तवानया चिन्तया । एतौ हि वत्सौ स्तन्यत्यागात्परेण भगवतो वाल्मीकेरर्पयिष्यामि । स एतयोः क्षत्रकृत्यं करिष्यति ।

(क) दिट्ठिआ अत्थदेवदाओ एदाओ । हा उज्जउत्त अज्जावि दे पसादा पडिप्फुरन्दि । (ख) भअवदीओ को एदाणं खत्तिओचिदं कम्म करिस्सदि ।

॥ १० ॥ **दिष्ट्येति** । एताः अस्त्रदेवताः । आनन्दहेतव इत्यर्थः । अद्याप्येवं दोषवादप्रयुक्तपरित्यागकालेऽपि ते प्रसादाः त्वदनुग्रहाः परिस्फुरन्ति प्रकाशन्ते । उक्तमासीत् । प्रथमाङ्क इति शेषः ॥ **नम इति** । वः परिग्रहाद्युष्मत्कर्तृकस्वीकारात् धन्याः स्मः क्षेमलाभयुक्ता भवामः । काले युद्धादिसमये ध्यातैरागन्तव्यमिति चिन्तितैः काले युद्धादिसमये वत्सयोरुपस्थेयं संनिधातव्यम् । युष्माभिरिति शेषः ॥ ११ ॥ **क्षुभिता इति** । क्षुभिताः क्षोभं प्राप्ताः । विस्मयः अपूर्ववस्तुसंदर्शनजन्यान्तःकरणविकारविशेषः । स चात्र गङ्गापतनतत्रत्यप्रसवजृम्भकप्राप्त्यादिमूलकः । आनन्दः स्वसंबन्धसंभावनार्हताप्रयुक्तप्रीतिविशेषः । ताभ्यां जर्जराः व्याकुलिताः । करुणस्य सीतावियोगजन्यदुःखातिशयस्य ऊर्मयः तरङ्गा मम कामपि दशामनिर्वाच्यामवस्थां कुर्वन्त्युत्पादयन्ति । ऊर्मिपदेन करुणस्य समुद्रत्वं व्यज्यते ॥ १२ ॥ **मोदस्व** मोदं प्राप्नुहि । इदानीं जृम्भकास्त्रलाभे । संवृत्तौ संजातौ । क्षत्रियोचितं क्षत्रियजात्यनुरूपं विधिमुपनयनसंस्कारादिशास्त्रार्थं कः कारयिष्यति ॥ **एषेति** । वसिष्ठशिष्याणां रघूणां वंशनन्दिनी संततेरानन्दहेतुः एषा सीतापि सुतयोः संस्कर्तारमुपनयनादिसंस्कारकाचार्यं न विन्दति न लभते । कष्टम् । दुःख्यत इत्यर्थः ॥ १३ ॥ **भद्रे** मङ्गलवति । **एतौ वत्सौ** ।

---

१ अनुध्यातैः. २ उपेतव्यम्. ३ संप्रति. ४ एतन्नास्ति क्वचित्. ५ शिष्याणां. ६ भद्रे. ७ वसिष्ठ एव ह्याचार्यो रघुवंशस्य संप्रति । स एव चानयोर्ब्रह्मक्षत्रकृत्यं करिष्यति ॥ टी॰. ८ भअवदि. ९ ॰चिदविहिं (॰चितविधिं).

यथा वसिष्ठाङ्गिरसावृषिः प्राचेतसस्तथा।
जनकानां रघूणां च वंशयोरुभयोर्गुरुः ॥ १४ ॥

रामः—सुविचिन्तितं भगवत्या।

लक्ष्मणः—आर्य सत्यं विज्ञापयामि तैस्तैरुपायैर्वत्सौ कुशलवावुत्प्रेक्षे।

एतौ हि जन्मसिद्धास्त्रौ प्राप्तप्राचेतसावुभौ।
आर्यतुल्याकृती वीरौ वयसा द्वादशाब्दिकौ ॥ १५ ॥

रामः—वत्स इत्येवाहं परिप्लवमानहृदयः प्रमुग्धोऽस्मि।

पृथिवी—एहि वत्से पवित्रीकुरु रसातलम्।

रामः—हा प्रिये लोकान्तरं गतासि।

सीता—नयतु मामात्मनोऽङ्गेषु विलयमम्बा। न शक्ताऽस्मीदृशं जीवलोकपरिवर्तमनुभवितुम्। (क)

रामः—किमुत्तरं स्यात्।

पृथिवी—मन्नियोगतः स्तन्यत्यागं यावत्पुत्रयोरवेक्षस्व। परेण तु यथा ते रोचिष्यते।

भागी०—एवं तावत्।

(क) णेदु मं अत्तणो अङ्गेसु विलअं अम्बा। ण सक्कम्हि ईदिसं जीअलोअप-रिवत्तं अणुभविदुम्।

द्वितीयान्तम्। स्तन्यत्यागात्परेण स्तन्यत्यागकालान्तरकाले। अर्पयिष्यामि विद्यादि-प्रदानार्थमिति शेषः। एतेन द्वितीयाङ्कविष्कम्भस्थं केनापि देवताविशेषेणेति वाक्यं व्याख्यातम्। [**वसिष्ठ इति**। ब्रह्म च क्षत्रं च ब्रह्मक्षत्रे। तयोरुचितं कृत्यं ब्राह्मणत्वजात्यनुगुणत्रय्यध्यापनं क्षत्रियत्वोचितधनुर्वेदाध्यापनं च करि-ष्यति।] **यथेति**। जनकानां रघूणां च उभयवंशयोः यथा वसिष्ठाङ्गिरसौ वसिष्ठशतानन्दौ गुरू तथा प्राचेतसः ऋषिर्गुरुः। इदं गङ्गावचनम् ॥ १४ ॥ तैस्तैरुपायैः बहुभिः हेतुभिः वत्सौ कुशलवौ उत्प्रेक्षे वत्सकुशलत्वेन अभिनेयशिशुद्वयं संभावयामि। हेतूनाह-**एतौ हीत्यादिना**। तन्त्रेणायं श्लोकः चतुष्टयपरः अभि-नेयशिश्वोः कुशलवयोश्च जन्मसिद्धास्त्रत्वादिकं समानं योज्यम्। वयसा जीवनकालेन हेतुना। द्वादशाब्दकौ द्वादशसंख्याकसंवत्सरयुक्तौ। अभिनेयशिश्वोरप्यभिनयकालापे-क्षया द्वादशाब्दकत्वं बोध्यम् ॥ १५ ॥ **वत्साविति**। परिप्लवमानहृदयस्तरलहृदयः। प्रमुग्धोऽस्मि प्रमूढोऽस्मि। रसातलमधोभुवनम्। लोकान्तरमन्यं लोकम्। विलयं

---

१ इमौ वत्सौ. २ जातौ–उभौ–प्राचेतसान्मुनेः। वीरौ संप्राप्तसंस्कारौ. ३ वत्सावि०. ४ यथा रोचि० तथा करिष्यामि; यथा रोचते तथा करिष्यासि. ५ गङ्गा. ६ नाम. ७ सक्कम्मि (सहाऽस्मि); सहिस्सं. ८ ०अस्स परिभवं.

(इति निष्क्रान्ते देव्यौ सीता च ।)[1]

रामः—कथं विलय एव वैदेह्याः संपन्नः[2] । हा देवि दण्डकारण्यवासप्रियसखि हा चारित्रदेवते लोकान्तरं पर्यवस्थितासि ।

(इति मूर्च्छति ।)

लक्ष्मणः—भगवन्वाल्मीके परित्रायस्व परित्रायस्व । एष[3] ते काव्यार्थः ।

(नेपथ्ये ।)

अपनी[4]यतामातोद्यम् । भो भोः सजङ्गमस्थावराः प्राणभृतो मर्त्या[5]मर्त्याः पश्यतेदानीं महर्षिणा भगवता वाल्मीकिनाऽभ्यनुज्ञातं पवित्रमाश्चर्यम् ।

लक्ष्मणः—(विलोक्य ।)

मन्थादिव क्षुभ्यति गाङ्गमम्भो
व्याप्तं च देवर्षिभिरन्तरिक्षम् ।
आश्चर्यमार्या सह देवताभ्यां
गङ्गामहीभ्यां सलिलादु[6]देति ॥ १६ ॥

(पुनर्नेपथ्ये ।)

अरुन्धति जगद्वन्द्ये गङ्गापृथ्व्यौ जुषस्व[7] नौ ।
अर्पितेयं त[8]वावाभ्यां सीता पुण्यव्रता वधूः ॥ १७ ॥

तिरोहितत्वम् । जीवलोकस्य परिभवं जीवलोककर्तृकतिरस्कारम् । उत्तरं पृथिव्याः प्रतिवचनं किं स्यात् । उत्तरमनन्तरभावि वा । मन्नियोगतः मदादेशेन स्तन्यत्यागं यावत्स्तन्यत्यागमभिव्याप्य पुत्रयोरवेक्षस्व पुत्रौ पश्येत्यर्थः । परेण तु पुरस्तात्तु यथा रोचिष्यते येन प्रकारेण रुचिर्भविष्यति ते तथाहं करिष्यामीत्यर्थः । एवं तावदेवमेव देव्यौ गङ्गापृथिव्यौ । निष्क्रान्ते रङ्गस्थानादिति शेषः । लोकान्तरे पर्यवसितासि । पर्यवसानं विश्रान्तिः । लोकान्तरमेव गतासीति प्रतिपन्नं निश्चितम् । स्तन्यत्यागात्परत्र रसातलगमनस्य पृथिव्याभ्यनुज्ञातत्वात् द्वादशानां वत्सराणामतीतत्वाच्च लोकान्तरं गतासीत्येतावन्निश्चितमिति भावः । एष ते काव्यार्थः । पर्याप्तं दृष्ट इति शेषः । इतः परं निवर्तितव्यमिति हृदयम् । आतोद्यं नृत्तगीतसमुदायः । अपनीयतां निवर्त्यताम् । मर्त्यामर्त्या देवमनुष्यात्मका जङ्गमस्थावरात्मकाश्च प्राणभृतः । वृक्षादीनामपि प्राणवत्त्वात्स्थावरोक्तिरविरुद्धा । वाल्मीकिनाऽभ्यनुज्ञातं करुणाद्भुतरसमित्यत्राद्भुतपदेन प्रकाश्यत्वेन बोधितं पवित्रं निर्दोषमाश्चर्यं पश्यत । **मन्थादिवेति** । गाङ्गमम्भः मन्थादिव मन्थनादिव क्षुभ्यति क्षोभं प्राप्नोति । अन्तरिक्षं देवैः ऋषिभिश्च व्याप्तम् । कौतुकादिति भावः । आर्या सीता देवताभ्यां गङ्गामहीभ्यां सह सलिलादुपैति प्राप्नोति ॥ १६ ॥ **नेपथ्ये इति । अरुन्धतीति** । नौ द्वितीयाद्विवचनम् । गङ्गापृथ्व्यौ जुषस्व जानीहि नौ । जुषस्व प्रीयस्व । तव वधूः स्नुषा इयं सीता आवाभ्यां तवार्पिता ॥ १७ ॥

---

१ निष्क्रान्ता गङ्गापृथिवीसीताः. २ कथं प्रतिपन्नमेव तावत् ।...न्तरे—न्तरं पर्यवसितासि. ३ एष किं. ४ अपनीयतां; आतोद्यकम्. ५ मर्त्याः. ६ उपैति. ७ भजस्व. ८ तवाभ्यासे—शे.

लक्ष्मणः—अहो[1] आश्चर्यमाश्चर्यम्। आर्य पश्य पश्य। (विलोक्य।) कष्टमद्यापि नोच्छ्वसित्यार्यः।

(ततः प्रविशत्यरुन्धती सीता च।)

अरुन्धती—

त्वरस्व वत्से वैदेहि मुञ्च शालीनशीलताम्।
एहि जीवय मे वत्सं प्रिय[2]स्पर्शेन पाणिना ॥ १८ ॥

सीता—(ससंभ्रमं स्पृशन्ती[3]।) समाश्वसितु समाश्वसित्वार्यपुत्रः। (क)

रामः—(समाश्वस्य सानन्दम्।) भोः किमेतत्। (दृष्ट्वा सहर्षाद्भुतम्।) कथं देवी[4]। (सलज्जम्।) अये अम्बा मेऽरुन्धती सर्वे च प्रहृष्यन्त ऋष्यशृङ्गशान्तादयोऽस्मद्गुरवः।

अरुन्धती—वत्स एषा भगवती भगीरथगृहदेवता सुप्रसन्ना गङ्गा।

(नेपथ्ये।)

जगत्पते रामचन्द्र स्मर्यतामालेख्यदर्शने मां प्रत्यात्मनो वचनं यथा-सा त्वमम्ब स्नुषायामरुन्धतीव सीतायां शिवानुध्यानपरा भवेति तत्रानृणास्मि जाता।

अरुन्धती—इयं ते श्वश्रूर्भगवती वसुंधरा।

(पुनर्नेपथ्ये।)

उक्तमासीदायुष्मता वत्सायाः परित्यागे यथा भगवति वसुंधरे श्लाघ्यां दुहितरमवेक्षस्व जानकीमिति। तदधुना कृतवचनास्मि प्रभोर्वत्सस्येति।

रामः—कथं[10] कृतमहापरा[11]धो भगवती[12]भ्यामनुकम्पितः। [13]प्रणमामि वः।

(क) समस्ससदु समस्ससदु अज्जउत्तो।

आर्ये इति [पाठान्तरे] अरुन्धतीं प्रति संबोधनम्। नोच्छ्वसिति उच्छ्वासं न प्राप्नोति ॥ **त्वरस्वेति**। शालीनशीलतामधृष्टस्वभावत्वं मुञ्च त्यज। सौम्यस्पर्शेन चन्द्रवच्छीतलेन पाणिना मे वत्सं जीवय सप्राणं कुरु ॥ १८ ॥ एतत्सीतास्पर्शरूपं किं किंहेतुकम्। कथं देवी जानकी। विस्मयद्योतकः कथंशब्दः। लज्जा मनःसंकोचः स चेहारुन्धतीदर्शनात्। भागीरथी भगीरथानीता रघुकुलदेवता देवी दीप्तिशालिनी सुप्रसन्ना अनुग्रहं कृतवती। आलेख्यदर्शने चित्रदर्शने। आत्मवचनं त्वद्वचनम्।

---

१ दिष्ट्या अहो. २ सौम्य. ३ मुपसृत्य; ०सृत्य रामं स्पृशन्ती. ४ देवी जानकी; देवी सलज्जा। अम्बा मे अरु०, सर्वे च ऋष्यशृङ्गादयो गुरवः; अये देवी।...कथं अम्बा अरु० प्रहृष्यद्०-शान्तासमेता गुरवः. ५ एष भागीरथीरघुकुलदेवता देवी गङ्गा सुप्रसन्ना. ६ रामभद्र. ७ एतन्नास्ति क्वचित्. ८ उक्तं च पूर्वमायुष्मता वत्सापरित्यागे. ९ प्रभो वत्सायाम्, तदनृणास्मि प्रभो वत्सायामिति. १० कृतापराधोऽपि भगवति त्वयानुकम्पयितव्यो रामः प्रणमति. ११ ०धोऽपि. १२ भग०...म्पितो रामः; कृतमहापराधो भगवति त्वयानुकम्पितो रामः. १३ इति प्रणमति.

अरुन्धती—भो भोः पौरजानपदाः इयमधुना भगवतीभ्यां जाह्नवीवसुंधराभ्यामेवं प्रश[1]स्यमाना ममारुन्धत्याः समर्पिता पूर्वं च भगवता वैश्वानरेण निर्णीतपुण्यचारित्रा सब्रह्मकैश्च देवैः संस्तुता सा[2]वित्रकुलवधूर्देवयजनसंभवा सीतादेवी परिगृह्यतामिति कथमिह भवन्तो मन्यन्ते ।

लक्ष्मणः—आर्य एवमा[3]र्ययाऽरुन्धत्या निर्भर्त्सिताः पौ[4]रजानपदाः कृत्स्नश्च भूतग्राम आर्यां नमस्कुर्वन्ति । लोकपालाः सप्तर्षयश्च पुष्पवृष्टिभिरुपतिष्ठन्ते ।

अरुन्धती—जगत्पते रामचन्द्र ।

नियोजय यथाधर्मं प्रियां त्वं धर्मचारिणीम् ।
हिरण्मय्याः प्रतिकृतेः पु[5]ण्यां प्रकृतिमध्वरे ॥ १९ ॥

सीता—(स्वगतम् ।) जानात्यार्यपुत्रः सीताया दुःखं परिमार्ष्टुम् । (क)

रामः—यथा भगवत्यादिशति ।

लक्ष्मणः—कृतार्थोऽस्मि ।

सीता—प्रत्युज्जीवितास्मि । (ख)

(क) [6]जाणादि अज्जउत्तो सीदा[7]या दुक्खं [8]पडिमज्जिदुम् । (ख) प[9]च्चुज्जीविदम्हि ।

अनृणास्मि निर्यातितर्णास्मि । ऋणं ह्यवश्यप्रतिविधेयमिति सादृश्यादेवमुक्तम् । आयुष्मता । त्वयेति शेषः । वसुंधरायै वसुंधरां बोधयितुमुक्तमासीदिति वचनं जातम् । श्लाघ्यां दुहितरमवेक्षस्व जानकीमितीदं वस्तु उक्तमासीदिति कर्मणि क्तो वा ज्ञेयः । कृतवचनास्मि । उच्यत इति वचनः उक्तार्थः कृतः अनुष्ठितः उक्तार्थो यया तथोक्तास्मि । अनुकम्पायितव्य इति दयाविषयः कर्तव्य इति प्रणमति प्रकर्षेण नमस्यति । पौराः पुरवासिनः । जानपदाः देशवासिनः । एवं प्रशस्यमाना 'आवयोरपि यत्सङ्गात्पवित्रत्वं प्रकृष्यते' इत्यभिष्टुता । पूर्वं रावणवधानन्तरकाले । वैश्वानरेणाग्निना । निर्णीतपुण्यचारित्रा निश्चितपातिव्रत्या । परिगृह्यतां राज्ञीत्वेन स्वीक्रियताम् । इहास्मिन्नर्थे कथं मन्यन्ते किं वो मतमिति भावः । भूतग्रामः गोबलीवर्दन्यायेन पौरजानपदातिरिक्ताः ग्राह्याः । आर्यां सीतां नमस्कुर्वन्ति । लोकपालाः इन्द्रादयः । सप्तर्षय अत्र्यादयः । पुष्पवृष्टिभिः करणैरुपतिष्ठन्ते पूजयन्ति । आर्यामित्यनुषङ्गः ॥ **नियोजयेति** । प्रियां त्वद्विषयकप्रीतियुक्ताम् । धर्मचारिणीं धर्मानुष्ठानशीलाम् । अध्वरे यागे । हिरण्मय्याः प्रतिकृतेः प्रतिमायाः पुण्यां पावनीं प्रकृतिं प्रतिमां सीतां यथाधर्मं नियोजयाज्ञापय । पुण्यामित्यनेन "यस्य भार्या विदूरस्था पतिता दूषिताऽथ वा । अनिच्छुः प्रतिकूला वा" इत्याद्युदासः ॥ १९ ॥ यथा भगवत्यादिशति । तथास्त्विति शेषः । कृतार्थोऽस्मि

---

१ प्रशस्य ममा०. २ सवितृकुल० ०संभवा परिगृह्यत इति कथं भव०. ३ मम्बया. ४ प्रजाः. ५ पुण्यप्रकृतिम्. ६ अवि जाणादि. ७ सीदादुक्खं. ८ पम०. ९ जीवि०.

लक्ष्मणः——आर्ये एष निर्लज्जो लक्ष्मणः प्रणमति ।

सीता——वत्स ईदृशस्त्वं चिरं जीव । (क)

अरुन्धती——भगवन्वाल्मीके उपनीयेतामिमौ सीतागर्भसंभवौ रामभद्रस्य पुत्रकौ कुशलवौ । (इति निष्क्रान्ता ।)

रामलक्ष्मणौ——दिष्ट्या तथैवैतत् ।

सीता——(सबाष्पाकुला ।) कुत्र मम पुत्रकौ । (ख)

(ततः प्रविशति वाल्मीकिः कुशलवौ च ।)

वाल्मीकिः——वत्सौ कुशलवौ एष वां रघुपतिः पिता एष लक्ष्मणः कनिष्ठतातः । एषा सीता जननी । एष राजर्षिर्जनको मातामहः ।

सीता——(सहर्षकरुणाद्भुतं विलोक्य ।) कथं तातः । (ग)

कुशलवौ——हा तात हा अम्ब हा मातामह ।

रामलक्ष्मणौ——(सहर्षमालिङ्ग्य ।) ननु वत्सौ पुण्यैः प्राप्तौ स्थः ।

सीता——एहि जात कुश एहि जात लव चिरस्य परिष्वजेथां मां पुनर्जन्मान्तरगतां जननीम् । (घ)

कुशलवौ——(तथा कृत्वा ।) धन्यौ स्वः ।

सीता——भगवन् एषाहं प्रणमामि । (ङ)

वाल्मीकिः——वत्से ईदृश्येव चिरं भूयाः ।

(**क**) वच्छ ईदिसो तुमं चिरं जीअ । (**ख**) कहिं मे पुत्तआ । (**ग**) कहं तादो । (**घ**) एहि जाद कुस एहि जाद लव चिरस्स परिस्सजह मं पुणो जम्मन्तरगदं जणणिम् । (**ङ**) भअवं एसा हं पणमामि ।

सीतारामयोः समागमरूपप्रयोजनसिद्धिमानस्मि । त्यागस्य स्वद्वारकत्वादेवमुक्तम् । प्रत्युज्जीवितास्मि ' यस्त्वया सह स सर्गः ' इत्युक्तरामसमागमात्मकपुनरुज्जीवनवती कृतास्मि । ईदृशः सन् चिरं जीव मम पत्युश्च समागमं परमं श्रेयो मन्वानः सन् चिरं जीव । रामभद्रस्य उपनय रामभद्रसमीपं प्रापय । दिष्ट्या तथैवैतत् । एतत्कुशलवोत्पत्त्यादिकं तथैव पूर्वमस्मच्चिन्तितप्रकारेणैव । आसीदिति शेषः । क्व तौ पुत्रौ । इदं वाल्मीकिप्रवेशसूचकम् । मातामहः मातुः पिता । मातृपितृभ्यां पितरि डामहच् । कथं जातौ कुशलवौ । जातौ कथमिति चित्तविकासे ॥ **हा तातेत्यादि** । सर्वत्र हाशब्दो हर्षद्योतकः । ननु वत्सौ युवां प्राप्तौ स्थः । ननु वत्साविति संबोधनम् । चिरस्य परिष्वजेथां बहुकालमालिङ्गतम् । न तु यत्किंचित्क्षणालिङ्गनेन तृप्तिरिति भावः । परिष्वजेथामिति लोट्मध्यमद्विवचनम् । लोकान्तराद्रसातलात् । तथा कृत्वा आलिङ्ग्य । धन्यौ स्वः प्रशस्तौ भवावः । एवमेव चिरं भूयाः एवमेव पत्यपत्याभ्यां

---

१ उपनयेदानीं. २ तथैव तत्. ३ सबाष्पाकुलं; बाष्पाकृतम्. ४ एष रघु० पिता युवयोः. ५ सीतादेवी ज०. ६ रामः. ७ युवां. ८ वि तुमं. ९ लोअन्दरगदं; लोअन्दरादो आअदम्.

सीता—अम्हहे तातः कुलगुरुरार्याजनः सभर्तृका चार्या शान्तादेवी सलक्ष्मणाः सुप्रसन्ना आर्यपुत्रचरणाः समं कुशलवावपि दृश्यन्ते तन्निर्भराऽस्म्यानन्देन । (क)

(नेपथ्ये कलकलः ।)

वाल्मीकिः–(उत्थायावलोक्य च ।) उत्खातलवणो मधुरेश्वरः प्राप्तः ।

लक्ष्मणः––सानुषङ्गाणि कल्याणानि ।

रामः––सर्वमिदमनुभवन्नपि न प्रत्येमि । यद्वा प्रकृतिरियमभ्युदयानाम् ।

वाल्मीकिः—रामभद्र उच्यतां किं ते भूयः प्रियमुपकरोमि ।

रामः—अतः परमपि प्रियमस्ति । तथाऽपीदमस्तु––

पाप्मभ्यश्च पुनाति वर्धयति च श्रेयांसि सेयं कथा
मङ्गल्या च मनोहरा च जगतो मातेव गङ्गेव च ।
तामेतां परिभावयन्त्वभिनयैर्विन्यस्तरूपां बुधाः
शब्दब्रह्मविदः कवेः परिणतां प्राज्ञस्य वाणीमिमाम् ॥ २० ॥

(क) अम्महे तादो कुलगुरू अज्जाअणो सभत्तुआ अ अज्जा सन्तादेवी सलक्खणा सुप्पसण्णा अज्जउत्तचलणा समं कुशलवा वि दीसन्ति ता णिब्भरह्मि आणन्देण ।

संगतैव भूयाः । नेपथ्ये । उत्खातः उन्मूलितः लवणः लवणनामकासुरो येन तथोक्तः । मधुरायाः तन्नाम्न्या नगर्या ईश्वरः स्वामी । शत्रुघ्न इत्यर्थः । अस्यापि प्रथमाङ्कारब्धप्रयोजनत्वान्निर्वहणे निवेशः । कलत्रपुत्रसमागमादिश्रेयांसि सानुषङ्गाणि । अनुषज्यते अनुसंबध्यते यदित्यनुषङ्गं मङ्गलान्तरम् । कर्मणि घञ् । संबन्धमनुवर्तिष्यत इत्याचार्यभगवत्पतञ्जलिप्रयोगेण नपुंसकत्वम् । संपत्संपदमनुबध्नातीति मङ्गलान्तरसहितानीत्यर्थः । शत्रुवधतद्राज्यप्राप्त्योश्च श्रेयस्त्वादनुभवन्नपि साक्षात्कुर्वन्नपि न प्रत्येमि नियतमिति न विश्वसिमि । **यद्वेति** । न मद्दोष इति भावः । इयमनियता इत्ययं प्रत्ययः । अभ्युदयानां श्रेयसां प्रकृतिः स्वभावः । विधेयप्राधान्यात्स्त्रीत्वम् । भूयः पुत्रकलत्रसमर्पणात्परमिष्टं किमुपहरामि उपहारीकरोमि । इदमेव सर्वथा ऋषयः श्रेयो विधास्यन्तीति प्रथमाङ्के सूचितम् । अतः परमपि उक्तादन्यदपि । किं त्विदं भरतवाक्यमस्तु । एवं सत्यपि वक्ष्यमाणं भरतवचनमस्तु भवनार्हम् । अर्हे लोट् । **पाप्मभ्य इति** । इयं च प्रशस्तिः । सा प्रसिद्धा इयं बुद्धिस्था कथा रामायणात्मकवाक्यप्रबन्धरूपा कथा । 'कथ वाक्यप्रबन्धे' इति धातुः । सा च वाल्मीकीयचतुर्विंशतिसहस्रिका । पाप्मभ्यः दुरितेभ्यः जगत्पुनाति विभाजयति । जगत इति षष्ठ्यन्तं विपरिणम्य योजनीयम् । पूङ् धातुः यद्यपि दुरितविभजनात्मक-

---

१ उपहरामि. २ किं त्विदं भरतवाक्यमस्तु. ३ पापेभ्यश्च. ४ पुनातु वर्धयतु च...येयं. ५ माङ्गल्या. ६ वाल्मीकेः. ७ परिणतप्रज्ञस्य.

(इति निष्क्रान्ताः सर्वे ।)

इति संमेलनं नाम सप्तमोऽङ्कः ।

इति महाकविश्रीभवभूतिविरचितं उत्तररामचरितं नाम नाटकं समाप्तम् ।

दोषनिर्हरणवाची तथापि पाप्मभ्यः पुनातीति 'स कीचकैर्मारुतपूर्णरन्ध्रैः' इतिवद् व्याख्येयम् । जगतः श्रेयांसि पुत्रमित्रादीनि वर्धयति मोक्षपर्यन्तानि उत्तरोत्तरमधिकानि करोति । अत्र कुटुम्बवृद्धिं धनधान्यवृद्धिं इत्यादिश्लोकद्वयमनुसंधेयम् । मातेव गङ्गेव माङ्गल्या मनोहरा च । माता हि दुःखविस्मारिणी सुखदा च भवति । गङ्गा च पापनाशनी मोक्षदा च भवति । तद्वद्रामायणमपीति भावः । शब्दब्रह्मविदः शब्द एव ब्रह्म परिच्छिन्नत्वापरिच्छिन्नत्वाभ्यां परब्रह्मसाम्यात्तद्रूपणम् । तद्विदन्तीति शब्दब्रह्मविदः । बुधाः सहृदयाः । अभिनयाः सात्त्विकाङ्गिकाहार्यवाचिकभेदेन चतुर्विधाः । अभिनयैरितीत्थंभूतलक्षणे तृतीया । अभिनयविशिष्टो यो विन्यासः रचनाविशिष्टयं च प्रतिपादकत्वरूपं विन्यस्तं विन्यासेन निष्पन्नं यस्यास्तथोक्ताम् । शरीरं चेहानुपूर्वी । प्राज्ञस्य सर्वज्ञशिरोमणेः कवेः भवभूतिकवेः इमां वाणीं परिणतामेनामुत्तररामचरितनाटकरूपभवभूतिवागात्मना यः परिणामः तद्वतीमेनां श्रीरामायणात्मककथां परिभावयन्तु परितश्चिन्तयन्तु । 'भू अवकल्कने' । अवकल्कनं चिन्तनमित्युक्तम् । इयं कथा श्रेयांसि वर्धयति एनां परिभावयन्त्वित्यन्वादेशादेनादेशः । वाल्मीकिवागेव भवभूतिवागात्मना परिणतेत्युक्तिः । उत्तररामचरितस्य गाम्भीर्यमाधुर्ये लभ्येते । परिभावयन्त्वित्यनेन 'बद्धा यदर्पणरसेन विमर्दपूर्वम्' इति श्लोकार्थो ध्वनितः । परिपूर्वकस्य 'भू सत्तायाम्' इति पठितस्यैवावज्ञानार्थकत्वमिति नास्य तत्प्रसक्तिः । शब्दब्रह्मविदो बुधाः अभिनयैः सह विन्यस्तरूपां प्राज्ञस्य कवेरिमां वाणीं परिणतामेनां परिभावयन्त्विति योजना । एतेन 'एनाम्' 'इमाम्' इत्यनयोर्न पौनरुक्त्यम् । अभेदसंबन्धेनान्वयवाचकयोरिव प्रकृतिविकृतिवाचकयोरपि समानविभक्तिकत्वनियमादुभयोर्द्वितीयान्तत्वम् । एवं साङ्गं नाटकं वृत्तम् ॥ २० ॥

यद्यप्यत्राखिलं किंचित्कविनानेन वध्यते ।
निरङ्कुशतया तत्तु समाधेयं मनीषिभिः ॥
कोशव्याकरणे नात्र लिखिते ग्रन्थगौरवात् ।
भावस्य तु गभीरत्वात्स कश्चित्कथितो मया ॥
भवभूतेः कवीन्द्रस्य क्व गम्भीरो गिरां भरः ।
क्व मे मतिरतिस्वल्पा सहायोऽत्र हयाननः ॥
अनवरतभावनाभिर्योऽर्थः क्लेशान्मया लब्धः ।
तस्य प्रकाशनीयं व्याख्या विदधातु कौतुकं सुधियाम् ॥

इति श्रीवाधूलवीरराघवविरचितायां भवभूतिभावतलस्पर्शिनीसमाख्यायामुत्तररामचरितव्याख्यायां सप्तमोऽङ्कः ।

समाप्तमिदं नाटकम् ।

उत्तररामचरितस्थसुभाषितसंग्रहः ।

I.–Sentences. Page.

II.–S'lokas. Page.

अन्तःकरणतत्त्वस्य दम्पत्योः स्नेहसंश्रयात्।
आनन्दग्रन्थिरेकोऽयमपत्यमिति बध्यते॥ 77

अहेतुः पक्षपातो यस्तस्य नास्ति प्रतिक्रिया।
स हि स्नेहात्मकस्तन्तुरन्तर्मर्माणि सीव्यति॥ 133

आविर्भूतज्योतिषां ब्राह्मणानां ये व्याहारास्तेषु मा संशयो भूत्।
भद्रा ह्येषां वाचि लक्ष्मीर्निषक्ता नैते वाचं विप्लुतार्थां वदन्ति॥ 112

ऋषयो राक्षसीमाहुर्वाचमुन्मत्तदृप्तयोः।
सा योनिः सर्ववैराणां सा हि लोकस्य निर्ऋतिः॥ 137

कामान्दुग्धे विप्रकर्षत्यलक्ष्मीं कीर्तिं सूते दुष्कृतं या हिनस्ति।
तां चाप्येतां मातरं मङ्गलानां धेनुं धीराः सूनृतां वाचमाहुः॥ 137

चिरं ध्यात्वा ध्यात्वा निहित इव निर्माय पुरतः प्रवासे चाश्वासं न खलु
न करोति प्रियजनः। जगज्जीर्णारण्यं भवति च कलत्रेऽप्युपरते। 159

न किंचिदपि कुर्वाणः सौख्यैर्दुःखान्यपोहति।
तत्तस्य किमपि द्रव्यं यो हि यस्य प्रियो जनः॥ 59,142

न तेजस्तेजस्वी प्रसृतमपरेषां विषहते स तस्य स्वो भावः प्रकृतिनि-
यतत्वादकृतकः। मयूखैरश्रान्तं तपति यदि देवो दिनकरः
किमाग्नेयो ग्रावा निकृत इव तेजांसि वमति॥ 147

पूरोत्पीडे तटाकस्य परीवाहः प्रतिक्रिया।
शोकक्षोभे च हृदयं प्रलापैरेव धार्यते॥ 83

प्रियप्राया वृत्तिर्विनयमधुरो वाचि नियमः प्रकृत्या कल्याणी मतिरनवगीतः
परिचयः। पुरो वा पश्चाद्वा तदिदमविपर्यासितरसं रहस्यं साधूना-
मनुपधि विशुद्धं विजयते॥ 48

लौकिकानां हि साधूनामर्थं वागनुवर्तते।
ऋषीणां पुनराद्यानां वाचमर्थोऽनुधावति॥ 12

वज्रादपि कठोराणि मृदूनि कुसुमादपि।
लोकोत्तराणां चेतांसि को नु विज्ञातुमर्हति॥ 53

वितरति गुरुः प्राज्ञे विद्यां यथैव तथा जडे न च खलु तयोर्ज्ञाने शक्तिं
करोत्यपहन्ति वा। भवति च पुनर्भूयान्भेदः फलं प्रति तद्यथा
प्रभवति शुचिर्बिम्बग्राहे मणिर्न मृदां चयः॥ 50

व्यतिषजति पदार्थानान्तरः कोऽपि हेतुर्न खलु बहिरुपाधीन्प्रीतयः संश्रयन्ते।
विकसति हि पतङ्गस्योदये पुण्डरीकं द्रवति च हिमरश्मावुद्गते चन्द्रकान्तः॥ 146

संतानवाहीन्यपि मानुषाणां दुःखानि सद्बन्धुवियोगजानि।
दृष्टे जने प्रेयसि दुःसहानि स्रोतःसहस्रैरिव संप्लवन्ते॥ 106

सर्वथा व्यवहर्तव्यं कुतो ह्यवचनीयता।
यथा स्त्रीणां तथा वाचां साधुत्वे दुर्जनो जनः॥ 7

उत्तररामचरितस्थश्लोकानां सूची ।

UTTARARA'MACHARITA.

ACT I.

(Prelude).

We adddress this salutation to the bards of old; our homage also to that Divine Speech, who is a portion of the Supreme Soul, and immortal.* (1)

(After the Benediction).

MANAGER—No more of prolixity. Let me address the respectable gentlemen (assembled) to-day at the fair of the Divine Kálapriyanátha: let it be known to your honours—There is, as you know well, an illustrious scion of Kaśyapa's race, bearing the distinctive title of 'Śrîkaṇṭha,' versed in (the sciences of) Grammar, Mîmáṃsá and Logic, Bhavabhúti by name, and son of Jâtukarṇî.

'Whom, a Bráhmaṇa, the goddess of Speech follows like one enslaved (obedient to his will—quite in his power); Uttararámacharita, (a play) composed by him, will (now) be represented'. (2)

Here am I turned into a man of that time (contemporary of Ráma) and a resident of Ayodhyá, as my business requires me to be. *(Casting a glance around).* Holloa, if this is the coronation-season of the great king Ráma, the destructive comet of the race of Pulastya, when joyous songs with music should go on continuously day and night, how is it that the public stalls are silent to-day?

(Enter an ACTOR *).*

ACTOR—Your honour, His Majesty has sent back to their homes those magnanimous monkeys and Ràkshasas, his allies in the war of Laṅká, as also the Bráhmaṇa and royal sages that had come from various quarters to offer their greetings, in whose honour festivities had continued for so many days.

MANAGER—Ah, this must be the reason.

ACTOR—And this other thing :—

---

* With the reading चिन्देम in the 2nd line—

Having addressed our salutation to the ancient poets, we pray for this, that we may obtain Divine Speech who is immortal and a phase of the Supreme Spirit.

The queens, the mothers of Ráma, have gone to be present at a sacrifice, with Arundhatî at their head, to the hermitage of their son-in-law, under the guidance of Vasishṭha. (3)

Manager—I am a stranger (here) and so I ask—who may this son-in-law be ?

Actor—

King Das'aratha begot a daughter, S'ántá by name, whom he gave in adoption to king Lomapáda. (4)

Ṛishyaśṛiṅga, the son of Vibhâṇḍaka, espoused her. He instituted a sacrifice lasting for twelve years. At his solicitation the elderly matrons have gone there, leaving (here) Jânakî, their daughter-in-law, though advanced in pregnancy.

Manager—Why concern ourselves more with this ! Come, let us be present at the royal gate, as befits the duties of our profession.

Actor—Let Your Honour then think of some excellent (blameless) mode of addressing the king when we approach him.

Manager—We should do our best to do our duty ; whence can there be exemption from blame ? People are wicked (have an evil tongue) as regards the purity of language, just as well as the chastity of women. (5)

Actor—Exceedingly wicked, you ought to say,

Since people speak ill even of the divine (or, the queen,) princess of Mithilá. Her residence in the house of the Râkshasa serves them as a basis ; but they distrust her ordeal (purification) in the fire. (6)

Manager—It will be a sad thing if this scandalous talk reaches the King.

Actor—The sages and the gods will, in every way, do good ! (*Walking about*). Where is the king, Oh ! (*Listening*). Thus say the people—

Janaka, who had come through affection to felicitate Râma, is gone to-day to Videha after having passed these days in festivities ; and to console the queen, disconsolate on that account, the king leaves his judgement-seat and enters the inner apartment. (7)

(*Exeunt both*).

End of the Prelude.

(*Enter* RA'MA *and* SÎTA' seated).

RA'MA—Queen, daughter of the king of Videha, cheer up. For thy esteemed father cannot (of his own will) leave us.

But the necessary performance of holy rites takes off his freedom. The home-life of those who keep the sacred fires is fettered with restraints (obstacles). (8)

SÎTA'—I know it, my lord, I know it. But separations from one's beloved connexions cause, nevertheless, affliction.

RA'MA—Just so. These are the worldly incidents piercing the vital parts of the heart, disgusted with which the wise leave all objects of desire and find rest in the forest.

(*Enter the* CHAMBERLAIN).

CHAMB.—Dear Ráma—(*Interrupting himself here, with confusion*). Your Majesty,

RA'MA—(*With a smile*). Venerable man, to address me as 'Dear Ráma' well becomes the servant of my father. Address me, therefore, as is your wont.

CHAMB.—Sire, Ashṭâvakra has arrived from the hermitage of Ṛishyaśṛiṅga.

SÎTA'—Venerable Kañchukin, why tarry then?

RA'MA—Send him in at once.

(*Exit* KANCHUKÎ).

(*Enter* ASHTA'VAKRA).

ASHTA'.—Hail to you both!

RA'MA—Revered Sir, I salute you. Please take your seat here.

SÎTA'—Venerable sir, I bow to you. Are my elders, together with their son-in-law, doing well, as also noble Śântá?

RA'MA—Is the revered Ṛishyaśṛiṅga, my brother-in-law, a habitual drinker of Soma all safe? And also the noble Śántá?

SÎTA'—Do they remember us?

ASHTA'.—(*Sitting down*). Yes, of course. Queen, his reverence Vasishṭha sends you this message—

The all supporting goddess Earth gave thee birth; king Janaka, Prajápati's peer, is thy father; and, O delightful one, thou art the daughter-in-law of those kings whose race has Savitṛi for its progenitor and me for its spiritual adviser. (9)

What else but this can I wish thee then? Mayest thou be the mother of a hero.

RA'MA—We are blessed.

The speech of ordinary sages follows sense; while sense attaches itself to the utterances of primeval sages. (10)

ASHTA'.—Moreover, the revered Arundhatî, the elderly queens and Śántá, repeatedly asked me to deliver this message, that whatever pregnancy-hankering Sítá may have, it should be necessarily fulfilled, without loss of time.

RA'MA—All that she says will be done.

ASHTA'.—And Ṛishyaśṛiṅga, the husband of her sister-in-law, sends this message to the queen:—Dear child, you were not brought as you are in a high state of pregnancy: and dear Ráma too was left there for your diversion. I, therefore, wish to see you with a son on your lap.

RA'MA—(*With a smile of joy mingled with blush*). May it be so! Has not the venerable Vasishṭha sent me some message?

ASHTA'.—Let it be heard.

We are detained (here) on account of the sacrifice of our son-in-law. You are only a youth, and have recently ascended the throne; be you intent on satisfying your subjects. The glory arising from that is the highest treasure of your race. (11)

RA'MA—It will be done as the venerable Vasishṭha advises.

Affection (friendship), mercy, personal happiness, nay, even Jânakî—giving up (sacrificing) these for the satisfaction of my people, I shall feel no pain. (12)

SĪTA'—Hence, indeed, is my lord the upholder of Raghu's race.

(*Exit*).

ASHTA'.—(*Rising and walking about*). Oh, prince Lakshmaṇa is here!

(*Enter* LAKSHMAṆA).

LAK.—Victory, victory to your Highness! Sire, that painter has, according to your instructions, portrayed your honour's life on this picture-wall.

RA'MA—You know, my boy, how to divert the queen in her melancholy mood. Upto what event then has he represented it?

LAK.—As far as the queen's purification in the fire.

RA'MA—Tush: (*In a conciliatory tone*).

What has she, who is pure by her very birth, to do with other purifying things? Holy water and fire need no purification from other sources. (13)

Queen, sprung from sacrificial ground, forgive us. This reproach will last through life.

What a hard lot it is that people have to be appeased by those who regard (the good name of) their family as their treasure! Therefore, what ill we have said of you does not, indeed, befit you. The natural place of a sweet-smelling flower is on the head: and not under trampling feet. (14)

SÎTA'—Let it be, my dear, let it be. Come away. Let us enjoy a sight of your life. (*They rise and move about*).

LAK.—Here is the painting.

SÎTA'—(*Marking with attention*). Who are these stationed above in a compact line that seem to praise my Lord?

LAK.—These are the well-known Jṛimbhaka missiles with their mysterious charms which were handed down from the revered Kṛis'ás'va to sage Viśvâmitra and presented by him to my revered brother on the occasion of the destruction of Tâṭaká.

RA'MA—Offer your veneration, Queen, to these heavenly missiles.

The primeval instructors, Brahmá and others, having practised penance for upwards of a thousand years for the benefit of Righteousness (or, the world, as the Com. takes it) beheld these as (the manifestations of) their own spiritual energies (*lit.* of the form of religious austerities). (15)

SÎTA'—My homage to these.

RA'MA—They will, by every means, wait on your progeny.

SÎTA'—I am blessed.

LAK.—Here is the account (the events that occurred) at Mithilá.

SÎTA'—Oh, here is my lord painted, distinguished by a grace of form swarthy like an opening young blue lotus, lovely, glossy and strong; with his blue and graceful splendour gazed at steadfastly by my wondering father, as he (my lord) snapped the bow of S'iva with little concern; and with a roundish face pretty on account of his locks (playing about).

LAK.—Behold, lady, behold.

Here is your father with S'atánanda, son of Gotama, the priest of the Janaka family, honouring his kinsmen, Vasishṭha and others. (16)

RA'MA—It is a scene worth seeing.

To whom is not welcome the kinship between the families of Janaka and Raghu, wherein the son of Kuśika became the donor and receiver in his own person? (17)

Sîta'—Here are you, four brothers, having your tonsure ceremony performed just at the time and gone through the rite of matrimony. I feel as if I stood just in the same spot and at the very moment.

Ra'ma—

Meseems the hour is present now, when, O fair-faced one, this your hand with the beautiful nuptial string fastened upon it, being joined with mine by the son of Gotama, thrilled me with joy, as if it were a great festival in a bodily form. (18)

Lak.—This is your ladyship; this is noble Máṇḍavî; and this our daughter-in-law Srutakîrti.

Sîta'—And son, who is this other one?

Lak.—(*With a blushful smile, aside*). Ah, her ladyship asks me about U'rmilâ: Well, I will direct her attention to another quarter. (*Aloud*). See this worthy sight. Ṭhis, too, is revered Bhârgava.

Sîta'—(*With alarm*). I shudder.

Ra'ma—I salute thee, saint.

Lak.—Lady, see, see. Here is he by his lordship—

[*Interrupting him here*—

Ra'ma—(*Wishing to divert attention*). Son, there is much yet to be seen. Show us the other scenes.

Sîta'—(*With a look of affection and deep respect*). This noble modesty highly becomes you, my lord.

Lak.—Here are we arrived at Ayodhyâ.

Ra'ma—(*Tearfully*). I remember it, Oh, I remember it.

Then my dear father was still alive, we were fresh from marriage and were tenderly taken care of by our mothers; gone are those days! (19)

This Jánakî too, then,

A (mere) child, with a countenance of lovely appearance on account of her budding teeth and a few tiny and fairy curls playing about the temples, gave delight to my mothers by her sweet limbs, extremely charming, vying with the moonlight and possessed of artless grace. (20)

Lak.—This is Manthará.

Ra'ma—(*Quickly showing elsewhere*). Queen, Princess of Videha,

This is that Iṅgudî tree in the town of Sriṅgavera where we formerly met our affectionate friend (Guha), king of the Nishádas. (21)

LAK.—(*With a smile, to himself*). Ah, he skipped over the account of our second mother.

SÎTA'—Oh, this is the scence of our tying up our matted hair.

LAK.—

That holy vow of leading a life in the woods, which the descendants of the Ikshváku race practised when aged and after devolving their royalty on their sons, was undertaken by my lord in his youth! (22)

SÎTA'—Here is the revered Bhágîrathí, with her lucid and purifying waters.

RA'MA—Divine river, tutelary goddess of Raghu's race, my homage to thee.

It was when sprinkled over with thy waters that Bhagîratha, of yore, having practised austerities, quite heedless of bodily anguish, raised to heaven his great-grandfathers, long after they had been reduced to ashes by the fierce wrath of Kapila, when at the sacrifice of Sagara they had excavated the earth while engaged in the search of the horse. (23)

Be thou who art such, O mother, devoted, as Arundhatî is, to the well-being of Sîtá, thy daughter-in-law.

LAK.—This is the banian tree named Śyáma, on the bank of the Kâlindî, by the side of the road leading to Chitrakûṭa, to which our attention was called by the *Bháradvája* birds (or, which was shown by Bháradvája).

RA'MA—(*Looks at it longingly*).

SÎTA'—Does my lord remember this region?

RA'MA—How can I forget it, my dear?

(That region) where you sank into sleep, having reposed on my bosom your limbs lovely though wearied and drooping from fatigue of the journey, soothingly pressed by close embraces and languid like a crushed lotus-stalk. (24)

LAK.—Here is the obstruction caused by Virádha at the entrance of the Vindhya forest.

SÎTA'—Let us have done with that. I will just see how we entered the Southern forest, my lord holding over me with his own hand a palm-leaf-umbrella to keep off the sun.

RA'MA—

These are the penance-groves on the banks of the mountain-brooks with hermits dwelling under the trees, wherein tranquil settlers (anchorites), who regard the rights of hospitality as their highest duty and who live upon handfuls of wild rice, have their homes. (25)

LAK.—Here is the mountain Prasravaṇa, situated in the middle of Janasthána, with its sombre view rendered darker by the ever-drizzling clouds and having its caves resounding with the roar of the Godâvarî wending its way through the surrounding forest, blue, glossy and dense, on account of the thickly growing clumps of trees.

RA'MA—

Do you remember, fair-bodied one, the days which we passed on the mountain happily, on account of Lakshmaṇa ministering to our comfort; do your remember the Godâvarî with its sweet water, and also our rambles in its environs? (26)

Moreover,

(Here) while we talked at random on this thing and that in very gentle tones, resting closely together, cheek to cheek, and one arm of each engaged in a close embrace, the night itself ended without our noticing how the watches flew. (27)

LAK.—Here is Śúrpaṇakhá in the Pañchavaṭî.

SÍTA'—Oh, my lord, for the last time I see you.

RA'MA—You, afraid of separation, this is a picture!

SÎTA'—Be it as it may. A wicked person causes uneasiness (alarm).

RA'MA—Holloa, the incidents at Janasthána appear as if they were taking place just now.

LAK.—

Here is what (the mischief that) was so wrought by the wicked Râkshasas by using the trick of the golden deer that it smarts us even though avenged. In the dreary Janasthâna, even the stones wept, even the heart of the adamant broke, by the actions of my revered brother in which his senses were overpowered. (28)

SÎTA'—(*With tears, to herself*). My lord, joy of Raghu's family, on my account you were thus afflicted!

LAK.—(*Looking at Râma*; *feelingly*).

This flow of your tears, falling down in streams like a shattered necklace of pearls, rolls on the ground in broken drops; though checked, your emotion, swelling the heart by its excess, betrays itself to others by the throbbing of the lower lip and the nostrils. (29)

R'AMA—Dear brother,

The fire of grief arising from the separation of my beloved, however fierce (intense), was at that time borne by me through the desire for retaliation; but now, reviving in my breast, it causes agony like a wound festering in the vital part of my heart. (30)

SÎTA'—Alas, alas! I too fancy myself to be bereaved of my lord on acount of the intensity of my anguish.

LAK.—(*To himself*). Well, let me divert their attention to another scene. (*Looking at the painting*; *aloud*). Here is the representation of the actions and the manly deeds of the revered father Jaṭâyu, king of the vultures, as old as one Manu.

SÎTA'—Alas, father, your fatherly love was fully borne out.

RA'MA—Alas, father, descendant of Kas'yapa, lord of the birds, where can there possibly be born again a great and holy saint like yourself?

LAK.—This is that part of the Daṇḍaka forest, to the west of Janasthâna, called Kuñjavân, inhabited by the headless demon Danu. This is the site of Mataṅga's hermitage on mount Ṛishymúka; this is the pious female ascetic of the S'abara tribe, called Sramaṇâ; this is the lake Pampâ, noted for its lotuses.

SÎTA'—Here it was, as I was told, that my lord wept aloud and bitterly, his courage and rage being undermined.

RA'MA—Queen, this is a delightful lake.

In this lake the tracts full of white lotuses, with their broad stalks waving, being shaken by the wings of the Mallikâksha birds singing indistinctly through hilarity, were seen by me in the intervals of the falling and rising of tears, as being full of blue lotuses. (31)

LAK.—This is he, the venerable Hanumân.

SÎTA'—This is he, the magnanimous Māruti, a mighty benefactor by his rescue of the world of mortals long sunk in despair.

RA'MA—

Happily it is he, of mighty arms, ever the new delight of Añjanâ, by whose valour both the worlds and we were blessed (or, attained our object). (32)

SÎTA'—Son, what is the name of this mountain having peacocks dancing vehemently on the blooming *Kadamba* trees, where under a tree, my lord is painted as swooning supported by you, weeping aloud, his beauty fading and his majesty and grace only remaining.

LAK.—

This is that well-known mountain called Mâlyavân, odorous with the flowering *kakubha* trees, to the summit of which clings a fresh cloud, blue and glossy.

RA'MA—

Desist from it, dear brother, desist from it ; I cannot stand it any more : I feel as if that separation from Jânakî has come upon me again. (33)

LAK.—Hereafter are represented the countless achievements, each more wonderful than the other, of his lordship and of the noble monkeys and *Râkshasas*. But the lady is tired; I, therefore, beg that you should take rest.

SÎTA'—My lord, I have a thing to say, a desire being produced in me by the sight of the painting.

RA'MA—You are welcome to speak it out.

SÎTA'—I feel (wish) that I should once more wander in those serene and majestic sylvan avenues, and that I should again bathe in the divine Ganges, a plunge in which is so purifying, gladdening and cooling.

RA'MA—Dear Lakshmaṇa !

LAK.—Here I am.

RA'MA—The elders have just sent word that her desires should be fulfilled without delay. Prepare (therefore) a carriage that moves lightly and does not jolt.

SÎTA'—My lord, you too should accompany me there.

RA'MA—O you hard-hearted, do you need tell me this ?

SÎTA'—Then I am glad at it.

LAK.—As your lordship commands.

[*Exit.*

RA'MA—Let us sit (or, lie down) here awhile, my dear, near the threshhold of the window.

SÎTA'—Let it be so. I am really overpowered by the sleep brought on by the exertion.

RA'MA—Then recline closely upon me that you should sleep (well).

Cast thy arm, covered with the particles of perspiration caused by the fatigue and excitement, round my neck, inspiring new life into me as it were, and possessed of the grace of a necklace of moon-gems melting under the kiss of the lunar rays. (34)

(*Helping her to do so, with delight*). My dear, what is this !

I cannot determine whether it is pleasure or pain, whether stupor or sleep ; whether the working of poison, or rapturous joy : at every touch of thine a certain sensation comes upon me, which, stupefying all my senses, now bewilders my consciousness, now paralyses it. (35)

SÎTA'—It is your constant love for me ; what else could it be ?

RA'MA—

These thy sweet words, O lotus-eyed one, cause the withered flower of my life to bloom, gladden me, lull all my senses into peace, serve as nectar to the ears and as a sovereign balm to the heart. (36)

SÎTA'—You sweet-speaker, come, let us lie down for rest. (*Looks about for something to sleep on*).

RA'MA—What are you searching for, my dear ?

Ever since the time of our marriage, whether in the house or in the wilderness, in the days of childhood and thereafter in those of youth, this arm of Râma has been thy pillow, lulling you to sleep and not resorted to by any other woman. (37)

SÎTA'—(*Gesticulating that she sleeps*). It is so, my lord it is so. (*Sleeps*).

RA'MA—How now, she, of pleasing address, has gone to sleep on my bosom ! (*Gazing upon her*).

She is the very Lakshmî in my house, and a pencil of nectar to my eyes ; her touch is a thick sandal-paste to my body ; this her arm twined round my neck is as cooling and smooth as a pearl-string ; what about her would not be pleasing (only),* but separation from her is exceedingly unbearable. (38)

(*Enter* DOOR-KEEPER).

There has approached, sire,—

RA'MA—Oh, who ?

DOOR-KEEPER—Durmukha, Your Majesty's personal attendant.

---

* With the reading यदि पुनरसह्यो न विरहः—
If there would be no separation again from her which is unbearable.

RA'MA—(*To himself*). Durmukha, the attendant of the harem ! He was commissioned by me to ascertain secretly the thoughts of the townsmen and the country-folk. (*Aloud*). Let him come in.

[*Exit* DOOR KEEPER.

(*Enter* DURMUKHA).

DUR.—(*To himself*). Oh, how can I communicate to his lordship such inconceivable slanderous talk of the people with regard to queen Sîtá ? Or, such is the bounden duty of me, unlucky that I am !

SÎTA'—(*Talks in her sleep*). O my lord, my delight, where are you ?

RA'MA—Oh, it is the same thought of separation produced in the Queen by the sight of the painting and causing uneasiness that is disturbing her sleep.

(*Touches her body affectionately*).

Happy is that fortunate man who, somehow, obtains that one thing (*viz.* pure, matchless love) which is the same in happiness or misery, which adapts itself to all conditions, where the heart finds its solace, the flavour of which is unaffected by old age, and which matures, as time removes the veil (of reservedness), into permanent deep affection. (39)

DUR.—(*Approaching*). Victory to Your Majesty !

RA'MA—Speak out what you have collected.

DUR.—The inhabitants of the city and the country praise Your Majesty, saying—'The good king Rāma has made us forget the great king Daśaratha.'

RA'MA—This is simply praise. Say if they discover any defect in me, so that it may be removed.

DUR.—(*Tearfully*). May Your Majesty listen. (*Whispers into his ear*)—Something like this.

RA'MA—Oh, terrible is the fall of this thunderbolt of words ! (*Faints*).

DUR.—Take heart, my lord.

RA'MA—(*Recovering*).

Alas, alas ! Fie upon the infamy attaching to one's stay in another's house ! For, the same with regard to Sitá, though extinguished by miraculous means, has again spread in all directions, as the evil turn of fortune would have it, like the poison of a mad dog. (Or, alas, alas, woe, woe ! The infamy attaching to Sitâ on account of her stay in the enemy's house which, though wiped off &c.) (40)

What am I, a miserable wretch, to do in this case? (*Reflecting, pitifully*). Or, what else (is to be done)?

By any means to satisfy the people is the self-imposed duty of the good; and the same was fulfilled by my father quitting me and his life together. (41)

It was also just now that the revered Vasishṭha sent me a message (to this effect).

Moreover,

Woe to me, a cursed being, if that noble, unspotted character, which was conspicuously maintained by the kings of the solar race, the best of mortals, were to be tarnished by a foul scandal in connexion with me! (42)

Alas, Queen, sprung from sacrificial ground, you who hallowed the earth by accepting it as your birth-place, you, joy of the race of Janaka and Nimi, and amiable with virtues, commended by Fire, Vasishṭha and Arundhatî, O you to whom Ráma is all your life, my dear companion in the great forest, a darling of your father, and moderate in speech, how is it that one thus graced should meet with such a fate!

By you the worlds are holy; but unholy are the words of the people with regard to you. In you the world finds a helper, but you fall a helpless victim!! (43)

(*To* Durmukha). Durmukha, say to Lakshmaṇa—This your new king thus commands you. (*Into his ear*). Thus, thus.

Dur.—Alas; how is it that by hearing the mere words of wicked men, Your Majesty has decided to act thus ungenerously towards the queen who was purified by fire and in whose womb is lodged the pure progeny of the race of Raghu?

Ra'ma—Tush! How can the people of the town and the country be wicked!

The race of Ikshváku is loved by the people; but unfortunately there was a cause of slander; and as for the miracle at the time of her purification, who could believe it, since it took place at a very remote place? (44)

Go, then.

Dur.—Alas, my Queen!

[*Exit*.

Ra'ma—Alas, how woeful! I have become a cruel man, the perpetrator of a very execrable deed.

Through a pretext I am handing over to death this my beloved whom I have brought up from her childhood and who has never dwelt away from me through affection, just as a butcher does a domestic bird. (45)

Why then do I, a sinner, not fit to be touched, defile the Queen? (*So slowly raises the head of Sîtâ and pulls away his arm*).

Leave me, O innocent one, who am a unique Châṇḍâla by my atrocious deeds. You are clinging to a deadly poisonous tree, taking it for a sandal one. (46)

(*Rising*). Alas! The world of mortals is now a changed scene to me; the purpose of Râma's life is at an end to-day; the world has become a void, a decayed forest; worldly life is without interest; my very body an abode of misery; I am forlorn; what shall I do? What course is open to me? Or rather,

Consciousness has been put in Râma simply that he should feel (experience) pain; my life has been acting the part of a nail of adamant driven into the heart. (47)

O mother Arundhatî, O venerable Vasishṭha and Viśvâmitra, O divine Fire, O goddess, the supporter of all creatures, O father Janaka, O father, O mothers, O dear friend Sugrîva, O gentle Hanúmân, O my great benefactor Bibhîshaṇa, lord of Laṅkà, O friend Trijaṭá, you have been deluded, you have been insulted by cursed Râma. Or who am I (what right have I) to call on them now?

For, these high-souled persons are, I think, as it were, polluted with sin when named by me an ungrateful villain. (48)

I, who,

Having discarded my beloved wife, the ornament of my house, gone to sleep having reclined on my bosom without any misgivings and heavy with the developed fœtus, trembling with fear, ruthlessly cast her off like an offering to the beasts of prey. (49)

(*Placing the feet of Sîtâ on his head*). Queen, O my queen, now for the last time Râma touches your lotus-like feet with his head. (*Weeps*).

(*Behind the scenes*).

Help! Help! The Bráhmaṇas in distress!

RA'MA—Ascertain, Oh, what it is.

(*Again behind the scenes*).

Harassed by the demon Lavaṇa, the multitude of sages, of austere penance, living on the banks of the Yamunâ, has approached thee for protection. (50)

RA'MA—What, troubles from demons yet! Let me yet once send Śatrughna for the destruction of this wicked son of Kumbhînasî. (*Advancing a few steps and then coming back*). Alas, queen, how will you fare in this condition? O mother Earth, do thou take care of thy very noble daughter, Jánakî,

(That Jánakî) who is the sole blessing of the families of Janaka and Raghu and whom, of holy character, thou broughtest forth in the holy sacrificial ground. (51)

[*Exit, weeping*.

SÎTA'—O my gentle lord, where are you? (*Rises hastily*). Oh, fie, fie. Deluded by an evil dream I call out to my lord. (*Looking about*). Alas, alas, my lord has gone away leaving me alone fast asleep. What can this be? Well, I will get angry with him if I am master of myself when I see him. Who waits here?

(*Enter* DURMUKHA).

DUR.—Queen, prince Lakshmaṇa says—The carriage is ready; Your Highness should mount it.

SÎTA'—Here I mount it. (*Rising and walking forth*). My heavy fœtus throbs. Let us walk gently.

DUR.—This way, this way, Queen.

SÎTA'—A bow to those whose wealth is their penance (sages)! My homage to the guardian Deities of the Raghu race! My veneration to the lotus-feet of my lord! Reverence to all my elders!

(*Exeunt Omnes*).

END OF ACT I., STYLED

'*The Exhibition of the Pictures.*'

ACT II.

(*Behind the curtains*).

Welcome to the female ascetic!

(*Enter a* FEMALE ASCETIC *in a traveller's costume*).

FE. ASC—Ah, the sylvan deity here waits on me with an offering containing fruits, flowers and leaves.

(*Having entered*).

SYL. DEI.—(*Offering the oblation*).

Enjoy this forest just as you wish ; this is a happy day for me. It is only with difficulty and by the force of merit, that the good come to have the company of good men. The shade of trees, water, and whatever is suitable food for penance-life, whether fruits or roots—all that is quite at your disposal here. (1)

FE. ASC.—What shall I say to this ?

A behaviour full of kindness, a restraint over speech pleasing by its modesty, a mind naturally prone to do good, and a friendship irreproachable—triumphant is this secret of the life of the good, of a sweetness not altered by time past or future, guiltless and pure. (2)

(*Both sit down*).

SYL. DEI.—Whom am I to know your ladyship for ?

FE. ASC.—I am A'treyî (of the family of Atri).

SYL. DEI.—Noble A'treyî, where do you come here from ? What makes you seek the groves of Daṇḍaka ?

A'TREYÍ—In this tract there dwell many scholars versed in the Vedánta lore, Agastya the foremost of them. To learn from them the principles of Vedânta I have wandered to this place from the abode (*lit.* side) of Válmîki. (3)

SYL. DEI.—When other sages too wait upon that ancient teacher of Brahma, the sage Práchetasa, for a complete study of Brahma-lore, what means all this trouble of a long journey on the part of your ladyship ?

A'TREYÍ—There is a great impediment to study there ; and that is why I have undertaken this long journey.

SYL. DEI.—What sort of impediment (you mean) ?

A'TREYÍ—A couple of boys, marvellous in every way and of an age when they could just have been weaned, were presented to the sage by some distinguished deity. Those boys win the affection not only of the sages but also of creatures animate and inanimate.

SYL. DEI.—Do you know their names ?

A'TREYI'—That very goddess, they say, told their names to be Kuśa and Lava and also described their power.

SYL. DEI.—What sort of power ?

A'TREYI'—They possess, it is said, the Jṛimbhaka weapons together with their secret spells, from their very birth.

Syl. Dei.—Helloa, this is really wonderful!

A'treyî—The Venerable Válmîki, having actually undertaken the duties of a nurse towards them, brought them up and watched over them. When their tonsure-ceremony was performed, he carefully instructed them in all the three lores except the Vedas. Just after that, in their eleventh year from conception, he invested them with the sacred thread according to the rite proper for the Kshatriya class, and taught them the three Vedas. There is no possibility of persons like me studying with these two possessing a very acute intellect and a strong memory. For,

The instructor imparts knowledge to the talented scholar just as he does to the dull; he does not, indeed, give them nor does he take away from them the talent for learning; and yet there is a very great difference as to the result. (It happens thus (the explanation is this):—a bright gem can take in an image; not so a heap (lump) of earth. (4)

Syl. Dei.—This is the obstruction in learning (you referred to).

A'treyî—There is another too.

Syl. Dei.—Which is the other one?

A'treyî—Thereafter once the Bráhmaṇa sage went to the river Tamasá to bathe (and offer the midday prayers). There he saw that one out of a pair of herons was being shot by a hunter. He then uttered the divine words of blameless composition, which suddenly manifested themselves to him and which took the form of the Anushṭubh metre—

"Thou shalt not obtain a position of honour, O fowler, for everlasting years, since thou hast killed one of the pair of the herons, maddened with passion."* (5)

Syl. Dei.—Wonderful! A new revelation of metre different from that of the Veda.

A'treyî—Then just at the time, the divine Brahmá, the procreator of beings, appearing before the revered sage to whom Brahma in the form of speech had been revealed, said—"Sage, thou art enlightened in the *S'abda* from of Brahma; describe, therefore, the life of Ràma. The prophetic eye of thy genius will have its vision never obstructed; thou

* Side-meaning—Lord of Lakshmî (Râma), thou hast obtained eternal glory, since thou didst kill one (Râvaṇa) of the pair of Rákshasas stupefied by Love.

art the first poet." With these words he vanished. Thereafter the venerable son of Prachetas (Válmîki) composed the history of Rámáyaṇa, the first manifestation of Divine speech in that garb in the mortal world.

Syl. Dei.—Ah, then the world has been graced.

A'treyî—Hence it was I said that there was a hindrance to our study.

Syl. Dei.—That is right.

A'treyî—I have had rest, friend. Now tell me the way to the hermitage of Agastya.

Syl Dei.—Start, from here enter the Pañchavaṭî and proceed on your way by the bank of the Godávarî.

A'treyí—(*With tears*). Can this be the penance-forest, this the Pañchavaṭí, and this river too the Godávarî? Is this mountain Prasravaṇa and thou Vásantí, the nymph of the forest?

Syl. Dei.—Everything is as you mention it.

A'treyî—Alas, child Jânakí,

This is the number of thy dear associates, theme of your occasional talks, which now being seen actually presents thee to our view though existing only in name. (6)

Va'santî—(*With alarm, to herself*). What, 'existing in name' she said! (*Aloud*). Revered lady, what great misfortune has befallen Queen Sîtá?

A'treyí—Not only a great misfortune but with calumny too! (*Whispers in her ear*). Thus, thus.

Va's.—Alas, what a cruel blow of fate!

A'tre.—Friend, take heart, take heart.

Va's.—Alas, dear friend, alas, noble lady! That such should be your lot! O friend, Râma! Or enough of you. Noble A'treyî, have you any intelligence as to what became of Queen Sîtâ after Lakahmaṇa abandoned her and returned from the forest?

A'tre.—No, no intelligence whatsoever.

Va's.—Oh, misery! How could this have happened when the eminent descendants of Raghu were guided by Arundhatî and Vasishṭha and the aged Queens were still alive?

A'tre.—The elder persons were at the hermitage of Ṛishyaśṛiṅga then. Now that sacrificial session lasting for twelve years has been concluded. Ṛishyaśṛiṅga bade farewell to all the elders having duly honoured them. Then the revered Arundhatî said that she would not go to Ayodhyâ, destitute as it was then of her daughter-in-law. To this the mothers of Râma gave their consent. And the venerable Vasishṭha, in approval of the same, clearly declared that they would go to the hermitage of Vâlmîki and live there.

VA'S.—Now, how is the king engaged at present?

A'TRE.—That king has commenced a horse-sacrifice.

VA'S.—Oh, fie! He has married too?

A'TRE.—Heaven forbid! No, no.

VA'S.—Who then is his consort in the sacrifice?

A'TRE.—A gold image of Sîtá.

VA'S.—How strange, Oh!

Harder even than adamant and softer than a flower are the hearts of super-eminent persons; whs can correctly guage them? (7)

A'TRE.—The sacrificial horse consecreted by Vâmadeva has been let loose and its guardians appointed according to the sacred rules. Chandraketu, the son of Lakshmaṇa, initiated into the use of the heavenly weapons, has been sent as their commander, accompanied by a force composed of the four divisions.

VA'S.—(*With tears of affection and wonder*). Even the son of Prince Lakshmaṇa! O mother, I have got new life now.

A'TRE.—About this time a Brâhmaṇa threw the body of his dead son before the gate of the king's palace, and, beating his bosom, loudly proclaimed an outrage upon the Bráhmaṇas. Then, while compassionate Râma was reflecting upon some fault of his own, knowing as he did that without some misconduct on the part of the king no premature death could happen among the subjects, an aerial voice was heard all at once.

"A Śúdra, S'ambúka by name, has been practising religious austerities on the earth; you ought to cut off his head, O Ráma; kill him and restore the Bráhmaṇa to life." (8)

As soon as he heard this, the lord of the earth, with a drawn sword in hand, ascended the aerial vehicle Pushpaka and began to move in all quarters and bye-quarters in search of the Śûdra ascetic.

VA'S.—A smoke-inhaling Śûdra, S'ambúka by name, practises penance in this very Janasthána. Can it be that noble Ráma may once more grace this forest?

A'TRE.—Friend, I go now.

VA'S.—Revered A'treyî, be it so; but the day has far advanced.

The trees on the banks having nests of birds on them are honouring the Godávarí with their flowers having their stems loosened by the heat and dropping down on account of the violent shaking caused by the elephants rubbing their itching temples against them, the trees, the barks of which have insects drawn out of them with their beaks by birds scratching on them (for food) in the shade, and on which there are flocks of wearied pigeons and the wild fowls that are cooing. (9)

(They walk about and depart).

END OF THE PURE VISHKAMBHAKA.

(Enter Râma seated in his Pushpaka, his sword raised with a feeling of compassion).

RA'MA—

O right hand, strike the sword on the S'ûdra ascetic that the dead boy of the Bráhmaṇa might revive: thou art a limb of Ráma clever (able) enough to exile Sîtá languishing under the very heavy load of the fœtus; whence couldst thou have mercy? (10)

(Striking with great reluctance). I have done a deed befitting Ráma. I hope the Bráhmaṇa boy will come back to life.

(Enter a HEAVENLY PERSON*).*

HEA. PER.—Victory, victory to the king!

When you who can grant protection even against Yama have been the punisher, that (Bráhmaṇa) boy has revived while I am thus exalted. Behold in me Śambûka bowing his head to your feet. Even death at the hands of the good leads to salvation. (11)

RA'MA—Both the events please us. Do you then enjoy the reward of your austere penance.

May those luminous worlds, full of bliss, called the Vairâjas, be thine for ever—the worlds where there are self-rejoicings and celestial pleasures and where there are also holy treasures. (12)

S'A.—All this greatness is due to your favour only. Of what avail is penance here? Or rather, my penance has done me a great service.

That you, the lord of beings and protector, who ought to be sought after in this world, have come here seeking me, a poor *Vṛishala*, having traversed hundreds of Yojanas, is the favour of penance ; or else, where was the chance of your coming again from Ayodhyā to this Daṇḍaka forest ? (13)

RA'MA—What, can this be Daṇḍakā ? (*Casting a glance around*). How now !

Here of a lovely dark and there arid with their frightful extent, filling up the quarters at different places with the murmur of brooks and interspersed with holy places, hermitages, hills, rivers, valleys and woods—these are the tracts of the Daṇḍaká forest meeting my view, the sites of which have been familiar to me. (14)

S'A.—This is Daṇḍakā assuredly. While living here, your lordship, formerly, verily

Killed in battle fourteen thousand demons, given to cruel practices, and three othess, Khara, Dúshaṇa and Trimúrdhan. (15)

By which act even people of the country, of my stamp, can roam fearlessly in this Janasthána, the abode of hermits.

RA'MA—This is not only Daṇḍaká, but Janasthâna also !

S'A.—Certainly. These are, verily, the vast forests on the borders of Janasthána stretching in the southren direction, the caverns of the mountains in which are crowded with the herds of furious and fierce beasts (of prey) and which (thereby) cause the hair to stand on end.

Moreover,

In some places noiseless and calm, in others resounding with the frightful roar of beasts, having wild fires enkindled by the breathings of hideous huge snakes lying down at pleasure and with a little water sparkling in the ravines, these are the borders (of the forests) wherein the thirsty lizards are drinking the sweat of monstrous pythons. (16)

R'AMA—

I see Janasthâna, once the abode of Khara, and (with it) behold the past occurrences, as if they were happening now before my eyes. (17)

(*Looking all around*). The princess of Videha was entirely fond of delightful gardens (or, groves) ; and these are those dreary (pathless) woods ! What can be more frightful than this ? (*With tears*).

"I will live with you in the forests fragrant with honey (floral juice)"—thus she said and did take delight in these; of that sort (so deep) was that love of hers. (18)

(A beloved person) without doing anything whatever, removes sorrows by delights. Whoever is a beloved person of one, that is his indescribable treasure. (19)

S'AMB.—Then enough of these which are painful to approach. May your noble self now see these peaceful and majestic middle forests which are surrounded by border-regions possessing the soft (gentle) beauty of the necks of peacocks screaming through passion, which are adorned with the clusters of young trees affording dark thick shade and densely situated, and which have in them the herds of deer of different species roaming fearlessly (*lit.* that are not agitated with fear).

Here flow the brooks with their crystalline waters cool and scented with the flowers of the *Vánîra* creepers bending under the impassioned birds perching on them, and with their many branches resounding as they stumble through the clusters of Jambû trees dark with the ripened wealth of their berries. (20)

Moreover,

Herein the growls of young bears living in the caves being prolonged (or swelling) by their echoes attain intensity; and the cool, pungent, but fragrant odour of the exudations from the joints of the S'allakî trees broken and scattered about by the elephants spreads all round. (21)

RA'MA—(*Checking his tears*). Friend, may thy path be favourable to you! Mayest thou attain the path of gods that thou mayest reach the worlds of bliss!

S'AMB.—Having first saluted the sage Agastya, the ancient expounder of Brahma, I will enter the everlasting region

RA'MA—

To-day I have seen again the very same forest wherein we formerly lived for a long time, both as hermits and householders, devoted to our proper duties and also tasting the flavour of worldly pleasures. (22)

These are the very mountains with peacocks uttering their notes; these are the same forest-sites with impassioned deer therein; and these two are the very same river-banks lined with the beautiful *Vañjula* creepers and the densely growing dark reeds (*Nichulas*). (23)

And that mountain here which can be discerned from afar, looking like a line of clouds (or, which looks like &c. although in the vicinity), that is Prasravaṇa, where the Godâvarî flows by. (24)

On the towering peak of this very mountain, the king of Vultures had his residence; and at its foot we two lived happily in those (so very well remembered) leafy huts, there, where the wood region is delightful on account of the singing birds warbling in it, the beauty of its dark trees being reflected in the waters of the Godávarî. (25)

Here, therefore, must be that Pañchavatî where there are spots which, on account of our long stay there, were the witnesses of our manifold acts of excessive confidence (familiarity), and where also dwells a forest-nymph, Vàsantí by name, a dear friend of my beloved.

Like dreadful venom circulating about, which begins to operate after a long time with virulence, or like the infixed point of an arrow shaken off by some force (or, somehow when in motion), or like an ulcer with flesh overgrown, bursting in the vital part of the heart, my grief, being intensified, torments me afresh and distracts me. (26)

Yet I will see these tracts, once so familiar to me. (*Observing carefully*). Oh, how the situation of the ground has changed! For,

Where formerly there was the current of a river, there is now a sandy bank; the density and the thinness of trees have been exchanged; seen after a very long time, I think the forest to be a different one: but the situation of the mountains assures me that it is the same. (27)

On, my love for the Pañchavaṭî forcibly draws me to it though I wish to avoid it. (*Feelingly*).

How can wicked Ràma, after having destroyed his beloved, now alone visit that Pañchavaṭî or go away without having honoured it, wherein he passed those days in her company as if in his own house, and with protracted talks upon his adventures in which he ever lived afterwards. (28)

(*Enter* S'AMBU'KA).

S'AMB.—Victory to Your Majesty! My lord, the venerable Agastya, having heard of your near presence from me, sends you this message:—"The good Lopàmudrá, having made preparations for the auspicious rites to be performed at the time of your alighting from the heavenly car, has been waiting for you; and with her all the sages, too. You should, therefore, honour us with your visit. You can then go back to your country in the swift Pushpaka car and be ready for the horse-sacrifice."

RA'MA—As the venerable sage commands.

S'AMB.—Your lordship then may direct the Pushpaka hither.

RA'MA—(*Guiding the* Pushpaka *that way*). Revered Pañchavaṭî, forgive Ràma this momentary transgression of duty on account of his regard for the elders.

S'AMB.—See, see, my lord.

This is the mountain *Krauñchâvata* with its flights of crows sitting silent in the vast clumps of the bamboo trees resounding with the hootings of the flocks of owls* crying in their bowery homes; upon this, frightened by the notes of the peacocks roaming about, the snakes coil higher round the branches of the old sandal trees. (29)

Moreover,

These are those (well-known) southern mountains with their peaks darkened by the clouds resting on their points, and with the waters of the Godávarî roaring and splashing in their caves; and these are those holy confluences of rivers with deep waters awful with the tumult of the waves rushing forth in wild confusion on account of their dashing against one another. (30)

(*Exeunt Both*).

END OF ACT II., STYLED

'The Entrance into the Pañchavaṭî.'

ACT III.

(*Enter* TWO RIVERS).

ONE—Friend, Muralà, why do you seem to be in a hurry?

MURALA'—Friend Tamasà, I am sent by Lopàmudrá, the wife of the venerable Agastya, to Godàvarî, the best of rivers,

---

* With the reading उभ्र—owls in their rumbling, bowery homes.

to deliver this message:—You know that after his abandonment of our daughter-in-law (Sîtà),

Ráma's feeling of sorrow, which does not break out on account of his gravity but which causes poignant pain inside, is like the boiling (of a drug) in a closed pot. (1)

In consequence of the torment caused by the continuous grief arising from the befalling of the calamity on a beloved person of that sort (*i.e.*, Sítà), and which has gone to excess, good Ráma is now exceedingly emaciated. My heart trembled within me to its root when I saw him. Now, as he will be returning, dear Ráma is sure to see those spots in the Pañchavaṭí, which were the witnesses of his confidential sports in the company of his wife. While good Ràma is there, we have to fear great risks of his straying from his nature at every step in his present condition, owing to the violent agitation caused by his excessive and wide-reaching grief, though he is naturally firm-minded. Venerable Godâvarî, you should, therefore, be watchful in that case (be attentive to him)

Do you then refresh the soul (spirits) of Ràma every time he swoons, by the breezes (coming) from your waves, gently, gently urged forth, cool by the particles of the spray (of water) and wafting with them the odours of the lotus-filaments. (2)

TAMASA'—(Such) kind attention is but worthy of her affection. But there is at hand to-day a radical means of restoring Ràma to life.

MURALA'—How do you mean ?

TAMASA'—Listen. When formerly, as I hear, Laskhmaṇa returned from the skirt of the penance-grove of Vàlmîki having left her there, Queen Sîta, when she began to suffer from the pangs of travail, threw herself into the stream of the Ganges on account of the poignancy of the pain. Just there and then she gave birth to twin sons. There she was attended upon by the divine Pṛithvî and Bhâgîrathi and taken to the nether world. The goddess Gaṅgà entrutsted the two boys, when they had been weaned from the breast, to the great sage Pràchetasa in person.

MURALA'—(*With astonishment*).

Even the adverse turn of fortune of such persons proves ery wonderful, since divine personages like these come to minister to their wants. (3)

Tamasa'—Now the revered Bhàgírathí, having heard from the lips of Sarayú of the expected visit of dear Ràma to Janasthàna in connexion with the S'ambúka incident, had the same apprehension which the revered Lopàmudrá had already entertained in her affection, and came, together with Sitá, to Godàvarí on the plea of some domestic customary observance.

Murala'—It was a wise forethought on the part of the revered Bhàgírathî. For, verily, as long as good Ràma was in his capital, enaged in the various affairs conducive to the prosperity of the world, his internal distractions were checked. But, as he is not so occupied now and has no other companion but his grief, his entrance into the Pañchavaṭî will be a serious calamity. How is queen Sîtà then to comfort Ràma?

Tamasa'—Having this object in view the revered Bhàgîrathí said to her—'Child Sitā, born of the sacrificial ground, to-day is to be the cermony of tying the auspicious knot corresponding to the twelfth year of the long-lived Kus'a and Lava. Do thou, therefore, worship, with flowers collected with thy own hands, thy primeval father-in-law, the divine Sun, the progenitor of such an extensive race of royal sages, taking its name after Manu, and the destroyer of sin. Through my favour, even the sylvan deities shall not see thee moving on the earth, much less the mortals.' To me also she said—'Tamasá, child Jánakî has already a great affection for thee; be thou, therefore, her companion.' I will, therefore, act according to her bidding.

Murala'—I, too, will communicate this account to the revered Lopámudrá. I think good Ràma has arrived, too.

Tamasa'—There, having issued from a pool of the Godàvarî, is she,

The daughter of Janaka, her countenance charming owing to its pallid and emaciated cheeks and her loosened braids waving about, coming to the wood like the very image of pity, or rather like the pain of separation incarnate. (4)

Murala'—Here, indeed, is she,

Like a pretty sprout forcibly plucked off from its stem, the terrible and long grief, drying up the flower of her heart, parches up her very pale and emaciated body, as does the autumnal sun the innermost leaf of the Ketaka flower. (5)

(They turn round and exeunt).

Pure Vishkambhaka.

(*Behind the Scenes*).

A great mishap, a great mishap!

(*Enter* Sìtà *engaged in gathering flowers, listening with pity and anxiety*).

SÎTA'—Ah, I think it is my dear friend Vàsantî that speaks.

(*Again behind the Scenes*).

That young one of an elephant, which was formerly reared by queen Sîtà (by being fed), as he danced before her, with the tips of tender leaves of the Śallakî tree gathered with her own hands—

SÎTA'—What of him?

(*Again behind the Scenes*).

That same one (now a grown-up elephant) has been attacked through pride and engaged by another powerful lordly elephant as he was sporting with his mate in the water. (6)

SÎTA'—(*In confusion*; *going forward a few steps*). Save, my lord, save that boy of mine. (*Gesticulating recollection with dejection*). Alas, alas! Unfortunate that I am, the same words to which I had been familiar for a long time stand foremost on my lips (*lit.* closely follow me) at the sight of the Pañchavatî. Alas, my lord! (*She faints*).

(*Enter* TAMASA').

TAMA.—Cheer up, child, cheer up.

O sovereign of balloons, halt just here.

SÎTA'—(*Having come back to her senses*; *with fear and joy*). Ah, whence is this sound of words deep and loud like the rumbling of water-laden clouds, which, filling up the cavities of my ears, at once inspires even me, an unlucky creature, with life!

TAMASA'—(*With tears of affection*). O child,

Why are you thus agitated and anxious at a sound indistinct and coming from an unknown source, like a peahen at (the rumbling) of a cloud? (7)

SÎTA'—O revered one, how do you call it indistinct? I for myself recognized from correspondence of the voice that it was my lord who spoke.

TAMASA'—I hear that the King of the Ikshvàku race has come to Janasthàna to punish, as the rumour goes, the Śûdra ascetic.

Sîta'—I am glad to see that the King does not neglect his royal duties.

(*Behind the Scenes*).

These are the slopes of the mountain in the vicinity of which flows the Godàvarî, abounding in rills and caverns, where even the trees and the deer were my relations and whereon I dwelt for a long time in the company of my beloved. (8)

Sîta'—(*Looking forth*). What ho ! It is my lord himself with a body weak, emaciated and pale like the disc of the moon at dawn, and recognizable only by his gentle and serene majesty. Revered Tamasá, support me. (*She falls into the arms of* Tamasa' *and faints*).

Tamasa'—(*Supporting her*). Daughter, take heart, take heart.

(*Behind the Scenes*).

By this sight of the Pañchavaṭî,

A stupor, as though it were a column of smoke of the fire of my grief (so long) concealed within but about to break out fiercely to-day, envelops me at first. (9)

O my dear Jánakî !

Tam.—This it is that was feared by the elders.

Sîta'—(*Coming to herself*). Oh, how is this !

(*Again behind the Scenes*).

O Queen, my beloved companion during my residence in the Daṇḍaka forest, and Princess of Videha ! (*Swoons*).

Sîta'—Alas, alas, ! Having called out to me, a cursed being, my lord has swooned, his dark lotus-eyes being closed. Alas, how he is stretched on the ground helplessly on account of his breath being suspended ! Save, save, O revered Tamasà; call him back to life.

Tamasa'—

Rather you yourself, O gentle princess, restore the lord of the world to life; for the touch of your hand is dear to him, and in it he takes extreme delight. (10)

Sîta'—Come what may; I will act as your reverence says. (*Exit in haste*).

(*Then is discovered* Ra'ma *fallen on the ground cheering and reviving being touch d by* Sîta' *in tears*).

Sîta'—(*Somewhat rejoiced*). I think the life of the three worlds has come back.

RA'MA—Oh, joy, what can this be!

Can this be a trickling all round (of the balmy juice) of the leaves of Harichandana (the heavenly tree or a kind of fragrant sandal), or is this a sprinkling resulting from (with the quintessence of) the sproutlike lunar rays being squeezed, or is this the juice of the vivifying drug re-animating my scorched life, that is besprinkled over my heart! (11)

Moreover,

This is certainly the same touch formerly experienced by me that at once revived and lulled my heart, and which now, having quickly dispelled my swoon caused by grief, benumbs my body again by its gladdening influence. (12)

SÎTA'—(*Withdrawing, with trepidation and fear*). This much even is much for me at present.

RA'MA—(*Siting up*). Can it not be that I am favoured by the queen Sîtâ in the kindness of her heart!

SÎTA'—Oh, fie! Will my lord now seek me?

RA'MA—Well, let me see.

SÎTA'—Revered Tamasà, let us move away. If the king sees me he will be more angry with me for having approached him without leave.

TAM.—O my child, by the favour of Bhàgîrathî you are invisible even to the wood-nymphs.

SÎTA'—Ah, I remember it, it is so.

RA'MA—O dear Jànakî!

SÎTA'—(*Faltering through emotion*). My lord, this your speech is not in accord with (against) what has taken place. (*With tears*). Or rather, why should I, steel-hearted, be relentless towards my lord whose sight is difficult and not possible to obtain even in another life, who has been affectionate just towards me, an unfortunate woman and has thus spoken? I know his heart and he knows mine.

RA'MA—(*Looking all round, in despair*). Alas, there is nothing here.

SÎTA'—Venerable Tamasà, though he abandoned me without any cause in that way, yet I know not what the feelings of my heart are when I see him in this plight.

TAMASA'—I know them, child, I know them.

Indifferent through despair, ruffled by harsh treatment, paralysed as it were on account of the sudden meeting in this long separation, pleased by its inherent goodness, and deeply affected by the touching words of your husband, your heart appears to melt with love, as it were, at this moment. (13)

RA'MA—Queen,

Your touch, cooling and delightful through affection, as though it were your favour incarnate, still gladdens me; but where are you yourself, O delightful one? (14)

SíTA'—These, indeed, are the mellifluous utterances of my lord, disclosing an unfathomable depth of affection and overflowing with delight, by hearing (or, having confidence in) which I highly esteem my existence though (rendered) painful by the dart of unjust (*lit.* causeless) abandonment.

RA'MA—Or whence can my beloved be here! Surely this must be Ràma's delusion caused by his cleverness in constantly entertaining thoughts about her.

(*Behind the Scenes*).

Oh, a great calamity! a great calamity! (*Then is heard the first half of the stanza 'Whom* QUEEN SíTA', *with handfuls &c.'*).

RA'MA—(*With sympathy and eagerness*). What of him?

(*Again behind the Scenes, the second half, 'With his mate &c.' is heard*).

SíTA'—Who will now go to his rescue!

RA'MA—Where is he, where is that wicked one, that attacks the fondling of my dear wife, with his mate? (*He rises*).

(*Enter* VA'SANTî *in flurry*).

VA'S.—How, His Majesty Ráma (the delight of the Raghu race)!

SîTA'—Ah, my dear friend Vàsantî!

VA'S.—Victory to Your Majesty!

RA'MA—(*Eying her*). Holloa! Vásantî, my wife's dear companion!

VA'S.—Sire, make haste, make haste. Descend from here to the Godàvarî by the Sítátírtha (stairs sacred to Sítà) lying to the south of Jaṭàyu's peak and rescue the child of the Queen.

SíTA'—Alas, father Jaṭàyu, dreary appears this Janasthána without you.

RA'MA—Oh, these allusions to past events do, indeed, cut my heart to the quick.

VA'S.—This way, my lord, this way.

SÎTA'—Revered lady, do you think even the sylvan deities do not see me?

TAMASA'—O child, the divine power of the goddess Mandâkinî surpasses that of all others; why do you entertain a doubt then?

SÎTA'—Let us follow them then. (*They then walk round*).

RA'MA—Revered Godâvarî, I bow to thee.

VA'S.—(*Observing*). Sire, rejoice at the victory won by the Queen's son with his mate.

RA'MA—Let my boy of long life ever triumph.

SÎTA'—Oh, my dear boy has turned out such.

RA'MA—O Queen, you are to be congratulated.

This your son, O fair-bodied one, now a subduer of rut-shedding elephants, who, with his tender tusk smooth like the shoots of a lotus-stalk just growing, used to pull off the Lavalî-sprout from the root of your ear, has become the abode of everything that is a blessing in his blooming youth. (15)

SÎTA'—May this my son live long and in the inseparable company of this his lovely mate.

RA'MA—Friend Vâsantî, see, see. Our dear son has even learnt the art of pleasing his mate.

Every time she finished the repast of the mouthfuls of lotus-stalks plucked off in sport he gave her trunkfuls of water scented with the blooming lotuses; he afterwards besprinkled her with the shower of spray from his trunk, and then at the end (of the bath) he held over her, through affection, a lotus-leaf with a straight stalk as an umbrella. (16)

SÎTA'—Revered Tamasâ, as for this (elephant) he has grown so much; but I do not know how much those my sons, Kuśa and Lava, have grown by this time.

TAMA.—As this is, so they must be too.

SÎTA'—So unlucky I am that I suffer continual separation not only from my lord but also from my two sons.

TAMA.—This was fated.

SÎTA'—Or, why have I given birth to sons, since my lord did not kiss their clean lotus-like faces, such as they are, with their cheeks bright on account of their teeth, a little sparse, tender, and white with a smile continuously blooming on them, accompanied by sweet lisping, and decked with locks?

TAM.—This will come to pass by the favour of the gods.

SíTA'—Revered Tamasâ, my breasts are heaving and overflowing with milk as I am thus put in mind of my sons, and their father too is close by. I have thus become a worldly woman for a moment.

TAMA.—Need this be said! A child is, indeed, the highest pitch of the excess of love; it is the strongest link that connects the parents.

On account of its being the abode (centre) of their affection, a child is the one knot of joy that unites the principles of the hearts of the husband and wife. (17)

VA's.—May your lordship see this way too.

Here, perched on the Kadamba tree, with his crest upraised and looking like a crown of gems, is shrieking in the company of his mate that peacock whom with new-fledged feathers beautifully waving, your beloved wife nourished day by day. (18)

SíTA'—(*With eagerness and tears of affection*). It is he, it is he!

RA'MA—Revel, my boy, revel.

SîTA'—Do so.

RA'MA—

With a heart melting with affection do I remember you as a son, as my fair wife made you dance to the beatings of her tender (*lit.* sprout-like) hands, enhancing by the quick and clever play of her eye-brows the beauty of her eyes that rolled round in their lids (sockets) as you moved circuitously. (19)

Oh, even animals regard familiarity.

This *Kadamba* tree displaying a few flowers was reared by my beloved.

SîTA'—(*Observing carefully*). Well has my lord recognized it!

RA'MA—

This mountain-peacock remembers the queen since he feels great delight on it as in the company of a relative. (20)

V'AS.—Please take your seat here, Sire.

(RA'MA *sits down*).

VA's.—This is the same stone-slab situated in the middle of the plantain-grove which served as a bed to you in the company of your beloved; and since, seated on this, Sitâ often gave grass to these deer, they do not leave it. (21)

RA'MA—I cannot bear to look at this even.

(*So he weeps and sits elsewhere*).

SÎTA'—Friend Vâsanti, what is this that you have done by showing this to my lord and to me! Alas, alas! My lord is the same; this is the very Pañchavaṭî forest; this is the same dear Vásantî; these are the very (quite unaltered) sites in the forest of the Godâvarí, the witnesses of our various confidential sports; these are the same deer, birds and trees, that were just like children (to us); and I, too, am the same: and yet all this though seen has ceased to exist, as it were, for me, a luckless creature! Oh, such is the revolution that the world has undergone (in my case)!!

VA'S.—Dear Sítá, how don't you see the condition of Ráma:–

He, who giving delight to our eyes by his limbs, lovely like a fresh(-blown) blue lotus, was ever new to us though seen at pleasure and continually; even he, with his senses enfeebled, his complexion turned pale and his body emaciated through grief can now be recognized but with great difficulty as the same: and yet he is charming to the sight. (22)

SÎTA'—I see it, friend, I see it.

TAMASA'—Enjoy the sight of your husband.

SÎTA'—Oh, Destiny! Who had imagined even in a dream that he would be separated from me and I from him! I will, therefore, look, for a while, as much as my tears will allow, at my kind husband as if come from a second existence. (*So she remains gazing upon him*).

TAMASA'—(*Clasping her, with tears*).

Pouring down tears of joy and grief that gush forth in floods, and wide-opened and dilated through vehement longing, your sight, like a stream of milk, charming by its excessive whiteness, seems to bathe the lord of your heart by shedding upon him a rain of affection. (23)

VA'S.—

Let the trees dripping floral juice offer their oblation of flowers and fruits; let the sylvan zephyrs blow, wafting the sweet odour of blooming lotuses; and let the birds with melodious voices incessantly pour forth their sweet songs; for here has king Ráma come again in person to this wood.

RA'MA—Come, dear Vâsantî; please sit down here. (24)

VA'S.—(*Sitting, tearfully*). Sire, is prince Lakshmana well?

RA'MA—(*Not hearing it*).

When I see the trees, birds and fawns whom the princess of Mithilá reared with water, wild rice and grass (respectively), offered with her own lotus-like hands, a certain emotion rises within me as if it were the liquid of my heart and capable of breaking even a stone. (25)

VA'S.—Great King, I ask if prince Lakshmana is quite well.

RA'MA—(*To himself*). Ah, she calls me 'great king'; this is a cold title of address; while her question, asked in a faltering voice, regards Lakshmaṇa's welfare only. So I think she is acquainted with the Sîtâ affair. (*Aloud*). Oh yes, my boy is all right.

VA'S.—(*Weeping*). My lord, what more can I say? You are ruthless.

SÎTA'—Friend Vásantî, why should you speak in this strain? My lord deserves kind treatment at the hands of all, and particularly at my dear friend's.

VA'S.—

You are my life, you are my second heart; you are the moonlight to my eyes and the ambrosia to my limbs-You flattered your guileless wife with hundreds of such loving expressions, and *her* you--Or peace! Why talk more of this? (26) (*She faints*).

TAMASA'—It is but natural that she should thus break off in her speech and faint.

RA'MA—Take courage, friend, take courage.

VA'S.—(*Coming to herself*). Why then was this unworthy act done by your lordship?

SÎTA'—Desist Vâsantî, desist from this.

RA'MA—Because people would not bear it.

VA'S.—For what reason?

RA'MA—They themselves know something.

TAMA.—The rebuke comes too late.

VA'S.—O you hard-hearted one, fame is dear to you, as I hear; but what infamy, I ask, can be more dreadful than this? What became of the fawn-eyed maid in the wilderness? Tell me, my lord—what do you think of her fate? (27)

SÎTA'—You yourself, dear Vásantî, are hard-hearted and ruthless, since you thus inflame my lord already burning with grief.

TAMA.—It is her affection and grief that speak thus.

RA'MA—Friend what else could I think?

Of her with eyes quickly rolling like those of a frightened fawn, one year old, and dull by the burden of her throbbing fœtus, the slender bodily frame, made of moonlight as it were and soft like a tender young lotus-stalk, must surely have been destroyed by beasts of prey. (28)

SÎTA'—I am alive, my husband, here I am alive.

RA'MA—Oh, my dear Jánakî!

SÎTA'—Alas! Alas! My husband weeps bitterly (giving free vent to his grief) as if he is another (an ordinary) man.

TAMASA'—Child, this is but proper; people under affliction must extinguish their grief (seek relief by weeping).

When a tank is full to the brim an outlet is the only remedy. When the mind is agitated (tossed) by sorrow it is sustained only by lamentations. (29)

This is especially the case with dear Râma to whom life has been exceedingly painful in many ways.

With an attentive mind he has to govern this world according to the rules of administration; his grief for his dear wife withers his body as heat does a flower; having himself abandoned her he cannot easily have the relief coming from lamentation; but to-day he can breathe a sigh of relief and thus lamentation is, indeed, a gain to him. (30)

RA'MA—What misery, Oh!

My heart breaks under its heavy anguish, but does not go into twain; my languid frame falls a victim to (*lit.* bears) swoons, but leaves not consciousness; the inward fire (of sorrow) inflames my body, but parts not life asunder. (31)

SÎTA'—Your state is such.

RA'MA—O ye citizens and countrymen!

Verily you did not approve of the queen's staying in my house and, therefore, I abandoned her in a forest like straw; nor did I mourn her loss. But the various objects of long familiarity move me; and so being helpless, I weep to-day; please forgive me. (32)

VA'S.—(*To herself*). His excess of grief has reached its climax. (*Aloud*). My lord, have recourse to courage now, when matters have already taken their turn.

RA'MA—Friend, what means this talk of courage?

It is the twelfth year since the world was bereft of Sîtá; her very name has been blotted out; and yet it is not that Rama has ceased to exist. (33)

Sîta'—These words of my husband make me faint (with emotion).

Tama.—Just so, my child.

So full of affection and yet terrible with grief, these cannot be highly gratifying words; these are the showers of honey that pour upon you but mixed with (burning) poison. (34)

Ra'ma—O Vásantî, have I not, indeed,

Borne the dart of sorrow in my heart causing poignant pain and corroding the vital parts, like a red-hot dart driven athwart into my breast or the venomous bite of a serpent? (35)

Sîta'—Thus have I, luckless that I am, again become a source of affliction to my lord!

Ra'ma—Though I have thus manned my heart so that it should remain perfectly at rest, yet the agitation now caused in me at the sight of the various dear and familiar objects is quite irresistible.

Whatever effort I, somehow, put forth to check the outburst of the sentiment of grief set in wild commotion, undermining that, some strange emotion forcibly spreads over (overpowers) me, as the flood of water rushing with irresistible fury does a dam of sand. (36)

Sîta'—My heart is somehow bewildered, its own sorrows being forgotten, on account of the stirring of my husband's grief, the fury of which is irresistible and terrible.

V'as.—(*To herself*). His Majesty has got into a painful condition. I will, therefore, change the topic (divert his attention). (*Aloud*). Let Your Majesty honour these spots of Janasthâna of long familiarity by a look at them.

Ra'ma—Just as you say. (*With these words he rises and walks round*).

Sîta'—I think the remedy thought of by my dear friend to divert his grief will simply inflame it.

Va's.—(*Pitifully*). Sire, sire.

In this very bower of creepers you waited for her with your eyes directed to (fixed on) her path; while she tarried long on the sandy-bank of the Godâvarí, her curiosity being excited by (watching) the swans; and, when while returning she saw that you appeared to be displeased, through timidity she folded her hands gracefully in salutation which looked like a lotus-bud. (37)

SÎTA'—You are cruel, Vásantî, you are cruel; since by thus constantly shaking the dart (of grief) thrust deep into the vital part of the heart you torture me, unlucky woman, and my lord, again and again.

RA'MA—O ruthless Jànakí, you appear to be present here and there and yet you do not take compassion on me.

Alas, alas, my Queen! My heart bursts; the frame of my body gives way (falls to pieces); I deem the world a void: I burn from within with an ever-consuming flame; my inward soul, writhing with pain and helpless, seems to sinks into impenetrable darkness; and a universal stupor paralyses all my senses; what am I, an ill-starred being, to do? (38). (*Faints*).

SÎTA'—Woe, woe! My husband has swooned again.

VA's—Compose yourself, sire, compose yourself.

SÎTA'—My dear, alas, I am undone since on account of me, a luckless creature, there again and again comes over you, who are the support of the welfare of the whole world of the living, a change of state, which is terrible by its endangering your life.

TAMA.—Child, take cheer, take cheer. Again the touch of your hand alone is the remedy for reviving dear Ràma.

VA's.—How does he not recover yet! O my dear friend Sìtà, where are you? Restore to consciousness the lord of your life.

(SÎTA' *hurriedly approaches* RA'MA *and touches him on the heart and the forehead*).

VA's.—O joy (*lit.* fortunately), dear Ràma has regained consciousness.

RA'MA—

Anointing the constituents of my body from within as well as from without with ointments formed of nectar as it were, a pleasant touch suddenly calling me back to life brings on an insensibility of a different nature, due to joy. (39).

(*His eyes still closed in felicity*). Dear Vásantî, fortune now smiles upon you.

VA's.—How, sire?

RA'MA—Friend, what else? Jànakî is again with me.

VA's.—Ah, lord Râma, where is she?

RA'MA—(*Shows that he experiences her felicitous touch*) Lo, here she is before me.

VA'S.—Alas, my lord, why do you burn me, luckless that I am, with these ravings, terrible because of their cutting me to the quick, when I have been already consumed by the fire of grief?

SÎTA'—I wish to withdraw. But then this my hand, which is perspiring and lying about helplessly and which trembles continuously, refuses, as it were, to obey me, being as if held fast by adamantine glue by the touch of my lord which is gladdening and refreshing on account of long attachment and which at once dispels my torment though long and agonising.

RA'MA—Friend, how can you talk of ravings?

The hand which, bearing the marriage-bracelet, was formerly seized by me at the time of the nuptial rite, and which had been long familiar to me by its touches to be had at will and cooling like nectar.

SÎTA'—My lord, you are now just the same again.

RA'MA—

That same hand of her, refreshing (or, delight-giving) like a mass of snow and resembling a tender *Lavalî* sprout have I obtained now. (40).

(With these words he grasps it).

SÎTA'—Oh, fie, fie! Infatuated by the touch of my lord I have surely committed a blunder.

RA'MA—Friend Vàsantí, joy has paralysed my senses; excitement has overpowered me; do you, therefore, hold her.

VA'S.—Oh, pity! This is simply insanity.

(SÎTA' *quickly snatches away her hand and withdraws).*

RA'MA—Woe, woe! What a piece of carelessness!

Her benumbed sprout-like (tender) hand, trembling and perspiring has, all of a sudden, slipped off from my hand also turned heavy, shaking and perspiring. (41).

SÎTA'—Alas, alas! With his eyes now unsteady, now fixed, now stupefied and now rolling about, he is not yet able to compose himself.

TAMASA'—*(Looking at* SÎTA' *with affection and a smile of curiosity).*

By the pleasurable sensation caused by the touch of her beloved lord, my dear child is covered with perspiration, with her hair standing on end and bodily frame trembling; thus resembling the twig of a Kadamba tree, with buds shooting out, shaken by the breeze and besprinkled by the new shower. (42).

SÎTA'—(*To herself*). Ah, having thus lost control over my heart I am ashamed in the presence of Tamasà; what will be her thoughts to behold this repudiation and yet such an affection on my part!

RA'MA—(*Casting a glance all round*). Ha, what! She is surely not here. You, heartless Sîtà!

SÎTA'—Really I am heartless, since I yet live though I behold you in this plight.

RA'MA—Where are you, my Queen? Take compassion on me. It does not behove you to abandon me in such a state.

SÎTA'—O my lord, this is the reverse of the truth.

VA'S.—Have mercy on me, my lord. By your own uncommon fortitude compose your heart whose delusion has gone to its excess. Whence could my dear friend be here?

RA'MA—Clearly she is not here. How else could even Vàsantî fail to see her? Could this, indeed, be a dream? But then I am not asleep. How could Ràma get sleep? All things considered, this must be his reverence Delusion, created by my various fancies, that again and again pursues me hard.

SÎTA'—It is I, a cruel woman, that have deluded my lord.

VA'S.—Sire, see, see.

This is the iron-chariot of Ràvaṇa shattered by Jaṭàyu; and yonder are the goblin-faced mules (now) remaining only in skeletons; here it was that your foe cut off the wings of Jaṭàyu from their roots and then jumped into the sky bearing with him Sîtà struggling for liberty, looking like a cloud with lightning flashing within. (43).

SÎTA'—(*With alarm*). My lord, father (Jatàyu) is being slain, and I, too, am carried off. Help, help!

RA'MA—(*Rising in haste*). Thou wretch, the robber of Sîtà, and of my father's life, where canst thou escape?

VA'S.—O my lord, the destructive comet to the race of the demons, is there yet scope for your wrath?

SÎTA'—Ah, I too was out of my wits!

RA'MA—Quite of a different sort is my present calamity!

That (my first) separation from my fair-eyed beloved, which, owing to the existence of means, afforded constant diversion, and gave rise to the sentiment of wonder in the world by the conflicts between the warriors, was to be terminated at the destruction of the enemy; but how is this separation to be borne silently, being endless and also irremediable? (44).

SÎTA'—This separation endless! Alas, I am undone, ill-starred that I am.

RA'MA—Oh, misfortune!

Where are you, my darling, at a place where my friendship with the lord of monkeys avails not; where the valour of the monkeys is of no use; where even the intellect of Jàmbavat comes to naught; to which even the son of Wind can have no access; to which Nala, the son of Viśvakarman, too, cannot open a path, and which is inaccessible even to the shafts of the son of Sumitrà? (45).

SÎTA'—I set a high value on that my former separation.

RA'MA—Dear Vásantî, Ràma's seeing his friends at present will simply cause pain to them; how long shall I keep you weeping then? Allow me, therefore, to go.

SÎTA'—(*Fainting from excitement and embracing* TAMA.). Revered Tamasá, how now, my lord is going, indeed! (*She swoons*).

TAMASA'—Dear child, take comfort, take comfort. To the revered Bhâgîrathî let us go, too, to celebrate with her the auspicious birth-day rites of the long living Kus'a and Lava.

SÎTA'—Revered one, be pleased. Let me behold, even for a moment, the person whose sight it is not easy to obtain.

RA'MA—I have now an associate in my performance of the As'vamedha—

SÎTA'—(*With agitation*). Who, my lord?

RA'MA—A gold image of Sîtâ.

SÎTA'—(*Breathing a sigh of relief, tearfully*). My lord, you are yourself now. Oh, now my lord has extracted the dart of shame arising from my repudiation.

RA'MA—I will divert my eyes smeared with tears just by looking at it.

SÎTA'—Blessed is she who is thus honoured by my lord, and who, diverting him, has become the stay of hope of the world of mortals.

TAM—(*Embracing her with a smile and tears of affection*). O my dear child, you have thus sung your own praise.

SÎTA'—(*Casts down her face with a blush and to herself*). Oh, the revered Tamasâ laughs at me.

VA'S.—This meeting is a great favour upon me. Let your departure now be such as to cause no hindrance in your undertakings.

SÎTA'—Va'santî is now acting adversely towards me.

TAM.—Come, child; let us go.

SÎTA'—(*Sorrowfully*). Let us do so.

TAM.—Or rather, how can you go away, you

Who cannot withdraw even with heart-rending efforts, your eyes which are riveted as it were upon your lord, and are dilated through the desire of seeing him? (46).

SÎTA'—My repeated bow to the lotus-like feet of my lord, a sight of which is obtained with extraordinary merit. (*She swoons*).

VA'S.—Take cheer, dear child, take cheer.

SÎTA'—(*Recovering*) How long can the full moon be seen through enveloping clouds?

TAMA.—How wonderful is the variety of incidents!

The one sentiment of pathos, divided by a diversity of causes, undergoes different variations, as water assumes the different conditions of eddies, bubbles and waves, and it is all, nevertheless, but water. (47).

RA'MA—O prince of balloons, come here.

(*All rise.*)

TAM. & VA'S.—(*To* SÎTA' and RA'MA *respectively*).

May the Earth, the divine river (Ganges) together with divinities like ourselves, that mighty preceptor, the originator of metres, and the sage Vasishṭha, too, accompanied by Arundhatî, grant you blessings that you may attain the highest good! (48).

(*Exeunt omnes*).

END OF ACT III.

ACT IV.

(*Enter* TWO ASCETIC BOYS.)

FIRST—Saudhâtaki, behold the beauty which the venerable Vâlmîki's hermitage presents to-day on account of the numerous guests that have arrived and the special preparations that are being made in their honour. For,

The deer of the penance-grove drinks to his satisfaction the warm and savoury scum of the boiled rice after his mate that has recently brought forth young has drunk of it; while there is diffused all round the aroma of boiling vegetables mixed with jujube fruit, followed gently by the spreading fragrance of the cooked rice mixed with ghee. (1).

Sau.—Welcome are the grey-bearded folks of various descriptions who have been the cause of this special holiday !

First—(*Laughing*). There must be some unusual reason for this your respect for the elders, Saudhâtaki.

Sau.—O Dâṇḍâyana, what is the name of the guest that has come to-day bringing with him a great company of old ladies ?

Da'.—Tush, no joking. This is the revered Vasishṭha that has arrived from the hermitage of Ṛishyasṛiṅga, leading the queens of the great king Das'aratha, with Arundhatî at their head. How do you thus prattle then ?

Sau.—Oh, Vaśishṭha !

Da'.—Yes, he.

Sau.—I, however, thought he was a tiger or a wolf.

Da'.—What disrespectful language this !

Sau.—Since as soon as he came he greedily feasted upon that poor tawny calf.

Da'.—In acceptance of the holy text—"The *Madhuparka* (an offering of curds &c. mixed with honey) should be accompanied with a dish of flesh-meat"—householders offer a heifer, a big bull or a goat to a Śrotriya (a learned Brâhmaṇa) coming as a guest. And the writers on holy law enjoin this duty.

Sau.—Oh, you are caught.

Da'.—How so ?

Sau.—For, when the worshipful Vasishṭha arrived, the heifer was slaughtered. But to-day, when the royal sage Janaka came, the revered Válmîki offered the Madhuparka with simple curds and honey, while he let off the heifer.

Da.—The holy sages prescribe this mode of reception only in the case of those who have not abstained from flesh; but the revered Janaka has abstained from flesh.

Sau.—For what reason ?

Da'.—The moment he heard of the sad calamity that overtook queen Sîtâ, he took to the life of an anchorite; and it is some years since he has been practising religious austerities in the penance-grove of Chandradvîpa.

SAU.—Why then has he come here ?

DA'.—To pay a visit to the revered Vâlmîki, his old and intimate friend.

SAU. —Has he had an interview with his kinsmen to-day or not ?

DA'.—It was only just now that the holy Vasishṭha sent the revered Arundhatî to queen Kausalyâ with the message that she should come in person and see king Janaka.

SAU.—Just as these old folks have met together so let us too join our comrades and enjoy this joyous holiday by playing together. (*So they turn round*).

DA'. —This is the aged royal sage Janaka, an expounder of Brahma, who, having paid his respects to the revered Vâlmîki and Vasishṭha, has now sat down at the root of a tree outside the hermitage ; he,

Who has been consumed by the (fire of) grief for Sîtâ abiding in his heart, like an old tree with fire spreading within. (2).

(*Exeunt Both*).

END OF THE MIXED VISHKAMBHAKA.

(*Enter* JANAKA).

JANAKA—

My grief caused by that serious, bitter, heart-piercing and painful calamity which befell my child, intense and continuous, does not cease even after a long time, but, as if fresh, keeps on cutting my vitals, like a keen, sharp-toothed and new saw. (3).

What hard luck! My accursed body with its vital fluids sapped by old age, unbearable grief and still more by such penances as Parâka, Sâṃtapana and others, and thus deprived of its support, does not fall yet. The sages hold that those who commit suicide are condemned to those worlds where no sun shines, and which are shrouded in eternal darkness. Though many a year has elapsed the agonizing emotion of grief which is clearly felt every moment on account of my constant brooding over it does not cease, as if ever-new. O child, Sîtâ, sprung from holy ground, such has been your doom that I cannot even give free vent to my tears through shame. Alas, daughter,

I remember your lotus-like face, when a child, with its irregular weepings or smiles, with a few tender budding teeth shining therein and with its faltering, incoherent and sweet babbling. (4).

O revered Earth you are very hard-hearted, indeed !

How did you bear, O cruel one, the destruction in that manner of that daughter of yours, whose greatness you, the holy fire, the sages, Vasishtha's wife and Gaṅgá, nay, even the divine Sun, the progenitor of Raghu's race. himself knew ; whom you brought forth as the Goddess of Speech did learning; and who herself was of divine rank like any of the preceding ? (5).

(*Behind the Scenes.*)

This way, this way, your reverence and great Queen.

JANAKA—(*Looking*). Oh here comes Arundhatî, the way being shown by Gṛishṭi. (*Rising*). But whom did he address as 'great Queen' ? (*Observing carefully*). Ah, ah ! How is it that she is my dear friend Kausalyá, the lawfully wedded wife of the great king Das'aratha ? Who can recognize her as the same ?

She was like the goddess of wealth in the palace of Das'aratha ; or, why use a comparison,—the goddess of wealth herself. But alas, Oh pity ! She is altogether changed in obedience to the will of fate, looking like some embodiment of grief. Oh sad end ! (6).

This is another accursed change of conditions.

The sight of that very person, who was, in former days, a festivity incarnate to me, is now as unbearable as salt applied to a sore. (7).

(*Then enter* ARUNDHATÎ, KAUSALYA' *and* KANCHUKÎ).

ARUN.—I say, it was the advice of your preceptor that you should go in person and see Janaka. I too was sent with the same object. What means then this hesitation on your part at every step ?

KANCH.—Queen, I request you to calm yourself and act according to the revered Vasishṭha's behest.

KAU.—Since I have to see the king of Mithilá at such a time, all my griefs thicken upon me simultaneously ; I am therefore unable to compose my heart the ties of which are shattered to their roots.

ARUN.—What doubt is there about this !

The sorrows of men sprung from the separation of their beloved kinsmen, though continuing ceaselessly, become unbearable at the sight of a dear person and flow, as it were, in a thousand streams. (8).

KAU.—How can we, indeed, show our face to the royal sage when such a fate has overtaken our dear daughter-in-law?

ARUND.—

This is your noble kinsman, the upholder of the Janaka family, to whom the sage Yâjñavalkya taught the whole of the sacred lore. (9).

KAU.—This is the royal sage, the delight of the great king's heart and the father of my dear daughter-in-law. Alas, alas! I am carried back to those days which afforded unmixed pleasure. O Destiny! All that is no more.

JANAKA—(*Approaching*). Revered Arundhatî, Janaka, of Videha, bows to you.

With my head bent low to the surface of the earth I bow to your reverence, as to the divine Ushas, adorable to the world and the source of blessings to the three worlds, you by whom your husband, though a repository of holy lustre, and though the most to be revered of even the primeval sages, regards himself as purified. (10).

ARUN.—May the Supreme Light be manifest to thee! May the God that blazes and stands beyound the reach of darkness purify thee!

JAN.—Noble Gṛishṭi, is it all well with the mother of the Protector of men?

KANCH.—(*To himself*). We have been unsparingly and very bitterly reproached. (*Aloud*). Royal sage, it does not behove you to afflict the Queen who has been already exceedingly grieved and who, in her anger for this very incident, has long avoided the sight of the moonlike face of dear Ráma. It was surely some lamentable misfortune of Ráma. For, hearing that same dreadful slander was spreading everywhere among the citizens and the country-folk, who being mean-minded, would not believe in the purification by fire, his Honour committed that piece of cruelty.

JAN.—(*Wrathfully*). Ah, of what significance is this fire in purifying my offspring! Oh misfortune! Already insulted by Ráma we have been again contemned by the mob raving like this!

ARUN.—(*Sorrowfully*). Exactly so. To speak of fire in connexion with our dear child is an insult. The word Sítá speaks enough. Alas, daughter!

Whether thou art to me a child or a pupil, be that as it may; the super-eminence of thy purity consolidates my affection for thee; thy childhood or womanhood is not the consideration; verily thou art adorable to the (three) worlds: in the case of (or, with) the virtuous, merits are the object of reverence; neither (their) sex nor (their) age. (11).

KAU.—Oh, my agonies revive. (*She faints*).

JAN.—Oh misery, what is this?

ARUN.—Royal sage, what else could it be?

That king, that happiness, that knot of children, and those days—all this stood before her mind's eye at the sight of you, her friend, in the hour of this terrible calamity; and then she fainted: for the heart of matrons is as tender as a flower. (12).

JAN.—Alas, alas! I have become cruel in every way, since I do not receive affectionately the beloved wife of my dear friend, seen after a long time.

He was a desirable relation, a dear friend, the very heart, joy in a visible form; nay, the entire fruit of existence, my body, my soul, or any other thing more precious than this: what was not the noble and great king Daśaratha to me! (13).

Alas, this is that very Kausalya!

Whenever there was any serious discord in private between the husband and wife, I was the person to whom they severally communicated their complaints, and then their pacification or exasperation was a matter resting with me. But enough of these recollections, since, overpowering the heart, they burn me. (14).

ARUN.—Oh hard luck! Her heart has become motionless on account of her breath being long suspended.

JAN.—Oh dear friend! (*He besprinkles her with the water in his gourd*).

KANCH.—

Fortune, having at first, like a well-disposed friend, manifested an unmixed favourableness, but again becoming terrible by the sudden reverse, intensifies, alas, the anguish of the mind. (15).

KAU.—(*Recovering*). O child Jánakí, where are you? I remember that engaging lotus-like countenance of yours graced solely with the singular beauty imparted by marriage and with a pure smile playing upon it. Brighten my lap once more, dear child, with your limbs lovely like glittering moon-light! The great King would always say—This is the daughter-in-law of our mighty ancestors of the race of Raghu, but as Janaka's daughter she is only a daughter to us.

KANCH.—It was as the Queen says.

Though the King had five children, the enemy of Subáhu (Ráma) was his special favourite; and of his four daughters-in-law Sitá was as dear to him as his daughter Śàntá. (16).

JAN.—O dear friend, great king Das'aratha, thus did you attract the heart in every way! How can I forget you?

It is customary for the parents of the bride to honour the kinsmen of their son-in-law; but in our connexion your respectful treatment of me was a reversal of that order; you who were such are snatched away by Death, as also that cause of our connexion: fie upon the life of me, a sinful wretch, in the horrible hell of this world! (17).

KAU.—Dear Jánakí, what am I to do! My cursed life is firmly fastened with an indelible adamantine glue and will not leave me.

ARUN.—Take consolation, Princess; you should also in the meanwhile stop your tears. Moreover, don't you remember what your family preceptor said at the hermitage of Ṛishyaśṛiṅga, that what was fated to happen took place, but that the result would be blissful?

KAU.—How can I expect such a thing, whose all hopes are past fulfilment?

ARUN.—Do you think then, royal daughter, that it was a false utterance? Look not at it, noble Princess, in another light. It is bound (so) to happen.

Let no doubt be entertained with regard to the utterances of Bráhmaṇas to whom the Supreme Light has been revealed. Good luck resides in their speech. They utter not words of false import. (18).

(*A confused noise behind the scenes; all listen*).

JAN.—Oh, to-day being a holiday on account of the arrival of the distinguished guests, it is the youngsters at school that are making a row, being briskly at play.

KAU.—How easily is happiness attained in childhood! (*Observing*). Hollo! Who is this boy in their midst that delights my eyes with his limbs firm, lovely, and tender, that disclose the grace of dear Ràma?

ARUN.—(*Aside, with tears of joy*). This must be that secret, the very nectar to my ears, communicated to me by Bhágîrathî. But I do not know which of the two, Kus'a and Lava of long life, that boy is. (*Aloud*).

Of a lovely dark like the petals of a blue lotus, decked with forelocks, of pure grace, embellishing, as it were, with beauty the assemblage of boys, and appearing like my dear Ráma once more restored to childhood, who may this be that being seen all at once delights my eyes, as with nectareous collyrium? (19)

KAN.—I think the boy must undoubtedly be of Kshatriya extraction in a student's stage of life.

JAN.—It is just so. For,

He has on his back a pair of quivers, the feathers of the arrows in which reach his crest; his breast has the tiny holy mark of sacred ashes; he wears the *ruru* skin; his lower garment dyed with red madder is held fast by a girdle of Mûrvá grass; and in one hand he has a bow with a rosary of Rudrákshas, in the other a *pippala* staff. (20).

Revered Arundhatî, what is your guess? Where may he have come from?

ARUN.—We have just come to-day.

JAN.—Venerable Gṛishṭi, my curiosity is intense. Go, therefore, to the revered Válmîki himself, and ask him. Say also to the boy that some elderly persons here wish to see him.

KANCH.—As your lordship commands. [*Exit.*

KAU.—What think you? That he will come, being thus addressed?

JAN.—Can noble conduct belie such grace of form?

KAU.—(*Observing*). How wonderful! Having with modesty listened to the words of Gṛishṭi and dismissed the boys of the ascetics, that boy has already started hitherwards.

JAN.—(*Eying him for a long time*). Oh this is something wonderful!

There is in him an excess of noble qualities mellowed by modesty and innocence common to childhood, capable of being perceived (marked) by the discerning and not by the vulgar. This being so prominent attracts my mind though rendered dull by bewilderment, just as a tiny piece of the loadstone does iron. (21).

LAVA—(*Entering*). How shall I, of my own motion, address my salutation to these persons whose names, rank and family I do not know, although they command my respect? (*Deliberating*). This mode of address is unobjectionable, as the elders say. (*Approaches respectfully*). Here Lava bows his head to you all in succession.

ARUN. and JAN.—Blessed boy, may you live long!

KAU.—Dear child, live long!

ARUN.—Come here, dear boy. (*Seating* Lava *on her lap, to herself*). Not alone my lap has been filled up, but also the cherished desire of my heart has been fulfilled after a long time.

KAU.—Dear child, come here too. (*Taking him on her lap*). Oh wonder! He resembles dear Ráma not only by his bodily frame that has the dusky bright of a garland of blue lotuses a little oppened, but also by his voice very deep like the note of a royal swan whose throat has been rendered melodious by its feeding on the filaments of lotuses. Why, even the touch of the body of my dear child, soft like the interior of a fully developed lotus, is of the same sort. Dear boy, let mee see the lotus of your face. (*She raises his chin, looks at him carefully, and with tears of emotion*). Royal sage, do you not see; if his face be closely observed it bears a resemblance to the moon-like face of our daughter Sîtá?

JAN.—I see it, dear friend, I see it.

KAU.—Oh! My mind, as if frenzied, suggests to me something like this.

JAN.—

In this child clearly appear to be perfecty mirrored in their entirety the same form and the same splendour of my dear daughter and the eminent descendent of Raghu (Ram'a); there also the same voice, that same natural modesty, and also the same awe-inspiring majesty. Alas, Destiny! how does my mind, being agitated, run along wild paths! (22).

KAU.—Dear child, have you a mother, and do you remember your father?

LAVA—No, no.

Kau.—To whom do you belong then?

Lava—To the revered Válmíki.

Kau.—My dear boy, tell all that is proper to be told.

Lava—I know but this much.

(Behind the Scenes.)

Ye soldiers, here this prince Chandraketu commands you that no one shall transgress the bounds of the hermitage.

Arun. and **Jan.**—Ah, Prince Chandraketu has arrived on account of his being the guardian of the sacrificial horse, and we shall see him this day. Oh lucky day!

Kau.—'The son of Lakshmaṇa commands'—these are words sweet as nectar that I hear.

Lava—Noble sir, who is this Chandraketu, may I ask?

Jan.—You know Rama and Lakshmaṇa, the sons of Daśaratha?

Lava—These two are the very heroes of the Rámáyaṇa; are they not?

Jan.—Just so.

Lava—How then can I not know them?

Jan.—Chandraketu is the son of that Lakshmaṇa.

Lava—He is the son of U'rmilà, then, and the grandson of the royal sage, king of Mithilá.

Arund.—(*Laughing*). Oh, the boy has shown his deep acquaintance with the story.

Jan.—(*Reflecting*). If you are so conversant with that history, then tell us, we ask you, what the names of the children of those sons of Daśaratha are and born of what mother each.

Lava—This chapter of the story has not been heard by us or by any one else before.

Jan.—What, has the poet not yet written that portion?

Lava—He has, but has not yet published it. Part of it has been composed as a separate work being full of sentiment, and adapted to theatrical exhibition. That composition written with his own hand, he has sent to the venerable sage Bharata, the writer of the Aphorisms on Music (singing, dancing and instrumental music).

Jan.—With what object?

Lava—That the revered sage, it is said, may have it performed on the stage by the heavenly nymphs.

Jan.—All this has the deepest interest for us.

LAVA—Great is the interest (*lit.* care) which the revered Vàlmîki has evinced in that work. For he sent the manuscript to the hermitage of Bharata by some pupils, and my brother was despatched, bow in hand, as their escort, to ward off any casualty.

KAU.—Child, have you a brother too?

LAVA—Yes, the noble Kus'a.

KAU.—He must be your senior, as your words show.

LAVA—Exactly. He is, indeed, elder by order of birth.

JAN.—What, are you, of long life, twins?

LAVA—Quite so.

JAN.—Child, tell me what sort of termination the story has.

LAVA—That Lakshmaṇa returned after he had left queen Sità sprung from sacrificial ground, all alone in the forest when her time of travail was near, she being banished by the king, afraid of the false scandals of the people.

KAU.—Alas, child, with a countenance lovely as the moon, what sad end of the wicked pastime of Fate suddenly overtook the blossom of your body, forlorn and alone!

JAN.—Ah daughter,

Having experienced that insult and the dreadful forest, as also those pains at the time of labour, surely you must have often remembered me as your protector, in your fright, as the eaters-of-raw-meat thronged round you from all sides. (23).

LAVA—(*To Arundhati*). Noble lady, who are these two?

ARÚN.—This is Kausalyá, and this Janaka.

LAVA—(*Surveys them with reverence, sorrow and wonder*).

JAN.—Oh, the cruelty of the wicked citizens! Oh, the rashness of king Ràma!

As I have been long brooding over this terrible blow of the thunderbolt in the form of this calamity, it is now time for my wrath to blaze up, with a sudden outburst, with bow or with curse.

KAU—(*With dismay and trepidation*). Help, help, revered lady; pacify the angry royal sage.

LAVA—Such is mostly the state of mind of spirited men who have received an insult.

ARUN.—King, Ràma is your son; and the poor subjects must be protected. (24).

JAN.—But no, peace be with either of them as far as Ráma is concerned; for he is my treasure in the form of a son; while the town-people are chiefly composed of Bráhmanas, children, old and decrepit persons and women. (25).

(*Enter*)

BOYS—(*In excitement*). Friend, we have heard of a certain animal which they call a horse in the country; the same we have seen with our eyes to-day.

LAVA—They speak of the 'horse' in treatises on zoology and warfare; tell me then how it looks.

BOYS—Listen:

Behind it has a huge tail which it shakes constantly; its neck is long and it has four hoofs (like other animals); it eats grass and throws out balls of dung each as big as a mango. But why describe it thus? It is going farther and farther off; come, come; let us follow it up. (26).

(*With these words they approach and pull him by his deer's skin and hands.*)

LAVA—(*With curiosity, hesitation and modesty*) Noble sirs, look here, they are dragging me away. (*He runs with haste*).

ARUN. & JAN.—May our dear child satisfy his curiosity.

KAU.—Revered lady, I feel I shall not live if the boy be out my sight (*i. e.* without his company); let us, therefore, go to another spot and see the boy as he goes. Long may he live!

ARUN.—Quick of foot, the nimble boy has gone far already; how is he to be seen?

KANCH.—(*Entering*). The revered Válmîki says that your honours will know it at the proper time.

JAN.—This is something extremely mysterious; Revered Arundhatî, friend Kausalyá, noble Grishṭi, let us go ourselves and see his reverence Práchetasa. (*Exeunt the* ELDERS).

(*Enter*)

THE BOYS—Behold, Prince, that wonderful object.

LAVA—I see it and know what it is. Surely it is a sacrificial horse.

BOYS—How do you know that?

LAVA—You fools, surely you must have read it also in the chapter (on horse-sacrifices). Don't you see that the guards are cuirassiers, lancers and quiver-bearers numbering a hundred in each division? This army appears mostly to consist of such troops. If you do not believe me, go and ask them.

BOYS—Hollo, soldiers, why does this horse roam about thus guarded?

LAVA—(*Wistfully; to himself*). Oh, a horse-sacrifice is, as is well-known, the mighty and sublime test of the supreme power of the world-conquering king that casts all other kings into the shade.

(*Behind the scenes*).

This horse, this banner, or rather, this war-cry, belongs to the one supreme hero of the seven worlds, the destroyer of the race of Rávaṇa. [See notes, however]. (27).

LAVA—(*With an air of disdain*). Ah, these words are exciting.

BOYS—What is to be said? The Prince is clever, indeed!

LAVA—Hollow! ho! Are there no Kshatriyas in the world that you should proclaim thus?

(*Behind the scenes*).

Ah, whence can there be Kshatriyas (worthy of the name) before (as compared to) the great king!

LAVA—Fie upon you impudent babblers!

If they (the Kshatriyas) are, they do exist; but what means this threatening proclamation? Or rather, why utter these words? Here I carry off that (boasted) banner of yours. (28).

Hollo, comrades, surround the horse and drive it (homeward) with clods of earth. Let the poor thing graze among the roebucks.

(*Enter* a man *full of haughty pride*).

MAN—A truce to this rashness! What is it that thou hast said? These battalians of armed men are stern and merciless; they brook not an insolent word even from a child. Prince Chandraketu is a destroyer of foes. Therefore make off quickly by this thick row of trees ere he arrives, whose heart has been attracted by the sight of these wonderful forests.

BOYS—Prince, have done with the horse. The lines of soldiers with flashing weapons threaten you, while the hermitage is far away. Come, therefore, let us scamper off, bounding like the deer.

LAVA—(*Smiling*). What, their weapons are flashing, you say? (*He strings his bow*).

Let this bow of mine, with its sharp jaws in the form of its points encircled by the tongue-like string, and sending forth a terrific, deep and hoarse sound (like the grinding of the teeth) resemble by its frightful cavity the gaping of the horrible (*lit.* machine-like) mouth of the god of death, grinning when about to make a meal of the world. (29).

(*All walk on in proper order and depart.*)

END OF ACT IV.

ACT V.

Ye soldiers, succour has, indeed, come to us now.

Verily here comes Chandraketu, on hearing of our fight, in his speeding chariot drawn by the fleet steeds which are galloping, being urged on by Sumantra, with his flag-staff of the Kovidàra wood shaking by the jolting (of the car). (1).

(*Enter in a chariot driven by* SUMANTRA, CHANDRAKETU *bow-in-hand, and with a feeling of joy and hurry mingled with wonder*).

CHAN.—Noble Sumantra, see, see:

Here is the warrior-boy, of unknown extraction, with his beautiful countenance glowing with slight anger, and his five locks all in a flutter, being in the van of battle, showering on the troops a hail-storm of arrows from his bow the points of which are ever resounding with its twang. (2).

Wonderful, wonderful!

The ascetic-boy rouses my curiosity, as he stands there, single-handed, like some new and still unknown scion of Raghu's race, in the midst of the body of the troops, scattering in all directions thousands of shafts glowing as they cleave, with a terrible clash, the temple-joints of the elephants. (3).

SUMANTRA—Long-lived one,

As I behold the boy who far outdoes the prowess alike of the gods and of the demons, and possesses similar features, I am reminded of Ráma, wielding the bow when he worked destruction upon the foes of the sacrifice of Kuśika's son (Vis'vámitra). (4).

CHAND.—My heart feels shame when I see so many warriors exerting their strength against a single youth.

For, this boy, who is single-handed, is surrounded by our forces wielding various weapons in their sturdy and huge hands, which flash forth in the thick of the raging battle, with their chariots resounding with the jingle of gold bells and with their cloud-like elephants raining down showers of rut. (5).

SUM.—Prince, of what avail are these against him even when united; what then (would be their condition) if they were fighting separately?

CHAND.—Make haste, noble one, make haste. Terrible is the havoc that he has commenced among our followers For,

Sending forth the twang of his bow, that swells with the loud sounds of the kettle-drums, and grates fearfully against the ears of the elephant-herds roaring in the mountain-caverns, the hero makes the ground, with the numerous heads and headless trunks frightfully dancing about, appear as if bespattered with the morsels from the horrible mouth of the god of death when satiated. (6).

SUM.—(*To himself*). How should I allow dear Chandraketu to engage in a single combat with a hero of such a type? (*Reflecting*). But we have grown old in the house of Ikshváku. Besides, what alternative is there when fighting has become necessary?

CHAN.—(*With a mingled feeling of astonishment, shame, and confusion*). Oh, fie! My troops are retreating on every side.

SUM.—(*Driving forth the chariot*). Prince of long life, the hero is now within reach of your voice.

CHAND.—(*Forgetfully*). Noble one, what did our heralds say, was his name?

SUM.—Lava.

CHAND.—Hollo Lava, of strong arms, what have you to do with these soldiers? Here am I; advance against me; let valour measure itself with valour. (7).

SUM.—Prince, lo, lo!

The warrior-lad being challenged by you desists from the slaughter of the army like the proud cub of a lion from the slaying of elephant-herds on hearing the roar of clouds. (8).

(*Enter* Lava *with bold and haughty strides*).

LAVA—Bravo, prince, bravo! You are trully a descendant of Ikshvàku. Here I turn to you now.

(*A great noise behind the curtains*).

LAVA—(*Turning back with firm steps*). How now? These generals, although overpowered, now turn back and surround me, being intent on battling! Fie upon you, miscreants!

Let the deep and tumultuous uproar of the army, rising from all sides like the tide of the ocean lashed by the hurricanes of doomsday, be swallowed up by the stupendous flames of my fierce wrath, the counterpart of the submarine fire raging furiously when struck against by the mountains. (9).

(*Moves round rapidly*).

CHAND.—Youth,

I love you for your wonderful and surpassing qualities. You are therefore my friend, and so whatever belongs to me belongs to you also. Why do you slay then your own followers? This Chandraketu here is, indeed, the touch-stone for your haughtiness. (10).

LAVA—(*Turning back with joy and haste*). Oh, how lucid and yet bold is the heroic language of this high-souled prince of the solar race! Why then trouble myself with these? I will first honour him.

(*Behind the scenes, a noise again*).

LAVA—(*With wrath and disdain*). Ah, I am annoyed by these villains who would not allow me to speak with the hero. (*Advances towards them*).

CHAND.—Noble charioteer, see a sight worth seeing:

With his glance fixed on me with pride mingled with curiosity, with his bow raised, and followed from behind by the troops, he resembles a cloud carrying the rain-bow and agitated either way, being beaten by a blast from both the sides. (11).

SUM.—The prince alone knows how to look at him even. I for myself am simply paralysed with wonder.

CHAND.—O ye princes!

Shame to you and shame to us as well! Since you have thus girt up your loins to battle with this boy—you innumerable and mounted on elephants, horses and chariots, he alone and on foot; you closely clad in steel, he wearing only the holy deer-skin; you his seniors in age, and he with a body lovely on account of his tender age. (12)

LAVA—(*With pain*). Ah, what! He shows pity! (*Reflecting*). Well, to avoid loss of time I will just paralyse the forces with the Jṛimbhaka missiles. (*He remains in meditation*).

SUM.—Ho, how is it that the tumultous uproar of our army ceases all of a sudden?

LAVA—I shall now see that boaster.

SUM.—(*With confusion*). Prince, I think that boy has invoked the Jṛimbhaka missile.

CHAN.—What doubt can there be as to this?

A dreadful combination, as if of darkness and lightning, baffles the eye, although directed towards an object, as it is lit up and suddenly obscured; moreover, this army stands motionless as if painted in a picture; verily it is the Jṛimbhaka missile, of unlimited power, that is at work. (13).

Wonderful, wonderful!

The sky is being filled up with the Jṛimbhaka missiles which have the pitchy dark of the mass of darkness collected in the vaults of *Pâtâla*, and whose blazing splendour resembles the tawny lustre of brass glowing when heated, as if with the peaks of mount Vindhya, tossed about by the strong and terrible hurricanes at the time of the universal destruction, and having their gorges filled up with the clouds blending with the tawny lightning. (14)

SUM.—But where could he have learnt the lore of these weapons from?

CHAN.—I think from the revered Pràchetasa.

SUM.—It can not be so, with regard to missiles, and particularly with the Jṛimbhaka missiles.

These were the offspring of Kṛiśâs'va; from him they passed to Kauśika; he handed them down to dear Râma and with him they rest now. (15)

CHAN.—Other sages, too, whose minds are pervaded with the light of *Sattva* and who have beheld the holy *mantras*, see everything.

SUM.—Prince, be on your guard; the eminent hero has turned up again.

THE PRINCES—(*To each other*). O, how noble-looking this prince is! (*They behold each other with love and affection*).

Can it be the fortuitous conversation or the excess of excellences, or a time-honoured friendship formed in some previous life, or my relationship with him owing to the will of providence, not yet known to me, that my heart feels drawn toward him at the first sight? (16)

SUM.—Mostly it is the characteristic of living beings that some one feels an ardent love for another, which men of the world call 'the friendship of the stars' or 'the love which the eye begets.' This love the wise declare to be spontaneous and unaccountable.

That attachment which springs up without a cause cannot be counteracted; it is a thread formed of affection which links together the inner hearts. (17)

THE PRINCES—(*With reference to each other*). How can I shoot the arrows at his body lovely like a polished *rájapaṭṭa* (a gem or silken garment) at the sight of which my limbs are covered with the hair standing on end through my longing to embrace him? (18)

But what other course is there than taking up the weapon against one who has displayed such a fierce spirit of heroism? What is also the use of that weapon which is not directed against an antagonist of such a type? And what will he himself say of me if I am not inclined to fight, when the weapons are already brandished? Stern, indeed, is the warrior's duty that obstructs the operation of love! (19)

SUM.—(*Marking* LAVA, *with tears to himself*). My heart, why dost thou indulge in fancies?

That which was the seed of our hope was nipped in the bud by Fate; when the creeper is already cut off, where is the possibility of its bearing the blossoms? (20)

CHAND.—Venerable Sumantra, I alight from the chariot.

SUM.—And for what purpose?

CHAND.—In the first place this heroic youth will be honoured; secondly, O noble one, I shall thus be properly observing the martial law; for the canonists say that men in chariots shall not advance against those on foot.

SUM.—(*To himself*). Alas! I am now thrown into a fix.

How can a man like myself go against a right course of action, or how can he permit an act solely grounded on adventure? (21)

CHAND.—When my revered fathers consult your honour, the dear companion of their sire, in matters of doubt, why should your noble self hesitate?

SUM.—Prince of long life, your intention is quite consistent with the laws of duty.

This is the martial law, this is the time-honoured ordinance; and this is certainly the heroic course of conduct pursued by the lions in the race of the (most eminent) Raghus. (22)

CHAND.—The noble one only can speak so.

Your honour alone knows the history, the holy chronicles, the canons of law, and also the customary pratices of the Raghu family. (23)

SUM.—(*Embraces him with tears of affection*).

Dear child, how few have been the days since dear Lakshmaṇa, your father, even though the slayer of Indrajit, was born! And his child now follows the course of a warrior. All hail to the family of Das'aratha which has thus attained its stability! (24)

CHAND.—(*Painfully*).

What stability can our race have when the eldest of the Raghus (Ràma) is unrepresented (without progeny) !—with this grief are our three other fathers smitten. (25)

SUM.—Alas ! The words of Chandraketu pierce the very vitals of the heart

LAVA—Strange, how divided are my feelings !

As the lotus-plant rejoices at the rise of the moon, so do mine eyes at his sight; and yet this my arm which lovingly holds the ponderous bow with its string resounding with the fierce sound of its twang and manifests such a strong and fierce spirit of war, is eager for the fight. (26)

CHAND.—(*Descends from the chariot*). Noble sir, Chandraketu of the solar race salutes you.

SUM.—May the eternal God, the divine Boar, grant thee, for thy welfare, a lustre, invincible, holy and majestic, such as Kakutstha possessed. (27)

Moreover,

In the ensuing fight, may the divine Sun, who is the progenitor of thy race, give thee energy (*lit.* keep thee cheerful); may the son of Mitra and Varuṇa (Vasishṭha), who is the spiritual guide even of thy sires, bless thee; may the strength of Indra and Vishṇu, of Agni and Marut, and of the divine Eagle, be thine; and may the magic twang of the bows of Ràma and Lakshmaṇa grant thee victory ! (28)

LAVA—Prince, you certainly appear exceedingly well when seated in the chariot. Enough, enough of this extreme regard.

CHAND.—Well, then, the noble warrior too should mount another chariot.

LAVA—Noble one (Sumantra), seat the prince in the chariot.

SUM.—You, too, comply with the request of dear Chandraketu.

LAVA—What hesitation can there be in using one's proper implements? But we, living in the forest, are not accustomed to move in chariots.

SUM.—Dear son, you know how to act in a manner befitting pride and politeness. If the sovereign of Ikshvàku race were to see you, such as you are, his heart would melt with affection.

LAVA—Noble sir, that royal sage is reported to be a noble man. (*With a feeling of shame*).

We too are certainly not so disposed as to put obstacles into the performance of sacrifices. Who, in this world, does not highly esteem that king for his virtues? But those words of the guardians of the horse, dreadful on account of the insult they meant to the whole *Kshatriya* race, roused my anger. (29)

CHAND.—(*With a smile*). What! You are wroth even at the superiority of my father!

LAVA—Wroth or no is a different matter. But I ask this much:—We hear that king of the Raghu race is self-restrained. He is not arrogant, they say, nor are his subjects so. Why then do his people utter diabolical words?

The sages call the language of the conceited and the arrogant as infernal. That is the source of all enmity and the bane of the world. (30)

On this account they condemn it, while they extol the other (of the opposite sort).

The wise call truthful and agreeable speech a cow, the mother of all blessings; a cow that grants desires, removes misery, begets fame and destroys sin. (31)

SUM.—Oh, this youth is of a refined character being the disciple of Vàlmîki. He speaks nobly owing to his education under the sage.

LAVA—And now, Chandraketu, as to your question if I am indignant at your father's superiority of valour: I ask you—Are all the accomplishments of a warrior confined to one individual?

SUM.—Surely you do not know the king of the Ikshvâku race and hence you speak in this strain. Desist, therefore, from your bold talk.

True that you have displayed your valour by your slaughter of the troops, but you ought not to blurt out such language with regard to the victor of Jamadagni. (32)

LAVA—(*With a laugh*). Noble sir, what means this bragging that the king is the victor of the son of Jamadagni!

It is a natural fact that the strength of the Bràhmaṇa lies in his tongue, while the strength of arm belongs to the Kshatriya alone. Jâmadagnya was a Bráhmaṇa who wielded arms, and if he was subdued, where is the ground for praising that king? (33)

CHAND.—(*With almost a pang*). Venerable Sumantra, have done with this exchange of words.

He must be some extraordinary and novel incarnation of valour, that has come down now, since he does not esteem even the noble son of Bhṛigu a hero, and does not know even the holy exploits of my father competent to grant immunity from danger to all the seven worlds. (34)

LAVA—Who, indeed, does not know the heroic acts and the greatness of the Raghu king? And yet there is something that should be said. Or, God forbid!

He is old and his actions should not be scrutinized; let him be alone; why dwell on his doings? He is great in the world and his fame unblemished even though he killed the wife of Sunda (Tàḍakà)! And the three steps which he had to pace back without turning his face in his fight with Khara and the dexterity he displayed in slaying the son of Indra (Válí) are also facts well known to the world. (35)

CHAND.—Ha, you violate all rules of propriety since you traduce my father; you are growing too bold.

LAVA.—Holloa, he now scowls at me!

SUM.—Their anger is ablaze! For,

The tremor caused by rage agitates the knots of their hair; their eyes, which somewhat resemble the leaf of a red lotus, are turning deeper red; and by the knitting of their eye-brows which have suddenly commenced their play, their faces bear resemblance to the moon with the spot brought into prominence or to the lotus with bees hovering about. (36)

THE TWO LADS—Let us then repair to a spot suitable for fighting.

(*Exeunt Omnes*).

END OF ACT V.

ACT VI.

(*Enter a pair of resplendent* Vidyádharas *in an aerial vehicle*).

VID.—Oh! Wonderful, indeed, are the heroic deeds of these two princes of the solar race that have suddenly closed in fearful combat and have displayed their martial volour; the gods and demons are in utter bewilderment with extreme wonder at them. For, look, my dear, look at them.

There is raging wonderfully the fight, striking terror into the whole world, between the two (combatants) with their locks constantly fluttering, showering arrows by stretching their bows whose bells are ringing like the clash of tinkling bracelets and which send forth a frightful sound on account of their booming huge strings and points. (1)

And to announce good fortune to both, the gentle and deep sound of the celestial drum is going forth like the rumbling of a thunder-cloud. (2)

Let us therefore pour down on these two eminent warriors a continual shower of flowers the mass of which will be charming, being thickly intermixed with the lovely full-blown golden lotuses, and which will be gratifying (to the senses) by the honey of the numerous fresh and jewel-like buds of the trees of paradise.

VIDYA'DHARÎ—But why has the sky, all of a sudden, turned tawny as if with the streaks of lightning flashing out of season?

VID.—Can it be then that to-day

Śiva has opened his (third) eye on the forehead, emitting a dazzling lustre like that of the sun whirled round on his moving wheel by Tvashṭṛi? (3)

(*Reflecting*). Ah, I have it. It is the fiery missile discharged by prince Chandraketu, his anger being provoked. From it comes this fall of voluminous sparks of fire. For now,

The multitudes of the aerial cars have withdrawn with their banners and chauries chequered by being slightly burnt; while these flames, as they spread about the borders of the silken flag-cloths, appear for a moment like the streaks of saffron (4)

Wonderful! His reverence the fire has actually spread round, terrible by its sparks bursting forth with a fearful hissing sound like that of the thunderbolt when breaking into pieces, and awe-inspiring with its masses of raging flames spreading about (*lit.* licking on) in wild confusion. Its heat is very fierce on all sides. I will, therefore, screen my wife with my body and retreat to some great distance. (*Does accordingly*).

VIDYADHARI'—Happily has the heat been warded off from me when it had just begun to affect me, by this touch of my lord's body, thrilling, soft, agreeable and cooling, like spotless pearls, and causing my eyes to close and roll about with delight.

VID.—Ah, what have I done! Or,

Whatever person is beloved by another, he is his indescribable treasure. He removes sufferings, without doing anything himself, by the delights (of his mere presence). (5)

VIDYA'DHARÎ—Ah, whence is the sky overcast with clouds, dark like the necks of impassioned peacocks and decked with the playful lightnings continuously flashing forth?

VID.—Holloa, hey! This must be the effect of Varuṇa's missile employed by Prince Lava. How now, the fiery missile has been quenched by the thousands of streams of water pouring down in continuous succession.

VIDYA'DHARÎ—Oh, how I welcome it!

VID.—Ah, ah! Everything pushed to an extreme leads to disaster. For, the whole animal creation is quaking as if being closely wrapped up in darkness, deepened by the pealing clouds thrown into agitation by a series of hurricanes as at the destruction-time of the universe, as if it were rolling in the horrid cavity of the mouth of Death, wide opened to make one meal of the whole world, or as if it were shut up in the belly of Nàráyaṇa, when at the close of a *yuga* he sleeps his sleep of meditation, with all the passages of his body closed. Well done, Chandraketu! Well done! Rightly have you discharged the Wind-missile. For,

The wind has entirely (*lit.* to some unknown region) banished the clouds, though numerous, as the means of right knowledge dispels all the illusions superimposed on Brahma. (6)

VIDYA'DHARÎ—But who is this, my dear, that is causing his celestial vehicle to alight between these two princes, waving the end of his upper garment with his hand raised up in haste, and ordering them from afar to desist from fighting with sweet and loving words?

VID.—(*Observing*). Fortunately it is the Raghu king on his return from his killing of S'ambûka.

Having heard the tranquil words of the great personage and having out of respect for him desisted from the work of fighting, Lava stands peaceful, while Chandraketu bows down to him. May the monarch be happy on account of his union with his sons! (7)

Come then, let us depart.

[*Exeunt both.*

END OF THE MIXED VISHKAMBHAKA.

(*Enter* RA'MA, LAVA, and CHANDRAKETU *in a bowing posture*).

RA'MA—(*Alighting from the Pushpaka*).

Chandraketu, you the moon of the solar race, come quickly and give me a close embrace; let the fire that burns in my mind be quenched by your limbs cooling like the flakes of snow. (8)

(*Raising him up and embracing him with tears of affection*). Is it all well with you, the wielder of celestial weapons?

CHAND.—It is well with me, now that I have fortunately come in contact with Lava, of wonderful exploits and lovely to sight. I, therefore, request that my father should look upon this eminently brave warrior with an equally affectionate eye as on me, or even still more.

RA'MA—(*Marking* LAVA *closely*). I am glad that this comrade of my dear child has an appearance exceedingly serene, lovely and auspicious.

He is, as it were, the science of archery appearing in a corporeal form to safeguard the worlds; or martial duty become incarnate for the protection of the treasure of Vedic observances; or he seems to be the sum of all powers or the collection of all virtues; ay, the very store of the meritorious actions of the world standing out in a visible shape. (9)

LAVA—(*To himself*). Oh, how purifying and majestic is the appearance of this magnanimous personage!

He is the one great asylum of comfort, affection and devotion; and the grace of supreme Duty, as it were, moving in a bodily form. (10)

Oh, wonder!

At his sight all hostility has suddenly ceased, and a feeling full of joy spreads (over me); that arrogance has vanished somewhere, and modesty makes me humble; I am subdued to him, strangely fascinated. Or rather, the magnanimous possess some supreme excellence like the holy places. (11)

RA'MA—How is it that he at once assuages my sorrow and wins the affection of my inward soul from some mysterious cause? Or that love, and that it should be dependent on some perceptible cause, is a contradictory assertion.

Some unknown internal cause links together objects; affections do not, indeed, depend upon external accidents; for the lotus blooms at the rise of the sun, and the moonstone melts when the moon rises. (12)

LAVA—Chandraketu, who is this?

CHAND.—Dear friend, he is my revered father

LAVA—Then he bears the same relation to me by the law of relationship, since you have called me your dear companion. But there are four revered heroes of the story of the Râmâyaṇa who are entitled to this mode of address by you. Give me, therefore, the exact relation.

CHAND.—Then know him to be my eldest father.

LAVA—(*With joy*). what, he is Raghunâtha himself? Oh happy luck! The day has auspiciously dawned for me to-day since I behold this king. (*Marking him with modesty and curiosity*). Father, Lava the disciple of Vâlmîki, bows to you.

RA'MA—Long-lived one, come, come. (*He embraces him affectionately*). Dear boy, enough, enough of this excessive modesty. Embrace me pressingly again and again.

Your touch, fleshy, soft and tender, like the inner leaf of a well-developed lotus and cooling like the nectar oozing from the moon, or sandal-juice, gladdens me. (13)

LAVA—(*To himself*). Such disinterested affection he has for me! But I in my ignorance showed hostility towards this very personage, inasmuch as I pushed my obstinacy to the very extremity of taking up arms. (*Aloud*). Revered father, pardon the childish folly of Lava.

RA'MA—What fault has my dear child committed?

CHAND.—When he heard the proclamation of my father's exploits from the keepers of the horse, he played the hero.

RA'MA—This is creditable to a *Kshatriya*.

A man of might does not brook the might of others getting ascendancy; it is his innate disposition, being inherent in his constitution, and not acquired. If the divine sun blazes incessantly with his beams, why does the fire-crystal shoot forth its rays as if insulted? (14)

CHAND.—Indignation, too, appears graceful in this great warrior alone. For let my revered father behold how the troops are motionless all round and rooted to the spot on account of the stupefying missile employed by my dear friend.

RA'MA—Dear Lava, withdraw the missile; and you too. Chandraketu, console the troops that are feeling ashamed at their motionless state.

LAVA—As my revered father commands.

(*He remains in meditation*).

CHAND.—As you order. [*Exit.*

LAVA—Father, the missile has ceased to operate.

RA'MA—Dear child, missiles have secret charms for their employment and withdrawal, and their knowledge is obtained by traditional instruction.

The primeval instructors &c. (15) (See p. 5).

Now the venerable Kṛis'às'va communicated the occult science of these missiles to Kaus'ika, who had been his disciple for over a thousand years and he transmitted it to me. This is the order of transmission. And now I ask, from whom did my child receive his instructions ?

LAVA—The missiles revealed themselves to us both spontaneously.

RA'MA—(*Reflecting*). What cannot be possible ? This may be (due to) some singular greatness, the result of the ripened fruit of excellent merit. But how do you use the dual ?

LAVA—We are two brothers, twin-born.

RA'MA—Who is then the other ?

(*Behind the scenes*).

Dàṇḍàyàna,

Was there a fight as I heard between Lava, of long life, and the troops of the king ? What do you say, friend, that there was one ? Let then, to-day, the title of 'Imperial King' cease to exist in the world; and let also the fires arising from the weapons of the Kshatriyas be extinguished. (16)

RA'MA—But who is this of a complexion dark-blue like sapphire, that by his very voice covers me with horripilation, making me thereby resemble a *Kadamba* tree that puts forth buds in joy on hearing the deep roar of a fresh blue cloud ? (17)

LAVA—This is that my elder brother, the noble Kus'a, who has now returned from the hermitage of Bharata.

RA'MA—(*With eagerness*). Dear child, here do you call him of long life.

LAVA—So I will. (*He walks about*).

(*Enter* KUS'A).

KUS'A—(*Touching his bow with curiosity, joy and fortitude*).

If there would be a fight with the kings of the solar race, who from the time of the revered Manu, the son of Vivasvat, have granted protection from danger to Indra and who have kept the fire of their natural martial vigour ever blazing for the destruction of the haughty, then blessed will be this bow of mine, with its string lighted up with the flames of the fierce rays shooting forth from the blazing missiles. (18)

(*Walks forth in a warlike attitude*).

RA'MA—There is an extraordinary excess of manliness in this *Kshatriya* youth.

His eye bids defiance to (*lit.* treats as straw) the essence of the power of the three worlds; his bold and proud gait bends down, as it were, the earth; and though yet in his boyhood, he possesses the hugeness of a mountain; who is this that is advancing, Martial spirit or Pride itself? (19)

LAVA—(*Approaching*). Victory to my revered brother!

KUS'A—Long-lived one, what is this talk going round about a fight?

LAVA—Oh, it is a trifling matter. My revered brother, however, should give up his haughty bearing and behave modestly.

KUS'A—For what reason?

LAVA—Because we have here his majesty, the lord of the Raghu (or Ráma). He loves us and is longing for your company.

KUS'A—(*Surmisingly*). That hero of the story of Râmâyaṇa, the protector of the Vedic treasure (or the world)?

LAVA—Yes, he.

KUS'A—He is a magnanimous person, whose sight is holy and covetable. But I can not yet make up my mind as to how we should approach him.

LAVA—Just as we would a father.

KUS'A—How, indeed, can this be?

LAVA—The very noble and gentle Chandraketu, the son of U'rmilá, treats me with affection, calling me his dear friend. On account of this connexion, this royal sage becomes our spiritual father.

KUS'A—Now humility, even towards a Kshatriya, will not be objectionable.

(*Both walk forth*).

LAVA—See this great man, dear brother, the supreme excellence of whose manifold and uncommon achievements is clearly perceptible from his noble mien, majesty and serene dignity.

KUS'A—(*Closely observing*). Oh, how gracious his form and how sanctifying his majesty ! In a right place, indeed, has the author of the Rámáyaṇa employed the Goddess of speeech. (20)

(*Approaching*). Father, Kus'a, the disciple of Práchetasa, salutes you.

RA'MA—Come, come, long may you live !

This person longs with paternal affection to embrace you whose bodily frame is as lovely as a cloud filled with water. (21)

(*Embracing him ; to himself*). What then, can this boy be my child ?

He seems, as it were, to be the very essence of my body flowing forth from every limb through affection ; or rather my very life appearing in a visible form outside my body ; he is fashioned as it were from the oozings of my heart melting through intense joy ; since as I embrace him he appears to besprinkle my body with a stream of nectar. (22)

LAVA—Father, the sun is shining right on the forehead. My father, therefore, should be pleased to take a seat for a while in the shade of the S'ála trees.

RA'MA—As my child likes.

(*All walk round and sit down according to rank*).

RA'MA—(*To himself*).

Oh, though combined with modesty, the general deportment of Kus'a and Lava, such as their gait, their mode of standing and sitting, and so on, foreshadows universal sovereignty. (23)

The artless graces of beauty set off their resplendent forms lovely in each part, just as the heart-bewitching rays do a spotless gem, or the drops of floral honey the full-blown lotus. (24)

I also observe in these two boys an almost complete resemblance to the princes of Raghu's race.

Their body is dark-blue like the neck of a full-grown pigeon with the shoulders (neck) well-turned like those of a bull ; their gaze is steady like that of a lion in good spirit, and their voice is deep like that of a drum beaten on an auspicious occasion. (25)

(*Surveys them closely*). Oh, their bodies not only resemble mine,

But to a careful eye are clearly visible in these two boys the various resemblances to Janaka's daughter : nay, there stands once more before my eyes that very countenance of my beloved, lovely like a fresh-blown lotus. (26)

The same is the stamp of their lips, enchanting with the beauty of the teeth that disclose a pearly whiteness, and the same too is the beauty of their ears ; and although their eyes are red and blue, yet they possess the same grace. (27)

And this is the wood inhabited by Vàlmîki, where, as I hear, the queen was abandoned. This is their form, and this their age and majesty. And the fact that the missiles disclosed themselves to them of their own accord makes me thus reflect :—Can it be my permission to the missiles at the time of our looking at the pictures that has taken effect ? For we have heard that even our ancestors did not get a knowledge of these missiles without traditional information. This over-great delight of my heart, too, assures my mind tossed about by doubts. That they are twins also greatly agrees with my own experience. For I had often marked that the queen in her pregnancy was blessed with twins.

(*With tears*).

For, when the love that had already taken root had grown with our growing familiarity, it was I who first perceived with the gentle touch of my hand the double character of the fœtus in her womb as we were alone, she with her eyes closed from a sense of natural bashfulness though feeling perfectly at ease; and it was after some days that she herself came to know the same. (28)

(*Having wept*). What, shall I ask them in some way?

LAVA—Father, what is this?

The shower of tears has lent to your face, the blessing of the world, the loveliness of a lotus besprinkled with dew-drops. (29)

KUS'A—Ah, my boy,

What possibly would not be a source of grief to the lord of the Raghus when separated from queen Sîtá? Verily on the loss of a beloved the whole world becomes a wilderness. His great love, so well known, and this endless separation! Why do you then ask thus as if you have not studied the Râmāyaṇa? (30)

RA'MA—(*To himself*). Oh they speak indifferently. Enough of questioning. Foolish heart, what means this sudden emotion which agitates you with affection? Having thus betrayed the anguish of my heart I have become an object of pity even to these boys. Well, I will conceal my emotion. (*Aloud*). Boys, there is a much talked of work, entitled the Rámáyaṇa, an outcome of Válmîki's poetic genius (*lit.*, language) and a panegyric of the solar race. Out of curiosity I wish to know something in it.

KUS'A—We have learnt the whole of that composition. These two *s'lokas*, however, are now present to my memory from the last chapter of the part descriptive of (Ráma's) boyhood.

RA'MA—Repeat them, dear boy!

KUS'A—

Sîtá was naturally an object of affection to the high-souled Ráma; and she increased that affection by her virtues alone. (31)

Similarly, Ráma was dearer to Sîtá than even her life: it is their (individual) heart that knows the mutual love. (32)

RA'MA—Oh pity! Exceedingly painful is this blow to the vital parts of my heart. Alas, Queen! So it was, then. Oh, the incidents of worldly life, unpleasant on account of the sudden reverses and terminating in disappointments, cause affliction.

Where is that unbounded joy, intensified by unparalleled love, where the mutual love, and where those passionate enjoyments of deep interest! Where again is that union of hearts whether in weal or woe! Nevertheless this life moves in me, the accursed one does not vanish! (33)

Oh, pity!

I am reminded of that time, so painful to remember, which is able at once to unfold (conjure up in my memory) the thousand virtues of my beloved. (34)

Then it was that the bud-like breasts of the fawn-eyed one, that had just made their appearance, expanded a little after some days; (a time) when love, intense by the combination of youth, affection and longing, displays itself working boldly in the heart but gently in body. (35)

LAVA—And this is the stanza addressed by the sovereign of the Raghu race to queen Sîtà, while they sported in the forest adjoining the Chitrakúṭa mountain and the river Mandákinî—

For you is set here, as it were, this stone-slab before us, round which the Kesara tree has poured, as it were, a rain of flowers. (36)

RA'MA—(*With a smile of shame and a feeling of affection and pathos*). Very innocent, indeed, are boys, especially those who live in a forest. Alas, Queen, do you remember that spot, the witness of our acts of great intimacy at that time? Alas, oh pity!

I remember her face, as it was cooled by the perspiration caused by fatigue, with its beautiful moon-like forehead overhung with her tresses dishevelled by the gently blowing breezes from the Mandàkini, with its cheeks bright, not being marked with saffron-paint, and engaging with its well-formed ears charming in their unadorned state. (37)

(*Remains as if paralysed*; *then pitiously*).

What wonder, ho!

A beloved person, pictured and placed before the mind as it were, after long-continued meditation, does, indeed, give consolation even in separation: but when fancy ceases, the world appears like a desolate wilderness; and then the heart is, as it were, burnt by being placed on a heap of burning chaff. (38)

(*A voice behind the curtains*).

Alarmed on hearing of the strife between the boys, Vasishṭha, Válmîki, the queens of Das'aratha, and Janaka, together with Arundhatî, with their bodies worn out by old age, are coming tardily, being overpowered by fatigue on account of the great distance of the hermitage, though speeding on with their minds. (39)

RA'MA—What ! Revered Arundhatî, Vasishṭha, my mothers, and Janaka too, all here ! O ill luck ! How can I see them ? (*Looking forth piteously*). Alas, that fate should bring Janaka too here is a stroke of the thunderbolt to me, an unlucky being !

Why am I not torn into a thousand pieces when thus seeing my father's friend in such a condition, after the dreadful calamity has taken place, having (once) seen him, in the company of my father, on the festive occasion of the auspicious wedding of their children, attended by Vasishṭha and others, delighted at the desirability of the alliance; or rather, what is not Ràma capable of doing? (40)

(*Behind the curtains*).

Alas, alas, oh pity !

Having seen, all of a sudden, the lord of the Raghus in such a condition, with his majestic appearance only left to him, his distressed mothers have fallen into a strong swoon just after the recovery to consciousness of Janaka who was the first to faint. (41)

RA'MA—O father, O mothers, O Janaka !

Out of place is your compassion for me, a sinner, who was cruel to her who was the sole blessing of the families of the Raghus and Janakas. (42)

I will, however, pay my respects to them. (*With these words he rises*).

KUS'A and LAVA—This way, father, this way.

(*They walk round overpowered with pity*).

[*Exeunt omnes.*

END OF ACT VI.,

Styled 'The Recognition of the Sons'.

ACT VII.

(*Enter* LAKSHMANA.)

LAK.—Holloa, ho! To-day, indeed, the venerable Vàlmîki, having invited, together with us, the subjects including the Bràhmaṇas, the Kshatriyas, and the other inhabitants of the city and the country, has caused to be assembled here, by his power, the whole collection of beings, animate and inanimate (their spirits) as well as the multitude of the principal gods, demons, animals and serpents. And his lordship (Ráma) said to me—"We are invited by the revered Válmîki to witness the performance of his own play by the heavenly nymphs. You, therefore, go to the theatre on the bank of the Ganges and seat the audience." And I have seated the whole assemblage of mortals and immortals in their proper places. But here,

Comes his lordship, in this very direction, out of respect for Válmîki—he, who lives the very austere life of an ascetic, though still dwelling in the hermitage of his kingdom. (1)

(*Then enter* RA'MA)

RA'MA—Dear Lakshmaṇa, have the spectators taken their seats?

LAK.—Yes, they have.

RA'MA—Now these two boys, Kus'a and Lava, should have a seat of honour like that of prince Chandraketu.

LAK.—I have already provided such for them, full aware of your lordship's affection for them. Here is a royal seat spread out. Your lordship should sit down on it.

RA'MA—(*Sits down*).

LAK.—Holloa, actors, commence the play.

SU'TRADHA'RA—(*Entering*). Hear ye! His reverence, the truth-speaking Válmîki, thus informs the animate and the inanimate world—Here is something which I perceived with the unerring eye of a sage as purifying and exciting the sentiments of pathos and wonder, and then wove into a poetic composition. You should attend to it out of respect for the Muses (or with कार्ये *v. l.*—respect for the sublime theme).

RA'MA—This is what is meant. The great sages have beheld the laws by intuition. The perceptions of these revered seers which are fraught with the highest truth and beyond foulness never prove false, and therefore ought not to be called in question.

(*Behind the curtains*).

Alas my lord, alas prince Lakshmaṇa, as I am here alone, unfortunate and helpless, with the pains of labour approaching, and all hope gone, the wild animals are eagerly looking out to devour me. I, therefore, a luckless creature, will throw myself into the Bhâgîrathî.

LAK.—(*To himself*). Alas, alas! This is something quite unexpected.

SU'TRA.—

The Queen, the daughter of the all-supporting Earth, abandoned by the King in the great wilderness, is throwing herself into the Ganges in the agonies of child-birth. (2)

[*Exit.*

(*End of Prologue.*)

RA'MA—(*In alarm*). Queen, queen, wait a moment.

LAK.—My lord, this is a play.

RA'MA—Alas Queen, dear companion during my residence in the Daṇḍaka forest, this calamity has befallen you on account of Râma.

LAK.—My lord, just look at the performance.

RA'MA—Here I am ready, framed of adamant as I am.

(*Enter* SÎTA', *supported by* PṚITHIVI' *and* GANGA', *each with a boy in her lap*).

RA'MA—Dear Lakshmaṇa, I sink, as it were, into a powerful gloom, the nature and cause of which are unintelligible to me. Bear me up.

THE TWO GODDESSES—

Take comfort, O blessed one! Good luck greets thee, princess of Videha! Thou hast brought forth, beneath the waters, twin sons, the upholders of Raghu's race. (3)

SÎTA'—(*Regaining her senses*). Happily have I given birth to two sons. Alas, my lord! (*She faints*).

LAK.—(*Falling at Râma's feet*). My lord, my lord, good luck has smiled upon us. The race of Raghu has a blessed offspring. (*Looking at him*). Alas, alas! His lordship has fainted, overwhelmed with the flow of tears that burst forth. (*He fans him*).

PṚITHIVI'—Child, take cheer.

SÎTA'.—(*Regaining her senses*). Revered one, who are you and who is this?

PṚI.—This is Bhágîrathî, the tutelary goddess of the Raghu family.

SÎTA'—My homage to you, goddess!

BHA'.—Do you obtain an abundance of blessings befitting your virtuous life.

LAK.—We are highly blessed!

BHA'.—This is your mother, Earth.

SÎTA'—Alas, mother, you have seen me in this plight.

PṚI.—Come, my darling, come, my daughter.

(*She embraces* SÎTA' *and swoons*).

LAK.—(*With joy*). Fortunately has the Queen been favoured by Gaṅgà and Pṛithivî.

RA'MA—(*Observing*). This is more touching, indeed.

BHA'.—All-triumphant is parental affection, since even the all-supporting Earth is pained. Or rather, common to all (universal) is this thread of worldly life (*viz.*, affection), the knot of infatuation of the mind, which exists within (exerts a secret influence on) sentient beings and is not to be counteracted. Goddess Earth (the supporter of creatures), child Vaidehî, take heart, take heart.

PṚI.—Goddess, how can I take heart, being the mother of Sîtá?

I bore her long stay in the midst of the Rákshasas; but her second exile is extremely unbearable.

BHA'G.—

Who is, indeed, able to close the gates of a creature's destiny when about to bear fruit. (4)

PṚI.—Revered Bhágîrathî, you have worthily spoken. Or rather, was this proper on the part of dear Ràma.

He showed no regard for the hand which he, as a youth, had firmly seized in his boyhood; nor did he show any for me, nor for Janka, nor for Fire, nor for her dutiful conduct, nor for his offspring. (5)

SÎTA'—Ah, I am put in mind of my lord.

PṚI.—Ah, whom do you call your lord?

SÎTA'—(*With a blush and with tears*). Or, as my mother calls him.

RA'MA—Mother Earth, such am I.

BHA'G.—Goddess Earth, you are the very body (main-stay) of the world. Why then do you get angry with him as if you did not know him properly?

A dreadful scandal spread among the people; as for the purification by the fiery ordeal it took place in Laṅká; how could the people *here* believe it? While to keep contented the whole world is the family inheritance of the descendants of Ikshváku: being in such a fix what was the boy to do? (6)

LAK.—Deities have an unobstructed knowledge of the minds of creatures.

GANGA'—Nevertheless here I fold my hands to you.

RA'MA—Mother, your favours on the family of Bhagîratha have been uninterrupted.

PṚI.—Goddess, I am always favourably disposed towards you. But I speak thus on account of the vehemence of affection bearing down irresistibly upon me. Not that I do not know Ráma's love for Sîtà.

Having abandoned my daughter, as ill-luck would have it, with a burning heart, he now lives by his uncommon fortitude and the meritorious acts of his subjects. (7)

RA'MA—Verily, parents have a tender affection for the children.

SÎTA'—(*Weeping and with folded hands*). Let my mother absorb me into her own self.

RA'MA—What else could she say!

BHA'G.—Heaven forbid! May you live for thousands of years!

PṚI.—Daughter, you have to look after your sons.

SÎTA'—I am without a protector; what then have I to do with them?

RA'MA—Heart, thou art made of adamant.

BHA'G.—How could you be without a protector when your lord lives?

SÎTA'—What sort of a lord have I, an unfortunate creature!

THE TWO GODDESSES—

Why do you speak disparagingly of yourself, you who are the blessing of the world and by being associated with whom even our own sanctity increases? (8)

LAK.—Hear this, my lord.

RA'MA—Let the people hear it.

(*A noise behind the scenes*).

RA'MA—Something very marvellous is going to happen.

SÎTA'—How is it that the sky is ablaze?

THE TWO GODDESSES—Ah, we have it,

Those very weapons are manifesting themselves, along with the Jṛimbhakas, whose order of transmission is from Kṛiśàs'va to Kaus'ika and from Kaus'ika to Ràma. (9)

(Behind the scenes).

Queen Sìtà, our homage to thee; thy sons are our resort, since king Ràma, the delight of Raghu's race, so commanded us on the occasion of his looking at the painting. (10)

SÎTA'—Happily these are the presiding deities of the missiles. Ah, my lord, your favours are still shining upon us.

LAK.—Your lordship had said that they would by all means wait upon her offspring.

THE TWO GODDESSES—

A bow to you, mighty missiles! Blessed are we by your favour! You should attend upon the boys when meditated upon in the hour of need. May you fare well! (11)

RA'MA—

The waves of emotion mixed with the mingled feelings of wonder and joy being set in agitation now hurl me into an indescribable state. (12)

THE TWO GODDESSES—Rejoice, daughter, rejoice. Your sons have now become like dear Ràma.

SÎTA'—Divine ones, who will perform in their case the rites proper for the warrior class?

RA'MA—

Alas, even Sìtà, the delight of the race of the Raghus who are guarded by Vasishṭha, finds no one to perform the ceremonies of her sons. (13)

BHA'G.—Child, why trouble yourself with this thought? When these boys are weaned I will entrust them to the venerable Vàlmîki who will perform for them the necessary rites.

Just as Vasishṭha and Aṅgirasa are, so is the sage Vàlmîki the spiritual guide of the families of Janaka and Raghu. (14)

RA'MA—It is well thought of by the revered goddess.

LAK.—I really tell you, my lord, that from these various circumstances I see that these two boys are Kus'a and Lava.

For these two warriors had the missiles from their very birth, both were under Práchetasa, they resemble your lordship and are twelve years in age. (15)

RA'MA—Dear brother, my heart too being tossed by similar thoughts, I am quite bewildered.

PRI.—Come child, sanctify the surface of the earth.

RA'MA—Ah my dear, you are gone to the other world.

SÎTA—Let my mother take me up in her bosom. I can no more put up with such vicissitudes of the world of the living.

R'AMA—What will the answer be ?

PṚI.—At my command take care of the boys until they are weaned. Thereafter you may have your wishes.

GANGA'—Just so.

(Exeunt the two DEITIES *with* SÎTA').

R'AMA—What, the princess of Videha has altogether disappeared ? Alas Queen, dear companion in the exile of Daṇḍaka, O goddess of virtue, you have departed to the next world ! *(He swoons.)*

LAK.—Save, save, O venerable Vàlmîki. Is this the gist of your piece ?

(Behind the scenes.)

Remove the musical instruments. O you living beings, movable and immovable, mortals and immortals, behold now a holy miracle ordained by the great sage, the venerable Vâlmîki.

LAK.—*(Looking forth)*.

The water of the Ganges is agitated as if from churning ; the sky is filled up with divine sages ; and Oh, wonder, there emerges from the water the Queen, along with the goddesses Gaṅgà and Pṛithivî. (16)

(Again behind the scenes).

O Arundhatî, adorable to the world, know us to be Gaṅgà and Pṛithivî : here we make over to you your daughter-in-law, Sîtà, of virtuous character. (17)

LAK.—Oh, wonderful, wonderful ! See, see, my lord ! *(Observing)*. Alas, his lordship does not recover yet !

(Enter ARUNDHATÎ *and* SÎTA'.)

ARUN.—

Hasten, O princess of Videha ; leave aside your bashfulness ; come and vivify my son by the agreeable touch of your hand. (18)

SÎTA'—*(Touching him in great haste)*. Cheer up, my lord, cheer up.

RA'MA—*(Having regained consciousness, joyfully)*. Oh, what is this ? *(Seeing her, with joy and wonder)*. Oh, the Queen ! *(With a feeling of shame)*. Oh, my mother Arundhatî and all my elders, Ṛishyas'ṛiṅga, Śàntá and others, are here in rejoicings!

ARUN.—Here is the divine Gaṅgà, the tutelary goddess of Bhagîratha's house, graciously disposed.

(*Behind the scenes.*)

Lord of the world, Rámachandra, remember your words addressed to me at the time you were looking at the painting, *viz.*, 'Be thou, O mother, ever devoted, like Arundhatî, to the welfare of Sîtà, your daughter-in-law', and I have fulfilled that obligation.

ARUN.—Here is your mother-in-law, the revered Earth.

(*Behind the scenes, again*).

The long-lived one had said at the time of the banishment of my dear daughter—Revered Vasundharà, look after the well-being of your noble daughter, Jànakî,—and I have acted up to those royal words of my son.

RA'MA—How, your reverences still favour me though I have committed a great crime! I bow to you.

ARUN.—Ye citizens and countrymen, here is Queen Sîtá, born of the sacrificial ground and daughter-in-law in the solar family, who has now been thus praised by the goddesses Gaṅgá and Vasundhará, whose pure character had been formerly established by the divine Fire and who has been eulogized by Brahmá and the other gods—made over to me, Arundhatî. What do you think as to her being accepted now?

LAK.—My lord, thus upbraided by the revered Arundhatî, the people of the city and the country, and the multitude of beings, pay their homage to the Queen, while the guardians of the world and the seven sages are honouring her with showers of flowers.

ARUN.—Lord of the world, Ràmachandra,

Install as your associate in the sacrifice your beloved and virtuous wife, the holy original of the gold image. (19)

SÎTA'—(*To herself*). My lord knows how to wipe away Sîtá's sorrow.

RA'MA—As your reverence commands.

LAK.—I have gained my object.

SÎTA'—I breathe again.

LAK.—Queen, here does shameless Lakshmaṇa bow to you.

SÎTA'—May you live long, such as you are!

ARUN.—Revered Vàlmíki, let Kus'a and Lava, the sons of good RA'MA, born of Sîtá's womb, be presented now. (*With these words exit*).

RA'MA and LAK.—Thank God, it is as we thought it.

SÎTA'—(*Overwhelmed with tears*). Where are those my sons? (*Then enter* VA'LMI'KI *with* KUS'A *and* LAVA).

VA'L.—Dear Kus'a and Lava, here is the lord of Raghus, your father; here is Lakshmaṇa, your uncle; this is Sîtá, your mother, and this is the royal sage Janaka, your maternal grandfather.

SÎTA'—(*Looking at him with a mingled feeling of joy, sorrow and wonder*). How, my father!

KUS'A and LAVA—O father, O mother, O grandfather!

RAM'A and LAK.—(*Embracing them with joy*). Now, boys, you are obtained by merit.

SÎTA'—Come my darling Kus'a, come my boy Lava, embrace for a long time, your mother, who have obtained another existence.

KUS'A and LAVA—(*Doing accordingly*). Blessed are we!

SÎTA'—Venerable sir, I salute you.

VA'L.—Child, mayest thou long be in this happy state!

SÎTA'—O blessed day! Here I see my father, our family preceptor, the elderly matrons, the noble S'ántá with her consort, my revered lord, together with Lakshmaṇa, graciously disposed, and with them all, Kus'a and Lava. So I am overwhemed with joy.

(*A confused noise behind the scenes*).

V'AL.—(*Rising and observing*). Oh, the lord of Mathurâ (S'atrughna) has arrived after having slain Lavaṇa.

LAK.—Good fortunes come in train!

RA'MA—Though enjoying all this I cannot be sure of that. Or rather, such is the nature of prosperity.

VA'L.—Good Râma, tell me what further favour I shall bestow upon you.

RA'MA—Can there be anything further to be wished for! Nevertheless let there be this:—

This story (the Râmâyaṇa) the well-known one, which leads to bliss and is heart-ravishing, purifies from sins and increases blessings. May the wise revolve in their minds this composition (thus) developed (here) in a dramatic form (*lit.*, a poem characterized by gesticulations), that same one composed by the learned Vālmîki, who had perceived the Brahma in the form of words. (20)

(*Exevnt Omnes*).

END OF ACT VII.,

Styled 'The Final Union'.

NOTES.

ACT I.

P. 1. उत्तररामचरितम्—*Lit.* 'an account of the latter part of Râma's life,' signifies 'the play of that name' as embodying that account, by अभेदोपचार or the rhetorical transference of an epithet. *Cf.* शारीरकं, the title of Śaṃkarâchârya's Bhâshya on the Ved. Sût., on which Dikshit remarks शारीरकं भाष्यमिति त्वभेदोपचारात् ; or उत्त० लक्षणया तद्वर्णनं यस्मिन् ।

इदं कविभ्यः &c.—Following the convention of Sanskrit writers on poetics the poet opens his play with what is termed the *Nándî*. See p. 3. This constitutes the Maṅgala of Sanskrit writers, which removes obstacles in the way of the writer and ensures success. इदं—qualifies नमोवाकं; see below, सामान्ये नपुंसकम्. कविभ्यः पूर्वेभ्यः—Such as Válmîki, Vyàsa and others, the originators and institutors of the science of poetry. Kálidása, too, makes a similar reference to the पूर्वसूरिs in his Ragh. I. 4. Some take कविभ्यः to refer to Vâlmîki alone, the plural being used आदरार्थे (to show respect). But this does not seem to be natural and is not necessary. The Com. Lakshmaṇa and Vîra. (also in the alternate interpretation he suggests), take इदं कविभ्यः as one word (see com. p. 2. l. 19); but this is unnatural. नमोवाकं—नम इति शब्दस्य वाकमुक्तिं, the expression 'a bow to'. वाक is a *mas.* noun derived from वच्+अ (घञ्) added भावे (see com. p. 2 l. 29), the च् being changed to क् by चोः कुः Páṇ. VIII. 2. 30. नमोवाकं नमोवचनं; वचेर्घञ् Tattvabodhinî. The नमस्कृति is कायिक as shown by इदं and वाचिक as indicated by प्रशास्महे (wish for, *i. e.* address) निर्दिशामः. नमःशब्दस्य वचनं कुर्महे इत्यर्थः । Śekhara. The ultimate sense is नमःशब्दस्योच्चारणपूर्वकं तान्स्तुमः । We praise them by folding our hands and uttering the words 'Our veneration to you.' The reading नमोवाक्यं is meaningless, as नमः is not a वाक्य, unless we supply अस्तु after नमः. The root शास् with आ in the sense of 'to wish' is given as A'tm. (आङ्शासु इच्छायाम्). How does the poet use it in the A'tm. with प्र then? The rule about आ is not absolute:— आङ्पूर्वत्वं प्रायिकं तेन नमोवाकं प्रशास्महे इति सिद्धं; Sid.-Kau. The Com. Gh. interprets these two lines as containing a salutation to Gaṇapati, quoting the Vedic passage गणपतिं हवामहे कविं कवीनाम् &c. (कवये गणपतये इत्यर्थः). But this is far-fetched.

वन्देमहि &c.—Next he salutes the goddess of speech (that he should succeed in his undertaking and win the applause of the audience). तां—*that i. e.* who is well-known. अमृतां—imperishable, immortal. The goddess of speech is immortal as being a phase of the Supreme Spirit. The poet further on uses the word शब्दब्रह्म; see p. 54. आत्मनः—A'tman used by itself generally means 'the Supreme Soul.' When the distinction between the Supreme Soul and the individual one is to be marked, the words पर and प्रत्यच् are respectively prefixed to it. कलाम्—कला इव तां what looks like a portion of; a phase of. *Cf.* काव्यालापाश्च ये केचिद्गीतकान्यखिलानि च। शब्दमूर्तिधरस्यैते विष्णोरंशा महात्मनः॥ V. P. I. 22. 84.; see also com. Vîra. proposes several other interpretations of this śl. which are far-fetched.

2nd half—विन्देम देवतां &c. *V. l.* In this case इदं in the first half refers to the prayer expressed in the 2nd; नमोवाकं must be taken adverbially; नम इति वाकः (उक्तिः) यस्मिन्कर्मणि तद्यथा तथा in a manner in which the word नमः is uttered, *i. e.* having uttered &c.; or it may be taken as a gerund in अम् (णमुल्) from वच्, नम इत्युक्त्वा. प्रशास्महे—we wish, pray for—that we may obtain Divine speech *i. e.* power of expression, command of language. With this reading the first line fits in better with the 2nd; and yet this reading does not seem to be genuine. We cannot expect the poet to make such a prayer (for though put in the mouth of the Sûtra., it is really an expression of his own wish) in the face of his assertion यं ब्रह्माणं &c. immediately after this, and his usual utterances of confidence in his power elsewhere (वश्यवाचः कवेर्वाक्यं Mv. I. 4, Mál.-Mádh. I. 7 &c.). Also what is the propriety of the epithets देवतां and आत्मनः कलाम् then ? They are out of place unless a salutation is offered to the goddess of learning. Again with this reading the Nândî has eleven *padas* only instead of twelve. It is also in the fitness of things that the poet should salute Válmîki and also the divine speech that was revealed to him before he described the Rámáyaṇa, (see p. 53 *infra*) as he too had to do the same thing. We, however, leave this question an open one.

P. 3. नान्दी—आशीर्नमस्क्रियारूपः श्लोकः काव्यार्थसूचकः । नान्दीति कथ्यते । Bharata. नन्दन्ति देवता अस्यास्तस्मान्नान्दीति कीर्तिता। It is so called because it is the cause of delight to the gods (as well as to actors, &c.). The Nândi or the Benediction forms the first part of the Prelude and is termed 'the Pûrvaranga.'

In it the protection of the tutelary deity is generally invoked in favour of the audience or the actors. Sometimes a short prayer is added to the benediction or even substituted for it. The Nândî may consist of eight, twelve or eighteen *Padas*; see com. p. 3, यत्राहुमि: &c. which gives the convention about the length of the Nândî. The term पद् is variously defined; if it be taken to mean a foot of a Śloka, it may consist of one or more stanzas; the best writers scarcely go beyond one or two. The present Nándî is made to conform to the convention by taking पद् in its usual acceptance of a grammatical word. It has twelve Padas. With the other reading प्र must be separated from प्रशास्महे (उपसर्गतिङन्तयो: समासाभावेन) to get the number twelve. According to the def. of the Nándî given above it should give an indication of the subject-matter of the plot. Thus the words आत्मन: कला refer to Ràma and Sîtá; वन्देमहि च &c. to the people's repentance and their bowing to Sîtâ leading to her re-union with Râma through the favour of Vâlmîki to whom reference is made in the first line. See com.

नान्द्यन्ते सूत्रधार:—This stage-direction is put after the Nándî, agreeably to Hindu prejudices, though it has puzzled many a commentator. It is the Sûtradhâra (unless otherwise directed) who recites the Nândî according to the text of Bharata—'The Sûtradhâra should recite the Nândî in a tone neither high nor low &c.' But his name is not put before the Nândî, as nothing but auspicious words can introduce a work. For a full discussion of this question see our notes on Śàk. or Vik. It is also not unlikely that it was the intention of the original writers, though the commentators have failed to mark it, to discriminate between the real and assumed character of the Sûtradhàra, who repeated the Benediction in his proper character as a Bráhmaṇa, which he often was, and then carried on the dialogue of the Prelude as the manager of the theatrical company.

कालप्रियनाथस्य—All the three plays of Bhavabhûti are mentioned as being represented at the shrine of Kála., by which term the poet probably refers to the god Śiva in his own town (Padmapura). It seems, in ancient India it was usual to exhibit dramatic performances at some fair or on the occasion of some festival. (See Rat.).

आर्यमिश्रान्—The honourable or respectable gentlemen. The title आर्य corresponds to the modern 'gentleman'; for the qualifications of an A'rya, *cf.* Bharata as quoted by Jag.—कुलं

शीलं दया दानं धर्मः सत्यं कृतज्ञता । अद्रोह इति येष्वेतत्तानार्यान्संप्रचक्षते ॥ मिश्र—is simply used as an honorific suffix; see com. also; it is sometimes added to the names of great scholars, as मण्डनमिश्र. अत्रभवन्तः—Your honours. अत्र and तत्र are prefixed to the pronoun भवत् to show respect; अत्रभवान् refers to a person near at hand, and तत्रभवान् to one not present.

श्रीकण्ठ०—श्रीः सरस्वती, or 'ऋचो यजूंषि सामानि सा हि श्रीरमृता सती' इत्युक्तलक्षणा वाग् वा कण्ठे यस्य. This was Bhavabhûti's paternal name according to the commentators. भवभूति—The Com. accounts for the name in two ways, which see. The words नाम and लाञ्छन, however, show that the reverse is true. भवभूति was the poet's proper name (his birth being probably the result of Śiva's favour) and his exceptional poetical abilities afterwards gained for him the distinctive appellation of Śrîkaṇṭha. पद०—see com; पद *lit.* 'a grammatical form' stands for Grammar; वाक्य or a logical statement or a syllogism for 'Logic or Nyáya'; and प्रमाण or authoritative statement for the two Mîmáṃsás, Pûrva and Uttara. जातुकर्णी—जतुकर्णगोत्रप्रसूता. The mention of the name of the poet is in accordance with Bharata's precept—प्रसाद्य रङ्गं विधिवत् कवेर्नाम च कीर्तयेत् । प्रस्तावनां ततः कुर्यात् काव्यप्रख्यापनाश्रयाम् ॥. Nâṭ. V. 154. It was necessary in those days of scanty means of circulation to announce to the people the name and scholarship of the writer of a play; only then a good audience was attracted.

P. 4. ब्रह्माणं—The word is purposely used instead of ब्राह्मण. In the first place it shows that Bhavabhûti was a rigid performer of the six duties of a Bráhmaṇa (see com.), *viz.* यजन, याजन; अध्ययन, अध्यापन; दान and प्रतिग्रह; secondly it implies comparison to the God Brahmá whose wife सरस्वती is. वश्या—one entirely in the power of another; one having no free will or independence of action; a servant girl. The fig. is Upamá. Some construe ब्रह्माणमिव यं &c., but then this would be liable to the fault of दूरान्वय. The Com. reads वश्येवान्ववर्तत and says वश्या सत्येव विधिप्रतिषेधार्हा (who could be ordered or forbidden by him) &c.; for his other subtleties of construction see com. With this comp. वश्यवाचः कवेर्वाक्यं, Mv. I. 4. उत्तरं &c.—The present play is a sequel to the Mv., wherein the poet has depicted the events of Ráma's life previous to his installation on the throne of Ayodhyá after his conquest of Laṅkà.

P. 5. कार्यवशादायोध्यकः—an inhabitant of Ayodhà on account of some business, *i. e.* he was not a native of Ayodhya.

as will appear further on, but one gone there on some special business. कार्य does not mean 'the business of the play', although the com. says प्रयोगानुरोधात्; for it does not explain his वैदेशिकत्व. See p. 6 (वैदेशिकोऽस्मीति &c.). आयोध्यक means belonging to Ayodhyá; see com. It is formed from अयोध्या and the aff. वुञ् (अक) which is added to a word denoting a locality and having य for its penultimate. See Sid.-Kau. on Pàṇ. IV. 2. 121, 125.

पौलस्त्य—Rávaṇa, the son of Viśravas, the son of Pulastya, one of the ten Prajápatis. See Rámá. Sun. K. 23. 6. 8. कुल—refers to Rávaṇa's sons and brother Kumbhakarṇa and sister Śúrpaṇakhá. ०धूमकेतोः—The destructive fire to. *Cf.* नन्दकुलकाननधूमकेतोः Mud. I. 10. धूमः लिङ्गं चिह्नं वा अस्य. धूमकेतु may also mean a comet (which is commonly regarded as the harbinger of some coming calamity; *cf.* Kum. II. 32). रात्रिंदिवं-रात्रौ च दिवा च irregular Dvandva; day and night, without a break. असंहता०—आनन्दार्था आनन्दसूचिका वा नान्दी आनन्द०, असंहता आनन्दनान्दी यस्मिन्. नान्दी—Joyous songs together with instrumental music. According to some नान्दी means 'the symphonious sound of twelve tabors beaten simultaneously' (एकदा द्वादशमृदङ्गघोषो नान्दी इति रङ्गराजः). अभिषेक०—Vîra. reads पट्टाभि०, where पट्ट means 'a fillet or tiara made of gold worn at the time of the coronation;' see Ragh. XVIII. 44; पट्टप्रधानः अभिषेकः पट्टाभिषेकः; a comp. of the शाकपार्थिवादि class. विश्रान्तचार०—चारणs are wandering minstrels or singers; or actors. Vîra. reads चारचरणानि and explains विश्रान्तं चाराणामधिकारिपुरुषाणां (government officers) चरणं movement येषु; for other interpretations, see com. चत्वरस्थानानि—Public stalls or squares; चत्वर (Mará. चवाठा) is a place where four roads meet. It also means 'a courtyard'; the courtyards of houses.

भाव—The Sûtradhára is so addressed in dramas. It means 'the learned one'; भावो विद्वान् Ak. स्वगृहान्मा०—may be separated as ०गृहात् from his palace; or स्वगृहान् acc. pl., to their homes. But in this case we should rather expect स्वगृहाणि; besides, there is no propriety of saying 'to their houses.'

P. 6. प्लवंग—प्लवेन गच्छति इति one that goes by leaps; a monkey; fr. गम् by adding अ (खच्) before which a nasal is inserted; by adding (अ) प्लवग also. समाजनोप०—See com.; who waited upon him to greet or to offer their hearty congratulations. The other reading समाजोप० 'who waited upon him in groups or in the assembly or at the coronation' does not seem to be original, and is not appropriate. संभाज् 10. P· (probably derived from सं + भज् cau.) combines in itself the idea of respect with joy (प्रीतिदर्शनयोः). It is again used in I. 7. ०दिगन्तपावनाः—*V. l.* the purifiers of different regions by reason of their holiness. This reading is not appropriate here; but the purifying influence of the sages and other holy personages is often referred to by Sanskrit poets; *cf.* संचारपूतानि दिगन्तराणि &c. Ragh. II. 15; Kum. VI. 60, 61; पुण्यानि हि नामग्रहणान्यपि महामुनीनां किं पुनर्दर्शनानि । Kâd. p. 77. ब्रह्मर्षयः &c.—Seven classes of Ṛishis are generally mentioned. They are Ṛishi, Maharshi, Paramarshi, Devarshi, Brahmarshi, Kándarshi and Śrutarshi. A king who leads a hermit's life, being a Kshatriya, ranks below a ṛishi. आः—Interj. implying 'recollection' here· In some edd. this speech is omitted, the previous speech being continued as संप्रति हि वसिष्ठ &c. then सू०—एवमेतत् । नटः-वैदेशिकोऽस्मीति &c. But this is not right; it is the Sûtradhára who is a stranger in Ayodhyá and not the Naṭa, as is clear from his very question किमिति विश्रान्तचारणानि &c. and from the words of the Naṭa अतिदुर्जन इति वक्तव्यं—देव्या etc. (which show that he knew the people of Ayo. very well) further on. Had the Sûtra. been a native of Ayodhyá he would have known it.

वसिष्ठः—The family priest of the solar race, the son of Brahmá in one life, and of Mitra and Varuṇa in another. See note on Nimi p. 39. राघव०-*V. l.* राघव properly means 'a descendant of Raghu.' As Ráma was the most distinguished of the Raghus, the term here applies to him. यज्ञे—For being present at; the loc. indicates object or purpose; or सति may be supplied after यज्ञे, यज्ञे सति there being a sacrifice; see com. अपत्यकृतिका—see com.; or अपत्याय कृतिः acceptance यस्याः. We have कृतकतनयः in Megh. II. 8. रोमपाद—Lomapâda was a king of Aṅga. See Râm. Bâl. 11; also 7, 9, 10. The Râmâ.* seems to say that शान्ता was the daughter of Romapáda; see Bâl. 9; but the Vish. P. distinctly says that she was Das'aratha's daughter (यस्मादजपुत्रो दशरथः शान्तां नाम कन्यामनपत्याय दुहितृत्वे नियुयोज) (Vish. P. IV. 18.)

* In the com. accompanying I's'varachandra's ed., verses are quoted from the Râmâ. Bâl. Canto X. to show that Loma. who was without issue adopted S'ânta' as his daughter (अपुत्रस्त्वङ्गराजो वै लोमपाद इति श्रुतः । स राजानं दशरथं प्रार्थयिष्यति भूमिपः ॥......दास्यते तां तदा कन्यां शान्तामङ्गाधिपाय सः । &c.); but these are not found in the Bombay ed. of the Ráma'.

P. 7. विभाण्डकसुत: &c.—Vibhâṇḍaka was a descendant of Kaśyapa. ऋष्य०—so called because he had a small horn on his forehead. When a great drought devastated the country of Anga, its king Lomapâda. by the advice of the Bráhmaṇas, caused ऋष्य० to be brought to his country by means of seductive damsels, and gave his daughter, Śântà, in marriage to him. Ṛish. was pleased and rain fell in copious showers. It was this Ṛishya. who performed for Daśaratha the Putrakâmeshṭi. द्वादशवार्षिकं—lasting for twelve years; see com. which quotes Páṇ. V. 1. 80. The aff. ठञ् (इक) has a past sense as well as future; as मासं भूतो मासिको व्याधिः, मासं भावी मासिक उत्सवः । Sid.-Kau. Here the Sattra was just commenced, as is clear from A'treyî's words in the second Act–संप्रति परिसमाप्तं &c.; see p. 52. तदनुरोधात्—in compliance with this request. उत्कोर—developed. ०गर्भां—advanced in pregnancy. Sîtâ does not seem to have been far advanced in pregnancy, as in the message from Arundhatî and the old queens brought by Ashṭávakra, reference is made to her pregnancy desires, which a woman has in the earlier stage of pregnancy up to the fifth month.

स्वजातिसमयेन—According to the duties of our class, which lie in singing songs in praise of the king. समय–customary duties (आचार). उपतिष्ठाव:—wait upon. By the Vârttika 'उपाद्देवपूजा–संगतिकरण–मित्रकरण–पथिष्विति वाच्यम्', स्था with उप ought to be A'tm. The Com. defends the Paras. by supposing Râma to be a mortal; but if the view that a king is a portion of God (*cf.* Kâlid.–स्तुत्यं स्तुतिभिरर्थ्याभिरुपतस्थे सरस्वती । Ragh. IV. 6) be followed, the Paras. is to be defended by the Várt. वा लिप्सायाम्.

उपस्थानस्तोत्र०—उपस्थानार्था स्तोत्रपद्धतिः; पद्धति mode of expression, composition (with which they may approach the king). उपस्थान-waiting upon for the purpose of pleasing.

मारिष—*Lit.* a patient (मर्षणान्मारिषः) or good man. Also a term of address (used by the Sûtra. when speaking to the chief actor or Pa'ripa'rśvika); see D.-R. II. 69.

सर्वथा &c.—He means—It is ours to do our duty properly. It is useless to seek exemption or freedom from blame; for we can never find it in this world situated as it is (so full of wicked men). व्यवहर्तव्ये—*V. l.* The cons. will be-व्यवहर्तव्ये (in matters to be transacted) सर्वथा (in every respect, absolutely *i. e.* from which one can not hope to escape) अवचनीयता कुतः। न कश्चिदपीत्यर्थः । But this is not as forcible as the reading in the text. यथा &c.—The fig. is अर्थान्तरन्यास. वाचां साधुत्वे—Perhaps this is intended as a fling against his adverse critics by the poet; *cf.* ये नाम केचिदिह नः प्रथयन्त्यवज्ञां Mâl.-Mâdh. I. 6. दुर्जनः—*i. e.* doing discredit to their humanity. *Cf.* the following in which women and speech are compared—सरसाः कान्तिहारिण्यो नानाश्लेषविचक्षणाः । भवन्ति कस्यचित्पुण्यैर्मुखे वाचो गृहे स्त्रियः ॥ Mark how ingeniously and yet imperceptibly the poet is introducing the audience to the public slander about Sîtâ, which is the turning-point in the play.

P. 8. देव्याः—Mark the appropriateness of the term. Even Sîtâ's divine origin does not shield her from blame. वैदेह्याः—is also emphatic. She, the daughter of Janaka, ought to have been above all such blame. सापवादः—talking scandalously जनः—The people. According to the Râmâ. it was only a washerman who blamed Râma for admitting Sîtâ in his house; but the poet makes the people at large talk ill of her, probably to show that Râma had sufficient ground to take the step he took in abandoning Sîtâ. रक्षोगृह॰—This reading is preferable to ॰गृहे स्थितिः; for, symmetry requires it; ॰गृहस्थिति better corresponds to अग्निशुद्धि. तु—brings out very vividly the folly of the people. They easily believe the one but disbelieve the other. *Cf.* चितां मे कुरु सौमित्रे व्यसनस्यास्य भेषजम् । मिथ्यापवादोपहता नाहं जीवितुमुत्सहे ।......अधोमुखं स्थितं रामं ततः कृत्वा प्रदक्षिणम् । उपावर्तत वैदेही दीप्यमानं हुताशनम् ॥.........यथा मां शुद्धचारित्रं दुष्टां जानाति राघवः । तथा लोकस्य साक्षी मां सर्वतः पातु पावकः ॥ एवमुक्त्वा तु वैदेही परिक्रम्य हुताशनम् । विवेश ज्वलनं दीप्तं निःशंकेनान्तरात्मना ॥ Canto 116; विधूयाथ चितां तां तु वैदेहीं हव्यवाहनः । उत्तस्थौ मूर्तिमानाशु गृहीत्वा जनकात्मजाम् ॥......अब्रवीत्तु तदा रामं साक्षी लोकस्य पावकः । एषा ते राम वैदेही पापमस्यां न विद्यते ॥ 118-2.5. For the full account see Râmâ. Yudh. K. Cantos 115-118.

After the recovery of Sítá from *Rávaṇa*, Râma welcomed her coldly, and after intimating some suspicions unfavourable to her chastity, (तद्गच्छ त्वानुजानेऽद्य यथेष्टं जनकात्मजे । एता दश दिशो भद्रे कार्यमस्ति न मे त्वया ॥ कः पुमांस्तु कुले जातः स्त्रियं परगृहोषिताम् । तेजस्वी पुनरादद्यात्सुहृल्लोभेन चेतसा ॥ Râma. Yudh. K. 115. 18-19) refused to receive her ; on which Sîtâ determined to commit herself to the test of fire. Having entered the fire prepared for this purpose in the presence of the gods and of *Das'aratha*, the deceased father of Ráma, it proved innocuous, and *Agni*, its deity, restored to Râma his bride unhurt, and declared her purified by the ordeal she had undergone. *Das'aratha* also bore testimony to Sítá's virtue, and Râma's doubts being thus dissipated, he joyfully received his bride.—*Uttara.- Ra'mâyaṇa.*

According to the *Brahmavaivarta Purâṇa*, Sîtâ herself was not carried off by *Ràvaṇa*, her shadow or *Chha'ya'* being substituted by *Agni* for her substance. It was this semblance, also, that entered the fire, in order to give *Agni* an opportunity of restoring the original to Râma. The *Padma-Purâṇa* (*Pa'ta'la-Khaṇḍa*) dispenses with the ordeal, but brings forward *Agni*, *Va'yu*, *Varuṇa*, *Brahma'* and *Das'aratha* to swear to Sîtá's innocence; *Brahmá* further consoles Ráma by declaring it was necessary Sîtâ should have been carried off by *Ra'vana*, as his rape of a virtuous woman was the only cause of destruction to which he was subject, agreeably to the curse denounced upon him by *Nala-Kûvara*, and the previous boon conferred upon him by *Brahmá*. In the *Uttara-Khaṇḍa* of the same *Pura'ṇa* she enters into the fire as in the other authorities. (Wilson.)

P. 9. किंवदन्ती—a scandal, slander. कोपि कुत्सितो वा वादः ; or 'किं वदन्ति' (what do the people say) इत्याख्यायमाना (in which there is such inquiry). स्यन्देत—will flow to *i. e.* gradually reach the ears of. सर्वथा—श्रेयोवि०—is a distant indication of Sîtá's final restoration with her son and the happy termination of the plot. The two speeches of the Sûtra. and of the actor also contain the Bîja of the plot. See com.

भो भोः &c.—This is a speech addressed आकाशे as remarked by the com., although there is no stage direction to that effect. When a character asks a question to a character or characters, not present on the stage, shows that he hears a reply, and reproduces it, it is called an आकाशभाषित ; see com.

सभाजयितुं—*Cf.* देवं सभाजयितुमागताः S'a'k. p. 121. जनक—king of Videha. He was the foster father of Sîtâ, having found her, an infant, in the ground ploughed for sacrificial purposes. Hence Sîtâ possessed the patronymic Vaidehî. Janaka was known for his great piety and good works and was deeply read in the Vedantic lore. The sage Yâjñavalkya was his spiritual guide. See *infra* IV. 9. विदेह—The country which lay to the north-east of Magadha. Its capital Mithilâ is the same as Janakapura in Nepal, north of Madhuvâṇî. विमनसः—विगतं unsettled, distracted मनोऽस्याः । धर्मासन—Judgment-seat (धर्म law, आसन seat). This is also called कार्यासन (Vik. II.), व्यवहारासन (Ragh. VIII. 18) &c. धर्मासनात्—leaving the judgment-seat; the abl. is ल्यब्लोपे (०सनं विहाय). नरेन्द्रः—Here Râma's entry on the stage is indicated according to the canon of dramaturgy—"No character shall enter the stage without previous intimation to the audience."

प्रस्तावना—For def. see com. p. 3. That is आमुख or प्रस्ता० wherein the Sûtradhâra holds conversation with नटी, or विदूषक or some actor, indicative of the matter in hand. It is of five kinds of which the present is of the प्रयोगातिशय kind. See Sah.-Dar. IV. 36.

ततः प्रविशति &c.—This is a technical expression. It is not possible for Râma to walk seated, but he is discovered seated on the stage when the curtain is lifted up. **न शक्नुवन्ति**—Râma means that Janaka's departure was not an act of will but of necessity. **गुरवः**—The pl. used out of respect. *Cf.* आज्ञा गुरूणां ह्यविचारणीया । Ragh. XIV. 46.

नित्यत्वं—does not mean here 'daily performance'; for in that case Janaka could not have stayed at Râma's palace even for a day; but the necessary performance of rites at stated or fixed periods (नियमेन भवं नित्यं) such as दर्शपूर्णमासेष्टि, &c., नित्यत्व being equivalent to नियतत्व. The acts (कर्माणि) enjoined upon a person are of three kinds—नित्य, नैमित्तिक and काम्य. The नित्य acts are those which, when not performed, lead to sin, such as संध्यावन्दन, वैश्वदेव &c.; the नैमित्तिकs are those which ought to be performed on stated occasions, such as at the time of the birth of a child, &c. The काम्यs, as their name implies, are those which are to be performed for the accomplishment of some object, as the पुत्रकामेष्टि. Lak. explains अनुष्ठाने नित्यास्तत्परा अनुष्ठाननित्या अध्यात्मनित्या इति वत् । तेषां भावस्तत्त्वं धर्मैकप्रवणतेत्यर्थः । But this is not a good way, as it does not explain the स्वातन्त्र्यापकर्षण. Gh. reads ०नित्यत्वात्—which is not good; for in this case the construction becomes involved; गृहस्थता must be taken as the subject of अपकर्षति; besides, हि remains unexplained. अपकर्षति—takes away, denies them (the independence to act in domestic matters as they like). **आहिताग्नीनां**—Three fires are usually consecrated, *viz.* दक्षिणाग्निर्गार्हपत्याहवनीयौ त्रयोऽग्नयः । Amara. The perpetual fire is kept burning in the *Kuṇḍa* called गार्हपत्य, from which it is taken to the other *Kundas* as required. **संकटा**—full of, beset with; from कट् with सम् to cover fully and अच्; or सं an obstacle and कट added स्वार्थे. **प्रत्यवाय**—fr. इ or अय् to go, with प्रति and अव; an obstacle, such as अनुष्ठाननित्यत्व &c.; or the sin caused by the non-performance of obligatory acts, as the Com. takes it. वीरहा वा एष देवानां भवति योऽग्निमुद्वासयते । इति श्रुतेः । The same śloka occurs in Mv. (IV. 33). **गृहस्थता**—The life of a householder, domestic as well as religious.

P. 10. **अज्जउत्त**—आर्यपुत्र the son of the father-in-law; a term used in dramas by a wife when addressing or speaking about her husband. **संसारभावा:**—such worldly incidents as separations from beloved persons, &c. The Com. reads भागा: (the portions of happiness or misery that fall to a man's lot), but this has no propriety. Gh. and Lak. read भोगा: pleasures, enjoyments, which also does not suit the context. Râma is here referring to Sîtâ's separation from her father, which is not a भोग. Besides, pleasures do not pierce the vital parts of the heart. **बीभत्समान**—Pres. p. of बीभत्सते the desiderative base of बधृ, to be disgusted with. For the ab. येभ्य: see com.; बधृ takes the desi. aff. स in the sense of चित्तविकार (see the Vârt. quoted in the com.), something at which the mind revolts. **मनीषिन्**—मनीषा अस्यास्तीति; a talented man. According to Malli. (who follows Bhâshya) मनस ईषिण: those who reach everything by their mind; those whose intellect can penetrate everything. A comp. of the पृषोदरादि class.

कञ्चुकी—So called from the long white cloak he wore. Bharata calls him कञ्चुकीय (the form काञ्चुकेय is also met with in Bhâsa's dramas). He was generally an old Bráhmaṇa, truthful, free from the influence of passion, and a clever man of business; *cf.* ये विप्रा: सत्यसंपन्ना: कामदोषविवर्जिता: । ज्ञानविज्ञानकुशला: कञ्चुकीयास्तु ते स्मृता: ॥ Bharata XXIV. 58; see also com. **रामभद्र**—'Child Ráma.' This form of address has a blessing implied in it and bespeaks seniority or superiority on the part of the speaker. The Kañchukin at first addresses Râma as was his wont when Daśaratha lived and Ráma was only a prince; but suddenly remembering that Râma was now a crowned king, he corrects himself and addresses him as महाराज 'My Lord'. **आर्य**—The Kañchukin is always a respectable character in Sanskrit plays. He is never treated as an ordinary menial. **उपचार**—a form or mode of address. This shows Râma's modesty, as well as his courtesy, to his servants. Wilson remarks on this passage-The mode here adopted of delineating Ráma's kindly disposition is very Shakespearian.

अष्टावक्र—*Lit.* crooked in eight limbs; see com. The penultimate अ of अष्टन् is lengthened only when the whole is a name; (otherwise अष्टपुत्र:). A celebrated Brâhmaṇa, son of the great sage Kahoḍa. His father who had married a daughter of his preceptor Uddâlaka, was so devoted to his holy studies that he neglected his wife even when she was far advanced in pregnancy. The son while yet in the womb blamed his father for this neglect of her. The sage became very angry at this impertinence and condemned his son to be born crooked. यस्मात्कुक्षौ वर्तमानो ब्रवीषि तस्माद्वक्रो भवितास्यष्टकृत्वः। Mb. By his father's favour, however, he afterwards became perfectly straight (by having bathed in the river Samanyâ).

P. 11. सोमपीथी—सोमस्य पीथं पानमस्यास्ति; the form सोमपीती—सोमस्य पीतं पानमस्यास्तीति–also occurs. One who habitually drinks Soma; a constant performer of *Somayâga*. आवुत्तः—भगिनीपतिः (Amara.) a brother-in-law. Vîra. reads भावुकः the blissful one. उपविश्य—the questions were asked so rapidly that he had no time to sit. The additional epithet कुलगुरु after देवि is dropped as out of place here.

विश्वंभरा—विश्वं बिभर्ति इति that which supports the world, the earth. From विश्व+भृ+अ (खच्) before which a nasal comes in; similarly रथंतरं साम, पतिंवरा कन्या, अरिंदमः; see Pâṇ. III. 2. 46. प्रजापतिसमः—Janaka is compared to Brahmâ on account of his great knowledge. He figures in the Upanishads as a *Brahmavittama* and *Brahmanishṭha* king and a great patron of learning. He was also जीवन्मुक्त, *i. e.* one who had obtained मोक्ष while living; *cf.* अभयं वै जनक प्राप्तोसि, Bṛih. Up. IV. 2·4. तेषां—such illustrious kings as Dasaratha, Aja, Raghu, &c. नन्दिनी—*Lit.* 'The delighter.' The word shows that the birth of a daughter was as much a source of delight as that of a son in ancient times. गुरु—(1) the progenitor; (2) the spiritual guide.

P. 12. किमन्यत् &c.—Vasishṭha says this, because, being the daughter-in-law of the solar kings and daughter of Janaka, Sîtâ had every comfort at command, so that the only wish he could express with regard to her was to wish that she should give birth to a hero. *Cf.* Ragh. V. 35. वीरप्रसवा—A blessing much prized by the Kshatriya ladies. *Cf.* अपाण्डितं क्षत्रकुलाङ्गनानां न वीरसूशब्दमकामयेताम्। Ragh. XIV. 4.

साधु—साध्नोति धर्मं; fr. साध्+उ Uṇâdi, a righteous man, a saint. ऋषीणां—is opposed to साधूनां, आद्य to लौकिक. The Ṛishis being the repositories of penance have the power to control the workings of Destiny and so their utterances come to be fulfilled whatever they may be; see com. They being आद्य are unfettered by the laws which govern the ordinary world; while ordinary saints have first carefully to ascertain the meaning of what they wish to say and then give utterance to it, lest their saying might not come true. For a very similar idea, *cf.* वरः खलु एष न आशीः and प्रागभिप्रेतसिद्धिः पश्चाद्दर्शनं, तव प्रसादस्य पुरस्तु संपदः । Śák. VII.

गर्भदोहदः—दोहं आकर्षं ददाति इति दोहदः *m. n.*; दोहदः पुंनपुंसकं Rabhasakos'a. Though given in Amara as a syn. of इच्छा, it usually means a pregnancy desire ; *cf.* Viśva गर्भमात्रेपि दोहदम्; and so the addition of गर्भ is unnecessary ; dissolve गर्भकृतः दोहदः गर्भदोहदः. Vîra. reads गर्भदोहृदोदयः the appearance of pregnancy longings; दौहृद a pregnancy desire, fr. द्विहृद् (substituted for द्विहृदया) a pregnant woman, who has two hearts—one her own, one of the child in the womb. See Malli. on Ragh. III. 1 and our note thereon. अचिरान्मानयितव्यः—On the necessity of gratifying the pregnancy-hankerings of a woman, see Malli. on Ragh. III. 6. यदेषा—whatever she tells. यद्येषा *v. l.*—if she tells, which she might not do out of modesty. This at first sight seems to be a better reading, as it brings out Sîtá's modesty, and has support from न मे ह्रिया शंसति किंचिदीप्सितं &c. Ragh. III. 5; and still we have preferred यदेषा ; for the context requires Ráma's readiness to accede to the wish expressed in the message; it does not look at all polite to make it conditional. Again, it is the duty of the husband to ask and know the desire of his wife even though she does not tell it of her own accord.

P. 14. वत्से &c., वत्सोपि रामभद्रः &c. Ṛishya. addresses Ráma and Sîtá thus, as he was an elderly kinsman, being the husband of Śántâ, Ráma's elder sister. आदिष्टोस्मि—Mark the humility of Râma. He does not say संदिष्टम्. बालः—The propriety of this word is explained in the com. तस्माद्यशः—Gh. reads स्वस्मात् (यशः) for तस्मात् which he renders by आत्मनः; यत् (since) वः यशः स्वस्मात् परमं धनं glory is a treasure higher than your own selves; but with this reading the construction becomes awkward. The good of the subjects was the first thing the kings of the solar race had at their heart ; *cf.* Ragh. I. 18, 22, and *infra* śl. 14. This message of Vasiṣṭha serves as an incentive to Ráma to come to the decision he did on hearing of the slander about Sîta'.

P. 15. मैत्रावरुणिः—The son of मित्रावरुण ; for the comp. see Gr. § 193. The story of the birth of Vasishṭha is thus given by Sâyaṇâchârya in his com. on Ṛig. VIII. 33. 11—(उतासि मैत्रावरुणो वसिष्ठो &c.) तयोरादित्ययोः (मित्रावरुणयोः) सत्रे दृष्ट्वाप्सरसमुर्वशीम् । रेतश्च-

स्कन्द तत्कुम्भे न्यपतद्वासतीवरे ॥ तेनैव तु मुहूर्तेन वीर्यवन्तौ तपस्विनौ । अगस्त्यश्च वसिष्ठश्च तत्रर्षी संबभूवतुः ॥ बहुधा पतितं रेतः कलशे च जले स्थले । स्थले वसिष्ठस्तु मुनिः संभूत ऋषिसत्तमः ॥ See also Ráma. Uttara-K. Canto 57, 6-7.

स्नेहं &c.—No nobler sentiment has perhaps escaped any other lips. Ràma prized the good of his subjects above every earthly pleasure. In fact Ràma's sense of duty as king had entirely banished all idea of self from his mind. Nay, it was a pleasure to him to subordinate personal comfort to the weal and satisfaction of his subjects. यदि वा &c.—a forecast of the future abandonment of Sîtá. Herein appears the Bîja of the Play. जानकी—mark the propriety of the word; he does not say Sîtà. The reference to Janaka's name shows that he would face even the anger of that monarch, but mind public good. See com. लोकस्य—लोकानां *V. l.*—is abandoned as लोकस्य appears to have been the original reading since Ráma says further on लोको न मृष्यतीति; see p. 82. नास्ति मे व्यथा—*Cf.* अपि स्वदेहात्किमुतेन्द्रियार्थाद्यशोधनानां हि यशो गरीयः । Ragh. XIV. 36. त्यजन्त्यसून् शर्म च मानिनो वरं &c. Nai. 1. 50. तेजस्विनः सुखमसूनपि संत्यजन्ति सत्यव्रतव्यसनिनो न पुनः प्रतिज्ञाम् । Bha. Nît. 110.

अत एव &c.—This shows Sîtá's uncommon affection and reverence for her husband. She, noble-minded and well-bred, not only does not resent the words of her husband uttered to her face, but on the contrary congratulates him for having uttered them. Like her husband she also attached the highest importance to Ráma's duty as a sovereign. *Cf.* her words further on दिष्ट्या अपरिहीनराजधर्मः &c. p. 69. राघवकुल०—See com.; *cf.* अल्पसुमणयिनां रघोः कुले न व्यहन्यत कदाचिदर्थिता । Ragh. XI. 2. विश्राम्यताम्—Let Ashtâ.—be seen to rest; *i.e.* let refreshments be given to him so that his fatigue is removed.

वीथिका—seems to mean here a long wall, or a terrace serving as a picture-gallery. It cannot mean 'a scroll of paper' as some take it. For we see further on that Ràma and Sîtá leave their seat and go to have a look at the painting. Had it been a picture-roll or board Lakshmaṇa could have easily brought it with him. शान्तं पापम्—*Lit.* 'let the evil be pacified (warded off).' This expression is used when one says something undesirable and which the hearer does not like to have said; it in equivalet to 'hush, no reference to that.' ससान्त्ववचनम्—Ráma knew that Lakshmaṇa's reference to Sîtá's purification would cause pain to her and unsettle her and speaks in a manner that would please.

जानासि &c.—A *Kâku* seems to be intended on these words so as to convey to Lakshmaṇa a suggestion that he should not allude to anything likely to hurt the feelings of Sîtá. The poet, of course, as suits his purpose, makes Lakshmaṇa misunderstand his brother's meaning. He takes the words to be a compliment paid to him for his timely suggestion. दुर्मनायमाना—pre. p. of दुर्मनाय् Âtm., a denom. from दुर्मनस्. Sîtá was ill at ease because of her father's departure; see com.

P. 16. उत्पत्ति०—She was born like a divine being and not like an ordinary mortal. किमस्याः—Janaka, further on, makes a similar remark; *cf. infra* p. 110. See also Com.'s remark किं तु पावका चेति सूच्यते । अपि मां पावयेत्साध्वी &c. तीर्थोदकं—तीर्थ by itself means holy water (ऋषिजुष्टजलं); निपानागमयोस्तीर्थमृषिजुष्टजले गुरौ । Amara.; but here it means simply 'holy' as remarked by the Com.; see com. The Śloka is nearly repeated in Mv. See IV. 27. Ráma means by this to convey to Sîtá his real estimate of her character; that she was made to undergo the fire—ordeal was simply for the conviction of the people that they might not raise scandals.

देवयजन०—देवा इज्यन्ते अत्र इति देवयजनं a piece of ground set apart for sacrificial purposes ; तस्मात्संभवो यस्याः सा ०संभवा. सीता derived her name from *Sîtá* 'ploughed ground.' *Cf.* अथ लोकेश्वरी लक्ष्मीर्जनकस्य पुरे स्वतः । ...... सीतामुखे समुत्पन्ना बालभावेन सुन्दरी । सीतामुखोद्भवात्सीता इत्यस्यै नाम चाकरोत् । Pad. Pur., and लाङ्गलोल्लिख्यमानाया यज्ञभूमेः समुद्गता । सीतेयमूर्मिला चेति द्वितीया जनकात्मजा । Mv. I. 20. जीवितावधिः—जीवितमवधिर्यस्य whose limit is the duration of life, *i. e.* lasting as long as you will live. For Lak. referred to it just now; other people might also do it in future. प्रवादः—प्रणामः *v. l.* is quite out of place. If we adopt this reading जीवितावधिः becomes meaningless. Râma begins in a pleading tone, gently refers to the प्रवाद that is inevitable, and asks her not to mind that. We have again a reflex of this further on when Râma says जातं च दैवाद्वचनीयबीजं I. 44. Again, if we read प्रवाद here, then only the first line of the next śl. becomes appropriate.

कष्टं &c.—What a hard lot ! People have to be humoured, and cannot be punished for what they might say, by those &c. The reading कष्टः is not good. It cannot properly qualify जनः; it must be taken in the sense of कष्टप्रद. Vîra. reads क्लिष्टः, which also does not yield a happy sense; for it will then refer to Sîtá and will mean 'we have to please you because you suffered affliction (and not on account of any intrinsic merit on your part)—which is nonsense. तन्नो is preferable to तन्मे. नः—by us. नैसर्गिकी &c.—Râma means that although he knew that the treatment Sîtâ received was as unnatural and foolish as the trampling down of a sweet-smelling flower under feet, yet he had to do it. *Cf.* Mâl.-Mâdh. IX. 51. ताडनानि—is preferable to ताडितानि as better corresponding with the noun स्थितिः.

P. 17. सरहस्य०—*Rahasya* is the mystic charm (or, charms, to be secretly taught) which endows a missile with its proper potency or makes it cease to operate. जृम्भका०—For a description of the power of these famous weapons, *cf.* V. 13, 14, further on, and Mv. pp. 30, 33 (Nir. Ed.). These are also called the sons of Kṛiśâśva (cf. *infra* V. 15) and are described as moving and assuming any form at will (कृशाश्वतनयान्राम भास्वरान्कामरूपिण :। प्रतीच्छ मम भद्रं ते पात्रभूतोसि राघव ॥ Râm. I. 28). These were 100 in number. Their special property, as their name implies w s to cause insensibility; see Râm. I. 26–28.

कृशाश्वात्—Kṛiśâśva is the name of a king of the solar race, an ancestor of Râma. But evidently he could not have been intended here. A Muni or Devarshi so named was the husband of Jayá and Vijayâ, (according to the Râmâyaṇa, but of Archî and Dhishanâ according to the B. P.), two daughters of Daksha. Kṛiśâśva is also the author of a work on dramatic representation and dancing, whence Kris'âśvin is given in Amarai as a word for an actor or dancer. The sage is anterior to Páṇini, as the latter refers to him in IV. 3. 111. For Kaus'ika see विश्वामित्र in A. Dic. उपसंक्रान्तानि—came to be handed over to Vis'vâmitra.' with their secret charms.

ताटका—Was the daughter of Suketu, a Yaksha, and wife of the *Daitya* Sunda. She was changed into the form of a *Râkshasî* after her husband's death by the curse of Agastya. Her destruction was the first exploit of Râma when going with Visvâmitra to protect his sacrifices. See Ragh. XI. 15–20. प्रसादीकृतानि &c.–*Cf.* यानि हि भगवतः कृशाश्वादुरुचर्याव्रतैरधी तस्य सरहस्यजृम्भकप्रयोगसंहारस्य दिव्यास्त्रमन्त्रपारायणस्य वियातत्त्वबीजानि तानि मत्प्रसादादर्थतः शब्दात्मना च रामभद्रस्य संप्रति प्रकाशन्ताम् । Mv. I.

P. 18. ब्रह्मादय: &c.—This is the same as Mv. I. 42. ब्रह्महिताय-ब्रह्म properly means the Veda; hence the Vedic law governing human life ; *cf.* ब्रह्मकोषस्य *infra* VI. 9. परःसहस्रा–:सहस्रात्पराः । पर being a word of the पारस्करादि group takes स् after it. सहस्र takes परनिपात being included under the राजदन्तादि group. See Gr. § 198. एतानि—Here Râma speaks of missiles in general, as the Jṛimbhakas are said to have originated with कृशाश्व ; see above, note on जृम्भक. अपश्यन्—has a technical meaning. The charms of these were revealed to them. The ऋषिs are considered as मन्त्रद्रष्टारः the seers of the Vedic Mantras (*i. e.* to whom the Mantras were revealed intuitively), and not as the creators of them (मन्त्रकर्तारः). गुरव :—instructors in and fathers of the different sciences and arts.

सर्वथेदार्णि &c.—एदाणं—is gen. pl. There is no dat. in Prakrit; so in translating into Sanskrit we must substitute the dat. for the gen. as required by the rules of grammar. This, as we shall see further on, proves to be a boon and not merely a blessing (वरः न आशीः). *Cf. infra* VII. 10 and Lakshmaṇa's speech. वृत्तान्तः— *i. e.* representation of the occurences at Mithilâ (Janaka's capital). अम्महे—a particle expressing wonder or surprise, like अहो.

Some read शोभमान (shining, resplendent) after मसृण. मांसल—fat, great, hence muscular. अनादर०—without concern, *i.* easily. शंकरशरासन—This was the bow of S'iva which was made for him by Visvakarman and which he wielded victoriously against the other gods at Daksha's sacrifice, but without success against Vishṇu. He then deposited it with Devarâta, an ancestor of Janaka. *Cf.* Ragh. XI. 76. When Sîtá was to be married it was declared that he who would wield this bow would get her hand. When all failed to lift it up, Râma rose up, easily lifted it up, and broke it while laying on the string. *Cf.* लीलया स धनुर्मध्ये जग्राह वचनान्मुनेः । आरोपयत्स धर्मात्मा सलीलमिव तद्धनुः ॥ आरोपयित्वा मौर्वीं च पूरयामास तद्धनुः । तद्बभञ्ज धनुर्मध्ये नरश्रेष्ठो महायशाः ॥ Rám. Bâl. Canto 67. शिखण्ड—शिखा-भिर्ड्यते इति । The side-locks which boys wear and which are taken off at the time of marriage. बालानां तु शिखा प्रोक्ता काकपक्षः शिखण्डकः Haláyudha.

P. 19. शतानन्द—The son of Gotama and Ahalyá and the well-known family-priest of the Janaka family. जनकानां-जनक was also the name of the family, like Raghu.

द्रष्टव्यमेतत्—एतत् refers to the scene painted. Ráma means that the scene is worth seeing, for it represents the alliance of the two families. Vîra. reads सुश्लिष्टं ; but it has no propriety here. It was a past thing represented. Again Ráma says this in response to Lak.'s आर्ये पश्य पश्य, which leaves no doubt as to the original reading.

P. 20. गोदानमङ्गल—गावः लोमानि दीयन्ते छिद्यन्तेऽस्मिन् इति गोदान तदेव मङ्गलम् ; the auspicious ceremony of cutting the hair previous to marriage, generally performed in the 16th year in the case of a Bràhmaṇa and in the 22nd in the case of a Kshatriya. It was also called केशान्त, केशान्तश्चैव षोडशे । Yâj. I. 36. The Com. R. (according to Mr. Kane) says—विवाहात् प्राक् गोवितरणरूपः (in the form of giving cows to the Bràhmaṇas) मङ्गलहेतुः क्षत्रियाणामाचारविशेषः । And Mr. Kane thinks that the Rámá. supports this meaning ; but it does not ; the last two ślokas of the quotation hé gives in support of his remark go against him—they are गवां शतसहस्राणि चत्वारि पुरुषर्षभ : ॥ वित्तमन्यच्च सुबहु द्विजेभ्यो रघुनन्दनः । ददौ गोदानमुद्दिश्य पुत्राणां पुत्रवत्सलः ॥ स सुतैः कृतगोदानैर्वृतः सनृपतिस्तदा । &c. This shows that the giving of cows was a part of the Godána ceremony. See com. on the slokas also. See Malli. on Ragh. III. 33. and our note ad loc. ; also Manu. II. 65.

विवाहदीक्षिताः—विवाह एव दीक्षा विवाहदीक्षा the vow of marriage, (and not the ceremony initiatory to marriage), the marriage ceremony; for this sense *cf.* अथास्य गोदानविधेरनन्तरं विवाहदीक्षां निरवर्तयद्गुरुः । Ragh. III. 33. विवाहदीक्षा एषां संजाता ते विवाहदीक्षिताः । The marriage scene was painted there—the princes seizing the hands of their brides, &c.

आगृहीत°—आ does not seem to have any special sense here, though the Com. attaches such to it. कङ्कण seems to mean the marriage string tied round the wrist. The last two lines occur also in Mâl.—Mâd. IX. 9. Gh. explains आदराद्गृहीतश्चासौ कमनीयकङ्कणः च which was respectfully seized by me and which had a charming bracelet on.

P. 21. आर्या &c.—Lakshmaṇa speaks respectfully of Sìtá and Mâṇḍavî as they were the wives of his elder brothers Râma and Bharata. Śatrughna being his younger brother stood in the relation of a son to him and so he calls his wife वधूः (a daughter-in-law). Sîtâ and Ûrmilá were the daughters of Janaka (Sîradhvaja) and Mâṇḍavî and Śrutakîrtî of Kuśadhvaja, Janaka's younger brother. Râma was the eldest brother. Bharata was born after him and after that were born Lak. and Śatrughna. भरतो नाम कैकेय्यां जज्ञे सत्यपराक्रमः अथ लक्ष्मणशत्रुघ्नौ सुमित्राऽजनयत्सुतौ । Bâl. K. XVIII. 13, 14.

आत्मगतं—अपवार्य *V. l.* तद्भवेदपवारितम् । रहस्यं तु यदन्यस्य परावृत्य प्रकाश्यते ॥ Sâh.-D. The stage-direction here ought to be स्वगतम् or आत्म० (which is opposed to प्रकाशम्). अपवार्य is used when a character turns aside and says something secret to a character to the exclusion of others. Here Lak. speaks to himself. There is none on the stage to whom he could have said that. भार्गवः—भृगोः गोत्रापत्यं पुमान् a descendant of Bhṛigu. He was the son of Jamadagni, son of Ṛichîka. As he was a pupil of Śiva he was highly incensed at Râma's having broken his bow and intercepted him as he was returning to Ayodhyâ with his father and brothers. But as the Vaishṇava power passed over to Râma as soon as he (Râma) took up his bow, he acknowledged himself to be vanquished and retired to a life of devotion.

ससंभ्रमम्—The very name of Bhârgava was a terror to the Kshatriyas of his time. When he confronted Daśaratha, as he was returning to Ayodhyâ after Râma's marriage, Sîtâ was with him; and she was then frightened along with the other ladies. Now as she heard the name of Bhárgava suddenly she was agitated and frightened.

साक्षेपम्—interrupting him, so as to divert attention or change the topic. आक्षेपेण सहितम् ; this is preferable to साधिक्षेपं *v. l.*—fault-findingly, with disapproval (of his speech). Mark the modesty of Ráma. He knew that Lak. would refer to Paraśuráma's defeat by him and did not allow him to finish his speech. He did not like that the discomfiture of a great personage like Para. should be dwelt upon. Sîtâ was agreeably struck by this magnanimity of Ráma and looked at him with reverence. अयोध्यां—*i. e.* of course from Videha. तातपादेषु—This is the respectful way of referring to one's father. मातृभिः &c.—This is also a great blessing.

P. 22. प्रसन्नु &c.—The Com.'s readings are not good. The poet represents Sîtâ as a child (शिशुः) at the time of her marriage (*cf. infra* VII. 5); and this is in keeping with the Râmâ., for it appears from Sîtâ's speech addressed to Rávaṇa in the disguise of an ascetic that she was six years old when married; *cf.* उषित्वा द्वादश समा इक्ष्वाकूणां निवेशने ।...... (4) अष्टादश हि वर्षाणि मम जन्मनि गण्यते ।......(॥). See Araṇ. K. Canto 4. प्रसन्नु०—The first line is rather ambiguous. It is generally and naturally taken as qualifying दशनमुकुलैः. दशनाः (teeth) मुकुला इव दशनमुकुलाः bud-like teeth. प्रतनु॰—प्रतनवश्च ते विरलाश्च ; very tiny or small and isolated—grown apart. But here प्र has no force. The teeth were not extremely small ; it goes against दशनमुकुलैः ; they were bud-like, *i. e.* a little bulging in the middle, and hence appeared विरल. So it is better to translate प्रतनुविरलैः as 'not very much apart' (प्रतनु यथा तथा विरलैः). The reading पतन॰ adopted by some does not suit the context at all. पतन means the falling of (the teeth); now to make the teeth appear विरल we shall have to suppose that every other tooth had fallen off, which is absurd. How can the face be मुग्धालोक if the teeth had gaps between them ? no poet will like to describe such a face. The fact is that Sîtâ being a śiśu none of the teeth had fallen; they were very tiny and a little apart.

प्रान्तोन्मी॰—प्रान्ते उन्मीलन्तः मनोहराः कुन्तला येषां, which had her charming hair waving about their sides. But how could the hair have played by the sides of the teeth ? Were they exposed to view. Certainly not. So we have to understand by प्रान्त that part of the cheek which comes near the teeth. It is better therefore to take the first line independently. प्रतनुविरलैः &c. कुन्तलैः मुग्धालोकं (see trans). In this case प्रान्तो॰ will mean प्रान्तेषु at their ends or tips उन्मीलन्तः waving, spreading about (being acted on by the wind) अत एव मनोहराः कुन्तलाः तैः. But against this cons. also two objections can be urged. The first is that प्रतनु॰ cannot be fitly taken with कुन्तलैः; such hair is not a mark of beauty. But this may be removed by adopting the reading पतनविरलैः, her ringlets fell down on her cheeks and so were विरल. The other is—we should expect a च in the second line. To avoid this R. construes प्रतनु॰ मनोहरकुन्तलैः प्रान्तोन्मीलत् प्रान्तयोः पार्श्वयोः गण्डयोरिति यावत् । उन्मीलत् शोभमानं looking graceful. The च, however, can be easily supplied. The Com. Vîra. reads दशनकुसुमैः a comparison which is unusual ; teeth cannot be fitly composed to flowers. He also reads मनोहरकुड्मलैः and says उन्मीलच्छब्दः प्ररोहद्दन्तपरः ; he means that the new teeth that were just appearing by the sides of the other teeth looked like buds, which is also absurd. The reading मन्दालोकं adopted by Gh. is bad, being quite inappropriate.

ललित॰—exceedingly lovely. The repetition (वीप्सा) shows excess. ज्योत्स्ना॰—*i. e.* full of लावण्य; *cf.* त्वं कौमुदी नयनयोः &c. further on. For the meaning of प्राय see com. R. translates ज्योत्स्नाप्रायैः by ज्योत्स्नासदृशैः bright or lustrous like the moon-light. अकृत्रिम०—कार्येण निर्वृत्तः कृत्रिमः (fr. कृ+त्रिम); artificial; the aff. त्रि which always has म added to it is added to roots having an indicatory डु (as कृ, पच् &c.). See Páṇ. III. 3. 88. न कृत्रिमाः अकृत्रिमा; अ० विभ्रमाः graceful action येषां. अकृत्रिम suggests innocence natural to childhood. अम्बानां—अङ्गानां v. l. is not good. As Ráma refers to his mothers in the previous verse, it is natural that he should refer to Sîtâ's being fondled by them on their laps, especially as she was a pretty child. अङ्गकैः her tender (or lovely) limbs. The Com. takes the क in the sence of दयनीयत्व fit to be treated tenderly ; it may be taken also अल्पार्थे, the अल्पत्व referring to the absence of fulness to be imparted by youth.

P. 23. मन्थरा—the knavish hunch-backed maid of Kaikeyî who instigated her mistress against Râma. See Ayod. K. Canto 7. इङ्गुदी०—cf. आससाद महाबाहुः शृङ्गवेरपुरं प्रति ॥ 26...सुमन्त्रमब्रवीत्सूतमिहैवाद्य वसामहे ॥ अविदूरादयं नद्या बहुपुष्पप्रवालवान् । सुमहानिङ्गुदीवृक्षो वसामोऽत्रैव सारथे ॥ 27, 28, Rámá. Ayodh. K. शृङ्गवेर—a town on the Ganges near the modern Mirzapur inhabited by Nishâdas or wild tribes. निषादपति—this was Guha. He was very useful to Râma and assisted him, Lakshmaṇa and Sîtâ, in being ferried over the Ganges in their journey southwards. He was the king of the Nishádas (name of one of the wild aboriginal tribes of India). स्निग्धेन—cf. तत्र राजा गुहो नाम रामस्यात्मसमः सखा । निषादजात्यो बलवान्स्थपतिश्चेति विश्रुतः ॥ Ibid 33.

जटासंयमन०—Before Ráma crossed the Ganges, he and Lakshmaṇa took off their royal garments and put on a dress more suited to the life they had to lead thereafter. To get the hair matted Râma applied the sap of a banian tree to it, which he ordered Guha to bring for him. See Râmá. Ayo. K. Canto 52. 61–69, 71.

रघुकुलदेवते—for Gaṅgá was propitiated and brought down by Bhagîratha; see p. 189 where she is called भगीरथगृहदेवता.

पुत्रसंक्रान्तलक्ष्मीकैः —Such was the custom of the kings of the Ikshâku race who were strict followers of the Vedic laws. Cf. मुनिवनतरुच्छायां देव्या तया सह शिश्रिये गलितवयसामिक्ष्वाकूणामिदं हि कुलव्रतम् ॥ Ragh. III. 70 and Malli on it; also Ragh. VII. 71. Mark the use of the word संक्रान्त. The goddess of royalty had passed to their sons already; see Com.'s remarks. Cf. Ragh. III. 36; V. 38. Or संक्रान्त may be taken in the causal sense (अन्तर्भावितण्यर्थ); पुत्रे संक्रान्ता संक्रामिता लक्ष्मीः यैः.

इक्ष्वा०—इक्ष्वाश्च ते इक्ष्वाकवः (the descendants of Ik.) च. इक्ष्वाकोः राज्ञः गोत्रापत्यानि पुमांसः इक्ष्वाकवः. The aff. अ (अञ्) is dropped when the word is used in the plural and females are not meant; see Pâṇ. II. 4. 62; but the sing. will be ऐक्ष्वाकः. आरण्यक०—अरण्ये भवः आरण्यकः an ascetic living in a forest; आरण्यकानां व्रतं आरण्यव्रतं; fr. अरण्य + अक (वुञ्) by अरण्यान्मनुष्ये । Pâṇ. VI. 2. 129. आरण्यकं—*v. l.* आरण्यकानामिदमारण्यकम्. This s'l. occurs in the Mv. (IV. 51) with the reading त्वया तत्क्षीरकण्ठेन प्राप्त०.

P. 24. उर्वीभिदः—उर्वीं भिन्दन्ति इति तान्; qualifies प्रपितामहान्. अमर्षात्—through anger. पुरा प्रपितामहान्—The story of Bhagîratha who brought down the Ganges from heaven and purified his ancestors is too well-known to need any mention here. Sagara had two wives; केशिनी, daughter of the king of Vidarbha, and सुमति, the daughter of Kaśyapa and sister of Suparṇa (Vainateya). As he had no son he practised penance on the mountain Himâlaya and got two boons from the sage Bhṛigu. By virtue of one Keśinî got one son, असमञ्जस by name, who was to perpetuate the line; by the other Sumati got 60,000 sons. Asamañjasa's son was Aṃśumân, his son Dilîpa and his son Bhagîratha. Thus according to historical authority, the sons of Sagara were the great-grandfathers of Bhagîratha himself, and not of his father; and so the reading पितुः प्रपितामहान् is faulty and must therefore be rejected. The reading पितुश्च पितामहान् will do, but the च has no force. When Sagara began the last Aśvamedha sacrifice, Indra stole the horse. The 60,000 sons of Sagara were directed by their father to find out the horse. Not finding the horse on earth they dug down to the nether world, and found the horse grazing by the side of Kapila. They assailed the sage, calling him the thief, and were reduced to ashes by him through wrath. As the sons did not return in time, Aṃśumân was sent in search of them. He found the ashes of his uncles and wanted to offer obsequial water to them. He was told by Vainateya (his maternal uncle) that his uncles could go to heaven only if their ashes could be washed in the holy water of the Ganges. None was, however, able to cause the descent of the Ganges from heaven to earth, except Bhagîratha. For his account, see Rám. 38. 44 ; Bhág. P. IX. 8, 9. भरद्वाजावेदितः—described or pointed out by. वेदिताचित्र—*v.l.* ; here वेदित qualifies चित्रकूट.

०तनूतापं—Adv. comp.; अगणित: not minded तन्वा: ताप: यस्मिन्कर्मणि । ०पातं *v. l.* is not so good; it means 'not minding even the fall of his body'; but Bhagî. wanted to live; he was prepared to suffer any bodily torment to achieve his object. ०ताप:—*v. l.* is good; it qualifies भगीरथ:. उदधीधरत्—The Com. reads उदतीतरत् which is the Aor. 3rd pers sing. of तॄ *cau.* with उद्. Mr. Kaņe prefers this reading for the reason that it better agrees with the Râmâ. and quotes—अथ तद्भस्मनां राशिं गङ्गासलिलमुत्तमम् । प्लावयत्पूतपाप्मानः स्वर्गं प्राप्ता रघूत्तम । Canto 43; तारिता नरशार्दूल दिवं याताश्च देववत् । Canto 44. But the idea expressed by प्लावयत् or तारिता is expressed here already by स्पृष्टानद्भिः; so we have retained उददीधरत्. This śl. is written in the Hariņî metre which is suited to the air of plaintiveness it breathes. Gaṅgâ has to rescue the sons of Râma from death in future. See *infra* VII. 2.

शिवानु०—शिवस्य अनुध्यानं शिवा०, तत्परं यस्याः ; this is preferable to शिवानुध्याना *v. l.*; for then we have recourse to a Vyadhikaraņa Bah.; see com.; the dissolution शिवमनुध्यानं यस्याः does not bring out the sense prominently. The purpose served by this request will be seen in the further development of the plot; see p. 189. The sage Bhâradvâja resided at Prayâga and received Râma, Lak. and Sîtâ in his hermitage there which was then and afterwards much celebrated and 'where a temple dedicated to him still exists' (Wilson). See Ayod. K. 54, 55. In some places he is said to be the son of Bṛihaspati and the authorship of many hymns of the Ṛigveda is ascribed to him.

चित्रकूट—Lit. with variegated peaks. Chitrakûṭa is the name of a hill to the south of the Yamunâ and situated in the district now called Chitrakota or Chatarkot, about fifty miles south-east of Bundelkhand. According to the Râma. it was ten krośas from the confluence of the Ganges and the Yamunâ. *cf.* दश क्रोशा इतस्तात गिरिर्यस्मिन्निवत्स्यसि । ...चित्रकूट इति ख्यातो गन्धमादनसंनिभः ॥ Râmâ. 54, 28, 29. It was the first habitation of Râma in his exile, according to the Râmâyaņa, and then the seat of Vâlmîki's hermitage. Many temples and shrines dedicated to Râma and Lakshmaņa exist in the district; the heights abound with monkeys and some of the wild fruits there are still called Sîtâphalas.

वटः श्यामः—It is thus described by Kâlidâsa—(त्वया पुरस्तादुपयाचितो यः सोऽयं वटः श्याम इति प्रतीतः । राशिर्मणीनामिव गारुडानां सपद्म-

रागः फलितो विभाति ॥ Ragh. XIII. 53. See also Malli. thereon. This *vaṭa* is known as *Akshayya* (imperishable) *vaṭa* which has long been famed at Allahabad. Râma, with his brother and wife, rested under the shade of this tree after crossing the Yamunâ. This *vaṭa* was then in open space and on the opposite side of the river to that where it is now traditionally worshipped. कालिन्दी is the river Yamunâ, so called from being the daughter of Kalinda, a name of the sun (or, of the mountain from which it rises).

P. 25. अलस &c.—Bhavabhûti in this and other similar stanzas makes the nearest approach to Kálidâsa as the describer of Śriṅgâra, but this he does in order to intensify the sentiment of Karuṇa (Pathos) which he delineates so successfully and with a masterly hand in the present play. अलस—dull; लुलित—crushed, unnerved, languid : अलसानि च तानि लुलितानि च अत एव मुग्धानि (graceful) ; Sîtâ looked more graceful in her languid condition. ललित *v. l.* is not happy ; if ललित be taken to mean 'lovely,' that idea is expressed by मुग्ध. ललितेन मुग्धानि is not a good way ; for what sportiveness can Sîtá show when fatigued by the journey? संजात—संपात *v. l.* is not good, it has to be twisted into the sense of 'rapid movement.' ०संवाहनानि—दत्तं संवाहनं (pressing, shampooing) अङ्गमर्दनं येभ्यः । see com. मृणाली—a lotus-stalk. अङ्कानि—drooping limbs.

विराध०—A hideous demon, the son of Kâla and S'atahradá. He, by his penance, obtained a boon from Brahmâ, which made him invulnerable. Encountering Ráma, Lak. and Sîtâ, he seized the last and was trying to run away with her, when he was attacked by the two brothers with sharp arrows. Though shorn of his arms he could not, however, be killed and so the two brothers buried him alive. This being effected, there arose from the place a handsome person, who declared himself to be the Gandharva named Tumburu and thanked Ráma for his release from the accursed form to which he was condemned by Kubera. See Rámâ. III. ch.s 2-6. संरोधः—संवादः *v. l.* 'meeting with,' it does not mean 'conversation with,' as it cannot be painted.

आर्यपुत्र०—स्वहस्तधृत is better than हस्तधृत. ०आरम्भम्—आरम्भ means an undertaking, an act (आरभ्यते इति); for this sense *cf.* विततबहुतरारम्भयत्नाः परार्थे । Bh. N. ०दक्षिणारण्यपथिकत्वं—*v. l.* my being a traveller in my passage through &c. पन्थानं नित्यं गच्छतीति पथिकः one habitually a traveller. The Com. reads

अत्याहितं ०पथिकत्वं *i. e.* which led to great calamity. Gh. reads अक्षिभ्यां (with my own eyes) दक्षिणा०. These readings are inappropriate. Ráma and the party were not simply to travel through the D. forest; but they had to stay in it.

वैखानस—Anchorites ; householders in the third stage of life, living in forests. The name is derived from विखनस्, an ancient sage who seems to have written a work on the duties of वानप्रस्थ ; *cf.* हरदत्त on गौतमधर्मसूत्र III. 2—वैखानसो वानप्रस्थः। विखनसा प्रोक्तेन मार्गेण वर्तते इति। तेन हि स आश्रमः प्राधान्येन प्रतिपादितः। (quoted by Mr. Káne).

P. 26. **आतिथेयपरमाः**—आतिथेयं (अतिथिषु साधु) hospitality परमं the highest object or duty येषां ; आति० fr. आतिथि + एय (ढञ् by पथ्यतिथिवसतिस्वपतेर्ढञ्। Páṇ. IV. 4. 104 ; so पथि साधु पाथेयं, स्वापतेयं धनं &c.). **शमिनः**—शम एषां विद्यते इति शमिनः those who practise self-restraint; men with passions controlled. This is put in to show that although they were गृहिणः (living with their wives) they were शमिनः ; this is better than यमिनः, for *yamas* may be practised even by ordinary people. *Cf.* शमप्रधानेषु तपोधनेषु Śâk. II. 7. नीवारमुष्टि०—See com.; the propriety of the word मुष्टि is this :—they did not live a life of luxury there ; but cooked measured corn just sufficient to sustain life.

अनोकह—is strangely derived:—अनसः शकटस्य अकं गतिं हन्तीति. Dissolve—अविरलाः (growing thickly) च ते अनोकहाश्च तेषां निवहेन निरन्तरं (crowded or dense with) स्निग्धं नीलं च परिसरारण्यं (परिसरे भवमरण्यं) तस्मिन् परिणद्धा या गोदावरी तया मुखराणि कन्दराणि यस्य. **परिसर**—may also mean extent, in which case we may dissolve ०निरन्तरः स्निग्धः नीलश्च परिसरो यस्य तादृशमरण्यं &c. ०मुखकन्दरः *v. l.* must be explained as done by the Com.—'the caves of which have the Godávarî at their entrance'—a reading not as good as the one in the text. सतत &c.—सततमभिष्यन्दमाना ये मेघाः तैः मेदुरितः नीलिमा यस्य. **परिणद्ध**—Widening, spreading (परिणद्धा विस्तृतिमापन्ना); 'परिणाहो विशालता' Ak. It is not a good way to take परिणद्ध in the sense of 'encircled' or 'surrounded by'; it does not explain the मुखरत्व of the caves. **मेदुरित**—softened, or intensified; p. p. p. of मेदुरय् a denom. verb from मेदुर (thick or unctuous). **जनस्थान**—A part of the Daṇḍaka forest, so called probably because it was a safer place for human habitation, being less haunted by demons. It is generally supposed to be near Nasik. Some hold that it was much lower down the course of the Godávarî—rather towards its mouth. This passage occurs in the Mv. Act V. after Śl. 15.

प्रतिविहित &c.—लक्ष्मणेन प्रतिविहिता या सपर्या (attendance on, service) तया सुस्थयोः-we who were at ease on account of Lakshmaṇa attending to our comfort. सरसतीरां—*v. l.* with banks full of watery places or charming. तदुपान्तेषु—तस्याः उपान्तेषु in the adjoining spots of.

P. 27. किमपि &c.—The prevailing sentiment of the śloka is संभोगशृङ्गार and is quoted in the D.-R. as an instance of it. Its स्थायिभाव or permanent feeling is Rati, indicated by आसत्ति, अशिथिलपरिरम्भ, &c. आसत्तियोगात्—on account of our close contact. We have preferred this reading to आसक्ति; it is meant to explain मन्दं मन्दं and अविरलितक०; it is the reading found in D.-R. also. With आसक्ति, योग has no propriety; आसक्ति (deep love) itself spoils the poetic charm. It is better left understood. अशिथिल—See com.; दोस् is *m. n.* It is changed to दोषन् optionally from the Acc. pl.; hence ०दोष्णोः. रात्रिरेव व्यरंसीत्—The night only ended and not our conversation. The sing. is जाती—many a night was passed like that. There is a curious anecdote about this reading. Tradition says that Bhavabhúti first wrote एवं, but altered the reading afterwards at the suggestion of Kâlidâsa. (See Intro.). Whatever credit may be due to this tradition, the altered reading is certainly an improvement upon the original (if the poet wrote it so at all).

पञ्चवटी—A place in the great Daṇḍakâraṇya, generally identified with the place of that name near the source of the Godávarî. Râma passed here a long period of his exile. It derives its name probably from the five fig trees, *viz.* *As'vattha*, *Bilva*, *Vaṭa*, *Dhâtṛi*, and *As'oka*. शूर्पणखा—*Lit.* having nails like a winnowing basket; शूर्पाणीव नखानि यस्याः सा; mark the fem. ending; the fem. ई is not added when the comp. is a name; see Gr. § 330. She was a sister of Rávaṇa living at the time with her brothers, Khara and Dûshaṇa, in the Daṇḍaka forest. See A. Dict.

एत्तावत्ते &c.—At the very mention of Śûrpaṇakhâ's name all her past experiences were conjured up in Sîtâ's mind:—When S'ûrpaṇakhâ saw Râma she was struck with his beauty and coming up to him asked him to marry her. Ráma said that he was already married, and so told her in jest to marry Lakshmaṇa, who told her that he was a mere servant of Râma, and that it would not be fit for her to marry a servant; she would do well therefore to go back to Râma and marry him. She then came back to Ràma, and saying that she would devour Sîtâ, his human wife, rushed towards her with that intention. Ráma then shielded Sîtâ and told Lakshmaṇa to deform her. Whereupon Lakshmaṇa drew his sword and cut off her nose and ears. See Râmà. Ara. K. 17-18. Sîtâ thought that Śûrpaṇakhâ might eat her up and so she would no more see Ràma. Or this may be explained in another way; Sîtá remembered how Śûr. bore to Rávaṇa the report of the destruction of Khara and others and how she was carried away by the latter &c. and she thus exclaimed. Rama's remark अयि विप्रयोगत्रस्ते &c. shows that the latter explanation is preferable.

P. 28. कनकहरिण &c.—कनकहरिण एव छद्म तस्य विधिना व्यापारेण. Mârîcha, son of Táḍakâ, assumed the form of a charming golden deer at the instigation of Rávaṇa, and wandered about Ràma's hut. Sîtá, fascinated by its form, pressed Ráma to pursue it and to capture it anyhow. Ráma chased the apparent deer and was attracted far away by it. When hit by the arrow of Ráma, Mârîcha resumed his own form and before he was dead, uttered, imitating Ráma's accent, the words-' O Sîtá, O Lakshmaṇa.' Sîtâ, on hearing these words and fearing some mishap to Ráma, pressed Lakshmaṇa to go to his brother's rescue. In the meantime Rávaṇa came disguised as an ascetic and carried away Sîtâ. क्षालितं—washed away, *i. e.* avenged by Rávaṇa being totally destroyed. विकल०—The grief caused to Ráma was so great that all his senses were overpowered. विकलकरणैः—*V. l.* विकलानि च तानि करणानि च तैः; here विकल does not properly fit in well with चरित; for it means विगता कला येभ्यः तानि; not in their proper form; not as they should be; so we shall have recourse to the secondary sense 'full of distraction' &c. करुणकरुणैः *v. l.*—exceedingly piteous. The वीप्सा expresses excess. अपि ग्रावा रोदित्यपि &c.-Here the poet sounds the key-note of his poetic achievement in the present work, *viz* his development of the sentiment of Pathos. In fact the words put in the mouth of Lakshmaṇa, though not exaggerating the facts, form the poet's own judgement on the success of his work as a करुणरसप्रधान काव्य; and this his view has been supported by other critics; *cf.* Govardhana'cha'rya—भवभूतेः संबन्धाद्भूधरभूरेव भारती भाति । एतत्कृतकारुण्ये किमन्यथा रोदिति ग्रावा ॥

साकूतं—feelingly, with emotion.

अयं ते &c.—In this Śloka the two qualities of Ráma as a hero, *viz.* his स्थैर्य and his सहृदयत्व, are brought out. आवेगः—

the flow of grief, agitation. परेषां—the Pot. p. participle may be used with the Instr. or the Gen. of the agent of the action denoted by it. भरं—*Lit.* its weight, hence, excess. चिरध्मात०—*V. l.* which has caused the heart to swell for a long time.

P. 29. प्रियजन—*i. e.* Sîtá. प्रतिकृति०-*cf.* III. 44. विपच्यमानः—being developed, gaining strength. The com. takes this with Agni as well as व्रण. रणरणकः—fr. रण् to sound; रणशब्दस्तत्प्रकारः । प्रकारे द्वित्वम् ।

मन्वन्तरपुराण—for comp. see Com.; or °न्तरे पुराणः. As old as the present Manu, *scil.* वैवस्वत. मन्वन्तर—is the period of time during which one Manu presides over creation. A Kalpa is divided into fourteen such *Manvantaras*, each comprising a little over 71 *Mahâyugas*. A Mahâyuga is equal to the four *yugas* put together, *i. e.* 4,320,000 human years. तातजटायुषः—Jatâyu was the son of Aruṇa and Śyenî (see Mv. V. 6) and the younger brother of Sampáti. See Râmà. Ara. K. 4. 32, 33. He was thus of divine origin and preternatural longevity. Jaṭâyu had once saved the life of Das'aratha and from that time they had been connected by ties of the closest friendship. Hence Ráma speaks of him as तात. When Rávaṇa carried off Sîtâ, Jaṭāyu opposed him and tried to rescue her, but was overpowered and left mortally wounded. Hence Sîtâ makes the following remark. उदाहरण-a representation or manifestation in words or painting; for the former *cf.* Vik. pp. 22, 51 &c.

निर्व्यूढ—p. p. p. of वह् with निर् and वि; fully carried or borne out; proved true. *Cf.* निर्व्यूढः संभावनाभारो बुद्धरक्षितायाः. Mâl.-Mâdh. VII.; निर्व्यूढं कापालिकत्वं *Ibid.* IV. काश्यप-Jaṭâyu was the grandson of Kas'yapa, the father of Aruṇa. तीर्थ—a holy personage, one exercising a sanctifying influence upon others, as Jatâyu was. तर्थिभूतस्य *V. l.*—of one in the position of a teacher.

जनस्थानस्य पश्चि०—Having performed the obsequies of Jaṭâyu, Ráma travelled a little to the west of Janasthána and then to the south. After going for 3 Krośas from Janasthána, Ráma and Lakshmaṇa entered the क्रौञ्चारण्य. When travelling towards the east they passed beyond the Krauñchàraṇya, they met the demon Danu near the hermitage of the sage मतङ्ग. दनुकबन्ध- Danu is said to have been a son of the goddess Śrî, according to another account a grandson of Danu, a daughter of Daksha and wife of Kaśyapa, (according to the Mah.-

Bhâr. he was a Gandharva named Viśvávasu,) cursed to be a Rákshasa by the sage Sthúlaśiras, from which hateful form he was to be delivered by Ràma. In a fight with Indra the latter struck him with his thunderbolt and drove his head into his body, whence he came to be called Danukabandha (the headless monster). *Cf.* Mv. V. 34. When he seized Ráma and Lakshmaṇa with the object of devouring them, they extricated themselves from his grasp by cutting off his arms. When thus wounded he asked them who they were; and, on being informed of their names, he rejoiced at the prospect of his being freed from the accursed form and requested Râma to burn his body, which done, he rose from the fire as a pure heavenly being and counselled Ráma to seek the friendship of Sugríva. See Ràmáyaṇa, Ar. 69-72. Wilson says—

"This *Kabandha* or headless monster is possibly the original of the Anthropophagi of the East, and the "men whose heads do grow beneath their shoulders." He is described as vast as a mountain, of a sable hue, without legs; but with arms a league long, a formidable mouth in his belly, and a single eye of vast dimensions in his breast".

ऋष्यमूक—See Ar. 72, 11-12; for Matanga, see Ar. 73. According to Prof. H. H. Wilson, the mountain Ṛishyamúka, the lake Pampà, and the other scenes referred to here, are still known by the same appellations in the neighbourhood of the town of Anagundi, the ancient capital of the monkey-chiefs on the Tuṅgabhadrâ. "On the ascent to the mountain occurs the forest of *Mataṅga*, or the *Meghaprabha* wood, in which the trees never wither and the flowers never fade. The saint and his disciples had long disappeared; but his hermitage had remained inaccessible to noxious or inimical beings, and the cooking utensils left by him awaited, in perfect order, the arrival of Râma, being destined for his accommodation." Wilson.

श्रमणा &c.—also called श्रमणी in the Rámâ. सिद्धा—सिद्धयोगा who had obtained miraculous powers (Siddhis) by means of *Yoga*, such as the power to be small or great &c.; see A. Dic. under सिद्धि; or it may mean 'who had obtained the entire fruit of her penance.' The reading सिद्धशबरी is not supported by the Râmâ.; *cf.* तो दृष्ट्वा तु तदा सिद्धा समुत्थाय कृताञ्जलिः । पादौ जग्राह रामस्य लक्ष्मणस्य च धीमतः ॥ Ar. 74. 6; and अहं हि श्रमणा नाम सिद्धा शबरतापसी ।मतङ्गाश्रमवास्तव्या रामान्वेषिण्युपागता ॥

Mv. V. 27. Again, सिद्धा, when compounded, does not bring out the idea of her Siddhi so prominently, as when used independently. This Śramaṇâ was a devoted attendant of Mataṅga's disciples and an ardent devotee of Râma. She worshipped Râma when he came to her hermitage with Lakshmaṇa. She informed him how she was told by the sages that she would go to heaven after welcoming Râma as a guest and how she had been anxiously awaiting his arrival for that purpose; she then threw herself into blazing fire and went to heaven having assumed a resplendent form. See Ar. 74.

पम्पा—Name of a celebrated lake which is considered the same as the river Pennair, near which stands the Ṛishyamúka mountain. The river is known to rise in tanks; the northern part especially forms a stone-tank in the centre of Chandradurga. This was probably the original Pampá and Chandradurga the Ṛishyamúka mountain. Subsequently the name was transferred from the tank to the river which rose from it. See A. Dic.

P. 30. विच्छिन्ना०—विच्छिन्ने (utterly destroyed) अमर्षश्च धीरत्वं च यस्मिन्कर्मणि तद्यथा तथा; विसृष्टा० *v. l.* where विसृष्ट means 'given up'. अमर्ष०—Indignation leading one to take prompt action against the offender. It is one of the 33 *Vyabhichâribhâvas.* See Sáh.-D. or our Sáh.-Sár.-Saṃg. p. 47. किल—as I was told; because Sîtá being a prisoner in Laṅká could not have known it personally. प्रमुक्त०—प्रमुक्तः कण्ठः यस्मिन्कर्मणि तद्यथा तथा; very loudly. रुदितमासीत्—*Cf.* स तां दृष्ट्वा ततः पम्पां रामः सौमित्रिणा सह। विललाप च तेजस्वी रामो दशरथात्मजः॥ Ar. 75-22. रमणीयं &c.–Pampá is described in the Râmâ. as a beautiful lake with its transparent water chequered with lotuses and the ducks and geese playing upon its surface. Water-birds of radiant plumage crowded it, while its banks were green with fruit-laden trees, waving to and fro and diffusing their fragrance all round. *Cf.* Ragh. XIII. 30. Bâṇa has also described this lake in his Kádambarî.

मदकल०—मदेन कलाः (uttering indistinct but sweet notes) मदकलाः; now see Com. मल्लिकाक्ष०—A species of swans with beak and legs of a darkish colour. बाष्पाम्भः &c.—In the interval of the falling down of the tears (already formed in the eyes) and the rising up of new ones. कुवलयिनः—The idea is this:—As Râma's eyes were bedimmed with the moisture of tears, he could not take a clear view of the spots covered with white lotuses when he opened his eyes. These appeared darkish to him and the confusion was helped on by the exposed legs and beaks of the geese, so that he saw the spots as if they were covered with beds of blue lotuses. For the various meanings proposed see com.; one or two of these are far-fetched. The first three lines occur in Mál.-Mádh. IX. 14.

हनूमान्—He was the son of Marut (the god Vâyu) by Añjanâ, wife of a monkey named Kesarî. According to another account he was a portion of Śiva. On one occasion his *hanu* was broken by the thunderbolt of Indra and hence his name; मत्करोत्सृष्टवज्रेण हनुरस्य यथा हतः । नाम्नैव कपिशार्दूलो भविता हनुमानिति ॥ Râmâ. Uttarak. Adh. 41. चिरनिर्विण्ण &c.—the world that had long groaned under the oppression of Rávaṇa and his legions. Sîtâ makes this remark on the conspicuous part played by Mâruti in the Laṅká war and the final destruction of Râvaṇa. Had he not brought the potent herb from the mountain ऋषभ (see Yud 74), Lakshmaṇa, who was mortally wounded by Râvaṇa's Śakti, could not have lived. Ráma could not have survived the shock, and Râvaṇa's destruction would have been impossible. चिरनिर्व्यूढ &c.—*v. l.* चिरात् निर्व्यूढं जीवलोकस्य प्रत्युद्धरणं &c. But the reading in the text is better. According to the Com. Sîtá here refers to herself; see his remarks; but this would go against Sîtá's modesty. Again, Râma's next speech clearly shows that this is not the poet's meaning.

P. 31. अञ्जना—the mother of Hanûmat. कृतिनः—प्रशस्तं कृतमेषामस्तीति who have gained our object nobly; hence, happy, blessed. वयं च भुवनानि च—Râma adds वयं in order to supplement Sîtá's remark which referred to Mâruti's services in general. See com. This shows his great regard for Mâruti.

कुसुमित०—कुसुमान्येषां संजातानीति कुसुमिता ये कदम्बतरवस्तेषु ताण्डविना (having their dance) बर्हिणः (peacocks) येषु । ताण्डविताः—ताण्डवमेषां संजातमिति; or ताण्डववन्तः कृताः p. p. p. of the denom. fr. ताण्डववत्, वत् being dropped. अनुभाव०—is the dignity or majesty of mien with which a person impresses or strikes another with awe. *Cf.* Ragh. I. 37. सौभाग्य—collective grace. अनुभावसौभाग्ये यद्वा अनुभावस्य सौभाग्यं (excellence, excess) एव परिशेषो यस्यास्तादृशी चासौ धूसरा च &c.

P. 32. माल्यवान्—This is described as a minor mountain-range in the neighbourhood of किष्किन्धा. See Kish. K. VI. 1, 28, 9. It must be in the neighbourhood of Anagundi. Kálidása also has described this mountain. *Cf.* Ragh. XIII. 26–29. नीलः

स्निग्ध: &c —*Cf.* Mv. V. 42. यस्मैतस्मात् &c.—Because it was the sight of this mountain that had affected Râma very deeply in his bereavement. *Cf.* the stanzas from the Ragh. and Mv. referred to above (नवं पयो यत्र घनैर्मया च त्वद्विप्रयोगाश्रु समं विसृष्टम् &c.) प्रत्यावृत्त:—a sort of presentiment of the future separation from Sîtâ. पुनरिव—is obviously preferable to पुनरपि ; अपि has no force after प्रत्यावृत्त:. This shows the tender-heartedness of Râma.

उत्तरोत्तराणि—उत्तरस्मादुत्तराणि represented in a series ; or, one excelling the other. कर्माश्चर्याणि—कर्माणि च तान्याश्चर्याणि च; or कर्मसु आश्चर्याणि a comp. सुप्सुपा. प्रसन्नगम्भीर—*i.e.* delightful and abound ing in scenes. पवित्रनिर्मल &c. *v. l.*—निर्मल pure (purifying). अस्खलित०—अस्खलित: सुखश्च संपातो यस्य. As Sîtâ was advanced in pregnancy, such a precaution was all the more necessary.

P. 33. कठिनहृदये—Ráma gently rebukes Sîtâ for having entertained a doubt in the matter. He would have accompained her unasked. ०नोपकण्ठे—Because there they could get a refreshing breeze. वातायनावर्तके—in the recess or screened place near. अपवर्तक also means the same thing. But there is no reason why Ráma should ask Sîtá to sit or sleep in a place shut up from all sides. The hall they were in was a public one and the windows could not have been furnished with अपवरकs. संविष्टौ—may mean 'seated'; or 'sleeping'; for this *cf.* संविष्ट: कुशशयने निशां निनाय Ragh. I. 95. निरन्तरम्—निर्गतमन्तरं यस्मिन्कर्मणि तद्यथा तथा. शयनाय—शयितुम्.

जीवयन्निव &c—The fig. of speech is Upamá. The points of similarity are that both are slender and long, covered with drops, and gladdening. साध्वस—fear caused by the dreadful sights. साध्वसं च श्रमश्च ताभ्यां जनितो य: स्वेदस्तस्य बिन्दव: तै: सहित: ससाध्वस:; यद्वा ससाध्वसो य: श्रम: &c. ऐन्दव०—इन्दोरिमे ऐन्दवा ये मयूखास्तै: चुम्बिता अत एव स्यन्दिनो ये चन्द्रमणयस्तेषां हारस्येव विभ्रमो यस्य । This śl. (with the reading समूढसाध्वस &c.) occurs in Mâl.-Mádh. VIII. 3.

सुखमिति &c.—Because the result of both is an equal insensibility to any other perception. प्रमोह—प्रबोध *v. l.* with समुन्मीलति in the last line appears to be better at first sight, as it gives a better contrast with निद्रा ; but it must be rejected, as it goes against परिमूढेन्द्रियगण, while प्रमोह better agrees with विषविसर्प. Here also the pervading sentiment is संभोगशृङ्गार. It is quoted in the D.-R. as an instance of this, as also of the *Vyabhichâribhâva* मोह. *Cf.* with this Mál.-Mádh. I. 33, where

Mádhava describes the state of his mind on his first seeing Málatí. समुन्मीलयति *v. l.* is bad, as it goes against the context.

P. 34. स्थिरप्रसादा—This reply beautifully expresses Sîtâ's modesty. She means that it was his unchanging love for her that made him say so.

विकासनानि—Which cause to bloom; in this and in other similar epithets in this stanza the affix अन is added कर्तरि. सकलेन्द्रिय॰—Here प्रलय, one of the *Sâttvika bhâvas,* is expressed.

P. 35. सुवचनानि—Here their refreshing property is left to be understood. In Mâl.-Mádh. VI. 8, wherein the first two lines are the same as here, we have वचोमृतानि, which better explains their विकासनत्व &c. सरोरुहाक्षि—The fem. is क्षी when आक्षि refers to an animate object. रसायनानि—Powerful elixirs to the mind. रसायन properly means that in which रस or mercury is made firm and endowed with medical properties. Mercury when so prepared was considered to have the power of prolonging life and granting exemption from old age. Hence the word came to mean any powerful preparation acting as an *elixir vitæ, i. e.* refreshing or gratifying the mind. See com. The fig. in this stanza is Rûpaka.

प्रियंवद—Sîtâ thus addresses her husband lovingly. प्रियं वदतीति प्रियंवदः; a nasal comes in, as required by the aff. खच् (अ) when added to वद् after प्रिय and वश; see com.; similarly वंशवद.

शैशवे—As Daśaratha and Kausalyâ knew that Râma and Sîtâ were divine beings, they were allowed such liberty even in childhood. It was natural for Ràma to forget his human character when alone with Sîtâ, and to ask her to sleep using his arm as a pillow. स्वापहेतु—inducing sleep, which lulled you to sleep. अनुपाश्रितः—not resorted to by any other woman (as it was imposible for any one to do it); *cf.* for the idea अनन्यभाजं पतिमाप्नुहीति &c. Kum. III. 63. Prof. Belvalkar is inaccurate, if not wrong, in translating it as 'on which no other woman has a claim.'

P. 36. प्रसुप्तैव—एव shows Râma's surprise at the quickness with which Sîtá sank into sleep.

गेहे लक्ष्मीः—*Cf.* IV. 6. अमृतवर्तिः—a pencil of nectar thickened, serving as an eye-salve. As Amṛita is supposed to possess the highest property of pleasure giving, such expressions as अमृतवर्ति, अमृताञ्जनशलाका &c. are common enough.

भवं बाहु: &c.—Mark the poet's power of description. The idea in the last two lines of śl. 34 is again clothed here in a beautiful garb. This śl. contains a series of Rûpakas in its first three lines, and is cited by Vâmana in his Káv. S. V. IV. 3. 6 किमस्या: &c.—This line is full of variants. The reading यदि परमसह्यस्तु विरह: is capable of a three-fold interpretation: (1) यदि तु विरह: परमसह्य: स्यात्तर्हि अस्या: किं न प्रेय: 'what of her would not be highly endearing, if only her separation could be extremely bearable?' In this case, however, तु and परम are quite inappropriate. (2) अस्या: किं न प्रेय:; यदि तु विरह: स्यात् स एव परम् असह्य: 'what of her would not be highly pleasing?—but if there be separation, that alone would be extremely unbearable.' This also is not satisfactory, as तु does not fit in well. (3) Râma wanted to say किमस्या न प्रेय: यदि तु विरह: न स्यात्; but at such a time the idea of separation was too much for him to bear; and so, instead of completing the line, he pauses a little, and breaks out into विरहस्तु परम् असह्य: 'but her separation is extremely unbearable.' यदि पुनरसह्यो न विरह:—This reading, though it was adopted in the text of the second Ed., is abandoned though simpler and better, as it has no MS. authority. It is proposed by Vîr. as an emendation. यदि पुनरसह्यस्तु विरह: *v. l.* requires a straining; यदि तु पुन: असह्य: विरह: स्यात्सर्वमेवेदमप्रियतरं स्यात् is the best sense that could be given to the reading, we think. There is one more variant, which also gives a good sense and is easier, *viz.* किमपरमसह्यस्तु विरह: 'why add more words? everything about her has a charm; her separation only cannot be borne.'

देव उपस्थित:—The preceding śl. and this speech are quoted in the D.-R. as an instance of *Gaṇḍa* (a sort of premonition) called a kind of *Patâkâsthána* by the author of the S.-D. It consists in so introducing the words of a different character as to be syntactically connected with the speech of the character already on the stage, and to have a distinct bearing on them, though utterd with a different import. Thus here the word उपस्थित:, which means 'has arrived', is so brought in after Ráma's soliloquy, that its first sound conveys to him the ominous import of 'is impending,' and he being thus rudely shocked with the idea of separation from Sîtá, asks in alarm the question 'अयि क:'. Such words are generally supposed to presage good or evil. Here they foreshadow the coming separation of Sîtâ. This poetical device is common enough in Sanskrit Plays; *cf.* Veṇî. after the words दुर्योधनः—पर्याप्तमेव करभोरु ममोरुयुग्मम्-प्रविश्य कञ्चुकी-भग्नं भीमेन; Mud. IV. राक्षसः—अपि नाम चाणक्यबटुः-श्रोता०-जयतु-रा०-अतिसंधातुं शक्यः स्यात्-दौ०-अमात्यः; also चा०—अपि नाम दुरात्मा राक्षसो गृह्येत। सि०—अज्ज गहीदो &c. *Ibid.* I.

दुर्मुखः—The name is well selected for the tidings he has to communicate. It is the poet's creation. According to Kálidása and Râmâ. the spy appointed for that purpose was भद्र by name. पप्रच्छ भद्रं विजितारिभद्रः Ragh. XIV. 31. The reading अपसर्पितुम्—found in Mb. is grammatically inaccurate, the regular form is सर्तुं or सप्तुम्. अथ वा नियोगः &c.—*cf.* Kañchukî's speech at S'ák. p. 121. Here नियोग means the appointed task which must be done; *cf.* for the thought न वञ्चनीयाः प्रभवोऽनुजीविभिः Kir. I. 4.

P. 37. उत्स्वप्नायते—A denom. from उत्स्वप्न (one who experiences a dream.) विरहभावना—The revolving of the idea of separation in her mind. परामृशन्—touching, passing his hand over.

अद्वैतं &c.—What a grand ideal of conjugal love the poet gives us here! Ráma's words are not an effusion of youthful passion untried or inexperienced but passion tempered down by experience and long association. It is impossible to describe a husband's love and regard for his wife more effectively or naturally than the poet has done here. अद्वैतं—अविद्यमानं द्वैतं यस्मिन् which remains the same—unaltered—under opposing circumstances. द्वयोर्भावः द्विता तत्र भवं द्वैतं; or द्वे इते यस्मात्तत् द्वीतं तत्र भवं द्वैतं. Mr. Káne takes अद्वैतं independently, making the four clauses qualify it. He translates अद्वैतं by "identity of happiness and misery." But if taken thus, the 2nd and third lines lose their propriety; for, what has old age to do with its Rasa? Why is आवरणात्यय necessary for its परिणति? Again, the clause भद्रं तस्य सुमानुषस्य remains unconnected, and will have to be taken as parenthetical. It is, therefore, better to take अद्वैतं as an adj. qualifying प्रेम which we get from the context. यद् may be easily supplied. Vîr., who reads अनुगतं, construes—यत्सर्वास्ववस्थासु सुखदुःखयोः अद्वैतमनुगतं, which is not happy. विश्रामः—According to Pâṇ., विश्रम is the correct form, Vṛiddhi being forbidden before घञ् (अ) by VI. 3. 123. The poets, however, freely use the form; *cf.* Śák. II. 6; see com; or we may defend the form by adding अ (ण्) स्वार्थे, by including it in the पञ्चादि group, although not actually mentioned in it. भद्रं &c.—construe येन तदेकमानिर्वचनीयं प्रेमरूपं वस्तु कथमपि प्राप्यते तस्य सुमानुषस्य मनुष्येषु धन्यस्य भद्रम्; see trans. With the reading प्रेम for तस्य, the sense becomes simpler; but then भद्रं, after what is said in the previous three lines, has no propriety. Again it has no MS. authority. The reading प्रार्थ्यते has no propriety; कथमपि has no force in that case. If it is to be sought after, why seek it with difficulty? Stanza quoted in the D.-R. as an instance of an अनुकूल hero who is एकनायिक, with the reading भद्रं तस्य सुमानुषस्य in the fourth line.

P. 38. अर्थवादः—अर्थ्यते इत्यर्थः तस्य वादः *lit.* the mention or specification of the object (for which a thing is done). It is a term occurring along with विधि in the Bráhmaṇas and the Púrvamímáṃsá, and means what is said by way of commending a *vidhi* or sacred precept, such as स्वर्गकामो ज्योतिष्टोमेन यजेत. See A. Dic. Hence secondarily it means 'something said in praise of a thing,' and finally, 'praise or eulogy'. दोष—may be in his public or private life. प्रतिविधीयते Lit.—measures may be taken to counteract or remedy it; *i. e.* may be removed.

P. 39. हा हा धिक् &c.—This may be a general remark, or may be taken in connexion with वैदेही. अद्भुतैरुपायैः—This refers to the terrible ordeal of fire through which Sîtâ had to pass before she could be received by her husband as his wife. She came out of the fire unharmed and brighter than before, her purity being attested to by the God of fire himself. The rdeal was done in the presence of Daśaratha and many gods who had come down from heaven for that purpose. आलर्क—fr. अलर्क a mad dog. संजातगरप्रयोगः अल्यते वार्यते दशनभयादलर्कः उन्मत्तः श्वा। Kshîra. on Ak. The poison of a mad dog does not operate all at once after the bite, but shows itself several weeks or even one or two years after the time of infection, when it spreads through the whole system.

सतां—is emphatic; of good rulers (and not असतां). Ráma does not call his people wicked, nor does he blame them; but says that such a conduct on their part was natural; *cf.* I 44, *infra.* केनापि कार्येण—by doing anything, although it entails misery; *i. e.* by every means. पूरितं—there was लोकाराधन in the exile of Ráma; for the people would have censured him for not keeping his word. Also because the demons had to be killed and the world to be rid of that pestilence. पूजितं *v. l.*—honoured (by being observed).

शीर्णं—implies absence of stain. *Cf.* जज्वाल लोकस्थितये स राजा । Bhaṭṭi. I. 4. मत्संबन्धात्—on account of my connexion with it, *i. e.* my not taking action to remedy it. The reading मत्संबन्धा is not good; it leads to an awkward Bah.; मया संबन्धो यस्या or मम संबन्धो यस्याः; मत्संबद्धा 'connected with me' is not objectionable. Ráma's dread of infamy will appear from the following—अकीर्तिर्यस्य गीयेत लोके भूतस्य कस्यचित् । पतत्येवाधमाँल्लोकान्यावच्छब्दः प्रकीर्त्यते ॥ Râmá. Uttar. K. 45-12. कश्मलं—fr कश् to go and अल, before which म् is inserted by Uṇâdi I. 109; foul, ignominious. *Cf.* Ragh. XIV. 37.

P. 40. निमि—The founder of the Janaka family and a son of Ikshváku. He was cursed by Vasishṭha to lose his corporeal form; and he in his turn pronounced a similar imprecation on the sage. Both quitted their bodily forms. Vasishṭha was born again as the son of Mitra and Varuṇa; but Nimi did not like to be restored to a bodily form, although the gods were willing to enable him to do so; they, however, gave him a boon by which he was placed on the eyes of all people. See V. P. IV. 5. *Cf.* नेत्रेषु सर्वभूतानां वायुभूतश्चरिष्यसि । त्वत्कृते च निमिष्यन्ति चक्षूंषि पृथिवीपते ॥ Rámá. Uttar. K. 57 तातप्रिये—*Cf. infra* IV. 16. राममयजीविते—whose life is Râma alone. Here मय is added स्वार्थे; राम एव जीवितं यस्याः. स्तोकवादिनि—*Cf.* सत्याय मितभाषिणां Ragh. I. 7. कथमेवंविधायाः &c.—*Cf.* ईदृशीमाकृतिमनभिभवनीयां &c. Kád. p. 219.

त्वया जगन्ति &c.—पुण्यानि rendered holy or blessed. विपत्स्यसे—Ràma had by this time made up his mind as to how to act. So destruction was sure in her case; see com. The fig. here is विषम (the incongruity between cause and effect).

P. 41. नूतनः राजा—Mark the sarcasm of the expression. The new king, who (unlike his predecessors) can pass any order, which must not be disputed, but strictly obeyed. संतान—संतन्यते इति संतानः, fr. तन् with सम् and घञ्; it may mean 'progeny or 'continuation' as the affix is added करणे or भावे. Here of course the former sense is intended. अनार्य—*Lit.* something not worthy of an A'rya; hence, an act of cruelty, &c. अध्यवसितं—determined upon. अतिदूर—*scil.* in Lanká.

P. 42. बीभत्स—loathsome on account of its cruelty.

सौहदात्—सुहृदः भावः सौहदम्; fr. सुहृद् + अण्; so this is grammatically irregular. Both सौहार्द and सौहृद, however, occur in literature; *cf.* for the latter सखीजनस्ते किमुतार्द्रसौहृदः । Vik. I. 9; निसर्गसौहृदेन Mâl.-Mâdh. I.; यत्सौहृदादपि जनाः शिथिलीभवन्ति Mk. I. 13. Jagaddhara thus comments on the form—By the Sûtra हृद्भग सिन्ध्वन्ते पूर्वपदस्य च । Pâṇ. VII. 3. 19 (*i. e.* in the case of a compound word ending in हृद् &c. Vṛiddhi of the first vowel takes place in both the members) the proper form should be सौहार्द; how do you justify सौहृद then? उच्यते—हृदित्यादौ प्रतिपदोक्तस्य (the word that is mentioned) हृदयस्य हृल्लेखेति हृदादेशस्य आदिवृद्धिः (and not of the independent word हृद्); यद्वा संज्ञापूर्वको विधिरनित्यः इति वचनादुभयपदवृद्धेरनित्यत्वम् । See our note on the word, Mâl.-Mâdh. p. 8. Vâmana derives it from सुहृदय by adding अण् before which हृदय is changed to हृद् and the आदिवृद्धि is got by तद्धितेषु अचामादेः । Páṇ. VII. 2. 117. See Káv. S. V. 2. 83. अपृथगाश्रयां-So great was their love that Râma and Sîtâ were never apart after their marriage. *Cf.* śl. 37, *supra*. अपृथगाशया *v. l.*—one in heart, never holding conflicting thoughts or opinions. This reading, though better as far as Sîtâ is concerned (see notes on p. 32), is not adopted here as it cannot apply to गृहशकुन्तिका also. छद्मना—Because he was to send her away under the pretext of gratifying her desire. सौनिक—also शौनिक a butcher; सूना प्राणिवधस्थानं तज्जीविकात्वेनास्त्यस्य; fr. सूना + ठक् (इक). सौनिके—*v. l.* is not good; it will have to be taken in the sense of the Dative; 'as one gives......to a butcher.' गृहशकुन्तिका—गृहे पालिता शकुन्तिका; Sâkapârthivâdi.

स्वैरं—wilfully, *i. e.* at once; or, gently.

कर्मचां०—कर्मणा चाण्डालः a Chaṇḍála (*i. e.* a man of atrocious deeds) by acts, not by birth. Vasishṭha mentions four classes of these, *viz.* असूयकः पिशुनश्च कृतघ्नो दीर्घरोषकः । चत्वारः कर्मचाण्डाला जन्मतश्चापि पञ्चमः ॥ Ráma calls himself अपूर्व because he is not one of these. A Chaṇḍâla does not cast off his wife, much less one who is dutiful, and still less when she is pregnant. मुग्ध—innocent, unsuspecting; one that can be easily duped. विपाक—may mean 'fruit' or 'result.'

P. 43. विपर्यस्त:—In Sîtâ's company the world was all a source of joy and happiness to him; now it is the reverse of it. See the Com.'s remarks. जीर्ण०—implies absence of delightful spots and scenes. *Cf. supra* 30, प्रियानाशे &c. कष्ट०—full of—destined to suffer—hardships; the Com. reads काष्ठप्रायं, which seems to be a better reading. कष्टप्रायं would better agree with जीवितम्. अशरणः—Because there is no help for the present calamity.

दुःखसंवेदनाय—That he should not only experience but feel the pangs of sorrow. वज्रकीलायितं—P. p. p. of the denom. from वज्रकील (वज्रकीलमिवाचरति वज्रकीलायते); 'have acted the part of adamantine nails which can never be extracted;' *i. e.* life has been so infixed that it cannot escape. हृदि स्थिरैः *v. l.* is not so good, as the idea of स्थिरत्व is expressed by वज्रकील. See the com. which explains how Ráma had to suffer misery from early youth. His determined abandonment of Sîtâ would be the crowning blow of misery, and he therefore wishes that life had better left him; but it persists in continuing in him.

P. 44. सखि त्रिजटे—Trijaṭâ was an old female demon appointed by Rávaṇa to watch over Sîtá when kept as a captive in the Aśoka-Vaniká. She treated Sîtá very kindly and asked the other Rákshasîs to do so when they threatened by telling her that they would eat her flesh. It was owing to her that Sîtâ could support her life in her separation. For these kind services of Trijaṭâ to Sîtá, Râma addresses her as a friend. See Rámâ. Ar. K. 27.

मुषिताः—see com.; the *dravya* is of course Sîtâ. परिभूताः—insulted; *i. e.* of course by his unworthy conduct. Râma thinks that Sîtâ was a sacred treasure committed to his care by the above-named personages. He, however, has shown himself to be unworthy of the trust reposed in him, being thus guilty of the blackest ingratitude (कृतघ्नेन in the next sl.). ते हि &c.—The fig. is Utpreksbá.

विस्रम्भात् &c.—This explains how Ráma is कृतघ्न and पाप. Here Râma represents himself as cruel, proceeding in a sort of climax, each of विस्रम्भ, लब्धनिद्रस्य &c. serving to augment his cruelty more and more क्रव्यादेभ्यः—to eaters of raw flesh; this marks the culminating point. आतङ्क (*fr.* तञ्च् with आ to coagulate or contract)—properly means bodily distress or pain; hence, secondarily, what causes such distress; mental disquietude, fear.

पश्चिमः—last (पश्चाद्भवः). अपश्चिमः *v. l.* means the same thing; नास्ति पश्चिमः यस्य having no other subsequent or last, which is itself the last; *cf.* अनुत्तम Hit. I. अपश्चिम often occurs in plays. Nâg. IV. p. 88.

P. 45. अब्रह्मण्य—ब्रह्मणः हितं ब्रह्मण्यं न ब्रह्मण्यमब्रह्मण्यं something calamitous to the Bráhmaṇas (which ought not to take place). Hence used as a cry for protection or help against a calamity. कल्पीनां &c.—the first half occurs in Rámà. Uttar. K. 60. 15. लवण—a demon, son of Madhu and Kumbhînasî, the sister of Rávaṇa and daughter of Viśravas.

He was the sovereign of Mathurâ which was previously called after his father Madhuvana. He had inherited from his father an invincible trident originally obtained from Śiva. *Cf.* Ragh. XV. 5; Râmâ. Utt. K. 61–63. The Com. reads दुरात्मनो माथुरस्य कु०, where माथुर means the lord of Madhurâ; मथुरा निवासोऽस्य; by सोऽस्य निवासः Pâṇ. IV. 3. 89.

शत्रुघ्नं &c.—The complaint of the sages and the dispatching of Śatrughna against the demon Lavaṇa were events subsequent to the abandonment of Sîtâ. But the poet puts them earlier here, furnishing Ràma an occasion to leave Sîtâ alone, and thereby to avoid a spectacle which would otherwise have been terribly painful to him. भगवति &c.—We shall see further on that this request of Râma is remembered and acceded to by the goddess Earth.

गोत्रमङ्गलं—*i. e.* on whom depended the happiness and well-being of the two families पुण्ये—is redundant after देवयजने. It is perhaps put in for alliteration; or the poet might be taken to mean अजीजनः अत एव पुण्ये.

दुःस्वप्नेन—She dreamt that Ráma had left her and gone away and so she woke up in alarm. एकाकिनी—एका एव, alone (with the idea of helplessness); एकादाकिनिच्चासहाये Pâṇ. V. 3. 52.

P. 46. यदि प्रभविष्यामि—Sîtâ was sure that her anger would melt away at the sight of her dear husband in spite of her wish to chide him for leaving her. This brings out her extreme love for Râma. आर्यपुत्र०—Mark the reverence in which Sítâ holds Râma. This utterance is very touching. She did not know what was in store for her.

ACT II.

P. 47. The second Act opens with a *Chúlikâ*. अन्तर्जवनिकासंस्थैश्चूलिकार्थस्य सूचनम् । Here the words स्वागतं &c. of the wood-nymph, who is behind the curtain, indicate the approach of Âtreyî. The Interlude is meant to acquaint the audience with the events intervening between the close of the 1st and the commencement of the 2nd Act, a knowledge of which is necessary for a proper understanding of the incidents represented in the 2nd Act. We shall see that an interval of 12 years separates the two Acts. फलकुसुम०—फलानि च कुसुमानि च पल्लवाश्च फल०वास्तैर्युक्तमर्घ्यं फल०; अर्घः पूजाविधिः

तदर्घमिदमर्घ्यं; from अर्घ + यत्; it is a respectful offering to a god or a respectable person and often consists of water in a *droṇa* or a vessel. In the case of ascetics it should have fruits, flowers and leaves added to it; *cf.* फलपल्लवपुष्पाढ्यं तापसेभ्योऽर्घ्यमाहरेत् । quoted by Gu °कुसुमगर्भेण पल्लवा° *v. l.*—फलकुसुमानि गर्भे यस्य तेन; पल्लवयुक्तेन अर्घ्येण पल्लवार्घ्येण उपतिष्ठते—honours, waits upon. For the A'tm. see com. and H. S. Gr. p. 412. विकीर्य—having offered from a distance; indec. of कॄ with वि; वितीर्य *v. l.* —having given. यथेच्छं—यथेच्छाभोग्यं *v. l.* यथेच्छ आसमन्तात् भोक्तुं योग्यं.

सतां संगः &c.—*Cf.* गृहानुपैतुं प्रणयादभीप्सवो भवन्ति नापुण्यकृतां मनीषिणः । Sis. I. 14. न परार्धीनमिह वः—A courteous way of saying भवदधीनम्; परस्मिन्नधि पराधीनम् अधि necessarily takes ईन (ख) when the latter member of a compound, by अध्युत्तरपदात् Pāṇ. V. 4. 7.

P. 48. विनयमधुरः—विनयेन मधुरः, and not necessitated by the observance of a vow. अविपर्यासित—not changing, *i. e.* of uniform nature. अनुपधि—अविद्यमानः उपधिर्यस्मिंस्तत्; उपधीयते आरोप्यतेऽनेन इति उपधिः *lit.* that by which something is falsely attributed to another; fraud. *Cf.* with this Mv. I. 12; for the different traits of good men's character referred to here, see Bh. Nî. 62-65.

कां पुनः &c.—The conversation here is not only very elegant but full of politeness and sweet address. अगस्त्य—Son of Mitra and Varuṇa conjointly, born along with Vasishṭha. See *supra*, note on Vasisṭha, p. 6, and A. Dic.

उद्गीथविदः—Adepts in the Vedánta lore. उद्गीयते इत्युद्गीथः is the second portion of the Sâmaveda, which the priest Udgâtṛi recites. It is also a designation of *Om*, the monosyllabic representation of (the triple-natured, Saguṇa) Brahma, also called प्रणव, and is mentioned as such in the Chhând. Up., as a Vidyá for the attainment of the knowledge of Brahma. The passage ओमित्युद्गीथं quoted by the Com. is from the Chhând. Up.; the दहरविद्या referred to by the Com. is also from the same Up., VIII. 1. 1. Dahara is the heart-lotus and the Brahma in it is the object of knowledge; see Bhâshya on Ved Sú. I. 3. 14-18. *Cf.* also प्रणवो धनुः शरो ह्यात्मा ब्रह्म तल्लक्ष्यमुच्यते । अप्रमत्तेन वेद्धव्यं शरवत्तन्मयो भवेत् ॥ Muṇḍ. Up. II. 2-4.

निगमान्तविद्या—the same as वेदान्तविद्या. निगच्छन्त्यनेनेति निगमश्छन्दः; *fr.* निगम् to attain knowledge. °विद्या—knowledge of Brahma as unfolded in the Upanishads which are contained in the

A'raṇyakas and thus form the last part of the Vedas. वेदान्ते परमं गुह्यं पुराकल्पे प्रचोदितम् । नाप्रशान्ताय दातव्यं नापुत्रायाशिष्याय वा पुनः ॥ Śve. Up. VI. 22. पार्श्व—पर्शूनां समूहः the rib-bones; hence, the side of an animal; and secondarily, vicinity. वाल्मीकि—So called from Valmîka or an ant-hill, full of the nests of termites, with which he was covered as he sat down repeating the word Mará, Mará; see A. Dic.

P. 49. प्राचेतस—Vâlmîki, who was the twelfth son of Prachetas or Varuṇa. ब्रह्मपारायण—Complete course of study of the Brahma philosophy. पारस्यायनं पारायणं; now see com. स्तन्यत्याग॰—स्तन्यस्य (of the mother's milk) त्यागः मात्रा परिमाणं यस्य. सचराचराणां v. l.—here सह is meaningless; who are the beings left out of the चर and अचर beings?

उपस्नेहयति—excites the affection of; denom. fr. उपस्नेह, to cause to melt with love. संविज्ञान—a correct knowledge of.

धात्रीकर्म वस्तुतः—having actually undertaken &c. This is the best reading. Some read ॰कर्मवस्तुतः—धात्रीकर्मैव वस्तु ततः; but here वस्तु has no propriety. धात्रीकर्मतः is the Com.'s reading; it means 'beginning from the duties of a nurse.' चौलकर्म—the ceremony of cutting the hair and keeping the locks and crest, which is done generally in the third year. *Cf.* चूडाकर्म द्विजातीनां सर्वेषामेव धर्मतः । प्रथमेऽब्दे तृतीये वा कर्तव्यं श्रुतिचोदनात् ॥ Manu. II. 35. वृत्तचूडौ v. l.-वृत्ता चूडा चूडाकर्म ययोः; whose tonsure-ceremony was performed. त्रयी—the Vedic lore; the three Vedas. *A dvija* is not entitled to read or study the Veda until his उपनयन ceremony is performed. The Com. remarks that by त्रयी we are to understand also the 6 *aṅgas*, or works accessory to the study of the Vedas. वर्जं (त्रयीं वर्जयित्वा)-is the gerund in अम् from वृज्. इतराः—others; *i. e.* the remaining three, the Vidyás being four, *viz.* आन्वीक्षिकी त्रयी वार्ता दण्डनीतिश्च शाश्वती । विद्याश्चतस्र एवैता लोकसंस्थितिहेतवः । Kâm. N. II. 2-2. तिस्रो विद्याः—See com.; according to some these are आन्वीक्षिकी (त्रयी) वार्ता दण्डनीतिश्च शाश्वती; Kám. Nît. II. 2. आन्वीक्षिकी is metaphysics (आत्मविद्या); वार्ता is agriculture, tending cattle &c.; and दण्डनीति is science of government.

P. 50. परिनिष्ठापिताः—*i. e.* they were well grounded (into them); p. p. p. of the denom. from निष्ठा (निष्ठापय्) or of the cau. of स्था with परिनि. गर्भैकादशे—for the *Upanayana* of a Kshatriya boy is to be performed in his eleventh year from conception. *Cf.* Manu. II.36 गर्भाष्टमेऽब्दे कुर्वीत ब्राह्मणस्योपनायनम् । गर्भादेकादशे राज्ञो गर्भात्तु द्वादशे विशः॥ क्षात्रेण कल्पेन-कल्प refers to the rites proper for a particular class. See Manu. II. 42-49. गुरुणा—Vàlmîki was their गुरु in the full sense of the term ; *cf.* स गुरुर्यः क्रियाः कृत्वा वेदमस्मै प्रयच्छति । Yàj. S. I. 34. प्रज्ञा—the faculty of understanding. मेधा—the retentive faculty or memory ; धीर्धारणावती मेधा Amara. ज्ञाने—*i. e.* ज्ञानग्रहणे power to grasp. मृदाद्यः *v.l.*—is not good; for मृद् will have to be taken in the secondary sense of non-reflecting objects. *Cf.* for the idea पात्रविशेषे न्यस्तं गुणान्तरं व्रजति शिल्पमाधातुः । Málav. I. 6. The fig. is दृष्टान्त.

माध्यंदिन०—The midday bath and the rites to be performed after a bath (माध्याह्नसंध्या). नहीं तमसा—This is in accordance with the Râmá.—स मुहूर्तं गते तस्मिन्देवलोकं मुनिः (*scil.* नारद, after praising Râma, Bál. K. 4. 3) तदा । जगाम तमसातीरं जाह्नव्यास्त्वविदूरतः ॥

आकस्मिक०—आकस्मिकः प्रत्यवभासः manifestation यस्याः ताम्. अव्यतिकीर्ण०—अव्यतिकीर्णाः (not confused or mixed up) वर्णाः यस्याः whose syllables were properly arranged, of faultless composition. अनुष्टुभेन छन्दसा—The Rámá. poetically asserts that the श्लोक was a transformation of Vál.'s शोक ; पादबद्धोऽक्षरसमस्तन्त्रीलयसमन्वितः । शोकार्तस्य प्रवृत्तो मे श्लोको भवतु नान्यथा ॥ Râmá. Bàl. II. *Cf.* also Kàlidása निषादविद्धाण्डजदर्शनोत्थः श्लोकत्वमापद्यत यस्य शोकः । Ragh. XV. 70. मा निषाद &c.—Râmá. Bál. II. 15. मा अगमः—the retention of अ is आर्ष. Some explain away the anomaly by supposing the particle used here to be मा and not माङ्. Our Com. gives a queer defence of this. प्रतिष्ठा—a position of happiness or bliss. समाः is fem. and is generally used in the plural. *Cf.* the translation of the stanza by Griffith:—

No fame be thine for endless time,
Because, base outcast, of thy crime,
Whose cruel hand was fain to slay,
One of this [illegible]ntle pair at play.

The Com. interpre[illegible]s the Śl. as indirectly referring to Râma. Thus—मानिषाद् means Ráma (मा Lakshmî, *i. e.* Sîtá, her incarnation, निषीदति resides अस्मिन्), he being an incarnation of Vishṇu. क्रौञ्च-(*lit.* going wrong, fr. कुञ्च कौटिल्याल्पीभावयोः)-मिथुन may refer either to Válî and Tárá or Râvaṇa and Mandodarî ; Râvaṇa was काममोहित with regard to Sîtâ. Here the fig. is श्लेष. For much interesting information in connexion with this Śl. the student may read Ráma's com. on it (in the orig. Râmáyaṇa).

P. 51. आम्नायात्—आम्नाय: the Veda; आम्नायते what is studied इति आम्नाय: by adding अ (घञ्); or उपदिशति धर्माधर्मौ इति by adding अ (ण). अन्य:...वतार:—other than; for although we find अनुष्टुभ् among the Vedic metres (गायत्री, उष्णिह्, अनुष्टुभ्, बृहती), it is not as regular as we find it in post-Vedic literature; e g. in the Rámá. The Anushṭubh of the Purushasûkta will serve as an instance of the former. The fifth and sixth letters ought to be respectively short and long in the अनु०; this we find reversed in the Veda; e. g. सहस्रशीर्षा पुरुष: . Hence the regular अनु० used by Vâlmîki is called नूतन: छन्दसामवतार:.

आविर्भूत०—(1) To whom the Brahma in the form of words had been revealed; or (2) through whom the Brahma &c. had manifested itself. Words, being a perceptible phase (expression) of the invisible and ever-existing Brahma, are called शब्दब्रह्म, being identified with it. भूतभावन:—भूतानि भावयति (creates) इति; who creates according to the laws of previous creation; see com., and *cf.* the Śruti सर्वं धाता यथापूर्वमकल्पयत्. अव्याहतज्योति:—whose light will be unimpeded, *i. e.* you will be able to describe most private conversations, deeds &c. *Cf.* रामस्य चरितं कृत्स्नं कुरु त्वमृषिसत्तम। 32; वैदेह्याश्चैव यद्वृत्तं प्रकाशं यदि वा रह: ॥ तच्चाप्यविदितं सर्वं विदितं ते भविष्यति। न ते वागनृता काव्ये काचिदत्र भविष्यति ॥ 34, 35. आर्षं—ऋषेरिदं *lit.* of a sage; hence, prophetic; the expression implies superhuman power. प्रातिभं चक्षु:—प्रतिभा the creative faculty, genius, which creates new ideas. प्रज्ञा नवनवोन्मेषशालिनी (distinguished by ever-new flashes) प्रतिभा मता। इति रुद्र:। as quoted by Bhá. Dik. in his com. on A. K. प्रतिभाया इदं प्रातिभं. विवर्त—In the Vedánta philosophy this means modification or development, which is illusory appearance. The difference between विवर्त and परिणाम is this, that in the former there is no complete change of the cause, while in the latter there is the entire destruction of form or nature of the original cause (प्रकृतिस्वरूपानुपमर्देन रूपान्तरोत्पत्तिर्विवर्त: ०पोपमर्देन......परिणाम:). Bhavabhûti seems to be a *Vivartavádî* and therefore belongs to that school of the Vedántins which regards the whole of the phenomenal world as a mere illusion, the only real entity being Brahma Thus जगत् is the Vivarta of Brahma which is its अधिष्ठान. Similarly the Rámáyaṇa is a Vivarta of the *Śabdabrahma.* Bhavabhûti seems to have used the word विवर्त here in the sense of a modification of form, as कुण्डल, कटक &c. are of gold. The illusory world appears to be real by Avidyá. The illusion is dispelled by सम्यग्ज्ञान. The poet refers to this doctrine twice again in this work:—(1) in III. 47, wherein आवर्त, बुद्बुद, तरङ्ग &c. are indicated as the Vivartas of water, while (2) in VI. 6 he speaks of Vidyá as dispelling all illusion and resolving the *Prapañcha* into Brahma. इतिहास—fr. इति ह पारंपर्योपदेशो अव्ययं (traditional account of former events) आस्ते अस्मिन् । Bh. Dik.; इति ह आसीदयम् इति इतिहासः । इतिः एवमर्थे हः किलार्थे Kshîrasvàmin.

मण्डितः—of course by the ornament, the new work of Válmîki. It is quite natural that the wood-nymph, who is a friend and admirer of Ráma and Sîtá, should make such a remark. पण्डित *v. l.*, meaning 'has grown wiser by the new production', is not a very appropriate reading.

P. 52. ०बन्धुवर्गः—शाखिवर्गः *v. l.* is bad, as the reference is to the penance-grove, the mountain प्र०, Vásantî etc. These are regarded as the Bandhus of Sîtâ; *cf.* यत्र द्रुमा अपि मृगा अपि बन्धवो मे *infra,* III. 8. नामधेयं—This is purposely used, so that Vâsantî might ask a question and Sîtâ's abandonment be introduced to the audience. प्रासङ्गिकी—प्रसङ्गादागता; incidental, brought in by the drift of the conversation.

वासन्ती—The poet uses the name of the deity from here as it is introduced to the audience now from the reply she gave to आत्रेयी's question अपि जन० वासन्ती त्वम्. अत्याहितं—a great calamity; अत्यन्तमाधीयते तन्निवृत्त्यर्थं मनो दीयते अस्मिन्निति. Vâsantî asked the question as she knew absolutely nothing about the affairs in Ayodhyá ever since Ráma returned to it with Sîtá after the déstruction of Râvaṇa. इति मूर्छति—shows the great affection she had for Sîtá, whose great friend she had been on account of her (Sîtâ's) long stay in Janasthâna. दारुण—fr. दृ to tear, is appropriate with निर्घात which means 'a terrible stroke' here. निर्घात properly means the clash of two contending winds: वायुना निहतो वायुर्गगनाच्च पतत्यधः । प्रचण्डघोरनिर्घोषो निर्घात इति बुध्यते ॥

महाभाग—महान् प्रशस्तः भागः यस्याः one to whose lot fall a very great number of blessings; hence, fortunate. In contrast with this stands ईदृशः निर्माणभागः । न हि—Nothing at all. हि adds force. अधिष्ठितेषु—superintended or led by. रघुकदम्बकेषु—The word कदम्बक like कुञ्जर &c. expresses excellence. वधू—उह्यते पितुर्गेहाद्भर्तृगेहमिति. This is by Uṇâdi I. 83.

P. 53. परिशुद्धा—clear in their import. क्रतु—करोति क्रियते वा इति क्रतुः fr. कृ+अतु by Uṇâdi I. 77. The most important thing that a man does; hence a sacrifice. *Cf.* Gr. *Kratos*, Zend *Khratu*. A Kratu is one in which an animal is necessarily killed, while a Yajña is one in which an animal may or may not be killed. अश्वमेधः—अश्वः मेध्यते हिंस्यते अत्र. This sacrifice was performed as a mark of universal sovereignty. The Com. reads राजक्रतुः which means the same thing (क्रतूनां राजा राजक्रतुः); see com. प्रक्रान्तः—is used in connexion with sacred rites for which previous preparations are necessary, and means the performance of preliminary ceremonies.

परिणीतं—The instituting of a sacrifice always pre-supposes the existence of पत्नी, the husband's partner in religious performances. Hence the question. हिरण्मयी—हिरण्यस्य विकारः (made of, a production of) हिरण्मयी; here मय (ट्) has this sense. ॰प्रतिकृतिः—This is mentioned in the Râmâ. also. काञ्चनीं मम पत्नीं च दीक्षायां ज्ञांश्च कर्मणि। Uttar. K. 91. 25.

वज्रादपि &c.—To please the people Râma made his heart as hard as adamant, while at the same time he had the deepest affection for her, as was evinced by his remaining unmarried and using her image only when required to do so. लोकोत्तराणां—अतिशयेनोद्गता उत्तराः लोकेषु उत्तराः लोकोत्तराः supremely eminent, extraordinary. *Cf.* for a similar idea संपत्सु महतां चित्तं भवत्युत्पलकोमलम्। आपत्सु च महाशैलशिलासंघातकर्कशम्॥ Bh. Nî. 66.

वामदेव—Name of a sage often mentioned along with Vasishṭha in the Râmâyaṇa. Vâmadeva is also the Ṛishi of almost all the hymns of the 4th Maṇḍala of the Ṛigveda. See Dowson's Class. Dic. Vámadeva was engaged to officiate at the sacrifice as Vasishṭha was not there. संप्रदाय—संप्रदानमिति; *lit.* the due transmitting of knowledge by a preceptor to his disciple (गुरुपरंपरागतसदुपदेशः); traditional knowledge or instruction. चतुरङ्ग—The old army consisted of four parts which are हस्त्यश्वरथपत्तयः, elephants, chariots, cavalry and infantry.

P. 54. हन्त—expresses joy. She was glad to hear that Lakshmaṇa at least had a son, if Ráma had no chance of getting any (as she thought). सोरस्ताडम्—उरसस्ताडः तेन सहितं यथा तथा। It may also be taken as a Namulanta; कृत्स्नमुरस्ताडयित्वा. This was what the Bráhmaṇa said:—रामस्य दुष्कृतं किंचिन्महदस्ति न संशयः। यथा हि विषयस्थानां बालानां मृत्युरागतः॥...... राजदोषैर्विपद्यन्ते प्रजा ह्यविधिपालिताः। असद्वृत्ते हि नृपतावकाले म्रियते जनः॥ Râmâ. Uttar. 73. 10, 16. अपचार—misconduct, transgression of duty. Malli. translates this by वर्णधर्मव्यतिकर. See his com. on Ragh. XV. 47. Ràma admits the justice of the Bráhmaṇa's words; see Uttar. K. 76. 11. **अशरीरिणी**—incorporeal, from heaven. There is no reference to this in the Râmâyaṇa, though Kâlidâsa makes mention of it; *cf.* Ragh. quoted above. According to the Râmâyaṇa, Nârada counsels Ráma as to what was to be done. See Uttar. K. 74.

वृषल:—stands here for a शूद्र, as appears from Vásantî's speech below. A Śûdra was not authorized to read the Veda or to practise religious austerities, as that was the duty assigned to the Brâhmaṇa class. **तप्यते**—तप् 4 A'. to practise penance. **शीर्षच्छेद्य:**—शीर्षच्छेदमर्हतीति; ०च्छेद + य (यत्); see com. **आकृष्ट०**—आकृष्ट: कृपाण: आकृष्टकृपाण: स पाणौ यस्य. **पुष्पकं**—This was the celebrated aerial car wrested from his brother Kubera by Râvaṇa. When Ráma returned to Ayodhyâ from Laṅkâ seated in it after Râvaṇa's destruction, he allowed it to go back to its proper owner, Kubera, asking it to come back to him whenever thought of. See Uttar. 41. **विदिश:**—bye-quarters; the quarters between the principal ones. दिग्भ्यां विनिर्गता विदिक् । दिशोर्मध्ये विदिक् स्त्रियाम् Amara. **अपि नाम**—I wish that. Here अपि has the sense of संभावना. **नाम** is generally added to अपि in this sense. The two particles are used when the speaker intends that some desired thing should happen and when there is a likelihood or hope that it would so happen. *Cf.* अपि नाम तयो: कल्याणिनोरभिमत: पाणिग्रह: स्यात् । Mâl.-Mâdh. I.; अपि नाम कुलपतेरियमसवर्णक्षेत्रसंभवा स्यात् । Śák. I.&c. See A. G. 247.

कण्डूल—कण्डूर्विद्यतेऽस्य कण्डूल:. Construe:—कूले (स्थिता:) ०कीटत्वच: ०कुक्कुटकुला: कुलायद्रुमा: स्वकुसुमै: गोदावरीम् अर्चन्ति । कण्डूलानां ०पिण्डानां (the frontal globes) कषणेन (by the rubbing of) य: उत्कम्प: (trembling upwards) तेन &c.; see com. The fig. in the first two lines is उत्प्रेक्षा. See com.

P. 55. **अपस्किरमाण**—Pres. p. of कॄ with अप which is A'tm. in the sense of joy, maintenance, or building a nest; स् is inserted after अप when the meaning is to scratch for food &c. (as a quadruped or bird) and the root is A'tm.; 'अपाच्चतुष्पाच्छकुनिष्वालेखने' Páṇ. VI. I. 142. सुडपि हर्षादिष्वेव वक्तव्य: Várt. अपस्किरते वृषो हृष्ट: । कुक्कुटो भक्ष्यार्थी, श्वा आश्रयार्थी च । हर्षादिष्विति किम् । अपकिरति कुसुमम् । Sid-Kau. **विष्किर:**—विष्किर: शकुनिर्विकिरो वा Páṇ. VI. I. 150. **०कीटत्वच:**—a double Bah. **कुल**—सजातीयै: कुलम् Amara; applied to a group of animals of the same species. **कुलायद्रुमा:**—कुलाययुक्ता: द्रुमा: । मध्यमपदलो० स० (of the शाकपार्थिवादि class). Mark the alliterations in this stanza. Mark also how each word in the last line begins with क्.

विष्कम्भक—वृत्तवर्तिष्यमाणानां कथांशानां निदर्शकः । संक्षिप्तार्थस्तु विष्कम्भो मध्यपात्रप्रयोजितः । एकानेककृतः शुद्धः संकीर्णो नीचमध्यमैः ॥ D.-R. The विष्क० is an interlude at the beginning of an act of a drama carriedon by one or more characters, middling or inferior, who connect the main story of the drama with the minor parts of the plot by briefly explaining to the audience what has already occurred, and what is likely to happen later on. It is of two kinds, शुद्ध and संकीर्ण, the former when the characters carrying on the dialogue are of the middle class, and the latter when one or more of them are of the inferior class.

दक्षिण:—Right (also, kind); the word is purposely used; Ráma means to say that it is not kind to the Śúdra ascetic. जीवातवे—For restoring to life; dat. of जीवातु life, revival (properly of the Vedic inf.). रामस्य &c.—If this be regarded as the हेतु for striking, the fig. is Kâvyaliṅga. दुर्वह०—निर्भर० *v. l.* is not very appropriate with गर्भ; it must be taken to mean 'greatly developed'.

P. 56. कृतं रामसदृशं कर्म &c.—An act befitting Ráma (who had the cruelty to abandon an innocent wife even when pregnant). See com. This as well as the previous stanza shows that Sîtá's exile was an act quite against Ráma's will and weighed heavily on his mind.

दण्डधारः—दण्डं धारयतीति ; the inflicter of punishment, a king. The word is purposely used here; 'you granted safety to the Bráhmaṇa boy against Yama by punishing me, the offender.' इयसृद्धिः—*i. e.* his being elevated to a divine form. संजीवितः &c.—*Cf.* यस्मिन् मुहूर्ते काकुत्स्थ शूद्रोयं विनिपातितः । तास्मिन्मुहूर्ते बालोसौ जीवेन समयुज्यत ॥ Uttar. 76.15. सत्सङ्गजानि &c.—The fig. is *Arthântaranyâsa*. *Cf.* for a similar thought समुन्नयन्भूतिमनार्यसंगमाद्वरं विरोधोऽपि समं महात्मभिः । Kir. I. 8.

आनन्द—inward or spiritual joy. मोद—joy due to external objects (विषयसुखं); see com. पुण्याः (संपदः):—because not used for sinful purposes. पुण्याभि०—संभवाः *v. l.* qualifies आनन्दाः and मोदाः; पुण्यात् अभिसंभवो येषां which are born of, *i. e.* spring from, religious merit. वैराजाः—विराजः ब्रह्मण इमे, the brilliant region called ब्रह्मलोक or सत्यलोक souls translated to which are exempt from further birth. This is the seventh and the highest world, the other six being भूः, भुवः, स्वः, महः, जनः and तपस्. It is not destroyed even at the time of Pralaya. At a Pralaya the lower four worlds are destroyed; see Vish. P. II.7. Or, this may be the celestial region occupied by the Vairájas, the first gods or the Pitṛis of that name referred to by the Vâyupuráṇa, whose forms are composed of spiritual (तेजस्) and not of elementary substance. लोकाः सांतानिका नाम यत्र तिष्ठन्ति भास्वराः । ते वैराजा इति ख्याता देवानां दिवि देवताः ॥ शिवाः—ध्रुवाः v. l. everlasting, i. e. the residence therein.

प्रसादात्—प्रसादोपायः v. l. प्रसादः उपायः यस्य coming from your favour ; this is not a good reading. प्रसादोपादानः v. l.—प्रसादः उपादानं direct cause यस्य ; due to your favour. Perhaps this may be the original reading ; *cf.* प्रकृष्टपुण्यपरिपाकोपादान एष महिमा । Mv. IV. प्रसादादेव—solely on account of your favour-simply because *you* killed me. He explains this in the next śl.

अन्वेष्टव्यः—*Cf.* य आत्मा अपहतपाप्मा...सोऽन्वेष्टव्यः स विजिज्ञासितव्यः । Chhá. Up. VIII. 7-1; अभ्यासनिगृहीतेन मनसा हृदयाश्रयम् । ज्योतिर्मयं विचिन्वन्ति योगिनस्त्वां विमुक्तये ॥ Ragh. X. 23. भूतनाथः—Ráma is identified here with the Supreme Spirit. The Com. reads लोकनाथः; but भूत॰ is more in accord with the श्रुति quoted by him. Constr.—भुवने अन्वेष्टव्यः शरण्यः—भूतनाथः (त्वं) मां वृषलकम् अन्विष्यन् योजनानां शतानि क्रान्त्वा यदिह प्राप्तः असि सः &c. वृषलक—the क is कुत्सार्थे. Out of modesty he speaks disparagingly of himself. वृषल is a man of mixed parentage.

P. 57. किं नाम दण्ड॰—Râma had asked the Pushpaka to take him to the place where the Śûdra ascetic was. It brought him to the place ; but in the confusion of mind caused by his having to kill an ascetic, Râma did not mark the region ; and hence the question. क्वचित्-अपरतः—Here there, in one place,—in another. आभोग—widee xtent, expanse. भीषण—because of its great expanse. भीषणः आभोगस्तेन रूक्षाः not pleasant to look at; or भीषण आभोगो येषां ते च ते रूक्षाः sterile च. तीर्थाश्रम॰—तीर्थानि च आश्रमाश्च......कान्ताराश्च तैः मिश्राः । ॰गर्भ॰ v. l.—॰सरितः गर्भे येषां ते च कान्तारमिश्राश्च ; or गर्भभूताः कान्ताराः गर्भकान्ताराः small woods तैर्मिश्राः । The constr. may also be एते॰ भागाः परिचितभुवः संदृश्यन्ते. These regions appear to have their spots familiar to me.

रक्षसां &c.—The reading चतुर्दश &c. is according to Ar. K. 26.35. The reading चतुर्दश च राक्षसाः is in better accord with the detailed account of the Rámâ. When Śûrpaṇakhâ told Khara how she was maimed by Lakshmaṇa and asked him to take revenge on Ráma and Lak., he at first sent fourteen Rákshasas against them, but they were all killed by Râma. He then sent his general दूषण with 14000 Rákshasas against Ráma, but with the same result. The remaining two Khara and Triśiras also came and were killed. See Ar. K. 21, 8, 9. दूषण०—The comp. should rather be ०मूर्धाः; see com. where the comp. is defended by the general principle—'The rules about the change of the endings of compounds are not absolutely binding (अनित्यत्वात्).' The Com. also suggests another way, which. see Khara, the half brother of Râvaṇa was the principal general of the Râkshasa force stationed in South India. दूषण and त्रिशिरस् were under him. See Râmá. III. 20-30. This śl. occurs in Mv. (V-13).

P. 58. सिद्धक्षेत्रे—the abode of ascetics seeking Siddhi, or the place where Siddhi is attained. अकुतोभयः—नास्ति कुतः भयं यस्मिन्; a comp. of the मयूरव्यंसकादि class.

रोमहर्षण—Causing the hair to stand on end (owing to fright). उन्मत्ताश्च ते चण्डाश्च श्वापदाः । शुनः पदानि इव पदानि येषां ते श्वापदाः । तेषां कुलानि (the herds of the different classes of ferocious beasts) तैः संकुलानि गिरिगह्वराणि येषु । जनस्थानपर्यन्ते दीर्घारण्यानि ।

निष्कूज &c.—सीमानः the border grounds सन्ति । कीदृश्यः । क्वचित् निष्कूजाः (see com.) च ताः स्तिमिताश्च । स्तिमित implies absence of wind, so that not a leaf was astir; क्वचित् प्रोच्चण्डः सत्त्वानां स्वनः यासु । स्वेच्छया सुप्ता गभीराश्च ते घोराश्च यद्वा गभीरं यथा तथा घोराः घोरन्तः (deep-snoring) ये भुजगास्तेषां श्वासैः प्रदीप्ता अग्नयो यासु । गभीरभोग—v. l. गभीरः भोगः body येषां; but here गभीर is not appropriate with भोग; it cannot mean here 'hood' as the snakes were asleep. ०घोष—गभीरः घोषः येषां which made a deep hissing sound (when breathing). प्रदर—a crevice, a ditch. प्रतिसूर्यक—a lizard, a chameleon. अजगर—अजं गिरति इति, a huge serpent of the boa kind. In this sl. भयानक and बीभत्स are slightly displayed

पश्यामि च-च—Just as I see &c.; the two चs show that the two actions take place simultaneously.

प्रियारामा—one to whom beautiful gardens or delightful groves were dear in every way (when in Ayodhyâ); and yet for me she came to the forest. प्रियरामा—v. l. प्रियो रामो यस्याः who loved Ráma in every way (and yet I had the cruelty to abandon her). कान्तार is used here in the sense of a dreary and frightful forest. किमतः परं—अतः here refers to the sight of the woods.

इतीहारमतेवासौ—इति इह अरमत एव असौ; एव is emphatic—inspite of the fierceness of the forest. इतिहारमतेवासौ v. l.; here इतिह is a particle indicating a past event; or हा may be taken separately; thus alas ! did she &c. The other variants are:—(1) इतीवारमतीवासौ; here the two इवs have no propriety;

आरमति again is in the present tense. (2) इति चारमतेवासौ ; here इव must be taken in the sense of एव. (3) इति हा रमते सीता is also a good reading. In this case हा expresses sorrow, रमते being Present tense used for the Past. (4) इतीवारमतेहासौ *v. l.* may be separated as इति इव आ (समन्तात्) अरमत इह असौ. Thus did she seem to sport here; here इव has no propriety, or we may separate as इति इव आरमते ह असौ ; but here ह is merely an expletive; again, रम् with आ is Par.; so we cannot have आरमते. Other variants need no explanation. स्नेहस्तस्याः &c.—He means:—So deep was her love for me that she gave up even her fondness for strolling in beautiful gardens, and preferred to come with me to these frightful forests and lived here happily with me. *Cf.* what she said to Ráma when going to the forest—सुखं वने निवत्स्यामि यथैव भवने पितुः ।......शुश्रूषमाणा ते नित्यं नियता ब्रह्मचारिणी । सह रंस्ये त्वया वीर वनेषु मधुगन्धिषु ॥ स्वर्गेऽपि च विना वासो भविता यदि राघव । त्वया मम नरव्याघ्र नाहं तमपि रोचये ॥ Ayod. K. 27. 12-13-14.

P. 59. न किंचिदपि—Here Ráma explains why Sitâ longed to live with him in the forest and how she found pleasure there. Though Râma did nothing special towards contributing to Sîtâ's happiness, yet by being merely in his company she bore lightly all the hardships of a forest life. See com. सौख्यैः—*i. e.* of course caused by his presence.

दुरासदैः—*Lit.* difficult to approach; hence, causing pain. छवि—colour. पर्यन्तैः—border-spots covered with verdant grass &c. on account of which they resembled the peacock's neck. बहलच्छाय०—अविरलं निविष्टा नीला बहला छाया येषां ते ०छायाः तरुणतरवः तेषां षण्डैः &c.; or, after the Com. who reads छायातरु:०, अविरलं निविष्टा ये नीला बहलाश्च छाया० &c. महानुभावः—Noble or magnanimous one. मध्यमारण्यकानि—Śambûka first referred to the forests on the borders of the Janasthána ; but, as they were an unwelcome sight to Râma, he next directs his attention to the forests in the middle. श्वापद० महारण्यानि *v l.* is not good. The reading in the text is better as contrasted with ०पर्यन्तदीर्घारण्यानि.

इह समद &c.—This and the following stanza occur also in Mv.; see V. 40, 41. The principal sentence is इह निर्झरिण्यः वहन्ति. समदैः शकुन्तैः आक्रान्ता या वानीरवीरुधस्तासां प्रसवैः flowers सुरभीणि च शीतानि स्वच्छानि च तोयानि यासां. वानीरमुक्त० *v. l.*—flowers let down by. फलभरस्य परिणामेन (ripening) श्यामा या जम्बवस्तासां निकुञ्जेषु यस्स्खलनं तेन मुखराणि &c. See com.

कुहर—कुहराणि (caves) भजन्ते कुहरभाजस्तेषां. स्त्यान—thickness, magnitude. भावप्रधानो निर्देशः. अम्बूकृत—A noise resembling the splashing of water or that made at the time of spitting; hence, a growl. अम्बूशब्द उपचारात्तद्धति । अनम्बु अम्बु अकारि अम्बूकृतम्.

सल्लकी—(also called गजभक्ष्या) is a tree much liked by elephants. *Cf.* Vik. IV. 23. इभ०—इभैर्दलितास्च ते विकीर्णाश्च ये ग्रन्थयः knots or joints तेषां निष्यन्दः तस्य गन्धः । The śl. occurs also in the Mál.-Mádh. (IX. 6).

P. 60. देवयानः—*Lit.* that by which the gods go. The Com. refers to Bg. VIII. 24 (see also 25, 26) where Śrídhara understands by fire &c. the path indicated by a deity presiding over each of these. In this he follows Śaṃkaráchârya who remarks that 'fire' here means a deity presiding over time. This is the better of the two paths, *viz.* देवयान and पितृयान, attainable only by the knowledge of truth (सत्येन पन्था विततो देवयानः), mentioned in the Chhándogya and the Kaushîtaki Upanishads and in the Brahmasûtrabháshya on Ved. Sût. IV. 2. 21, 3. 1. 2, and by which a विद्वान्, free from sin or merit, goes to the world of Brahmá, from which there is no return. The reading शिवास्ते पन्थानो देवयानाः is not good, for the pl. goes against it; the path is one. Again, शिवास्ते पन्थानः सन्तु is the phrase often used when a person sets out on a journey. यावत्—First, before doing anything else.

शाश्वतं पदं—The abode of Brahmá, where residence is eternal; *i. e.* those who go there by the देवयान path never return to the world of mortals, but remain there in the state of मुक्त for ever. *Cf.* स एतान् ब्रह्म गमयति एष देवपथो ब्रह्मपथ एतेन प्रतिपद्यमाना इमं मानवमावर्तं नावर्तन्ते । Chhân. Up. IV. 15. 6. See also Gîtâ XV. 4.

आरण्यकाश्च गृहिणश्च—Here also the two चs show क्रिययाः यौगपद्यम्; living the life of hermits(such as living on fruits etc.) and of householders (as he had his wife with him). अरण्ये भवः आरण्यकः *Lit.* one living in a forest from birth. The affix वुञ् (अक) is added to a few words. See Várt. on Pâṇ. IV. 2. 129. रताः स्वधर्मे—Willingly doing our duty as Kshatriyas; *i. e.* protecting the sages, offering daily worship to the deities and the departed fore-fathers &c. रसज्ञाः—*i. e.* we also tasted.

मञ्जु—fr. मञ्ज् to sound; properly, what is grateful or pleasing to the ear; hence, beautiful in general. *Cf.* मनोहर which is used in connexion with the ears or eyes. आ may have a diminutive force here; or take आ समन्तात् मञ्जवः वञ्जुलतराः वञ्जुला लताश्च या येषु तानि. ०वञ्जुलकवानि *v. l.*—आमञ्जूनि वञ्जुलेषु कतानि येषु on which there were the charming chirpings of birds on Vañjula creepers. आमन्द्रमञ्जुलरुतानि v. l.—on which there were warblings of birds that were slightly deep and charming. नीरन्ध्र—without intervening spaces; i. e. in thick numbers.

आरादपि—although near. आरात् means दूर as well as समीप. But the use of अपि and अयं shows that the latter meaning is intended here. Generally a hill appears to have a blue hue like that of clouds from a distance. But the mountain, though near, looked to be so, being blue; see *supra* p. 26 where it is described and said to be situated in Janasthána. According to the Rámá. it was near Kishkindhá; see Kish. 27. K. प्रस्रवण—So called because of its many streams.

तेषु—so familar to us. पर्णोटज—उटज (उटेभ्यः जायते) itself means a leafy hut; but here it means simply a hut, a cottage. पयसि—is connected with वितत &c.; so this is an instance of एकदेशीयान्वय. अनोकह—a tree. मुखर—noisy with. वनान्त—a forest-region; अन्तशब्दः स्वरूपवाची। 'अन्तः स्वरूपे निकटे प्रान्ते निश्चयनाशयोः ' इति हेमः.

विविध°—विविधा ये विस्रम्भातिप्रसङ्गाः acts of excessive confidence तेषां साक्षिणः.

P. 61. चिराद्वे°—goes also with शोक. चिरोद्वेगारम्भी v.l. (चिरादुद्वेगं mental worry आरभते असौ) is not very appropriate. संवेग—Violent speed or motion. प्रचल—निहित v. l. is also not appropriate, and mars the beauty of the simile. The sorrow was there gaining strength like the point of an arrow once driven into the heart. The point is now shaken off and causes intense pain. रूढग्रन्थिः—*Cf. supra* I. 30. This shows that the wound was not properly healed. The fig. here is Málopamá. घनीभूतः—अघनः घनः संपन्नः. At the sight of Pañchavaṭi and by all the past memories being revived by it, Ráma's sorrow reached its climax as it were and overpowered him. मूर्छयति च—नूतन इव v. l. The former is more in keeping with Bhavabhûti's manner of putting things. Again घनीभूत implies intensity and after that नूतन has no propriety.

अनवस्थितः—not situated as it was, changed. संनिवेशः—the situation, the position, of scenes or the landscape.

विपर्यास—from अस् with वि and परि to reverse, to overturn. घन°—घनभावः विरलभावः च विपर्यासं यातः density has given place to thinness and thinness to density. बुद्धिं द्रढयति—assures; *lit.* confirms or fixes my idea or belief ; a denominative from दृढ

Kshemendra in his औचित्यविचारचर्चा cites this śl. as an instance of देशौचित्य.

यथा—पुनः v. l. in which case the first sentence stops at नीताः, and पुनः स्वे गृहे goes with what follows, and is perhaps a better reading.

P. 62. विलोकयतु—*cf.* I. 48. असंभाव्य—without showing my regard for it, *i. e.* honouring it with a visit.

अवतरणमङ्गल—The religious ceremony performed at the time of receiving a distinguished person, a bridegroom &c. which consists in waving auspicious lights around him by way of respect, or for warding off evil, &c.

वत्सला—वत्से कामोऽस्या अस्तीति; fr. वत्स+ल a *matub* aff.; see Pāṇ. V. 2. 98. This implies motherly affection for Ráma on her part. लोपामुद्रा—wife of Agastya and (अयोनिसंभवा) daughter of a king of Vidarbha. See A. Dic. सर्वे च आगस्त्यायनाः—v.l. the descendants of Aga.; अगस्त्यगोत्रापत्यानि; fr. अगस्त्य and aff. आयन added अपत्यार्थे. See Páṇ. IV. 1. 99. In the Rámâ. also Ráma goes to see Aga. after he kills Śambūka, and obtains from him a resplendent ornament (दिव्याभरण); see Uttar. K. 76. Rag. XV. 55. उपरोध-Properly means obstruction or restraint; hence, what causes obstruction or imposes restraint; regard for.

P. 63. कूजत् &c.—कुआ एव कुटीराः कुअकुटीराः; कुटीर means 'a small hut (ह्रस्वा कुटी)', from कुटी+aff र. कौशिकानां घटाः कौशिकघटाः; कुअकुटीरेषु कौशि॰ कुअ...घटाः; कूजन्त्यः च ताः कुअ...कौशिकघटाश्च तासां घूत्काराः; तद्वन्तः ये कीचकाः तेषां स्तम्बाः clumps तेषामाडम्बराः तेन &c. See com. The reading गुञ्जत्, which refers to a gentle sound, does not suit the context at all, even if we take गुञ्जन्तः as separately qualifying कीचकाः. The Com takes गुञ्जत्कुअकुटीराः separately as going with कीचकाः; but then गुञ्जत् by what means? and how can the *guñjana* be heard when the owls were hooting? Again, कौशिक॰ hangs loose in this case; where were the owls? So कूजत् is the best reading; it also gives better alliteration with कुअ. कीचक—bamboos which produce musical sounds as the wind passes through them; वेणवः कीचकास्ते स्युर्ये स्वनन्त्यनिलोद्धताः। Amar. स्तम्ब—clumps or stems. आडम्बर—a great display, a vast mass. मौकुलि—a crow. The Com. Gh. takes स्तम्बाडम्बर as स्तम्बेषु अडम्बराः गर्वरहिताः (अत एव मूकाः &c.); but this is not a happy rendering. The crows were silent through fear. प्रचलाकिन्—A peacock; fr. प्रचलाक a peacock's tail; सोऽस्यास्तीति. उद्वेल्लन्ति—wriggle up and do not leave the trees. This shows how fond they are of the trees. रोहिण—a kind of sanda with strong odour. पुराण—is taken because the sandal tree when old has greater fragrance. रौहिण—v. l. is explained as रोहिण एव रौहिणः by adding अ (अण्) स्वार्थे, like प्रज्ञ एव प्राज्ञः. कुम्भीनसाः—कुम्भीव नासिका येषां; by Pâṇ. V. 4. 118, नासिका at the end of a Bah. becomes नस when not preceded by स्थूल and the whole is a name. Mark the alliterations. This is an instance of शब्दचित्र काव्य.

कुहरेषु—is connected with गद्गद &c.; see note on पयसि p. 64. मौलि—the top of a peak; see com.

मेघा°—मेघैः आलम्बिताः मौलयः येषां तानि मेघालम्बितमौलीनि (अत एव) नीलानि शिखराणि येषाम्. मौलि—the top of a peak; see com. संकुल—mixed. चलत्—rushing forth. उत्ताल—उद्गतः तालात् उत्तालः boisterous, formidable, majestic. *Cf.* Wilson's translation:—

" Far to the south extends
The lofty range of hills, whose towering peaks
Are diademed with clouds; whose central caverns
Roar loud with mighty waters, as from the earth
The springs of the *Godávarî* burst forth;
And at whose base the sacred conflux blends,
In one broad stream, the loud, encountering torrents."

ACT III.

The third Act opens with a dialogue between the (presiding deities of) the two rivers, Tamasá and Muralá, which is necessary to prepare the audience for the meeting of Sîtâ (who is unseen) and Râma, which forms the subject of the Act. The scene is laid in Pañchavaṭî.

P. 64. अनिर्भिन्नगभीरत्वात्—*V. l.* अनिर्भिन्नं च तद्गभीरत्वं च तस्मात् on account of his gravity not being pierced or overpowered. In this case the idea of 'and therefore not finding a passage out' has to be inferred; or it may mean अनिर्भिन्नश्चासौ गभीरश्च अनि° तस्य भावस्तस्मात् on account of it (Râma's grief) being unmanifested and deep. In this case गभीर goes with करुणरस and निर्भिन्नत्व remains unexplained. The reading in the text, therefore, is preferable. पुटपाक—refers to the particular process of heating drugs either by placing them in a closed earthen pot (sometimes two parts hermetically joined together) or wrapping them up in leaves and covering the whole with a thick layer of clay &c. प्रतीकाश—properly means a reflection &c., at the end of a comp. it means 'like, resembling;' स्युरुत्तरपदे त्वमी। निभसंकाशनीकाशप्रतीकाशोपमादयः। Ak. II. 10. 37. The comparison is an apt one; the meaning is that Râma's grief, which he could not communicate to any one else, caused him the severest pangs within and thus resembled medicinal herbs or ingredients heated in a closed pot, which undergo intense heat inside, but it is not felt from outside.

तथाविधेष्टजन—a person so passionately loved; *i. e.* Sîtâ; or तथाविध may go with कष्टविनिपात, a calamity of that kind befalling &c. प्रकर्ष—excess, intensity. दीर्घशोकसंतानेन—long (extending over a period of twelve years) and continuous sorrow. This is a bad reading; it is faulty in many ways; it is not संतान that is ०पातजन्म; it does not agree well with प्रकर्षगत; again, संतान does not cause emaciation, but संताप does. प्रमादस्थानानि—प्रमाद properly means carelessness (प्रमादोऽनवधानता Ak.); hence, the result of such carelessness, a calamity; here, danger to life.

सबन्धनं—together with its ties, *i. e.* to its very base. The Com. reads कुसुमसम० the tie of which is as delicate as that (the stem) of a flower. This is not a good reading as it has no propriety here. Perhaps it was suggested to some one by Vik. I. 6.

P. 65. वीचीवातैः—Some explain this as वीचीजनकैः वातैः. It is better to take the comp. as वीचिसंपृक्तैः. It is rather their contact with the waves than their वीचिजनकत्व that is referred to here; *cf.* Ragh. I. 43, XIII. 35. शीकर &c.—This epithet is redundant as the शीतकत्व is already suggested by वीचीवातैः itself. आकर्षद्भिः—drawing along; see com. सर्पेव इति—इति marks the end of the message from Lopâmudrâ sent to Godâvarî which began with जानास्येव यथा on the last page.

दाक्षिण्यं—Scrupulous anxiety. दक्षिण properly means one who has generous thoughts towards another, one attentive to the welfare of another. मौलिकः—मूलादागतः Pâṇ. IV. 3. 74. संवेगात्—owing to the vehemence of. अभ्युपपन्ना—approached with the desire to assist; attended. अभ्युपपत्तिरनुग्रहः Ak.; हितसंपादनाहितनिवारणप्रवृत्तिः Com.; अनयाभ्युपपत्यास्या जीवितमवलम्बस्व Śâk. III. स्तन्यत्यागात्—स्तने भवं स्तन्यं the mother's milk; तस्य त्यागः giving up its sucking &c. परेण—A grammatical inaccuracy; परेण being an adv. ending in एन requires the Acc. by the Sûtra एनपा द्वितीया Pâṇ. II. 3. 31. प्राचेतसस्य—Gen. for the Dat.

ईदृशानां—refers to Sítá only. विपाक—an unwelcome turn (of fortune); calamity. उपकरणीभाव—The state of being helping hands or serving as helping instruments; this is a च्वि-formation. एवंविध:—*scil.* Gaṅgá, Prithvi and Válmíki. आयाति—the wonder lies in the fact that even these served Sítá in her reverse of fortune.

सरयूमुखात्—As Sarayû flowed past Ayodhyá the poet makes its presiding deity tell Bhágírathí about the possible departure of Râma to Pañchavaṭî to punish Śambûka. व्यपदेश—*Lit.* giving out another than the true motive; a pretext.

P. 66. राजधानी०—The Com. reads राजनीतिस्थितस्य but it is not a good reading; it means—abiding by, attending to, state-policy. Here his stay in Ayodhyâ is contrasted with that in Pañchavaṭî. आभ्युदयिकै:—अभ्युदय + इक (ठक्); see com. नियत—Limited, checked, restrained; as most of his time was taken up by affairs of state. For a similar idea *cf.* कार्यान्तरितोत्कण्ठं दिनं मया नीतमनतिकृच्छ्रेण। Vik. III. 4 अन्यम—व्यग्रं विविधं विविधे वा अग्रमस्य. *Lit.* one differently (*i.e.* busily) occupied. शोक०—शोक एव शोकमात्रं; शोकमात्रं सहाय: यस्य। As there was nothing to occupy Râma's mind he was entirely at the mercy of his grief अत्र—*i. e.* with regard to his आश्वासन.

संवत्सरग्रन्थि(?)—This seems to be a ceremony performed on the birth-day of a person and consisting mainly in tying an auspicious knot to a string fastened on the wrist, on every birth-day, the number of knots being thus a register of the years passed by the person. Vîra. gives what he says is the traditional explanation. See com. According to some the string was tied round the neck. It seems that a string was tied round the wrist of a child and on the knot were placed such things as गुग्गुल, निम्ब, सिद्धार्थ (mustard seeds), दूर्वा and गोरोचना as a protection against the evil eye as appears from a quotation from the कृत्यचिन्तामणि given in the Nirṇayasindhu—गुडदुग्धतिलान्दद्याद्धस्ते मन्थौ च बन्धयेत्। गुग्गुलं निम्बसिद्धार्थदूर्वागोरोचनादिकम्॥ एतावत:—expresses the great length of the chain. Râma was 37th in descent from Vaivasvata. मानवस्द(?)—Sprung from Manu. This Manu, also called सत्यव्रत from his great purity, was the son of Vivasvat (the sun) and is considered the founder and the first king of Ayodhyâ. See Ragh. I. 11 and our note *ad loc* अरंहतपाप्मानं—The sun is spoken of specially as the dispeller of sin and the healer of diseases; see com.; the com. refers to the passages from the Chhánd.

Up. I. 6. 6 quoted in the Śaṃkarabhāshya on Ved. Sū. I. 1. 20. The passage is this-अथ य एषोऽन्तरादित्ये हिरण्मयः पुरुषो दृश्यते... आप्रणखात्सर्व एव सुवर्णः ॥६॥ तस्य यथा कप्यासं पुण्डरीकमेवमक्षिणी तस्योदिति नाम स एष सर्वेभ्यः पाप्मभ्य: उदितः उदेति ह वै सर्वेभ्यः पाप्मभ्यो य एवं वेद ॥७॥ प्रकृष्टप्रेमा—प्रकृष्टं प्रेम यस्याः सा. प्रत्यनन्तरीभव—*Lit.* be at her elbow; in close attendance upon; a च्वि-formation. अप्रत्यनन्तरा प्रत्यनन्तरा संपद्यते प्रत्यनन्तरीभवति.

P. 67. परिपाण्डु—extremely pale. दुर्बलं—emaciated. परिपाण्डू दुर्बलौ च कपोलौ ताभ्यां सुन्दरम्. विलोल—dishevelled. Sitâ had neither combed her hair nor braided it nor tied it into a knot. The figure of speech in this stanza is उत्प्रेक्षा. The reading विरहव्यथेव is not good, as in that case the fig. will be Rúpaka which cannot be properly explained.

इयं हि सा—This is she, indeed. The sentence ends here. Some connect these words with the first line of the next śl. 'Here is she like a pretty sprout cut off from its stem.' But this is not a good way. The poet's object is not to describe her loveliness here. सा also has no force. किसलयमिव is in apposition with शरीर in the 3rd line. Gh. distinctly says किसलयमिव स्थितम्। शरीरविशेषणमेतत्. The fault of दूरान्वय may be ignored. The परिपाण्डु शरीर is aptly compared to किसलय cut off from the stem which also withers up and gets palish.

हृदयकुसुम—हृदयं एव कुसुमं हृदयकुसुमं तत् शोषयति इति °शोषी. This shows that the शोक having withered up the flower of the heart attacks the body. घर्म—heat. The autumnal heat is more scorching than the summer heat. गर्भपत्रं—Which is extremely tender and pale and is readily parched up. शुद्धवि°—शुद्ध because both speak in Sanskrit and are not low characters.

P. 68. स्वकर कलित—shows Sitá's motherly affection for the cub. लोलः—dancing before her in joy to receive the mouthfuls. कलभक—क is added to excite pity. संनिपत्य—having suddenly rushed upon or attacked.

आर्यपुत्र—In her excitement Sitá utters the words which were foremost on her lips by habit, forgetting that she was then separated from her husband. She herself accounts for her mistake in the next speech. सवैक्लव्यम्—with overpowering grief. विमानराज—*i. e.* Pushpaka. समाश्वस्य—Mark how Sitâ revives on hearing the voice of Râma. साध्वसं च उल्लासश्च ताभ्यां सहितं यथा तथा। साध्वस—agitation, fear (because she was afraid to meet Râma). उल्लास—joy, because she heard the voice of Râma whom she still loved. ससाध्वसोत्कम्पो° *v. l.*

with joy and tremor caused by fear. जलभर०- जलस्य भर: जलभरस्तेन भरित: मेघ: स्तनितं तद्वत् मन्थर: मांसलश्च. मांसल— मांसमस्त्यस्य fleshy, stout; hence, anything great or large of its kind; here 'loud'. उच्छ्वासयति—revives; उत्सुकयाति *v. l.* makes me uneasy or anxious.

P. 69. निक्वाण—a musical sound. कुतस्त्येऽपि—त्य is added to some adverbs of place, e.g. क्वत्य, तत्रत्य, अत्रत्य etc. किमन्यत्केऽपि निनदे *v. l.* seems to be an emendation made by some one to get in the word किम् in the śl. which is not there. But the following speech of Sîtá shows that the word अपरिस्फुट was used in the śloka. चकितो०—चकितमुत्कण्ठितं च यथा तथा. स्तनयित्नु a cloud; fr. स्तन् to thunder, स्तनयतीति and the Uṇá. aff. इत्नु.

स्वरसंयोग—संयोग is used in the sense of संवाद. तपस्यत:— Gen. of the pres. p. of तपस्य a Den. verb from तपस् which is Paras.; see Gr. § 646. ऐक्ष्वाको राजा—As she bitterly resented the abandonment of Sîtâ by Râma, she does not wish to take his name, as in her opinion he is a king who would do stern justice but not be kind even to his wife. Sîtâ understands what she means and defends her husband by ejaculating दिष्ट्या &c.—She rejoices at Râma's scrupulous observance of his kingly duties. See our note on अत एव &c. *supra* p. 15.

गोदावरी०—गो० परिसरे यस्य. निजसौम्य०—The effect of the separation could not rob Râma of his natural gentle and noble demeanour. निजेन सौम्येन गम्भीरेण च अनुभाव एवानुभावमात्रं तेन प्रत्यभिज्ञेय: .

P. 70. उद्दामं—उद्गतं दाम restrain यस्मिन्कर्मणि तद्यथा तथा fiercely, violently. उत्पीड इव—उत्पीड an enveloping mass of; a very happy simile. *Cf.* furthur पूरोत्पीडे तडागस्य śl. 29. दुःखामे:— is a Rûpaka.

गुरुजनेन—*i. e.* by Lopâmudrâ and Bhágîrathî. कथमेतत्— Sîtâ is surprised to hear Ráma addressing her as प्रिये जानकि. She did not expect this after Râma's abandonment of her and after such length of time. आमीलन्नै०—आमीलत् नेत्रमेव नीलोत्पलं यस्य. निरुद्ध: suppressed य: नि:श्वासस्तेन नि:सहं सोढुमशक्यं droopingly यथा स्यात्तथा; see trans. The Com. takes निरुद्धनि:श्वासं as an adv. modifying नि:सहं, 'so helplessly as to have his respiration withheld, as not to be able to breathe.' This is also a good way.

कल्याणि—The epithet is purposely used. She has the power to exercise a benign and vivifying influence. एष— refers to Ráma. निरतो जन:—नित: नितरां रत: extremely fond of निषतो मर:—*v. l.* To which is [illegible], *i. e.* upon which entirely rests, this weighty task (responsibility) of restoring Râma to consciousness; this is also a good reading. Another reading is तत्रैव नियतो भव: which R. explains as तत्र तस्मिन् तव पाणिस्पर्शे एव भवः संजीवनं (being called back to consciousness) रामस्येति शेषः नियतः fixed. The only other noticeable reading is तत्रैव नियता भव be you confined to that alone; use that remedy alone, *viz.* touching him by the hand.

P. 71. साह्लादो०—आह्लादनेन सहितः साह्लादः उच्छ्वासो यस्य. जीवित त्रैलोक्यस्य—Sîtá in her excessive love for Ráma identifies his life with that of the three worlds. The welfare of the world, indeed, depended on the life of Ráma. She again gives expression to this thought when she observes सकलजीवलोकमङ्गलाधारस्य (p. 87) and या चार्यपुत्रं विनोदयन्ती आशानिबन्धनं जाता जीवलोकस्य p. 95.

आश्चोतनं—a trickling (of the juice) over all limbs (आ). हरिचन्दन—may be the heavenly tree of that name or a kind of very fragrant saudal; छेदे रक्तं कषे पीतं हरिचन्दनमुच्यते। तर्पणः—तर्पयतीति; here अन is added कर्तरि. करकन्दल—The tender sprouts of the lunar rays. आतस०—न्तरो: *v. l.* The comparison of life to a tree is not happy; तोषण has no propriety with तरु; पोषक would have been better; even the reading adopted in the text is not very satisfactory.

स्पर्शः पुरा &c.—supply अयं. परिमोहनः—stupefying; this is explained in the fourth line. परितोषणश्च *v.l.* is not good, as it goes against the next two lines. The stupefying effect of Sîtâ's touch is also referred to before; see *supra* तव स्पर्शे स्पर्शे मम हि परिमूढेन्द्रियगणो &c. I. 35. परिहृत्य-प्रतिहृत्य *v. l.* is better. आनन्दनेन-By the pleasurable sensation caused. Here the aff. ल्युट् (अन) is added भावे while in संजीवन and परिमोहन it is added कर्तरि (in the sense of the agent). As Râma experienced the touch of Sîtâ's hand after so many years, the joy caused by it had a benumbing effect on him. The fig. in the last two lines is विरोधाभास.

न खलु—indicates जिज्ञासा or inquiry. 'Can it not be that,' 'I hope I am.'

P. 72. राजाऽधिकं कोपि०—Sîtâ purposely uses the word राजा. She thinks that on seeing her there, Râma, remembering his stern duty as a king, might reprove her for coming into his presence without permission as she was taken to the forest at his express order.

अस्य वृत्तान्तस्य—Sîtâ refers to her unmerited banishment. वज्रमयी—see हिरण्मयी p. 53. वत्सल—moved with affection for. निरनुक्रोशा—Pitiless, unsympathetic. अनुक्रोशति &c. —see com.; it rather means 'to cry after,' *i. e.* out of sympathy for, another; hence to show pity &c. अहमेतस्य &c.—*Cf.* अस्या देव्या मनस्तस्मिंस्तस्य चास्यां प्रतिष्ठितम् । तेनेयं स च धर्मात्मा मुहूर्तमपि जीवति ॥ Râmâ. Sun. K. XV. 12.

P. 73. हृदयानुबन्ध—the state of the feelings of my heart.

तटस्थ—indifferent, not expecting a favourable issue. कलुषं—disturbed by anger, ruffled. विप्रिय°—in consequence of the disagreeable deed (her abandonment). घटनोत्तम्भितं—*V. l.* घटनेनोत्तम्भितं may be interpreted to mean (1) petrified or paralysed by the sudden meeting; or (2) supported, cheered up. करुणैः—stands for करुणप्रलापैः.

प्रसाद इव &c.—The fig. is Rûpaka.

P. 74. अगाध°—अगाधं यथा तथा दर्शिताः स्नेहस्य संभाराः यैः. अगाधमानसस्नेह°—*V. l.* is not good. मानस has no propriety; again, the comp. becomes awkward; it has to be solved as अगाधः मानसस्य दर्शितः स्नेहसंभारः यैः. आनन्द°—आनन्दं निष्यन्दन्ते इति. प्रत्यय–Here means 'knowledge' (gained by hearing); प्रत्ययोऽधीनशपथज्ञानविश्वासहेतुषु A. K. Or it may mean 'confidence' as the com. takes it. निष्कारण°—परित्याग एव शल्यं निष्कारण० तदस्य संजातमसौ ।

संकल्पाभ्यास—Constant revolving in the mind of the thought about Sîtâ. पाटव—cleverness in repeating the fancies. Here it simply intensifies the meaning of अभ्यास. उपादान—generative (material or immediate) cause. °दान—Generated by his too constant a brooding over the image of Sîtâ. *Cf.* युष्मत्प्रसादोपादानः *v. l. supra* p. 56. अभियोक्ष्यते—may be Pass. or Active : in the former case it will mean 'should be appointed' *i. e.* asked to rescue him; in the latter 'who would assail the the attacking elephant.' The former sense seems to be the one intended.

रघुनन्दनः—is perhaps sarcastic; he is रघुन° (one who would care for his race) and not जनकजानन्दन. सीतातीर्थ—a flight of steps or place of landing named after Sîtâ.

P. 75. °च्छिदः—मर्माविधः *v. l.* मर्माणि विध्यन्ति pierce इति. The अ of मर्मन् is lengthened by the rule नहि-वृति-वृषि-व्यधि-रुचि-सहि-तनुषु । Pâṇ. VI. 3. 116; *i. e.* the vowel of the first member of compounds having for their second member nouns derived by the aff. क्विप् (०) from the roots नह् &c. is lengthened; *e. g.* उपानत् . नीवृत् , प्रावृट् . मर्मावित् , नीरुक् &c. *Cf.* हृदयमर्माविधः खल्वमी कथोद्घाताः Mv. V.

कथोद्घाताः—Allusions to the past stories. **उद्घात**—Introduction; *cf.* आकुमारकथोद्घातं (mentioning forth of) Ragh. IV. 20.

प्रकृष्टं—higher; the idea of excess is expressed by the Abl. देवताभ्यः; प्रकृष्टतमं *v. l.* is bad; it should be प्रकृष्टतरं. **उद्गच्छत**—उद्गच्छन् बिसस्य किसलय इव स्निग्धः (glossy and charming) दन्ताङ्कुरः the budding tusk यस्य. **कर्णमूलात्**-Sîtâ used to wear as an ear-ornament a *lavalî* sprout, which hanging down from her ear used to be snatched away by the young elephant. कर्णपूरात्—*v. l.* is not a good reading. In this case we shall have to suppose that the पल्लव was worn over the ear—ornament, which is not—probable; perhaps she did not wear a *Karṇapûra* in her exile. **वत्कल्याणं** &c.—स मदमुचां वारणानां विजेता अयं तव पुत्रः यत् कल्याणं प्रकृष्ट-शौर्यवीर्यादि तस्य &c.; see com. He has become the abode (possessor) of all that is considered a blessing, *viz.* youthful beauty, vigour, a mate &c. The Com. Lakshmaṇa Sûri attaches a technical meaning to Kalyáṇa (which seems far-fetched). He says–अनेनास्य चतुर्थावस्थाप्राप्तिर्दर्शिता । तदेव तस्य स्त्रीकामसंभवात् । तथा च पालकाप्यं—'वारणीयप्रदेशेषु तरुणीष्वेव कामवान् । पक्षयोश्चापि कटयोः कर्णयोश्चापि दानवान् । चतुर्थ्यामपि कल्याणः ॥' इति । कल्याणमस्यास्तीति कल्याणस्तन्नामकः इत्यर्थः ।

कान्ता—कान्ताया अनुवृत्तौ चातुर्यं the skill or art of attending or acting up to the desires of the mate, gallantry. *Cf.* Mál.-Mádh. p. 192. This is explained in the next śloka.

लीलो॰—This Śl. occurs in the Mál.-Mádh. IX., being st. 34, with the reading न instead of यद् in the fourth line. **छेद**—end; at the end of, during the intervals. **गण्डूष॰**—गण्डूषपदेन स्वयं पीत्वा जलदानं ध्वनितम् Jagaddhara on Mál.-Mádh. **संपादिताः**—संपातिताः *v.l.* made to fall, is not good, as the idea of पातन is contained in संक्रान्ति. **पुष्यत्**—growing, developing; hence, blooming. पुष्यत् may also be taken with पुष्कर meaning the tip of the trunk (though not preferably); see com. The reading पुष्यत् is better, as it gives the meaning directly.

P. 76. **कामं**—To her satisfaction. **यत्**—यतः since; goes with every line; यतः एवं कृतं तस्मात्कान्तानुवृत्ति॰ &c. **अनराल**—not crooked, straight; अनरालं नालं यस्य तदनरालनालं अन॰ च तन्नलिनी-पत्रं च तदेव आतपत्रं तत्.

एतावता—एतत्परिमाणमस्य एतावान्. **तादृशमपि**—even though of that sort, *i. e* so charming. तादृशं *v. l* is perhaps better.

ईषद्विरल &c.—ईषद्विरलाश्च ते धवलाः कोमलाश्च ये दशनाः teeth तैरुज्ज्वलौ कपोलौ यस्य. **अनुबद्ध** always present मुग्धे engaging, charming काकलीविहसिते यस्मिन्. काकली babbling or lisping; it properly means a gentle sound; ईषत्कल: काकली; काकली तु कले सूक्ष्मे Amara. निबद्ध०—निबद्धः काकशिखण्डकः यस्मिन्. अङ्कु—*scil.* चुम्बितम्. उच्छ्वसित—throbbing. प्रस्नुतस्तनी—Such is described to be the effect of true maternal love. संसारिणी—*i. e.* one who lives in a house and has her husband and children about her.

P. 77. प्रकर्षपर्यन्त—The last limit of the excess of affection. For the meaning of प्रकर्ष *cf.* प्रकर्षमाधारवशं गुणानां Kir. III. 18. संश्लेषण--A connecting or fastening together of.

अन्तःकरणतत्त्व--अन्तःकरणमिति तत्त्वं. स्नेहसंश्रय—The common receptacle of affection. आनन्द०—Because the affection of both is centred in the child. अपत्य—is derived in two ways. (1) न पतन्ति पितरोऽनेन; for when the family becomes extinct the ancestors are supposed to fall (2) अपततं भवति पितुः सकाशादेत्य पृथक्ततं भवति; that which detaches itself, springs from the stock; a child. In this Śl. also by tying together (joining) अ from अन्तःकरण०, पत् from दम्पत्योः and यम् from अयम् we get the word अपत्यम्.

This stanza is highly sentimental and one of the masterpieces of the poet. It makes a tender appeal to the feelings. Bhavabhûti is always happy in describing young children and parental relation.

अनुदिवसं &c.—The reading in the foot-note, which is the reading of most of the editions, does not appear to be appropriate; while the reading herein adopted clearly shows the connexion of Sîtâ with the peacock. अनुदिवसं—दिवसे दिवसे इति Avya. मणिमुकुट इव—On account of its having a long and thin neck and a plumage variegated with different colours the peacock is compared to a crown. अतरुण &c. *v. l.*—here अतरुण has no appropriate sense unless it is explained as नास्ति तरुणो यस्मात्स तथा, गुरुरित्यर्थः. अचिर०—अचिराद् अचिरं वा निर्गतं come out मुग्धं लोलं च मुग्धलोलं बर्हं plumage यस्य। It means—This peacock with its freshly grown tail, charming and waving, (is shrieking) at the close of the festivity of dance due to excessive joy. कदम्बे—The peacock is often described as dancing on the Kadamba trees. नदति and वधूसखः imply youth in him. वधूसखः—वध्वाः सखा वधूसखः and not वधूः सखा यस्य; the poet intends here merely to convey the idea of साहचर्य; *cf.* महिषीसखः Ragh. I. 48.

भ्रमिषु—The circuitous or whirling movements of the peacock. कृतपुटान्त &c.—The Com. takes the whole as one word taking probobly त्वां as the object of मण्डयन्त्या. In this case the meaning is— (by Sîta) who adorned you with the play of her moving and beautiful eye-brows and her eyes which whirled round in &c.' It seems better, however, to divide the line as °वृत्ति चक्षुः &c. in which case चक्षुः becomes the object of मण्डयन्त्या, and the construction becomes easier and the meaning more charming. कृता पुटान्तः मण्डलावृत्तिः येन. चटुल—moving gracefully, hence beautiful; चतुर is perhaps better. ताण्डवे—rapid, sportive movements. करकिसलयतालैः—करौ किसलये इव तयोः तालैः by the clappings of her tender, sprout-like hands. ताल—keping musical time by striking together the palms.

P. 78. तिर्यञ्चोऽपि—Here Ráma indirectly blames himself since he, though endowed with reason, did not do the same, as he abandoned Sîtá not regarding at all his love for her.

स्मरति &c.—may be construed as (1) एष देव्याः गिरिमयूरः कदम्बं स्मरति यतः स्वजने (देवीसंबन्धात्) इव &c.; or, and this is better, एष गिरिमयूरः देव्याः स्मरति (remembers with pain); अधीगर्थदयेशामिति कर्मणि षष्ठी। यतः स्वजने &c., The tree and the peacock were both tended by Sîtá and so there was a relation (fraternity) between the two. स्वजनः may also be nom.; तस्याः स्वजन इव &c. The fig. of speech here is काव्यलिङ्ग in which either a sentence or a word is intended to give a reason for the statement made in the whole sentence.

कान्तासखस्य—see वधूसखः above. बहुशो यदेभ्यः—वनगोचरेभ्यः *v. l.* has no propriety; it means fawns living in the forest. ततो हारिणकैः—Another illustration of तिर्यञ्चोऽपि परिचयमनुरुध्यन्ते.

एतत्तदेव—नीरन्ध्रबालकदली *v. l.* in the midst of thickly growing young plantain trees. This reading is not good as the construction becomes rather involved. अत्र again cannot be properly construed. न विमुच्यते—supply सा as the subject. जातनिर्विशेषाः—जातेभ्यः सुतेभ्यः निर्गतः विशेषः येषां ते. *Cf.* सुतनिर्विशेषं Ragh. V. 6. जात°, however, implies that they were tended with greater care and tenderness than the word सुत° does.

P. 79. जीवलोकस्य परिवर्तः—The world has thus changed for me. जीवलोक has its usual meaning here; the परिवर्त spoken of is with reference to herself. She meansa--ll these once gave pleasure to me; but their sight causes pain to me now. परिणामः संवृत्तः—is not a good reading. परिणाम cannot be well construed with

संवृत्तः। परिवर्तः संवृत्तः will do. नवकुवलय &c.—Construe यः नः सततं स्वेच्छादृश्योऽपि ०स्निग्धैः अङ्गैः नयनोत्सवं ददत् नवो नव एव आसीत्.........स इति कथमपि उन्नेतव्यः तथापि दृशोः प्रियः। कुवलयं—कोः of the earth वलयमिव शोभाकरत्वात्। ०यवत् स्निग्धैः. The comparison has occurred before; see p. 18. नः स्वेच्छादृश्यः who could be seen by us at our will, *i.e.* at any time we liked. ते for नः is not a happy reading. It is natural that Vásantî should speak with reference to persons like herself rather than with reference to Sîtá. There is no charm at all in saying that Râma was also स्वेच्छादृश्य to Sîtâ alone. The clause ददन्नयनोत्सवं also goes against this reading. Why should Ráma have given to Sîtá नयनोत्सव only and not परिष्वङ्गाद्युत्सव? We can better understand ददन्नयनोत्सवं with reference to persons like Vásantî to whom Ráma's sight was easily obtainable. नवो नव एव—Râma's sight never cloyed them. No familiarity could impair its loveliness. *Cf.* क्षणे क्षणे यन्नवतामुपैति तदेव रूपं रमणीयतायाः। The reading नवं नवं which qualifies नयनोत्सवं gives by itself a good sense, but it is exposed to the charge of दूरान्वय. Again, the reading in the text more prominently expresses the contrast between सततं स्वेच्छादृश्यः and नवः नव एव. विकल—enervated, drooping. शुचा—goes with विकलकरणम्. कथमपि उन्नेतव्यः—With difficulty only it can be made out that &c.

जन्मान्तरात्—For Sîtâ had quite despaired of being reunited with Ráma in her present existence, as twelve years had already passed away. अनुलब्धदर्शना *v. l.*—अनुलब्धं दर्शनं यया who obtained a sight of him; here अनु has no propriety. Cons.—बाष्पमवसृजन्ती ०दीर्घा......ते दृष्टिः दुग्धकुल्या इव हृदयेशं स्नपयति· विलुलित—tossed or shaken about. आनन्दशोक०—आनन्द because she obtained a sight of Ráma, the cherished object of her heart; शोक because of the thought of her abandonment and the desolation in which she had lived and was to live after Ráma's separation again. तृष्णया—through your longing to see your lord. पक्ष्मल—*v. l.* having thick (beautiful) eyelashes. उत्तान—wide-stretched, dilated. *Cf. infra,* Śl. 46, ll. 1 and 2.

P. 80. धवलबहल—' white for the most part (धवलो बहलो यस्याः)'; Sîtá had large eyes so that the white portion was more prominently seen than the pupil. दुग्धकुल्या इव—The continuous gaze of Sîtá fixed on Ráma and shedding the fluid of affection is compared on account of the prominence of the white part of the eye to a stream of milk bathing Râma, as it were.

रचन्तु &c.—Here Vâsantî speaks of the kingly reception of Ráma due from the several sylvan agents. The idea was probably suggested by Kálidása's Ragh. II. 8-13. स्फुटित०—स्फुटितानि च तानि कमलानि तेषाम् आमोदः स्फुटितकमलामोदः तस्य प्रायः बाहुल्यं येषु ते. अविरलं—without a break, continuously or ceaselessly. रज्यत्कण्ठाः—रज्यन्तः कण्ठा येषां with their throats full of melody. रत्युत्कण्ठाः *v. l.* रत्या रामविषयकप्रेम्णा उत्कण्ठाः raising their necks through their deep affection for Ráma. स्वयं—Ràma has come of his own accord to do honour to the forest and hence the greater necessity to accord him such a greeting. For the idea of making trees do acts of hospitality *cf.* Nág I. 11.

अश्रुतिमभिनीय—The stage-direction is for the actor. Ráma of course did not hear Vásantî's question, being absorbed in other thoughts.

करकमल०—करकमलाभ्यां वितीर्णैः. तरुकुसुम &c.—The fig. in the first two lines is यथासंख्य. द्रव इव—The विकार on account of its affecting his whole body is looked upon as the liquid of his heart (*i. e.* to have liquefied his heart) and running through all his limbs. For a similar comparison see śl. 36, below. If द्रव is taken with प्रस्तरोद्भेदयोग्यः then the comp. must be taken as प्रस्तरस्योद्भेदस्तेन योग्या तुलना अस्यास्तीति comparable with the breaking of a stone. Here Râma compares his heart to a stone in hardness. And since the विकार melts even such a heart, its power must be very great. The commentators Vîra. and Lak. construe विकार with हृदयस्य ; Vîra. reads प्रस्रवोद्भेद 'capable of appearing as the oozing of the heart'; see com.

P. 81. ननु—may be here for emphasis or may have the sense of "calling in a conciliatory manner." निष्प्रणयं—निर्गतः प्रणयः यस्मात् void of affection. A cold mode of address. सौमित्रिमात्रे च—and not with reference to Sìtà. Vâsantî, as an intimate friend of Ráma and Sîtâ, should naturally have used some familiar term of address and asked about Sîtâ's welfare first of all. But since she did not do either, Râma concludes that she was secretly indignant at something and that nothing short of her knowledge of Sitâ's banishment could have made her so indignant. बाष्पस्ख०—बाष्पेण स्खलितानि अक्षराणि यस्मिन्. This and the following ślokas are good instances of the *Vaidharbhî* style which is marked by absence of long compounds, and of pathos. Bhava. generally uses a simple style, free from involved compounds, when he has to make an impression or to stir inward feelings. ०सीतावृत्तान्ता—विदितः सीताया वृत्तान्तो यस्याः. Ráma does not say सीतात्याग &c. The very idea of त्याग is too painful for him to bear. आम्—yes. प्रियार्हः—प्रियमर्हतीति.

अनुरुध्य—having pleased or flattered. मुग्धां—the innocent or simple one (because she easily believed in what you said). सामेव—दोहदपूरणव्याजेनारण्ये त्यक्तवानसीति वाक्यशेषः। शान्तं—To Vásantî also the thought of Sîtá's banishment is over-whelming, and instead of completing the sentence by adding 'and her you abandoned', she breaks off in the middle and exclaims शान्तम् &c. It is a masterly device of Bhavabhûti to put this rebuke in the mouth of Vásantî and not of Sîtá. Śl. quoted in the D.-R. as an instance of वाकेली (III. 17). The last two lines contain the fig. of speech called आक्षेप (the apparent denial or suppression of something intended to be said, for conveying some special sense).

P. 82. स्थाने—Because of her excessive affection for Sîtá. कस्य हेतोः—When the word हेतु is used to indicate reason or cause, the gen. is used. *Cf.* परिचितमपि ते विस्मृतं कस्य हेतोः' Mud. I. 1. स एव &c.—must be read with a काकु (a particular mode of pronouncing) so as to imply a taunt. Ráma does not mention the slander directly. The very thought was horrible to him. चिरात्—When it is too late. For the evil cannot be remedied now, Sîtá being abandoned 12 years ago.

कठोर यशः &c.—This is a sneer flung by Vásantî at Ráma. किल—I hear that you long for fame. But, O lover of fame, what infamy could be greater than this? She means to say—In trying to save your reputation you exposed yourself to a greater infamy by abandoning your loving wife. कथय नाथ &c.—Vásantî is purposely seeking to awaken sympathy in Ráma for Sîtá by thus appealing to his feeling of pity. बत—expresses either sorrow or pity (अनुकम्पा).

स्वमेव दारुणा &c.—Since Ráma was already grieved it was certainly cruel on the part of Vásantî to have teased him any more. प्रणय एवं &c.—Tamasá means to say that Vâsantî was then entirely in the power of her emotion; she was acting under the impulses of her deep affection for Sîtâ and her sorrow.

त्रस्तैकहायन &c.—एकं हायनं year यस्य स एकहायनः such a deer is naturally more timid; त्रस्त एकहायनः यः कुरङ्गस्तस्य इव विलोला दृष्टिः

यस्याः सा। अनेन हृष्टेरतितरलता सूचिता. So in Mál.-Mádh. वस्तैकहायनकुरङ्गविलोलदृष्टेरास्लिष्टवत्यमृतसंवलितैरिवाङ्गैः। IV. 8. परिस्फुरित &c.—expresses her utter helplessness. मृदुबाल—मृदु with बालमृणाल is redundant; *v. l.* मृदुमुग्ध avoids the redundancy, but does not seem to be original मृदु may be taken with अङ्ग०; मृदुश्च बाल० कल्पा च. विलुप्ता—Râma's tenderness of heart does not allow him to say भक्षिता. This brings out Râma's extreme love for Sítá; *cf.* अतिस्नेहः पापशङ्की.

ध्रिये—I live, I am not destroyed (Pres. Active of ध्रृ 6 Â.).

P. 83. सांप्रतिक—संप्रति तस्येदं proper for the present time, hence proper, fit; from संप्रति and aff ठक् (इक).

परीवाहः—जलं परिवहत्यनेन an outlet or passage for water; उपसर्गस्य घञि इति वा दीर्घः; so परिवाह also. प्रतिक्रिया—the remedy to prevent it from bursting its banks.

विशेषतो राम०—is connected with सांप्रतिकम्. Some omit the word यस्य and read विशेषतो राम० बहुतर०; but then the sentence hangs loosely, without connexion with the preceding. बहुतर०—प्रकारैः कष्टः Tat.; or Bah.; see com. जीवलोक—The mortal world as existing for him; his life in this world. The कष्टत्व is explained in the next Śloka.

पाल्यं—For, क्षत्रियाणामयं धर्मो यत्प्रजापरिपालनम्. अभियुक्तेन मनसा—with a mind wholly devoted to it. The meaning is that it was not possible for Râma to neglect his duty as a king even for a moment. *Cf.* Śâk. V. 6. विलपन०—विलपनमेव विनोदः or विलपनेन विनोदः. असुलभः—Not that Râma could not have found relief by weeping, but that he could not have done so with any propriety. उच्छ्वासः—breathing that gives him relief. ननु &c.—It is indeed a gain that Râma should thus unburden himself to-day, for that will keep up his life in future.

दलति—breaks; for the intran. use *cf. supra* अपि दलति वज्रस्य हृदयं I. 28. गाढोद्वेगं—गाढः उद्वेगः यस्य. The reading गाढोद्वेगः subverts the symmetry of construction of the four lines and must be rejected. For then हृदयं becomes the Acc. (गाढो० हृदयं दलति) and we shall have to supply हृदयं again as Nom. to भिद्यते. द्विधा &c.—that would have put an end to my tortures. There is विरोधाभास here (यद्दलति तन्न भिद्यते) as also in the following lines. The Virodha is removed by taking दलति in a metaphorical sense. विकलः—shattered, drooping. स्थिरे मोहे दुःखाज्ञानात्कृतार्थः स्यामिति भावः। तदिहाध्यात्मिकविपद्द्वयमुक्तम्। Jag. 'अन्तरेण हि दलने यादृशी व्यथा स्यात्तादृशी व्यथा हृदि वर्तते।......यदि

मोहः कथमेवं जानासीत्यत्रोत्तरं चेतनां......तु न मुञ्चत्येवेत्याशयः ।' Tripurâri on Mâl.-Mâdh. भस्मसात्—does not entirely reduce it to ashes. साति: कार्त्स्न्ये । तथात्वे दुःखाज्ञानमेव स्यादित्याशयः । अनेनाधिभौतिकी विपदुक्ता । तदिह व्याधिदशायां मोहादय उक्ताः । इह कायावच्छिन्न आत्मा कायपदेनोक्तः । अन्यथा मोहस्यात्मधर्मतया कायेऽसंभव इत्यवधेयम् । Jag. on Mâl-Mâdh. This stanza is the same as Mâl.-Mâdh. IX. 12.

P. 84.—तृणमिव stands in contrast with the high regard he had for the people's satisfaction. ते ते भावाः—The various scenes and incidents. परिद्रव०—The Com. reads तथा द्रव०; the reading परिभ्रमयन्ति does not suit the context. इदं—refers to the क्रिया expressed by रुद्यते. 'Here I weep.' अशरणै:—I am quite helpless. प्रसीदत—take a generous view of the matter and do not blame me. अद्याप्येवं *V. l.*—construe अद्यापि with प्रसीदत. Take compassion upon me even now.

आपूर्ण—filling up (swelling) from all sides—well expresses the magnitude of his sorrow. मन्युसंभारस्य—The collection of, *i. e.* accumulated grief. The reading शोकसागरस्य is better as better agreeing with आपूरणं. अवगूर्णं(शोकसागरस्य) *v. l.*—The word is not of common occurrence. It means 'an eddy' (आवर्तः), or 'rising or swelling up of.' अतिक्रान्ते—in a matter that is past. धैर्यमव०—For lamentation would not mend matters. न च—here च has a disjunctive force. And yet it is not that &c. द्वौ नञौ प्रकृतार्थं द्रढयतः । The two negatives strengthen the affirmation by precluding a possible negation; *cf.* संभाव्यनिषेधनिवर्तने द्वौ प्रतिषेधौ । Vâm. Kâv. Sût. V. I. 9. नैताः &c.—सविषाः—The sorrow corresponds to the विष. The fig. here is *Apahnuti*, which is defined by Mammaṭa as प्रकृतं यन्निषिध्यान्यत्साध्यते सा त्वपह्नुतिः । A figure in which the real character of the thing in question is denied and that of another similar to it is superimposed upon it or ascribed to it. तिरश्चीन—तिर्यगेव तिरश्चीनं ; स्वार्थे खः (ईन); obliquely. अलातशल्य-A heated or fiery dart. अलात—a fire-brand. प्रत्युप्त—thrust in; p. p. p. of वप् with प्रति. कृन्तत्—corroding, cutting away.

P. 85. अतिनिष्कम्प०—अतिनिष्कम्पं यथा तथा (so as not to shake) स्तम्भितमन्तःकरणं येन तस्य. It is not a good way to take the comp. as ०निष्कम्पं च तत्स्तम्भितं च ; for if it was अति० there was no necessity for steadying it. संस्तुत—परिचित (familiar).

लोलो०—लोलश्चासो उल्लोलश्च or लोलादुल्लोलः तथा क्षुभितः exceedingly or furiously rising up, agitated ; or लोला उल्लोला महोर्मयो यत्र

ताहृक् क्षुभितं यस्य; now see com. उज्जृम्भणं—its swelling up; outburst. वेलोल्लोल *v. l.* वेलाया उल्लोल: वेलोल्लोलश्चासौ क्षुभित: agitated and gone beyond bounds; this is also a good reading. ०करणो० *v. l.* is not a good reading. It means लोलानि क्षुभितानि करणानि or लोलं क्षुभितं करणं अन्तःकरणं तथा तस्य वा उज्जृम्भणं the agitation of the senses; but this is against the context. Râma here speaks of his effort to check the outburst of sorrow and not his senses. Gh. and Lak. read हेलोल्लोल—easily agitated. This is not a good reading. करुण--the permanent sentiment (स्थायिभाव) of grief. This is compared to a body of water, while चेतोविकार is compared to rushing waters and the यत्न to a dam तोयस्येव—the fig. is Upamâ. सैकतं—made of sand; from सिकता and aff. अ (अण्) added in this sense by सिकताशर्कराभ्यां च । Pán. V. 2. 104; so शार्करः. कोऽपि—indescribable.

दुर्वार०—see com.; दुर्वारश्चासौ दारुणश्च is more natural. आरम्भ—operations of. दुःखसंक्षोभ—stirring up, agitation of grief. परिमुषित०—on seeing Ráma's pitiable condition caused by overwhelming grief Sîtâ forgot her own sorrow and was alarmed, not knowing (प्रमुग्ध) what the consequence would be. प्रमुग्ध—entirely bewildered. कष्टमभ्यापन्नः—has got into a painful state.

P. 86. संदीपनः--संदीपयतीति; अन added कर्तरि. The reading in the foot-note means—My dear friend considers the very excitants of grief as remedies for relieving his sorrow.

अस्मिन्नेव &c.—The description here is very touching. तन्मार्ग०-तस्याः मार्गः तन्मार्गः the way by which she was to return. चिरमभूत्—loitered, tarried long. सैकत—सिकताः सन्त्यत्र सैकतं a sandy bank, a bank. दुर्मनायितं—दुर्मना इव आचरति दुर्मनायते तथाभूतं offended, displeased, vexed; fr. दुर्मनस् + क्यच् (य) before which स् is dropped and the preceding vowel is lengthened. *Cf.* दुर्मनायमाना p. 15. इव—Râma was not really angry; but Sîtâ in her womanish timidity fancied that he was angry. कातर्यात्—ईषत्तरति स्वकार्यसिद्धिं गच्छतीति कातरः तस्य भावः कातर्यं timidity of heart, tenderness of feeling. प्रणामाञ्जलिः–a folding of hands in salutation, *i. e.* supplication to propitiate you; see com. This śl. is quoted in D.--R. as an instance of प्रणयमान. हृदय०—हृदयमर्मणि गूढं यत् शल्यं तस्य संघट्टनैः चालनैः by repeatedly shaking the dart fixed deep into the vital part of the heart. The dart of sorrow was shaken by pointed references to past events and scenes.

P. 87. हा हा देवि &c.—Mark how Râma's sorrow grows in intensity. This s'l. is one of the poet's masterpieces. *Cf.*

supra 31. Therein Ráma said that his heart refused to break, but now it is about to break; and so with the rest. ध्वंसते &c.—The frame of the body *i. e.* the joints are shattered (as it were). अविरलज्वालं *v. l.*—with dense flames. See com. सीदन्—Agonizing, writhing with pain. अत एव विधुरः helpless. विष्वङ्—may be adj. or adv.; in the first case it means 'affecting all senses'; in the latter 'from all sides', 'completely.' स्थगयति—paralyses all my senses. This stanza is nearly the same as Mâl.-Mâdh. IX. 20 (with the reading मातर्मातर्दलति हृ॰). इति मूर्च्छति—Râma felt a kind of stupor gently coming over him and he faints finally.

सकलजीवलोक &c.—Râma could truly be called मङ्गलाधार of the whole world. ॰लोकमङ्गल्यजन्मलाभस्य *v. l.*—whose birth (life) is auspicious (a blessing) to the world. संशयित॰—See com.; terrible because it endangers or threatens your life. दशापरिणाम—the change of condition.

संभावय—Revive him or bring him back to life.

P. 88. प्रलेप—balmy or soothing unguents or ointments. शरीरधातून्-The principal constituents of the body. These are त्वक्, अस्थि, असृज्, मांस, मेदस्, मज्जा and शुक्र. He, of course, means the whole body internally and externally. आनन्दात्—through joy. अपरविधं—अपरा विधा यस्य—different from the one I was experiencing. The fig. in the first line is Utpreksha. Or आनन्दात् may be taken with अपर॰--not differing from, identical with, joy.

कथमिव—इव has here the sense of 'possibly,' 'I should like to know.' मर्मच्छेद॰—मर्मच्छेदेन दारुणैः.

चिरसद्भाव—सद्भाव good feeling, attachment, चिर॰ love of long standing, *i. e.* deep. The Com. reads चिरप्रणयसंभार accumulated love of long standing. The reading चिरप्रणयस्वभाव does not give a good sense.

P. 89. हरता—उल्लाघयता *v. l.*—Lessening. लाघय्—is a Denom. fr. लघु. वज्रलेप—a kind of cement which gets as hard as adamant when dried and fixes together things indelibly. For its preparation see Brih. S. LVII. स्विद्यत्—perspiring (on account of the touch of her husband). Here स्वेद, one of the eight Sâttvika *Bhâvas*, is mentioned. The *Sâttvikabhâvas* or the external manifestations of the feelings due to सत्त्व are eight in number; स्तम्भः स्वेदोऽथ रोमाञ्चः स्वरभङ्गोऽथ वेपथुः । वैवर्ण्यमश्रु प्रलय इत्यष्टौ सात्त्विका स्मृताः ॥ निःसहविपर्यस्त—निःसहं

unbearably यथा तथा विपर्यस्त: lying helplessly on, completely paralysed. This indicates जडता. वेपनशील:—indicates वेपथु or tremor.

कङ्कण—The मङ्गलसूत्र or the auspicious string tied round the wrist at the time of marriage. स्वेच्छास्पर्शै: &c.—The Instr. may be उपलक्षणार्था (स्पर्शैरुपलक्षितो यो मम परिचित:) or करणे. The Com. reads सुधासूतै: पादै: &c.—This requires a twisting of sense to suit the context. सुधासूति: means the moon (see com.; or सुधाया: सूति: the source of); which was familiar with (a friend of) *i. e.* similar to the rays of the moon; as cool as nectar. But the idea of शिशिरत्व is expressed in the next line; so the reading in the text is preferable. स एवैतानी°—She means—'you give the same pleasure to me now, by holding my hand, as you did when you seized it at the time of marriage and afterwards when we were together.' निकरौपम्य°—°पम्येन सुभग: lovely, pleasure-giving; being similar to. For this sense of सुभग *cf.* सुभगसलिलावगाहा: Śák. I. p. 7. तुहिनकरको°—where करका means 'hail;' but there is no propriety of करका after तुहिन. The reading तद्दितरकरौपम्य of the commentators hardly gives any good sense, notwithstanding Vîra.'s remark सत्यकरसादृश्यं &c.; see com. ललित—tender. कन्दल—sprout. °निभ: expresses its softness.

प्रमादो मे &c.—in that she allowed her hand to be grasped by Ráma.

P. 90. निर्मीलित—*lit.* closed; *i. e.* deprived of their power of perception, benumbed.

साध्वस—agitation due to emotion. सखे तावत् त्वमपि *v. l.*—you too support her (along with me), is not a good reading; Ráma was not at all able to support her. उन्माद:—Madness, insanity. Vâsantî was not able to see Sîtá and so what Ráma said she believed to be the raving of madness. प्रमाद:—carelessness; because he allowed the hand to be drawn off.

करपल्लव:—कर: पल्लव इव. जड:—benumbed with sensation, cold. For the constr. see com.

In this stanza the Sâttvikabhávas जडता, प्रकम्प (वेपथु) and स्वेद are again mentioned. These are the external manifestations of रति, the Sthâyibhâva of शृङ्गार, which they help to strengthen here. This शृङ्गार too is accessory to and is meant to enhance the करुण which is the prevailing sentiment of this Act.

अनवस्थित—unsteady; or, not restored to their natural state. Now unsteady, now fixed; now unable to perceive, now rolling &c. अनुबद्धबहुघूर्णमानवेदनं &c. *V. l.* (see foot-note) 'I do not compose myself, whose torments are continuous, many and revolving, even now.' This reading, which is adopted by Vîra. seems to be better. In the previous śl. there is no mention of Ráma's eyes as rolling. He was also conscious, though agitated. Sîtá wanted simply to bring him back to consciousness. She blames herself in her previous speech for not withdrawing her hand after this was done. And now she finds fault with herself for not steadying her mind. In the next speech of Tamasâ there is a reference to this helpless condition of Sîtâ while in Sîtâ's speech which follows she actually says that she is ashamed of her helpless state. Gh. reads अनवस्थितस्तिमितघूर्णमानं (who am unsteady, dull and rolling) अविरलवेदनं (and whose agony is continuous) &c. which is also equally good.

रोमाञ्चित—रोमाञ्चा अस्य संजातास्तद्. This is another of the Sâttvikabhávas. सस्वेद०—स्वेदेन सहितं सस्वेदं ; सस्वेदं च रोमाञ्चितं च कम्पितं च अङ्गं यस्याः सा. These are the usual effects manifested by a woman at the touch of her lover. The form would be ०ताङ्गा also (and preferably).

मरुन्नवाम्भः०—मरुच्च नवाम्भश्च मरुन्नवाम्भसी ताभ्यां यथाक्रमं प्रविधुता चासौ सिक्ता च। The comp. is faulty since there is nothing to indicate the order of the construction. This is an instance of what is called in English 'Hyperbalon' or the transposition of words. This is a *Púrṇopamá*. The rain-drops correspond to the particles of perspiration, the agitation caused by the wind to प्रकम्प, and the buds (कोरक) to the *româñcha*.. Poets represent the Kadamba tree as putting forth buds when sprinkled over by the new rain-drops, or there is a rumbling of clouds; *Cf. infra* VI. 17, and घनराजिनूतनपयःसमुक्षणक्षणबद्धकन्दलकदम्बडम्बरः। Mâl. Mâdh. III. 7; Kum. III. 68.

आत्मना—हेतुना on account of. लज्जापिता—P. p. p. of the denom. from लज्जा. एष परित्यागः &c.—Such is the unmerited repudiation (under which I am smarting) and yet such is the intensity of my affection for him.

P. 91. विपरीतं &c.—Sitá means that it was he who had abandoned her; not that she had forsaken him.

लोकोत्तरेण—लोकेषु उत्तरं the best or most conspicuous लोकोत्तरं तेन. अतिभूमि०—०मिं (the highest pitch, excess) गतः विप्रलम्भः

delusion यस्य. **कुतो रामस्य निद्रा**—For the pain of separation always keeps him awake; see com.

अनेक॰—अनेकवारं परिकल्पनाभिर्निर्मितः constantly created or called up by my fancy. **भगवान्**—applied to विप्र॰ ironically.

P. 92. **कार्ष्णायस:**—made of iron (अयस् here-metal in general); see com.; कृष्णं च तदयः कृष्णायसं. अ is added to the final. **पिशाच**—पिशितमाचामति, अश्नाति वा; in both the cases the comp. is पृषोदरादि; a fiend, a goblin. **कङ्काल**—a skeleton, bones. **खरा:**—The mules yoked to Râvaṇa's car. **खड्ग॰**—see com.; this may also be taken (and perhaps preferably) as an adj. qualifying अरिः (खड्गेन छिन्ना जटायोः पक्षतिः येन). पक्षस्य मूलं पक्षतिः (पक्ष + ति indicating the root, by Páṇ. V. 2. 25). **जटायु:**—जटा पक्षमूलमेवायुर्यस्य (also जटायुस्); or जटया यातीति जटायुः। मृगय्वादित्वात् कुप्रत्ययः। **चलन्तीं**—struggling; and hence like व्याकुलवि॰. ज्वलन्तीं *V. l.*—burning with rage or her splendour. But this is not necessary. Sítá herself was bright-looking like lightning. चलन्तीं is necessary to complete the comparison. **अन्तश्चर्याकुल॰**—व्याकुला flashing; see com. for the propriety of the comparison. **अभि**—may also be taken as an adv. (to उदस्थात्). अविद्यमाना भीः यस्मिन् कर्मणि तद्यथा तथा fearlessly. But this does not seem natural. *Cf.* काञ्चनोरश्छदान् दिव्यान्पिशाचवदनान्खरान्। तांश्चास्य जवसंपन्नाञ्जघान समरे बली॥.........तस्य व्यायच्छमानस्य रामस्यार्थे स रावणः। पक्षौ पादौ च पार्श्वौ च खड्गमुद्धृत्य सोऽच्छिनत्॥ Ar. K 51; Sítá is thus described—सा तु तां राम रामेति रुदतीं लक्ष्मणेति च। जगामादाय चाकाशं रावणो राक्षसेश्वरः॥ तप्ताभरणवर्णाङ्गी पीतकौशेयवासिनी। रराज राजपुत्री तु विद्युत्सौदामनी यथा॥ &c.; see. Ar. K. 52, 13, 14 &c.

आर्यपुत्र &c.—Sítá here forgets that these were past events. So this is an instance of विस्मृति, one of the 33 Vyabhichári-bhávas. Ráma in his agitation forgets that it was a past event and rises up in hurry, as if it were happening then.

तात—*i. e.* Jaṭâyu. **राक्षसकुल॰**—*cf.* पौलस्त्यकुल॰ p. 5. प्रलयधूमकेतु a Madhyamapadalopî comp.; see com. **मन्युविषय:**—For Rávaṇa and his followers were all killed. **अन्य एवायं**—Of a different sort. **विपर्यय**—calamity; an evil course of destiny. The reading अन्वर्थः &c. has no propriety. Besides, it cannot be a proper reply to what Vásantî says in her last speech. That speech makes no allusion to प्रलाप. Ráma simply understands the word मन्यु in the sense of grief and explains why he should grieve now (अतः अस्ति मन्युविषयः).

विनोद—The dispelling of grief, recreation. The reading ॰कर: should have been preferred. *Cf.* I. 30, ll. 1, 2.

विमर्द—collisions, fightings. अद्भुतरसः—The Com explains how the Vîra Rasa gives rise to the Adbhuta Rasa. रिपुघातावधिः—which terminated with the destruction of the enemy. Ráma means that the former separation differed from the present one in two main points:—(1) in the former there was hope that it would come to an end one day, while in the present one there is none such (as Sîtâ is dead, as he believed her to be); (2) the former had remedies, resorting to which it could have been brought to an end, while the present one is irremediable. Construe the last line as अयं तु निरवधिरप्रतिविधः च अतः कथं तूष्णीं सह्यः। This reading is preferable to those in the foot-note as it better expresses the contrast between the first वियोग which was प्रतिविधेय and रिपुघातावधि and the second which is अप्रतिविध and निरवधि. This speech of Ráma serves to develop the विप्रलम्भशृङ्गार.

P. 93. निरवधिरिति—Ráma said निरवधि under the impression that Sîtá was no more. She, however, is alarmed to hear this actually from Râma's lips. For it dispels even the last shred of hope that she might have fondly cherished in her heart, of being sometime re-united with her husband, as she thinks that he is determined to stick permanently to his original resolve.

जाम्बवत्—A monkey chief (supposed to be a chief of bears). He was of signal service to Ráma during the Lankâ-war. He was famous for his medical skill. It was he who asked Hanûmat to go to the mounain Himâlaya to bring the potent herbs for curing the wounds of and to restore to consciousness the whole army when struck down and rendered senseless by the missile of Indrajit; see Yud. K. Ch. 74. नल—was the son of Viśvakarman and noted for his proficiency in engineering. *Cf.* अयं सौम्य नलो नाम तनयो विश्वकर्मणः। पित्रा दत्तवरः श्रीमान्प्रीतिमान् विश्वकर्मणः। एष सेतुं महोत्साहः करोतु मयि, वानरः। तमहं धारयिष्यामि यथा ह्येष पिता तथा॥ Rámâ. Yud. 22, 41, 42. अविषये—which is not the province of, *i. e.* which is beyond the reach of; see Mv. VI. 20. अविषयः *v. l.* is not so good; in this case we have to supply यः अवि० तत्र; it also violates symmetry, as we have यत्र in the first three lines. बहुमानितास्मि—*Lit.* I am made to think highly of; for she then lived every day on the hope of being rescued from the clutches of the enemy and being restored to her lord. ०विरहे—*v. l.* is not good; it means—"I was much honoured or esteemed in my former separation", which goes against the spirit of the above Śl.

P. 94. वर्षवर्धनमङ्गल—वर्षस्य वर्धनं तस्य मङ्गलानि the auspicious rites performed on every birth-day for the prolongation of life; see also com. अस्ति चेदानीं—This is a continuation of Ráma's speech on the last page. It ends with तत्रापि तावद् बाष्पदिग्धं चक्षुर्विनोदयामि. The student should bear in mind that Sîtâ and Tamasá are not present on the stage so far as Râma is concerned. सोत्कम्पम्—Sîtá of course heard these words with a shock. They came upon her like a thunder-bolt. सोच्छ्वासास्रम्—The following words of Ráma, however, not only banish all doubt from Sîtá's mind as to his having married again, but strengthen her belief that Ráma yet loved her with the same unabated warmth and constancy. She breathes a sigh of relief on hearing the words, which also bring tears of joy to her eyes. आर्यपुत्र &c.—All misunderstanding being removed Ráma is again to Sîtá what he once was to her, the same loving, tender-hearted husband.

P. 95. हिरण्मयी &c.—On this Wilson remarks: "Thus in the *Alcestis* of *Euripides*, *Admetus*. in order to console himself for the loss of his spouse, declares that,

> " By the hand of skilful artists framed,
> Her image shall be placed upon my couch."

The spirit with which Ra'ma has the image of Sita' formed is much more worthy of a hero and a King. In all his conduct, indeed, he is vastly superior to *Admetus*, and in the delineation of a situation in some respects similar, the Hindu poet is equally superior to the Grecian. "

उत्खातमिदानीं—For the declaration was made in the hearing of her friends, Tamasá and Vásantî.

तत्रापि—'Even there' (referring to Sita''s image). जीवलोकस्य—For the welfare of the world depended on the long life of Ráma which in its turn depended on the comfort Ráma could derive by looking at the image. This ejaculation of Sîtâ in her exultation serves as a basis for Tamasá to crack a joke. व्यतिकर:—meeting, visit.

P. 96. प्रतिकूला—For she assented to Râma's departure.

प्रत्युप्त—rivetted or fixed upon. मर्मच्छेद॰—implies the great tension of effort. आकर्षो न &c.—*Lit*. ' the withdrawing of which is not completed, *i. e.* effected, (even) with efforts cutting the vital parts. The reading of the com., मर्मच्छेदोपमेयत्नैः संनिकर्षो नि॰, does not give a clear sense ; it means—' its contact is checked (*i.e.* it is separated—withdrawn—from him) with efforts resembling the cutting of the vitals, *i. e.* which can be done with efforts as painful as the cutting &c.

कियच्चिरं &c.—Here Sitá compares Ráma to the full moon that cannot long be seen when the overcasting clouds hide it for the whole night from view. Sità means that it was only under fortunate circumstances that she obtained a short-lived sight of her beloved Ráma, and that she was therefore bound to be content with that much.

P. 97. संविधानकं—has a double meaning here: (1) it is apparently used in the sense of the the proper arrangement of diverse incidents (causes and effects) leading to one issue. Thus Tamasá refers to the various actions of and the sentiments put forth by Ráma and Sítá–now giving rise to Karuṇa, now Sriṅgára, and now to Adbhuta, but all merging again into the one permanent sentiment of Karuṇa ; (2) secondly, it means the judicious arrangement of the various incidents in a play or the *dénouement* of the plot. The śl. that follows serves as a key-note to the whole play. In fact the poet, telling us here that Karuna is the underlying sentiment throughout this drama, really refers to his own uncommon poetic skill which enables him to make the Sriṅgára, Adbhuta and other Rasas, with their proper *Bhávas* (Sáttvika, Vyabhichárí, &c.) and *Vibhávas* subservient to the development of the Karuna Rasa. And there is no doubt that the poet has described here in a masterly style शोक, the Stháyibháva of Karuna. For Rasa and other technical terms, see Introd.

एको रस:—Here Karuna (*i. e.* इष्टजनवियोगजन्यशोक:—the Stháyibháva of Karuṇa) is compared to the ocean. निमित्तभेदात्—According to the diversity of the causes and attendant circumstances. These are:—Ráma and Sitá, the *Alambanas* (the supports as it were on which the Rasa is grounded), their respective virtues &c. are the excitants (उद्दीपकविभावs), their tremblings, swoonings &c. are the *A'nubhavas* and joy, forgetfulness, anxiety &c. are the accessories or Vyabhichá-ribhávas. भिन्न—diversified. विवर्तान्—changes or different manifestations of form. See com. ; also *supra*, our note on विवर्त p. 54. आवर्त—eddies. बुद्बुद—bubbles. तरङ्ग—waves. विकारान्—The word विकार seems to be used here in the sense of 'different phases or manifestations of the same thing unaltered and to which they are finally reduced.' *Cf. infra* VI. 6. The illustration of water and its bubbles &c. often occurs in the

Bhâshya of Śmankarâchârya on the Ved.—Sût. ; *cf.* तथा हि समुद्रादुदकात्मनोऽनन्यत्वेऽपि तद्विकाराणां फेनवीचितरङ्गबुद्बुदादीनामितरेतरविभाग इतरेतरसंश्लेषादिलक्षणश्च व्यवहार उपलभ्यते । सलिलमेव &c.—As all these are finally reduced to water, so the various feelings and sentiments that appear and disappear on the ocean of Karuna give rise to the Karunarasa which they serve to embellish.

P. 98. तमसावासन्त्यौ—It should be remembered that तमसा and सीता were invisible to Vásantî and Râma. So the same śl. is put in the mouths of Tamasâ and Vâsantí. अमरसिन्धु:—The Gangel.. कुलपति:—was one who fed and trained up a large number of disciples (कुल). *Cf.* मुनीनां दशसाहस्रं योऽन्नदानादिपोषणात् । अध्यापयति विप्रर्षिः स वै कुलपतिः स्मृतः ॥ आद्यः &c.—Válmiki. अनुयाता॰ See com. वितरतु—Tamasá and Vâsantî being divinities were authorized to give such a blessing. See commentary. *Cf.* भद्रं भद्रं वितर भगवन्भूयसे मङ्गलाय । Mál.-Mád. I. 3. It will be seen from the VIIth. Act that all the personages mentioned here contribute to the fulfilment of the wish expressed herein.

ACT IV.

The fourth Act opens with an Interlude which is intended to relieve the tension of feeling caused by the highly-wrought pathos of the preceding Act. It announces to the audience the arrival and meeting, at the hermitage of Válmîki, of Vasishtha, Arundhatî and Kausalyá as settled at the close of the 2nd Act, and of Janaka who, together with Lava, one of the two sons of Ráma entrusted to Válmîki's care, form the principal characters of the Act.

P. 99. भूयिष्ठ॰—For the comp. see com. संनिधापित:—caused to be assembled at. समधिकारम्भ—special or unusual preparations.

मण्ड *m. n.*—The scum (gruel) of boiled rice. प्रसूतप्रिया॰—read प्रसूतप्रिया as the former is ungrammatical. अभ्यधिकं—the surplus of what remains after. पर्याप्तं—to his heart's content. स्फुरत्-rising or spreading about. मनाक्—a little. भक्त—cooked rice. सर्पिष्मत्—seasoned with ghee. ॰शाकपचनामोद:—शाकस्य पचनं पाकस्तस्यामोद: the exceedingly grateful smell of.

P 100. स्वागतं &c. Here are introduced two pupils, one of whom, Saudhátaki, is more jocose of the two, and belongs to the class of pupils who are humorous and given to joking, while Dáṇḍáyana represents the type of boys who are more serious and take a sober view of things. Saudh. welcomes the arrival of the guests as he gets a holidy and, as is in keeping with his humorous disposition, says स्वागतं &c जीर्णकूर्चानां-' the grey-bearded old folks;' said of Vasishtha, Janaka and others in joke. आगतं &c. *V. l.*—construe अनध्यायकारणमागतं &c.; or आगतं may be a noun, आगतमागमनं अनध्यायकारणं सविशेषभूतम् their coming has been the special cause; or their arrival, the cause of our holiday, has a speciality about it. सविशेषं भूतं a comp. सुप्सुपा. बहुमानहेतुः—this is of course said ironically. धिक् प्रहसनं—Away with your jesting.

P. 101. परापतितेनैव—As soon as he came; no sooner did he arrive than. मडमडायिता—greedily devoured; a nominal verb formed from मडमड, a word formed by onomatopœia; see however, com.

मधुपर्कः—मधुना पृच्यत इति. It is a respectful offering, made to a guest or the bride-groom or a distinguished visitor, so called because its principal ingredient is honey;*cf* मधु सर्पिर्जलं क्षौद्रं सिता चेतेश्च पञ्चभिः । प्रोच्यते मधुपर्कः । आम्नाय—आमनति धर्माधर्मौ इति आ०; the Veda; also, any Vedic injunction. बहुमन्यमानाः—obeying, observing. श्रोत्रिय—a learned Bráhmaṇa: *cf.* जन्मना ब्राह्मणो ज्ञेयः संस्कारैर्द्विज उच्यते । विद्यया याति विप्रत्वं त्रिभिः श्रोत्रिय उच्यते ॥ वत्सतरी—a heifer (two years old); वत्सतर (a weaned calf) marks a stage between वत्स and महोक्ष (a grown-up bull). See our note on Ragh. III. 32. निर्वपन्ति—Kill with a view to offer the flesh of. गृहमेधिनः—Malli. on Ragh. I. 7 very properly explains this as गृहैर्दारैर्मेधन्ते संगच्छन्ते इति, marriage being essential for the discharge of the religious duties attendant on a householder's stage of life. Some derive it from गृहमेध, the daily sacrifice which a householder has to perform. धर्मसूत्रकाराः—Sûtra is an aphorism or a concise saying having much meaning compressed in it; it is defined as स्वल्पाक्षरमसंदिग्धं सारवद्विश्वतोमुखम् । अस्तोभमनवद्यं च सूत्रं सूत्रविदो विदुः ॥ The Sûtras are divided into श्रौत or कल्प सूत्रs which treat of the sacrificial ritual, *e. g.* the दर्श and पौर्णमासेष्टि,and स्मार्त or गृह्य सूत्रs regulating the domestic life, *i. e.* giving rules for the various castes and A'sramas, for the performance of the Saṃskâras,such as उपनयन and the like. समामनन्ति—Lay down as sanctioned by the Veda.

निगृहीतोसि—You are well caught (as making a statement that goes against you). निग्रहस्थान is a technical term in

Nyáya philosophy meaning 'the place of defeat,' and is the last of the sixteen categories mentioned by Gautama. He explains this in the next speech.

विशसिता—killed; p. p. p. of शस् with वि, 1 P., to kill. वत्सतरी पुनर्विसर्जिता—From this it appears that the calf or so was required to be present at the time of receiving a distinguished guest, the same being slaughtered afterwards.

P. 102. अनिवृत्त०-मांसादनिवृत्ताः अनिवृत्तमांसाः-a comp. of the राजदन्तादि class, in which the proper order of words is reversed. एष कल्पः—This mode of reception, *viz.* समांसः मधुपर्कः. तादृशं—*i. e.* so calamitous. वैखानसः—see *supra* p. 25. A Vânaprastha must give up eating flesh; *cf.* स्थलजौदकशाकानि पुष्पमूलफलानि च। मेध्यवृक्षोद्भवान्यद्यात्स्नेहांश्च फलसंभवान् ॥वर्जयेन्मधु मांसं च भौमानि कवकानि च। Manu. VI. 13-14. संबन्धिनीभिः—The wives of Dasaratha. संभावयावः—honour, enjoy. मानयावः *V. l.*—means the same thing.

P. 103. अनुषक्तः—Closely adhering or clinging to. जरत्—ज्वलन् *v. l.* 'burning,' is not a good reading; for the burning was from within and not exposed to the view. Again, an old tree well compares with जनक who is old and is more likely to have fire within. दुरित—a calamity. विषक्त—firmly clung or fixed into; hence, caused. पटु—sharp enough to affect even me, an ascetic. धारावाही—The poet often compares continuous sorrow to a stream; *cf.* संतानवाहीनि further on (śl. 8). ककच—क इति कचति (produces the harsh sound Kra) a saw.

दुरासद—difficult to be brought within reach; hence, difficult to be borne, irresistible; *cf.* Mv. I. पराक—a kind of expiatory penance. It consists in abstaining from food for twelve days, with the mind and the organs of sense properly restrained. *Cf.* यतात्मनोऽप्रमत्तस्य द्वादशाहमभोजनम्। पराको नाम कृच्छ्रोऽयं सर्वपापापनोदनः॥ Manu. XI. 215. सांतपन—Another kind of penance. It consists in living upon each of the पञ्चगव्य(गोमूत्र &c.) a day and upon कुशोदक (water purified by Kuśa grass being dipped into it) the sixth day. गोमूत्रं गोमयं क्षीरं दधि सर्पिः कुशोदकम्। एकैकं प्रत्यहं पीत्वा अहोरात्रमभोजनम्। कृच्छ्रः सांतपनो नाम सर्वपापप्रणाशनः॥ Yâj.; *cf.* also Manu. XI. 212. ०प्रभृतिभिः—Chándráyaṇa, Prájápatya and others are meant. रस—the vital fluids, blood, marrow, &c. अनवष्टम्भः—lacking the necessary elements for sustaining life. दग्धदेहः—दग्ध when so prefixed means 'cursed, wretched.' *Cf.* हतक which is used at the end of a word.

शोषितान्तःशरीरधातोरवष्टम्भ एव महान् अद्यापि &c. *V. l.*—Great is the support (sustaining power) of me, the vital ingredints of whose body are dried up, since &c. Some read धातुः अनुपयुज्य-मानः not used for worldly purposes, which has become useless. अन्धतामिस्राः—अन्धं तामिस्रं येषु—shrouded in perpetual darkness. *Cf.* the passage from the ईशावास्योपनिषद् quoted in the com. The reading असुर्याः (असुराणामिमे) seems to be preferable, since असूर्या is tautological after अन्ध०. प्रतिविधीयन्ते—are assigned to, provided or destined for. परिभावना—The Com. takes this to mean 'thinking or brooding over it': but it rather appears to mean 'feeling, its revolving in the mind or making itself constantly felt.' अयि मातः—Janaka first speaks of Sîtá with reverence, the uppermost thought in his mind being her divine origin. Or, मातः may have been used as a term of endearment, like तात. ०भाग—doom, destined portion.

अनियत &c.—What a beautiful picture of Sîta''s childhood the Śloka gives! Bhavabhûti is always happy in describing child-hood. अनियत—whimsical, not due to any definite cause-वदनकमलकं—is a Rûpaka. असमञ्जस—सम्यगओऽत्र; or संगतमञ्जसा तत्त्वमत्र। ह्रस्वो नपुंसके इति ह्रस्वत्वम्. This stanza occurs in Mâl.-Mâdh. X. 2. *Cf.* Śâk. आलक्ष्यदन्तमुकुलाननिमित्तहासैरव्यक्तवर्णरमणीय-वचःप्रवृत्तीन्। &c. VII. 17. For the fig. of speech see com.

अतिदृढासि—You are extremely firm (and, hard-hearted). The words imply a rebuke; see com. त्वं—supply वेत्सि; here the verb विदुः must be taken with each Nominative, as remarked by the Com., with the necessary change of number; otherwise we should expect the verb in the 2nd person, instead of in the third as विदुः is. See com. कुलगुरुः—may refer to Vasishṭha. But it naturally goes with भास्करः (the god Sun, the progenitor of the race). In this case we must suppose Vasishṭha as included under मुनयः in the first line. तद्वत्—तत् may refer to Vidyá (Sarasvatî) or the deities mentioned before *viz.*, Fire, Gaṅgá &c. Perhaps the poet wrote त्वद्वत्. The reading शुद्धिं गतायाः पुनः appears to be a good reading at first, as lending force to the argument. But Janaka's words further on कोऽयमग्निर्नामास्मत्प्रसूतिपरिशोधने &c. (see p. 108) preclude the possibility of its being a genuine or a proper reading. It seems from those words that Jan. would not have even tolerated the idea of अग्निशुद्धि, much less referred to it. तथा विप्रसनं—Janaka is labouring under the belief that Sitá is no more in existence. वृष्टि—see com.

यथा श्रीः—Janaka at first speaks of Kau. by using an Upamá. But since the comparison failed to express adequately his admiration of her, he, as if dissatisfied with it, corrects himself and identifies her with Śrí, thus using a Rúpaka. कष्टं बत—expresses his intense sorrow. किमपि भूतं—Some indistinguishable or indescribable being. विपाकः—may mean an adverse change or turn of fortune. *Cf. supra* III. 3 and 12 below.

P. 106. अनभ्यवसायः—Want of resolution. अभ्यवसाय means 'a determined or resolute effort'. Kau. staggered at every step and seemed to be unwilling to proceed. This called forth the remark. The reading महानध्यवसायः also means the same, though in a roundabout way. What means this great effort on your part to proceed with us—*i. e.* why are you thus hesitating at every step. सर्वाणि दुःखानि—all the griefs lodged .in my heart. उद्वर्तमान—Being torn or plucked up.

संतानवाहीन्यपि—वहन्तीति वाहीनि; now see com. Though flowing continuously or ceaselessly (and hence the original fund of sorrow being gradually exhausted they ought neither to be दुःसह nor स्रोतःसहस्रैः प्लवमान). There is implied विरोधाभास. It is removed by दृष्टे जने प्रेयसि which explains whence the new impetus comes. सद्बन्धु°—सन् बन्धुः सद्बन्धुः a good *i. e.* dearly loved relative. संबन्धि° *v. l.* is not good; as the grief caused by separation from any and every kinsman cannot be संतानवाहि. दृष्टे जने &c —*Cf.* स्वजनस्य हि दुःखमग्रतो विवृतद्वारमिवोपजायते Kum. IV. 26. संप्लवन्ते—flow forth, spring up.

एवं गते—When such has been the fate of, when such a sad calamity has overtaken her.

याज्ञवल्क्य—A great sage and philosopher of great antiquity, and also the teacher of a portion of the Yajurveda. He is constantly mentioned in the Bṛi. Up. as the preceptor and adviser of king Janaka. *Cf.* Bṛi. Up. IV. 2. 11 &c. He is also the author of a Smṛiti or code of laws, called after him and next in importance only to the code of Manu. ब्रह्मपारायणं—पारस्यायनं पारायणं going to the opposite end, complete study of the Veda (ब्रह्म) including the Upanishads. जगौ—sang *i e.* expounded.

P. 107. अनिर्वेदरमणीयात्—giving unmixed delight, wherein our happiness was complete, there being nothing to mar it. The reading संभावितास्मि &c. (see ft.-note) does not give a good 'sense.,' It means—I am honoured (with a visit by Jana.) on a day free from any occasion for great joy; *i. e.* on a day when there is cause for sorrow. But this does not suit the sentence that precedes, while the words that follow become meaningless after this.

सीरध्वजः—Janaka. The line of the Janakas had the mark of a plough (सीर) on their flag. "He is called 'Síradhvaja' because his daughter Sítá sprang up ready formed from the furrow when he was ploughing the ground and preparing for a sacrifice to obtain offspring". (Dowson.) पूतंमन्यः—आत्मानं पूतं मन्यते पूतंमन्यः; also पूतमानी (by adding इन्). The म् comes after पूत by the rule आत्ममाने खश्च। Pán. III. 2. 83. The aff. खश् is added to मन् in combination with a case-termination when the object of thought is self. See Sid K. on the Sûtra. म् is added to a word ending in a vowel before a word taking an affix having an indicatory ख (.as खश्). माङ्गल्या—मङ्गले साधुः (capable of strewing blessings on) मङ्गल्या by adding य (यत्) according to तत्र साधुः Páṇ. IV. 4. 98. This reading is better. माङ्गल्या may be derived from माङ्गल (मङ्गलमेव माङ्गलं by adding अण् स्वार्थे) and then adding यत् (माङ्गले साधुः). देवीमुषसं—Ushas, the *Aurora* of the Latins and the *Eros* of the Greeks, is the goddess of the morning, and one of the deities of the Ṛigveda. Some of the hymns addressed to her are among the most beautiful ones. The Sun is regarded as her lover and is spoken of as following her as a man does his love. सूर्यो देवीमुषसं रोचमानां मर्यो न योषामभ्येति पश्चात्। RV. I. 115. 2. इव—the Upamâ here is based on श्लेष. In the case of Ushas the महतः निधिः is the Sun; the epithets are common to both.

परं ज्योतिः—The Supreme Light of Brahman. *Cf.* एष संप्रसादः ......परं ज्योतिः &c. Ch. Up. VIII. 3. 4; also तद्देवा ज्योतिषां ज्योतिः—(उपासते) &c.; see also Mu. Up. II. 2. 9; अक्षरं ज्योतिः *v. l.*—न क्षरतीति अक्षरं that Imperishable Light (Supreme Brahman). *Cf.* अथ परा यया तदक्षरमधिगम्यते। Muṇḍ. I. 1, 5; एतस्य वा अक्षरस्य प्रशासने गार्गि सूर्याचन्द्रमसौ विधृतौ तिष्ठतः &c. Bṛi. Up. III. 8. 9. परोरजाः—रजसः परः beyond the quality of रजस् or sin; a comp. of the राजदन्तादि class; Vîr. accounts for the change of the अ of पर to ओ by taking it as a comp. of the पृषोदरादि class (*i. e.* irregular); or पर being a word of the पारस्करादि group may take स् after it. *Cf.* the Śruti—एष वाव स परोरजा इति होवाच। य एष तपति। परोरजसां—beyond all foulness or passions; see com. and the Śruti cited there.

अनामयं—This is in accordance with the precept of Manu—ब्राह्मणं कुशलं पृच्छेत्क्षत्रबन्धुमनामयम् । II. 127. प्रजापालकस्य—and not प्रियापालकस्य. Mark the sarcastic allusion to Râma's abandonment of his innocent wife. He is regardful of the interest or well-being of his *subjects*, and not of his dutiful *wife*. निरवशेष—Entirely, in every respect.

P. 108. अनल्पका:—Very mean. कोऽयमग्निर्नाम &c.—Janaka bitterly resents the very idea that Sîtâ, his own offspring, needed purification. What was fire before his daughter, purity incarnate, and the most perfect model of womanly virtues! पुनः परिभूयामहे—For to call in question the purity of an offspring of Janaka's race was the grossest insult that could ever have been offered him. परिलघुनि—insignificant in every way. *Cf.* I. 13 and IV. 5. where Sîtâ is called a goddess. Arundhatî's next speech fully brings out the force of Janaka's remark.

स्त्रैण—womanhood. ननु—is for emphasis. It does not matter, that is not the consideration. For पदं हि सर्वत्र गुणैर्निधीयते Ragh. III. 62. *Cf.* न धर्मवृद्धेषु वयः समीक्ष्यते; and स्त्रीपुमानित्यनास्थैषा वृत्तं हि महितं सताम् । Kum. V. 16, VI. 12. गुणाः &c.—She supports her speech by a general statement. The figure here is, therefore, Arthântarányasa. न च &c.—The two चs and नs show that the two, whether taken singly or together, signify little.

P. 109 उन्मीलन्ति—expand, increase.

अथ—And then, *i. e.* on being aware of her present miserable condition and the contrast between those happy old days. पुरंध्रीणां—पुरं गेहं धारयतीति पुरंध्रिः or ध्री, a comp. of the पृषोदरादि class. Properly, a woman whose husband and sons are living. Here used in the sense of virtuous ladies.

P. 110. दूषितं—any fault in domestic or love matters. उपालभ्य०—Each blamed me for not interfering in the matter This explains to what extent he enjoyed the confidence of both. विधिः—the adoption of the proper measure. अवस्कन्द्य—from स्कन्द् with अव 1. P. to attack, to overpower.

एकरसां—Of uniform or unmixed flavour. *Cf.* Kau.'s speech on p. 107 (स्मारितास्मि &c.). अकाण्ड—नास्ति काण्ड उचितावसरो यस्य तदकाण्डं तेन; काण्ड—a division of time; or अप्रशस्तः काण्डः अकाण्डः. अकाण्डे—at an improper time or opportunity. विवर्तनं—change of front, adverse turn. विदीपयति—augments, makes more acute or keen. *Cf.* Māl.-Mâdh. IV. 7.

एक—Sole, chief. प्रस्फुरत्—playing upon. शुद्ध—pure, guiltless or artless. आस्फुरत्—shining all round. जाते—dear child. जात—a child newly born and to be tenderly taken care of; hence used in the Voc. as a term of endearment. उद्द्योतय—Because her lovely complexion shed a moon-light-like splendour all round.

P. 111. महत्तर—अतिशयेन महान्. A principal or chief person; a most respectable man.

पञ्चप्रसूतेः—*i. e.* the four sons and Śàntá. सुबाहुः—A demon, brother of Màricha, slain by Ráma, at Viśvàmitra's sacrifice. *Cf.* Ragh. XI. 29. The reading तथैव नान्या...यथैव सीता is bad, as the construction becomes involved or strained; for we shall have to construe यथा सीता प्रिया तनूजा तथा वधूचतुष्के अन्या प्रिया तनूजा न.

P. 112. संबन्धे—*i. e.* आवयोः संबन्धे. संबन्धबीजं—Sità. ०बन्धनिश्चलं—दृढं यथा तथा वज्रलेपेन घटितः बन्धः यस्य तद् दृढबन्धं अत एव निश्चलं; ०प्रतिबद्धनि०—*v. l.* वज्रलेपेन प्रतिबद्धं अत एव निश्चलं; here प्रति has no propriety. उपजातमेव—it did come to pass.

उदर्क—end; may be derived from अर्क् , अर्च् , or ऋच् with उत् to praise &c., and the aff. घञ् (अ); उदर्क्य-र्च्य-ते ; उदृच्यते वा इति. कल्याण उदर्कः यस्य तत्कल्याणोदर्कम्. She bids her take courage by reminding her of Vasishtha's prophetic words which must come true. अतिक्रान्त०—Past hope; or impossible to be fulfilled (com.). Since all reasonable time had passed it was natural for Kau. to think that it would be hoping against hope to expect a favourable issue. मृषोद्यं—मृषा उद्यते इति मिथ्यावचनं false utterance; fr. मृषा + वद् and क्यप् (य), व taking Samprasàraṇa. See Páṇ III. I. 114 तत—refers to Vasishtha's words भवितव्यं तथा......भविष्यति above.

आविर्भूतज्योतिषां—ज्योतिस् the Supreme Light or light of Brahma-explains why they are able to see the future correctly. *Cf.* the Vedic passage quoted in the com. The full text of the passage is—सक्तुमिव तितउना पुनन्तो यत्र धीरा मनसा वाचमक्रत। अत्रा सखायः सख्यानि जानते भद्रैषां लक्ष्मीर्निहिताधिवाचि ॥ Ṛv. X. 71. 2.

P. 113. विप्लुतार्था—विप्लुतः (sunk into or washed off by flood; hence, false) अर्थः यस्याः ताम्.

शिष्टानध्यायः—शिष्टनिमित्तकः अनध्यायः a holiday in honour of the arrival of distinguished persons. उद्धतं—boisterously. अस्खलितं *v. l.* without restraint or obstacle (अविद्यमानं स्खलितं यस्मिन्कर्मणि).

सावष्टम्भ—Full of firmness or dignity, stately. अपवार्य—This stage-direction is wrong. The speech of Arudhati is

स्वगत. It is not intended for any one else, as is clear from the context.

इदं नाम तत् &c.—It appears that Bhâgîrathî had already disclosed to Arundhatî the fact of Sîtâ's being still alive and of the birth of her two sons, Kus'a and Lava.

P. 114 कुवलय°—°दलवत् स्निग्ध: glossy, pleasing to sight चासौ श्यामश्च. पुनरिव—पुनरपि v. l. has no properity. The fig. is Utprekshá. क्षत्रियब्रह्मचारी—A Kshatriya-boy in a student's stage of life. ब्रह्म वेद: तदध्ययनार्थं व्रतमप्युपचारात् ब्रह्म; the act of living at the Guru's house for the study of the Veda; तच्चरितुं शीलमस्य ब्रह्मचारी.

चूडा°—This stanza gives the characteristic signs of a क्षत्रियब्रह्मचारी. कङ्कपत्र—The feathers of a heron with which arrows were furnished. भस्मस्तोक°—See com.; or स्तोकं भस्म भस्मस्तोकं तद् लाञ्छनं यस्य. स्तोक takes परनिपात in a Karm,; see Pán. II. I. 65. रौरवी—रुरो: (a kind of deer) इयं. See Ragh. III. 31.

मौर्वी—मूर्वाया इयं (अवयवार्थे अण्) मूर्वाया विकार: । made of the *Murva* grass. माञ्जिष्ठकं—मञ्जिष्ठया रक्तं माञ्जिष्ठं dyed with madder; तेन रक्तं रागात् इत्यण्; माञ्जिष्ठमेव माञ्जिष्ठकम्. कार्मुकं—कर्मणे प्रभवति इति fr. कर्मन् and aff. उक (ञ्). अपर:—besides the two. अपरे *V. l.*—in the other hand. These are the usual accoutrements of a Kshatriya Brahmachârin. *Cf.* कार्ष्णरौरववास्तानि चर्माणि ब्रह्मचारिण: । वसीरन्नानुपूर्व्येण शाणक्षौमाविकानि च । क्षत्रियस्य तु मौर्वी ज्या वैश्यस्य शणतान्तवी । ब्राह्मणो बैल्वपालाशौ क्षत्रियो वाटखादिरौ &c. Manu. II. 40. 45. Although Manu says ब्राह्मणो बैल्वपालाशौ it is not absolutely binding; for Gautama says—वार्क्षं ब्राह्मणस्य माञ्जिष्ठहारिद्रे इतरयोर्बैल्वपालाशौ &c. If we take अयं as subject, धत्ते as predicate and तूणीद्वयं, उर:, त्वचं, अधोवास: &c. as accusatives, with the reading दण्डं तथा पैप्पलं we shall get the fig. of क्रियादीपक. The fig. of अनुमान or Rhetorical Inference is also implied. This sl. occurs in Mv. I. 28.

उत्प्रेक्षसे—Conjecture, guess. अथैव &c.—She evades to give a direct reply to him but leaves it to be understood that she was equally ignorant of the fact. Perhaps she does so at the desire of Bhâgîrathi, who knowing the desire of Válmîki in the matter, must have told her to keep the matter secret for some time.

P. 115. भिद्येत वा &c.—Janaka means that the boy's noble look was a sure guarantee for his possession of good manners, and that he would therefore readily accede to their wish. The idea that grace of form and nobility of conduct must generally be found together is often expressed by Sanskrit poets; *cf.* कमलानां मनोहराणामपि रूपादिसंवदति शीलम् Mud. I. 19; न ह्याकृतिः सुसदृशं विजहाति वृत्तं Mrich. IX. 16; यत्राकृतिस्तत्र गुणा वसन्ति Subhâshita.

निशामित—heard. किमपि—Something unaccountable, strange. मौग्ध्य—मुग्धस्य भावः मौग्ध्यं, childish innocence or simplicity.

मसृण—softened by, delightful with. विदग्धः—properly 'well burnt'; hence, bright, and then, bright in intellect, of keen or acute preception. संमोहस्थिरमपि—Here स्थिर means 'rendered dull,' incapable of being easily affected by any emotion, by besilderment. But the महिम्नामतिशय is बलवान् and hence it attracts the mind. The reading संमोहः स्थिरमपि is bad; it is probably due to the carelessness of some scribe. In the first place why should there be संमोह at the sight of the boy, and even if there was, why should it be बलवान्? Again, संमोह cannot be fitly compared with अयस्कान्त; for it does not attract, but stupefies the mind. संमोदः—*v. l.* great joy (caused by the sight of the boy). एष—this that I feel, takes possession of my heart. एव *v. l.*—here the substitution of एव for एष does not improve the sense; for एव has no propriety. Again the cause of the joy is not stated. So the reading in the text is the best. परिलघु—Quick in its action, or tiny.

क्रम—respective position; e. he did not know whom to salute first. स्वतः—by myself, *i. e.* without being guided by some one. It will be better to read सतः for स्वतः (although they are deserving of salutation). अविरुद्ध—not opposed to good manners, unobjectionable. पर्याय—a series or succession of *cf.* एष वो रामशिरसा प्रणामपर्यायः Mv. IV.

P. 116. ईष०-दं a little, slightly विकसत् पनीलोत्पलं &c. कषायरक्त tuneful, sweet-sounding. *Cf.* चूताङ्कुरास्वादकषायकण्ठः Kum. III. 32. अनुहरति—Mr. Ghâte contends that this should be अनुहरते. But that does not seem to be intended. For by the Vârt. हरतेर्गतताच्छील्ये, हृ is Âtm. only when one imitates the modes of action &c. of one's parents by habit, which cannot be meant here as Kau. is not sure of Lava's origin from Râma.

रामभद्रमनुहरति &c.—Read रामभद्रस्य; हृ with अनु, like कृ, governs the Gen; *cf.* ताच्छील्ये किम् मातुरनुहरति । Sid.-Kau. on the Vârt. हरतेर्गतताच्छील्ये. पक्ष्मल—*Lit.* fibrous; hence soft and diffusing gladness or sending a thrill all round. आकूत—emotion or wonder.

P. 117. उन्मत्ती०—As if gone mad; for her idea was that Sitâ was dead. निपुणं—attentively, carefully.

इतोमुखं—of such import, *viz.* the boy's resemblance to Râma and Sîtâ expressed i- her last speech and the possibility of his being their son. रघूद्वह—The best of the Raghus; or उद्वह may mean 'a scion of'; उद्वह (उद्वहतीति) one who continues or bears up (raises to eminence) a family. संपूर्णप्रति०—The readings here are not satisfactory. As the line stands we must take सा एव निखिला आकृतिः and सा एव निखिला द्युतिः as the subjects of प्रतिबिम्बिता, and take the clauses सा वाणी &c. separately. The Com. reads संवृत्तिः. This simplifies the construction; for we can in this case take the first sentence as ending with प्रतिबिम्बिता, and take the clauses सैवाकृतिः &c. as an explanation of that statement. But the difficulty is about the meaning of संवृत्ति; the Com. translates it by संपर्कः-संबन्धः, probably meaning thereby 'the blending of the features of'. The reading संपृक्ता does not mend matters. It means 'blended', and qualifies आकृतिः and द्युतिः. पुण्यानुभावः—holy or purifying, majestic lustre. अनुभाव means here the majestic appearance which strikes another with awe and reverence. उत्पथैः—along wild or wrong paths. Janaka believed Sîtá to be dead ; and howsoever the boy resembled his daughter and Ráma he could not see how he could be their son. Therefore he blames his mind for entertaining what could be nothing more than a sweet fancy. पारिप्लवं—may be adj. or abverb. कथयितव्यं—What is reasonable to be said ; *i. e.* answer our question directly.

P. 118. अभ्यर्ण—adjoining; lying about. It is the p. p. p. of अर्द् with अभि when the sense is 'not very far off' by अभेश्चाविदूर्ये। Pâṇ. VII. 2. 25. नातिदूरं नासन्नं वा। अभ्यर्दितमन्यत्। Sid-.Kau. वत्स &c.—Mark the nobility of the mind of Janaka and Kausalyá. They have the same affection for the son of Lahshmaṇa that they would have had for the sons of Ráma, had he any. यदि स्वमिहाद्यः &c.—Janaka has yet some faint hope that the boy might turn out to be his daughter's offspring, in the course of the details he would give.

P. 119. प्रविभाग—a subdivision. संदर्भान्तरेण—written in the form of a different composition. अभिनेयार्थः कृतः—Adapted to dramatic representation. This is an invention of the poet. Se- our introduction to the VII. Act. भरतस्य—Bharata, the reputed sage and father of the Sanskrit drama. His work is known as नाट्यशास्त्र. The extant नाट्य० has 37 chapters and contains over 5000 ślokas mostly in the

Anushṭubh metre, with a few prose passages here and there. Kálidása also refers to Bharata as नाट्याचार्य-representing plays on the heavenly stage with the help of the Apsarasas. *cf* मुनिना भरतेन यः प्रयोगो भवतीष्वष्टरसाश्रयो नियुक्तः । ललिताभिनयं तमद्य भर्ता मरुतां द्रष्टुमनाः सलोकपालः । Vik. II. 18. तौर्यत्रिक-also called नाट्य, is the triple science and art of dancing, singing and instrumental music. तौर्यत्रिकं नृत्यगीतवाद्यं नाट्यमिदं त्रयम् । Ak. तूर्ये मुरजादि तत्र भवं तौर्यं instrumental sound; त्रयः अंशा अस्य त्रिकं (Pán. V. 1. 22) तौर्योपलक्षितं त्रिकं तौर्यत्रिकम्. सूत्रकारस्य—These Sûtras of Bharaṭa are known as the Nâṭyasútras of Bharata. तस्मिन्-scil. संदर्भे. आस्था—Care, regard. आनुयात्रिकः– ... त्रा गमनं सा प्रयोजनं (object, purpose) अस्य; ठञ् (the aff. इक) being added in this sense. प्रमाद—a mishap, an accident. आर्यः—This indicated that Kuśa was his elder brother. प्रसवानुक्रमेण—the order of birth. This leads Jan. to infer that they were twins.

P. 120. पर्यन्त—the limit or concluding portion of the story. Mark how Jan. and Kau. are anxious to elicit some information from the boy that would unfold the mystery of his birth and indicate his connexion with Ráma and Sítá.

च नवं--The reading वचनं is not so good. For it may refer to the words of the people, but we do not know from the play what those words were. नवं च *V. l.*—here च is out of place. क्रव्यात्--क्रव्यं raw meat अदन्ति क्रव्यादः; beasts of prey. क्षिप्रकारिता—क्षिप्रं करोति तस्य भावः rashness or precipitancy of action.

P. 121. वैशस--properly destruction, slaughter; hence, great distress or calamity. उत्पश्यतः--means here मनसि विभावयतः revolving in the mind. For its usual sense *cf.* Ragh. II. 60. धगु--The sound of the sudden bursting forth of a fire. Hence, here, suddenly, quickly. झटिति *v. l.*—at once, quickly; but the former is more forcible. चापेन शापेन वा—Janaka as a Râjarshi could use both these weapons. As a veteran Kshatriya warrior he could use his bow. By virtue of his power arising from long-practised penance he could effectively curse any one like a Brâhmaṇa.

सभयकम्पम्--Kausalyá, well conscious of this power of Janaka, is alarmed at the thought that he, acting under the impulse of his anger, might pronounce an imprecation on her dear Râma and his subjects and thus destroy them at once, and she naturally appeals to Arundhatî to interfere, as the only person able to pacify the angry royal sage.

एतद्धि &c.—These words are put into the mouth of Arundhatî in many editions, but they do not accord well with the following line. Nor is Arun. expected to say aught that would even indirectly inflame the anger of Janaka. एतत् refers to what Jan. says in his previous speech. प्राय: चित्तं should be taken as two different words. Construe परिभूतानां प्राय: एतत् एतत्प्रकारकं चित्तं such is the state of mind; *i. e.* inclined to show anger; or चित्त may mean 'resolution' (निश्चय:, 'चित्तं निश्चय उच्यते') हि. See also the Com.'s interpretation, which is equally good. If these words are really spoken by Arund., then we must supply किं तु to make the second line intelligible. राजन्नपत्यं &c.—Here Arun. refers to Râma and the subjects because these two were responsible for Sîtâ's abandonment. तदुभयं—*viz.* चाप and शाप. यत्—since. पुत्रभाण्डं—पुत्ररूपं भाण्डं a precious possession, a treasure. *Cf.* Mv. II. 43. भूयिष्ठ &c.- भूयिष्ठानि: द्विजा:......स्त्रैणं a multitude of women च यस्मिन्; and hence they are to be pitied. अनुश्रूयते—Known by heresay.

P. 122. पशुसमाम्नाय—According to the Com. this means 'that portion of the Veda which deals with a horse-sacrifice.' In translating this passage we have taken the word in the wider sense of a scientific treatise on animals. सांग्रामिकं—A treatise on the science of war. विपुलं--Thick and long. अजस्रं constantly; here an adv.; fr. जसु with अ and the aff. र (जसिर्नञ्पूर्वः क्रियासातत्ये वर्तते । Sid.-Kau.). आम्रमात्राः—आम्रं मात्रा प्रमाणं येषां. This is an instance of the fig. of स्वभावोक्ति or the simple and lifelike description of a thing. It is also हास्यरसपोषक. सकौतुको०—Lava as a boy had a curiosity to see the horse like the other boys. But at the same time, as a well-bred boy he could not leave the elders abruptly; so he felt also a sort of constraint (उपरोध); he had to take their leave to go; or the उपरोध may be from the boys. ०पराध०—*V. l.* with curiosity, a sense of being guilty, &c.-not a good reading. भगवति—जानामि &c.—The Com. reads before this—अरण्यगर्भरूपा &c. (see foot-note) which means:—you and I have been gladdened by him with his beauty and words like those of a forester. अरण्यं गर्भे यस्य having a forest in its interior; *i. e.* sylvan. न जीवाम्येव—Kau. being the nearest relative of the boy is most affected by his sight.

P. 123. अतिगम्भीर—Very important or serious (since Válmîki even refused to satisfy their curiosity and kept it mysterious). आश्वमेधिक:—see com.; or अश्वमेध: प्रयोजनमस्य·

तत्काण्डे—i. e. the portion of the Veda treating of the Aśvamedha sacrifice. प्रत्येकं—(एकैकस्मिन्बलभागे) in each body of troops परिवृत:-surrounded by soldiers. ऊर्जस्वल:—अतिशयित: ऊर्जः energy, valour, pre-eminence अस्यास्तीति fr. ऊर्ज or ऊर्जस् and वल (a *matub* aff.) pre-eminent, powerful. उत्कर्षनिष्कर्ष—The essence of greatness or pre-eminent dignity. ०निकष:—*V. l.* the touch-stone for testing the greatness of. This reading is bad as the adjectives ऊर्जस्वल and ०परिभावी cannot be well construed with निकष.

अयमश्व:—Better read योयमश्व: with the Com. It is a reply to the question किंप्रयोजन: &c. The reply is य: अयं (that you see before you) अश्व: इयं पताका is the banner of (that distinguishes him as). वीरघोषणा--वीरस्य वीरत्वस्य घोषणा a proclamation of the valour of. सप्तलोक—सप्तावयवो लोक: सप्तलोक:; a comp. of the शाकपार्थिवादि class (the comp. must be so taken; otherwise we should expect सप्तलोकी); तस्मिन् एकवीरस्य—एक: अद्वितीय: (sole, undisputed; hence chief &c.) वीरस्तस्य. This is a departure from Páṇ. Accoding to Páṇ. II. 1. 58 (see H. G. § 222. g) the form should be वीरैक. But the form एकवीर is found used by many authors. Bhattoji Dikshit, therefore, remarks—कथमेकवीर इति how do you accout for the form एकवीर—We reply बहुलग्रहणाद्भविष्यति supposing that the rule operates in most cases only (and not in a few.) This Śl. along with the 29th is quoted by क्षेमेन्द्र in his औचित्यविचारचर्चा as illustrative of प्रबन्धार्थौचित्य with the remark अत्रार्थे रामायणकथातिक्रमेण नूतनोत्प्रेक्षिता रामतनयस्य सहजविक्रमानुसारिणी शौर्योत्कर्षभूमि: परप्रतापस्पर्शासहिष्णुता प्रबन्धस्य रसबन्धुरामौचित्यच्छायां प्रयच्छति ।.

P. 124. प्रति—before i. e. in comparison with.

ते-The real Kshatriyas. This must refer to 'क्षत्रिया:'; it cannot grammatically refer to महाराज:. The pl. cannot be also taken as used आदरार्थे ; for लव does not speak respectfully about Ráma in the pl. in his dialogue with Chand. How can he suddenly do it here? सन्त्येव-They do exist. Your assertion to the contrary cannot blot out their existence from the face of the earth. But again what means this. विभीषिका—Threatening? तां—that boasted (banner of yours). शरसंबाधां—*v. l.* assailing it with a shower of arrows (if necessary). But the following speech of Lava does not support this reading; again the horse was alone and could have been easily led away.

लोष्टै: &c.—shows his utter disregard of their boastful proclamation. रोहित—a kind of deer. वराक:—the poor thing.

तीक्ष्ण—harsh, fierce. नीरस–cruel, without feeling. आयुधीय—आयुधेन जीवन्तीति आयुधीया: those who live by means of weapons; warriors. Fr. आयुध+ईय (छ); it also takes ठन्, आयुधिकः. अरिवि०—The destroyer of his enemies; *i. e.* will never spare them. दुर्दान्त: *V. l.*—is difficut to subdue or check. This is not so forcible as अरि० आक्षिप्तहृदय:—his mind being attracted by.

P. 125. हरिणप्लुतैः—हरिणानामिव प्लुतै: bounding like the deer.

ज्याजिह्वया—see com. We may also take the comp. as ज्या जिह्वा इव; but the Com's. way is better, as the bent bow is compared to the yawing mouth of Yama. This is connected with वलयित०; so this is what is called एकदेशी अन्वय वलयित &c.—Better say वलयिते उत्कटे formidable कोटी एव दंष्ट्रे यस्य. उद्गारि०—उद्गारि issuing forth घोर: &c. घोष: यस्य.

वक्त्रयन्त्र—horrible mouth. विडम्बि—imitating. विकट–formidable, large enough to inspire fear. We may separate विकटोदरं from ०विडम्बि; let the bow be one whose formidable cavity will imitate &c. The bow with the space between the string and the bent staff is compared to the mouth of Yama opened wide in yawning, on account of the work of destruction it was going to commence. Mark the alliterations in the stanza. The metre is not well adapted to the heroic sentiment (वीररस) expressed in the stanza.

ACT V.

The scene of this Act, too, is laid in the neighbourhood of Válmîki's hermitage. The two princes, Lava and Chandraketu, meet each other and express their mutual admiration. The dialogue is marked by a true spirit of chivalry and extreme courtesy. Lava, however, incidentally passes some adverse remarks on Ráma's actions. This inflames the spirit of Chandraketu and a battle becomes inevitable. A special feature of this Act is that it contains no Prákrit passage.

P. 126. भो भो &c.—is a Chûlikâ; see com. अवलम्बनं—The being supported. त्वरित०—त्वरितं यथा तथा सुमन्त्रेण (the charioteer of Daśaratha) नुद्यमाना: ज्यावल्गन्त: gallopping प्रजवना वाजिन: यस्य. The reading प्रोद्वेल्लत् and प्रोद्वलगत् mean the same thing. उद्घात०—उद्घातेन by the jolting प्रचलित: कोविदारयुक्त: कतुर्यस्य. प्रधनं—fight. Mark the पादान्तयमक (a kind of शब्दालंकार).

साद्भुत—अद्भुतेन सहितौ हर्षसंभ्रमौ यस्य. अद्भुत (wonder) at Lava's exploit; हर्ष at his having come across such a hero; संभ्रम because of the havoc Lava was making among the troops.

कलित—that he had come to have. **किंचित्कोप**—because Lava treated with little concern the troops though united against him. See com.; अविरत॰—see com.; or अविरतः constantly sounding यः गुणस्तेन गुञ्जन्त्यौ कोटी यस्य.

प्रवितत्गुण—The high-streched string. **समरशिरसि**—being in the van of the fight. **चञ्चत्पञ्च॰**—चञ्चन्त्यः waving about (on account of his rapid movements) पञ्च चूडा यस्य. As a Kshatriya boy he had five crests. From this it seems that Lava had his head uncovered (not protected by a helmet). **शरतुषारं**—a shower of arrows. The comparison to a cloud is implied. See com.

एकः—united, single-handed. **सैन्यकाये**—The array of the forces. **काय**—a multitude or assemblage of. **संभ्रकोपात्** *V. l.*—is not good as Lava is said to be only slightly angry in the previous śl. **रघुवंशस्य प्ररोहः**—a scion or offshoot. There is a *double entente* on वंश which means a family and a bamboo. The poet identifies the Raghu family with a bamboo tree, thus using a रूपक or metaphor. **नव इव प्ररोहः**—is an Utpreksha.

P. 127. **टंकार**—the clashing sound of. See com. for the compound; or it may be taken as ॰कपोलग्रन्थि च टंकारघोरं च ज्वलितं च शरसहस्रं यस्य whose thousands of arrows shatter &c., which are terrible by the twang of the bow, and which are blazing.

तुल्यरूपं—having a form similar to that of Ráma. The reading तवेन तु॰ is bad. For तव must refer to चन्द्रकेतु. So it will be absurd for Sumantra to say—I remember Ráma on seeing this boy similar in form to you.

कुशिकसुत—Vis'vámitra. According to the geneology of Vis'vá. given in the Rámá., he was the son of Gádhi, the son of Kus'anábha who was the son of Kuśa, born of Brahmá (ब्रह्मयोनिजः). So Viśvá. was not the son of कुशिक but of Gádhi, and a descendant of कुश, कौशिक being the family name. He himself says to Ráma—कस्यचित्त्वथ कालस्य कुशनामस्य धीमतः। जज्ञे परमधर्मिष्ठो गाधिरित्येव नामतः। स पिता मम काकुत्स्थ गाधिः परमधार्मिकः। कुशवंशप्रसूतोऽस्मि कौशिको रघुनन्दन ॥ **मखद्विषां प्रमाथे**—Subáhu and Márícha were the leaders of the demons who disturbed the sacrifices of Viśvámitra See Ragh. XI. 27-30.

धृतधनुर्षं—धृतं धनुः येन. Properly this should be ०धन्वानं; *cf.* उदीर्णधन्वा below, śl. 11; but such deviations from Páṇ. are defended by the general principle—"The rules about the changes of the finals of compounds are not always binding." (समासान्तविधेरनित्यत्वात्). स्मरामि The fig. is स्मृतिमत् which Mammaṭa defines as यथानुभवमर्थस्य दृष्टे तत्सदृशे स्मृतिः । स्मरणम् ; *i. e.*, the recollection of something already known at the sight of another similar to it.

एकमुद्दिश्य—एकमधिकृत्य many uniting their efforts against one.

समरभार—The brunt of the battle; तत्र भूरि स्फुरन्ति करालानि fierce च तानि करकन्दलीभिः huge hands कलितानि च wielded or grasped, शस्त्रजालानि येषां. Vîra. reads मदभरेण for समरभार. This goes with भूरिस्फुरत् and means 'through the highly-wrought intoxication of (fervour for) fighting'. समरभारभूमि *v. l.*—means the place where the battle rages fiercest. अमन्दमद०—अमन्दः profusely flowing मद एव दुर्दिनं येषां तादृशा द्विरदा वारिदा इव (an Upamá) द्विरदवारिदा येषु तेः The comparison of the array of elephants to drizzling clouds is commonly to be met with in the description of battles by Sanskrit poets. द्विरदडामरैः *v. l.* frightful or terrific with. ०डम्बरैः—with the majestic display of. The sentiment of the stanza is Adbhuta. व्यस्तैः—singly, each one by himself. अस्माकं—goes with आश्रितजन०. प्रमाथः—प्रमारः *v. l.* destruction.

घटा—a collection. निस्तीर्ण—given. कर्णज्वरं—pain to the ear. This may also be taken adverbially; 'in a manner to produce a feverish sensation.' आध्मातं—augmented, intensified.

P. 128. वेल्लत्—moving about as they were thrown with great force and had yet life in them. रुण्ड—the trunk of the body. मुण्ड—The head severed from the body. तृष्यत्—blood-thirsty. In translating this we have followed the reading तृप्यत् which is better. विघस—The remnant or residue of food, the mouthfuls thrown out from his mouth by Kála after he had got his fill; mark the alliterations. The sentiment of the stanza is a blending of *Vîra* and *Adbhuta*. The fig. is Utprekshâ.

द्वंद्व०—द्वंद्वस्य संप्रहारः a duel, a single fight. अथ वा &c.—*i. e.* I know the ways and practices of the family and what they are capable of achieving. I cannot, therefore, dissuade Chandraketu from fight. ०संभ्रमं—संभ्रम because he wanted to maintain the prestige of his race. वाग्विषयीभूत—has come within hearing or the range of your voice. It may also mean 'the subject of your talk'.

तेजस्तेजसि शाम्यतु—महान्महत्येव करोति विक्रममिति भावः. तेजः—heroic lustre, valour.

उपहूत—challenged for fighting. स्तनयित्नु—a cloud; fr. स्तन् + इत्नु. अवमर्द—destruction, slaughter. ०सिंहशावः—Because the lion fancies the cloud to be some mightier foe. *Cf.* अनुहुंकुरुते घनध्वनिं न हि गोमायुरुतानि केसरी Śiś. XVI. 25; and किमपेक्ष्य फलं पयोधरान्ध्वनतः प्रार्थयते मृगाधिपः। प्रकृतिः खलु सा महीयसः सहते नान्यसमुन्नतिं यया॥ Kir. II. 21.

P. 129. धीरोद्धत०—with bold and haughty steps; this is preferable to त्वरितोद्धतक्रमः. *Cf.* further on धीरोद्धता नमयतीव &c. VI. 19. See com. also. ऐक्ष्वाकः—Because of his heroic conduct. सावष्टम्भम्—with firmness; courageously. युद्धाभिसारिणः—Bent on fighting. जाल्मान्—rash; courting their own death. जाल्मोऽसमीक्ष्यकारी स्यात् Ak.

वडवावक्त्रहुतभुक्—the submarine fire. *Lit.* the fire issuing from the mouth of the mare. The sons of Kártavîrya, wishing to destroy the descendants of भृगु, killed even the children in the womb. One of the women of the family, in order to preserve her embryo secreted it in her thigh (ऊरु) whence the child when born was called और्व. On beholding him the sons of Kártavîrya were struck with blindness, and his wrath gave rise to a flame which threatened to consume the whole world. But at the intercession of his Pitṛis he cast it into the ocean where it remained with the face of a horse. See also our note on Ragh. IX. 82, XIII. 4. शैला०—शैल may not necessarily refer to Mandâra. क्रोधार्चि०—क्रोधाग्निज्वाला०. घन—deep. तुमुल—mixed, confused. The meaning is—As the submarine fire when stirred up checks the overflow of oceanic waters so let the fierce working of my wrath put down the tumult of the army. आस्फालित—tossed up, agitated or thrown into commotion.

गुणातिशय—गुणानामतिशयः excellence of your virtues.

प्रसन्न—clear and pleasing; this refers to the first half of the Śl., while कर्कशा refers to the last time प्रयुक्ति—प्रयोगः employment or use of. विकर्तन—the sun. विशेषेण कर्तनमस्य। विश्वकर्मणा यन्त्रोल्लिखितत्वात्. For the allusion see Ragh. VI. 32 and our note thereon; or विकर्तयति भक्तरोगान्.

P. 130. निर्वेद—Vexation. कदर्थितः—annoyed, troubled; or led to do an improper act, or to act wickedly, as she Com. takes it. This is p. p. p. of the denom. from कदर्थ; कुत्सितः अर्थः कदर्थः तद्वान् कृतः; मतुबन्तात् णिच्.

उदीर्ण—raised. द्वेधा समुद्धत: agitated, blowing य: मरुत् तेन चञ्चलस्य. मघवत: अयं माघवत: चाप: तस्य धर: तस्य. The darkish and valiant Lava approaching Chandra., but drawn back by the army assailing him from behind, is fitly compared to a cloud with the rain-bow on it and tossed alternately by opposite winds. The fig. is निदर्शना which is described as निदर्शना । अभवन्वस्तुसंबन्ध उपमापरिकल्पक: । "That is नि० which consists in an inconceivable connexion of things implying a comparison." कुमार एवैनं &c.—Here Sumantra very deftly praises the extraordinary prowess of Lava and at the same time encourages Chand. by hinting that he was not a whit inferior in prowess to him.

पदातावत्रैकस्मिन्—should be अत्रैकस्मिन् पदातौ for the sake of symmetry. So there is प्रक्रमभङ्ग. पादाभ्यामतति गच्छतीति पदाति: । मेध्यचर्म एवोत्तरीयमस्य; *i. e.* who is not protected by an armour even. कालज्येष्ठै: कालेन ज्येष्ठै:. बद्धपरिकर:—That you have girt up your loins, *i. e.* are bent upon fighting with him resolutely Chand. beholds the inequality of the fight--that so many of his warriorss should unitedly fight with a boy—and feels ashamed. It was against the rules of chivalry. The fig. is विरोध.

सोन्माथं—उन्माथ pain that upset the peace of his mind. He resented the very idea of pity.

P. 131. प्रगल्भं—प्रगल्भते इति, fr. गल्भ् धार्ष्ट्ये; used in its literal sense of 'a bold man.' आमन्त्रितं—Called in, invoked; *i. e.* made to manifest itself by repeating its proper mantra. व्यतिकर इव—The missile, it seems, first produced darkness followed by dazzling flashes of lightning and then lulled into sleep the opposing army. The following śl. gives an idea of its power. प्रणिहित—directed to an object. मस्तमुक्तं—now obscured, now dazzled. For the first half of the stanza compare Mál.-Mádh. IX. 52. लिखित-drawn in a picture. अमितवीर्यं—whose power cannot be measured, *i. e.* is unbounded.

कुञ्ज—a cavern. The nether world is supposed to be full of darkness. आरकूट-*m. n.* brass; उत्तप्तं &c. (see com.) कपिलज्योतिर्वत् ज्वलन्ती दीप्तिर्येषाम्. कल्पाक्षेप—the destruction of the universe. कठोर—forcible, violent. मीलन् &c.—मीलन्तो gathering मेघास्तडितश्च तै: कडाराणि tawny कुहराणि caverns or valleys येषां तै:. The fig. in the śl. may be Upamá or Utprekshá.

नैतदेवं &c—Because Vàlmîki was not known to be conversant with the lore of using the missiles. संप्रदाय—traditional handing down of knowledge.

P. 132. स्थिता अपि—here अपि has the force of एव. इति for अपि is out of place, as the śl. is introduced by यत:. The other reading व्यवस्थिता: gives a good sense.

प्रचीयमान—growing, accumulating. सत्त्व—is the best of the three qualities सत्त्व, रजस् and तमस् and its excess qualifies one for divine revelation. प्रवीर:—प्रतिवीर *V. l.*, the opposing warrior.

यदृच्छासंवाद:—a fortuitous or casual meeting. संवाद:—may also mean 'conversation'. Herein the princes state the various possible causes to explain why they feel drawn to each other. जन्मान्तर०—जन्मान्तरे निबिडं यथा तथा बद्ध:; *cf.* मनो हि जन्मान्तरसंगतिज्ञं । Ragh. VIII. 15 and तच्चेतसा स्मरति नूनमबोधपूर्वं भावस्थिराणि जननान्तरसौहृदानि । Śák. V. 2.

अवधानं—fixity. My heart rests on him lovingly; is firmly drawn to him. रसमयी—full of flavour, ardent. उपचार—mode of expression or explanation. तारामैत्रकं—friendship of the stars *i. e.* spontaneous or causeless friendship. It is a belief that persons born under the influence of the same constellation or a friendly position of stars have a natural liking or affinity for each other. *Cf.* Mál.—Mádh. VII. 4. चक्षूराग:—the love which the eye begets, *i. e.* which springs up at the sight of each other. *Cf.* Mál.—Mádh. VI. 15. अप्रतिसंख्येय—That cannot be accounted for or comprehended. अनिबन्धनं—अविद्यमानं निबन्धनं यस्य. आमनन्ति—*scil.* sages like वात्स्यायन. तदप्रतिसंख्येयनिबन्धनं प्रमाणं—*v. l.* seems to mean 'sages consider as an authority (for recognizing) the love, the cause of which is incapable of being correctly known or ascertained.'

P. 133. पक्षपात—attachment, affection. प्रतिक्रिया—prevention; it cannot be avoided. स्नेहात्मक—स्नेहरूप in the form of affection.

मसृणित—polished, rendered glossy. राजपट्ट—a kind of superior silk garment. कदम्ब—The multitude of. It may also mean buds of the Kadamba tree (पुलका: कदम्बानीव); for this comparison, see *supra*, III. 42.

आक्रान्त०—one who has got. कठोर—full, perfect. समय—The settled or conventional course of conduct, the time-honoured duty.

हृदय—&c.—On marking Lava's features Sumantra thought him to be the son of Ráma and Sítà; but on recollecting how Sítâ had met her end he saw how ill-founded his hopes were and hence his following remark. परिकल्पसे—fanciest in a different (strange) way; परिप्लवसे *v. l.*—gettest perturbed. The former is better. बीजं—*i. e.* Sítá. लतायां &c.—The fig. is दृष्टान्त.

P. 134. न रथिनः &c.—*Cf.* रथी च रथिना सार्धं पदातिश्च पदातिना। कुञ्जरस्थो गजस्थेन योद्धव्यो भृगुनन्दन ॥ Chaturvarga—Chintámaṇi. न्याय्यं-न्यायादनपेतं keeping to justice ; right. साहसैकरसां—*Lit* whose sole essence is rashness. *i. e.* which is wholly hazardous. कथं अभिजानातु—For he saw danger in Chandraketu's doing so.

चारित्र—Conduct, manner of action; fr. चर् + Uṇ. aff. णित्रन् (इत्र); or चरित्रमेव चारित्रं, स्वार्थे अण्. अप्रतिरूप—unequalled in excellence. प्रतिरूप—*v. l.* proper, worthy of.

इतिहास--History so modelled as to teach moral lessons. धर्मार्थकाममोक्षाणामुपदेशसमन्वितम्। पूर्ववृत्तं कथायुक्तमितिहासं प्रचक्षते ॥ पुराण--The special feature of a Puráṇa is that it treats of the five topics—सर्गश्च प्रतिसर्गश्च वंशो मन्वतराणि च। वंशानुचरितं चैव पुराणं पञ्चलक्षणम् ॥ The term इतिहास is generally taken to refer to the रामायण and the महाभारत, but as Chandraketu is the speaker here, the reference must be to the historical works then in existence. धर्मप्रवच॰—see com. कुलस्थिति-Family observances, the peculiar usages and practices of a family.

P. 135. दिष्ट्या गतं—Sumantra rejoices to see Chandraketu so dutiful. अप्रतिष्ठे—For he had no issue.

रसक्रमः—the rising of feelings; the sentiments of love and heroism were simultaneously present in his heart. ययेन्दो&c.—The sentiment of the first two lines is Rati and the style Kais'ikí, the words being full of soft consonants.

टणत्कार &c.—टणत्कारेण क्रूरं क्वणितं यस्य तादृशो यो गुणस्तेन गुञ्जद् गुरुधनुस्तत्र धृतः प्रेमा येन. गुञ्जत् is superfluous, so there is the fault of redundance. विकच--manifested. विकराल-fierce.-उल्बण intense. विकट-विकराल-व्रणमुखः *v. l.*--विकटानि किकरालानि च व्रणमुखानि यस्य having on it large and fierce open wounds; or विकटाः व्रणाः मुखे अग्रे यस्य. This does not seem to be a likely reading, as no mention is made before or after this of Lava's arm being wounded. Again, had it been seriously wounded it could not have been कलहकाम. The sentiment in these two lines is Vîra, and hence the predominence of harsh sounds in them

P. 136 ऊर्जस्वल—powerful. ककुत्स्थ—This was Puraṃjaya, an ancestor of Ráma. Being requested by Indra to assist him in his fight with the demons he promised to do so, provided the former became a bull and bore him on his back. Indra consented and the king vanquished the demons, seated on the hump of Indra in the form of a bull. Hence his name. श्रेयसे—The Dat. is तादर्थ्ये, *i. e.* for achieving the purpose or object for which an act is done, by the Vârt. तादर्थ्ये चतुर्थी वाच्या. परिक्ल्पताम्—should endow you with; governs मह:. वराह:—The divine Boar, the third incarnation of Vishṇu. He is invoked here as he was the first to gain victory over the first demon (Hiraṇyáksha), who was most powerful and oppressive and who had carried the earth to the bottom of the sea. "The reason of the invocation of Varáha" says Mr. Kàne, "may also be found in the fact that many royal houses had adopted the Boar or Garuḍa as their tutelary deity, as can be seen from the seals on copperplate grants and inscriptions."

धिनोतु—please you, give you enegry. मैत्रावरुण:—This name occurs in the Veda; *cf.* उतासि मैत्रावरुणो वसिष्ठोर्वश्या ब्रह्मन्मनसोऽधिजात: ॥ Ṛig. VII. 33. 11. Also मैत्रावरुणि:; see *supra,* p. 15. आग्निमारुतं—अग्रामरुतो: इदम्. सुपर्ण—Garuḍa. The name is thus accounted for in the Mahâbhârata:—एतत्पत्रं त्यजाम्येकं यस्यान्तं नोपलप्स्यसे ॥ २१ ॥ न च वज्रनिपातेन रुजा मेऽस्तीह काचन । एवमुक्त्वा तत: पत्रमुत्ससर्ज स पक्षिराट् ॥ २२ ॥ तदुत्सृष्टमभिप्रेक्ष्य तस्य पर्णमनुत्तमम् । हृष्टानि सर्वभूतानि नाम चक्रुर्गरुत्मत: ॥ २३ ॥ सुरूपं पत्रमालक्ष्य सुपर्णोऽयं भवत्विति । A'di P. ch. 34. All these deities are known for their supreme prowess.

स्वेषु—Lava is speaking as a Kshatriya and so he calls the chariot &c. his proper implements (उपकरण). रथचर्या—The manœuvres; movements of a chariot.

P. 137. क्रतुप्रतिघातिन:—In the habit of obstructing sacrifices. क्रतुद्विषतांमरो *v. l.*—towards the destroyer of the enemies to sacrifices (the demons), *i. e.* Ráma. This reading will have special propriety here: it will make Lava mean 'we too would not have made Ráma our enemy by so acting.' स व्याहार,—refers to the declaration योयमश्व: &c. and महाराजं प्रति कुत: क्षत्रिया: of the warriors. अमर्ष:—non-endurance, jealousy: jealous anger. But आमर्ष means 'anger.' दान्त—self-restrained, किल—as I hear. दृप्त—concei ed.

निर्ऋते—The bane of, the source of the misery of. स्याद् लक्ष्मीस्तु निर्ऋति: । Amara; नियता ऋतिर्घृणा यस्या: । निष्क्रान्ता ऋते: सन्मार्गादिति Kshîras. According to the Mbh. she is regarded as the wife of Adharma and the mother of Bhaya, Mahábhaya and Mṛityu, while the Márk. P. regards her as the daughter of Adharma and Himsá and the mother of Bhaya and Naraka.

सूनृत—truthful and agreeable; सूनृतं मङ्गलेऽपि स्यात्प्रियसत्ये वचस्यपि। Cf. सत्यं ब्रूयात्प्रियं ब्रूयान्न ब्रूयात्सत्यमप्रियम् । प्रियं च नानृतं ब्रूयादेष धर्मः सनातनः ॥ Manu. IV, 138.

अभ्युपपन्न—proper, becoming. आभिसंपन्न V. l.—what is right. आर्षेण संस्कारेण—With the polishing or refinement he has received from the sage. The Com. reads अभ्युपपन्नामर्षेण which means 'through just resentment.' दुष्कृत: etc.–The Com. reads (दुर्हृदो) निष्फलाति extirpates, utterly destroys. व्यवस्थितविषयः—Limited or confined to one individual, monopolized by one, i. e. not existing at all in any other person than Ràma.

P. 138. अतिप्रसङ्ग—Transgressing the limits of propriety or decorum; impudence. ओजायितं—Denom from ओजस् martial spirit (ओजस्वी इव आचरति ओजायते): 'you have displayed your heroism' (ओजस्विता दर्शिता). दमनः—The conqueror of; अन added कर्तरि. निर्बन्धं—Persistent ill talk or obstinacy in talking against. उच्चैर्वाद—Boastful assertion, bragging.

सिद्धं ह्येतद &c.—Cf. the Tándya-Bráhmaṇa तस्माद् ब्राह्मणो मुखेन वीर्यं करोति मुखतो हि सृष्टः &c. ब्राह्मणः—The word is emphatic; a Bráhmaṇa is naturally unfit for wielding weapons skilfully. शान्ते—was humbled.

सोन्माथं—with writhing pain or pang; or with convulsive agitation.

वृद्धास्ते &c.—In this s'loka Lava refers to some incidents that would seem to detract from Râma's reputation as a great hero. The pl. ते is used out of mock respect. तिष्ठन्तु किं वर्ण्यते—This is what is called in English the fig. of 'Aposiopesis.' सुन्दस्त्री—Táḍakà, Here Lava hints that Ráma did what was forbidden by the Śástra. This ought to have impaired his reputation as a warrior, but on the contrary he passes for a great man.

P. 139. अपराङ्मुखानि—Said ironically. When Khara attacked Râma unexpectedly with great impetuosity, Râma had to fall back three steps in order to get time to draw his bow. See Ràmá. Ar. K. Ch. 30. 23. इन्द्रसूनु—Vâlî. While Válî and Sugrîva were engaged in a duel, Ráma shot an arrow at Vâlî from behind a tree as previously arranged, and killed him. The sarcasm of this speech is plain enough. Chandraketu especially felt the keen sting of this allusion which cast a direct slur on Ráma's conduct as a warrior. Śl. quoted in D.—R. as an instance of Drava (गुरुतिरस्कृतिः), one of the *aṅgas* of Avamarsha Samdhi. This reference by the poet to the weak points in the career of his hero is condemned as improper by Kshemendra in his औचित्यविचारचर्चा. He says—अत्र अप्रधानस्य रामसूनोः कुमारलवस्य......वीररसोद्दीपनाय......प्रधाननायकगतस्य धीररसस्य ताडकादमनखररणापसरण.........वालिव्यापादनादिजनविहितापवादप्रतिपादनेन स्ववचसा कविना विनाशः कृत इत्यनुचितमेतत्। Vis'vanátha also condemns this when he says यत्स्यादनुचितं वस्तु नायकस्य रसस्य वा। विरुद्धं तत्परित्याज्यमन्यथा वा प्रकल्पयेत्॥ अनुचितमितिवृत्तं यथा रामस्य छद्मना वालिवधः। तच्चोदात्तराघवे नोक्तमेव। वीरचरिते तु वाली रामवधार्थमागतो रामेण हत इति अन्यथा कृतः। S.—D. VI. 50.

आः—indicates anger. भ्रुकुटीधरः &c.—He knits his brow against me; frowns upon me. भ्रुकुटिमुखः *V. l.*—'casts a frowing look at me' is not so forcible as the reading in the text. आकूतज—caused by emotion or a ruffled state of the heart; see *infra*, V. 35. क्रोधोद्धतो० *V. l.* (see foot-note)—Tremor caused by wrath has seized the whole of their body violently shaking their hair. कोकनदं—a red lotus. छदः—a petal. उद्भट-Prominent, clearly displayed. For the fig. see com. विमर्दक्षमा—suitable for a fight.

ACT VI.

The sixth Act opens with an Interlude which describes the combat between the two princes indicated at the close of the last Act. [A rule of Bharata forbids a fight from being actually represented on the stage.] Râma's timely arrival puts an end to the fight. The principal event in the Act is Râma's meeting with Kusa and Lava. As Ráma is beginning to think the latter to be his sons from the conversation that ensues, Janaka and party are announced and the Act closes. The scene is laid in the vicinity of Válmîki's hermitage.

P. 140. अत्यद्भुत &c.—अत्यद्भुतेन उद्भ्रान्ताः flurried देवासुरा येषु. झणत् &c.—झणत् झणत् इति यत् कंकणानां क्वणितं तद्वत्क्वणितं यासां ताः झ...क्वणिताः (a comp. like उद्गमुख or चन्द्रकान्ति; Bah.) किंकिण्यः यस्मिन् तत्. ध्वनद् &c.—ध्वनन् यः गुरुः गुणः, अटन्यौ the two ends च ताभिः कृतः &c. करालः—fierce, harsh. स्तनयित्नु—a thundering cloud. विचित्राय मङ्गलाय *v. l.*—For diverse (manifold) welfare. Here विचित्र has no propriety (as it primarily means a combination of things opposed in their nature). अमन्द्रं—अमन्द *v. l.* not gentle, deep.

प्रवीर०—प्रकृष्टो वीरो Prâdi Tat. अनवरतं—ceaselessly. अविरल &c. —अविरलैः कनकमयानि कमलानि कनककमलानि तैः कमनीया संहतिः

mass वस्त्र. अविरलमिलित—*v. l.* dissolve अविरलं मिलिता विकचानां कमलानां संहतिर्यस्मिन् भ्रमरतरु॰--मणिसदृशा मुकुला मणिमुकुलाः jewel-like buds ; भ्रमरतरूणां ये तरुणा· fresh मणिमुकुलास्तेषां निकरस्य यो मकरन्दस्तेन सुन्दरः. तडिच्छटा—The streaks of lightning. कडार—tawny, brown.

P. 141. त्वाष्ट्रयन्त्र--त्वष्टुरिदं त्वाष्ट्रं belonging to Tvashṭri; त्वाष्ट्रस्य यन्त्रस्य भ्रमिभिः भ्रान्तः whirled round मार्तण्डः तस्य ज्योतिर्वदुज्ज्वलः· qualifies पुटभेद्. This alludes to the story of संज्ञा the wife of the sun and daughter of Viśvakarman or Tvashṭri. संज्ञा could not bear the overpowering splendour of her husband and retired into the forest. On knowing this her father placed the sun on his lathe with his consent and trimmed off a portion of his bright disc. He could, however, succeed in reducing only one-eighth of the sun's splendour. See notes to Ragh. VI. 32. ॰ज्योतिरुज्ज्वलः—to take this as one word is not good. For here the aspect of the sky is fancied to be aglow with the opening of the third eye of Śiva which is again compared to the lustre of the sun ground on the lathe of Tvashṭru. This is not happy. So it is better to take the two lines separately taking उज्ज्वलं as used predicatively उज्ज्वलं ॰ज्योतिः किम्; पुटभेदः किम् as forming two Utprekshás; see com· ललाट &c.-an awkward comp. पुटभेदः—The opening of the eye-lids. नीललोहित-Śiva; नीलः कण्ठे, लोहितो जटासु. Or according to the Skanda-P.—नीलं येन ममाङ्गं तु रसाक्तं लोहितं शिखा। नीललोहित इत्येव ततोऽहं परिकीर्तितः ॥ The third eye of Śiva is supposed to be always closed, lest its fire might burn the universe. *Cf.* Mudr. I. 2.

आग्नेयं—अग्निर्देवता अस्य presided over by fire; fr. अग्नि and एय (ढक्). अवदग्धः॰—अवदग्धानि अत एव कर्बुरितानि केतवश्चामराणि च येषाम्. The white silken cloths and chauries of the aerial cars being slightly burnt by the fire presented a variegated appearance. The description here is lifelike and clearly indicates the poet's power of description. ध्वजांशुक॰—ध्वजाः अंशुकान्येव पटाः अंशुकपटाश्च; see com.; here अंशुक has the secondary meaning of 'a garment of excellent texture, fine.' कुङ्कुमच्छुरण-tinging or colouring with saffron. विभ्रम—शोभा or भ्रान्ति. The banner clothes tinged with the glare of the upwards-preading flames appeared to a looker-on at a distance as if they had been coloured with saffron. The figure is निदर्शना. The Com. reads दहति &c.; see foot-note. नवकिंशुकद्युति॰ means—'which has the grace of, appears like, the splendour of, a fresh Kimśuka flower.

His reading does not seem to be appropriate. For in this case सविभ्रम has no force after स्रुति; and दहति also is meaningless. For, the gods hurrying away with their balloons had placed their flags out of the reach of the flames. Nor can the Vîdyâdharas refer to any hostile army on earth as Lava had none such.

उच्चण्ड &c.—उच्चण्ड: frightful य: वज्रखण्डस्य अवस्फोट: breaking up (*i. e.* the clap of thunder) तद्वत् पटु: loud रव: येषां तादृशै: स्फुलिङ्गै: sparks गुरु: awful.

उत्ताल°—उत्तालेन stupendous तुमुलेन mixed, confused च लेलिह्यानानां licking (pre. p. of the Frequentative of लिह्) उज्ज्वलन्तीनां ज्वालानां संभारेण mass भैरव: terrible. उषसि बुध्यते kindled इति उषर्बुध: fire. **अङ्गनाछाय**—अंशुकेना° *v. l.* is not genuine, as is shown by the following speech of the विद्याधरी.

P. 142. **स्निग्ध**—*lit.* unctuous, hence pleasing, agreeable. **मांसल**—*lit.* fat (owing to his bulky body). **आनन्द°**—आनन्देन मन्दं gently यथा तथा मुकुलिते closed घूर्णमाने च लोचने यस्या: । आनन्दसंदलितघूर्णमानवेदनाया: *v. l.*—whose spreading (increasing) pain is destroyed (removed) by joy. **अल्पम्** उदित: अल्पो°. just manifested, slightly affecting. **अविरल** &c.—अविरला विलोला घूर्णमाना च या विद्युल्लता तस्या: विलासै: मण्डिता: तै: । **प्रलय** &c.—प्रलये या वातावलयस्तासां क्षोभेण &c. **मेदुर**—deepened. **एकवार°**—एकवारेण विश्वस्य ग्रसनार्थं विकटं wide-opened विकरालं fierce यद् &c ; see com.

P. 143. **योगनिद्रा**—sleep of meditation (which is a state between जागृति and सुषुप्ति); see Ragh. X. 14, and अनुयुगान्तोचितयोगनिद्र: संहृत्य लोकान् पुरुषोऽधिशेते । *ibid.* XIII. 6.

विद्याकल्पेन—resembling विद्या correct knowledge; see com.; when referring to ब्रह्म it means (विद्या ब्रह्मविद्या एव कल्प: means तेन) by means of the knowledge of the true nature of Brahma and the world. **विवर्त**—see note on the word, *Supra*. III. 43. According to the Vedânta as expounded by Śaṃkarâchârya, प्रपञ्च is विवर्त an illusory appearance, ब्रह्म its अधिष्ठान being the only real entity. All illusions are dispelled by a correct knowledge of Brahma (the वस्तु). *Cf.* यत्र त्वस्य सर्वमात्मैवाभूत्तत्केन कं पश्येत् &c Bṛih. Up. IV. 14. See Bhâshya on Ved. Sût. II. 1. 14.

ससंभ्रम—ससंभ्रममुत्क्षिप्तेन करेण भ्रमित: उत्तरीयस्याञ्चलो येन (a sign for discontinuing the fight). **संगदितं**—शब्दै:......संविहितं *V. l*—Words uttered by. **संप्रहार**—fighting.

P. 144. कुलचन्द्र--चन्द्र when thus used means 'excellent, pre-eminent.' There is a sort of pathos in Râma's thus addressing the son of Lakshmaṇa. चन्द्र indicates power to gladden and to cool. चन्द्रकेतो--This is लाटानुप्रास (the repetition of the same word in different connexions). तुहि-नशकल०—suggests that Râma expected Chan. to be calm and not to be seized by the feverish anxiety caused by the fight. शममुपयातु चित्तदाह:--indicates the superiority of the दिनकर-कुलचन्द्र to the ordinary चन्द्र (who does not allay the inner heat). दिव्यास्त्र०--दिव्यास्त्राणां धर: देह: यस्य. This is equivalent to दिव्यास्त्रधरस्य तव देहस्य. The reading of the Com. is clearer in this respect.

अपि नाम--asks a question mixed with hope. It is all well &c. I hope it is.

कुशलं—Mark the nobility of Chandraketu's speech. महावी-रप्रकाण्डं—प्रशस्तो महावीर: महावीरप्रकाण्डं. प्रकाण्ड means originally 'a wellgrown (excellent) trunk of a tree; hence when used at the end of a comp. it means 'excellent;' प्रशंसावचनैश्च इति समास:. *Cf.* मतल्लिकामचर्चिकाप्रकाण्डमुद्धतल्लजो । प्रशस्तवाचकान्यमूनि । Ak. I. 4. 27. These words are नियतलिङ्ग, *i. e.* they retain their own gender unaltered; as ब्राह्मणमतल्लिका. वीरमनरालसाहसं *V. l.*--whose heroism is straightforward (free from trickery).

P. 145. परिणत: कायवान्—construe कायवान् परिणत: has become incarnate. We have here both फलोत्प्रेक्षा and वस्तूत्प्रेक्षा। ब्रह्मकोष—The treasure of the Vedas and the rites enjoined by them. It was the duty of the Kshatriyas to see that the Vedic rites were performed without hindrance—a duty which was scrupulously observed by ancient kings. The third and the fourth lines go together; सामर्थ्यानां समुदय: a collection इव आविर्भूय स्थित: &c.: निर्मीयन्ते इति निर्माणानि actions; जगत: पुण्यानि निर्माणानि तेषां राशि:. This śl. occurs in Mv. also (II. 40) where Vîra. says पुण्यैर्निर्मीयन्ते इति पुण्यनिर्माणानि पुण्यफलानीत्यर्थ: । कृत्यल्युटो बहुलमिति कर्मणि ल्युट्। भोजना: शालय इतिवत् । जगतां पुण्यनि-र्माणानि जगत्पुण्यनिर्माणानि । So this may also mean 'the aggregate of the fruits (results) of the meritorious deeds of the worlds'. The stanza contains a series of Utprekshâs (मालोत्प्रेक्षा).

आश्वास—what inspires confidence (which relieves anxiety); *cf.* विश्वसनीयता in अहो दीप्तिमतोऽपि विश्वसनीयतास्य राज्ञो वपुष: Śâk. II. प्रकृष्ट-most eminent, or existing in its entirety. प्रसाद:-purity, grace. मूर्तिसंचर:--मूर्त्या संचर: अस्य ; moving about by means of, *i. e.* appearing in a bodily form. कर्तृकरणे कृता बहुलमिति तृतीया-समासः. This word occurs in Mv. I. 10. The fig. is Utpreksha.

अस्मिन्दृष्टे इतीति—must be taken with each clause. विश्रान्तः-is laid at rest, ceased to exist. रसः निर्वृतिघनः—A feeling full of intense joy. प्रह्वयति—*lit.* makes me bend, *i. e.*, act humbly or submissively; this is a denom. from प्रह्व. महार्घः—of great value, precious (used figuratively); hence, most noble or praiseworthy. अतिशयः—Supreme excellence, extraordinary virtue. The fig. is अर्थान्तरन्यास with an Upamâ involved therein. This stanza is another instance of Bhavabhúti's descriptive power. Śloka quoted in D.-R. as an instance of Śakti, one of the *aṅgas* of Avamarsha-Saṃdhi.

P. 146. एककरे—*adv.* meaning 'at once.' ०विश्रामं—should be grammatically विश्रमं. See com. on विश्रामो हृदयस्य &c. p. 3. It may, somehow, be defended as विश्रम एव विश्रामः by affixing अण् स्वार्थे, by प्रज्ञादिभ्योऽण् (as प्रज्ञ एव प्राज्ञः), though this word is not actually included in that group. See our note on the word at Śâk. II. 6.

निमित्तसव्यपेक्षः—व्यपेक्षया expectancy सह वर्तते सव्यपेक्षः; निमित्तेन सव्यपेक्षः . निमित्त of course means here 'an external (बाह्य or दृष्ट) cause, as is clear from कुतोपि निमित्तात् and आन्तरः कोपि हेतुः in the next śloka. विप्रतिषिद्ध—Contradictory. Supply a च after this to make the contradiction more prominent. The च is already found in the Mâl. Mâdh. where this passage and the following śloka both occur. Love, and that it should depend upon some external cause,' &c. The meaning is that true love cannot depend upon an external cause, since it must vanish as soon as the cause disappears; it must be spontaneous. *Cf.* Jagaddhara—निमित्तमिह द्वयं बाह्यमाभ्यन्तरं च । तदिह बाह्यहेत्वपेक्षः स्नेहोऽस्थिर एव । निमित्तनिवृत्तौ तन्निवृत्तेरावश्यकत्वात् । अत आन्तरनिमित्तापेक्षैव स्नेहस्येति भावः ।

व्यतिषजति—links or joins together. बहिरुपाधीन्—external conditions or accidents, such as beauty of person &c. पुण्डरीक—means here पद्म a day-lotus. The figure is अर्थान्तरन्यास (विशेषेण सामान्यसमर्थनरूप); see Jag. on Mâl.-Mâdh; according to some it is दृष्टान्त.

धर्मतः—by duty which requires one to treat a friend's father as one's own father. व्यपदेश०—title of address. गर्भच्छद—The internal leaf. पीन—*lit.* fat or stout; hence thrilling; *cf.* मांसल above, p. 142.

P. 147. चन्द्र—Mr. Ghâte interprets this as 'camphor', but camphor can have no निष्यन्द. Probably he means an unguent of sandal mixed with camphor.

एभ्य:—The Dat. is indefensible; we should expect the Acc. by क्रुधद्रुहोरुपसृष्टयोः कर्म. The Com.'s explanation is inadequate. Perhaps the poet wrote अति द्रुग्धं. The reading एभ्यः द्रोग्धुमज्ञेनायुधपरिग्रहः कृतः is free from this fault. But it does not express Lava's idea so forcibly as the former. दुर्योग:—inconsiderateness, bad resolve. अनुयात्रिक—see p. 119.

स्वः भाव:-his characteristic, innate, disposition. प्रकृतिनियतत्वात्-being inherent in or an inseparable property of his nature. किमाश्रेयो &c.—The fig. is Arthántaranyása. *Cf* यदचेतनोऽपि पादैः स्पृष्टः प्रज्वलति सवितुरिनकान्तः। तत्तेजस्वी पुरुषः परकृतनिकृतिं कथं सहते॥ Bhar. Nît. 37; also Kir. I. 43.

P. 148. अमर्ष—Anger; non-endurance; *cf.* अमर्षशून्येन Kir. I. 33. The word is used in a slightly different sense (jealous anger) at p. 137. विलक्षितानि-driven out of their wits, abashed.

आम्नायवान्ति—आम्नाय means the same thing as संप्रदाय, the particular formula handed down by tradition. ब्रह्मादय: &c.—The verse has already occurred; see I. 15. उपनिषद्—any mystical lore that is secretly communicated by the Guru to his disciple. From सद् with उप and नि to sit near (knowledge which a pupil derives by sitting near his preceptor in solitude). मन्त्रपारायणो॰ *v. l*—the knowledge of mastering the mystical charms. But here पारायण has no sense; it must be taken by *Lakshaṇá* to mean 'all the mantras.' परःसहस्र॰—सहस्रात्पराः परःसहस्राः ये संवत्सराः तानन्तेवासी who had been his pupil for more than a thousand years.

P. 149. प्रकृष्ट—Exalted, of a superior order. उपादान—a cause. It generally means 'immediate or material cause.' See p. 74 and notes.

किमात्थ &c.—This is an instance of what is called आकाशभाषित in Sanskrit dramas. It is a speech addressed to a character not present on the stage. It is defined as किं ब्रवीष्येवमित्यादि विना पात्रं ब्रवीति यत्। श्रुत्वेवानुक्तमप्येकस्तत्स्यादाकाशभाषितम्॥ Das.-R. अधिराज:—अधिको राजा a Prádi Sam. शस्त्रशिख॰—शिखी has no special propriety here; it is used for alliteration.

मेचक—dark blue. नवनील॰—नीलश्चासो नीरधरश्च नील॰, नवः यः नील॰ तस्य यद् धीरं गर्जितं तदेव क्षणः festive occasion, joy, तेन बद्धाः कुड्मला येन स नव॰ कदम्बस्तस्येव डम्बरः यस्य। तत्सदृश इत्यर्थः।

क्षण may also be taken in the sense of 'moment, instant,' गर्जितस्य क्षणस्तस्मिन् &c. भरताश्रमात्—See p. 119, Lava's speech.

वृत्तेन्द्राभय०—We learn from the Puráṇas that the kings of the solar race had been of constant assistance to Indra in his wars with the demons. *Cf.* our note on Kakutstha, Ragh. VI. 71. Even Râma had undertaken the war with Rávaṇa for the purpose of liberating Indra and other gods from the clutches of that demon. वैवस्वतात्—The reference here is to the seventh Manu, the son of Vivasvat or Sun and the progenitor of the solar race. He was the first king of Ayodhyá.- इक्ष्वाकूणां &c.—*Cf.* Ragh. I. 25, 28, IV. 35 &c.

P. 150. नीराजित--with the light waved about, illuminated or lighted up; p. p. p. of राज् cau. with निर्. नीराजन is a waving of light usually before an idol, and occasionally before a successful king returning home, and so on. It was also a cere-mony performed by kings or generals before starting on a campaign in the month of Âśvina, when lights were waved also before horses, elephants, &c.; see our note on Ragh. IV. 25; *cf.* Var. Bṛih. Saṃ. Ch. 44. क्षीरस्वामी explains this as नीरस्य शान्त्युदकस्य अजनं क्षेपोत्र नीराजनं वाहनायुधादेर्निःशेषेण राजनं वात्र ।.

विकटं—in a proud or haughty manner. पौरुषातिरेकः—Excess of manly power or heroism.

तृणीकृत—अतृणं तृणं संपद्यमानः कृतः तृणीकृतः. सत्त्वसार—The best or concentrated energies of. धीरा—steady, dignified. नमयतीव &c.—The fig. is उत्प्रेक्षा. वीरो रसः &c.—The fig. is संशयालंकार. Śl. quoted in D.-R. and S.-D. as an instance of Vilása.

उत्कण्ठते—Denom. from उत्कण्ठ (eagerly longing); is used with the Gen. or Dat.

P. 151. ब्रह्मकोष--see above, Śl. 9. आशंसनीय--To be desired or wished for. उपसदन—The proper form of approaching. धर्मतातः--धर्मेण प्राप्तः तातः, the relation following from that of friendship. अनवनीयः—अनिन्द्यः not blameable. This remark of Kuśa is quite in keeping with his true chivalrous spirit. For though it was no dishonour to him to bend before a worthy Bráhmaṇa, as a true Kshatriya he could not have done so before a Kshatriya, as that would have been acknowledging his superiority in power, &c.

प्रासादिक—amiable, winning (*lit.* always inclined to favour). व्यवीवृतत्—caused to exist, *i. e.* employed in the composition of Aor. of the Cau. of वृत् with वि. This appears to be the genuine reading; for the poet himself calls his Râmâyaṇa a विषत of शब्दब्रह्म ; see *supra.* p. 51. अवीवृधत्—*v. l.* increased ; Aor. of the cau. of वृध् ; this is not appropriate.

P. 152. संहननं—The build or frame of the body. सिंहसंहनन *V. l.*—handsome make ; वराङ्गरूपोपेतो यः सिंहसंहननो हि सः । Amara. सिंहं श्रेष्ठं संहननं यस्य ; संहननेन सिंह इति वा. This reading also will do as well. This line occurs also in Mv. II. 45.

अङ्गादङ्गात्—*i. e.* from every limb. निजस्नेह०—It will be better to read निजः. स्नेहजः देहसारः—The essence of the body due to affection. निजो देहजः स्नेहसारः—The essence of my affection flowing from my body. This is not a good reading, as the words अङ्गादङ्गात् सुतः show that it is the देहसार that is meant. *Cf.* the Śruti quoted by the Com. Its full text is—अङ्गादङ्गात्संभवसि हृदयादभिजायसे । आत्मा वै पुत्रनामासि स जीव शरदः शतम्॥ धातुः—The element of. The stanza contains four Utprekshâs.

ललाटंतप—उपपदसमासः; see com. The rule is असूर्यललाटयोर्दृशितपोः । Pâṇ. III. 2. 36. खश् (अ) is added to दृश् and तप् respectively after असूर्य and ललाट ; so असूर्यंपश्याः राजदाराः. A nasal is added to the first member when a termination having an indicatory ख् is added to the root. ०च्छाये—छाया बाहुल्ये इति नपुंसकत्वम्.

P. 153. वत्सस्य—संप्रदानस्य शेषत्वविवक्षायां षष्ठी. प्रश्रययोगेपि—For the force of अपि *cf.* note on राजन्येपि प्रश्रयः above. भावाः—Actions, ways of behaviour.

अविहितसिद्धाः—नास्ति विहितं विधानं यस्मिन्कर्मणि तद्यथा तथा without artificial means सिद्धाः । स्वभावसिद्धा इत्यर्थः. लक्ष्मीविलासाः—The graces of beauty. प्रतिकल०—कलायां कलायामिति । केतयन्ति—disclose or set off, adorn. The Com. reads ०रमणीयां कान्तिमुद्भेदयन्ति which makes the construction difficult ; and he has to explain the presence of the other object कान्ति by taking उद्भेदयन्ति as a verb governing two objects, but without authority. The reading of the first line वपुरवियुतसिद्धाः avoids this difficulty. The cons. is—वपुरवियुतसिद्धाः लक्ष्मीविलासाः कमनीयां ०कान्तिमुद्भेदयन्ति. The graces of their beauty which are inseparable from the body (वपुषा अवियुताः वपुरवियुताश्च ते सिद्धाश्च) and natural, give rise to (unfold) a complexion &c. But this is not a happy reading. For वपुः better compares with रत्न or पद्म having कान्ति. चन्द्रं for रत्नं is not a good reading. ते—well-known.

०च्छाया—The collective appearance, bodily resemblance.

कठोर—Fully developed. सुवन्धुर—well-turned or curved; hence—beautifully formed. अवन्धुरांसयोः—*V. l.* having अवन्धुरौ (not depressed, covered with flesh) muscular अंसौ shoulders ययोः—must be connected with अनयोः. अवन्धुरांसकं *V. l.*—is bad, as it involves tautology. Ślokas 24, 25 give the characteristic marks of a *Samrâṭ*.

P. 154. अनुरूपं—अनुरूपस्य भावः (भावप्रधानो निर्देशः) resemblance. उन्नेय—To be made out; observable. मुक्ता°—मुक्तावत् like pearls अच्छा ये दन्ताः तेषां छव्या सुन्दरा. °वन्धुरा *V. l.*—*Lit.* with the rays (छवि) spreading out like teeth; hence, brightened or illuminated with. कर्णपाशः—प्रशस्तः कर्णः कर्णपाशः a beautiful ear. पाश coming after केश means 'a collection,' while after कर्ण it has the sense of 'beautiful.' पाशस्तु मृगपक्ष्यादिबन्धने। कर्णान्ते शोभनार्थः स्यात्कचान्ते निकरार्थकः। छात्राद्यन्ते च निन्दार्थः। इति हेमः। नेत्रे रक्तनीले—red (as they were warriors) and blue. Sîtâ's were नील (dark) only. सौभाग्यगुणः—The excellence of beauty.

तत्र विमृशामि—I think over it. °प्रासङ्गिकं—(permission) given on the occasion of. उद्भूतं—Come to pass has taken effect. संप्लवमान—swimming in, overwhelmed with, doubts. विस्रम्भयते—inspires confidence; cau. of स्रम्भ् (or श्रम्भ्) with वि I. A'. to confide in. *Cf.* सतां हि संदेहपदेषु वस्तुषु प्रमाणमन्तःकरणप्रवृत्तयः। Śák. I. 22. The joy which Râma's heart felt assured him that he was right in his conjecture. The Com. reads-अयं विस्मयसंप्लवमान &c., which means—'This excess of pleasure and grief floating on-full of-wonder, is the delusion of (deludes) my heart.' But this does not agree well with what follows. आत्मसंवादः—reassurance of what I myself felt, a confirmation of my own experience. द्विधा प्रतिपन्नः—was ascertained or found to be consisting of two parts.

P. 155. विकास—properly, unfolding; hence, development, growth. जडदृश्—with eyes dull, not seeing clearly, *i. e.* half closed. परामर्शकलया—by a gentle or skilful touch; कला may mean 'skill.'

अवश्याय—dew-drops. The fig. is निदर्शना.

सीतादेव्याः......रघुपतेः—From the use of these terms it appears that the boys were kept in the dark as regards their real parentage and their relation with the personages of the Râmâyaṇa. They did not even know that Sîtá was their mother. The whole mystery is unravelled when the boys are introduced to their parents at the close of the drama. प्रियप्रायो &c.—is an *arthántaranyása* strengthening the statement in the first line.

तटस्थित:—Because the boys spoke as if they were strangers to Sîtá, and consequently to Râma also. Had Kus'a spoken of Sîtá as मातुः or जनन्याः, Râma would have concluded that they were her sons. स्नेहपरिप्लव—overwhelmed with, pervaded by, affection. पारिप्लवः विकारः *v. l.*—an excited state of feeling. But पारिप्लव (चञ्चल) does not well fit in with विकार. The Com. reads संप्लवाधिकारः—This act of jumping to (at once entertaining). निर्निबन्ध०—any object of desire; see com.; 'with the agitation of my heart thus broken out, *i. e.* manifested.'

P. 156. अन्तरयामि—I shall conceal my agitation, collect myself. निष्यन्द-*lit.* the flow or essence of; hence, the production or outcome of. आवृत्तः—repeated, studied. प्रकृत्यैव &c.—The slokas found in the extant rec. of the Ràmá. are प्रिया तु सीता रामस्य दाराः पितृकृता इति । गुणाद्रूपगुणाच्चापि प्रीतिर्भूयोऽभिवर्धते । तस्याश्च भर्ता द्विगुणं हृदये परिवर्तते । अन्तर्गतमपि व्यक्तमाख्याति हृदयं हृदा ॥ Bál.-K. 17. 26, 27. The Com. reads the fist śl. nearly as in the Rámá. See foot-note.

वज्रपात-a blow to. निरन्वयविपर्यास० -निरन्वयः (निर्गतः अन्वयः यस्मात्) causeless, unaccountable, *i. e.* sudden, विपर्यास change reverses; तेन विरसवृत्ति—unpleasant, disagreeable. विप्रलम्भ—non-fulfilment of one's wishes. पर्यवसायिन्—ending in वि०, illusory; or विप्रलम्भ may meau 'separation'; see com.

P. 157. बहुल—great, most pleasing by or abounding in. अन्योन्यं यत्नाः—*v. l.* efforts to please each other. कौतुकरसाः—enjoyment of delights; or, eagerness or fondness for delights, as the Com. takes it. प्राणः—used in the sense of जीव or मुख्य प्राण, and hence the singular.

एकोन्मीलन &c.—एकं एकदेव वा यदुन्मीलनं तत्र पेशलः. उन्मीलन does not mean 'development' here, but unfolding, presenting to the mind; पेशलः—clever or skilled in, able to. The readfng क्रमो० lessens the force of the idea. All the qualities of Sîtâ rise up in his memory all at once.

P. 158. तदा—At that time, *viz.* that referred to in slokas 31, 32 above; *v. l.* यदा is not good; the स्तनमुकुल was already विस्तारि then आकूत—a longing for each other, emotion यत्र—यस्मिन्काले. मन्दाकिनी—This is not the Ganges, but some small river in the vicinity of Chitrakúṭa, as that mountain was, according to the Rámá., about ten Krośas from Prayága. *Cf.* अथ शैलाद्विनिष्क्रम्य मैथिलीं कोशलेश्वरः । अदर्शयच्छुभजलां रम्यां मन्दाकिनीं नदीम् ॥ Ayod.-K. 95. 1. त्वदर्थमिव...प्रवृष्ट इव—For the Kesara tree is very rich in flowers which fall down all round. The fig. is. उत्प्रेक्षा. This Śloka occurs in the Rámâyaṇa in a chapter which the Nirṇayasâgar edition gives as प्रक्षिप्त between chapters 95 and 96 of the Ayodhyá-Kaṇḍa, with the reading त्वदर्थमिह विन्यस्ता त्वियं श्लक्ष्णसमा शिला । यस्याः पार्श्वे तरुः पुष्पैः मवि (वृ) ष्ट इव केसरैः ॥ See Com.'s remark.

मुग्धः—Because in their boyish innocence they did not know that those allusions would cause pain to Ráma's mind.

P. 159. प्रसृत &c.—प्रसृतः यः मन्दः मन्दाकिनीसंबन्धी मरुत् तेन तालिता ये अलकाः curly hair तैः व्याकुला obscured, covered ललाटचन्द्रस्य द्युतिर्यस्मिन्. अकुंकुम &c.—see the Com.'s remark. उत्प्रेक्ष्यते—is pictured, *i. e.* appears vividly before my mind's eye. निराभरण &c.—*i. e.* it was आभरणस्याभरणं; not that ornaments graced it, but on the contrary impaired its beauty.

प्रवासे—when out on a journey; in separation. विकल्पव्युपरमे-When the fabric of fancy is dissolved, when the image worked up by fancy vanishes. कुकूलानां—is appropriate. The heart is burnt as it were on a fire, which is slow but intense and steady in its action.

P. 160. विदूराभ्रमतया—explains भ्रमजडाः which in its turn explains चिरेणागच्छन्ति. विश्लथजटाः *v. l.*—with their matted hair loosened.

जुष्टे—shared by, in which they took part. महावैशसे—The extremely cruel deed, *i. e.* Sîtá's destruction. रामेण किं दुष्करम्—This is one of the many reflections by Râma on his own cruel action which ever afterwards had been constantly haunting and pricking his mind. See note on कृतं रामसदृशं कर्म p. 56.

अनुभावे—his majestic appearance. See *supra*, p. 33. प्रथमप्रमूढ &c.—This bears testimony to Janaka's tender-heartedness towards, and extreme affection for, Ráma. Though he was wroth with Ràma for his exile of Sitâ, his anger melted away as soon as he saw the emaciated figure of Râma and fell into a swoon. विधुर—विगता धूः कार्यभारः यस्य: unnerved, languid; hence, afflicted, overpowered with emotion. The reading प्रथमप्रबुद्धजनकप्रबोधिताः means—made aware about Ráma by Janaka who recognized him first; see com. It is not a good reading, for it is not possible that Janaka should know Ráma before his own mother.

ACT VII.

A peculiar feature of this Act is that it opens with a drama composed by Vâlmîki and represented on the stage by heavenly damsels before an audience composed of Ráma, Lakshmaṇa, the citizens of Ayodhyâ and the principal inhabitants of the three worlds. This plan is adopted by Vâlmîki in order to bring home to the minds of the subjects of Ráma the innocence of Sitá and their own guilt in doubting her chastity. This purpose is well served and the Act closes with the final union of Ráma, Sîtâ and their two sons, and is in this respect comparable with the last Act of Kálidása's Śàkuntala wherein also we find the happy union of the hero with his son and wife long after she had been repudiated in a state of pregnancy. The scene of this Act also is laid in the neighbourhood of Vâlmîki's hermitage.

P. 162. सब्रह्मक्षत्र०—The separate mention of ब्रह्म and क्षत्र is by the ब्राह्मणवसिष्ठन्याय or the गोबलीवर्दन्याय. नायकनिकाय—निकाय is a collection of beings having similar qualities &c.; *cf.* पशूनां समजोऽन्येषां समाजोऽथ सधर्मिणाम् । स्वान्निकायः । Amara. स्थावरः—*i. e.* their presiding deities. We have already met with such in the persons of Tamasá, Muralà and others. भूतग्रामः–ग्राम when at the end of a compound means 'a collection or multitude.' आतोद्यस्थान—आसमन्तात्तुद्यते ताड्यते आतोद्यं a musical instrument ; ०स्थान a place were musical instruments are played upon; hence, here, 'a theatre.'

राज्याश्रम—is a Rûpaka-Samâsa. The meaning is—Though he lived a strictly pious life he could have married a second wife after his exile of Sîtá, at least for the performance of religous rites and for progeny, without violating the rules of that life; and yet he did not do so but lived the abstemious life of an ascetic. This brings out the force of अपि. We know from the Raghuvaṃśa that the kings of the solar race always lived a semi-ascetic life considering their kingdom a hermitage. *Cf.* राज्याश्रममुनिं मुनिः Ragh. I. 58.

वाल्मीकिगौरवात्—Ráma did care to see plays acted. But he was coming to see this play, the nature of which he did not know, out of respect for Vâlmîki. प्राश्निकाः *V. l.*—*Lit.* those who are fit to ask questions (and discuss a matter); judges (of the merits and demerits of a performanee); from प्रश्न + इक (ठक्) by तदर्हति Pâṇ. V. I. 63. There were persons of high literary attainments and were given seats on the stage. See com.

स्थानप्रतिपत्ति—a seat of honour. For this sense of प्रतिपत्ति comp. Ragh. XIV. 22; सामान्यप्रतिपत्तिपूर्वकं Śâk. IV. 17.

P. 163. प्रत्यय-knowledge of; it may also mean 'confidence.' See Com.'s remark. It seems that no throne was placed for Râma, as the celestials were to come to witness the play; but a rich seat, such as a carpet, was spread out for him to sit upon. भूतार्थवादी—one who speaks things as they happened; hence, a truth-speaker. It is a हेतुगर्भविशे०; his words, therefore, must not be distrusted. *Cf.* Vâlmîki's address to Râma-प्रचेतसोऽहं दशमः पुत्रो राघवनन्दन। न स्मराम्यनृतं वाक्यमिमौ तु तव पुत्रको॥ बहुवर्षसहस्राणि तपश्चर्या मया कृता। नोपाश्नीयां फलं तस्या दुष्टेयं यदि मैथिली॥ मनसा कर्मणा वाचा भूतपूर्वं न किल्बिषम्। तस्याहं फलमश्नामि अपापा मैथिली यदि॥ Uttara-Kâṇḍa, Ch. 97. 18-20. आर्षेण चक्षुषा—This is put in to exclude the possibility of its being perceived wrongly. किंचित् and काव्यगौरवात् bespeak modesty on Vâmîki's part. कार्यगौ० *v. l.* is better.

P. 164. एतदुक्तं भवति—This is what is meant. साक्षात्कृत०-This is a significant epithet. It means—The sages are the beholders of holy law (*i. e.* they know it intuitively) and therefore they know how to decide what is right and what is wrong. The expression seems to have occured to the poet from the following passage of the Nirukta—साक्षात्कृतधर्माण ऋषयो बभूवुस्तेऽवरेभ्योऽसाक्षात्कृतधर्मभ्य उपदेशेन मन्त्रान्संप्रादुः। Chap. I. अमृतसाराणि—having for their essence the knowledge of Brahma or Moksha (the eternal truth). The meaning 'ambrosial' is inappropriate. अमृतंभराणि *V. l.*—possessing, full of, अमृत the knowledge of Brahma. अमृतं भराणि अमृतंभराणि; see com. परोरजांसि—beyond foulness, clear; their inward eye is never bedimmed by foulness, but always perceives clearly. व्याहन्यन्ते—are obstructed, prove false. अन्यद्—something quite unexpected.

P. 165. हताशां—हता already destroyed आशा यस्याः सा having no hope, helpless. अपमवेक्षस्व &c.—Râma in his agitation caused by his overpowering love for his wife forgets that it was a dramatic representation, and believing that the event was just happening thus exclaims. लक्ष्मणमवेक्षस्व—*v. l.* Look to, have regard for, Lakshmaṇa. In this case the meaning will be—As I abandoned you without cause, you have just reason to be angry with me and so you won't care for me. But have regard for Lak. at least who served you like a son in our exile and who would be extremely grieved at your loss. See com. प्रबन्धार्थ—The representation. उत्सङ्गित—taken in the lap; p. p. p. of the denom. from उत्सङ्ग. The दारक are the infants brought by the dramatist to represent Kuśa and Lava, who were sitting near Râma. अनिबन्धनं—causeless, unaccountable; hence, sudden. अन्धतमसं—अन्धयतीति अन्धं; अन्धं च तत्तमः. अ is added to the final of तमस् after अव, सम् and अन्ध. The Com.'s reading does not give a good sense.

P. 166. कल्याणप्ररोह:—Now it is कल्याणप्ररोह; this is an echo of the sentiment expressed by Chandraketu in V. 25. Also, a blessing is implied in this. उचित—उपचित *v. l.* collected, laid in store. कल्याणसंपदं—excellent blessings.

P. 167. अभ्युपपन्ना—Favoured. इति जितमपत्यस्नेहेन—*Cf.* Śák. IV. 6. मोहग्रन्थि:—the knot of infatuation. It is this affection that ties down men to the world. It spreads a delusion over the mind and prevents it from seeing the real nature of things. This refers to the doctrine of Mâyá which makes men believe the unreal world to be real. गूढग्रन्थि:—*v. l.* means the secret tie which binds together the two (the parent and the offspring). मूढग्रन्थि, another reading, is bad. as मूढ cannot be taken with ग्रन्थि without some twisting of sense. It does not seem to be the Com.'s reading (though found in the com.) from the plain way in which he explains it. अनुपप्लव:—which nothing can overpower (cut off). उपप्लव: *v. l.*—which overpowers sentient beings. सीतां प्रसूय—when I am the mother of Sítá, how can I not feel for her? सोढ:—With एक: *v. l.* the meaning will be एक: राक्षसमध्यवास: दुःसहः द्वितीयस्तु सुदुःसहः. The reading तु for च is preferable.

पाकाभिमुखस्य—for the idea *cf.* अथ वा भवितव्यानां द्वाराणि भवन्ति सर्वत्र। Śák. I. 15; देवी च सिद्धिरपि लङ्घयितुं न शक्या। Mṛich. VI. 2.

P. 168. सदृशमुक्तम्—This is ironical. She does not accept the philosophy of Bhâgírathí as is apparent from her next question.

प्रमाणीकृत:—Considered an authority against his decision. She means to say that Râma would have found reason to alter his decision, had he shown the slightest regard for any one of these. अनुवृत्ति—her obedient conduct.

शरीरमसि—and so you ought to know the thoughts and inward feelings of all. Here शरीर is used in the secondary sense of 'the support of,' that which upholds it (the body with the soul), as the mere body is incapable of feeling.

इक्ष्वाकूणां &c.–*Cf.* I. 41. इह विषमे—In this difficulty, being in such a fix. *Cf.* Ragh. XIV. 34. तदतिगहनं—*v. l.* and that is a very hard thing to do. Here तद् refers to यद् in the preceding line. The reading तमसि विषमे is not very intelligible unless तमसि be taken in the secondary sense of 'perplexity of the mind.' The reading in the text is certainly preferable.

P. 169. अन्तःप्रकाशः—Inner light., *i. e.* knowledge of the inward feelings and thoughts of others.

तथाऽप्येष मे अञ्जलिः—Mark the tender-heartedness of Gaṅgā. She entirely identifies herself with the race of Bhagîratha and folds her hands to Prithivî to implore her forgiveness. In some editions these words are put into the mouth of Lakshmaṇa, but as such they are quite out of place, nor is then Prithivî's reply to Gaṅgâ, त्वियं प्रसन्नास्मि वः, intelligible. आपातदुःसहः०—unbearable in its first charge or onset, overpowering at the first attack; qualifies संवेग (agitation due to affection).

गर्भरूपेषु—गर्भ a new-born child; ०रूपेषु—those who are to them in the relation of children to be tenderly taken care of.

विलय—disappearance, merging into. *Cf.* यथाऽहं राघवादन्यं मनसाऽपि न चिन्तये । तथा मे माधवी देवी विवरं दातुमर्हति ॥ 14 &c., Rámá. Uttar.-K. Ch. 97 ; also Ragh. XV. 81, where Sîtâ seriously contemplates the step. अपेक्षणीयौ &c.—A departure from the Râmâyaṇa. According to it, as soon as Sîtá made the request the earth opened and from the chasm a celestial throne, adorned with bright jewels, came out with the goddess पृथ्वी seated thereon. She placed Sîtâ on her lap and entered the earth with her again, while the gods showered flowers on her. तामासनगतां दृष्ट्वा प्रविशन्तीं रसातलम् । पुष्पवृष्टिरविच्छिन्ना दिव्या सीतामवाकिरत् ॥. See Intro.

P. 170. प्रकृष्यते—is enhanced.

P. 171. वत्सयोः—कर्मणि षष्ठी. विस्मय०-विस्मय at the strangeness of events, आनन्द at the prospect of progeny. जर्जरः—broken through, intermixed with. करुणोर्मयः—The waves of pathos The comparison to the sea, which is implied herein, shows that the sentiment of Karuṇa is all-pervading.

वसिष्ठगुरूणां—*Cf.* Ragh. I. 60-64.

P. 172. आङ्गिरस—is Śatánanda, the son of Gautama (a descendant of Aṅgiras) and family-priest of the Janaka family.

उपायैः—used in the sense of हेतु, means or circumstances leading to conviction. These are given in the next couplet. द्वादशाब्दिको—द्वादश अब्दान् भूतो twelve years old. 'तमधीष्टो भृतो भूतो भावी' (Páṇ. V. 1. 80) इति ठञ् (इक) प्रमुग्धः—at a loss to decide. पर्यङ्कीकुरु—*Cf. supra* śl. 8. Prithivî merely wanted Sîtá to sit down. Ráma, however, understands this to be a permission to Sîtá to enter the bowels of the earth, and hence exclaims लोकान्तरं गतासि. मन्नियोगतः—at my command.

P. 173. चारित्र—virtuous conduct.

काव्यार्थः—The desired or final end of a poem. Lakshmaṇa asks Válmîki if he wrote his Kávya simply for such a tragic end. Here ends the गर्भनाटक. देवर्षि०—देवाश्च ऋषयश्च तेः; or देवर्षि one of the seven kinds of saints. See our note on राजर्षि, Vik. p. 12. पुण्यव्रता—of virtuous or holy conduct.

P. 174. शालीन०—शालाप्रवेशमर्हति शालीनः अधृष्टः; *lit.* one deserving to be in the house; hence, modest. खञ् is added in this sense by 'शालीनकौपीने अधृष्टाकार्ययोः' Páṇ. V. 2. 20. ०शीलता—habitual or natural bashfulness. जगत्पते—This explains why she obeyed his order. आत्मनो वचनं—refers to p. 45. अनृणा—अविद्यमानं ऋणं यस्याः सा. उत्क्रमासीद्वायु०—See p. 45.

P. 175. लोकपालाः—इन्द्रो वह्निः पितृपतिर्नैर्ऋतो वरुणो मरुत्। कुबेर ईशः पतयः पूर्वादीनां दिशां क्रमात् ॥ Amara. सप्तर्षयः—these are मरीचि, अत्रि, अङ्गिरस्, पुलस्त्य, पुलह, क्रतु and वसिष्ठ. उपतिष्ठन्ते—The A'tm. shows that Sitá was treated as a deity. स्था takes A'tm. by the Várt. उपाद्देवपूजासंगतिकरण &c. धर्मचारिणी—धर्मं चरितुं शीलमस्याः or धर्मं पुण्यमवश्यं चरतीति. हिरण्मयी—हिरण्यस्य विकारो हिरण्मयी. प्रकृति—the original of a thing.

कृतार्थोऽस्मि—Mark how Lakshmaṇa takes sincere delight in the re-union of Ráma and Sîtá. It was the one object of his life to behold his brother and sister-in-law live in perfect happiness.

P. 176. निर्लज्जः लक्ष्मणः—Mark the modesty of Lakshmaṇa. Though he accompanied Sîtá to the forest and left her there expressly at the stern command of his brother, still he thinks that he was in some measure guilty, and calls himself निर्लज्ज in that he came forth to bow to her now. ईदृशस्त्वं—you who feel in this way, *i. e.* who bear such affection for me; see also com. The reading ईदृशोऽपि is bad; it means 'although you are such Sità will not say anything that will displease Lakshmaṇa.' Gh. reads वत्ससदृशत्वं ; but वत्ससदृश has no propriety here.

पुनर्जन्मान्तर॰—Who have again entered upon a new existence. लोकान्तरगतां v. l.—that had (almost) gone to the other world. ईदृश्येव—see com.

P. 177. उत्खातलवण:—For Lavaṇa see notes to p. 45. We know from the first that Śatrughna was sent by Râma to destroy Lavaṇa ; now he returns after twelve years. मधुरेश्वर:—After Śatrughna killed Lavaṇa, he founded, on the scene of his victory, a city which he named Mathurâ or Madhurâ. *Cf.* Ragh. XV. 28; also Bhâg. P. शत्रुघ्नश्च मधोः पुत्रो लवणं नाम राक्षसम् । हत्वा मधुवने चक्रे मथुरां नाम वै पुरीम् ॥. Śatrughna was, after this, installed king of Madhurâ by Râma as already promised. सानुषङ्गाणि—Closely following one another, or coming in close succession. अनुषङ्ग—close contact, conjunction. न प्रत्येमि—According to the Com., this means—'I have no faith in their stability or permanence (from past experiences).' प्रकृतिरियं—*i. e.* their unpermanence, transitoriness. Or better, न प्रत्येमि I am not aware of anything, so much overwhelmed with good fortunes I am. In this case इति प्रकृतिः will mean—to overwhelm one by coming upon one in such rapid succession.

इदमस्तु—This is the भरतवाक्य or the concluding stanza of a drama containing a benediction, so called because it is sung by the Bharata (actor) divesting himself of his dramatic character. For herein he refers to the conditions and people of his own time.

सेयं कथा—*i. e.* the story of Ráma's life as given in the Râmâyaṇa. पुनाति and वर्धयति are preferable to पुनातु and वर्धयतु as the perusal of the Râmâyaṇa was believed to be purifying long before the time of Bhavabhúti. मङ्गल्या च मनोहरा च—qualifies कथा and also माता and गङ्गा; see com.

परिभावयन्तु—Revolve in their minds, reflect on; *i. e.* read and enjoy. अभिनयैः विन्यस्तरूपां—cast in the form of a drama; *lit.* in a form marked by, *i. e.* capable of being represented by gesticulations. शब्दब्रह्मविदः कवेः—Here the poet, though outwardly referring to Vâlmîki, makes an allusion to himself also. The Com. takes शब्दब्रह्मविदः as qualifying बुधाः. It is better taken with कवेः; *cf. supra*, आविर्भूतशब्दब्रह्मप्रकाशः &c. p. 51. In the third and fourth lines the words एतां and इमां occur, and one of them seems to be redundant. The redundancy, however, can be got over by construing the lines as—बुधाः प्राज्ञस्य शब्दब्रह्मविदः कवेः (वाल्मीकेः) तां एतां (कथां) अभिनयैः विन्यस्तरूपां इमां परिणतां (which is developed or has assumed the form of) वाणीं (this composition) परिभावयन्तु. See translation. Another meaning also is intended by the poet:—तामिताां (वाल्मीकेः कथां) प्राज्ञस्य शब्दब्रह्मविदः कवेः (भवभूतेः) अभिनयैः विन्यस्तरूपां परिणतां (matured, refined) इमां वाणीं परिभावयन्तु—'May the wise consider that this story (of Vâlmîki) is the same as this perfect composition of the erudite poet Bhavabhûti who knew the Brahma in the form of words.' What the poet means is that his play also is as ennobling and purifying as the work of Vâlmîki, the same being invested with dramatic interest, with the suggestion that he is also as great a writer as Vâlmîki. And Bhavabhûti is not far wrong in this estimate of himself. *Cf.* the opinion of Râjaśekhara—बभूव वल्मीकिभवः पुरा &c., quoted in the Introd. परिणतप्रज्ञस्य—*V. l.* with his genius matured or perfected. The statement is amply borne out by the merits of the drama.

APPENDICES.

No. I.

THE METRES USED IN THE PLAY, THEIR DEFINITIONS AND SCHEMES.

1. Sanskrit Verse is regulated by quantity, and not by accent as in English. A पद्य or stanza consists of four पादs or quarters. A *Páda* is regulated by the number of syllables (अक्षरs) or syllabic instants (मात्राs). When the *pâdas* are all in one metre, it is called a सम वृत्त, to which type most of the metres conform; those are अर्धसम वृत्तs wherein the first *pâda* corresponds with the third and the second with the fourth, called respectively the odd and the even *pádas*. A third class is विषम वृत्तs, which are very rare.

2. The vowels अ, इ, उ, ऋ and ऌ are short, and the rest long. The quantity of a syllable is determined by its vowel. A syllable with a short vowel is called लघु (light), and one with a long vowel is called गुरु (heavy).

3. But a लघु syllable becomes गुरु if it is followed by an *Anusvâra* or a *Visarga*, or a conjunct consonant, or when it occurs at the end of a *pâda*.*

4. Three successive syllables form a गण (foot); marking a short syllable as ⏑ and a long one as—, the different गणs, which are eight in number, may be exhibited as follows† :—

य ⏑ — —; र — ⏑ —; त — — ⏑; भ — ⏑ ⏑; ज ⏑ — ⏑; स ⏑ ⏑ —; म — — —; and न ⏑ ⏑ ⏑. A short syllable is often indicated in the Definition by the letter ल and a long one by ग.

5. The Uttararámacharita contains in all 19 varieties of metres, which we give below in alphabetical order :—

अनुष्टुभ्—(also called श्लोक) Def. श्लोके षष्ठं गुरु ज्ञेयं सर्वत्र लघु पञ्चमम्। द्विचतुःपादयोर्ह्रस्वं सप्तमं दीर्घमन्ययोः ॥. There are many variations of this metre, but the one defined is the commonest. Each *pâda* of it consists of eight syllables, of which the sixth is long and the fifth short, and the seventh

---

*सानुस्वारश्च दीर्घश्च विसर्गी च गुरुर्भवेत् ।
वर्णः संयोगपूर्वश्च तथा पादान्तगोऽपि वा ॥
आदिमध्यावसानेषु यरता यान्ति लाघवम् ।
भजसा गौरवं यान्ति मनौ तु गुरुलाघवम् ॥

in the 2nd and 4th *pádas* is short and in the 1st and 3rd *pâdas* long. The rest of the syllables may be either short or long. This is the shortest metre in general use, and is easily recognizable. *Examples*—I. 1, 2, 3, 4 &c.

आर्या—Def. यस्याः प्रथमे पादे द्वादश मात्रास्तथा तृतीयेऽपि । अष्टादश द्वितीये चतुर्थके पञ्चदश साऽऽर्या ॥. This belongs to the class of metres regulated by the number of मात्राs or syllabic instants. The four *pâdas* contain respectively 12, 18, 12 and 15 *mâtrâs*. Ex.—III. 41; VI. 13.

इन्द्रवज्रा—Def. स्यादिन्द्रवज्रा यदि तौ जगौ गः ।. 11 Syllables. Scheme—त, त, ज, ग, ग. *Ex.*—I. 11, 44; II. 3; IV. 8; VII. 4, 16.

उपजाति—Def. [स्यादिन्द्रवज्रा यदि तौ जगौ गः । उपेन्द्रवज्रा जतजास्ततो गौ ॥] अनन्तरोदीरितलक्ष्मभाजौ पादौ यदीयावुपजातयस्ताः ॥ [इत्थं किलान्यास्वपि मिश्रितासु वदन्ति जातिष्विदमेव नाम ॥]. An Upajáti is a mixture of one or more *pádas* of इन्द्रवज्रा (see above) with one or more of उपेन्द्रवज्रा (11 Syll., Sch.–ज, त, ज, ग, ग) so as to form one stanza. A mixture of other metres also in this manner is called an Upajáti The student is recommended to scan and find out in each case whether a *pâda* is in Indravajrâ or Upendravajrà *Ex.*—I. 5; II. 6; III. 35, 42; IV. 16; VI. 15, 27.

[उपेन्द्रवज्रा—See Upajáti above].

[औपच्छन्दसिक—See Málabhâriṇî below].

द्रुतविलम्बित—Def. द्रुतविलम्बितमाह नभौ भरौ ।. 12 Syllables. Scheme-न, भ, भ, र. *Ex.*—III. 27; VI. 15.

पुष्पिताग्रा—Def. अयुजि नयुगरेफतो यकारो युजि च नजौ जरगाश्च पुष्पिताग्रा ॥. Odd *pâdas*–12 Syllables. Sch.—न, न, र, य. Even *pâdas*–13 Syllables. Sch.—न, ज, ज, र, ग. This is an अर्धसम वृत्त. *Ex.*—III. 18, 20; IV. 4; V. 4; VI. 8.

पृथ्वी—Def. जसौ जसयला वसुग्रहयतिश्च पृथ्वी गुरुः ।. 17 Syllables. Sch.—ज, स, ज, स, य, ल, ग. The pause occurs after the eighth syllable. *Ex.*—V. 5; VI. 1, 37.

प्रहर्षिणी—Def. म्नाशाभिर्मनजरगाः प्रहर्षिणीयम् ।. 13 Syllables. Scheme म, न, ज, र, ग. The pause occurs after the third syllable *Ex.*—I. 30, 31, 40, 49; III. 39 ; V. 1, 18.

मञ्जुभाषिणी—Def. सजसा जगौ च यदि मञ्जुभाषिणी । 13 Syllables. Sch.–स, ज, स, ज, ग. *Ex.*–I. 18; III. 4; VI. 4, 17, 41.

मन्दाक्रान्ता—Def. मन्दाक्रान्ता जलधिषडगैर्म्भौ नतौ ताद्गुरू चेत् ।. 17 Syllables. Sch.—म भ, न, त, त, ग, ग. The pauses occur after the fourth and the tenth syllables. *Ex.*—I. 33 ; II. 13, 14, 25; III. 6, 15, 36, 38; IV. 26; V. 12; VI. 9, 22; VII. 6.

मालभारिणी—(Also called औपच्छन्दसिक, of which it forms a special variety) Def. विषमे ससजा गुरू समे चेत्सभरा येन तु मालभारिणीयम् ॥. Odd *páda*-11 Syllables. Sch.-स, स, ज, ग, ग. Even *pâda*-12 Syllables. Sch.-स, भ, र, य. This is an अर्धसम वृत्त. *Ex.*-V. 8.

मालिनी—Def. ननमयययुतेयं मालिनी भोगिलोकैः ।. 15 Syllables. Sch.—न, न, म, य, य. The pause occurs after the eighth syllable. *Ex.*—I. 24, 26, 27 ; II. 20, 21 ; III. 5, 19, 23, 25, 48 ; V. 2, 3, 13; VI. 12, 24, 26.

रथोद्धता—Def. रान्नराविह रथोद्धता लगौ ।. 11 Syllables. Sch.—र, न, र, ल, ग. *Ex.*—I. 34, 37, 45.

वंशस्थ—Def. जतौ तु वंशस्थमुदीरितं जरौ ।. 12 Syllables. Sch.—ज, त, ज, र. *Ex.*—VI. 25.

वसन्ततिलका—Def. उक्ता वसन्ततिलका तभजा जगौ गः ।. 14 Syllables. Sch.—त, भ, ज, ज, ग, ग. *Ex.*—I. 7, 9, 14, 25, 36; II. 10, 11, 22, 23 ; III. 8, 11, 12, 21, 26, 28, 47; IV. 6, 23, 29 ; V. 10, 11, 24, 34 ; VI. 7, 16, 19.

शार्दूलविक्रीडित—Def. सूर्याश्वैर्यदि मः सजौ सततगाः शार्दूलविक्रीडितम् ।. 19 Syllables. Sch.—म, स, ज, स, त, त, ग. The pause occurs after the twelfth syllable. *Ex.*—I. 39 ; II. 9, 16, 28, 29, 30 ; III. 16, 37, 43, 45 ; IV. 1, 5, 17, 20, 22, 25 ; V. 6, 14, 19, 28, 35, 36 ; VI. 18, 40 ; VII. 20.

शालिनी—Def. मात्तौ गौ चेच्छालिनी भोगिलोकैः ।. 11 Syllables. Sch.—म, त, त, ग, ग. The pause occurs after the fourth syllable. *Ex.*—I. 42; III. 2; IV. 18; V. 31, 33.

शिखरिणी—Def. रसै रुद्रैश्छिन्ना यमनसभला गः शिखरिणी ।. 17 Syllables. Sch.—य, म, न, स, भ, ल, ग. The pause occurs after the sixth syllable. *Ex.*—I. 28, 29, 35, 38; II. 1, 2, 26, 27; III. 13, 30, 40, 44; IV. 3, 10, 11, 12, 13, 14, 21; V. 9, 16, 26; VI. 11, 14, 28, 30, 33, 35, 38, 39.

हरिणी—Def. नसमरसला गः षड्वेदैर्हयैर्हरिणी मता ।. 17 Syllables. Sch.—न, स, म, र, स, ल, ग. The pauses occur after the sixth and the tenth syllables. *Ex.*—I. 20, 23; II. 4; III. 22, 24, 31, 32; IV. 19; V. 29.

No. 11

BOMBAY UNIVERSITY EXAMINATION PAPERS.

(*N. B. Questions repeated are omitted*).

1891.

I. Translate into English:—(1) अत्याहतज्योतिरार्षं ते प्रातिभं चक्षुः । (2) विपर्यासं यातो घनविरलभावः क्षितिरुहाम् । (3) इत्यादिभिः प्रियशतैरनुरुध्य मुग्धां तामेव शान्तमथ वा किमिवोत्तरेण । (4) याज्ञवल्क्यो मुनिर्यस्मै ब्रह्मपारायणं जगौ । (5) प्रसादे कोपे वा तवनु मदधीनो विधिरभूत् । (6) सुलभसौख्यं तावद्बालत्वं भवति । (7) अश्व इति पशुसमाम्नाये साङ्ग्रामिके च पठ्यते । (8) तदपि खलु मे स व्याहारस्तुरंगमरक्षिणां विकृतिमखिलक्षत्राक्षेपप्रचण्डतयाऽकरोत् । (9) अहो निरन्वयविपर्यासविरसवृत्तयो विप्रलम्भपर्यवसायिनस्तापयन्ति संसारवृत्तान्ताः । (10) तामेतां परिभावयन्त्वभिनयैर्विन्यस्तरूपां (*v. l.* ०रूपा) बुधाः शब्दब्रह्मविदः कवेः परिणतप्रज्ञस्य वाणीमिमाम् ।. II. Explain the meanings of the following expressions :—पदवाक्यप्रमाणतत्त्वज्ञः; अर्थवादः; विवर्तः; पुटपाकः. III. Discuss the different readings in the following lines :—(*a*) यच्चाद्भुतं कर्म विशुद्धिकाले प्रत्येतु कस्तत् द्युति (*v. l.* भुवि) दूरवृत्तम् । (*b*) अन्तःप्रसुप्त (*v. l.* प्रसृप्त) दहनो ज्वलन्निव वनस्पतिः । (*c*) अरुन्धतीजनकौ—अये मेध्याश्वरक्षाप्रसङ्गात् (*v. l.* ०रक्षापदेशात्) उपागतो वत्सश्चन्द्रकेतुरद्य द्रष्टव्यः । अहो सुदिवसः । (*d*) आश्चर्यमार्या सह देवताभ्यां गङ्गामहीभ्यां सलिलादुपैति (*v. l.* ०दुदेति) ।. IV. Give a brief sketch in English of Bhavabhûti's description of the Daṇḍaka forest

1899.

I. Translate into English :—(*a*) भ्रमिषु कृतपुटान्त० &c. III. 19. (*b*) संख्यातीतैर्द्विरगतुरग० &c. V. 12. II. "Bhavabhúti, as a rule, adapts his style to the sentiment." Illustrate this remark by quotations from the play. III: (*a*) Explain the allusion in यानि त्रीण्यकुतोभयान्यपि पदान्यासन्खरायोधने यद्वा कौशलमिन्द्रसूनुनिधने तत्राप्यभिज्ञो जनः । V. 35. (*b*) Write grammatical notes on:—अगणिततनूतापं तप्त्वा; ओजायितम्; अब्रह्मण्यम्; द्वादशवार्षिकम्; सोमपीथिन्. IV. Explain fully, giving the context where necessary:—(*a*) अये मध्यमाम्बावृत्तान्तोऽन्तरित आर्येण । (*b*) अन्वर्थ एवायमधुना प्रलापो वर्तते । (*c*) वियाकल्पेन मरुता मेघानां भूयसामपि । ब्रह्मणीव विवर्तानां क्वापि विप्रलयः कृतः ॥ VI. 6. V. Describe the character of Ráma as painted by Bhavabhûti, supporting your answer by quotations.

1901.

I. Discuss the merits and defects of the Uttararámacharita. II. Translate into English:—(*a*) सस्वेदरोमाञ्चित॰ &c. III. 42; (*b*) अपत्ये यत्तादृग्दुरित° &c. IV. 3. Dissolve and name the compounds सस्वेद॰ and मरुन्नवाम्भः॰ in (*a*), and name the metres. III. Explain with reference to the context:—(*a*) स्थाने खलु वाक्यनिवृत्तिर्मोहश्च। (*b*) वृद्धास्ते न विचारणीयचरिताः। (*c*) चित्रमाम्नाया-दन्यो नूतनश्छन्दसामवतारः। (*d*) मया पुनर्ज्ञातं व्याघ्रो वा वृको वैष इति। IV. (*a*) Give the meanings of ब्रह्मकोष, व्यतिकर, प्रचलाकिन् and हरि. (*b*) Derive निर्ऋति, सौनिक and तौर्यत्रिक. (*c*) Write grammatical notes on क्षेण, अपास्किरमाण, हिरण्मयी and परःसहस्र.

1903.

I Translate into English:—(1) श्रमाम्बुशिशिरी° &c. VI. 37; (2) पाप्मभ्यश्च पुनाति &c. VII. 20. II. Explain fully, with reference to the context:—(*a*) अस्त्येतत्, आर्यपुत्र अस्त्येतत्। (*b*) कथं नामधेयाभिरयाह। (*c*) गुरुजनोपरोधात्क्षणं क्षम्यतामतिक्रमो रामस्य। (*d*) अहो संविधानकम्। (*e*) अयं पुनरविरुद्धः प्रकार इति वृद्धेभ्यः श्रूयते। (*f*) तं हि धर्मं धर्मसूत्रकाराः समामनन्ति। III. Make a few remarks on the language, ideas and sentiments of the Uttararáma-charita. IV. (*a*) What was the position of (i) Women, and (ii) Brahmins in the age of Ráma as depicted by Bhavabhúti? (*b*) Describe in English the exterior of a क्षत्रियब्रह्मचारिन्. (*c*) Write grammatical notes on अग्निमारुत, धिनोतु, ग्रथयति, स्निग्ध and मौलिक.

1905.

I. Translate into English:—(*a*) कूजत्कुञ्जकुटीर° &c. II. 29; (*b*) यया पूतंमन्यो निधिरपि &c. IV. 10; (*c*) हन्त हन्त भोः... ...प्रवेपते। (See pp. 142-143). II. Explain the propriety of the following with reference to the context and the whole play:—(*a*) एते हि हृदयमर्मच्छिदः संसारभावाः। (*b*) हा आर्यपुत्र पतावन्ते दर्शनम्। (*c*) हन्त मिश्रीकृतो रसो वर्तते। (*d*) सर्वथा व्यवहर्तव्ये कुतो ह्यवचनीयता। III. (*a*) Show the harmony between the first Act and the last. (*b*) Why has the third Act been called छाया?

1909.

I. Translate into English:—(*a*) अद्वैतं सुखदुःखयो॰ &c. I. 39. (*b*) कष्टमेवं नाम जरया...आक्रन्दितुमपि न शक्यते। (See pp. 103-104). II. Explain with reference to the context:—(*a*) किमस्या न प्रेयो यदि परमसह्यस्तु विरहः (*v. l.* यदि पुनरसह्यो न विरहः, किमपरमसह्यस्तु विरहः)। (*b*) भिद्यते वा सद्वृत्तमीदृशस्य निर्माणस्य। (*c*) नूनं संकल्पाभ्यासपाटवोपादान एष भ्रमो रामभद्रस्य। (*d*) कुतोऽतिक्रान्तमनोरथाया ममैतत्। (*e*) मुग्धहृदय

कोऽयमाकस्मिकस्ते स्नेहपरिप्लवो विकारः । III. "As the poet of nature and human passion and feeling generally, Bhavabhûti occupies a very high rank among Sanskrit authors." Justify and illustrate this remark from your play. IV. Explain clearly the idea in the verse ending with संवृत्ताः कुवलयिनो भुवो विभागाः (I. 31). *Or*, state in what sense Bhavabhûti uses the words विप्रलम्भ, व्यतिकर and वितर्त.

1911.

I. Translate into English :—चूडाचुम्बित° &c. VI. 20. Name the metre, and dissolve the compound भस्मस्तोकपवित्रलाञ्छनम्. II. Explain clearly with reference to the context :—(*a*) अर्थवाद एषः । दोषं तु कंचित्कथय येन प्रतिविधीयेत । (*b*) त्वाष्ट्रयन्त्रभ्रमि° &c. IV. 3. (*c*) अथ वा स्नेहश्च निमित्तसव्यपेक्षश्चेति विप्रतिषिद्धमेतत् । (*d*) अयि देव राक्षसकुलधूमकेतो अद्यापि ते मन्युविषयः । III. (*a*) Write grammatical and explanatory notes on :—वज्रकीलायितम् , पूर्तमन्यः, निगमान्तविद्या, त्रयीवर्जम्. (*b*) What do you know of the following from the Uttara. :—शान्ता, मधुपर्क, school holidays, भरत, the weak points in Râma's career, सूनृता वाक्? IV. Indicate the time taken by the action of the Uttar. *Or*, briefly point out the salient features of Râma's character, supporting your remarks with quotations.

1916.

I. Translate into English :—(*a*) अद्वैतं सुखदुःखयो° &c. I. 39; (*b*) स्निग्धश्यामाः क्वचिदपरतो &c. II. 14; (*c*) पातालोदरकुञ्ज° &c. V. 14. Name and dissolve the compounds सुखानुबन्ध्य (*a*), तीर्थाश्रमगिरिसरिद्गर्भकान्तारमिश्राः (*b*), and उत्तप्तस्फुरदारकूटकपिलज्योतिर्ज्वलद्दीप्तिभिः (*c*). Give the metre of (*b*), and its scheme. II. Discuss readings in the following :—(*a*) प्रतनुविरलैः (*v. l.* पतनविरलैः) प्रान्तोन्मीलन्मनोहर-कुन्तलैः (*v. l.* °मनोहरकुड्मलैः) दशनमुकुलैः (*v. l.* दशनकुसुमैः) मुग्धालोकं शिशुर्दधती मुखम् । (*b*) विकारश्चैतन्यं भ्रमयति च संमीलयति च (*v. l.* समुन्मीलयति च) ।. III. Give in your own words, in English or Sanskrit, the substance of the dialogue between Chandraketu and Lava. IV. Explain the following, giving the context :—(*a*) किं न संभाव्यते । कोऽपि प्रकृष्टपुण्यपरिपाकोपादानो महिमा स्यात् । (*b*) तदद्याप्युच्छ्वासो भवति ननु लाभो हि रुदितम् । (*c*) अन्धतामिस्रा ह्यसूर्या नाम ते लोकास्तेभ्यः प्रतिविधीयन्ते य आत्मघातिन इत्येवमृषयो मन्यन्ते । (*d*) किं व्यवस्थितविषयाः क्षात्रधर्माः । V. What change has the poet made in the catastrophe of the drama? Either justify or criticize that change.

Index of Important Words.

(The figures refer to the Pages of this Edition).